DATE DUE

NEW BOOK TO BE
CIRCULATED BEGINNING
JAN 2 2 1997

GAYLORD   PRINTED IN U.S.A.

Dexterity and Its Development

RESOURCES FOR ECOLOGICAL PSYCHOLOGY

A Series of Volumes Edited by:
Robert E. Shaw, William M. Mace, and Michael T. Turvey

Dexterity and Its Development

Edited by

Mark L. Latash
Pennsylvania State University

Michael T. Turvey
University of Connecticut
Haskins Laboratories, New Haven

With *On Dexterity and Its Development* by Nicholai A. Bernstein
Translated by Mark L. Latash

LAWRENCE ERLBAUM ASSOCIATES, PUBLISHERS
1996   Mahwah, New Jersey

Lawrence Erlbaum Associates, Inc., Publishers
10 Industrial Avenue
Mahwah, New Jersey 07430

Cover design by Gail Silverman

Library of Congress Cataloging-in-Publication Data

Dexterity and its development / edited by Mark L. Latash and Michael
T. Turvey.
    p.   cm.
    "With On dexterity and its development, by N. A. Bernstein,
translated [from the Russian] by Mark L. Latash."
    Includes bibliographical references and index.
    ISBN 0-8058-1646-1
    1. Motor ability. I. Latash, Mark L., 1953–   . II. Turvey,
Michael T. III. Bernshteĭn, N. A. (Nikolaĭ Aleksandrovich),
1896–1966. O lovkosti i ee razvitii. English.
QP303.D48 1996
612.7′6—dc20   95-38131
                                                            CIP

Books published by Lawrence Erlbaum Associates are printed on acid-free paper,
and their bindings are chosen for strength and durability.

Printed in the United States of America
10 9 8 7 6 5 4 3 2 1

Contents

PART II COMMENTARIES

Preface

You are about to begin reading a scientific book unusual in many respects. The first part of the volume is a translation from Russian of the book *On Dexterity and Its Development* written about 50 years ago by one of the greatest scientists of the 20th century, Nicholai Aleksandrovich Bernstein. This book was not published at the time it was written because of the internal political situation in the Union of Soviet Socialist Republics (you can read more about this period of Russian history in the chapter by I. M. Feigenberg and L. P. Latash). For a long time it was believed that the book had been destroyed; however, this was not the case. Fortunately, the severity of the laws of the Soviet Union was softened by their notorious ineffectiveness, and one of Bernstein's students, Professor I. M. Feigenberg, found the manuscript and restored the book. The book was eventually published in 1991, 25 years after the death of its author.

Very few scientific works remain interesting to the reader 50 years after they were written. This rule is particularly true for books in which the authors try to present the state of a scientific field in a popular style, understandable not only to professionals but also to people who are generally curious but lack the particular scientific background, including college and even high-school students. Bernstein's work, however, is a rare exception to this rule, and we are sure that you will enjoy it as much as it would have been enjoyed in the 1940s had it been published at that time.

Bernstein's original book, presented in Part I, was directed at a wide audience ranging from specialists in biomechanics and motor behavior to coaches, neurologists, physical therapists, athletes, and even inquisitive college and high-school students. Part II of this book provides both a historical and a contemporary perspective on Bernstein's ideas. One commentary was written by two authors well acquainted with Bernstein's life and times. Six additional commentaries were written by scientists close to current developments in the field of movement and dexterity. The authors were encouraged to follow the example set by Bernstein, that is, to write their contributions in a reader-friendly style and to avoid excessive jargon, mathematics, data, and extensive referencing. They tried to retain Bernstein's style in presenting new findings in the areas of biomechanics, motor control, and motor development in a way that would be both understandable to nonspecialists in these areas and informative for professionals working in different areas related to human movement.

Making the book accessible to an English-speaking audience presented the translator with a difficult task. Bernstein's language is very rich and lively and frequently humorous, yet it is never scientifically imprecise. So the translator's major difficulty was to preserve the colorful language of the original without sacrificing its scientific depth. The translator would like to thank his native-English-speaking colleagues and particularly Dr. Edward Reed for the very careful reading of various drafts of the translation and for making numerous suggestions and corrections.

We hope that this volume will be read with pleasure by all those interested in the origins and mechanisms of the production of voluntary movements, regardless of their educational and professional background. We also think that the unique history and composition of this book will make it helpful and attractive to historians and philosophers of science.

Now it is our pleasure to introduce you to this timeless masterpiece.

—Mark L. Latash
—Michael T. Turvey

Resources
for Ecological Psychology

Edited by
Robert E. Shaw, William M. Mace, and Michael T. Turvey

This series of volumes is dedicated to furthering the development of psychology as a branch of ecological science. In its broadest sense, ecology is a multidisciplinary approach to the study of living systems, their environments, and the reciprocity that has evolved between the two. Traditionally, ecological science emphasizes the study of the biological bases of *energy* transactions between animals and their physical environments across cellular, organismic, and population scales. Ecological psychology complements this traditional focus by emphasizing the study of *information* transactions between living systems and their environments, especially as they pertain to perceiving situations of significance to planning and execution of purposes activated in an environment.

The late James J. Gibson used the term *ecological psychology* to emphasize this animal-environment mutuality for the study of problems of perception. He believed that analyzing the environment to be perceived was just as much a part of the psychologist's task as analyzing animals themselves, and hence that the "physical" concepts applied to the environment and the "biological" and "psychological" concepts applied to organisms would have to be tailored to one another in a larger system of mutual constraint. His early interest in the applied problems of landing airplanes and driving automobiles led him to pioneer the study of the perceptual guidance of action.

The work of Nicholai Bernstein in biomechanics and physiology presents a complementary approach to problems of the coordination and control of movement. His work suggests that action, too, cannot be studied without reference to the environment, and that physical and biological concepts must be developed together. The coupling of Gibson's ideas with those of Bernstein forms a natural basis for looking at the traditional psychological topics of perceiving, acting, and knowing as activities of ecosystems rather than isolated animals.

The purpose of this series is to form a useful collection, a resource, for people who wish to learn about ecological psychology and for those who wish to contribute to its development. The series will include original research, collected papers, reports of conferences and symposia, theoretical monographs, technical handbooks, and works from the many disciplines relevant to ecological psychology.

Series Dedication

To James J. Gibson, whose pioneering work in ecological
psychology has opened new vistas in psychology and
related sciences, we respectfully dedicate this series.

Part I

On Dexterity and Its Development

N. A. Bernstein

Introduction

This book was written in response to a suggestion by the Administration of the Central Research Institute of Physical Culture. This suggestion contained two objectives: first, to present as strict and precise a definition and analysis of the complex psychophysical capacity of dexterity as possible; second, to provide a popular overview of the contemporary understanding of the nature of movement coordination, motor skill, exercise, and so forth, which are of very high practical importance for both professionals in the area of physical education and for all the numerous participants of the physical-culture drive in our country, an overview that should encourage genuine culture in all connotations of this word. Thus, the book was conceived as popular-scientific.

The need for popular-scientific literature is very strong in our country. It would be basically wrong to dismiss this kind of literature on the grounds that the Soviet Union does not need "semieducated" citizens and that its citizens should have an undisputed right and means to master special literature without the condescension and arrogance that are, as some claim, inevitably present in popular-science literature. This view is totally wrong.

The time when a scientist could be equally well oriented in all areas of the natural sciences passed, irreversibly, long ago. Even 200 years ago, it required the omnipotent genius of Lomonosov for such universality. In essence, he was the last representative of universal natural scientists. During the two centuries that separate us from Lomonosov, the volume and content of natural science have grown so immensely that scientists of our day spend all of their lives mastering the material of their major, narrow areas of specialization. Very few

Bernstein in the mid-1940s.

of them find enough time to follow the heavy flow of the scientific literature in order not to lag behind even in their own field. They are rarely able to find time to mull over other areas of their own science and even less time for other areas of natural science in general.

This overflowing stream of new information in all the branches of natural science and, directly related to its growth, the increasing differentiation of scientific and scientific-practical professions, create an increasing danger of turning their representatives into narrow specialists lacking any general horizon, blind to anything except the narrow path that they have chosen in life. This narrowing of the general perspective is dangerous not only because it deprives people of the irresistible beauty of wide general education but also because it teaches them not to see the forest behind the trees even in their narrow area; it emasculates creative thinking, impoverishes their work with respect to fresh ideas and wide perspectives. Jonathan Swift, also about 200 years ago, predicted the emergence of such "gelehrters" with blinkers on their eyes, blind, confused cranks; Swift sharply ridiculed them in his description of the Academy of Sciences on the Island of Lagado.

The role of popular-scientific literature is to overcome this danger. Let it be guarded by all the muses from condescending arrogance toward the reader, from the Horacius' *Odi profánum vulgus et arceo!* ("Hate the dark mob and drive it off!"). The popular-scientific author must approach the reader, not as an ignoramus, not as a vulgar mob, but as a colleague who needs to become acquainted with the basic facts and current conditions of an adjacent area of science, an acquaintance that the reader would never be able to achieve by studying the same problems in the mountains of original papers and special literature. The popular-scientific author strives to provide the reader with a wide perspective, one that is necessary for both theoretical and practical creativity in any area, and tries not to descend to some imaginary, unrespected lay reader but to elevate the colleague-reader from a different area to a bird's flight from where he is able to see the whole world.

A contemporary professional, whether a theoretician or a practician, should know everything about his own basic area and basic things about everything.

The area of theoretical linguistics related to popular-scientific writing is absolutely undeveloped. It is ruled by chaos, unclearness, and groping empiricism. If one wants to make a contribution to this kind of literature, being as serious and responsible as it deserves, the author must first of all realize how to start. As far as I am able to discern, there are three different styles in the contemporary popular-scientific literature.

Typical examples of one of them are widely available and well-known books including *Prosvyastcheniye* ("Enlightment"): *The World* by A. Meier, *The History of Earth* by I. Neymark, *The Human* by L. Ranke. Books of this kind are not much different from any textbooks or special literature, aside from taking into account the level of the targeted reader. Such authors do not try to entice the reader or to excite the reader's curiosity; any enticement and curiosity stem directly from the inherent interest of the theme and the subject themselves. Their style is dry, businesslike, based on a strict plan that is mostly defined by the dogmatics, not the didactics, of the subject.

The second style of popular-scientific literature may be called *Flammarion*. Widely known books by C. Flammarion on astronomy and cosmography are characterized mostly by two basic features. First, they continuously flirt with the reader, particularly with the female reader, whom the author, according to the ideas of the bourgeois society of the 19th century, depicts as an extremely prim, impatient, and ignorant person but for whom he does not spare any amount of gallantry. Second, the text is diluted. Undoubtedly, simplicity of discourse and percentage of dilution are not the same things; we are aware of many examples of very specialized and hard-to-understand scientific works that nonetheless contain about 90% of a useless, liquid solvent. From my view, such swelling of a book does not help any more than flirting with the readers of either gender.

The third style is the most recent one and most brightly illustrated by the books by P. De Kruif dedicated to the history of great inventions in medicine and biology. De Kruif's first and most talented book, *Microbe Hunters* is well known and very popular in our country. As far as I know, De Kruif was the first to introduce into popular-scientific literature a brave, impressionistic style, enriched with all the contemporary achievements of general stylistics. His text is rich with images, bright comparisons, and humor, and he sometimes ascends to the passionate enthusiasm of a zealot for science and advocate for the martyrs. He is helped by the historical aspect that is present in most of his books, whether it is history of a great invention with all its intricate complications or history of the life of a great scientist. In both cases, the narration is filled with dynamic and developing intrigue. The reader holds his breath to find out what will happen next and is eager to peek at the last page, as some young ladies do when reading a breathtaking novel. The title of the first book by De Kruif, *Microbe Hunters* by itself introduces the reader to his style and manner. De Kruif turns the history of the scientific struggle into a fascinating, adventurous novel without devaluing the described events and their significance.

The style of De Kruif has begun to find followers in the Soviet Union. For example, the bright essays of Tatyana Tess, which are dedicated to the most prominent contemporary Soviet scientists and which sometimes appear in the major newspapers, are undoubtedly influenced by the style of De Kruif. Also, the style of the essays of Larisa Reisner, who died an untimely death, have much in common with that of De Kruif.

I decided to use the style of De Kruif because of a number of its attractive features. The endeavor, however, turned out more complex because of the lack of plot dynamics. My problem was to apply this style to describing a theory, an area of science, with its somewhat inevitable lack of dynamics. The third essay ("On the Development of Movements") was the easiest one, exactly because of its historical nature, which gave me a chance to dramatize the fascinating canvas of movement evolution in the animal world up to human beings.

In the other essays, I decided to use the whole available spectrum of means developed and ordained by the theory of belles lettres, every artistic method that has been sanctioned by it. I am determined not to be afraid of any Russian word that is able to express the required ideas most accurately and vividly, even if that word is not included in the official (scientific and administrative) language. Furthermore, I extensively use different kinds of comparisons, from fleeting metaphors, lost somewhere inside subordinate clauses, to extensive parallels that occupy a full page.

My desire to make the text as lively as possible led to the inclusion of a number of narrative episodes, from fables and myths to realistic essays predominantly related to impressions from the Great Patriotic War (World War II). Finally, as for the illustrative material, I enjoy the full support of the publisher and introduced numerous drawings into the text. The book contains drawings whose content closely accompanies the material and also a number of scientific illustrations indirectly supporting the discourse (these are mostly drawings from areas of anatomy, zoology, and paleontology and photographs of the highest athletic achievements). I decided not to be afraid of including an element of humor in some cartoons, genially making fun of clumsiness and awkwardness or suggesting unrealistic examples of dexterity and skillfulness.

All these attempts in the area of popular-scientific literature are, perhaps, just one big mistake. Undoubtedly, however, there is a chance that at least a small grain of what has been found was found correctly. Indeed, only those who never search never err, and, on the other hand, not one of the (re)searchers ever expected to find something worthwhile at the first attempt.

Let me rely on harsh, albeit friendly, critique and on the reader's experience in pronouncing the final judgment.

What Is Dexterity?

RECONNAISSANCE AND BATTLES OF SCIENCE

Physiology long ago passed beyond being merely "the frog science." The subject grew both in size and in level of development. It addressed doves and chickens, then moved to cats and dogs. Later, a respectful place in the laboratories was taken by monkeys and apes. The persisting requirements of practice moved physiology closer and closer to human beings.

There was a time when the human was considered a unique being, a semigod. Any research into the human bodily structure and function was considered sacrilegious. Spontaneous scientific materialism took its position in science only about 300 years ago; at that time, the first frog was dissected. However, in current times, the depth of the abyss between humans and all other living beings has become apparent. Here, the subject was not human supernatural origin or immortal soul. The abyss was revealed by the inevitable, persisting requirements of everyday practice. Physiology of labor and physiology of physical exercise and sport emerged. What kind of labor can be studied in cats? What is common between the frog and the track-and-field athlete?

Thus, genuine human physiology and genuine human activity has developed and expanded. Scientists attacked one bastion after another, delving deeper and deeper into the mysteries of functions of the human body.

Development of each natural science, including physiology, might well be compared to a persistent victorious offense. The adversary—the unknown—is strong and is far from being defeated. Each inch of land has been captured only after fierce battles. The offense does not go smoothly. Sometimes, it is stopped for quite a while, as the opponents entrench and try to gather new forces. Sometimes, a seemingly captured area is taken back by the adversary—the unknown. This regression happens when a promising scientific theory is proved wrong, because its fundamental facts were misunderstood or misinterpreted. Nevertheless, the regiment of science knows only temporary upsets and misfortunes. Scientific offense is like ocean high tides: Each wave is only half a meter higher than the previous one, but wave after wave and minute after minute, they push the tide higher and higher. The difference from high tides is that the scientific offense does not end.

There are many common features between the development of science and the battlefield. There is a slow, methodical movement of the whole front when each step is taken once and forever. There are brave assaults, clever breakthroughs, which quickly penetrate deep into the area that had offered the most resistance for years. Such breakthroughs of genius in scientific battles include the discoveries of Nikolai Lobachevsky, Louis Pasteur, Dmitri Mendeleev, and Albert Einstein. In science, as in battles, an important role is played by short reconnaissance sallies deep into the enemy's rear. Such excursions are not attempts to capture and retain a new piece of territory. They can yield, however, important information on the deep enemy arrangements and help the main body of the army to reorganize prior to a major offensive operation by the whole front.

For a quarter of a century, I worked as a modest officer in the army of science, in the regiment of human physiology. During all these years, I took part only in the slow, systematic offensive actions of the science infantry. The suggestion that I write essays on the *physiology of dexterity* was the first reconnaissance assignment because this area had only a few bits of facts that were firmly established by scientific research. It seems to be the proper time to undertake such an intelligence action because life urges it. Was the choice of the officer lucky? How valuable is the collected material? These questions are not for me to answer. The intelligence report is here, in front of the reader, in form of a book. Let the reader make the decision.

PSYCHOPHYSICAL CAPACITIES

The banner of physical culture bears the names of four notions that are commonly addressed as psychophysical capacities: *force, speed, endurance,* and *dexterity.*

These four are quite unlike each other.

Force is virtually a purely physical feature of the body. It depends directly on the volume and quality of the muscles and only indirectly on other factors.

Speed is a more complex feature that combines elements of both physiology and psychology.

Endurance is even more complex. It is based on the cooperation of all the subsystems and organs of the body. It requires a high level of cooperation of metabolism among the working organs, transport system (the circulatory system, which delivers supplies and eliminates wastes), organ providers (respiration and digestion), and all the organs of higher command and control (the central nervous system). In fact, a hardy body should satisfy three conditions of endurance: It should have ample supplies of energy to spend when necessary. It should be able, at a proper time, to generously offer these supplies without sparing a single unit of energy. Finally, it should be able to spend the resources with a tight, sensible frugality so that they last for the maximal amount of useful work. Briefly, to possess endurance is to have much, to spend generously, and to pay miserly. Obviously, this capacity characterizes the complex organization of the body as a whole.

The degree of complexity is even higher for dexterity. One can hardly say what prevails in it—physical or psychic. At least, as we are going to see, dexterity is a *function of control*, and, therefore, the main role in dexterity is played by the *central nervous system*.

Dexterity stands aside from the other capacities in many aspects. It is certainly more flexible and more universal than any other capacity. Dexterity is a kind of currency for which all other currencies are readily traded. It is a trump suit that beats all other cards.

DEXTERITY—THE WINNER

Many myths, tales, and sagas glorify dexterity, the winner. However, this theme is best developed by an old Chinese-Tibetan fable, recited here in full:

All the inhabitants of forests, meadows, and mountains suffered from the cunning Monkey, but she treated most mercilessly three of them: the Elephant, the Camel, and the yellow-eyed Bunny. So, these three decided to go and bring a complaint to the Black Chieftain, the cave bear of the Himalayas.

The Black Chieftain listened to the plaintiffs and ordered the Monkey to compete with each of them according to the rules set by the plaintiffs. If the Monkey won all three competitions, she would be pardoned. If she lost just one, she would be sentenced to death.

The first was the mighty Elephant. He said, "Far-far away, there is a spring of magic water, Dun-Khe. But there is no way to the spring. The only path is blocked by sharp, heavy rocks, by thick thorny bushes. Here is my challenge: The one to be the first to reach the spring and bring a cup of magic water will be the winner." The Elephant relied on his enormous strength. He thought, "The Monkey will never be able to move the rocks or to push her way through the bushes. If she follows me, she will trail on the way back as well, and I shall hit her cup with my tail and spill the water."

And the Elephant moved forward. If there was a rock on his way, he pushed it aside with his mighty tusks. If bushes and trees blocked the path, interweaved more intricately than the strokes in the most complex Chinese hieroglyph, he pulled them out of the earth with his mighty trunk and threw them on the ground.

FIG. 1.

The Monkey never even thought of following the Elephant. She ran and jumped on the highest palm, looked around, and started to jump over and dive under the branches. Here, she clung with her tail, swung like a clock pendulum, and flew over a hundred yards. There, she hid her paws into her fur and slipped like a grass snake. She got to the magic spring Dun-Khe and rushed back to the Black Chieftain with a cup full with magic water. And during all the jumps and somersaults, she did not spill a drop from the cup!

The Monkey gave the magic water to the Black Chieftain. The Black Chieftain was mightily surprised and drew with a tooth on bamboo bark the first saint symbol of victory "Yi."

The yellow-eyed Bunny was the next to step forward. He said, "Can you see that mountain behind us? This is the mountain of miracles, Hamar. It takes eight days for a Man to circle it. The mountain has four slopes, the first one is of the black rock, the second one is of grey rock, the third one is of brown rock, and the fourth one, that we can see, is of golden rock. If you take a piece of rock from all four slopes and put them together, they will immediately glue into one magic rock that turns any rock into gold. But you need to collect all the rocks in one day; otherwise, they will not glue together. Many tried to get the magic rock of the Hamar mountain but all failed. You cannot climb the mountain because it is as smooth as glass and as slippery as ice. Here is my challenge: Whoever is the first to run around the mountain and bring a piece of rock from each of the four slopes to our Black Chieftain will be the winner."

The Bunny relied on his quick feet. He thought that the long-armed and long-footed Monkey would never be able to catch up with him.

And so the Bunny ran around the mountain as fast as he could. He was always fast, but this time he ran faster than ever. He ran faster than the swallow flies, than the mackerel swims.

The Monkey did not try to catch up with the Bunny. She rushed straight up the golden slope. She hung by her claws, swung through the air with her tail as

FIG. 2.

if it were a wing, crept like a snake, ran along the slope like a fly. She reached the top of the mountain, where all four slopes met, picked a piece of rock from each slope, and slid back like an avalanche. The Bunny was just half way around the mountain.

The Monkey gave all four rock pieces to the Black Chieftain. The Black Chieftain was even more surprised. He drew with a tooth on bamboo bark the second saint symbol of the victory "Ro."

The next was the Camel. He said, "Far away, beyond the great desert, there is an oasis where the magic flower Li grows. Whoever owns the flower should not be afraid of any black magic. But the way there is long and hard. There is nothing in the desert besides cactus trees and thorny bushes. My father traveled there when I was young, and only two camels from the whole caravan returned. I shall walk to the oasis and bring you, the Black Chieftain, the magic flower Li. I only implore you, please, for the sake of our ancestors, to destroy this nasty Monkey. So, this is my challenge: If the Monkey gets to the oasis faster than I do and brings you the magic flower, I shall forgive all her sins and bow my head in front of her. If she dies there of heat and exhaustion, that will only be her fault."

The Camel thought, "The frail Monkey will never be able to reach the oasis. I am the ruler of the desert, and I shall put all my strength into this feat. The path to the oasis is covered with horse and camel bones, so the Monkey will be no match to my endurance, and her tricks will not help her."

The Camel drank a lot of water, put two waterskins across his humps, and started to walk. This time, the Monkey did not wait and ran quickly into the desert.

There was just one path through the desert, and one should stick to it or be lost and die. The Monkey knew that the Camel would walk along the path. She ran to a group of high cacti and strong bushes. There she tied a tricky loop made of dry grass and small branches so that it crossed the path, climbed a high bush, and waited for the Camel. The Camel walked smoothly along the path and did not even notice the loop. He drew the loop so that it started to bend the bush

FIG. 3.

where the Monkey sat. Suddenly, the loop slipped off, the bush straightened and pushed the Monkey forward as from a sling. The Monkey flew through the air, helping with the feet, steering with the tail.

She flew not less than ninety thousand steps and landed on another high bush. The bush bent one way nearly to the ground, then the other way, and when it started to straighten, the Monkey let it go and flew again for another ninety thousand steps.

The Monkey landed on the path and saw another camel. So, she fixed another tricky loop in the camel's path. It took her less than a day to fly to the magic oasis at the very end of the desert.

And the way back was much easier.

When she picked the magic flower Li, all the ghosts of the desert became her servants. She ordered them to take her to the Black Chieftain's cave. A hot whirlwind took her and, in a minute, brought her across the desert. The Camel walked not more than a hundredth of the way.

The Black Chieftain, the cave bear of the Himalayas, was amazed. He took the magic flower Li from the Monkey and drew with a tooth on bamboo bark the third saint symbol of the victory "Ha."

The Monkey was pardoned and still lives happily in the forests and meadows.

Now, let us move from fables to real life, and ask master of sport I. Brazhnin, to share with us one of his childhood recollections:

It happened thirty years ago. All of Russia was crazy about French wrestling. The championships took place in each town, in each village, and even in each block where there were half a dozen of boys aged 10 to 15.

At that time, I was exactly at that age, was a local champion, and could follow for hours the huge Vanya Leshiy or Sarakaki, who performed at nights at the local circus.

Once, the whole crowd of us followed a famous wrester, Mkrtichev, who strolled along the Arkhangelsk streets. He was a huge bum, swarthy, fat, and very strong. He not only was a wrestler but also worked each night at the circus, lifting heavy weights, bending iron bars, tearing apart horseshoes, breaking copper coins, and doing a lot of tricks requiring amazing strength.

For us, Mkrtichev was a supernatural idol, and I followed him at a respectful distance, looking from all sides at the marvelous athlete.

Once, Mkrtichev walked to a goldsmith who employed an apprentice, one of the teenagers of our block, Monka. I had frequently dropped by as Monka's friend. So, I followed the famous athlete into the shop.

I don't remember how Monka started to talk about the circus strength shows, but at the end, Monka (who was 17 at the time, but was short and skinny, and did not look more than a 15-year-old) asked Mkrtichev to cut a three-kopeck coin with small scissors that were used by goldsmiths for cutting copper, silver, or tin.

Mkrtichev, who broke coins with his fingers in the circus, with a condescending smile took the scissors, the coin, and . . . after trying for the whole ten minutes, all sweating and confused, returned the coin and the scissors to Monka.

Then Monka took the scissors in his right hand, put the coin in them, and in three accurate and quick moves cut it into two. He did the same with a thicker five-kopeck coin. The famous athlete was able only to gape and shamefully hurried out of the shop. Since that time, I stopped following Mkrtichev—he was defeated.

WHY DO WE VALUE DEXTERITY?

Dexterity has always had an irresistible charm. We will later attempt to find the secret of its attraction. In any case, there is no argument that folk wisdom values it very highly. Starting with the famous Bible legend about the giant Goliath and young David, who defeated the giant with dexterity (this legend is amusingly repeated in the meeting of Monka and Mkrtichev), the epics, fairy tales, and proverbs of all peoples praise dexterity. There is enough serious material later in this book, so I recite one more fable, this time in a brief version.

The father sent his three sons to travel around the world and to learn wisdom. In three years, the sons were back and told the father that one of them had learned the skill of the barber, the second one had learned the profession of the blacksmith, and the third one had become a fencer.

The father asked them all to sit in front of the house and to wait for a chance to demonstrate their skills. The one who bested the brothers would inherit the house and all the valuables.

They sat for a short while and saw a hare hopping across the field.

"This one is just for me," said the barber. He took his instruments, ran after the hare, put foam on its muzzle, and shaved it cleanly without cutting the skin.

"Yes," said the father, "You are certainly a great master. If your brothers do not do something amazing, the house will be yours."

FIG. 4.

"Wait a minute, daddy," said the second son, the blacksmith.

And exactly at that time, a carriage appeared on the road pulled by a pair of trotters. The blacksmith grabbed his tools, ran after the carriage, tore off all eight horseshoes and replaced them with new ones without stopping the carriage.

"Wow," said the father, "I can see that you also did not waste your time. I don't know who is more dexterous of you two. Your brother will have a hard time catching his elder brothers."

He had just spoken these words, when it started to rain. The father and the two elder sons crawled under the bench while the third son, the fencer, remained outside. He drew out his sword and started to swing it over his head hitting away each drop of water. The rain grew harder and harder and eventually it started to pour. But the younger son just swung his sword quicker and quicker and managed to deflect each drop according to the perfect rules of fencing, so that he remained as dry as if he were sitting under an umbrella.

The father could not make a choice and divided his estate between all three sons. That was the only smart thing to do.

Let us once again compare this fable to real life. A return to childhood is not necessary: The last 5 years have supplied enough examples.

Once (it was at the beginning of the Great Patriotic War), our reconnaissance cavalry unit was encircled by the Germans, who were much more numerous.

The situation was very tense, and it was very hard to break the encirclement.

Among the cavalry unit was one circus rider. At the first shots, he staggered in the saddle and hung down from the horse, his head nearly touching the ground. The Germans thought that he had been killed and just accidentally strapped in the stirrups. They stopped paying attention to him and to his horse, who wandered across the field with the hanging dead body. But the rider was not even wounded. His horse understood him without words. Pretending to be dead, the rider led the horse across the enemy positions, and not only returned unharmed but also gathered very important intelligence information. When he decided that the reconnaissance was over, he straightened in the saddle and successfully returned.

What helped this hero to avoid death and to complete his task so brilliantly? Self-control, strength, endurance? Yes, but most of all, motor skill and quick wits—that is, dexterity.

Following is another example from thousands and thousands of feats by our brave soldiers during the Great Patriotic War.

The Nazis encircled a village house and were very close to capturing it. One of them hid behind the closed gates, put the barrel of his machine gun between the leaves, and poured fire at the house until its basement was captured by the Nazis. The last Soviet soldier who was still in the house ran to the attic. There was no way to retreat and it was obvious that in five minutes he would be captured by the enemies. There was no time to spare.

The soldier ran to the attic window. He took a hand grenade and threw it into the gates. Through the smoke, he saw the demolished gates and the stunned Nazi machine gunner. He jumped out of the window, made a somersault, and landed straight on the German soldier. Before the German could understand what was happening, his gun was grabbed by the Soviet soldier who shot the German and started pouring the machine-gun fire at the attic, where the pursuing Germans appeared. The Germans were stopped, and the short time break was enough for the other Soviet soldiers to come to the rescue.

I do not remember the name of the hero. He was neither Goliath nor Hercules. He was an average-built man, but, at a hard time, his athletic abilities and wits

FIG. 5.

saved him. In this example, his life and the whole situation were saved by dexterity.

What is so special about dexterity? Why is it so attractive and valued so highly? We are not mistaken in naming the following features:

First, and perhaps also most important, motor dexterity is a universal and very versatile capacity. One might say about a dexterous person that he or she does not burn in fire and does not drown in water. There is always a demand for dexterity, and it helps in many different situations. In professional skills and in labor movements? Certainly. In everyday life, in the garden, and at the farm? No argument. In gymnastics, track and field, sport games, and acrobatics? Everything there depends on dexterity. In a battle? The two previous examples from the thousands of situations have illustrated the importance of dexterity for a soldier. In this book, we shall see many examples illustrating the outstanding versatility of this capacity.

The second attractive feature of dexterity is its accessibility, which gives a person with an average constitution a chance at victory over a giant or an athlete. It is very encouraging that the Soviet and European records in pole vault, a physical exercise that is virtually totally built on dexterity, belong to N. G. Ozolin, a person of average height and not very athletic constitution. The following proverb applies to dexterity: "A golden speck is small but valuable."

FIG. 6.

Everyday experience indicates that dexterity is not an inborn, unchangeable capacity that is impossible to gain just as it is impossible to change one's inborn eye color. Dexterity is exercisable: One can develop it and induce its considerable growth. One need not have long legs and a powerful chest. It is sufficient to have an average body typical of an average, healthy human.

The next important feature of dexterity is that it is not a crude, physical capacity like force or endurance. It builds a bridge to the area of genuine intellect. First, there is wisdom in dexterity. It is an accumulation of life experiences in the field of movements and actions. For this reason, dexterity frequently increases with age and is preserved until later years more than other psychophysical capacities. Then, as with any capacity related to psychology, dexterity bears a reflection of the individual. All strong men have approximately the same kind of strength aside from quantitative differences and, perhaps, one of them may have stronger arms, whereas another may have a stronger back. Strength is kilograms, nothing more. Naturally, it is easy to develop its quantitative indices. Dexterity in each person is qualitatively different and unique. That's why it is the only psychophysical capacity that still lacks a quantitative measure. There are records in speed, in strength, and in endurance, but no one has been able to invent a competition that would provide champions and record holders in pure dexterity. Dexterity helps in a number of athletic endeavors, but its role is that of a director who stays behind the curtain while the prizes are being given to speed, or strength, or endurance. This position seemingly puts dexterity at a disadvantage, but, in fact, it elevates dexterity over all other capacities, making it particularly attractive.

In all my physiological essays, we speak about the *purely motor dexterity* leaving aside the areas in which the same notion is used for psychological abilities. However, drawing a distinct line between the two is difficult, and we shall see a number of examples in the book. Motor dexterity is a kind of "motor wits," but very frequently, this simplest form of wits steadily grows into mental wits, into inventiveness and technique. A skilled worker frequently starts with practicing his movements at the highest speed but then moves into their qualitative development and rationalization. The worker may eventually improve the design of his tools and equipment and develop inventive ideas. This side of dexterity, its intellectual basis, the fact that its development is enriched with deep mental penetration into the heart of the problems, is most enticing. For example, N. G. Ozolin, a Ph.D. in pedagogy and champion pole vaulter, reached his outstanding achievements by deep analysis of the physiological aspects and biomechanics of movements, mechanics of pole elasticity, and so forth.

WHAT IS DEXTERITY?

So, what is dexterity? Let us listen once again to I. Brazhnin:

> So, what is dexterity? In order to understand it, let us turn to the word's history. The word *dexterity* ("lovkost") is a derivative of the root *catch* ("lov").

The original meaning of this word relates to hunting, trapping, and fishing. Hunters were earlier called *trappers* ("lovtsy"). ("If there are beavers, there will be trappers." "The wild beast runs into the trapper.")

The hunting dogs were called trapping dogs, for example, beagles. Specially trained hunting birds—falcons and peregrines—were called trapping birds. The ability of these animals to catch the prey, to intercept it, to jump on the prey, and to seize hold of it was called *trapping skill* ("lovkost").

With time, the applicability of the word dexterity widened and included humans. However, its meaning has not changed. Dexterity still refers to quickness, agility, flexibility, and skillfulness of our body.

A great definition for the word "dexterity" is given by V. Dahl in his *Thesaurus*.

According to Dahl, dexterous means "harmonious in movements." And this is probably the most precise definition. Indeed, the harmony of movements defines a dexterous jumper, rider, or runner. Indeed, the ability to harmonize many small movements of arms, legs, and body into a whole movement providing the best result is dexterity.

I disagree with the definition by Dahl cited by Brazhnin. "Harmony in movements" is something characterizing good coordination in general, but good coordination and dexterity are obviously different. In order to be a skilled endurance walker one needs to have ideal motor coordination. But is there any dexterity? Perfect general coordination, "harmony in movements," is necessary for a sprinter, for a long-distance swimmer, and for a participant of team performance in rhythmic gymnastics. But the word *dexterity* does not fit these movements. In the sentences "He dexterously ran 1,000 meters" or "She dexterously swam the distance," the word *dexterously* is obviously misused, and further in the book, we are going to see why.

On the other hand, judging movements as harmonious is to a large extent subjective. I may think that Petrov is more harmonious whereas you prefer Sergeev, and it is as hard to agree on as which brand of ice cream tastes better. For a scientific definition, we need something more precise.

First of all, let us agree on the following. Dexterity, as we have already established, is a very complex psychophysical phenomenon. Folk wisdom, which created through the ages such language notions as bravery, pride, stinginess, and endurance, also separated a group of features into something called dexterity and gave it this name. To use just one word for this complex is practical, because its components frequently belong together and definitely have some kind of internal relationship. However, such separation and unification under one name is conventional. One cannot "discover" dexterity as it was possible to discover the function of the pancreas and the centers of speech in the brain. One cannot expect that dissecting a body and examining muscles, joints, and other structures under a microscope will reveal dexterity. The idea of discovering dexterity with new, sophisticated devices is as naive as the feelings of the simple-minded peasant who was fascinated that the astronomers had been able to discover the names of the stars by observing them through telescopes. One can study to any degree of precision all possible *features of dexterity*, but an agreement on what is going to be termed dexterity, what is going to be included in this notion, should be reached in advance, even with the inevitable conventionality and arbitrariness.

The definition of dexterity should *not be discovered but built*. In order to minimize conventionality and arbitrariness, one must follow certain general rules.

First, a correctly built definition of a notion such as dexterity should match as closely as possible its common usage in the language. The feeling for one's native language is very highly developed in every human, and he will immediately sense any false usage. The scientific definition should also be built in such a way that it precisely fits the imprecise but basically quite clear understanding of the word that is present in everyone.

Second, another requirement of the definition is that it should *give opportunity to detect dexterity and discern it* quickly and unambiguously from everything else that is not dexterity. We need to tie a thread to the notion of dexterity so that it can be pulled out for scrutiny at any time and so that we are sure that the thread will pull out only dexterity and not something else.

Third, a scientific definition is considered good if it helps one to penetrate the intrinsic nature of a phenomenon. It should *follow a general scientific theory* and help further develop the theory. Such a definition would be scientifically valuable, and its successful construction could by itself be a valuable contribution to science.

I reach a general definition of dexterity only in the final essay where we summarize all the essential and necessary signs of this capacity. For now, we will suggest a preliminary definition, one that complies at least with the first two requirements.

Throughout the following exposition, we should be able to detect always and precisely whether what is being discussed is dexterity or not.

The fable and nonfable examples already have something in common among them: In each example, we saw a quick and successful solution to a complex motor problem.

Let us take a couple of examples from physical culture and sports. Downhill skiing and slalom make high demands on a skier's dexterity. What is the difference between slalom and plain cross-country skiing, which does not require any particular dexterity? It is in a conglomerate of unexpected, unique complications in the external situation, in a quick succesion of motor tasks that are all unlike each other. A close analogy is presented by cross-country skiing across a complex terrain. Here, in contrast to slalom, each participant is free to choose not only different methods of overcoming the obstacles but also to run with one's unique style. This sport is also fully built on dexterity.

The common feature in all the examples becomes clearer. In all of them, dexterity is in *finding a motor solution for any situation and in any condition*. This feature is the essence of dexterity; it is what makes it different from simple harmony in movements. It is clear now why a sprinter or long-distance swimmer

FIG. 7.

22

does not need dexterity. In their activities, there are no unexpected complications of the motor task or of the external conditions that would require motor dexterity.

Let us use another way, similar to a well-known game where one of the players hides an object, and the other one must find it. The second player is guided to the hiding place with words like *cool, cold,* and *freezing* as he walks away from the hidden thing and *warm* and *hot* as he approaches it. Let us consider certain types of movements, indicating which of them have higher demand for dexterity.

Walking along a sidewalk? Cold. Walking with a load, walking when tired, walking when in a hurry, or walking along a muddy road? All of them, cold. Crossing a street with heavy traffic? Warmer. Walking with a cup of coffee or with a bowl of hot soup? Very hot.

Running along a track? Cold. Running in a competition in which victory is achieved not only by speed but also by tactics? Warmer. Running in place? Very cold. Barrier running? Warmer. Running across a swamp, over digs and holes? Hot. Running under enemy fire? Always very hot.

There are many more examples in the book, but everywhere, we see the same thing: *Demand for dexterity is not in the movements themselves but in the surrounding conditions.* There is no movement that would not place high demands on dexterity, given appropriate conditions. The conditions increase the complexity of a motor task or demand the emergence of an absolutely new motor task requiring motor wits. Walking on the floor does not require dexterity whereas walking on a rope does because it is much harder to walk on a rope successfully.

This aspect of motor wits, which is likely to be most important and characteristic for dexterity, is reflected in language. When a motor task in complicated and must be solved not straightforwardly but with motor dexterity, we say *izlovchitsya, prilovchitsya* ("to contrive"). When force does not help, *ulovka* ("a trick") does. When we master a motor skill and, with its help, overcome a complicated motor task, we say that we *nalovchilis* ("became proficient"). In all cases in which motor initiative or adjustment is required, there is a certain *tuning of the movements to an emergent task,* and the language finds an expression having the same root (*lov*) as the word *dexterity.*

Analysis of the complex capacity of dexterity and scientific reconnaissance into this important but poorly developed area will require deep analysis of the basis of motor control. In the next essay, we will learn the structure of our apparatus of movements and the *physiological principles of control* of movements in our body. Essay 3 is dedicated to the development of movements in the process of evolution. The general fact is that any complex event of life can be understood only from knowing the history of its emergence and development. For movements, in particular, there is a clear and precise developmental succession from animals to humans that influenced the way we control our movements. From there, I move to the *construction* of movements in humans (essay 4), and to successive *levels of motor control* for more and more complex human movements (essay 5). We then show the reader the physiological basis of control and of motor skill and the dynamics of skill development (essay 6). Finally, in the last essay we *meticulously and carefully scrutinize the notion of dexterity* according to all the accumulated material, to analyze the problem of its exercisability, and to give it a detailed definition.

I have tried to write in an easily readable accessible style. Particular attention was paid to explanations of all the terms when they are first used. I have also tried to develop the main idea methodically and successively, as is done in geometry. How successful I have been is for the reader to determine. However, because objectively the theme is not simple and contains numerous facts that are new for the reader who is not a neurophysiologist, I ask the reader to read the book in the order in which it was written without skipping any parts. Otherwise, some passages will naturally be unclear or confusing and will hinder correct understanding of the separate ideas and of the book as a whole.

And now—forward!

On Motor Control

In order to understand the physiological nature of the motor capacity called dexterity, one must first understand how movements are controlled in the human body. This seemingly natural and simple thing—control of movements, or as it is addressed in physiology, motor coordination, when analyzed by precise scientific methods—appears to be a complex and large enterprise that requires collective, organized participation of many physiological mechanisms.

In essay 3, we will see the reasons for the long process of the evolution and complication of this system and will discover how and by what means this development proceeded. First, however, we would like to answer questions which naturally arise: What are the reasons for this complex organization? What makes control of our body movements complex?

THE RICHNESS OF MOBILITY
OF HUMAN MOVEMENT ORGANS

Human movement apparatus, called the skeletal-articular-muscular system, has an unusually rich mobility. The main supporting structure of the body is the trunk with the neck, or, in essence, the vertebral column with its 25 intervertebral links and associated muscular apparatus. It is capable of various, nearly snakelike bends, twists, and winds. The human neck is far less impressive in its flexibility and mobility than are the necks of giraffes, ostriches, or swans, but it is not worse in providing accuracy and stability in shifts and turns of the

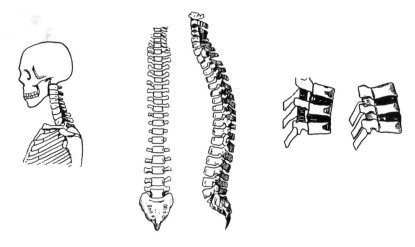

FIG. 1. *Left*–Cervical part of the vertebral column. *Center*–Human vertebral column from the front and from the left (intervertebral cartilage disks are not shown). *Right*–Mobility of the vertebrae.

FIG. 2. A schematic section of the hip ball joint.

central observation tower of the body, the head with its high-precision telescopes (eyes) and locators (ears).

Four multilink lever systems of extremities are connected to the trunk with ball-and-socket joints, which have a highly versatile ability to move. In humans, the joints of the upper extremities, which are most important for mobility, are connected to the body in a very mobile, loose way. These joints hang nearly exclusively on muscles. In fact, the major supporting bone of the arm, the scapula, is not connected to any of the other body bones.[1]

Let us first consider the simpler lower extremity. At the lower end of the long and firm femur is the knee, with its wide range of flexion and extension, which holds the record within the human body, about 140° of active and about

---

[1]Certainly, one cannot consider a contribution to its stability the fact that the scapula is connected by a small joint to the clavicle, which in turn connects to sternum, which in turn connects to the first rib, which in turn connects to the first vertebra!

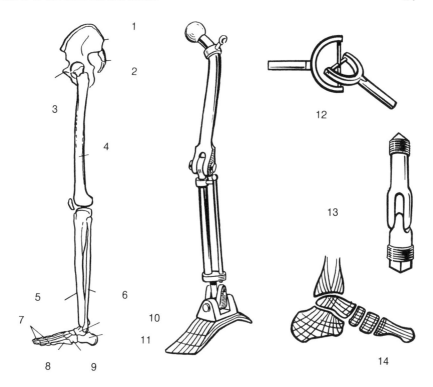

FIG. 3. *Left*–Skeleton of the human left leg. *Center*–Model reproducing joint mobility of the human leg. 1–Sacrum. 2–Coccyx. 3–Pelvic bones. 4–Thigh. 5–Tibia. 6–Fibula. 7–Phalanxes. 8–Metatarsus. 9–Tarsus. 10–Calcaneus. 11–Talus. 12–Hooke's hinge. 13–Joint with two degrees of freedom. 14–Schematic longitudinal section of the foot bones.

170° of passive motion range (for example, as when the knees bend in the squatting). *Active mobility* in a joint is due to the work of its own muscles, whereas *passive mobility* is due to other, external forces. A semibent knee joint allows small rotation of the tibia (by 40°–60°). At the leg's end there are two more joints, which are located, in humans, very close to each other and which create the ankle-joint system. It allows the foot to bend with respect to the tibia in all directions by 45°–55°, as with the well-known Hooke's joint.[2] The foot itself is an elastic arch consisting of numerous bones that is perfectly suited for bearing half of the weight of the body and, during running and jumping, for resisting strains that correspond to five or six times the body weight. However, its active mobility is nearly nonexistent. In animals that are "fed by their legs,"

---

[2]Such Hooke's or Cardan's joints are used, for example, in vehicles for connecting the fixed body of the transmission box to the wheel-bearing suspension, which is in turn connected to the springs and, therefore, should be mobile.

like wolves, tigers, and dogs and in fast, slender runners, like horses and deer, the question of which of the pairs of the extremities is more important for survival is not that obvious. The foot is transformed into a chain of flexibly suspended elements consisting, as in the horse, of four consecutive links actively participating in walking and running.

The upper links of human arms are not that different in their construction from those of animals. Only the ball-and-socket shoulder joint in humans is much more mobile. It allows wide movements sideways that are impossible, for example, in dogs and horses. Clear advantages of the human arm start below the elbow. The human arm, in close cooperation with and under control of the brain, introduced *labor* into Earth life. Labor itself, however, also introduced numerous changes and improvements into the arm structure. Only humans and apes have the ability to *pronate* and *supinate* the forearm and the hand. These are the movements we use when opening a door with the key or when winding the clock. The total range of motion of these movements is over 180°. The link between the forearm and the hand (the wrist joint) has its own two types of mobility, up-and-down mobility by 170° and right-and-left mobility by 60°. These two directions, together with pronation–supination, are equivalent to having the hand suspended on another ball-and-socket joint following the shoul-

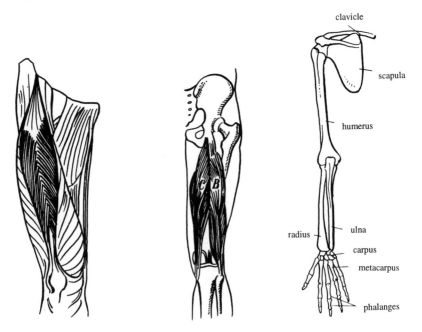

FIG. 4. *Left*–Muscles of the anterior thigh surface, with the rectus femoris, a knee extensor, singled out. *Center*–Muscles of the posterior thigh surface, with hip and knee flexors singled out: B–musculus biceps femoris; C–musculus semitendinosus. *Right*–Skeleton of the human left arm (posterior view).

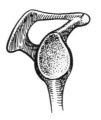

FIG. 5. Joint surfaces of the ball shoulder joint: *left*–the scapula surface; *right*–the shoulder surface.

der joint. According to the theory of mechanics, two such consecutively connected joints plus the elbow joint (flexion and extension in the elbow) not only give the hand the capability of taking any orientation and location in the accessible environment but also let it do so with a variety of positions of the intermediate links, shoulder, and forearm. Tightly grab a static handle or ledge. You will see that you can grab objects of virtually any shape and orientation and you will still be able to move the elbow, that is, to displace the shoulder and the forearm without moving the body or the scapula.

The skeleton of the hand is by itself a fine mosaic of 27 bones (not counting the volatile, miniscule bone elements). Here is a puzzle: Why do we need all 12 mobile joints between the small carpal and metacarpal bones if they all are ingrown into the thickness of the hand so that the fingers separate only from the beginning of the main phalanxes? Anyone who has shaken hands with someone who has paralysis of the hand would never ask this question. He will always remember the difference between the rigid, curved board he touched and the flexible hands that he knows from the experience of shaking hands with healthy people. Because of the ability of the thumb to counterpose itself to the fingers (the so-called opposable thumb), which is present only in humans and monkeys, *the hand becomes an organ of grasping and firm holding.* There is no loop or handle to which the hand cannot automatically adjust with a stunning, almost waxlike plasticity. Fingers and the thumb, aside from other hand components, have 15 joints, and if one counts all separate directions of active mobility in both directions (so-called *degrees of freedom*), the fingers of one hand have 20 of them. In purposeful, adaptive finger movements, in their quickness, accuracy, and dexterity, humans are many times superior to the most developed closely related animals. The flexible and rich

FIG. 6. *Left*–Limits of hand flexion and extension. *Right*–Wrist abduction and adduction.

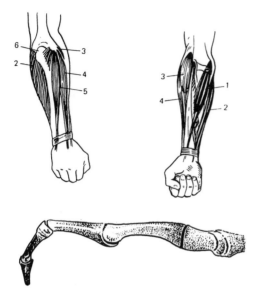

FIG. 7. Forearm muscles controlling
the wrist: 1, 2–radial and ulnar wrist
flexors; 3, 4–radial wrist extensors;
5–ulnar wrist extensors; 6–m.
brachioradialis.

FIG. 8. Metacarpal and phalangeal
bones of the middle finger.

mobility of the wrist, the base for the fingers and the thumb, makes the human
hand a brilliant tool deserving of the brain of its owner.

ON THE MOVEMENTS OF TONGUE AND EYES

Is there anything worth our attention to mobility, aside from the briefly discussed
properties of trunk, extremities, and neck? In quick and agile runners and jumpers
like foxes, beagles, squirrels, and kangaroos, it makes sense to note one more
important tool, the tail. But is there anything else in humans? The answer does
not usually immediately come to mind. Mounted on our head, however, we have
at least two devices whose rich and precise mobility is not less striking than that
of the hand and fingers. Let us consider them here.

Let us pass over the mandible with its strong and hardy muscles, a representative of the skeletal-articular-muscular apparatus within the head. Much
more interesting is the *glossopharingeal apparatus*. The tongue is basically a lump
of striated muscular fibers[3] that go in all directions. Its mobility is enormous
even in animals whose vocabulary may be limited to just one syllable, "moo,"
or "mee," or "miau." Such "vocabularies" fade when compared to the richness
of speech sounds produced by humans with an amazing, subconsciously controlled
precision and quickness by glossial and pharyngeal muscles in the *process of*

---

[3]As we see in essay 3, there are two types of muscular tissue in the bodies of vertebrates: very
small and weak smooth muscles located in the walls of internal organs and blood vessels, and striated
muscles that form all the voluntarily controlled muscular apparatus and also include the heart muscle,
quick, large, and strong.

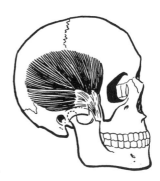

FIG. 9. M. temporalis.

speech. Unique, fine control of these soft organs that is required for human speech gave rise to the development of a particular, specialized cortical area in the left hemisphere of the human brain (discussed later). Injuries or strokes within this so-called Broca's area lead to a loss of the ability to speak, although voluntarily controlled mobility of the tongue and pharynx does not suffer. Note, by the way, that "speaking" birds like parrots do not have anything even resembling the speech area in the brain.

Another apparatus with an amazing mobility, whose complexity and vital importance are virtually unknown to many of us, is the eyes, a pair of eyeballs forming the organs of vision. The human apparatus of vision contains: (a) six pairs of muscles providing for concordant eye rotations when tracking an object; (b) two pairs of muscles that control the eye lens, the cornea (for those who like photography, we may say that these two muscular pairs focus the eyes); (c) two pairs of very thin and fragile muscles that control pupil dilation and contraction (once again, in the language of photography, these muscles control diaphragm of the objective depending on brightness of the scene); and (d) two pairs of muscles opening and closing the eyelids. These 24 muscles work in a precise coordination from early morning till late at night. Let us note that they work absolutely subconsciously and that up to 75% of their work proceeds without voluntary control. One third of the muscles (the second and third groups just described) do not allow any voluntary intervention into their work. It is easy to imagine that if all these two dozens of muscles required conscious attention as, for example, work of an observer using numerous gauges, this would require so much work that there would be no chance to control voluntary movements of other organs. Let us imagine, for a moment, a man who is passionately describing his feelings to an adored beauty while taking care that his eye movements do not lose the object of his feelings in the heat of the confession or do not see a poorly outlined spot in the place of the beautiful face. If we also remember the importance of correct eyeball movements for the assessment of distance to objects, the poor sufferer would have to concentrate all of his attention on eye movements if he did not want to hit the object of his passion while gesticulating or kiss an umbrella handle rather than the beautiful hand.

The collective work (or, as we say in physiology, *synergy*) of the eye muscular apparatus bears a very complex and important responsibility. According to the very deep and precise expression of the father of Russian physiology, I. M. Sechenov, we do *not just see* with our eyes but we *look*. In fact, the whole act of vision is active from the very beginning to the very end: we search with our eyes for an interesting object and track it by placing its image into the most sensitive and sharp area of the retina; we assess distance to an object based on strain in the eye muscles; we scan the object, "feel" it with our gaze, as if there were invisible tentacles stretching from the eyes to the object (as ancient scientists thought was the case).

In the process of looking, our eyes (a) move in any direction following a moving object; (b) move in a very coordinated fashion, either exactly parallel to each other or slowly diverging or converging; (c) purposefully converge in order to eliminate object doubling and to assess distance to an object (stereoscopic vision); (d) simultaneously focus the cornea; (e) at the same time, control the width of the pupil, providing the neural elements of the retina with the exact amount of light necessary for optimally sharp vision; and (f) as has been already noted, actively scan and feel the objects, lead the gaze along the lines in a book, and so forth. All these movements are performed simultaneously and concordantly, without confusing each other; very automatically but not in a machinelike manner; not according to an unchangeable standard, but with a highly developed and dexterous tuning.

THE MAIN DIFFICULTIES IN MOTOR CONTROL

In this brief survey of the mobile parts of our body, we have, only in our extremities and head-mounted devices, close to a hundred directions and types of mobility (degrees of freedom). If we add the snakelike flexibility of our neck and trunk, the resulting number is enormous. The reader can probably sense already the difficulty of control of such a multifaceted mobility, but probably does not yet realize what the major problem is. Let us look methodically into all the difficulties and try to reveal the most challenging ones.

If one takes into account that different movements in many joints take place simultaneously and that such unified movements as looking, walking, running, and throwing proceed in the form of finely tuned, cooperative synergies, one of the difficulties becomes immediately obvious in its full extent. How enormous would be the distribution of attention if all the elements of such complex movements were controlled separately with close attention to each of them! In some patients with brain injury resulting from tumor removal from certain brain areas, one can see the loss of the ability to control complex movements voluntarily. Such patients are nearly motionless; even the simplest movements, such as lifting an arm, require an enormous concentration of will and attention. Each of us, after being instructed to lift an arm, will immediately, involuntarily bring it down as a very natural movement. In patients with brain injuries, the lifted arm remains suspended. The patient must notice it and issue a special command for the arm to lower. In physiology, it is not infrequent that one of the complex autonomic systems that makes our life easier and that is vitally important is not noticed, is considered as something natural, until one sees a pathology in which this system ceases to function. Only in these cases does the great importance of such an intact system become brightly illumined and apparent. This happened with the described problem of distribution of attention among the dozens and hundreds of types of mobility and their precise coordination.

This is the first problem of controlling the motor apparatus of our body, but it is far from being the most important one.

The second, more serious problem is not that obvious at a first glance. It becomes more apparent if we turned attention from the human body to machines constructed by human hands. There are numerous machines that have diverse and versatile mobility, for example, a mobile crane derrick with a rotating and bending jib and machines with keyboards like typewriters and pianos. There is always, however, a human being by the side of these machines who with his movements continuously controls all the movements of the machines, with separate keys or levers. Thus, these machines are in fact groups of simpler machines. Movements of the simple subcomponents, a key in a typewriter connected to a lever of a certain letter or one of the ballbearings of the crane jib, are very simple and uniform. The amazing part in the functioning of these machines is the skill and dexterity of the operator, in his ability to perform many accurate and correct movements simultaneously. Thus, we have turned from machines back to the human being with the human's amazing capability of coordinated simultaneous movements in all the degrees of freedom. Let us now turn, for comparison, to automatic machines that work without continuous human control.

The world of automatic machines presents us with a stunning fact. Contemporary technology created machines of amazing complexity that are able by themselves, without human intervention, to perform various and quite complicated jobs. A large printing machine makes 50,000–100,000 newspaper copies in an hour, printing simultaneously on both sides of the paper, using two colors, collating the prints, and, if necessary, binding them. Such a machine is as big as a two-story house and contains dozens of shafts and cylinders with many hundreds of levers and pinions. A large multivalved, oil diesel engine is another example of a giant, powerful machine with hundreds of moving parts, racks, and pinions. Among the automatic machines, there are ones that can process, dry, and print films; make bottles; weave carpets with complex patterns; and so forth.

The most amazing thing is that all these huge machines with all the variety of their mobile parts have just *one degree of freedom*; that is, in technological language, they have *forced movement*. This term means that each moving point, each segment of the levers, each wheel or bearing moves along the same, precisely defined path. The shape of this path may be quite different; some of the components may move along a curved path, whereas others move along straight lines, and still others move along ovals, and so on; each and every point, however, never leaves its predefined trajectory. So, although very complex in their appearance and structure, machines have the simplest possible *mobility*. Automatic machines having parts with two degrees of freedom are very few (e.g., centrifugal controllers in steam engines). At the time of this writing, no artificial device has exceeded two degrees of freedom.

WHAT ARE TWO AND THREE DEGREES OF FREEDOM?

This reticence on the part of the engineers and designers is easy to explain. In machines with forced movement of all the parts, each point of the mechanism follows one and the same, unchangeable trajectory. Even if one of the parts was designed to have *two degrees of freedom*, it still would not have two or several possible trajectories. Instead this particular part would have the capability to wander across a *surface*, for example, the surface of a plane or the surface of a sphere. What is important, the part would be able to wander in any possible way, along any path or trajectory, with the only requirement not to leave the surface. If I take a pen and start drawing on a piece of paper, no matter how peculiar the figures I draw, I will never exceed the limitations imposed by two degrees of freedom if the contact between the tip of the pen and the paper remains unbroken. Therefore, this transition from one to two degrees of freedom means a huge qualitative leap from a single, exactly defined path, a trajectory, to an *infinite*, and quite arbitrary, *variety* of such paths. There are two degrees of freedom in the hand with respect to the forearm. Fix your right forearm in a stationary position, for example, firmly on a table, and form a pointer with the extended index finger, like those on road signs. You can still draw an unlimited number of shapes and figures in the air with the fingertip.

Three degrees of freedom provide even more possibilities, although the qualitative leap is not as great as between one to two degrees of freedom. A point on a body or an element of a machine with three degrees of freedom can move arbitrarily in a limited *section of space* (for example, this kind of mobility is present in a fingertip of a free arm). Let us clarify that, according to the laws of geometry, an absolutely free point, for example, a snowflake in the air, cannot have more than three degrees of freedom. Three degrees of freedom mean for a tangible point the possibility to move absolutely freely in a section of space that is practically accessible.

This fact, somewhat unknown to the general public, creates an abyss between forced, one-degree-of-freedom movements and the mobility of parts with two or three degrees of freedom. It also explains why engineers try to avoid anything that goes beyond forced movements. Two degrees of freedom, as compared to one, mean that a moving point or a part of a moving system attains *freedom of choice* of any of an infinite variety of accessible trajectories. Human beings are able *to make a choice* within the multitude of accessible trajectories and to explain the choice of a most appropriate trajectory for a given situation. But how can one force a machine to make a choice? It is important to note that even now there are an increasing number of machines which are able to make automatic choice (for example, various sorting or quality-control machines). The most common example is the public telephone containing a simple device that can quickly and sensitively distinguish between real and counterfeit ten-kopeck coins.

First, it is very important, for the purposes of this book, that all machines of this kind have a sensory organ whose readings lead the machine in making a choice. For example, in machines that sort cigars by their color, the role of the sensory organ is played by a photoelectric element sensitive to different hues of brown. Second, with very rare exceptions, these machines can distinguish between only a few possibilities, a coin lighter or heavier than normal, a cigar lighter or darker than the sample, and so forth. Therefore, these machines do not represent two degrees of freedom, which immediately gives the system an infinite multitude of options. Actually there is an amazing machine called a gyropilot, or automatic pilot. Such machines are mounted on large ships and represent a large and accurate compass (a gyrocompass) connected to powerful engines that control the rudder. In a gyrocompass, the sensory organ is the compass itself, and the ship that has two degrees of freedom (sea surface) automatically follows only one route defined by the compass. This is the only example of a machine that performs a *continuous choice* of path in the presence of actual two degrees of freedom that I was able to find. This example is very interesting because it clearly demonstrates that choice of a path can be performed only on the basis of continuous watching, that is, how the movements proceed according to the dictates of a vigilant "sensory organ." The example also clearly illustrates another difficulty in controlling the motor apparatus of our body, which we are going to analyze next.

HOW TO OVERCOME EXCESSIVE DEGREES OF FREEDOM?

The fact that just two degrees of freedom in a machine has become possible only during the technical revolution of the 20th century, at a time when we have mastered flying, television, and atomic energy, shows that this is not a simple matter. In human and animal bodies, however, joints with two degrees of freedom are among the relatively simple. All of the previous review has shown the boundless generosity of the body, which scatters dozens or even hundreds of degrees of freedom all over its limbs. We have already established that even in the case of only two degrees of freedom, choice of one or another definite trajectory is possible only when the movement is closely controlled by the sensory organs. Apparently, the immense richness of the moving organs, whose boundlessness we are just beginning to realize, can be mastered and used for our needs rather than leading to total anarchy only if each and every degree of freedom is tamed and bridled by a specialized sensory system that closely monitors it. The complexity of control necessitated by the variety of movable joints fades when compared to the second complication—the problem of overcoming the immense redundancy of the degrees of freedom that fill our bodies.

This complication, similarly to the first one, is represented by impressive examples in the area of pathological changes. We have already mentioned that many of the very complex physiological systems of a healthy organism escaped attention of scientists until they saw cases in which a system stopped functioning normally. This oversight is an unfortunate feature of our mentality: We see the importance of a system in the everyday life only by observing catastrophic consequences of its malfunctioning.

There is a very grave spinal cord disease related to syphilis. It leads to pathological changes in the conduction spinal systems that transmit muscular-articular sense. In the course of this disease (tabes dorsalis), a person loses the normal ability to know the position and movement of body parts with his eyes closed. The reader can conduct this simple experiment. With your eyes closed, ask another person to move your arm to a new position or your fingers slightly up or down. You will always be able to describe exactly what is happening with your arm or fingers. Moreover, what is particularly important, after looking at the arm or fingers, you will see that the posture corresponds exactly to how you imagined it. Sometime when your arm or leg "falls asleep," try to perform the same experiment before the sensitivity returns (before the prickles start). You will be greatly surprised to find that you have no idea where your "sleeping" limb is and, after opening your eyes, that it is positioned quite differently from what you expected.

Patients with tabes dorsalis experience a similar but much more serious condition. Blindfold such a patient, lift his arm, and ask him to keep the arm in the same position. The arm will fatigue and slowly and involuntarily lower after a minute or two. The patient will be sure that the arm is still high over the head and will be very much surprised when the blindfold is removed.

Without actually seeing these patients, it is hard to imagine how disrupted all their voluntary movements are. A patient with tabes dorsalis either cannot walk at all or walks with enormous effort, very slowly, using crutches, and only with open eyes. Vision substitutes, to a certain degree, the lost muscular-articular sense, taking the responsibility of the "sensory organ" discussed earlier. However, because its properties are different, vision does a very poor job. The ability to write is destroyed completely; the hands tremble with any attempt to do something; the more the patient tries to control them and calm them, the more they dance around.

Tabes dorsalis provided physicians with an insight into the complexity of the problem of controlling movements and what can happen when there is no mechanism for controlling the redundant degrees of freedom of our body. Let us mention that patients with tabes dorsalis do not have even a trace of paralysis; their muscle force is normal and, with open eyes, they are able to make any elementary movement in any of the joints. They have intact passive mobility (joint motion) and active mobility (muscle work), but the controllability of the motor apparatus is dramatically disrupted. The coachman was wounded and fell off the coach box; the four horses, having lost the control mechanism, rush the coach, full of frightened passengers, without a road or direction.

Apparently, when the body is healthy its sensory organs provide enough guarantees against such problems. On the other hand, the enormously excessive degrees of freedom, apparently give us considerable advantages.

Let us consider examples of instruments made by human hands. In many cases a more flexible instrument, which is certainly much more challenging to work with, has unquestionable advantages in its flexibility and fine results. An experienced master will always prefer an instrument with more degrees of freedom, that is, with fewer rails and props, than an instrument that might be easier to use but that also constrains the worker.

In the area of sports, the bicycle is an example. A bicycle is harder to control than a tricycle, but anyone who has mastered a bicycle will probably never want to ride a tricycle again. The bicycle is preferred, not because it is lighter, but because, in the hands of an experienced rider, it is more flexible and maneuverable, and, although this sounds strange, more stable than the tricycle. Another similar example is presented by skates: light children's skates with their wide blades are less flexible and maneuverable than the sharp-bladed, more challenging Norwegian running skates.

As for musical instruments, it is rather intriguing that relatively simple stringed instruments like balalaika have frets, which help a novice not to play out of tune. A more elaborate instrument of the same kind, a violin, does not have frets, and no maestro violinist would agree to play a violin with frets. The master does not need external "crutches" because he is more confident in his *hearing*, a sensory organ that always represents the basic reliable means of overcoming the excessive degrees of freedom.

Nature, as we have seen, went along the same route, avoiding frets and props in the movement apparatus and generously scattering around degrees of freedom. Nature does not make mistakes; and it did not make a mistake in this case, either.

PROBLEMS DUE TO MUSCLE ELASTICITY

We are rather close to giving a sufficiently complete answer to the opening question of this essay: What are the factors that make control of our motor apparatus, that we know from childhood, so complicated? It is necessary, however,

FIG. 10. Direction of forces in a muscle.

to mention one more complicating factor (complication three) that gives rise to new problems in controlling movements of the body. This complication is due to the *elastic properties of the muscles*.

In the next essay, we discuss the basic features of the human *engine*, the striated muscle, and consider its properties in more detail. Here, we are just going to touch on these properties to the extent necessary for the analysis of the main thesis of this essay.

Muscles of our motor apparatus deserve the name of *tissue* probably more than any other formations in our body. In fact, muscle tissue, which is similar to any tissue, consists of thin threads (muscular fibers); however, these threads do not interweave (with the exception of the heart muscle) but run parallel to each other like well-brushed hair. Extremely thin threads of skeletal muscles are not thicker than fine woman's hair and are elastic like rubber. Each of these fibers can *contract* under the influence of the muscle nerve, that is, become shorter (by 20%–30%) and stiffer, that is, more resistant to stretch. There are some differences between various muscle fibers, like the differences between different rubber tubes, thicker and thinner, stiffer and softer, and so forth, but these are not crucial. All the skeletal muscles consist of hundreds of such muscle fibers; and each fiber is an *elementary engine*. A whole, large muscle, for example, the biceps of the arm, can therefore be considered a multivalve machine with parallel cylinders. The only means for voluntary movements and active work in the body are these peculiar, elastic, contracting threads, multiplied by hundreds and thousands and connected from all sides to all possible mobile parts of the body.

It may seem that the particular structure of an engine moving a machine or a press is not of any particular importance. If it provides the necessary speed and power, its structure and source of energy supply, whether oil, gasoline, electricity, or steam, does not matter. This happens not to be the case. The unique properties of muscle fiber as the universal engine in the body are such that they cannot be ignored. The major problem in using a striated fiber as an engine is in that it *pulls* the bones (muscular fibers cannot push because of their softness), and the pulling force is *not stable and precise but elastic*.

The fact that muscle fibers can produce work in only one direction, that is, pull but not push, is not that unfortunate. Turning again to examples from

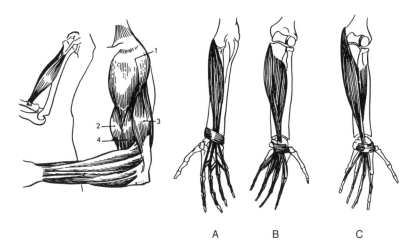

FIG. 11. *Left*–Muscles of the left shoulder: 1–deltoideus; 2–biceps; 3–triceps; 4–brachioradialis. *Above*–Separated biceps with its two heads. *Right*–Muscles controlling fingers: A–extensor digitorum communis, B–profundus, and C–sublimus.

technology, one finds that in an automobile engine, each cylinder can also work in only one direction; it can push but not pull. In machines, this disadvantage is overcome by placing at least two cylinders side by side; when one of them pushes, the other returns passively to position. Our joints have a similar apparatus, each of the directions of their mobility (which we have already agreed to call degree of freedom) is controlled by a pair of muscles with opposite directions of action, called *antagonist muscles*. For example, there are flexors and extensors of the elbow joint and flexors and extensors of fingers. When one of the muscles pulls the bone in its direction, the other muscle is passively stretched so that it is able to move the joint in the opposite direction. The mechanism is complicated by the *elastic resistance* of the muscular forces.

Let us imagine, for example, that the cylinders in an automobile engine are connected to the moving parts, not by strong metal shafts, but rather by elastic elements, such as spiral springs. Then, movements of the crankshaft will not closely and precisely follow movements in the cylinders but will depend on various other factors. If a car is moving downhill, the elastic spring will virtually not compress and will easily and quickly turn the crankshaft. If the car moves uphill, the cylinders may not even be able to move the crankshaft because all their power is used to compress the elastic connector. Smooth asphalt or viscous mud, tailwinds or head winds, and so on, will all be transferred from the wheels to the crankshaft that will do with the peripheral ends of the shafts whatever it wishes, whereas the central ends will move exactly in the rhythm of the engine. Maybe some of our female readers will prefer another example: Imagine that the horizontal shaft in a sewing machine, which connects the wheel to the

FIG. 12. Controlling movements of a heavy ball with two rubber bands. The lever is connected to the neck with a nonextendable cord to eliminate the effects of gravity.

leftmost box and transforms its rotation into up-and-down movements of the needle, is replaced with a rubber rod. If the cloth is thin and soft, the difference may not be noticed. If a seamstress starts sewing together two pieces of a heavy fabric, however, the needle will lodge and virtually stop moving. Although the seamstress may still be turning the wheel without noticing the difference, at some point, she sees that the machine is not sewing and removes the fabric. Unexpectedly, the shaft starts turning by itself, like a wound spring, and moves the needle up and down although the wheel is not turning. Let us leave the seamstress to treat her wounded finger and curse the stupid construction of the machine, and turn to a very simple experiment, which the reader can conduct. Attach to your belt a shaft with a load on its end, as shown in Figure 12. Now attach two long straps of rubber to the load. Take the free ends of the rubber straps into your hands and try to move the load accurately; for example, draw a square or your initials in the air. You will immediately see how hard the task is, how inaccurate the movements of the load are, and how erratically it behaves. Now close your eyes and ask another person how well you control the load without vision. Obviously the results will be quite discouraging, not much different from the movements of a patient with tabes dorsalis discussed earlier.

As stated and illustrated, control of movements with elastic attachments is very complex because the result will depend not only on the behavior of the engines but also on a number of other, uncontrolled factors. The engines may exert the same forces 10 consecutive times and cause 10 absolutely different movements. Control of such a system is possible *only if the system is continuously supervised by a sensory organ*; even then control requires considerable dexterity. Once again, the same principle that helped nature to overcome redundant degrees of freedom and even allowed a generous number of them to coexist, the principle of motor control based on sensory signals, is the saving principle that helps us out once again.

We may probably say that the third complication, the elastic properties of the muscles, is essentially quite similar to the previous complication. The fact that identical forces may in different trials lead to different movements means that the moving body does not display forced movement, that is, that *it has excessive degrees of freedom*. However, in this case, excessive degrees of freedom depend not on mobility of the body but on peculiarities of the forces acting on it. They should be differentiated and called *dynamic* (dynamics is the science of forces). Apparently, if the problem is solved in theory, there is not much difference between overcoming 100 *kinematic* degrees of freedom (kinematics is the science of mobility) or adding to them about 50 dynamic degrees of freedom.

WHAT IS MOTOR COORDINATION?

It is time to summarize the main conclusions of this essay. We have established that the control of the motor apparatus of our body is a complex, multifaceted problem that cannot be solved by the most sophisticated contemporary technology even in its most simplified version. Based on the nature of these complications, let us formulate an exhaustive definition of motor coordination: *Coordination is overcoming excessive degrees of freedom of our movement organs, that is, turning the movement organs into controllable systems.* As noted, the degrees of freedom can be both kinematic and dynamic.

Now, it is not hard to define the main principle that allows nature to assure control over skeletal-muscular moving apparatus, the principle that is being copied, with varying success, by the contemporary technology, the principle of motor control with sensory organs. Let us turn first, however, to one more example from technology, an example that suggests the best name for the principle. Let us discuss *precision artillery fire*.

A flying artillery shell is a body with a great amount of excessive degrees of freedom, resembling, in this respect, organs of the human body. Its movement in the air is far from being forced. Its flight is affected by changes in air density, wind, rising air flows, unavoidable imperfect location of its center of mass, and so on. Because of all these factors, even the most precise calculations and careful analysis of artillery tables cannot ensure its accurately hitting the target on the first attempt. Thus, a different approach is taken.

Somewhere, far from the artillery battery, there is an observer who communicates with the battery personnel by radio. The observer informs the battery personnel of the location of explosion of the first shell, how far it is from the target and in which direction. The commanding officer immediately translates this information into changes in the aim, and orders a second shot. It is followed by a second report from the observer (better, as a rule) and with new corrections. After the second correction, the aim is usually good enough so that real fire can start.

Let us use this good term for a similar situation in physiology, for the described principle of continuous motor adjustments based on information from sensory organs: *the principle of sensory corrections.* The role of the observer in artillery fire is played by different sensory organs of the body.

There is an interesting consequence of the principle of sensory corrections. It is common and customary to think that the *execution* of a voluntary movement is fully the responsibility of the motor systems of the body—muscles, as direct movers; motor nerves transferring motor impulses from the brain and spinal cord to the muscles; and brain motor centers as the source of the command for the motor impulses. On the contrary, the *sensory systems* of the body are not less busy than motor systems during execution of a movement. Continuous, corrective flows of signals are transmitted to the brain along sensory nerves of all possible modalities, including tactile, visual, muscular-articular, vestibular (from the ears, transmitting signals about the equilibrium), and others, informing the brain whether the movement has been initiated, whether it proceeds according to a plan, and whether corrections are necessary. During a movement, each contracting muscle excites some of the sensory mechanisms, which immediately inform the brain about it. Each burst of motor impulses directed *from the brain* to a muscle is a direct cause of another burst of impulses transmitted from sensory organs *to the brain.* Therefore, this inflow of sensory signals is tranformed into appropriate movement corrections; that is, the sensory signals become a cause of new motor impulses, corrected and appended, that rush from the *brain* to appropriate muscles. This closed, *circular* process is termed in physiology *reflex loop.* Damage to the loop at any point leads to total disruption of movements, as is corroborated by the rich material on diseases of the nervous system.

A few brief experiments by the reader convincingly illustrate how sensory correction of movements is performed and to what results it leads. Take a pen and write quickly on a piece of paper a row of the letter *m*, first with open eyes, then with closed eyes. You will not see a difference. Now, try the same with writing a word, for example, *coordination.* You will be successful again, but the difference becomes visible. Now, write the same word in block letters, again, first with the eyes open, then with the eyes closed. Finally, draw two small circles side by side and try to draw crosses inside the circles. I purposefully placed the tasks in an order corresponding to the decrease in accuracy of performance after visual corrections are switched off. The last task will certainly lead to total disaster unless you are exceptionally good at motor tasks and have practiced drawing with closed eyes. An analysis of the results of this simple experiment shows that the first task is virtually totally performed under control of the muscular-articular sensory apparatus and does not require visual control. The other tasks require more and more participation of visual control, and its elimination leads to deterioration of the movements.

It is also difficult to make accurate movements with cold hands, such as threading a needle or untying a knot. The problem here is not in the muscles because most of the muscles controlling finger movements are located in the forearm closer to the elbow, and therefore, are hidden in the sleeve. This fact is easily demonstrated by testing the muscle force with a dynamometer. A person can squeeze as strongly with cold hands as with warm hands. The cause of the motor deterioration is the weaker muscular-articular and tactile sensitivity in hands and fingers.

Each of us, who ties a necktie each morning, knows how confusing the operation is if done while looking in a mirror, unless we practice this skill while looking in a mirror. The reason is that the practiced movement is corrected by muscular-articular sensation, and interference of a strong, distracting visual control disrupts the well-practiced skill. This experiment is opposite of the first one, in which movements were disrupted by *switching off visual corrections*; here coordination is disrupted when *visual corrections are turned on*. As we will see in the remaining essays, there is a large number of well-practiced movement skills that break down under visual control.

MUSCULAR-ARTICULAR SENSE AND ITS ASSISTANTS

Muscular-articular sense is definitely the primary and most essential sense in most cases of motor control. All the various organs of this type of sensitivity are termed in physiology *the proprioceptive system*. (Proprioceptive sense means "sensing itself," that is, having a sense of one's own body). Sensory endings of proprioceptive organs are scattered all around the muscular fibers, tendons, and articular capsules. These endings (called *receptors*) send signals to the brain on the position of body links, joint angles, muscle forces, and so on.

The whole proprioceptive system is ruled by an organ that senses head position and movement in space, the *vestibular apparatus*, or ear labyrinth, which resides deep behind the temporal bone (in the inner ear on both sides). All the signals from this system give the brain exhaustive information on position of the body in space and also position and movement of different parts of the body. It is quite obvious that proprioception plays the first violin in sensory corrections and that its malfunctioning (as in the patients with tabes dorsalis) leads to the gravest and most poorly compensated disruptions of motor coordination.

The previous examples show that the proprioceptive system is not the only system controlling sensory corrections. Each type of sensitivity (perhaps even the solitary, confined tenant of the mouth, sense of taste) can be delegated proprioceptive responsibility. The central nervous system bases its decisions on expediency. If a certain sensory organ has in its repertoire certain sensory corrections that are best suited for a given movement, these organs are mobilized for providing corrections. Thus, all types of sensitivity sometimes play (to larger or smaller degrees) the role of *proprioceptors in a wide, functional meaning* of this term.

Vision is the most important sensory organ in humans. It participates in control of a huge variety of movements, mostly accurate hand movements, labor movements, and throwing movements requiring aiming (e.g., throwing at a target, shooting, soccer, tennis, etc.).

Hearing is less frequently mobilized by humans as a proprioceptive sense, but it is used together with other types of sensitivity by musicians, joiners, mechanics, assemblers, and so on. (Certainly, we do not mean here the execution of verbal commands.) In many animals, for example, in carnivores, hares, owls, and bats, hearing plays a dominant coordinative role. The same can be said about the sense of smell in many wild animals and hunting dogs.

Tactile sensitivity closely cooperates with vision and proprioception in most of the accurate body movements, in a large number of labor movements, and so forth. It is impossible to find the beginning and the end in the unbreakable union of these three types of sensitivity, to separate their roles in the correction of complex movements. Everyone knows how crucially important good tactile sensitivity is for surgeons, sculptors, tailors, grinders, and others. For people who are blind, tactile and proprioceptive sensitivity plays the most essential role in controlling all accessible movements.

In the next essays, we are going to discuss the differences between the combinations of sensitivity that subserve various motor tasks and various movement structures. These combinations provide a key to the correct physiological classification and systematization of movements. First, however, we need to tell the reader how movements emerged and developed in animals and humans.

The next essay will be devoted to this *history of movements*.

On the Origin of Movements

THE GREAT COMPETITION OF LIFE

No natural phenomenon can be understood without carefully considering how it emerged. The main reason is that everything in the world is a chain of causes and consequences, and most important, everything continuously changes, develops, and dies. Each fact in the world has its own biography, the study of which is vital for discussing that fact. Even among people, from the very best to the very worst representatives of humanity to understand the creations of a great poet, one needs to know the story of his life; in order to pronounce a fair sentence for a thief, one must analyze his miserable biography.

Everything lives and changes. Only 200 years ago, the universe itself was considered an embodiment of eternity and invariability. In fact, it is full of life and changing literally in front of our eyes. During the short life of astronomy, we have witnessed the birth of young, giant red stars, growing and acquiring brilliance. The photographic plates of the observatories show elderly stars that have already lived through their 20 billion years, ruby dwarfs, cooling and shrinking like hot metal in a foundry. Animate nature is even more replete with changes, and these changes help us understand the concealed meaning of events, because they are closer to us and we feel being a part of them. Thanks to works of the great founders of contemporary biology, we are aware of one of the major driving forces of these perpetual changes in nature. We know that these changes represent continuous development, continuous movement forward, and this development takes place in conditions of a harsh, merciless *struggle for life*. All the

45

FIG. 1. Evolution of life.

history of animate nature is a kind of competition among species trying to survive. In this competition everything weak and unsuccessful is mercilessly thrown away. All of the accidental, fortunate finds and "inventions" of nature that strengthen and support their owner cause the owner to win at this worldwide competition and eventually to become one of its numerous participants. We will see inventions from across nature, for example, the elongated body shape, striated muscles, and the pyramidal brain system, and how the owners of these biological novelties subjugated animals with outdated body structures and became, at various times, rulers of the animal kingdom. In the area of movements, we will be able to demonstrate how important such "technological revolutions" were for the victorious development of one or another class of animals and how each of these innovations led animals toward higher motor adaptability, better coordination, higher resourcefulness, quickness, and accuracy of movements, or, in other words, in the direction of increased motor dexterity.

Two basic sources of information provide insight into the history of animal life. The first one, the actual documentation about prehistoric life forms in the form of ancient fragments found during excavations of the Earth's layers, is most direct and reliable, but unfortunately, many of the organs of organisms that died long ago could not have survived even a fraction of the millenia that separate us from their owners. We would be limited to making only guesses concerning these organs if not for the second source of information, which we are going to consider now.

It was noticed a long time ago that highly developed animals demonstrate higher variability over the centuries. The higher mammals compose one of the youngest subclasses of animals on Earth, but they have managed to change dramatically during a few hundreds of the thousands of years of their existence, a very small time period in the framework of Earth history. During this time, a small hoofed animal, the size of a dog, the protohyppus, transformed into our friend and companion, the horse. Dogs changed even faster. As far as human beings are concerned, only several tens of thousands of years ago, during the glacier epochs, humans were quite different from contemporary humans in brain volume, facial features, and shape of the extremities. On the other hand, simple organisms stay virtually unchanged during millions of centuries. Even in the present time, some mollusks (cuttlefish) and crustacea do not differ considerably from fossils dating back to the Earth's adolescence. All these facts help us substitute actual history with the material provided by *comparative anatomy and comparative physiology* of animals. In fact, in all the cases, when we are able to compare data from both sources, they precisely correspond to and support each other. So, let us see what these two comparative sciences can reveal about the *origin and development of movements on Earth*. Let us start with two brief pieces of information that will cast some light on the subject.

THE SCALE AND THE CAST

Let us start with the scale. According to estimations by scientists, Earth has been in existence for about 2 billion years; life on Earth, starting from its simplest forms, has been here for approximately half this time. Neither of these numbers says anything to our imagination. Let us try a different approach.

In order to get a practical drawing of Earth, a geographical map, the cartographer usually draws the map smaller compared to the actual size of the Earth,

FIG. 2. Some scales.

reducing it by a factor of 10, 50, or 100 million. *Let us draw the history of Earth on a scale of 1:50,000,000*, where 100 years corresponds nearly exactly to 1 minute. Human life is 40–45 seconds long.

So, on this scale, the Earth is only 40 "years" old. It has quite a few wrinkles, huge mountain ridges, and white hair of Arctic and Antarctic snow. Perhaps it has more wrinkles and white hair than it should at the age of 40, but consider that its life was not easy; the whole history of great geological changes, shifts of seas and mountains, and volcanic activity witness its hardships. At the conception of the first glimpses of animate life, Earth is a 20-year-old woman, the best age for childbearing.

If we now make a drawing of mammals' closest relatives, vertebrates, the oldest representatives, *prehistoric fish*, emerged on Earth somewhere in the middle of the total time of animal life, about 10 "years" ago. About 2–4 "years" ago, the Earth was still ruled by reptiles, huge lizards, about which we will talk later.

The oldest *mammals* appeared on Earth not more than 2–3 "years" ago; the Earth gave birth to them as a middle-aged woman, spending the best 10 years of her life nursing invertebrates, worms, and mollusks. The highest mammals, carnivores, highly developed hoofed animals, and others have been in existence for only several "months." About 2 "weeks" ago, the first apes emerged. The oldest human being who deserves the name is not more than a "week" old. How insignificant are these time intervals compared to the total age of life on Earth!

"Yesterday" or "the day before yesterday" (150,000–300,000 years ago), there was terrible weather on Earth. The climate became very cold, and huge areas became covered with ice. Scientists call this the glacier period. At that time, 1 or 2 "days" ago, there appeared the first humans who lived in caves and who battled with stone axes and carefully preserved in their caves an accidentally found fire. The oldest of the truly historic documents—Egyptian and Assyrian inscriptions, the Great Pyramids, and the origins of Chinese history—date back slightly more than 1 "hour." The Christian epoch is about 20 "minutes" old, and the Renaissance (after the terrible stagnation of the middle ages) and the discovery of America are 4–5 "minutes" old. Our mind has been trying to penetrate the meaning of things and the history of 40 Earth "years" for not more than the last 5 "minutes." Should we expect to accomplish much during such a short time?

The second group of facts that will help in understanding the development of movement is a table of large classes into which scientists classify the animal kingdom, from the most ancient and simple organisms to the most highly developed animals. These classes are enumerated in Table 1 and discussed in more detail later.

TABLE 1
Classes of the Animal Kingdom

Class	Description/Examples	Notes
1. Protozoa	Unicellular, infinitesimally small animals	
2. Coelenterata	Coral polyps, sponges, goloturia, sea lilies	Many members of the second class live like plants, spending all of their life in one place. Their digestive cavity is baglike with only one opening that is used for both feeding and elimination. In the third class, a complete digestive canal is already apparent.
3. Echinodermata	Starfish	
4. Worms	Common worms, leeches, tapeworms	Members of the fourth and fifth classes have an elongated body with head (mouth) and tail ends. Their bodies exhibit a segmented structure, especially clear in worms. They do not have a skeleton; the only stiff element of the body is a transportable house or shell. Their slowness is proverbial.
5. Mollusks	Snails, cuttlefish, oysters	
6. Arthropods	Insects, crayfish, spiders, centipedes	These last two classes are very different from all the rest. They have segmented, mobile skeletons and actual extremities and are capable of quick, strong movements. They are the only ones (except for a few mollusks) that have a real central nervous system—a brain.
7. Vertebrates	Fish, frogs, lizards, birds, mammals	

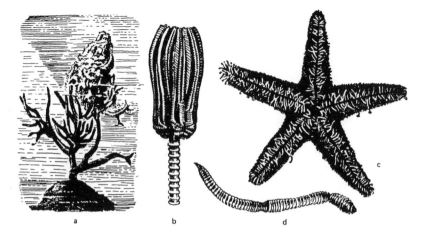

FIG. 3. a–Sponge. b–Sea lily (trias). c–starfish. d–annelida.

FIG. 4. Snail.

THE EMERGENCE OF LIFE AND EXCITABILITY

Now, having a scale and a classification, let us turn to a *history of movements* in the animal kingdom, *reconstructing* the infinitely remote past similarly to the way archaeologists draw plans and build models of long-vanished buildings and cities.

FIG. 5. *Left*–Squid. *Right*–Giant squid.

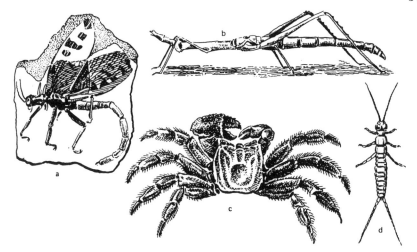

FIG. 6. a–Remnants of an insect of the coal period. b–Stick insect (*Proscopia scabra*). c–Sand crab. d–Microscopic insect (*Campodea*).

Even if a reconstruction of an ancient temple in Peru or a tomb in Babylon involves more imagination than documented facts, we are ready to forgive a scientist for the verisimilitude and persuasiveness. We are much more confident in our reconstruction of the history of movements because it is solidly based on facts.

Let us move through those immeasurably remote times, when the Earth slowly cooled and was covered by clouds and a hot salted soup of oceans. Various molecules and their pieces wandered across the ocean waters, collided with each other, joined each other in all possible combinations, and broke apart again. It looked as if the young Earth's chemistry tried its abilities. Earlier, when Earth was burning, any chemical compounds were as impossible as they would be in a hot oven.

But in this relatively cooler Earth, somewhere, in one of the places of the great ocean, maybe even only once during its existence, a collision of the pieces created a long, chain molecule that was crucially different from everything that had been formed before. Although the probability of the emergence of such a molecule was as low as all the cards in a shuffled deck occurring in the same order 100 consecutive times, there was enough time and space for all possible combinations to occur.[1] For the first time in Earth history, this wonderful molecule appeared to be more stable than all others. It was able not only to guard itself against accidental disintegration with special relationships and types of

---

[1]Certainly, one should not think that a live protein molecule or a live cell with its very complicated structure could emerge in one step as a result of just one wonderful event. The emergence of a molecular chain, discussed here, is certainly just one episode in a long chain of events that occurred consequently in the development of live substance. Such steps included the emergence and gradual complication of organic colloids (coatservats) containing nitrogen, sulphur, phosphorus, and iron, the formation of the original cellular protoplasma, and so forth.

bonds among its parts but also to promote emergence of *new molecules* that were in all respects identical to it. Its presence, by itself, forced other chemical pieces containing hydrogen, carbon, oxygen, and nitrogen to attach themselves temporarily to the parent molecule, move through it, and form exactly the same molecules. Someone living at that time would probably have called it a "molecule multiplicator." Through this process the notions of self-preservation and proliferation emerged on Earth together with the first *live particle*. Once it had been accidentally born in the Earth's waters, it could not disappear.

Over numerous centuries the inexperienced Earth wasted time on the development of the simplest unicellular animals (infusoria, paramecia, and rhizopoda) whose single cells tried to make life by moving their plaits and false-stalks, working alone to provide food, movement, preservation, and proliferation. A couple of million centuries later, during these 3–4 years of "scaled" time, multicellular organisms formed.

In a body consisting of many thousands of living cells, the cells cannot be identical because some of them are inside the body whereas others are on its surface. Here we witness *cell specialization*: Some cells, those on body surface, accommodate the carrying out the jobs of *excitability* and *sensitivity*; others, deep in the body, learn to change shapes, to *contract*, and to provide *primitive movements*. Let us call the former cells *receptive*, and the latter, *contractile* body elements.

In the warm waters of the prehistoric ocean are only representatives of the second and third classes (see Table 1), semianimals, semiplants with slow, lazy movements, as one stretching after sleep. Probably the first movements were spontaneous, originating from the cells' muscles themselves, and were not directed anywhere, but developed only because moving organisms had better chances than absolutely motionless organisms in the struggle for life.

Each physiological process is connected with a particular set of cellular, chemical processes. The receptive cells of the body's surface with their increased excitability took the responsibility for sensitivity and also secreted certain chemi-

FIG. 7. *Left*–Reconstruction of an ichthyosaurus. *Right*–Reconstruction of a flying reptile, rhamphorhynchus.

cal products of their metabolism in response to the action of external excitative factors including mechanical impacts, cold, heat, and so forth. It so happened that these products traveled with the liquids through the body to the vicinity of contractile, muscular cells. Clearly animals whose muscular cells accidentally happened to be excitable by these *receptive substances* had a very serious, even decisive, biological advantage. Whereas other organisms were able only to move spontaneously, in ways that could frequently be senseless or even harmful, the new organisms could *react* to external stimuli (for example, they could move directly to a potential prey or move away from a potential danger). This new phenomenon on Earth, *reactivity*, was initially nonselective, indiscriminate, dim, or, in physiological terms, diffuse. We can observe in some lower organisms such *diffuse excitability* and reactivity even now. It lies still until you touch it; when you touch it, it starts general, irregular body movements that are more pronounced in response to a stronger excitation.

This is how the first natural chemical excitatory substances for a muscle, the primitive *mediators* between the receptive body surface and muscles, were revealed. These substances still play a very important role in movements of the highest organisms including you and me. Each time we voluntarily contract a muscle, its nervous endings release a microscopical, tiny drop of a substance that is, in essence, 500 million years old.

In the succeeding generations, special channels for delivery of these chemical mediators developed gradually. However, before these channels had enough time to complete the construction of these "water communication lines" and provide selective delivery of mediators to certain muscular groups, another event took place whose biological significance was incomparably higher.

CONCEPTION OF THE NERVOUS SYSTEM

Each chemical reaction has an electrical *reflection*, that is, it is accompanied by changes in electric potential. We know that chemical affinity itself has an electrical nature (e.g., affinity of an acid to bind an alkali or of phosphorus to bind oxygen). This affinity is based on the well-known physical principle of mutual attraction of opposite electrical charges. The phenomenon of mediator excitation would not be possible without such an electrical basis. The excitation of receptive elements, the mediator action of muscular cells, and the reflective contraction of these cells were originally accompanied by small, hardly noticeable changes in electrical charges, most closely resembling electrical changes in the antenna of a radio receiving a signal from somewhere in New Zealand.

Here, when we first speak of *bioelectrical phenomena*, it makes sense to introduce a comfortable scale that can provide a clear picture of their actual magnitude. However, *in contrast to what we have done with the time scale*, we need large *amplifications* similar to the powerful amplifiers researchers use to deal with these signals in a laboratory.

FIG. 8. Comparison of scales that gives an idea about actual values of electrical voltage in nerves and muscles. On a conventional scale, 65 m = 1 volt. On this scale, Mount Everest corresponds to 120 volts of common voltage; the Eiffel Tower corresponds to the voltage of a pocket flashlight battery; the curve below the watch corresponds to voltage changes in a human neural fiber transmitting impulses.

According to the scale, let us make one volt 65 meters high (approximately the height of Hotel Moskva in Moscow). The voltage of a pocket flashlight battery equals, on this scale, the height of the Eiffel Tower in Paris; voltage of the common 120-volt power line equals the height of the highest mountain, Everest.

On this scale, changes of electrical potential during the functioning of our skeletal muscles equal *several centimeters*, and oscillations of the potential in muscles of those lower animals we discussed earlier and in the neural cells of human brain are not larger than the letters of the font used for printing this book. Biological currents running along our nerves correspond to the voltage of a flashlight as gooseflesh pimples to the Eiffel Tower. We hope that these comparisons help the reader imagine the scale of the events.

The importance of the last, seemingly secondary factor is enormous. To explain it, let us once again spell out how the great universal principle of selection, *natural selection* of the most fit organisms, worked. We shall meet it many times in the following discussions. So, let us bring it out of parentheses, as it is done in mathematics with a common factor for a number of members. Later, we shall just refer to it in brief form.

It so happened, as a result of accidental inborn changes that occured within certain limits in different species, that some of their muscular cells became excitable not only by a direct chemical action of a mediator but also by its electrical companion, an infinitesimally small electrical oscillation that had always accompanied the mediator. It is quite clear that species with electrically excitable muscles had an important advantage in the struggle for survival as compared to their less sensitive brothers. First, the electrical wave (or impulse) propagates at a much higher speed than a solution slowly soaking between the cells; therefore, the electrical impulse gives its owner the ability to react much more quickly. Second, the electrical impulse has a potential of being directed to one or another muscle group, whereas mediator-containing solution bathes the whole organism. It is not surprising, therefore, that nature's invention of the electrical (or telegraphic) principle of transferring excitatory impulses started to struggle vigorously for the commanding position. Those species who, for one reason or another, were deprived of this ability, died quickly and left descendants too weak to compete with the more advanced organisms. At first, electrical excitability was just a supplement to the main chemical process. Later, it became independent, and its transformation resembled the famous and very profound fairy tale by Hans Christian Andersen about a professor and his shadow. In this story, the shadow tears itself from the professor's feet and then manages to make a quick and successful court career; in a year the shadow returns to its former master, who was less fortunate, and suggests to him that he take the job of his own shadow.

Obviously, bioelectrical impulses first spread diffusely across the body. Step by step, fibers that demonstrated *better conduction* of these *biocurrents* separated (or, in a biological language, *differentiated*). Such fibers, or *fibrils*, represented long shoots of the cells. In all organisms, all tissues consist of cells and such shoots. Their development, feeding, and existence depend on cells that are, so to say, nourishing and supporting depots for the tissue elements. Those fibers that became specialized for transferring impulses (it is time to start calling them *neural impulses*) formed nets inside the organism, within which the life-sustaining cells were scattered. These modest nets with nonspecialized, scattered single cells could not even dream about the remote future when they would take the absolutely predominant position in the body as its *central nervous system*. For the time being, this barely noticeable messenger-attendant carried out its not very important function of transmitting messages from receptive to muscular cells, and at that time, no one could know that there was a marshal's baton hidden in its backpack. Specialization of the nutrient cells, relays, and primitive neural nets, that is, their transformation into actual neural cells with the formation of centralized *conglomerates* of such cells, called *neural knots* or *ganglia*, happened much later.

HOW THE MOUTH END OF THE BODY
BECAME ITS HEAD AND DOMINANT END

Now we are moving toward a new revolution, a new dialectic leap in the history of the development of movements and motor apparatus. The causes for this jump look very modest and insignificant. Such things frequently happen in nature: Seemingly insignificant causes sometimes lead to extremely important consequences. This unexpectedness is apparently the reason that even a very developed and sophisticated science has problems with exact predictions of future events, and exceptions from this rule are very rare (for example, astronomy with its predictions of solar eclipses). Put three billiards, 25 millimeters in diameter each, in one straight line at intervals of 1 meter. Then try to hit the first ball so that it directly hits the second ball so that the second ball similarly, hits the third ball straight on. Calculations show that if the first ball deviates from the ideal straight line by $\frac{1}{1000}$ that is, by 3.5 angular minutes, the second ball will automatically deviate by $\frac{1}{50}$ or by *more than 1 degree*, and the third ball will deviate from the required direction by 25 degrees, that is, by more than *one fourth of a right angle*. A similar avalanche-like accumulation of consequences of a seemingly insignificant event took place at one time during the evolution of movement.

The seemingly insignificant event was the emergence on Earth of elongated, sausagelike animals. The two classes described earlier (Classes 2 and 3 in Table 1) have symmetrical, spherical shapes with a mouth somewhere in the middle.

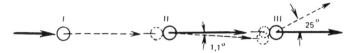

FIG. 9. Accumulation of error (angular discrepancy) during collisions of billiard balls.

The body shape of the simpler members, coelenterata, is less precisely defined; it is just a bag with one opening so the organism is forced to replace natural processes of waste elimination with regurgitation. The more developed echinodermata have a digestive canal, a radial body shape, and five elongated, symmetrical appendices.

Later, elongated animals (future worms and mollusks) developed, with a digestive tube spreading the whole length of the body with a mouth opening at one end and an anal opening at the other. The mouth end was what mattered. Obviously the mouth end is the *active* end of the body. It searches food; it is the first to meet prey or danger. The body usually moves *head first*.

Because of quite apparent reasons, sensitivity of body surface increases at this end (we will not again discuss in detail how accidental, favorable changes were preserved by natural selection). It is more important for the front end of the body than for any other part to quickly and discriminately feel the features of a touched object, an object to which it crawled. Sensitization of the primitive types of sensitivity (to touch, temperature, taste, and chemical composition), which can be given a common name of sensitivity of direct touch, is called *contact sensitivity*. In addition to contact sensitivity, the front, mouth end gives birth to the development of new, more elaborate sensory organs, or *receptors*. These new receptors can adequately be termed, using a common technical prefix, *telereceptors*. The prefix shared by this term and the words *telephone, telegraph, television*, and *telemechanics*, and so on, reveals its meaning: These are *long-range receptors*. Each of the primitive contact receptors changed and gave birth to one of the high-tech, long-range receptors. The organ of chemical sensitivity, taste, transformed into a chemical telereceptor, *sense of smell*. Sensitivity of the front end to touch refined and transformed into the sensitivity to low-amplitude, high-frequency vibrations transferred through the environment into an organ of *hearing* sounds that are nothing but oscillations or vibrations of air or water. And finally, the contact sensitivity to temperature first transformed into sensitivity to irradiation and then to sensitivity to irradiating energy of the most powerful part of the solar spectrum—light energy. Thus, *vision* emerged.

It is impossible to capture at once the importance of telereceptors for the development of the organism and its movements. First of all, they led to an *enormous growth of the space* in the world that was accessible to the animal's perception. The contact receptors are able to open, at most, several centimeters of the adjacent space to the animal. Telereceptors enlarge this area up to hundreds of meters. An animal that has only receptors of direct contact, that is, blind, deaf, and deprived of the sense of smell, does not feel prey unless it accidentally bumps into it and does not suspect danger even when it is just a few centimeters away. The advantages of species able to detect prey and danger at a distance of 100 meters are so obvious that they do not require explanation.

The consequences are another matter. If an animal is forced to live in a world of only those stimuli that directly touch it, its motor requirements become very limited as well. If it feels a painful touch on some part of the body, it moves only the hurting part by a local muscle contraction. It cannot feel food until it is just next to its mouth, so that a minor change in posture would suffice to capture the food. Elongated bodies of animals from the corresponding classes consist of segments that are very clearly seen in a worm or leech. When any of these stimuli acts on one of the body segments, it induces a purely local displacement of the affected segment, or at most, of a couple of its neighbors.

Imagine an animal from the same group but who already has telereceptors. If a prey or a danger is detected at tens of meters, *all the points of the body* are approximately at the same distance from it. Any local movements, then, are useless. It is necessary for the organism to move *the whole body* to an attractive object or away from a dangerous one. Consequently, perception by long-range receptors requires, not segmental body movements, but transfers of the whole body in space. In science, these movements are called *locomotions*. (Locomotions in humans include walking, running, swimming, and crawling, and also locomotor movements assisted by tools, such as skiing, skating, etc.).

It is easy to understand what kinds of requirements to *the nervous system* are presented by the new classes of movements. Although primitive segmental body movements can be sufficiently controlled by purely local reactions, at most involving two or three segments, a locomotor movement of the whole body through space requires a united, concordant activity of muscles of the whole body that transfers it in a required direction. Therefore, some centers are required that can assure such a harmonious, united choir of muscles of the whole body. Naturally, the place for these centers is somewhere at the front end, at the captain's bridge of the body, where the telereceptors are concentrated and provide the widest view of the environment. These centers unite contractions of all the muscles, or *integrate* them in a uniform rhythm and according to a uniform objective. These same centers also become leaders of the movement; that is, they take the initiative in deciding when and which movement to perform and what changes to introduce in its course.

One cannot ignore one more qualitative leap caused by the telereceptors. An attractive or menacing object detected at a large distance gives an animal *time* for a whole succession of planned movements. What is detected *from far away* is detected *in advance*. With these conditions, the animal can hide or find and prepare an ambush, it can develop a more or less complex strategy of attack or defense. Furthermore, this leads (again, through the mechanism of natural selection) to the development of *primitive memory*, by which the organism can remember a sequence of planned actions and not to mix up their order; *primitive intelligence*, which allows the animal to develop a sequence of actions; and, finally, *primitive dexterity*, which allows the animal to find an effective solution for the problem. All three abilities presume a more or less well functioning *brain*.

Thus, according to the inevitable logic of events, the mouth end of the body became, first, its front end, then equipped itself with high-tech telereceptors and became the head end, and, finally, transformed into the main end of the body. It so happened that the mouth created the telereceptors that created the brain.

DEFENSE OR OFFENSE?

We are getting closer to the event that played an extremely important role in the history of movement development.

We have already seen that, in the earliest period of animal development, when intelligence had not yet been engendered on Earth, the leading, commanding position in evolution was occupied by movements. For the sake of movements, telereceptors developed and refined their work, and the primitive brain was conceived. Because of these developments, a prominent change in the motor resources of animals, which we are going to discuss here, strongly influenced all the organs and systems in the animal body. One may even say that the whole future of animals was to a large extent defined by a revolutionary change that happened at that time.

Conditions of the struggle for survival and competition among the animals became more and more harsh. Life could not accommodate slow, soft-bodied, jellylike organisms whose mobility was similar to that of the hour hand of a clock.

Struggle and selection required innovations.

As in military technology, there were alternations of different strategies, from passive defense with armored bodies to active struggle with elaboration of the means of offense.

At first, it appeared that the first strategy, defense, was going to predominate. The highly developed, soft-bodied creatures, mollusks, started to develop shells, which could provide protection for the whole body of the animal. Apparently, this development did not help much and not for long because, at the next step of evolution, we see clear domination of the active principle, in the form of an event that we are going to discuss next. This event (this is the last introductory note) represented a huge dialectic leap toward absolutely new equipment for animal motor apparatus. Despite the deep abyss between the old and new movement organs covered with this leap and despite the total lack of any intermediate forms, this leap was certainly not instantaneous in time. Evolution always moves slowly, at least from our human perspective, and undoubtedly, it took more than a millenium for the new organs to achieve domination. (Dialectic leaps in evolution are always qualitative leaps but not necessarily instantaneous.)

This long period of time was not spent, however, on a gradual elaboration of new motor organs involving intermediate steps. We have already stressed that such intermediate forms did not exist. During this time, a semiaccidental change in a couple of animals evolved and, in hundreds of thousands of centuries, became common for a multimillion population.

MASTERING THE STRIATED MUSCLE

The basic event, crucial for the whole following revolution, was the emergence of *striated muscle*, or more precisely, of a striated muscular fiber, or even more precisely, of a microscopically small round plate the size of the red blood cell, that is, less than $\frac{1}{100}$ of a millimeter in diameter. Each muscular fiber consists of an enormous number of such plates alternating like beads. Each muscle of our skeletal-muscular apparatus consists of many thousands of such parallel fibers. The plates are termed *anisotropic discs*, let us abbreviate this name to muscular *anisoelements*.

Striated muscle (we shall see soon why it got its name) completely solved *the problem of speed and power*, the features that were so apparently lacking in the primitive, soft-bodied creatures. Muscles of the new type were able to contract with the speed of lightning; let us consider, for example, the wing movements of a fly or a mosquito that move at a frequency of several hundred per second. During contractions, striated muscles easily produce power thousands of times greater than that produced by ancient muscular cells (the smooth muscles) of the same weight.

It seems very probable that evolution just accidentally ran across the principle of striated muscle: This notion is supported, in particular, by the already noted total absence of any intermediate forms indicating a gradual, systematic development in this direction. The only exception is the striated *cardiac muscle* in vertebrates, which is older than skeletal muscles. However, the differences between the cardiac and skeletal muscles are so insignificant and, more important, all the basic, crucial new principles typical of the skeletal muscles are so fully represented in the cardiac muscle that the cardiac muscle cannot be considered an intermediate form. Apparently, the biological advantages of striated muscular tissue were so great that it was accepted immediately and victoriously spread over hundreds of thousands of species despite, as we will see, its significant drawbacks and inconveniences.

The emergence of the long-awaited quick and powerful engine gave rise to active and productive adaptive activity in organisms. Sluggish and weak smooth-muscled cells nicely coexisted with the soft and slack bodies of their owners. The situation changed when new, quick, and powerful contractions entered the scene. To put such a muscle into the body of a worm or jellyfish is like trying to load an artillery shell into a sausage skin. Stiff and sturdy lever systems became urgently

a   b

FIG. 10. Elements of a striated muscle fiber under a high-resolution microscope: a—when stretched; b—when contracted.

needed, systems that would provide the new muscles with both high mobility and points of force application for their brisk, powerful contractions.

Creation of these stiff lever systems by evolution proceeded in such a peculiar way that I would like to tell about it in the form of a short fable. We hope that, after everything that has been said about the principles of evolution, this fable will not lead to misunderstanding but instead provide a brighter and more lively exposition.

Life announced a great competition for the best support for striated muscle. The first prize was shared by two projects. At the first glance, they both solved the problem in ingenious and adequate ways, although their approaches were extremely different. The first project was submitted under the heading "Arthropoda," and the second one was called "Vertebrata." In both projects the striated muscle was considered as something given and was combined with rigid skeletons with mobile joints. Both probably complied with the rules of the competition.

The project Arthropoda was manifested by centipedes, spiders, crustacea, and all insects. Its idea was to use sturdy, empty *shells* that looked like knight's armor. The muscles were *inside* the hinged shells, spanning from one of the segments to another and moving the shells by action from inside. The shell covered the whole body of the animal (e.g., a crayfish) and served as an armor ingeniously uniting this function with the function of lever mobility. Moreover, the external shell skeletons perfectly solved *the problem of stability* in a way that did not require any help from the muscles. This can easily be demonstrated with a simple experiment. Place a cotton ball soaked in ether or benzene at the head of a crustacea or an insect. The anesthetized or even dead animal preserves its stability; it continues to stay in the position it was in before. Let us remind the reader, for comparison, that any anesthetized or dead vertebrate falls down. Thus, muscles in the Arthropoda were absolutely relieved of any secondary duties, like providing

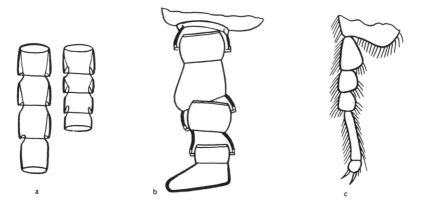

FIG. 11.   a–Consecutive segments of an arthropod shell: *left*–in a stretched state; *right*–in a contracted state. b–Schematic of a leg of an underwater diver's suit. c–Part of a bee leg (substantially amplified).

FIG. 12. Luring crab (*Gelasimus*).

support, and were busy with their main occupation for which striated muscle was best suited—*active contractions*. This purpose is reflected in its microscopical structure, which makes it considerably simpler than muscles in vertebrates.

The project Vertebrata, using the *skeletal-muscular apparatus of the vertebrates* solved the problem in a basically different, nearly opposite way. The rigid parts, *bones* are connected in chains and placed *in the middle of each of the body links*. *Muscles* cling to them from *outside*, from all the sides where they may be required by mobility. If joints cannot move in certain directions (e.g., the human elbow joint cannot move sideways), the extendable and tender muscular tissue is substituted with tougher tendons and ligaments. In any case, each joint *is fixed from all sides* with elastic rods, *muscles or ligaments*; this system of support is similar to that of high ship masts or antennas of radiotransmitters. At first glance, this method looks less convenient and less obvious than the one in insects. It also loads

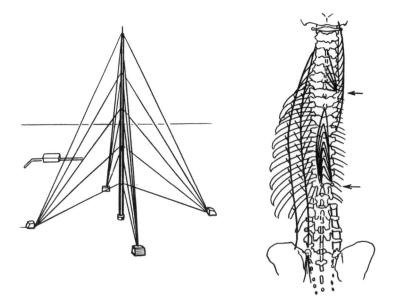

FIG. 13. *Left*–Mast with shrouds. *Right*–Schematic of spinal muscles acting on the principle of shrouds (muscular fibers marked by arrows are actually located at each vertebral level and are shown here for only two vertebrae).

the muscle, aside from its primary engine functions, with the function of *supportive* (called *static*) *work*. On the other hand, there is a clear gain in *flexibility*, both passive and active. Compare a crayfish and its clumsy armor to a fish or snake, flexible as their soft-bodied ancestors. Let us remember that the first vertebrates which entered the great competition of life were *fish*, which in fact did not have extremities. These organs developed later. At the very beginning of their existence, vertebrates consisted virtually of just a spine that carried on itself a multibone skull and a flexible thorax. The spine consisted of many segments flexibly connected to each other and provided the richness and freedom of bending.

DRAWBACKS OF THE STRIATED MUSCLE

One more fact supports our conclusion that the principle of striated muscle was accepted at once and nearly accidentally, although the biological necessity for it was ripe. It looks as if, after wandering into this principle, nature snatched at it and immediately, without any corrections or additions, used it for equipping mobile skeletons. The point is that detailed analysis of the physiology of striated muscle shows that it is not that convenient and that, in many respects, is quite inappropriate for its function. Apparently, its principle had something very attractive so that nature, at first, blindy believed in it, as if not seeing its very apparent drawbacks. Later, when the drawbacks became obvious, nature suddenly realized that some of the important "technical specifications" had not been met in the structure and functioning of the new muscle. (We hope once again that the reader will forgive the figurative embodiments that we are going to use in the next paragraph, but they will help us stress the most important facts.) Striated muscle, as it came from the hands of evolution, appeared in some very important aspects so poorly meeting its purpose that it was necessary to find quick compromises for making it useful. Besides, there was no alternative engine.

First, it appeared that the type of contraction of striated muscle, or, more precisely of its microscopically small active particle, its *anisoelement*, was absolutely inappropriate to fit the biological requirements. This type of contraction, as it is seen on contemporary sensitive recorders, is a *crude, brisk jerk*, so sudden and explosive that there is a real danger of breaking the attached bones. The compromise, developed as a method of coping with this absolutely inappropriate briskness, was to interlay the anisoelements with similarly tiny particles of elastic tendinous tissue (called *isoelements*). Under a microscope, the muscle fiber started to look like a pillar of 3-kopeck and 20-kopeck coins corresponding to alternating aniso- and isoelements. The isoelements play the role of *buffers* or *shock absorbers* for the violent jerks of the anisoelements: They stretch during the jerks and then shorten more smoothly and gradually, helping the muscle to perform its function. The aniso- and isoelements have different color and transparency, and their alternation in each fiber makes the muscle appear striated, thus its name.

FIG. 14. A column of alternating copper and silver coins, illustrating the appearance of muscular fiber through a microscope, when treated with acid and dissociated into Bowman disks.

Second, anisoelements are *absolutely unable to perform prolonged contractions*; moreover, they are unable to regulate the duration of the contractions.

The only thing that an anisoelement can do is to develop a very rapid explosion of force and contraction. In human muscles, this explosion does not last more than $\frac{1}{1000}$ of a second. Even worse, after each contractile explosion, the anisoelement tires or becomes exhausted, or something else happens that is still unknown to physiologists; it then needs time (two to three times longer than contraction time) to recuperate after a contraction and get ready to work again. Immediately after a burst of excitation, the anisoelement is absolutely nonexcitable even by the strongest, most demanding stimuli. Nothing of this sort happened with the good old, easily controllable, smooth muscle cell.

For nature to overcome this inconvenience of the anisoelements, another compromise was necessary. The nervous system learned to send to striated muscles a *series* of excitatory impulses that rushed one after another at a machine-gun rate (50–200 per second). Each burst of contraction of the anisoelement is still much shorter than the interval between two successive impulses, but here the isoelements help by prolonging each contraction. Other factors help the contractions of anisoelements to merge into smooth movements, including *viscosity* of a jellylike, semiliquid substance (called *sarcoplasm*) that fills the space between the elements; *elasticity* of tendons and ligaments; and inertia of the movement organs themselves.

The described high-frequency series of excitations (called *tetanus*) is the only way to repetitively contract a striated muscle fiber for a prolonged period of time or to sustain a contraction for more than $\frac{2}{100}$ of a second. One can compare a tetanic series of excitations to an alternating electric current that is able, despite its intermittent nature, to run electric doorbells and a number of other, more important instruments. You can hear that skeletal muscles actually drone like a buzzer by placing an ear to the strained biceps of your friend or by clenching your teeth so that your own temporal muscles start to buzz. This buzzing would not, by itself, be a serious drawback. It is much worse, however, that during each contraction a striated muscle *releases a burst of its chemical energy*, and this energy *cannot return to the muscle*, whether or not it is used for external mechanical work.

Even if a muscle is to *keep* a load at a certain height without lifting it, it can achieve this only by a *tetanus*, that is, hundreds of contraction bursts per second.

Each burst releases as much energy as would be required to quickly lift the load. Because in the absence of movement mechanical work is not being performed, the whole huge power produced by the muscle goes into useless heating.

But this is not all. Anisoelements are as unable to regulate the *force* of their contractions as they are unable to control their duration. If you stimulate a striated muscle fiber with electric current, you need to get to certain current values to make the fiber feel it and produce a contraction. After you move past this threshold, any further current increase will be unable to produce even 1% increase in force of the evoked fiber contraction. It will stay the same. This rule of the striated muscle function has a very picturesque name—"all or none." A similar rule applies in the shooting of a rifle. In order to make a shot one must pull the trigger with a force not less than a certain threshold. However, further increase in the force of pulling the trigger will increase neither the force nor the distance of the shot.

Thus, the force of a brief jerk, which is the only possible mode of functioning of the anisoelement, also cannot be regulated, and nature had to invent another adaptive compromise to reach some controllability. Each branch of a motor nerve sends its smaller branches to a group of 10–100 muscular fibers. Such a group is called *mion*.[2] Depending on its size, each muscle in the body consists of several dozens or hundreds of mions. The method of controlling its force of contraction is in engaging different numbers of mions. Switching the mions on and off is exactly the way by which the nervous system manages to achieve the amazing smoothness and fine control of changes in muscular forces, such as that in the gentle and accurate work of a nurse tending a wound or in the confident and precise movements of an engraver. We should mention, however, that the central nervous system has developed another, more subtle auxiliary method of controlling muscle force, which is discussed in essay 5.

The preceding were the numerous, auxiliary, and corrective mechanisms acquired by striated muscle to make its advantages realistically useful. If one thinks more about it, the whole situation is extremely atypical. Usually, selection and natural evolution modify and refine a new organ until it perfectly fits into its place. Consider, for example, the fascinating, vast system of digestive glands (studied in every detail by our great compatriot, I. P. Pavlov), perfectly suited for digestion of all kinds of food. Consider also the very sensitive and ingenious apparatus for controlling blood pressure in the blood vessels—the *sinuses* of the recently discovered sensitive devices in the aorta, close to the heart, and in the carotid arteries—that very sensitively react to any changes in vessel pressure. Compared to them, muscular tissue looks like a strange exception: It is crude

---

[2]The fiber of a motor nerve with its commanding neural cell in the spinal cord is called a *motoneuron*; the whole microscopically small aggregate of motoneuron plus mion is called a *moton*. In contemporary literature, the term *motor unit* has been established for the aggregate consisting of a motoneuron and muscular fibers innervated by its axon.

and very poorly suited for physiological needs; it was not modified or refined, but, rather, developed with plenty of compromises and different tricks. One may think of a farm manager who ordered a thresher but received a passenger car. The striated muscles of our body look like such a car equipped with homemade rope drives and wooden planks nailed to its bumpers.

ARTHROPODS IN A DEAD END

I have already mentioned that the comparison between the motor apparatus of arthropods and of vertebrates favors the simplicity and precision of the former. The only apparent advantage of the vertebrates is the flexible mobility of their bodies. Another advantage is not so obvious and needs a brief elaboration. At first glance, this advantage looks like a drawback. I am speaking now about the required active participation of the muscles in maintaining postural equilibrium, that is, in what is called *body statics*. For example, all six legs of an insect are attached to the thoracic segment of its body. Its body has its own shell-type stability and does not require additional muscular work. The human body is also connected to the extremities and supported by two of them, but it can preserve its vertical posture only by continuous contraction of all the muscles that brace it, like shrouds bracing a ship's mast. Although this system seems to be much harder to control, however, it provides the human (and any vertebrate) body with exceptional adaptability and maneuverability.

The only principle that succeeded in solving the problem of combining all the advantages of the soft-bodied creatures with a rigid-lever construction appropriate for transducing large forces was the basic principle of vertebrates. There is no argument that it is much harder to control such a "soft-stiff" system, but

FIG. 15. A termite queen surrounded by her court.

we have seen in the previous essay that a more challenging instrument with more degrees of freedom is less restrictive and is valued more highly by its master. A real master would, without regrets, let his son have such simplifying things as frets and supports together with the tricycle.

These unpretentious biological advantages of vertebrates did not hesitate to affect the course of future history of the animal world. Both huge classes, arthropods and vertebrates, rightfully shared the ruling positions on our planet, but then, the vertebrates left their competitors far behind. Moreover, the reason is not in absolute body dimensions, in which arthropods have never been able to catch up with vertebrates (the vertebrates set all the records in body dimensions during the next period of their development). It is much more important that arthropods hopelessly trailed vertebrates in their intellectual abilities and in the tightly-coupled-with-intellect area of movements. All the stories about the supposedly amazing intellect of insects are based on a couple of overused examples from the community life of termites and bees. More closely analyzed, these stories appear to be pure misunderstanding (according to such experts and authorities on insect life as J. Fabre, F. Lebbock, and others). These insects undoubtedly possess a specific and complex instinct that controls their actions. The nature of this instinct is absolutely unknown. There is an abyss, however, between instinct and intellect, an abyss similar to that between the crayfish's armored shell and the swan's neck or cat's body. The same insects that are able to build honeycombs with geometric precision, at eternally identical angles, or to organize "cowsheds" of plant louses near their anthills are totally confused to the point of a total loss of coordination when forced to act in minimally unpredictable conditions. It is striking and amazing when 10 termites seem to cooperate in dragging a straw to their hill. A more careful inspection, however, reveals that only 6 of them are actually pulling the straw to the hill while the other 4

FIG. 16. Ant tailors sewing their nests.

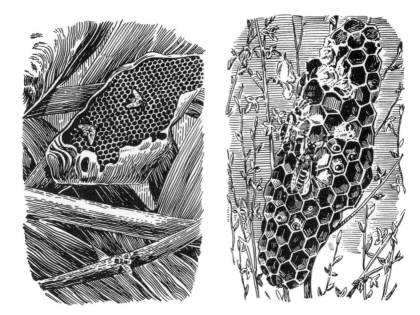

FIG. 17. *Left*–Wild wasp (*Polybia*) honeycombs. *Right*–Wild wasp (*Polistes gallica*) honeycombs.

are pulling in different directions and that the straw simply follows the stronger force. Turn a beetle on its back, place a fly without wings on the tip of a straw, block the main trail to an anthill with a narrow water stream, and so on. The first reaction of all these insects will be bewildered confusion; the second will comprise actions that are striking in their meaninglessness and clumsy stupidity. We have already said in essay 1 that the most essential *feature* of dexterity is *resourcefulness*, the ability to quickly and successfully solve a problem in an unexpected condition. Such resourcefulness is totally lacking in the behavior of arthropods. They may be exceptionally *quick* (a fly, a flea, a crab in the water, a hunting spider, etc.) because their bodies are equipped with striated muscles that are nearly free of viscous sarcoplasma, but it is a long way from quickness to dexterity. At least, this is the conclusion drawn by anyone butted in the stomach by a playing boy's head. After preferring the shell principle to the principle of multilevel flexibility, arthropods followed the chosen route with the absolute consistency. Evolution elaborated for insects complex and accurate instincts, as unchangeable as their shells, and created for their primitive, everyday life similar forms of behavior, monotonous, well-adjusted, and forever invariable as train tracks, but it also permanently closed to them the routes to individual adaptivity and accumulation of individual life experience. By doing so, evolution forever blocked for insects any prospects of intellectual progress.

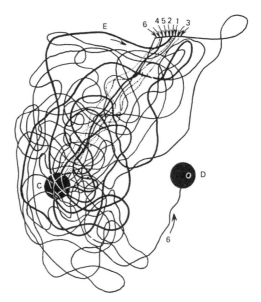

FIG. 18. Paths of six wandering termites who learned to walk from a starting point (A) to a feeding point (C) after the food was moved to a new location (D); only one termite eventually found the way (based on studies by F. Lebbock).

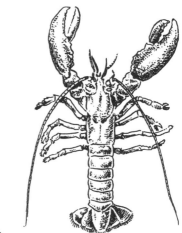

FIG. 19. Lobster.

EVOLUTION OF VERTEBRATES

To complete this essay, we must summarize the "modern" history of movements, the history that started after the "striated revolution" just described. Let us leave the arthropods at their dead end, where they arrived because of the drawbacks of their motor apparatus, and concentrate on vertebrates.

FIG. 20. *Above*–Imaginary landscape of the Jurassic period (an ichthyosaurus is
in the water, and an archeopterix is in the sky). *Below*—Reconstruction of a giant
reptile, stegosaurus, which lived in the territory of contemporary Europe about
100 million years ago (its length is 7.5 m, its height is 3.6 m, and its brain is the
size of a human fist).

The most important features of *neokinetic animals*[3] are striated muscular apparatus, a central nervous system, and a brain. The features are more or less
clearly seen in higher mollusks (e.g., cephalopods, cuttlefish, octopus, etc.), but

---

[3]Neokinetic means "referring to new movements." This term is used for the new motor organs
in their totality, including striated muscles, rigid multilink skeletons, explosive processes of excitation,
and so forth.

only vertebrates have incorporated these features with appropriate conditions for the impetus and unceasing development that is still in progress. This development, whose details we discuss somewhat later, eventually led to the brain and, in particular, to its youngest area, the so-called motor cortex, establishing a dictatorship over virtually all the physiological functions. This development is a new page in brain science that has just recently started to be written. A great Russian physiologist, K. M. Bykov, significantly contributed to its understanding. Each year, we discover more and more functions of our body that are controlled by the brain: metabolism, the control of blood physiochemical processes, the formation of blood, the struggle against contagious elements, and so forth. All of this looks very different from the plain fibers that had simply differentiated from the surrounding tissues through which the primitive electrochemical excitatory impulse tried to force its way.

Table 2 provides the consecutive order of the development of vertebrate classes. In order to assess their relative timing, let us again use a time scale 1:50,000,000 for better visualization.

The most ancient mammals emerged at the end of the period of the reptile kingdom, about 3 "years" ago. One "year" ago, the mammals already ruled the Earth; there was a large number of mammal species. The higher mammals (e.g., carnivorous, elephants, and early monkeys) are 3–6 "months" old. Apes and the most ancient human ancestor, so-called pithecanthropus, are about 2 "weeks" old. Human beings of the glacier periods, mammoth hunters, are less than 1 week old. For comparison of these actual time intervals with the naive notions of myths and with world religions, according to this time scale, God created the universe, according to the Old Testament, about 1.5 "hours" ago.

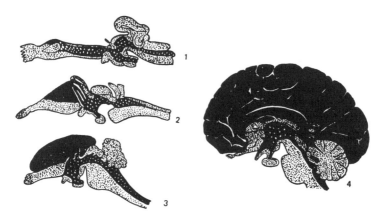

FIG. 21. Brain evolution from the lower fish to human (longitudinal sections shown): 1–ray (*Chimera*); 2–lizard (*Varanus*); 3–rabbit (*Lepus*); 4–human (scales are different). Light dotted areas indicate the most primitive brain areas; dark dashed lines indicate brain cavities (ventricles); black areas indicate the new brain (hemispheres).

TABLE 2

Classification of the Vertebrates

Class	Description/Examples	Notes
I. Fish	a. Ancient, prebone–lamprey, sharks, ray-fish, sturgeon b. More recent, with bone skeletons–perch, ruff, pike, flying fish	The ancient fish apparently appeared sometime during the third "decade" of the scale.
II. Amphibia	Frogs, tritons, acsolotl	In present times, only a few orders represent this previously numerous class. Reptiles are the last of the so-called cold-blooded vertebrates. It would be more precise to define the first three classes as animals with *variable body temperature* equal to the temperature of the environment. The first amphibia emerged on Earth about 15 "years" ago, the first reptiles about 6–8 years ago.
III. Reptiles	Snakes, turtles, lizards, crocodiles	
IV. Birds	a. Lower, hatched–kiwi, penguin, ostrich, chicken, ptarmigan b. Higher, nestling–swallow, owl, eagle	Birds gradually developed from flying reptiles. This process started about 5 years ago and lasted 3–4 years.

V. Mammals	a. Primitive, marsupial–platypus, kangaroo, numerous Australian marsupials
	b. Lower–insectivorous animals, rodents
	c. Higher–hooved, carnivorous, semimonkeys
	d. Highest–monkeys
	  1. Lower–pavian, marmoset
	  2. Higher–apes (in order of increasing closeness to humans–chimpanzee, orangutan, gorilla)
	e. Direct ancestors of human beings and contemporary humans	

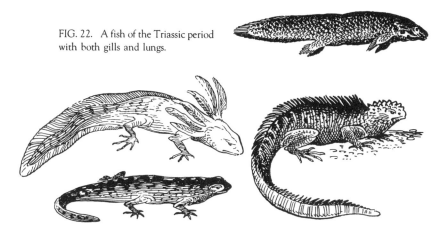

FIG. 22. A fish of the Triassic period with both gills and lungs.

FIG. 23. Development of an axolotl from larvae with gills to adult animal with lungs.

Birds and mammals together form a group of warm-blooded vertebrates, or more precisely, animals with a *constant body temperature*, one that is independent of external temperature. Because the rate of any chemical process increases dramatically with temperature, all of the processes in the bodies of warm-blooded animals (in particular the most interesting for the purposes here, processes in their nerves and muscles) are realized much more quickly and energetically than those in cold-blooded animals. (This fact is soon going to be very useful.)

SENSORY CORRECTIONS

Of all the animals, vertebrates found the best solution for the problem of adaptation and development. Let us begin this overview of their history with two more innovations that emerged and developed as direct consequences of the

FIG. 24.

FIG. 25. A representative of marsu-
pials, kangaroo.

emergence of striated muscle and the whole new motor principle, which we just
termed *neokinetic*. The first innovation was *sensory corrections* (carefully described
in the previous essay). Primitive animals without a skeleton and with slow,
smooth muscles and predominating local segmental movements did not need a
system of fine control of movements, which require continuous control from
sensory organs. Moreover, in order to compare a movement with its plan, and
this is the essence of the function of sensory corrections, an organism needs to
plan the movement in advance, that is, to have organs that are able to plan. If
you do not have a brain or memory (in any form) that is able to carry out in a
correct order parts of a complex sequence of movements or actions, how are you
going to perform comparison of the movement? What are the criteria for deciding
whether the movement is proceeding exactly as it was planned?

Finally, also note that the motor apparatus in the new, neokinetic animals
quickly became more and more difficult to control with the primitive means
that were available in worms or oysters. As we already mentioned, the long-range
sensory organs, telereceptors, brought to life transfer movements of the whole
body, that is, locomotions. Locomotions required organized, cooperative work
of the muscles of the whole body, in other words, synergies. Such work was an
orchestra searching for a conductor, the brain. Each musician of this large orchestra, each striated muscle, was a much less compliant and obedient instrument
than the ancient smooth-muscle cells. We have already discussed those complicated contrivances forced on the central nervous system in order to obtain from
these muscles prolonged contractions (tetanus) or smooth changes in force. It
was a collision of numerous factors: the increased speed and force of movements,
their range and complexity, whims of their major performer (the muscle), con-

FIG. 26. *Above*–Young gorilla. *Below*–Reconstruction of the head of a human ancestor (a Neanderthal).

tinuously increasing requirements for accuracy, and so forth. Combined with the factors described in the previous chapter (the extreme disobedience of mobile systems with multiple degrees of freedom and additional problems originating from muscle elasticity), more reasons for the urgent necessity of sensory corrections at this stage of evolution are not needed.

It is interesting to note that the reflex loop in primitive animals (also discussed previously) works quite differently from how it functions in us. Consider a worm that crawls to an obstacle or a snail that reaches the tip of a grass blade. When there are complications of this kind, these animals start rather animated, aimless searching movements in all directions. In the more highly developed neokinetic animals, *movements follow sensations*; that is, movements are directed and controlled by sensations. In the *lower* animals, the opposite is true: *Sensations are served and provided by movements.* Seemingly senseless and unorganized movements induce sensations, catch and grab them where they can. This mechanism of active "sensing" has been preserved in our bodies as well. It occurs in the functioning of our highest senses, vision and touch, in which a reflex-loop mechanism is a part of a complex, indivisible whole. In the next essays, we shall see other examples of how carefully our nervous system has preserved the most primitive mechanisms that look outrageously outdated and ready to be archived. This crude, primitive mechanism of sensations, which had developed long ago, long before sensory corrections, was revived, refined and updated, and merged with the sensory corrections to provide the function of our most highly developed sensory organs.

Moreover, the urgent need for sensory corrections found in higher animals became a new and very powerful factor pushing toward further development of the brain. As we are going to show, this necessity primarily promoted the development of the *sensory fields* (complex sensory conglomerates from very different sensory organs), which direct animal and human movements and help to orient them in space.

DEVELOPMENT OF EXTREMITIES

The second innovation that naturally followed the establishment of the neokinetic system with its joint levers and striated muscles was *the development of extremities*. In the lower, soft-bodied organisms, there were no extremities. At best, there sometimes emerged *pseudopodia* ("false extremities"), for example, rays of a starfish or snail's "leg," which is, in fact, a lower part of its body. Vertebrates also spent quite some time developing genuine extremities.

Rudiments of extremities in fish, side fins, do not work as propellers. While swimming, the fish works with its tail that acts as a propeller and with its odd back and belly fins, which screw into the water with winding movements. The side fins are mostly used as depth and, partially, direction rudders. These fins started to transform into real extremities only after the animal emerged from the water. At some stage of evolution, fish felt too crowded in rivers, seas, and oceans. Vertebrates attempted to conquer other of the Earth environmental elements, trying to get into the air (swallow fish and flying fish) or onto soil (crawling fish, amphibia fish, etc.).

FIG. 27.   A crawling fish from Africa (*Periophthaimus*).

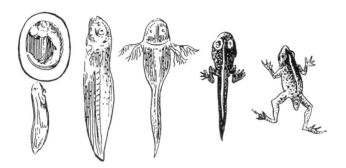

FIG. 28. Stages of frog metamorphosis.

Fish were followed by a class of vertebrates, amphibia (from Greek "having two lives"), which already had real extremities (legs) the skeletons of which preserved the radial or handlike shape they had had in fish fins. Evolution once again followed its traditions—avoiding drastic innovations and creating the new organs from the available material (legs from the side fins, lungs for breathing from the swimming bladder, etc.). Each species of the most common representative of amphibia, the frog, very illustratively repeats during its life the permanently imprinted history of water vertebrates moving onto solid ground. It starts life as a fish, even without fins, breathing through gills (tadpole); later, the gills disintegrate simultaneously with the emergence of the tail and feet.

Extremities were a very profound and important innovation. They emerged at a time when the ancient stimuli for segmental body structure had largely disappeared, and the development of extremities stepped over the ruins of this old principle of construction, which was still present in the most ancient part of the body, its trunk. This path of development explains, first, why the ex-

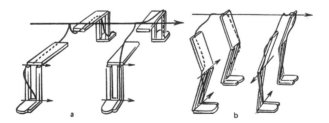

FIG. 29. A schematic of skeletal structures: a–in reptiles; b–in mammals. (1) Reptiles do not have anterior–posterior rotational mobility in the hip and shoulder joints; a lack forcing them to twist the whole body left and right when walking; (2) the existing configuration of mammal limbs emerged as a result of their turning toward each other; (3) correct orientation of the stepping part of the front paw (hand) required an additional crossing of the forearm bones (permanent pronation); rotational movements of the wrist and forearm (pronation and supination) are typical for humans and are absent in quadrupedal mammals.

tremities themselves do not show any signs of segmentation, as seen, for example, in the principle of innervation of their muscles. Second, we should note another, very important fact. Subsequent development in vertebrates of neokinetic, large motor synergies for transfer across space (locomotions), and, finally, of extremities as a modernized tool for such transfer, led to corresponding equipment of the central nervous system with special devices necessary for taking care of all these innovations. Comparative anatomy of the brain reveals that this series of novelties, more than any of the previous steps in the development, contributed to the development of a genuine centralization in the central nervous system, the emergence of the first formations that actually deserved the name of "*brain*." The oldest part of the central nervous system in vertebrates, the *spinal cord* (and also its direct continuation in the head, the so-called "spinal cord of the head," the medulla and brain stem) still patterns the segmental type of structure. New brain nuclei, which emerged during the "fish" period of evolution and were finalized in the first animal with legs, the frog, are already absolutely *unsegmented*. Their neural pathways control the spinal cord as a whole and, in particular, control all the extremities. Even more important, the activity of the highest brain structures controlling movements and locomotions (in the following essays, we are going to address it as Level B) in amphibia proceeds according to the rules of the neokinetic system, that is, with relatively high-voltage, quickly traveling signals, following the all-or-nothing law, and so forth. Older brain centers, which in amphibia retain control over trunk movements (Level A, according to our scheme), still work mostly according to the primitive motor laws, that is, with low-voltage, slow impulses, with a considerable role played by the ancient chemical signal transmission, and so forth. It is amazing that even human beings, whose brain differs from the frog's brain more than a great king's castle differs from a savage's shack, have a brain with separate representations of Level A and Level B that quite clearly separate control of the neck and trunk muscles from control of the extremities. To a large degree, the ancient,

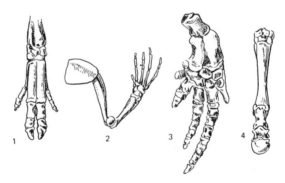

FIG. 30. Skeletons of the distal part of the forelimb (hands of different animals): 1–pig; 2–frog; 3–whale (the fin); 4–horse.

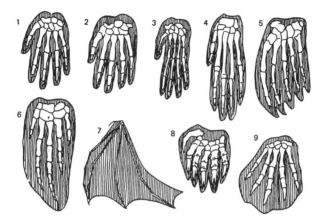

FIG. 31. Skeletons of mammal hands: 1–human; 2–gorilla; 3–orangutan; 4–dog; 5–seal; 6–dolphin; 7–bat; 8–hedgehog; 9–platypus.

FIG. 32. Animals with flying devices.

segmental, trunk Level A in humans still continues to work according to those primitive motor laws. The problem of levels is discussed in more detail in the next two essays.

ENRICHMENT OF MOVEMENTS

All the following development of movements in vertebrates was a continuous enrichment of the motor apparatus and abilities of animals from class to class and from year to year of our chronological table of evolution. This enrichment did not occur without a reason but also did not result from some inborn, internal "spring" that pushes animals toward continuous perfection. Movement enrichment was induced by the same merciless, cruel, and absolutely external reason— the *competition and struggle for life*. Animals felt crowded because of continuous proliferation. There was not enough food. Carnivorous species emerged, leaving it to other animals to search for appropriate feeding material and preferring to consume food in the already semiprocessed form of weaker animals. The latter developed means of self-defense, such as quick feet, protective color, armored skin, horns, and hoofs. Those who did not have such means of defense were the first to be eaten by the carnivorous, who did not suspect that, by doing so, they were improving the prey. Indeed, those species who were better defended, even accidentally, had better chances of surviving and of having descendants. The best defense was still rich and perfect motor abilities. The same law of competition hit the predators with the other end of the stick: Those who were less quick, less smart, and large-toothed risked dying of hunger, being unable to catch the improved-in-self-defense prey.

In this way, movements were enriched with respect to force, quickness, accuracy, and endurance. But this kind of enrichment was purely quantitative. More important are two other aspects of movements, which also improved progressively. First, *motor tasks* to be solved by an animal *became more and more complicated* and, simultaneously, *more and more variable*. The whole list of fish movements consists virtually of its main locomotion, swimming, plus a couple of simple hunting movements. In one of the least developed fish, the shark, hunting always consists of its swimming under a prey, turning belly-up (it fits it better), and opening its jaws. Amphibia, besides swimming, can also crawl, jump, and make sounds. Snakes are able to hide in ambush. How much more complex and variable are the chain hunting movements of carnivorous mammals! Here we see the fox's tricks, the keen search by a hunting dog, and the insidious ambush by a tiger stalking its prey. In the following discussion, we shall look in more detail into this side of movements, that is, of the complication of the problems.

The second aspect in the development of movements is a *continuous increase in the number of unexpected, unique problems* that needed to be solved by an animal immediately, "in real time." As we saw in the introductory essay, this is where a large demand for dexterity occurs. The motor menu of animals includes relatively fewer and fewer standard, always-identical movements that can be done automatically without thought or adjustment. One might assume that locomotions, transfers across space, are examples of such, always-standard movements. This is not true. When a fish swims inside an endless, homogeneous water medium, there are actually not too many stimuli for variability. Transfers across solid ground, however, are a different matter because they do not take place on fixed tracks. This environment has ditches and gullies; swamp hummocks and unpassable undergrowth; safe paths where one can freely jog and enemy-concealing forests where one must sneak without a sound, sensitizing all the telereceptors; and so on, and so on. Complex motor acts, absolutely impossible for a fish, fill the life of a highly developed mammal. The intensified struggle for life makes its existence full of unexpected events that require an ability to save hundredths of a second, immediately make a decision, and *accurately and dexterously* realize it. We shall see that this continuous increase in the number of unlearned movements and motor acts *is based* on a similarly *continuous development* of new, more complex brain areas, mostly, the *brain cortex*.

The first embryos of brain cortex are already apparent in higher reptiles, but only in the highest vertebrates, the mammals, does it take the commanding position and continue to develop further and further. Brain cortex is the organ with an unlimited capacity for *accumulating personal life experiences of an animal,* memorizing them, processing their meaning, and creating on this basis solutions for new, previously never-encountered tasks.

In the area of intellectual activity, this ability is smartness, wits, and cleverness; in the area of motor acts, we call the same ability dexterity. Not without reason, we may say about a man with outstanding dexterity, "How smart his movements are! How clever his hands are!"

PRIME OF THE REPTILE KINGDOM

The list of movements of the lowest vertebrates, the fish, consists nearly exclusively of swimming locomotions. Typical fish movements are smooth, wavy, monotonous synergies involving the whole body (from the head to the tail

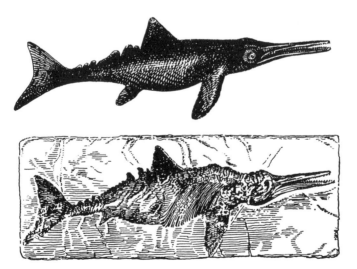

FIG. 33. *Below*–Remnants of an *Ichthyosaurus quadriscissus* with skin. *Above*–Its reconstruction.

propeller). These movements never stop, even when a fish remains in one place, even during sleep. Apparently, these extremely pitiful abilities are sufficient for the fish because its everyday life is sufficiently covered by them even in present times. The situation changed dramatically when the oceans started to become smaller and smaller while their inhabitants were becoming more and more numerous. Occupation of air and ground became an urgent necessity.

Let us not waste time on the second group of vertebrates, *amphibia*. In essence, they were merely an intermediate form and never dominated Earth in either number of individual animals or in number of species. For a long period of time, such a dominating role fell to the lot of *reptiles*, the next stage in the development of vertebrates. Reptiles were Earth's rulers much longer than their followers, mammals (this fact is clear from the numbers in the table of evolution of vertebrates). Mammals exterminated the reptiles quickly and surely (later we shall see why). A long time ago, there were numerous orders and species of reptiles, which ruled the sea, ground, and air. Only four orders have survived until the present time: lizards, turtles, snakes, and crocodiles. Apparently they are still trying to exact revenge on their conquerers, mammals, with cold ferocity and deadly poison, their last weapons.

Reptiles developed rapidly during the Triassic period. This period was their "early kingdom," when most of them still dwelt in water (such as the gigantic fish-lizard, ichthyosaurus, and a lizard with a swan neck, plesiosaurus). In the following Jurassic period, they already ruled all the spheres. Large-toothed, flying pterodactyls rushed through the air, probably with discordant, sharp cries. On the ground, the reptiles proliferated in enormous variety. One should note that reptiles were the first creatures to master ground and air, so there were no competitors, and this victory was not hard and did not require struggle or development of special, modernized organs for the struggle. In the still-warm greenhouse climate of the slowly cooling Earth, with its rich humus from the plants and with no dangerous enemies, the reptiles grew like huge mushrooms on manure, reaching enormous sizes that have never been repeated on Earth.

FIG. 34. *Left*–Skeleton and outline of the plesiosaurus body. *Right*–Its reconstruction.

FIG. 35. *Left*–Reconstruction of a rhamphorhynchus. *Right*–Skeleton of a pterodactyl.

FIG. 36. Reconstructions of crawling and flying ramphorhynchus.

During this Jurassic period, the "middle kingdom" of the reptiles, they reached their golden age. Paleontology, the science of fossil relics, has produced a complete album of the types of ground reptiles. Only very few of them actually crawled. There were herbivorous and carnivorous, small and large, rodent and insectivorous, catlike and elephant-like reptiles. Over those long millions of years, the Earth was populated by the giants, Brontosaurs and Atlantosaurs, whose length was several tens of meters and who could use three- and four-story buildings as house furniture. Compared to their older relatives, amphibia, reptiles of that time had a number of significant advantages. They had strong scale covers instead of the thin skin of frogs and newts. Their brain was enriched with one more level, a paired neural nucleus, the striatum (Level C1), which surpassed the Level B nuclei of amphibia and fish and which significantly increased their motor capabilities. Finally, their long-range sensory organs, telereceptors, started to create for themselves the first, most primitive areas of a brain formation with a very special structure. These formations were rudiments of a brain cortex, which was totally absent in those reptiles and which is still absent in their descendants. We have already mentioned an extremely important revolution in the status and significance of the brain coincided with the emergence of the brain cortex (we are going to discuss it later). The development of the brain cortex was different than that of the long-ago-developed striated muscle. Striated muscle, as we have seen, emerged abruptly, and its masters did not adjust and modify it according to their needs but rather obediently adjusted themselves to its difficult character, like Cinderella's sisters who tried to cut off their toes or heels to squeeze a foot into the shoe. In the case of the brain cortex, the situation is the opposite: Its development included extensive preparatory work, preliminary intermediate forms, searches, and so on. We know all this because the life history of the cortex has been preserved in the brains of contemporary animals and in our own brain. In the human brain, there are both the primitive motor nuclei of Levels A and B and the higher nuclei of reptiles. Now, they are ruled by much younger and more perfected brain structures. In the brain cortex, there are strange, "old-fashioned" areas, which have very few things in common with the structure of its larger part. When you study the human brain cortex under a microscope, you feel as if you are walking along different streets of a large, old town. Suddenly, during the walk, you get into a block with very unusual buildings that feel very ancient and that are unlike all other buildings in the town. This is approximately the impression one gets when looking through a microscope at the most ancient areas of the brain cortex, its olfactory areas, and, partly, its visual areas. These areas are directly connected to the main telereceptors of vision and smell. They emerged at the time of reptiles, first in the brain cortex, and were the original nucleus that was, during later millenia, encircled by a huge town of human brain cortex.

Motor resources of reptiles were much richer than those at the previous stage represented by fish; different reptile species of that time could run, fly, swim, and jump. Aside from mastering various kinds of locomotion, these animals were also able to inhibit and regulate their movements, in contrast to the ever-moving fish. They could stop and remain as motionless as a statue. They could move slowly and malleably as through viscous dough and could, when necessary, rush like an arrow or make precise, quick, aimed leaps. Finally, reptiles brilliantly mastered equilibrium, and some of them (small snakes and especially lizards) deserved the description of dexterous.

FIG. 37. Skeleton of a giant brontosaurus

FIG. 38. Reconstruction of a giant brontosaurus compared to a contemporary elephant.

FIG. 39. *Left*–Skeleton of a stegosaurus. *Right*–A reconstruction.

THE STRUGGLE FOR WORLD SUPREMACY

At the dawn of the next, Cretaceous period, reptiles still ruled the Earth, but this period was bound to be fatal for them. The history of this "new kingdom" of reptiles is a history of continuous, cruel, and exterminating wars in the air, in the sea, and on the ground, struggles that led to the convincing and irreversible elimination of reptiles from the governing positions and to their virtual extermination, with only the pitiful remnants still present today, remnants getting closer and closer to total and final extinction. They were ousted from the air by birds, their direct descendants, and they suffered their most crucial defeat on the ground from a young (at that time) branch of warm-blooded vertebrates, mammals, who possessed many undisputable advantages.

What were the reasons for the destruction of the kingdom of reptiles? There were several of them, and they are of direct interest for us, because they allow us to penetrate deeper into the nature of movements and motor coordination.

First, the gigantic size of the reptiles of the Jurassic and Cretaceous periods was by itself disastrous. As they say in physics, each reaction has its temperature coefficient; that is, it proceeds faster at higher temperatures. This principle is also true for the phenomena in the neuromuscular system. It is well known and has been accurately measured that the speed of transmission of the electrochemical excitatory signal, the neural impulse, differs greatly between cold-blooded and

FIG. 40. Jurassic reptiles (iguanodon, compsognathus, and pterodactyl) in a forest.

warm-blooded animals. A wave of excitation travels along frog nerves at a speed of 8–10 m/s, whereas it runs along cat or human nerves at a speed of 100–120 m/s. Moreover, it has been established that this speed depends only on the type of the nerve (motor nerves are the fastest) and on body temperature but not on size of the body. Therefore, it can be assumed with good reason that neural impulses propagated along the nerves of giant reptiles no faster than they do in contemporary frogs and crocodiles. Now, let us make a simple calculation.

Imagine that someone bit the hind paw of a 30-meter giant reptile, who felt the pain, jerked back the limb, and hit the attacker with it. In order for the pain to be felt, neural impulses must travel through the leg (6 meters), trunk (10 meters), and neck (10 meters). The total is 26 meters, or 3 seconds one way. Let us assign the same amount of time for the reactive motor command from the brain to reach leg muscles. We should also add at least 1 second for the reaction to take place in the brain. So, the total time from the moment of the bite to the beginning of a leg movement is 7 seconds, a long time if you look at your watch and patiently wait for the 7 seconds to elapse. We should not forget also about the time that was necessary for a 5-foot muscle to excite, contract, and move the towering leg.

Now, it is easy to imagine that if the attacker were a lion or a saber-toothed tiger of those times (machairodont) with a total length from a hind limb to the brain and back of about 3 meters and reaction time less than ⅓ of a second,

FIG. 41. Dawn of the mammal kingdom.

FIG. 42. Reconstruction of a mammoth.

such a warm-blooded carnivore would be able to gnaw off the leg completely before the reptile was able to feel anything and to make a decision. If we imagine ourselves witnessing such a fight, they might translate the long, drawn-out wail of a reptile being eaten alive as "I . . . se–e–e–em . . . to–o–o . . . be–e–e . . . bi–i–i–tte–e–en . . . by–y–y–y . . . so–o–o–omeo–o–o–ne!" The outcome of such a struggle is not hard to predict.

Skeleton relics of Jurassic and Cretaceous giant reptiles reveal that they had a tiny head on a long neck that fitted them no better than would a mouse's head. Most of this disproportionally small head was occupied by the facial skeleton and large-toothed jaws, so that the brain had only a tiny, narrow space. We understand it better taking into account that an animal, which needed to consult the brain about each movement and wait 7 seconds each time for a reply, would

FIG. 43. A battle between a carnivorous (*left*) and herbivorous (*right*) iguanodons of the Jurassic period.

be absolutely helpless even without meeting hairy carnivores. Apparently, most of their motor reactions were controlled by the spinal cord. This could significantly shorten the time of neural conduction down to 2–3 seconds. Indeed, many of those reptiles had an enlargement of the spine (receptacle of the spinal cord) in the lumbar-sacral area from which hind-limb nerves originated. This enlargement indicates that the spinal cord in this area was also considerably enlarged; it was even bigger than the brain. Certainly, this construction significantly limited the quality and variety of movements, because the modern brain nuclei, striata, could be consulted only in exceptional and in not very urgent situations. It may well be that this independence of the lumbar-sacral enlargement led to a particular walking rhythm of the hind limbs, a rhythm independent of the walking rhythm of the forelimbs. This gait must have created a strange picture to behold!

The second cause of destruction of the reptile kingdom was common for reptiles of all sizes. All of them, as a rule, laid eggs into warm soil or sand and did not hatch them. Their young ones hatched themselves so that each individual animal spent all its life, from hatching to death (except during brief mating periods) in absolute solitude. Such things as family, training, or sharing experience with the youngsters were unknown. Each of the tiny brains started to accumulate life experiences from the very beginning. The absence of a cortex (its rudiments were pitiful) made the brain very poorly suited for accumulating and processing such experiences.

FIG. 44. *Above*–Extinct crocodile, teleosaurus (note the extremely small skull volume). *Below*–Contemporary alligator and its eggs.

The new, young class of mammals, warm-blooded, spirited, with a very much enriched brain and corresponding motor repertoire, was too strong an adversary for the reptiles. The smaller, dexterous carnivores pounced on the slow and seemingly purposefully prepared meat mountains and, by rapacious hunting, quickly eliminated them.

MOTOR ACHIEVEMENTS OF BIRDS

For consistency, before addressing the most prominent advantage of mammals, their motor talent, let us provide here an overview of the gains of the immediately preceding class, the birds. The *striatum*, the highest motor nucleus in reptiles, reached in birds its peak of perfection. A high level of development was also reached by the *cerebellum*, an organ of equilibrium and of "controling one's own body," which progressed in parallel with the striatum. The striatum (Level C1) heads a complex neuromuscular system, which very gradually developed in vertebrates, stage after stage. These stages are the most ancient, Level A; a newer level, the pallidum (B), dominating in frogs; and eventually, the level of the striatum (C1), which reached its golden age in birds. These levels together form the *extrapyramidal motor system* (EMS). Its gradual development explains many features of its structure. First, all of its nuclei, or levels, relate to each other as bosses to employees; that is, they form what is called a hierarchy. Second, the consistent overgrowth of the brain with new stories allowed the younger levels not to grow new neural pathways to the muscles because such pathways to all the muscles were already available. As a result, a system (see Figure 2 on page 99) that truly deserves the description of multistoried emerged.

This figure shows that direct pathways (i.e., pathways without transfers) to muscular cells exist only from neural cells of the spinal cord, so to say, *precells* of all the motor nervous system. Neural pathways from Level A nuclei (rubral cells), transferring orders to muscles, connect only to the motor cells of the spinal cord which send new impulses along motor nerves to target muscles. Similarly, neural pathways from the Level B nuclei reach only the Level A nuclei, whereas pathways from the Level C1 nuclei reach only the Level B nuclei. In order for a command to go from the striatum to a muscle, four consecutive neural volleys must replace each other, C–B, B–A, A–spinal cord, and spinal cord–muscle. Despite all the advantages and power of striatum as a supreme motor center, this historically established device had a number of drawbacks. One of them, according to accurate measurements by Lorente-de-No and other scientists, is that each transfer of a neural volley requires *additional time* (in physiology, this time is called *synaptic delay*). This time is very short in warm-blooded animals. Naturally, it is longer in cold-blooded animals, and if it happens three or four times, it adds considerably to the already slow neural process.

The EMS achieved its peak in birds (in these generally small animals with very high body temperature, this shortcoming of the EMS was not felt nearly as much as it was in huge reptiles). Highly developed sensory organs in birds provided them with complete and perfect command of all the types of *locomotions*, running, flying, and clambering. All these movements are not the trunk type, as in fish and snakes, but are an evolutionary younger extremity type. The importance to flying of perfect, sensory-based control of equilibrium has become obvious since humans themselves started to fly. Regulation and inhibition of

FIG. 45. *Left*–Skeleton of an extinct ancestor of birds, archeopterix. *Right*–Reconstruction of an archeopterix in flight (note the clawed wings).

movements and the ability to alternate complete motionlessness, slow movements, and quick rushes started to develop in reptiles. In this area, birds have reached high perfection and diversity. Finally, the list of bird motor acts includes several absolutely specific movement classes that are not found in reptiles. First, birds have a number of complex instincts. Controlled by instinct, bird actions are sometimes so skillful, accurate, and perfect, that they create an impression of conscious activity based on cognition similar to labor movements of humans. This impression is absolutely wrong. Besides the fact that birds do not have the organ of cognition, the motor cortex, direct analysis undoubtedly shows a deep difference between those bird actions and similar, intellectual activity of human beings. For example, when a bird makes a complex, perfectly built nest, sometimes actually sewing it together, like the tailor bird, or when it finds a way to its nest through hundreds of kilometers guided by an absolutely unknown sense, it looks identical to meaningful chain actions of a skillful and knowledgeable human. However, it is sufficient to confuse a bird with an unexpected obstacle or complication, and all the depth of the difference becomes apparent. When it is necessary for a bird to make just one deviation from an unchangeable pattern, to consider some minor detail, to contrive somehow in a minimally unexpected situation, and so on, we immediately witness a reaction of disorganized confusion already observed in lower animals. Thus, all these impressive instincts of migration, building nests, and hatching and feeding nestlings are only at first glance similar to genuine intellectual activity, which is not afraid of such small obstacles.

These instincts do, however, indicate a high level of purposeful biological adaptation and clearly illustrate motor advantages of birds as compared to more ancient vertebrate classes.

Second, in a sharp contrast to reptiles, birds usually *live in families* and themselves educate their nestlings. The notion of *mother*, the idea of *motherhood* first emerged on Earth when the first bird hatched its first eggs. Aside from the deep fundamental importance of this event (we discuss it later), it associated with a new, wide enrichment of the list of movements: directly educational actions of feeding, taking care of the nestlings, preparing them to fly, and so on. Besides these, a "homemaking" bird has a wide repertoire of complex movements of its private toilet, for example, cleaning and oiling the feathers, cleaning the nest, and so forth. Birds also brought to life *expressive sounds* of attraction, alarm, and actual *songs*, replacing the deadly croaking of frogs. *Dance* was also born. In general, the motor "ceiling" of birds is immeasurably higher than in reptiles, and there is just one aspect in which this "ceiling" presses them down. The still virtually absent motor cortex makes even the most gifted and highly developed birds ill-suited for the accumulation of personal experiences, for mastering new, complex motor skills, and particularly for displaying dexterity during unexpected, unpredictable motor problems.

HOW THE PYRAMIDAL SYSTEM DEVOURED
THE EXTRAPYRAMIDAL ONE

Our assertion that the EMS, after developing to its limits, contained a number of deeply concealed biological inconveniences is not merely a guess. It is based on the fact that mammals, who took care of eliminating reptiles of the "obsolete" type, made a revolutionary step in the development of their brain-motor systems, which, first and foremost, radically culminated in the multistoried motor organization. Even in the most ancient and primitive *mammals, the brain cortex was much more fully expressed* than in birds and reptiles, and even more important, it started playing the primary role. The striatum and cerebellum, which had reached their peaks in birds, began to move backward in their development in mammals, and even, in a sense, to move into disuse. Mammal motor cortex already had representation of all the sensory organs, both proximal and remote.

We have discussed how *movements* were enriched by the gradual formation of new brain nuclei, taking command over the old ones. It is not clear how and why the emergence of new supreme nuclei and the formation of a multistoried hierarchical system helped the enormous qualitative increase in motor capabilities, but the fact itself is undeniable. Now, in the formation and development of the mammalian brain, we witness a similar process with respect to sensory organs.

For example, in fish and frogs, the pathway from eye retina to the brain centers of vision consists of just one step, a route without transfers. In humans

FIG. 46.   Skeleton and outline (*left*) and reconstruction (*right*) of an early ancestor of horse, *Anoplotherium* (size of a dog) from the Eocene epoch.

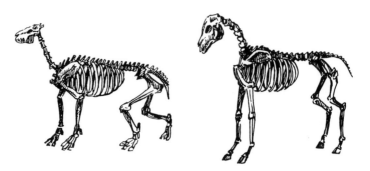

FIG. 47.   *Left*–Skeleton of an extinct perissodactyl animal similar to a contemporary llama. *Right*–Skeleton of a contemporary horse.

FIG. 48. Contemporary horse.

(bypassing other animals, for brevity), there are four steps from the eyes to the supreme visual cortical centers (termed Field 19); that is as many as in a fully developed EMS. In this area of higher sensory organs, the multistoried organization suggests a significant qualitative improvement. The slowing down in vision or hearing induced by the multistoried system is incomparably less dangerous than it would be for movements because of a very simple reason: The distance from the brain to a muscle somewhere in the foot is nearly 2 meters in humans and even greater in horses or elephants, whereas the eyes and ears are only centimeters away from the brain cortex.

In the process of the brain cortex becoming equipped with all the types of sensory signals in the most perfect form, the central power of controlling movements naturally shifted there as well, and all the inconveniences of remote and indirect connections between the brain and the muscles became more and more obvious. Here, in contrast to many other cases, life decided not to move along the route of gradual and careful adjustments but, rather, solved the problem in one move, similar to the cutting of the legendary Gordian knot. This is a unique case in the history of brain development. A *special neural pathway* grew from the cortical cells directly, without any transfers, to motor cells of the spinal cord. It was inadvertently called the *pyramidal neural tract*. This name originates from the early period of brain science and, by the way, explains the name *extrapyramidal* (i.e., nonpyramidal or outside-of-pyramidal) applied to the more ancient motor system of the brain.

A more or less detailed characterization of what the pyramidal motor system (PMS) brings to and does for movements in general and for dexterity in particular is presented in essay 5. Here, we are going to restrict ourselves to a few brief details so that it does not depart too far from the historical review.

First of all, to avoid any misunderstandings, we have to state unequivocally that the emergence and development of the PMS in no way meant the elimination of the ancient EMS. The decline of the EMS was limited to a minor decrease in dimension (involution) of its nuclei. When reptiles and birds developed the striatum, the pallidum was not eliminated but preserved with its list of movements, and new, more complex, accurate, and diverse movements controlled by the striatum were added to the list. Similarly, mammals preserved the EMS for movements (and elements of movements) that were performed by their

FIG. 49. Surinam marsupial with its brood.

remote anscestors. The new PMS, the own motor apparatus of brain cortex, which, as we have seen, established direct contacts with motor cells of the spinal cord without any intermediate steps, was used by mammals for absolutely new sets of movements and actions that were beyond the power of all the earlier motor nuclei. These new movements mostly included accurate, precise, and strong *targeted movements*, such as aiming, touching, grasping, accurate and strong *striking*, far and precise *throwing*, accurate and carefully planned *pressing*. These simple movements (and many others, see essay 5) gradually developed into numerous *meaningful chain actions*, such as the handling of *objects*, the using of *tools*, and, eventually, *meaningful labor*.

When compared to birds and especially to reptiles, mammals have relatively many more *singular, aimed movements* of attack, hunting, and so on. All these actions are not stereotyped, differing from one occasion to another and displaying very accurate and quick *adaptability*. They manifest progressive increase in an ability to quickly create *new, unlearned motor combinations* exactly fitting an emerging situation. If one borrows an analogy from the area of music, mammals perform fewer and fewer movements based on memory or written music and

FIG. 50. Apes: chimpanzee, gorilla, gibbon, orangutan (from *left* to *right*).

improvise more and more. This tendency explains their continuously increasing ability to acquire motor skills; they are more easily trainable. They have a larger number and variety of self-caring movements and toilet such as grooming, cleaning and sharpening claws, searching for parasites, preparing and processing food.

A permanent place in a mammal's everyday life is occupied by the family and the education of the young. Is there a person who has not seen a cat bringing to its kittens a semistrangled mouse to educate them? Is there anyone who has not witnessed a lioness or a tigress in a zoo generously but sensibly distributing "pedagogical" slaps to the cubs? Wolf, marmoset, and beaver females teach their litter about specific features of everyday life. Family also engenders a large number of emotional feelings and experiences that are unknown to reptiles: attachment, self-sacrifice, gratitude, obedience, and friendship. Actions that form an intermediate stage on the way to actual objective and chain actions become plentiful. These include various social games, the giving of examples with pedagogical objectives, the handling of objects, and so forth. Birds can use signal sounds and song sounds. In mammals, we see a number of expressive meaningful sounds, nearly words. How sensible and diverse are the sounds made by a smart dog in different situations! E. Seton-Thompson says the same about bears, I. Prishvin about beavers, Rudyard Kipling about seals. Facial expressions and expressive movements that have been totally absent in birds emerge. Each of us have seen the changeable and understandable (without words) "facial expressions" of a dog when it is happy, or shameful, or insulted.

Due to the functioning of the PMS, totality of mammal movements loses the specific, as if sticky and viscous, patterns of movements, the alternation of movements with statuelike, static postures typical of birds and reptiles. When a lizard or a turtle or a crocodile is motionless, it is actually motionless like a log. The same motionlessness is seen in a sitting parrot or owl. They all typically demonstrate slow, viscous movements of head and neck or clawed paws. These features of movements and motionlessness are very typical for the EMS. Interestingly, something similar can be observed in patients with brain diseases that lead to a relative overemphasis of the EMS and a weakening of the PMS. Movements of "pyramidal" animals, mammals, become more elastic, resembling movements of a spring. Mammals are never absolutely motionless. Their rest is always filled with watchful head and neck movements, the pricking and turning of ears, or with some other involuntary and habitual minor motor acts. A dog or a cat, stupefied by watching for a prey, appears as motionless and taut as a raised rifle cock. But observe what is going on with the tail. . . .

Now we have moved closer to the third and *most important reason* for the destruction of the reptile kingdom on Earth and for the consolidation of the still-lasting mammal kingdom. Reptiles lacked a cortex; their supreme motor system was the EMS. *Mammals introduced into the world the principle of brain cortex* with its unlimited abilities. The PMS became an exceptionally rich apparatus driving the warm-blooded striated muscles. Its most important advantages included quickness, strength, and accuracy of movements; the unlimited ability to accumulate personal life experiences (that was helped by the fact that parents accumulated experiences and taught them to their young); and the ability to create immediately, on the spot, new motor combinations like building houses from toy blocks or making words from typographical letter sets. On the outer, apparent side of the events that occurred during the Cretaceous period, warm-blooded mammals ate all the cold-blooded lizards. The internal side of the same events was much deeper and more important. Its essence, the PMS, devoured the EMS and asserted its status over the EMS remnants. Within 2 or 3 years (on the schematic historical time scale) of their appearance, mammals ruled all the animal world. For the last week or week and a half, the Earthly throne has been occupied by humans. Let us conclude this essay with a brief assessment of some of the more recent historical events on that same time scale. The brain of the world's ruler continuously enlarged and asserted its genuine domination over the world. About 1 hour ago, humans invented writing and thus started the historical period of their existence. Humans survived the terrible headache of the gloomy medieval stagnation of thought, and the healthy origins prevailed. Experimental studies of nature, genuine positivistic science, started about 5 "minutes" ago. Brain and nervous system physiology is in its second minute of existence. I ask my readers to forgive that discipline the important gaping omissions and numerous blank spots that still exist and that are quite natural for its young age.

On the Construction
of Movements

A MYTH ABOUT ZEUS AND THE MAN

Let us start this essay with a brief myth. Imagine that we have found the story among dusty manuscripts in a corner of an old secondhand book store:

> When Zeus created the living beings and placed them on Earth, he gave each of them brains that would best fit their owners. He gave the fish a brain that allowed it to swim, wriggle, and swallow the tasty, thick water. He gave the frog a brain that made it as bouncy as a wet rubber ball. He gave brains to the snake and to the turtle; he gave their share to the running, swimming, crawling, and flying birds that fill the sky. He also did not forget about the furry four-legged creatures, marsupials, rodents, and insectivores. He gave brains to the double-hoofed rhinoceros and to the single-hoofed horse, to the beaver and to the squirrel, to the walrus, seal, bear, and tiger, and even to the Bornean pot-bellied orangutan, and even to the gloomy African gorilla. . . . Man was the last to come.
>
> "Here," said Zeus with a touch of pride, giving the Man something looking like a pink paté on a plate. "You will be happy with what I give you. This is cortex of large hemispheres that I have endowed with many wonderful features. Look, this place will give you speech. That one will help you understand other people. This convolution will make you grammatical; that fissure will let you write; this corner will let you enjoy music; that part will make your right hand your trustworthy and reliable assistant and will let it master the most complex tools. All these things are for you, and for you only, my beloved child, and none of the other creatures will have them. Are you happy?"

"No, I am not," answered the Man. "I am sorry, Father, but you yourself made me so insatiable. I cannot restrict myself to only spiritual food. I do not want to live only a mental life, to be a young elder, a monk renouncing all the pleasures of life that you created so beautiful! Look at the horse, how strong his feet are and how endurant he is! Look at the eagle, how powerful his flight is, and how precisely he strikes his prey like your lightning, oh, Thunderer! Look at a swallow rushing through the air like an arrow. I also want to run, jump, climb, and even fly, damn it! Don't deprive me of all this!"

"Well," said Zeus, "I will also give you brains of the eagle and of the swallow. So, when you get tired of thinking, you will be able to run and to jump. When fighting your enemies, you will be as powerful as the eagle and as quick as the swallow. Are you happy now?"

"No, not yet," said Man. "I also need to be as flexible as the snake. I want my body to be able to curl and uncurl like a spring, I want my jumps to be not worse than those of the frog and the flea. I want my body to be free of fatigue and to feel myself as comfortable in all the elements as the fish in the water."

"You are asking too much, and I am getting bored," answered Zeus. "I shall give you brains of the fish and the frog, but this will be it. I have already spent on you five times as much time as on all other animals. But listen to what else I am going to say. So that you and all your descendants remember my generosity, each of your children and children of your children will, during their childhood, live through the lives of all those animals whose brains I gave you. Your life is long enough to spend some time as each of these creatures. There will be enough left for a real human life. And now, get lost."

And so, it happened, as Zeus, the Cloudmaster, the Father of all living on Earth, had said. Man starts his life as a fish and during nine months swims in mother's waters. Then, he arrives outside, he spreads his lungs but still kicks and wriggles helplessly as a fish on a shore and also croaks his "agoo" without any

FIG. 1.

sense or expression like a frog. After six months of life, his bird brain becomes mature; he learns how to sit and to stand, to maintain equilibrium, then to walk and to run, to quickly grab things and put them into his mouth. At the same time, he repeats words of the others without any sense, like a parrot. During the second year, his mammal brain ripens. His teeth grow, and this is a difference between birds and mammals. He starts to speak and understand the speech of others. Gradually, his forelimbs turn into hands. When a child learns how to use his hands not only to destroy things but also to use them, then he stops being a cub and turns into a Man. He is forced to sit behind a desk or a tool bench, and good-bye happy childhood!

This is what the myth about Zeus and Man says. Let us extract a scientific gain from it.

THE BRAIN SKYSCRAPER

The myth, or fable, is in many aspects correct as far as human movements are concerned. Some things should be expressed more precisely, and some things should be emphasized and analyzed more deeply.

First, it is true that the human brain is a multistoried building whose stories emerged successively, one after another. In essay 3, we have more or less carefully

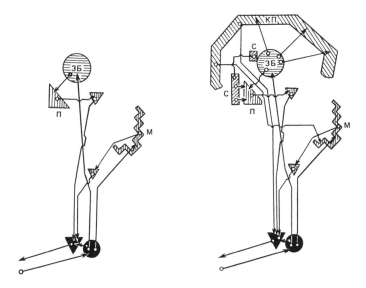

FIG. 2. Schematic of brain complication in the process of its development: П–pallidum; ЗБ–thalamus; C–striatum; M–cerebellum; КП–cortex. *Left*–A stage in the brain development corresponding to a fish or frog: *below* (black)–spinal nuclei; the upper centers include thalamus (sensory) and pallidum (motor). *Right*–Human brain with new levels—striatum and cortex.

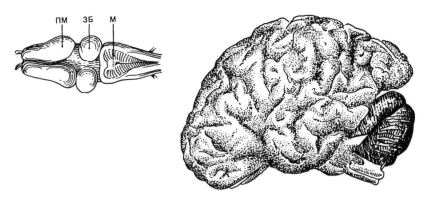

FIG. 3. *Left*–Frog brain (viewed from above): ПМ–motor nuclei (pallidum); ЗБ–sensory nuclei (thalamus); M–cerebellum. *Right*–Human brain.

traced the history of their emergence. The *lower department* of the adult human brain consists of neural nuclei corresponding to a frog's *pallidum*, its highest brain formation. (We do not address here the lower auxiliary centers of Level A, which are discussed in essay 5.) These nuclei obey the orders from the level of the *striatum*, which controls the brain motor structure in reptiles and birds. Even higher, there is the PMS of the brain cortex. This formation emerged even later and only in mammals. The brain cortex looks very different from all the other, older brain formations. It looks like a single, solid layer, which is crumpled and wrinkled with convolutions and fissures. These wrinkles emerged only because the cortex tried to grow as large as possible, but the cramped skull prevented it from doing so. However, if we forget about the fissures and convolutions and smooth out the cortex with an imaginary iron, we shall see a single, uniform, wide layer that covers the large hemispheres from all sides like a wide cloak. (In the early period of brain anatomy, the cortex was called *pallium cerebre*, "brain cloak.") However, if one considers the internal, historically developed structure of the brain cortex, it no longer looks that uniform. The most ancient (sensory) cortical rudiments emerged in the epoch of reptiles; these rudiments are still preserved in the human brain, retaining their structure and function. Later, in birds and in mammals, new cortical sections emerged and took their place near the old ones, as in a mosaic. Each of the new sections brought the possibility of a new function, and each of them has retained its "profession" in the human brain. They look very similar, and their deep distinctions can be seen only through a microscope. Despite the fact that these sections emerged side by side in the developing cortex and their edges merged together, the younger formations controlled the older ones as had happened in the more ancient brain structures. During the time of mammal evolution, already after the emergence of the PMS, at least two more motor systems managed to emerge in the brain. These systems are purely cortical, and they control the PMS similarly to the way the consecutive stories in the older EMS control each other. The highest

FIG. 4. An early, embryonic stage of the human brain development. At this stage, the brain looks like a tube with one dead end. During the next stages, the tube walls enlarge, and the tube separates into five balloons (shown with Roman numerals). Thin dashed lines outline centers (in the same form and location as in Fig. 2) that will develop from the balloons.

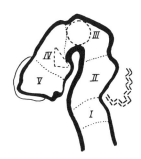

and youngest of these systems is present only in humans and provides humans an exclusive advantage over all other animals. These several stories, concealed in the seemingly single-layered cortex, tower over the multistoried EMS building and form, together with the EMS, a large brain skyscraper. We will see later what the function and the meaning of such a multistoried construction are.

THE PREMATURELY BORN FULL-TERM BABY

During my school years, one of my friends teased me and my classmates, assuring us that the English were born blind. We did not actually believe him, but this fable made us wonder why the young ones of our closest friends, dogs and cats, were born so helpless and incomplete. We sympathized with them. These thoughts combined with a somewhat proud confidence that everything was much better with the human being, the king of the nature. We did not suspect that, at the moment of birth, a human has not fewer but probably more unfinished parts in the central nervous system and that it takes not less than 2 years to totally eliminate all the structural deficiencies and to mature completely, like a tomato when picked green and placed at a sunny place to ripen. This brain maturation happens very slowly; system after system is activated at its precisely defined, particular time and enriches the child's motor abilities more and more. Therefore, the Zeus fable is correct in describing these facts.

We already mentioned in essay 3 a very interesting biological principle discovered by a well-known follower of Charles Darwin—Hèckel. Hèckel named this principle the *biogenetic law*. It would be more correct to call it a "custom of nature" rather than a "law of nature," because the laws of nature should be followed without exceptions, like the universal law of gravity.

The principle of Hèckel is similar to many other scientific principles related to live nature in that it is far from being universal. The only thing we can say is that it is certainly obeyed more frequently than it is violated.

The biogenetic custom of nature states that all the major steps of the process of evolutionary development of an animal, which were followed by its ancestors, will be repeated in summary form at the beginning of the development of each

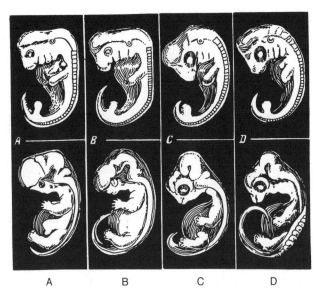

FIG. 5. Embryos of the human (A), dog (B), chicken (C), and turtle (D) embryos in the 4th week of development (upper row) and in the 6th–8th week of development. All the drawings are scaled so that the embryos are approximately the same size. All the drawings clearly show horizontal balloons of the neural tube similar to those in Fig. 4.

individual. In the process of formation and development, each individual appears to be recollecting, one after another, memories of the great past revolutions, by reproducing them briefly in itself. For example, the times when our very remote direct ancestor, who, very much like contemporary fish breathed through gills, had passed a long time ago. But even in our times, each human embryo has gills during the first weeks of gestation. Later, they are transformed into different things, including sublingual bone, auditory bones of the middle ear, the ear–throat Eustachian tube, and so on. The biogenetic principle applies very directly to motor neural systems and the movements themselves. So, the Zeus myth happens to be correct here as well.

The brain matures in a baby, story after story, in the same order in which it emerged in the animal world. A baby *is born* when its *pallidum* (Level B), the ceiling

FIG. 6.

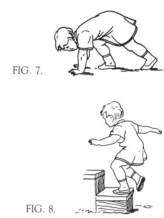

FIG. 7.

FIG. 8.

level of reptiles, is just finishing its development. Hence, babies cannot perform any movements beyond those available at this level. The situation is complicated even more by the fact that the more ancient, lower Level A, which controls the neck and trunk movements and posture (about which we are going to talk later) *has not had enough time to mature* and to start functioning *at the moment of birth*. Therefore, a newborn cannot control the main supporting structure of the body and the head, its trunk and neck, and cannot use its "dynamic struts," the extremities. The baby lies helplessly on its back, its trunk heavy and motionless and its four extremities capable only of chaotic kicking movements in all directions and absolutely without purpose. Moreover, there is one more complicating factor: The Level B can send its impulses to spinal motor cells and, through them, to muscles, only via nuclei of the lower Level A. Therefore, Level B is forced to sit idly and wait until Level A matures enough to allow motor impulses to pass through. The baby is thus deprived of *synergies* that accompany Level B, that is, the coordinated movements of a whole extremity or of all the extremities. Practically, during the first 2–3 months after birth, the baby has no motor coordination at all. Only at the end of the first 3 months of life do correct coordinated eye movements, turning from back to stomach, and other similar activities start to develop. At about 6 months, two levels of the brain start to function nearly simultaneously: the lowest Level A, which gives the baby a strengthened and coordinated trunk; and the striatum (Level C1), which enables the baby to sit, to stand up on its legs, later to crawl (one more biogenetic reminder about humans' four-legged ancestors!), and eventually, to walk and to run.

The development of the PMS is delayed even longer. Sensory cortical areas begin to work much earlier: The baby starts to recognize objects that it saw before, to understand words when being addressed, to develop preferences in gastronomy. The PMS gradually starts to reveal itself during the second half of the first year of life, after the striatum. The manifestations of its activity include the baby's grasping of objects, placing and moving things, pointing with a finger, and so on. At the same time, the first intelligible speech sounds emerge, usually those of request or command (e.g., "give"). Hand movements are still very inaccurate; the baby frequently misses its target by quite a margin, but until this time it has not even tried to perform movements like grasping or throwing—it did not have an instrument to do them! The difference between a baby past 6 months of life and one before 6 months is approximately the same as that between a person who has a bicycle and can barely ride it and a person who has no bicycle at all.

The higher cortical levels, which emerged during evolution after the PMS, mature later in a growing baby. The cortical system of actions (Level D), which we describe in essay 5, forms during the second year of life. First, this system enables a child, somehow, even very crudely, to handle objects: to eat with a spoon, to open a box, to draw with a crayon, to take off stockings. Second, it brings about a *new stage in speech development: naming objects*. This stage corresponds to a huge step forward in the development of the child's self. Soon, the child realizes its self, and then, for the first time, replaces an inexpressive "*Borya* wants" with a proud "*I* want!"

Although the process of *anatomical brain maturation* is complete at 2 years, general motor development is far from completion. One cannot speak about a more or less complete control over movements until the human is 14–15 years of age. Until this time, the teenager is clumsy in many aspects, tires quickly, uses a childish handwriting, and so forth. All this suggests that the *harmony in work* of all parts and sections of the brain (or, as physiologists call it, *functional maturation*) is delayed much longer than anatomical maturation. In essay 5, we shall present a brief review of motor development between the ages of 2 and 15 years. Here, however, it is necessary to explain more precisely the consequences and the effects on voluntary movements of the brain multistoried structure.

NEW PROBLEMS AND BRAIN DEVELOPMENT

We have seen already, in the essay on the history of movements, how the brain gradually became more complex. The struggle for life intensified and required a continuous increase in motor "armaments." Motor tasks, which the animal was forced to solve, became more complex and diverse. *Motor tasks* (motor needs) and the implacable necessity to move *more quickly, accurately, and dexterously* were the leading causes for the development of the brain and its accessories during all the millenia of evolution. The conditions might have changed only during the last, relatively very short period of time. In humans, because of the absolute dictatorial position of the brain, movements have lost their crucial role and retreated under the attack of labor and intellectual needs. In any case, this shift has taken place very recently, not more than a week ago on the schematic time scale.

So, intensification of the struggle for survival led to a gradual accumulation of similar motor tasks that were still beyond the animal's abilities. The necessity to find a solution inevitably grew with time. Animals had to meet the new, more complex motor requirements in order to survive. Meeting the new requirements had one major obstacle: the necessity to master *new sensory corrections*.

In the second essay, we described in detail sensory corrections as the basis for the control of movements of our body organs. In order to make an organ follow a brain command and do exactly what is required, the brain needs to have *continuous* control over the movement. This necessity means that the sensory organs (or receptors, as we call them in essay 3) must continuously send signals to the brain about the progress of the movement and thus enable the brain to introduce, without delay, required changes (*corrections*). Just *one redundant degree of freedom*—in excess of the single degree of freedom corresponding to movements along a fixed, unmodifiable path, without which there is no mobility—means an *infinite freedom of choice of movements*. That is why, *in order to control a movement*, each redundant degree of freedom must be saddled and bridled by an appropriate sensory correction. Apparently, the receptors must primarily be able to inform the brain about the most essential movement aspects, that is, those aspects whose wrong execution would lead not only to movement discoordination but also to its total disruption. For example, reptiles cannot use their forelimbs for anything except locomotion (transfer). On the other hand, mammals can use them for a variety of movements, more complex in both meaning and in diversity: to supply food, as dogs and wolves do; to slap opponents in the face like cats; to dig in the snow like a deer; to take and handle objects like a squirrel. The reptiles do not have such special nuances of perception, and, even more important, they do not possess those *united combinations* (*syntheses*) of different sensations (tactile, muscular-articular, visual, etc.) that are required to control such movements. Similarly, a 6-month-old baby, who is far from possessing all the adult corrections, cannot grasp an object that he sees and that obviously attracts him, a lack apparent from its energetic although ineffective flounderings. All the baby's attempts remain futile because it *does not have the mature combinations of sensations* that enable us, the adults to grasp immediately with a hand an object in any visible point in space.

We have already seen in essay 3 that brain development in vertebrates proceeded in discrete leaps, each one marking a qualitative enrichment of the brain. Each such leap or crucial moment in the development meant that a problem of mastering a new class of movements, which had been looming for a long time, was solved successfully. As a result, the central nervous system was acquiring a *new class of sensory corrections* corresponding to the new, urgent problems and suitable for solving them. The term *new class* meant either a direct, new feature of sensations or a new way of processing, comparing, estimating, and integrating those sensations. It is quite understandable that such a new class of sensory corrections required corresponding *new brain equipment*. Naturally, brain formation also proceeded, not through a gradual development, but in abrupt leaps with considerable qualitative changes. Each such leap in brain development gave rise to the building a new story, a new motor system, so that the whole process of brain development looks like a history of *consecutive additions* of new stories to a building. The human brain resembles a house that was originally built long ago with just one floor, according to the modest aspirations of its residents. The next generation of its inhabitants demanded more, their financial abilities also grew, fashions had changed, and so they built a second floor over the old one. They left all the utility rooms on the first floor and moved the main rooms to the second floor. A son of the owner of those times was an even wealthier and more enterprising person. He was not satisfied with the second floor with its bedroom, office, and chapel, where his old-fashioned father had spent all his life. The son wanted a study, a drawing room, and so on. He built a third floor over the two old ones but did not change much in the older floor design and maintenance, adjusting them only slightly to the new order of life and work. One can imagine that, when there are six or seven floors built consecutively one over another over the same number of generations of owners, the house will be very far from any architectural design or artistic unity. The same can be said about the human brain. It is extremely complicated, at least in the areas related to motor control; very capricious; and breaks down easily. Too many of its features need to be accounted for and justified by historical reasons. Anyone who has worked in a clinic for neurological patients can remember how depressing were the first impressions, created by the abundance and variety of brain disorders and the ease of their emergence. However, basic reconstruction of the human brain is not on the agenda here, and we will not waste time on fruitless regrets. Let us restrict ourselves to pointing out that there was an enormous job of adaptation and fitting together of the different brain parts. As a result of hundreds of years of adjustment of different brain parts of different ages, the human brain has eventually become a reasonably good and quite productive apparatus, when it is not sick or injured.

ENRICHMENT OF SENSORY IMPRESSIONS

So, each new leap in the development of brain motor systems was, first of all, an *acquisition of a key to a whole new class of motor tasks*, which had until then been inaccessible. We have seen how reptiles mastered many types of terrestrial locomotion and flying; how birds achieved complex and refined motor instincts; and how an increase in the motor abilities of mammals progressed at a rapid, continuously increasing pace, which included complex hunting, upbringing of the young ones, primitive building, and so forth. All these achievements, gained one by one, have always been based on the same foundation: *an improvement* and refinement *of sensory corrections*, that is, primarily, sensory perceptions, which form the basis for the corrections. The basis for each new class of corrections is always represented by *a new anatomical brain story*. This new structural level brings with it a new *set of movements*, a new set of mastered coordinations, which is appended to the previous one.

All this tightly interweaved and mutually interrelated phenomena—a new *class of tasks*, a new *type of corrections*, a new brain story, and, as a result of all this, *a new list of movements*—are called a new *physiological level of the construction of movements*.

In the next essay, we present brief sketches of the human levels of construction of movements, from the lowest to the supreme. Prior to that discussion, however, a couple of clarifications are necessary.

First, let us try to understand in which direction and how new *sensations*, which form the basis of new sensory corrections pertaining to the higher and more complex levels of construction, develop and improve. Unfortunately, our knowledge of how and what animals, especially the lowest animals, feel and to what extent their feelings are similar to ours, are in a very primitive state since we do not have a way of asking them. (An indirect and not always applicable way was developed by the famous Russian scientist I. P. Pavlov and his students in the form of the method of conditioned reflexes.)

Movements themselves, however, tell us about the enrichment of sensations and impressions. Each new step of movement evolution reflects, as a mirror does, an improvement in the functioning of sensory organs. If the feelings of animals are concealed from us because we cannot squeeze into the skull of a lizard or a gopher, the movements of these animals are quite open for any kind of scrutiny. Therefore, we are able to follow how both movements and the underlying signals of their sensory corrections become specialized, refined, and more meaningful. We have already seen such examples from the history of animal evolution and from the development of a human baby.

Studies have shown that perception is weaker, more restricted, and less acute in animals at the lower end of the evolution ladder, whereas perceptions created by the sensory organs of a highly developed brain are markedly precise, accurate, and clear. Consider, for example, why 7- and 8-year-old schoolchildren cannot read regular print and require a large font, although their vision is itself more acute than that in adults.

Second, a highly developed brain classifies and processes information from peripheral sensory organs in a quite different way from a less-developed brain. The highly developed brain does not simply give itself to an external flow of impressions but processes them, relates them to each other, quickly confronts them, and performs a skillful, very informative cross-examination. Similarly, an elderly, experienced physician needs simply to glance at a patient with his weak eyes to diagnose an old, neglected disease, whereas young medical students cannot do so with their young, acute eyes. Certainly, such comprehension of impressions takes place absolutely subconsciously and, to a large extent, involuntarily. There is even a special word for it, *intuition*, which, however, does not explain anything.

After such processing, perception of the external world certainly loses something; it becomes less fresh and direct, more schematic, and perhaps sometimes even biased. (A famous Milano astronomer of the 19th century, Sciaparelli, dedicated all his life to the studies of Mars and compiled very detailed maps of its surface. He saw through his mediocre telescope more details than we are able to discern now with the help of photography through powerful contemporary equipment. However, he also "saw" things that now have been proven not to exist on Mars, for example, double channels). On the other hand, perception emphasizes the basic meaning and essence of perceived events and is able to consider the world in fine detail.

The third specific feature of the development of sensory perception is most clearly reflected in corrections, that is, in the aspects of perception that are most closely related to motor coordination. Control of movements by more developed levels of motor coordination is characterized by a smaller share of the raw, direct impressions that come directly from certain sensory organs. Direct impressions are replaced by whole moulds or bars of sensations from different sensory organs that merge together to a state of total indiscrimination. Let us restrict ourselves to just one example of vision, how it functions in humans. If we were able to fix our eyes so that they would not be able to move, we would be unable to discern not only distance to or dimensions of objects but also their shape. We feel that we see directly through the eyes the distance to an object, its actual size, and its shape whereas, in fact, the perceptions that tell us about these features of the object are not of visual origin. Humans judge distance to visible objects by perceiving the strain of eye muscles required to merge two images of an object into one; it is impossible to perceive distance with just one eye. We define the shape and dimension of objects by outlining them with our eyes by placing the object, point by point, into the central area of the retina (*fovea*), and again muscular sensations tell us how big or small the object is and what its shape is, based on the amplitude and pattern of eye movements that have been required to outline the object. Sometimes, we subconsciously help ourselves by touching an object, that is, with tactile sensation. Everyone probably remembers the unpleasant necessity of restraining one's own hands in a sculpture museum, when they longed to touch the statues, and how our impressions suffered because touching was forbidden. As we are going to see further, a very important, dominating role *in the control* of our movements, particularly hand movements, is played by such unified, *synthetic* perceptions of space, distance, dimension, and shape of objects.

Finally, impressions and perceptions of a highly developed brain display one more interesting feature: They become *more active*. An eye does not simply see objects; it looks, examines, and scrutinizes them. An ear does not simply allow external sounds inside itself; it does not hear sounds but listens to them attentively, draws out the most important ones as if performing a selection among what it hears. The active nature of absorbing impressions into oneself is particularly brightly apparent when sensory organs need to utilize all their ability and art. This concerted effort happens, for example, in the blind, whose tactile perception substitutes, more or less successfully, for lost vision. Anyone who has watched people who are blind knows how actively they feel all interesting objects, such as a face or sculpture. In people who are not blind, this "feeling" activity of vision is not that striking but, as it has already been mentioned, plays an important role. It is not widely known that eye movements in humans are more diverse and their coordination more refined than in animals, including those animals that are superior to humans in visual acuity. This increase in the activity of sensory organs represents a resurrection, in a new form, of a very old, primitive mode of their functioning that had been present in worms and other soft-bodied creatures even before striated muscle and sensory corrections were born. However, now it reappears in a very different form and in a very close relationship with sensory corrections. Here we see an absolutely indisoluble and very complex tangle of interactions in which sensory signals (sensory corrections) modify and direct movements, while the movements modify and deepen the perceptions derived from the sensory organs. An analysis of this tangle, however, is likely to lead too far from the main path.

LISTS OF MOVEMENTS AND BACKGROUND LEVELS

We need to make one more introductory explanation concerning the levels of coordination and sets of movement belonging to each of them.

Assume that some particular species of animals has a supreme coordination level, that its motor ceiling is a Level X. After many centuries, a new species emerges that possesses a higher level, Y. The set of movements introduced by this higher level is added to the previous list, inherited from the ancestors, which had stopped at Level X. Does this mean that the addition of one new level of construction of movements (Y) adds exactly one new set of movements? The answer turns out to be no, so simple arithmetic does not apply here. The addition of a new level enriches movements to a larger extent because of the following reasons.

When a new, stronger, and more dexterous level develops and brings with it a whole new layer of movements, there are many movements of the older level whose essence exactly corresponds to those of the new level but that were inaccessible because of purely technical, secondary, but insuperable, reasons. Indeed, the new level has brought with it more powerful sensory corrections than those available before, corrections more accurate, more deeply penetrating into the meaning of movements, more active, and so on. However, these corrections do not cover everything that may be required to control each and every movement, cannot protect them from all sides. Here, then, it may happen that a missing correction for a complex movement is available at the old Level X.

FIG. 9. Nina Dumbadze, record holder and champion of the Union of Soviet Socialist Republics in discus throwing.

Clearly, we do not refer here to the most basic and responsible corrections whose absence would be equivalent to the disruption of the whole movement. However, it happens very frequently (and, as we are going to see, this is rather a rule than an exception) that although there are no problems with the basic, leading corrections, the movement, nevertheless, does not come out nicely, because many things, albeit secondary, are still lacking. In such cases, cooperation from a lower level (X) provides necessary help. In such a movement, the upper level (Y) takes the position of the leading level, that is, takes the responsibility for the most basic, vital corrections responsible for the meaning of the movement, for its success or failure. The lower level (X) takes the role of a lubricant in an engine. Its corrections make the movement easier, smoother, quicker, more expedient, more dexterous, and increases the probability of success. It is tempting to say that these auxiliary corrections provide the movement with its lining or background. Therefore, in such cases, we say that the lower level, X, takes for such a movement the role of a *background level*.

Let us consider two or three examples, which are long overdue. A boy ran and, while running, dexterously picked an apple from a tree. The movement of picking an apple requires a whole spectrum of corrections that are missing at the level that controls running and jumping. This movement (picking) is controlled by a higher level and by different brain structures. On the other hand, if the apple hangs too high, so that it is impossible to pick without taking a run, *the level* controlling the movement of picking becomes helpless *by itself* and requires help in form of a running start, that is, locomotion. In this example, the running start becomes an *auxiliary, or technical, lower, background level*, such as that we have just discussed. The upper level, so to speak, borrows from the lower one the auxiliary elements of the movement, the necessary corrections that it does not have.

The role of technical background corrections is even more apparent in such complex movements as discus throwing. The throwing movement, itself, is basically provided by the same level that played the leading role in the previous example. To perform the movement correctly and successfully, however, requires many various auxiliary corrections. It is necessary to maintain *correct tone*, that is, involuntary contraction of neck and trunk muscles. It is necessary to harmoniously execute an extensive *muscular synergy* of all the body muscles from the head to the feet, which provides a spiral winding up of the body and its successive unwinding, similar to the releasing of a spring. This movement also requires a *locomotion*, but one more complex than in the previous example: a running start and then a turn around.

All these background corrections are necessary for the primary, crucial throwing movement to be performed, as though it were riding on all the other submovements, and each of the background levels finds its corrections in another, lower level of construction of the movement. In this example, virtually all the levels happen to be involved in background activity. A cooperative and harmonious interaction among all of them is required so that the main objective of the whole movement—a discus throw—is achieved with maximal success, riding on all the background levels like a rider on a horse.

So, the emergence of a new level (Y) above an older level (X), aside from its direct set of movements, has led to the emergence of one more set that can be addressed as $\frac{Y}{X}$ and is the list of movements for which Level X supplies auxiliary, background corrections. After these examples, it is not necessary to specifically emphasize that *each* of the human levels can use for its technical, background needs *any* of the lower levels in any combination.

One should certainly not presume that such a complex and, at the same time, harmonious cooperation of a number of levels, that we have just unveiled with the help of examples, could emerge spontaneously, by itself. Each new type of movement requires *significant preparatory work* to form such a cooperation. This work is called *exercise* or *practice*. Events that take place during exercise include the collaboration of the most appropriate *technical background corrections* for a given movement and the *mutual adjustment* of all the background levels among themselves and in conjunction with the *leading level of this particular movement*. The collaboration of background corrections for a movement at the lower levels is also called *movement automation*; later we shall clearly see why. The problems of motor skill development, exercise, automation, and so on are discussed in a special essay of this book, essay 6.

THE SPINAL TRIGGERING APPARATUS

The level of spinal cord should probably be named the lowest and the most ancient human level of motor control. The primitive motor cells, which we discussed in essay 3, are located at this level, among conglomerates of neural cells. All motor impulses, that is, commands for contraction of certain muscles, that originate in brain motor centers can influence muscles only via these spinal cells.

Each muscle of our body consists of several tens or hundreds of thousands of small bunches of fibers, called *mions*. Each mion is approached by one thin fiber of a motor nerve, which branches at its end and makes contact with each of the mion's fibers. The motor neural fiber originates from one of the spinal primitive cells, which serves as a trigger for a certain mion. There are exactly as many thousands of mions as there are motor neural fibers and triggering neural cells in the spinal cord. These thousands of triggering cells form something like a keyboard representing exactly all the muscular equipment of the body. If it is necessary to activate mion N^a 17411, the triggering cell N^a 17411 must be activated.

As we have already mentioned, none of the impulses from the brain has direct access to muscles; these impulses act only on the keyboard of spinal triggering cells. Perfectly isolated from each other, neural fibers stretch from the brain along the spinal cord and terminate at different spinal levels, so that their branched ends come close to the spinal cells (keys). A motor impulse from one of the brain "floors," or levels, runs down along the spinal cord and excites the triggering cell of a mion whose activation is necessary at that particular time.

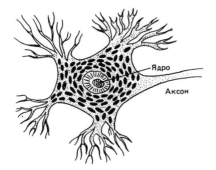

FIG. 10. Schematic drawing of a neural cell viewed through a micro-scope. The treelike branchings are dendrites.

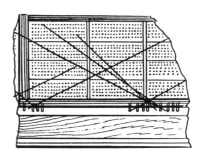

FIG. 11. A commutation board at a telephone station for connecting customers. Something similar takes place between the lower terminals of the brain neural cells and dendrites of the triggering cells.

A long time ago, in lower vertebrates, the spinal cord was rather independent. Sensory signals from the body surface immediately switched on triggering cells, giving rise to simple, monotonous movements. We already had a chance to mention in essay 3 that the spinal cord of the giant reptiles had a special enlargement at the area connected to the hind limbs, so the necessity of addressing the brain during most of the movements was avoided, a necessity that would considerably slow down the transmission.

All of this changed a long time ago in higher mammals and humans. In a healthy state, their spinal cords never perform independent movements. All the motor control shifted upward, to the brain motor centers. The basic, segmental principle of the spinal cord structure, in which each segment, from vertebra to vertebra, had some degree of independence, itself has become obsolete. Since the time when animals became quick and agile, when a vital role in their life was starting to be played by transfers from one place to another (locomotions), which required united, coordinated activity of all the body muscles under the supreme command of the brain, the segmental structure became an outdated, unnecessary trace of the past. Since that time, the spinal cord has gradually started to play the role of a simple impulse transducer, a triggering mechanism, as we have just defined it, and this transitory period is over in human beings.

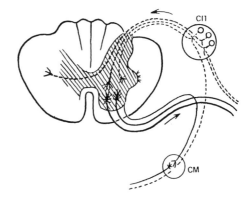

FIG. 12. Schematic cross section of the spinal cord at the level of one of the root pairs: dashed area–grey (neuronal) matter; surrounding white areas–white matter (conducting pathways); solid lines–motor neuronal pathways; dashed lines–sensory pathways; thin lines–sympathic fibers; CΠ–spinal, intervertebrate ganglion; CM–sympathic ganglion.

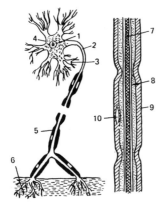

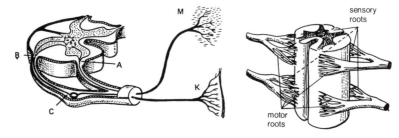

FIG. 13. Structure of a neuron (*left*) and axon (*right*): 1–neuronal nucleus; 2–axon; 3–dendrite; 4–neuronal soma; 5–membrane of a neural fiber; 6–terminal branches; 7–axon; 8–myelin membrane; 9–Schwann membrane; 10–membrane nucleus.

FIG. 14. *Left*–Scheme showing the structure of spinal roots and paths of peripheral neural fibers: A–place of an anterior root exit from the spinal cord (shown as a section); B–place of a dorsal root entrance; C–intervertebrate ganglion; M–muscle; K–skin. *Right*–Two spinal segments and spinal roots.

That is why *the level of the spinal cord has not survived in our bodies*: It died with the last Mohicans who still needed it in some form, the primitive reptiles.

Let us now turn to actual, still-existing levels of construction of movements in our central nervous system. We shall consider them, one by one, from the lowest and oldest to the highest, those that control the most complex, meaningful movements and actions. Certainly, in a volume like this, in which the question of movement construction is merely a necessary introduction to the main problem of dexterity, we shall only give very brief sketches of the levels that have been defined by the science of human movements.

Levels of Construction
of Movements

THE LEVEL OF TONE: LEVEL A

At a sign from the pilot, a parachutist climbed on a plane's wing. The wind was strong and gusty. The vast scenery below, filling the cup of the horizon up to its edges, seemed to tremble like springs. The instinctively clenched hands did not want to let go. The parachutist overcame his weakness, rolled himself into a ball, and dropped down.

The whine cut off like a shot fired. The man hit the soft pillows of air and dived like a swallow extending his body and tossing back his head.

He was experienced in delayed drops and calmly guarded himself against going into a spin, without any strain, just by moving his left arm. The body itself took the correct postures while the stopwatch counted the kilometers . . .

The sketch that starts this essay illustrates a rare example of Level A playing the role of the leading level. In an overwhelming majority of movements, Level A lets its younger brothers take the leading post but is itself never eliminated from action. Quite the opposite—one can hardly find movements that would not be based on this "background of all backgrounds." The fact that it is not readily obvious nicely fits the role of this level as a deep foundation for movements. Indeed, basements of buildings are also deeply concealed under the ground, and a savage or a child would not suspect their existence. This level plays a more or less purely defined leading role in those quick seconds of aerial phases of some (but not all) jumps: the starting jump, springboard jump into water, ski jump, and so forth. The rarity of its solo performances while the rest of the orchestra remains quiet is explained by its extremely old age. Level A and its movements are very valuable documents proving our direct lineage from the pra-mother fish, the eldest of the vertebrates. The rarity of this level's taking the leading role is directly related to the fact that only in exceptional cases do humans get into situations similar to the one in which fish spend all their days: *in an equilibrium with the environment, without the apparent action of gravity.* Obviously, this can happen with us only in very rare and brief moments of so-called free falls. For aquatic animals, such smooth movements (or not even actual movements but, rather, equilibrating stirs, twists, and curls) of the body are very appropriate. As stated in essay 3, Level A was a preextremity level that naturally specialized in *trunk and neck* muscles. It still remains a trunk-and-neck level, even in us, humans, whereas control of the extremities has been taken over by the younger levels starting with Level B.

Anyone who has paid careful attention to his body movements undoubtedly knows how different are the trunk–neck system of the body, on the one hand, and the equipment of the extremities, on the other hand. To see this difference clearly, one need only analyze such movements as throwing, long jump, mowing, gymnastic exercises, and so on. Smooth, elastic, enduring movements dominate the behavior of the trunk and neck, maintaining head equilibrium. They provide mobile, adaptive support, which is a mixture of equilibrium and movement, of statics and dynamics. This system has neatly been termed *statokinetics.* Movements of the extremities, on the other hand, are strong, abrupt, and frequently consist of alternations (there and back). They are absolutely and thoroughly dynamic.

The explanation of this fact once again originates from movement history. When life moved out of the water onto solid ground, there was a highly increased demand for rigid, abrupt, dry movements, like the ground itself. Smooth and volatile waterlike movements were pushed into the background. At the same time, the extremities were born, bringing with them a new, supreme Level B, which, from the very beginning, adapted to these new tools.

One might think that the essence of the apparent difference between the movements is in the difference between the bone and articular structures of trunk and extremities. The trunk–neck stalk consists of numerous, small vertebrae assembled in an elastic but not very mobile rod similar to a rubber stick. The

FIG. 1. Ski jump.

FIG. 2.

long and rigid links of extremities are connected with mobile ball joints, perfectly lubricated and moving virtually without friction. However, the origin of the difference between their movements is different. Undoubtedly, both skeletal-articular and neuromuscular systems developed in parallel, always exerting influence on each other, but the first violin was definitely played by the neuromuscular system. As a result of their mutual adjustment, nature managed to re-create in the trunk–neck system almost all the prevertebrate, ancient softness and flexibility. Arthropods, insects, and crayfish, could not even dream about anything of this kind. Only centipedes have something similar. Moreover, it is particularly interesting that this flexibility, *invertebrate* in its nature, found its place nowhere else but in the area of our *spinal column*.

According to the most crude scheme, Levels A and B divided the body territory according to this very principle: Level A took the spinal column and support; Level B took the movers (extremities). Obviously, this division is oversimplified, first, because the functioning of both levels in humans is under the control of the higher, cortical levels. Besides that, the division was complicated by the unavoidable interference between the levels. Level B was forced to participate in the functioning of *trunk muscles* because the primitive, weak means of Level A could not keep pace with the powerful and quick movements of the body and lagged behind the movements of the extremities. On the other hand, Level A found a very important function in control of movements of the extremities, so it took some of the primary roles, although only as a background level.

In a section of essay 3, "Drawbacks of the Striated Muscle," we discussed the extremely inconvenient features and character of the striated muscle, or more precisely, its *anisoelements*. The most important inconveniences mentioned include shot-like *crudeness of contractions*, their extremely *short duration*, and *the impossibility of controlling the force of the contractions*. We also mentioned a way to overcome the last inconvenience, namely, to methodically and progressively involve muscular fibers in an orderly way if a gradual force increase was required by the task and to gradually switch them off when a gradual drop of force was required. This indirect method resembles the gradual darkening in a theater: turning on and off groups of lamps. This method certainly yields an imperfect, steplike process, but separate mions are so small that the steps are imperceptible. However, this method is a very indirect one. In the same section of essay 3, we also discussed another, more refined method of controlling muscle force. Let us get back to it here.

First, it is necessary to mention that impulses from Level A, probably because of their historical age, are characterized by a domination of the primitive, chemical method of excitation (described in the first sections of essay 3). During the functioning of Level A, as in the good old days of smooth muscular cells and soft bodies, electrical impulses play an auxiliary, secondary role while the primary role is played by chemical *mediators*. The chemical mode of excitation transmission was abandoned long ago by the newer levels of movement construction, which switched to an electrical, telegraphic method of transmission. In the human body, the chemical mode is still preserved in internal organs equipped with smooth muscles, such as the stomach lining, intestines, and uterus. This same chemical method, quite unexpectedly, once again stepped forward and found itself a role in controlling the new, striated muscles. It turned out that it was possible to force a skeletal muscle to function in a very specific way. Impulses from Level A happened to be able to induce in this stubborn and disobedient muscle exactly the same smooth, slow, and economical contractions of medium force during stretching or shortening, typical of smooth muscles of soft-bodied animals and human internal organs. What is contracting this way in the striated muscle? Are these same anisoelements that explode like dynamite in response to impulses from other levels? Or is this the semiliquid substance, sarcoplasm, in which muscular fibers are submerged? The answer is still unknown, but the fact is nevertheless the fact. Physiologists have been forced to be satisfied with a chance to give these smooth, slow contractions with their fine force control a name. They were termed *tonic contractions*, and the mode of functioning of the striated muscle, which is similar to that of the smooth muscle, was termed *muscular tone*. Somehow, Level A is the only one of all the levels of the central nervous system that is able to force the striated muscle to speak this alien language. The muscle listens only to this level, creating for Level A a very important and solid position in the system of the levels. As it has been mentioned, the younger levels sometimes help Level A to control the neck and the trunk with their strong motor impulses, but Level A itself helps to a much higher degree the newer levels to control the extremities. It provides the muscles of the extremities with *tone*, that is, with what can be called *background contraction*. It provides movements with basic priming, which can be used by the newer and better differentiated levels for drawing patterns of quick, dexterous, and strong movements. But this is not all.

Scientists have recently found that muscle tone and tonic contractions are not the only things provided by impulses from Level A. Perhaps it is even more important that these impulses can very precisely *control the excitability* of both the triggering spinal cells and their mions. The properties of the striated muscle are such that a change in its excitability leads to a precisely defined change in the force it generates in response to impulses from the newer levels. Levels B and C (discussed later) may change the magnitude of their motor impulses as they wish, but, as we have seen in essay 3, *this will not produce any effect* on the muscle, guarded as it is from any such changes by the "all or none" law. If these impulses are not weaker than a certain minimum, each mion responds with a contraction of an invariable force. However, if Level A uses its language and says to a mion "stronger" or "weaker," if, in other words, it turns up the wick of the mion's triggering cell, the mion will obediently start responding to impulses from the upper levels with stronger or weaker contractions, or even die and stop working completely, as does a kerosene lamp when its wick is retracted.

This last fact plays an extremely important role in the coordination of movements. The power of Level A over muscle excitability is so great that it is able to completely inhibit the triggering spinal cells, or to *block* them from the descending motor impulses. The following extended example illustrates the importance of such blocking, which is related to an extremely important phenomenon.

Because *muscles* cannot push the bones but can only pull them, in other words, because muscles *have only unidirectional action*, each direction of mobility of our joints must naturally have a pair of muscles with opposite actions. For example, in the elbow joint, one muscle acts as a flexor (this is the well-known biceps),[1] and another one, on the back side of the shoulder, acts as an elbow extensor (because of its three heads, it has been named triceps). It is easy to understand, that the unimpeded work of the biceps requires that the extensor, the triceps, which stretches during elbow flexion, not pull in its direction as a stretched spring but, rather, yield meekly. The triceps will have its turn in the next phase of a movement, when it contracts and extends the elbow joint. Here, the flexor, the biceps, must ensure that it provides only a minimal burden with its elastic properties.

Here, the backstage work of Level A starts to play its role. It controls the triggering cells and mions of muscles with opposite actions, similarly to the way valve mechanisms of steam engines control the cylinders. Impulses from Level A act through the spinal cells on the excitability of muscles similarly to the way valve mechanisms turn on one of the cylinders while shutting off another one (or other ones). When it is necessary to switch off the extensor, the spinal cells of its mions become nonexcitable, and the extensor muscle tone drops; that is, its length and ability to lengthen increase. In the next phase of movement, the

---

[1]There is one more flexor muscle, brachioradialis, acting at the elbow joint together with the biceps. Its existence does not change anything in the physiological relations considered here.

opposite happens. It seems unnecessary to go into further explanation of why this hidden, preparatory background mechanism is necessary for a smooth and economical movement.

The general and particular importance of the background activity of Level A is particularly apparent in disorders when, due to some cause, it changes in some direction. In such cases, one can observe a general, constrained rigidity of the whole body; a deadly mask of a face deprived of any expression; scant movements that can hardly be initiated; or vice versa, an excessive looseness and relaxation in all the joints. With such a patient without muscle tone, it is easy to place both of his feet behind the neck or nearly to tie his whole body into a knot, but he himself cannot make any meaningful movement or even exert any moderate effort.

Here we should address the question of whether Level A has any *relation to dexterity* or any importance for it. Level A in humans *does not lead* any movements and, even with respect to body posture, is the leading level only in very special, exceptional cases. Apparently, therefore, this question is applicable only with respect to the *background function* of Level A. We need to find out if the degree of development or the perfection of the background corrections at Level A has any importance for dexterity.

Obviously, its importance is quite significant. A stooped body, flabby muscles, arms hanging alongside the body like laundry on a rope, easily induced dizziness are all somewhat exaggerated signs of what happens when Level A malfunctions, even if there are no underlying, irreversible anatomical brain injuries. To try to exhibit dexterity with such an apparatus is like trying to write with a broken pencil.

However, if one excessively extends the boundaries of the notion of dexterity, there is a danger of confusing dexterity with what is called *good coordination of movements*. However, these two notions are quite different, and it would be a shame to lose the strict definition of dexterity, which is valuable and helpful in many aspects. Therefore, it is necessary to state that good motor coordination is a prerequisite for dexterity, whereas ideal, precise functioning of the level of tone and posture (Level A) is a prerequisite for good motor coordination. In order to bake bread, one needs flour. In order to obtain flour, one needs to grow wheat, which, in turn, requires rain. However, it would be imprecise to say that one needs rain to bake bread. In the following discussion on the levels of motor coordination, we are going to meet more direct and apparent prerequisites for dexterity.

To conclude the description, one must add that actions at Level A, both in its leading and background roles, are virtually totally involuntary and largely evade consciousness. Level A is deep down, in the brain cellars, and we rarely descend to its level to observe and check its functioning with direct observation. Usually, it justifies our confidence, does not like interference in its business, and carries on its duty as reliably as the internal body organs. For example, the duodenum and the spleen also rarely report their work to our consciousness!

THE LEVEL OF MUSCULAR-ARTICULAR LINKS: LEVEL B

Its Structure

From the diary of an interstellar traveler:

> A remarkable machine, unlike any other I had seen before, was rushing towards me. It moved so quickly that it was difficult to see all its parts. It apparently did not have any wheels but nevertheless moved forward at an amazing speed. As I was able to see, its most important part was a pair of powerful, elastic rods, each one consisting of several segments. They changed their shape so quickly, stretched and retracted, extended and folded, flashing by each other and moving along peculiar arcs of such precision and beauty that it was impossible to penetrate into their essence and origin. How far is our technology from constructing such mechanisms!!!
>
> I was given a tube called a "time magnifier." Looking in it, I could see the movements of these objects slowed down and extended in time. Looking after the machine that rushed away, I could see it in more detail. Each rod moved along a complex curved arc and suddenly made a soft contact with the ground. Then, it looked as if lightning ran along the rod from the top to the bottom, the rod straightened and lifted off the ground with a powerful, resilient push, and rushed upwards again. In the upper part of the machine, there were two more similar rods, but smaller in size. As I was able to understand, the upper rods were connected with the lower ones by some kind of transmission and moved at the same rhythm. However, their direct purpose remained unknown to me.
>
> As I was told, the machine consisted of more than two hundred engines of different size and power, each one playing its own particular role. The controlling center was on the top of the machine, where electrical devices were located that automatically adjusted and harmonized the work of the hundreds of motors. Due to these controlling structures, the rods and levers were able to move along the complex curves that allowed the machine to move without wheels faster than wind.

I hope that the reader will pardon me for this minor mystification. This passage is not from the diary of an Earthling traveling to distant planets, but from the diary of a citizen of one of the planets, Sirius, traveling to Earth. What the Sirius traveler saw was merely a human sprinter. This brief sketch is an appropriate introduction to the description of the level of muscular-articular links—Level B.

The reader has already met the level of muscular-articular links or, in other words, the level of synergies, that we denote by the letter B. This level developed in order to subserve all possible *locomotions* on the ground, and later, in the air, when these types of locomotions became needed by the vertebrates. It is a contemporary and a partner of the *extremities*. Finally, it is the first level in vertebrates that started to use high-frequency sequences of impulses in order to

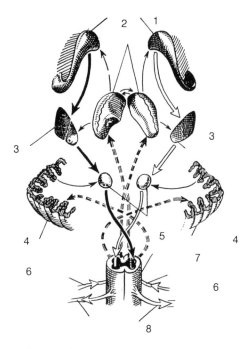

FIG. 3. Major sensory and motor nuclei of the extrapyramidal system, with a scheme of connections and conducting pathways. Motor pathways are shown with solid lines; sensory pathways are shown with dotted arrows. 1–Striatum. 2–Thalamus. 3–Pallidum. 4–Cerebellum. 5–Red nucleus. 6–Sensory root. 7–Spinal cord. 8–Motor root.

induce prolonged and strong contractions, called *tetani* described in the section "Drawbacks of the Striated Muscle" in essay 3.

Each level of construction of movements is a key to solving a particular *class of motor tasks*. As essay 3 explained, tasks related to both synergies of large muscle groups and to different locomotions emerged a long time ago; they are much older than any of the vertebrates and were born along with elongated body shapes and telereceptors. Level B originates from the same ancient times. It is a venerable elder who, in essence, is even older than Level A. Taking into account its age, one should not be surprised that during its long life, it has suffered many biological modifications. It dwelled in the frontal (head and thoracic) neural ganglia of arthropods. It found its new home in the neural nuclei of the mesencephalon in vertebrates, when these nuclei were still the supreme rulers of the whole central nervous system. Later, as we will see, it was forced to retreat and give up its position and heir's rights when the power was captured by the younger and stronger formations of the forebrain.

The history of brain development involves a prominent and steady process that has been called *encephalization*.[2] When the new superstructures were built

---

[2]The word *encephalization* originates from the Greek *encephalon* ("located in the head") meaning the brain. This word may be known to the reader from a commonly used word *encephalitis*, "brain inflammation."

in the brain, they took over functions that had earlier resided in the lower, older brain structures. Somewhat earlier, we had a chance to mention how the spinal cord had lost more and more of its independence. In a frog, the spinal cord is still able to control many complex and meaningful reflexes after the frog's decapitation. If chicken's head is quickly chopped off, the chicken is able to run about 100 steps and perhaps even to fly onto a low balcony. A cat whose spinal cord has been surgically separated from the brain cannot walk but still preserves one of the important background activities of walking, namely, alternating leg movements that can be observed if the cat's body is suspended in the air on straps. In humans, as indicated by observations of patients suffering from certain diseases, this alternating background stepping already requires an intact Level B, that is, intact middle sections of the brain.

Similarly, many of the functions owned by Level B for millions of years moved "upwards." Level B is still the *level of synergies* and muscular-articular links, but it is not the level of locomotion any longer, as it was long ago. In humans, it plays very important and responsible *background roles*, but a large portion of its functions, which it used to control in reptiles, has since that time migrated upward to the more modern and better equipped brain structures. We are going to find these functions in the next sections in Level C.

Let us now briefly overview the anatomical basis of Level B in humans. This overview is worthwhile because it very clearly reflects the principle of sensory corrections, which we have advanced as the main principle of motor coordination.

Motor neural nuclei of Level B, the pallidums, or "pale spheres," are located in the deepest regions of the brain. Their output motor nerves extend 2–3 cm downward to the red nuclei, like loaded cars from city warehouses to the nearest large railroad station somewhere in the suburbs. The red nuclei are the executive neural centers of the lower level (A). In addition to their main responsibilities, they also carry the additional load of transferring impulses from Level B further downward to the spinal trigger cells.

Certainly, the red nuclei do not leave the "loads" delivered from the pallidums "unopened"; they modify and process them. The red nuclei apparently send downward their own impulses to Level A, using one physiological way, or one language; whereas the transit impulses from Level B are sent in another language. Here, physiology still has much to find out.

Sensory (or receptor) centers of Level B are the largest of the brain nuclei (see Figure 5.). These centers are a pair of neural cell conglomerates with an old Latin name meaning "*visual prominence*," *thalamus*. The word *visual* is very misleading. It reflects the degree of ignorance of the past scientists who pioneered brain investigation and named all the formations they met. As later scientists discovered, the thalamus has only a very weak relation to visual nerves and vision.

The description of brain *center* fits the thalamus very well. It receives from all the parts of the body the neural pathways from *all peripheral exteroceptors* including the senses of touch, pressure, hot and cold, pain, and so forth, and all the *muscular-articular sensitivity* that we agreed, in essay 2, to call *proprioceptive*. All these signals enter the thalamus directly from sensory nerve endings in skin, muscles, tendons, and articular fascia, without any interruptions or intermediate relays. Thus, the thalamus receives all the sensory signals by the most direct and fastest way, firsthand.

Historically, the thalamus used to be even richer. In its structure, it resembles large world cities. Its history is similar to that of Moscow and New York, which gradually gave birth to numerous suburbs nearly merging with the cities them-selves and forming huge conglomerates (Greater Moscow, Greater New York, etc.). If one adds to the thalamus the numerous small adjacent neural nuclei, the system of "the Greater Thalamus" involves virtually all the body sensitivity, without exception. Thalamus's "suburbs" receive visual, auditory, and olfactory nerves; they also receive branches of nerves that connect the brain with the neural equipment of the internal organs, meaning that the Greater Thalamus receives internal sensory information as well.

It is easy to understand that, having all these direct and universal sensory connections, the thalamus has actually become the center of all the body receptor mechanisms, and no other brain structure can compete with it with respect to *sensory corrections*. When there were no telereceptors, striated muscles, or loco-motions more or less deserving this name, nature somehow managed without sensory corrections. However, when sensory corrections became vitally needed, evolution, first of all, created an organ that would perfectly fit this function. As a result, neither Level A nor any other of the higher levels is able to control such vast, all-embracing synergies as those controlled by Level B. Such move-ments as running, jumping, vaulting, gymnastic exercises, wrestling, swimming, and so on, are possible only because of the richness of information collected by the thalamus.

The unfaltering encephalization affected Level B as well. The neural pathways of the telereceptors from the organs of *vision, hearing, and smell* make a transfer in the thalamus and travel further upwards to the *brain cortex*, where they occupy vast, finely segregated territories. Contact sensitivity, including touch, pain, and muscular-articular sense, has also built pathways to the brain cortex and founded there their large representations, but they have nevertheless preserved *close re-lations with the major thalamic nuclei*, which are the first place where signals from different parts of the body arrive. As far as the long-range receptors are concerned, the thalamus of the higher mammals and humans is rather blind and deaf.

This last factor explains why the list of movements independently controlled by Level B has become shorter. This level has preserved its very influential position as a background level, a fact made clear from the aforementioned brief list of movements with large synergies that crucially depend on Level B. However, its "weak-sightedness" limits its chances of being the leading level.

Its Functions

In order to clearly understand the position and workload of Level B in humans, let us first consider its advantages and drawbacks.

The major advantage of this level has already been mentioned. It is the unique ability to control large muscle choirs, large synergies, an ability that has never been reproduced in any of the younger levels. We have intentionally stressed this ability in the opening passage describing a sprinter mistaken for a machine. After everything that was said in essay 2 about the problem of degrees of freedom, in particular about the fact that even powerful contemporary technology is just starting to master the second degree of freedom, it is easy to understand the amazement of an inexperienced observer watching a runner. Our problem is that we are used to an inexhaustable flow of miracles lavishly presented to our eyes by nature each and every hour. It seems that in order to regain the ability to be surprised, we must imagine ourselves tourists from Sirius. Perhaps it would not do us any harm to do this more frequently!

Movements, whose responsibility for control resides in other, higher levels, are incomparably more frugal with respect to the number of simultaneously engaged muscles, unless they borrow this ability from Level B by using it as a background level, for example, during different kinds of locomotions. The afore-mentioned specific ability of Level B makes it, so to speak, the main control desk with respect to all the muscles of the body. It plays the most important background role, and not only when all the hundreds of body muscles must be mobilized. It is not that arrogant. For example, it readily takes responsibility

FIG. 4. Finish of a 100-meter sprint.

even for synergies limited to muscles of one arm (for example, during writing, knitting, tying a knot with one hand, etc.).

Because of the very close relation between Level B and the whole receptor mechanism of the body, movements controlled from this level are always coherent and harmonious. They look graceful even in very ungraceful people. They are very well tuned, not only with respect to a certain moment of time. The same level can skillfully organize the time course of movements, that is, *control movement rhythm*, providing alternating activity of flexor and extensor muscles, and so forth. Another typical characteristic of the movements controlled by Level B is the exceptional, minted *identity* of consequent repetitions of a movement (called, movement *cycles*) during all possible rhythmical movements. Consecutive steps during walking or running are as similar as minted coins; the consecutive cycles during sawing, filing, mowing, or hammering, for example, are more alike than two drops of water.

This characteristic is closely related to the formation of *motor skills* and to the *automation* of movements, and we are going to get back to it in the next essay.

FIG. 5. Alexander Pugachevsky, record holder and champion of the Union of Soviet Socialist Republics in middle-distance running.

It seems that this level of muscular-articular links (B), which possesses such extremely rich possibilities, would be able to control a large number of various movements. It is prevented from doing so by the already mentioned drawback in its sensory information supply: *In humans, it has very poor connections with the telereceptors of vision and hearing*, whose neural pathways go to the higher levels. Therefore, as it is easy to imagine, it is well fit to provide fully the *internal consistency* of a movement, to coordinate behavior of all the muscles, to arrange necessary synergies, and so on. It is unable, however, to adjust such a complex and harmonious movement to changes in external conditions, to the actual environment.

For example, consider *walking*. Even during ordinary human bipedal walking, this motor act involves all four extremities, oscillating at a common rhythm. All the body muscles are involved either in providing support or in the basic dynamic activity of walking. If a human unexpectedly found himself or herself in boundless, interstellar space, Level B would probably be able to provide accurate execution of all the movements of normal walking in the absence of any environment. Unfortunately, in such a situation, walking would be meaningless. Actual, functional walking always takes place on some surface, in some direction, and in certain conditions. The ground may be solid, soft, slippery, or uneven; there may be a pebble, a puddle, a step, or a pothole on the road; during walking, there may be turns, slopes, wind blasts, or another oncoming pedestrian. It is necessary to react in a timely fashion and appropriately to all such events. First of all, one needs signals from the telereceptors. But, as we are going to see in the next section, the signals themselves are not the most important (people who are blind can walk without vision). What is most important is a particular organization of all the incoming impressions as a whole, something that is too much for Level B. Only such an organization can provide all the necessary sensory corrections.

Let us make one comparison that most clearly illustrates the role of Level B and its weak spots. In movements like walking or running, the function of this level is similar to that of an airplane mechanic who makes sure that all the major engines, auxiliary equipment, and control devices are functioning normally. The role of the leading level during walking and running (as we will see later, this role is played by Level C) is comparable to that of the pilot who flies the airplane along a certain route and levels it during deviations, turbulences, and wind blasts, without caring about what is actually going on inside the airplane's systems. Level B *is invaluable for internal movement control* when one of the *higher levels takes the responsibility for its external pilotage*.

As a typical background level, Level B mostly functions *without participation of consciousness*; this characteristic is typical for all the background corrections. Many of its functions proceed fully or partially *involuntarily*, although they are much more accessible for voluntary intervention than the deep "underground" background corrections of Level A. It is certainly unreasonable to expect the level of muscular-articular links to have in stock background, auxiliary corrections for all possible movements and skills acquired by a human during a lifetime.

FIG. 6. Tatyana Sevryukova, record holder and champion of the Union of Soviet Socialist Republics and Europe in the shot put.

This is not the fact. Level B in humans is well suited for the *accumulation of life experience*, for building new coordinative patterns and storing them in the treasury of motor memory. We consider this aspect in the next essay. In adults, Level B is overstocked with all possible background corrections developed in response to requests from the higher levels, which needed these corrections for certain motor skills. These background corrections "made to order" are called *automatisms*. It is not surprising that a mature Level B, enriched by numerous ordered background corrections, can easily find in its "library" perfectly appropriate, or, at the very worst, more or less appropriate corrections for those very few unusual movements that an adult human meets for the first time in his life. This attribute gives the human great maneuverability and aptitude for acquiring very diverse skills and also enhances the accessible means for quick decision making in any situation. A person with a better developed collection of background corrections in his library is much better equipped for *finding a quick motor solution for any situation*. As we saw in essay 1, this ability is the original, most basic definition of dexterity.

An analysis of the higher levels of motor coordination will show us that the motor abilities provided by a well-developed Level B do not contain dexterity by themselves but that they do provide its most vital prerequisites. Because the classification of movements is based on their levels of control, it is necessary to divide all the manifestations of dexterity into two large classes, one called *body dexterity* and the other *hand dexterity, object dexterity*, or *hand skill*. We shall see that the motor means of Level B form the vital basis for the first class and are one of the very important prerequisites for the second class. We are going to see clearly body dexterity for the first time at the next Level C. Level B, when left to itself or forced to rely in its work on a poorly functioning, helpless level of muscular-articular links, would be able to accomplish not more than the bravest and most skillful knight who takes part in a tournament riding a lame jade.

After all this, the reader will not be surprised to see a list of independent movements controlled by Level B naked like an autumn tree. Most of the movements that were once controlled from this level left it for the higher brain structures.

Which independent movements have been left to this level? Semivoluntary, semiconscious motor acts, most of which are less than moderately important. It still has facial expressions under its control:

> Rows of magical expressions
> of a lovely face.
> (A. Fet)

It still controls pantomime, or the language of body movements, those expressive involuntary gestures accompanying speech and behavior, which are rather rare in reserved peoples of the North and that overfill everyday life of active, spirited Southerners.

> "And what did you do with your hands, I wonder!" mentioned caustically Uncle Petr Ivanovich Aduev, describing to his nephew how he, according to the uncle's suspicion, announced his love. "Probably, spilled or broke something?"
> "Uncle, you *were* eavesdropping!" exclaimed the nephew in desperation because of the uncle's sagacity.
> "Yes, I was sitting there, behind a bush!"
> (I. A. Goncharov, *A Common Tale*)

Finally, Level B continues to control plastic movements belonging to this same group. We mean not the movements of Western European ball or folk dance, which are closer to locomotor acts, but rather the dance movements of the lazy East, leisurely and full of sweet langour, suddenly interrupted with passionate, eager aspiration. Then, there are movements of endearment, caress and fulfilled passion; movements of stretching the whole body and yawning; some of the free gymnastic exercises of the Müller system; and also a number of idiosyncratic, semiautomatic movements typical of an individual person, like scratching behind an ear, twisting a button, or playing with fingers like fat Uvar Ivanovich in *On the Eve* by Ivan Turgenev (the movements of this last group are, in their essence, very close to a dog's tail wagging). These movements compose a more or less complete list of what Level B can do.

The picture becomes quite different if we consider the list of Level B's *background performances*. Here, Level B changes dramatically, assumes a dignified air, and displays all the glamour and diversity of its talents. The style and meaning of its background activity is clear from the previous discussion. Enumeration of particular examples is more appropriate in the next sections, which present the characteristics of movements that are subserved by them.

THE LEVEL OF SPACE: LEVEL C

Its Structure

Another level of movement construction enters the lobby ready for scrutiny.

This is a very complex and interesting level. It deserves attention already because it is the first level to possess extensive, extremely rich sets of independent movements, not just background corrections as has been the case until now. Moreover, as we are going to see, this level provides the basis for many of the movements of interest to an athlete: virtually all movements in gymnastics, track-and-field, acrobatics, and many other areas of movement, not to mention the many background corrections which it provides for all the sport and athletic movements.

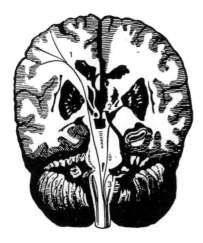

FIG. 7.   Vertical section of the brain in a plane behind the ears: 1–pyramidal tract; 2–pallidum pathway; 3–cerebellar pathway.

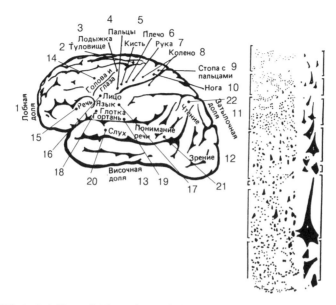

FIG. 8. *Left*–Human left hemisphere with the major cortical centers with numbers corresponding to the part of the body each controls: 1–frontal lobe; 2–trunk; 3–ankle; 4–fingers; 5–hand; 6–shoulder; 7–arm; 8–knee; 9–foot with toes; 10–leg; 11–occipital lobe; 12–vision; 13–temporal lobe; 14–head and eyes; 15–speech; 16–face; 17–tongue; 18–pharynx; 19–larynx; 20–hearing; 21–understanding of speech; 22–reading. *Right*–Section of the brain cortex in the area from which the pyramidal tract originates, magnified 40 times. The right edge shows samples of pyramidal cells at a larger magnification. Pyramidal axons start from the largest cells (Betz cells) in the fifth layer from the outer surface.

Level C in humans is not easy to unravel and understand at the first glance. It is much more complex in its structure and creates an impression of ambiguity and duality. It possesses two very different and totally independent *brain systems of motor neural centers* and two similarly dissimilar *systems of sensory signals*. Level C appears to occupy two different stories in the brain. However, it is certainly not a couple of levels but a single level displaying very solid, specific features that are not reproduced anywhere else.

As far as the duality is concerned, a careful analysis reveals that the situation is rather simple. Level C in humans is in a state of transition, in the middle of the process of *encephalization*. Just now, it is leaving the upper story of the EMS (known from our analysis of birds), the striatum, where it used to reside completely, prior to the emergence of the modern PMS in mammals. This process of its transition to a new apartment is so advanced that there are no doubts of its new address: All the lower subsystems of the cortical motor system (pyramidal system) have been fully occupied by it. Half of its posessions and furniture are still below, near the old fireplace, whereas the other half have been placed all over the vast space of the frontal central cortical gyri. Of course, contemporary scientists are unable to observe the dynamics of this transition-encephalization. Objective brain study is less that 150 years old, and such transitions require a comparable number of millenia. To notice such a transition is as impossible as seeing the movement of a clock's hour hand by looking at it during a fourth of a second. However, in another 100–200 thousand years, Level C in humans will undoubtedly become totally cortical and pyramidal, and the striatum will probably be used by the level of muscular-articular links (B). It will provide this level with better, more refined, and more precise mechanisms than those available to it now.

In most of the higher mammals who already have a PMS, Level C still resides mostly in the system of the striatum. In these animals (for example, cats and dogs), a complete experimental transection of the pyramidal tract on one side of the body leads only to a moderate lameness, which resolves completely after a certain time. In humans, disorders induced by a malfunctioning of the PMS (this happens frequently after so-called strokes) do not improve.

Let us look at how Level C functions. It was brought to life by a very old group of motor tasks whose common features suggest that it be called "the level of space." These motor tasks are certainly older than the PMS and even the striatum. This is the class of problems that emerged when vertebrates moved onto solid ground and into the air and also acquired extremities. Originally, this group of tasks was exclusively a class of locomotions but later developed into a class of tasks to handle external space in general. The necessity to have such a highly developed level of space became particularly urgent when the space became *vast*, due to *telereceptors*, and *accessible*, due to the strong levers of the *extremities* equipped with striated muscles. Encephalization moved this level from the pallidum to the striatum. During the last several pages of the history of evolution, this level started to feel rather crowded in the striatum as well, and now it is suspended between the earth and the sky, between EMS and PMS, sitting on two chairs.

Certainly, although the new cortical dwelling is much better and more spacious (examples of its movements are provided later), the level of space has managed very well in taking all the advantages from its present dual, intermediate situation. It uses for control of its movements *both motor systems*, extrapyramidal and pyramidal, with all the peculiarities and specific features of both. For sensory corrections, it also relies on sensory signals pertaining to both systems, which are very different in both composition and methods of processing raw sensory impressions. This duality creates for it *sensory libraries*, which are so rich that they can easily compete with those of Level B. Sensory information provided by the brain cortex to the *upper sublevel* of the level of space is particularly finely and precisely structured. Here we see vast *visual* and *auditory* areas (the former is in the occipital, and the latter is in the temporal cortical areas) and a particularly developed *tactile* area, reflecting in detail the whole surface of the body and located in close proximity to the pyramidal area. The brain cortex also contains a representation of *muscular-articular sensitivity*. The location of all these cortical areas is in the left part of Figure 8.

The pyramidal cortical *motor* area and the *sensory* area of tactile and muscu-lar-articular (proprioceptive) sensation are located in both hemispheres along both shores of a straight, deep ravine called the central or Roland's gyrus, the first one along the frontal edge and the second one along the back edge. Neural cells, where corresponding neural pathways originate and terminate, are not scattered randomly around these cortical areas. Quite the contrary—here rules a strict and rational order. The *sensory strip* exactly reflects the whole body from top to bottom, but in a twice-reversed pattern: The *left* part of the body is reflected in the *right* part of the brain, and vice versa, and in both right and left hemispheres, the body is reflected *upside down*.

Areas of the frontal *motor* strip are located exactly opposite the corresponding areas of the back sensory strip and exactly at the same level. For example, the small area containing neural cells that control hip muscles is located exactly "across the road" opposite an area representing sensitivity of skin and muscular-articular receptors of the hip.

Surface areas of the frontal, motor strip are *electrically excitable*. If one applies a weak electric current to the naked brain surface in the pyramidal area (this can be easily and absolutely harmlessly done in humans during brain surgery), one can obtain contractions of any muscle group of the body, carefully moving the ends of the electrodes from one point to another. Maps of the pyramidal area (similar to the one shown in Figure 7) were drawn in exactly this way.

However, the sensory signals that form the basis for sensory corrections of the level of space, are not used in a raw form. We have already discussed that, as we move from the lower to the higher levels, sensory signals become increas-ingly processed, and signals from different sources merge and interweave with numerous traces of earlier memories. This complex, finely structured *synthesis*, which forms the basis of Level C, is called the *space field*.

What Is the Space Field?

First of all, the space field is an exact, *objective* (i.e., corresponding to reality) *perception of external space* based on the cooperation of all the sensory organs, supported by the whole experience, guarded by memory.

Second, the space field is a kind of *ability to use the external space*. We can easily and without thinking place our finger at any point in space that we see or clearly imagine. This ability means that we are able to activate instantaneously a particular combination of muscles, in a particular sequence, and to particular degrees of force that are necessary for an immediate and perfect transition to the required point. Certainly, this ability to translate quickly from a language of a representation of a point in space into a language of required sequences of muscle activation (or a so-called muscle formula of the movement) is not specific to the hand or finger. We can equally as easily get to a point in space with the tip of a foot, the nose, the mouth, and so on, or with the tip of an object held in the hand or between the teeth. Somewhat more dexterity is required to get an object to any point in space with an accurate throw. This is what we call "*the ability to use space*," the second specific feature of the space field.

We need to say a few words about the basic features of the space field, features that are very important for analyzing the functioning of Level C of movement construction.

First, the space that we are able to use, in the sense just described, is *vast* and stretches far away in all directions from our body.

Second, we confidently perceive that space field as something *stationary*. When, for example, we turn around by 360°, we never have the feeling that the surrounding world is turning around us, although the raw, direct sensations from the sensory organs are telling us exactly that. Those cases when we feel that the surrounding world rather than we ourselves is turning around (for example, vertigo) are related to pathological distortions of the normal functioning of the level of space.

Third, we perceive the external space as absolutely *homogeneous*, identical in all its parts. As we know, our eyes display all objects in perspective. For example, close objects are seen as big, distant objects are seen as small, and parallel tracks appear to converge at a point on the horizon. Our tactile and muscular-articular senses also have unequal areas in space: There are more and less sensitive areas on the skin, with more densely or more sparsely distributed sensory points; muscle sense may also have a very different degree of sensitivity (depending on the position of the body and extremities, etc.). Despite all this, the internal processing of these raw impressions in the brain is so powerful that our consciousness gets a clear, integral *perception of the space field*, all the parts of which are as uniform as the figures in a geometry textbook. All the numerous distortions of reality that are contained in the raw information from sensory organs are eliminated and corrected so perfectly that we do not even suspect that many of them exist. Many of these distortions of reality (or sensory illusions) have been discovered only during the last century. This fact illustrates how perfectly the finalized, "clean copy" representation of the space field is rid of distortions before the representation enters the consciousness and starts to control sensory corrections of Level C.

The three most important features of the space field, its *spaciousness, stationariness, and homogeneity*, are supplemented by our abilities to clearly perceive *dimensions* of objects in space and *distances* between them, to clearly recognize *shapes* of the surrounding objects, to correctly judge *angles* and *directions*, to recognize and reproduce with movements (e.g., to draw) figures and shapes similar to each other, and so on.

Properties of Movements at Level C

Movements pertaining to Level C take place in the space field. Now, it will be easier for us to understand why these movements have their particular properties and not others.

These movements are very different from the smooth, harmonious synergies displayed in the windows of Level B. Movements of the level of space (if they are not overfilled with background corrections from Level B) are usually frugal and brief. They possess a somewhat businesslike dryness and do not involve large groups of muscle. They are, so to say, the chamber music of the muscles.

Typical movements of the space level are *aimed, transferring movements*. Many of them are singular. They always lead *from somewhere to somewhere and for some purpose*. They transfer the body from one place to another, overcome external forces, and move objects. These are the movements that point, take, move, pull, place, and throw. They all have a beginning and an end, a start and a finish, a raise and a throw or strike. They inevitably lead to a definite, ultimate result. Even in cases when these movements are repeated (e.g., hammering a nail, dealing cards, catching flies, etc.), their repetition is only superficial, referring to their external appearance, and they all imply a definite outcome: The whole nail will sooner or later be in the wall, all the cards will be dealt, and all the flies will be caught.

FIG. 9.

FIG. 10.

FIG. 11.

This feature of movements at Level C may be contrasted with the typical features of movements at Level B: Can one speak about the purpose of a smile or about the final objective of a yawn?

The second feature of movements controlled from Level C is not less prominent than their target nature. They are typically characterized by a certain degree of accuracy and precision. At least, the judgment of the quality of these movements is crucially dependent on how accurate and precise they are. One must be able to ride a bicycle along a narrow, straight plank or to hit or parry a ball with a racket so that its accuracy is comparable to that of the legendary William Tell or Odysseus. Consider Level B once more: What kind of accuracy can be expected from frowning brows or from the movements of a baby caressed by its mother?

On the other hand, the same aspect of movements at the level of space is revealed in another feature, one that has a direct *relation to dexterity*.

Pick up a small object, for example, a matchbox, from one and the same place several times, with quick, accurate movements, and try to observe your own movements. If you are afraid that observing yourself will distort your movements, observe those of another, without telling the person the reasons for this experiment.

You will inevitably see that the *terminal phases* of all the movements, that is, the moments of touching the object, very accurately converge on one point, like light rays meeting at the focal point. The *trajectories* of the hand from an initial flexed position to the target, however, will inadvertently be different, diverging from each other by more than a dozen centimeters.

It is not hard to guess the immediate *cause* of this fact. The most important, meaningful part of the movements is their termination—grasping the matchbox. This part is under the intent, watchful attention of the sensory corrections of Level C, which controls these movements. Intermediate parts of the movement do not matter for the outcome; therefore, the leading level remains indifferent to them.

It is much harder to understand how such a complete *indifference of sensory corrections* to the intermediate part of the movement *coexists with their extreme vigilance* at the terminal phase, because the end of any movement is hafted on its medial part, as the tip of a spear is hafted on its shaft. If the shaft of a spear is fragile and loose, what kind of accuracy can be expected from the tip?

FIG. 12. Taking a matchbox from the table.

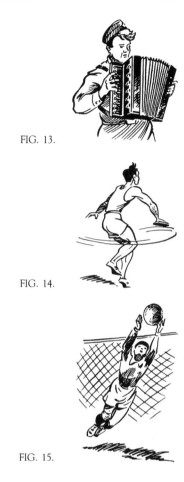

FIG. 13.

FIG. 14.

FIG. 15.

Without delving too deeply into this complex problem of neural mechanics, let us just briefly touch on the problem of *how this difficulty is actually solved*. We already mentioned earlier that the enormous experience collected day after day has elaborated in our brain, more specifically at Level C, a skill of quick and perfect *translation from a language of representation of a point in space into a language of muscle formula for a movement* leading to that particular point. Each point in space that can be reached by the extremities, is so well mastered that all the possible ways of reaching that point or of getting into it are equivalent. Thanks to this experience, processed and absorbed by the brain hemispheres, we reached, long ago, a complete interchangeability of all movements leading to the same spatial target. In those cases when it does not make a difference which of the thousands of muscle formulas leading to a spatial target are used, Level C activates the first available one.

This feature creates an essential difference between the behavior of corrections at Levels B and C. The level of muscular-articular links (B) always primarily cares about *its own body.* Its sensory systems continuously provide it with extensive information on the positions of different parts of the body, the force of individual muscles, joint angles, and so forth. Naturally, when this level constructs a movement, it starts from the *biomechanical aspect of the movement,* follows the most expedient and economical order of muscle involvement, and makes sure that it chooses the smoothest and most streamlined form of the movement from the infinite number of possibilities provided by the abundance of the degrees of freedom. Therefore, all of its movements are smooth, harmonious, and even gracious.

Level C is quite different. It builds its movements in the *space field,* starting from the location of a point in the space spread in front of one's eyes. As stated earlier, this space is external, that is, separate from and independent of our body. It is therefore clear why Level C corrections, guiding a movement, care only about how that movement fits the external, alien space outside the body. It does not care much about the biomechanical side of the movement, how joint angles will change, or even how comfortable or uncomfortable intermediate postures are. It knows one thing: There are enough degrees of freedom in an arm to place the wrist into any point of accessible space and by many paths. It is none of its business how joint angles actually group to reach the goal. Perhaps this is the reason for some of the awkwardness and dryness of the movements supervised by Level C.

However, we have paid this small price for the ability to control space, which gives us numerous advantages, advantages that certainly outweigh these minor shortcomings. This ability provides us a choice among, not tens or hundreds, but innumerable thousands of ways to a single, defined spatial target. When a movement proceeds without any complications (like taking a matchbox from a table), this wide choice results in an unintentional diversity of the less crucial movement components. If unexpected complications do occur in the course of a movement, however, Level C immediately mobilizes its vast resources (and it has quite a choice!). Where the level of muscular-articular links (B), with its perfect movement formulas ideally fitting the properties of muscles and joints, meets an impasse, the level of space (C) easily demonstrates its adaptivity and resourcefulness.

Adaptability and resourcefulness are also the source of the third characteristic feature of the level of space, *switchability.* It is relatively easy to enter a point in space not only with different movements of one and the same extremity but also with the right or left arm, elbow, tip of a foot, nose, and so on.

When we climb a mountain, we continuously switch to different types of locomotion, such as walking, crawling, clambering, hanging by the hands. A concertina player can very easily switch from one harmonious system to another, although the locations of different buttons and keys are different for different systems. A violinist can very easily play a viola, although doing so requires major changes in the movements of the left hand. Skiers know many different ways of making turns, of braking during descent, or of ascending a hill. The list of examples is virtually endless. All of them show that whenever the *level of space* enters the scene, it invariably brings with it *flexibility and maneuverability*. This feature, if properly developed, improves the movements considerably by making them more flexible, more skillful, and imbued with sterling dexterity.

Movements at the Level of Space

Compared to the meager list of independent movements controlled at the level of muscular-articular links (B), the complete list of movements controlled at the level of space (C) seems a bottomless sea. We are not referring here to the background corrections that Level C provides for some higher levels but to the completely independent motor acts. It is absolutely impossible to catalogue them. The only thing we can do is select, out of this abundance, several of the most important and typical groups which represent the major features of this level and describe a few typical examples from each group.

The *most ancient and basic* movements of the level of space, which apparently were the main reason for its emergence, are *locomotions*, transfers of the whole body in space from one place to another. It is certainly impossible to enumerate them all. At the head of their procession, we see the ancestors of all the types of terrestrial locomotion—*walking and running*. Each of these two primary locomotion patterns gives birth to whole families of their modifications—the military stride, tiptoeing, goose stepping, running over different distances, and so on. They are surrounded by numerous locomotions of other types: the ancestor of all the locomotions, swimming, and crawling, clambering, and on up to walking on all fours and on one's hands. All these locomotions contain numerous repetitions of the same movement *cycles* (these movements are sometimes described

FIG. 16.

FIG. 17. Natan Rokhlin, record holder of the Union of Soviet Socialist Republics
in high jump.

as "cyclic"). They are followed by singular, *noncyclic* locomotions, such as different
kinds of long jumps and high jumps, vaults, and so forth.

Humans perform all these kinds of locomotions by themselves and are able
to perform any of them unaided, without any special objects. Also in the procession of locomotions, we see transfers performed *with the help of* certain *objects*.
These include locomotions with the most simple assisting devices: skiing, skating,
roller skating, pole vaulting, and walking on stilts. Further, there are numerous
locomotions for transferring objects: carrying a load in one's arms or on one's
back and using a stretcher, wheelbarrow, sledge, cart, barge hauler's loop, and
so on. The reader has probably been unaware until now of such a large catalogue
of locomotor transfers.

All these locomotions are movements of the whole body, that is, movements
for which each muscle carries some load. It is quite understandable that the
demand for background corrections during such movements is rather high, particularly for the corrections from the level of muscular-articular links (B). These
complex, vast movements require a harmonious, perfectly timed interaction
among numerous joints and hundreds of muscles. Therefore, the muscular-articular level carries the lion's share of work. We may safely say that nine tenths
of the total muscular work during walking or running is controlled by this
background level, whereas not more than one tenth is controlled from the leading
level of these locomotions. This is not surprising. In a car or on a steamboat,
the muscular power of the driver is much less than the power of the engine.
However, these small-magnitude corrections, which control the whole move-

ment, bear most of the responsibility. Without them, a car, as well as a walking person, would immediately turn into a blind source of energy, aimless and even dangerous. Huge muscular synergies of Level B create the powerful and harmonious movement pattern that fascinated the tourist from Sirius, described earlier, but they would not be able to solve locomotor tasks if left to themselves. These tasks are always solved by the "pilotage" of the level of space—Level C.

The *second group* of Level C movements naturally includes similarly large movements that involve the *whole body in space*, just as those that we call locomotions, but these do not transfer the person from one place to another. This group mostly consists of various athletic, gymnastic, and dancing movements, such as various exercises on parallel and uneven bars, rings, horizontal bar, and trapeze and various vaults and somersaults. Acrobatics and ballet have also contributed considerably to this group of movements.

The muscular-articular background level has probably more trouble with this group of movements than with the first one. *Walking* along the streets, *running* after a tram, and *jumping* from a step are probably performed by everyone on a daily basis, but this is unlikely to be true about vaults and entrechats. The latter movements, aside from being far from common, also place greater demand on coordination. The necessary corrections and muscular synergies for these movements do not develop in a natural way during childhood, as happens with most

FIG. 18. *Left*–Nikolai Ozolin, record holder and champion of the Union of Soviet Socialist Republics and record holder of Europe in pole vault. *Right*–Alexandra Chudina, record holder and champion of the Union of Soviet Socialist Republics in high jump.

FIG. 19. Stepanchyonok, record holder and champion of the Union of Soviet Socialist Republics in sprint hurdles.

of the locomotions. Most of these corrections are more demanding and refined; they literally give humans many more headaches and need to be developed with special exercises. The larger a library of background corrections an individual has accumulated, at the muscular-articular level, the more skillful and resourceful the level of space (C) is in retrieving and using them and the better and faster the movements of this group will develop.

Now, let us move from the whole body to its parts. The *third group* of movements controlled by the level of space includes *accurate, targeted movements of arms* (and other organs) *in space*. Our arms and fingers can also "walk" and "run"; these movements have not been monopolized by the feet. The language is full of expressions that characterize the movements: "the fingers ran along the keys," "fluent fingers," "hands with the tool moved there and back." In the same group, we meet movements that stress, not quickness, but *accuracy*. These are the confident, aimed, simple movements that served as the first examples of movements at the level of space, movements that take, carry, grab, show something. They use numerous ways to move things, put them somewhere, throw them, and transfer them. The level of space cannot do anything more complex with objects. As we will soon see, this requires supervision by the higher *level of actions*. But to move things in space is a direct profession of Level C.

Different movements of this group use the background services of the muscular-articular level (B) to very different degrees. For example, in movements such as simple pointing, this level has virtually nothing to do. On the other hand, for finger locomotions of a pianist or an accordionist, it takes on as much responsibility for mutual adjustment of all the muscle contractions as it does during actual walking and running.

It is natural to move from moving objects to *overcoming resistance*. Here, in the *fourth group*, we are going to place different forceful movements. Let us not waste too much time on them, and present examples of five representatives that first come to mind: Lifting heavy objects from the ground, pulling oneself up on gymnastic rings, drawing a bow, athletic weight lifting, and turning the crank of a winch or the windlass of a well. Muscles work intensely in these kinds of activity; therefore, there is also much work for the background levels. Everyone knows how profoundly these movements can be improved by developing a skill.

Now, we are approaching one of the most interesting groups of movements of the level of space, the swinging-throwing, or *ballistic*, movements. This *fifth group* includes striking *movements*. In fact, if you think about it, striking with an axe or with a heavy sledgehammer with all one's might differs from the movement of throwing only in its final instant. If the fingers let the object go when it moves at the highest speed, the result is a throw. If the fingers do not perform this slight, additional movement, the result is a strike. Both groups of movements are closely related in their basic features: In both cases, the task is to accelerate an object to a maximal possible speed.

It is much more reasonable to break this group into two parts according to a different criterion. Some of the swinging-throwing movements mostly emphasize the *force* of a throw or strike. Other movements stress the accuracy of the movements. Examples of the first group include the striking of a hammer; weight jerking; shot putting; and discus, hammer, or grenade throwing. Examples of accurate ballistic movements include javelin or ball throwing at a target; movements during tennis, lapta (a Russian game very similar to baseball), gorodki (similar to skittles), and croquet; juggling movements; bayonet stabs; movements by a blacksmith, locksmith, upholsterer; fine striking movements by a carpenter, surgeon, mechanic.

The importance of a well-developed skill for ballistic movements is clear from the fact that the ability to strike and throw skillfully and accurately is very rare. Furthermore, because *a movement requires motor skill, it needs background corrections*—this fact we have already firmly established. Actually, the essence and basis of the swinging-throwing movements are in the finely adjusted synergies at Level B. Look carefully at the well-known difference in the throwing styles of boys and girls. A girl throws with virtually the same movement that she uses for pointing, only with a larger swing. Hers is simply an exaggerated pointing movement based on pure, straightforward corrections from the level of space. When a boy winds to the right like a spring and draws in the air a complex swinging curve outward, backward, and downward, and then rushes forward shooting the stone like a rocket, forcefully shifting his center of mass to the forward left foot, we see an extended, well-developed synergy of the muscular-articular level. Here, it is hard to say which muscles work harder, the right shoulder or the left hip muscles (the boy would not believe us about the latter).

The last, sixth group of movements controlled at the level of space includes everything that did not find its place in the previous groups. We need to mention various movements such as aiming, imitating, and mimicking. When a monkey mimics the movements of a man who performs in front of it a complex action with an object from the highest level, Level D that we are going to discuss next, the monkey is acting at its ceiling level, the level of space, and because of this reason, it cannot succeed:

"The spectacles refuse to work. . . ." (from "The Monkey and the Spectacles," a fable by I. A. Krylov.)

THE LEVEL OF ACTIONS: LEVEL D

What Are Actions?

Already in monkeys, there is a considerable separation of functions between arms and legs. . . . They use the former mainly for collecting and holding food, the way it has already been done by some of the lower mammals with their forelimbs. Some monkeys and apes use hands for building nests on the trees, or even, like chimpanzees, covers between the branches to hide from bad weather. They use their hands to grab cudgels to defend against enemies or bombard the enemies with fruits or rocks. When in captivity, they use their hands to perform a number of simple actions, imitating corresponding movements of humans. However, exactly in these movements, we can clearly see the huge difference between the underdeveloped arms of even man's closest relatives, the apes, and the human arm improved by the labor of hundreds of millenia. The number and basic location of arm bones and muscles are the same in apes and men, but nevertheless, a hand of an ancient savage was able to perform hundreds of jobs impossible for any ape. The ape's hand has never been able to make the crudest stone knife.

FIG. 20. *Left*–Female type of throwing. *Right*–Male type of throwing.

Until the first rock was turned by human hands into a knife, a long time should have passed, compared to which the historic period known to us seems small and insignificant. But the crucial step was made, *the hand became free* [i.e., became free of supporting and locomotor responsibilities] and could improve in its skill and dexterity. The acquired flexibility has been inherited and improved from generation to generation.

Thus, the arm is not only an organ of labor but *also its product*. Only thanks to labor, thanks to all its new operations, thanks to the inheritance of the acquired development of muscles, tendons, and, over longer periods, also bones, and thanks to the new ways of applying the inherited improvements to new, more complex operations, only thanks to all this, the human hand reached the high level of perfection that allowed it to bring to life the paintings of Raphael, the statues of Torvaldsen, and the music of Paganini.

Thanks to the cooperative work of the hands, organs of speech, and brain, not only in each individual separately, but in society, human beings acquired the ability to perform more and more complicated operations, to set higher and higher goals, and to reach them. The process of labor was becoming more and more diverse, perfect, and multi-faceted from generation to generation. (F. Engels, *Dialectics of Nature. The Role of Labor in Transition from Ape into Man*)

The *level of actions* (in neurophysiology, this level is also called the level of objective actions, of chain actions, of meaningful actions, and so on; from the following discussion, we shall see how well these terms fit this level), to which is assigned the letter *D*, differs significantly in many aspects from all the earlier described levels.

First of all, all three earlier levels, A, B, and C, together with their problems, originate from the deep past. The youngest of them, Level C dates back to the times of the origin of striated muscles and skeletons with joints. Following the law of encephalization, Level C continuously expanded and enriched the sphere of its tasks and moved forward within the brain, changing its "apartments" to more and more comfortable ones. At this point in time, Level C of the human brain is in the very midst of one of its moves in full swing; this time it moves into the motor cortex, a dwelling equipped with a good telephone (hearing) and television set (vision). However, despite this never-ceasing movement forward, according to all the signs, Level C has already moved over the peak in its development. For any of the movements characteristic for this level, one can easily name a mammal or even a bird that is superior to us humans in the ability to perform it perfectly. There are plenty of animals who can run faster and have more endurance than humans; many of them are better than we in clambering, jumping, swimming, controlling equilibrium, and so forth.

The situation is quite different with the level of *actions*, Level D. Its earlier rudiments may be seen only in the highest mammals, such as horses, dogs, and elephants. Apes possess considerably more of them, but even in apes, the *actions* are so few and rudimentary that Level D may rightfully and virtually without exaggeration be called *the human level*. Perhaps humans became human largely thanks to this level and in relation to it.

FIG. 21.

First of all, it is necessary to explain what we mean by *actions*. Actions are not simply movements. Most of them are whole sequences of movements that together solve a motor problem. Each such chain consists of different movements that replace each other systematically, leading one to a solution for the problem. All the movements, parts of such a chain, are related to each other by *meaning* of the problem. If you miss one of the links of the chain or mix up their order, you will fail to solve the problem.

Let us consider the very simple but impressive example of lighting up a cigarette. A smoker takes a cigarette pack out of his pocket, opens it, selects a cigarette, kneads it, and puts it between the lips; then he opens a matchbox; takes out a match; glances at it to check if its head is intact; turns the matchbox; strikes the match once or several times, as necessary, until it ignites; turns it so that the flame flares up; if necessary, protects it from wind; moves it close to the cigarette; sucks the match's flame into the cigarette; extinguishes the match; throws it away; and eventually puts all the things back where they belong.

Such an everyday trifle as lighting a cigarette turns out, perhaps quite unexpectedly for the reader, to consist of not less than 20 consecutive movements—links, all of which the smoker must perform, without omitting any of them, without changing their order, and, at the same time, adjusting to external conditions that are not always identical. Watch a smoker five or six times when he lights a cigarette: Although this action is very simple and very automatic, especially for seasoned smokers, each of the half dozen repetitions will differ somewhat from the others in both the list of the movements and in their number.

The same features can be seen in various other movements as well. In day-to-day life, humans put on clothes, sharpen a pencil, wash, shave, cook poached

FIG. 22.

eggs, make tea, make the bed, and so on. In professional life, there is a boundless abundance of actions: placing a part onto a machine tool, putting a thread through a sewing or spinning machine, turning, punching, forging, drilling, hardening, putting paper into a typewriter; all these are just an infinitesimally small group of actions selected at random from the ocean of professional labor. The area of sports provides a similarly long list: actions of a player running forward with the ball toward the opponent's goal; tactics of a long-distance runner; actions of a wrestler who tries to turn the opponent lying on the ground onto his back; actions of a driver of a racing car, and so on, and so on.

In all such actions and in those that the reader can easily add, there coexist two features already noted: a *chain structure* and *adaptive variability* in the composition and structure of the chains during repetitions of a task.

It is easy to explain why such a large proportion of motor acts from Level D have chain structure, consisting of a whole, frequently long row of consecutive events of different meaning and purpose. Motor tasks, which are one after another coming to be necessary, become more and more complicated in their meaning. This complication happens much faster than does the development and enrichment of the human motor apparatuses, that is, the extremities, which are the human's basic, natural tools. Even if one supplies them with auxiliary devices and the most refined corrections from the brain levels, a single movement would still be unable to provide and perform what is required by a motor task in each and every situation. This inability is obvious from the examples of actions already discussed.

The human hand is a vital and indispensable participant in virtually all the described actions and therefore, in its essence, should be a universal instrument suited for the most diverse activities. This is the direction in which it has developed in the process of evolution. During this process, it has undergone changes similar to those that constantly take place in technology. With respect to any type of machine tool, universality and versatility are inversely related to speed. A bolt, a nut, or a rack can be made on a universal lathe in several minutes using about 100 consecutive movements; however, the same lathe can be used for making bolts and nuts of any size and shape and also a countless number of other parts. At the same time, a highly specialized machine is able to make hundreds of nuts in a minute, spitting them out quicker than can be counted, but it can make only one kind of nut and nothing else. A gain in speed (and, sometimes, also a gain in quality) is being bought for the price of narrow and strict specialization.

There are very similar events taking place in the development of organisms. Those organs that, according to their function, can specialize in a clear and narrow fashion reach very high speeds by performing the standard, monotonous task in one step. For example, the reflex system of salivation works in this way by performing virtually instantaneously a refined and complex chemical analysis of food in the mouth and secreting saliva of a perfectly fitting chemical composition. In the motor area, for example, the mechanism of bearing a baby or the refined, very complex, automatic mechanism of coordinated movements of both eyes (see essay 2) work in this way. The diversity of jobs that the hand should be able to do cannot be met with anything but long, adaptively variable chains of more or less elementary actions.

The next characteristic *feature of actions* is that they are frequently *performed with an object*. This fact explains one of the terms used for this type of motor acts—*object actions*. Movements at the level of space (C) also frequently involve objects, but at that level, the action is usually restricted to simply moving an object from one place to another (to place, to reach, to get, to put into, to move toward, etc.) or applying certain force to an object (to press, to hit, to lift, to push, to throw, etc.).

Object actions, on the other hand, change the object more significantly; these changes are not restricted to a simple change in the object's location.

A cigarette lights up, an egg cooks, a photographic plate develops—all of these are chemical changes. A metal part is turned, a beard is trimmed, clay is turned into a bowl or a statue—these are changes in shape and dimension. A goal is scored; a queen takes a bishop or a rook; metal types in the hands of a typesetter form a text. In these last examples, the changes seem to be confined to a move; however, careful consideration reveals that this is not the case. If the task for the soccer players were to place the ball behind the goal line, taking it into the hands and carrying it there would be much easier and faster. If the essence of chess were in moving the pieces, then, first, the "blind" game without the board and pieces would not be considered chess; second, the pieces being moved by a 2-year-old sneaking into his father's office would be equivalent to Botvinnik's play; and, third, eventually the best spillikins player would automatically become chess champion.

In all these examples, it is clear that the moving of the objects has a concealed meaning, one that ties the movements into meaningful chains.

Here we need to mention one very interesting and typical feature of actions that also illustrates the accessible levels of action performance by different animals. Apparently, if actions forming a meaningful chain imply something more than just simple movements of the objects, then there may frequently occur intermediate movements within such a chain that move the object *in a wrong direction* in relation to its final destination.

If, for example, you need to unfasten a tight belt, it is first necessary to tighten it a little more. If you need to remove a cupping glass from the body, you should not pull it from the skin but insert a fingernail under it to let in air. If you want to pick an apple high on a tree, you should not jump in vain but rather walk away for a chair, step on it, and easily get your reward.

Let us see how animals or small children behave in such situations.

There is a plate with food behind a wire railing. A chicken (which does not possess the level of actions) sees it and starts to strive fussily along a straight line,

FIG. 23.

tries to fly over the railing, pecks the wire, and so on. A smart dog may "sin" at first with the "chicken sin" but then will turn around and *walk away from the food* to a place where it knows there is a gate. That is, the dog is able to switch *from the level of space to the level of actions*. Chickens and other similarly low animals have, by the way, one auxiliary type of behavior that undoubtedly has developed as a result of adaptation to life and that helps them out sometimes. The chicken starts to run excitedly all over the cage, thus increasing its chances of finding the gate *by pure chance*. It may happen that it actually runs through it. Monkeys made one more step forward in their development, compared to dogs; they are able to look for a tool, perhaps a stick, and to pull the food inside.

A child of 1½ years has received a large wooden egg that can be taken apart into two halves. He has seen such eggs before and knows, first, that the egg consists of two halves and, second, that there is a surprise inside that is as attractive to him as corn is for a chicken or a banana is for a monkey. But how can he open the egg? The child does, in essence, the same things as the chicken from the previous example. He puts into action *the level of space* (C), the highest of the levels to have matured at this age. Acting along similar lines, the chicken rushes toward the corn *along the same line* (a straight line) that it sees the corn. The child tries to open the egg, acting *along the same line* at which the halves should separate. Thus, the child starts to pull the halves with all his might from each other until, at some moment, they flow apart and the desired surprise flies in a third direction. Only considerably later, when the child has a mature and ready-to-work *level of actions* (D), will he realize that in such situations it is necessary *not to pull* the halves toward where they should eventually go but rather to turn or to rock them.

There are numerous examples of movements that lead in a wrong direction: a screw that can be extracted by *turning* but *not by pulling*; a suitcase lid with a lock that must first be *pressed down* in order to be released and *opened*; a hanging fruit that must be hit with a stick *from one's body* in order to get it; a soccer ball that is sometimes passed by a forward *to the left*, although the goals are *to the right*, because this direction is the shortest way to score the goal; a boat rudder that must be turned *counterclockwise* if one wants the boat to turn *clockwise*. All these movements are components of *chain actions*. All these and other similar movements are illogical from the view of simple, straightforward considerations of spatial relations, and all of them (or, at least, a great majority) are impossible for a small child or the smartest animal to perform.

FIG. 24.

In order to fully characterize actions, one must add that they include one more type of chain motor acts, maybe quite surprising to the reader—*speech*. If we consider it more attentively, we will realize that speech has all the essential, necessary features of chain actions. It represents a sequence of separate movements—links, in this particular case—movements of the tongue, lips, and vocal cords. Separate members of the chain are linked by a common meaning that cannot be reduced to moving something somewhere. Finally, many small modifications and deviations (in accent, intonation, pitch, etc.), which do not alter the meaning, are possible and actually occur all the time. A close relation between *labor movements controlled at Level D* and articulate speech was already emphasized by F. Engels in the same article from which I borrowed the earlier passage:

> First, labor, and later, together with it, articulate speech were the most important stimuli that helped the monkey's brain to gradually turn into human brain which, although being very similar in its structure, is superior to the former in its dimension and perfection.
>   The inverse action of the development of the brain and its subordinate senses, of the increasingly developing consciousness, and of the ability to think abstractly,

upon labor and language provided both with a new stimulus towards further development. (F. Engels, *Dialectics of Nature. The Role of Labor in Transition from
Ape into Man*)

Note that the so-called centers of speech in the brain cortex, namely, those
cortical areas whose injury immediately leads to the loss of the ability to speak
are parts of the same extensive cortical areas that represent the neuro-motor
apparatus of Level D.

Major Features

Now, having outlined the main features of *what we call actions*, we may return
to characterizing the level at which they are performed.

Its first sharp difference from the previous levels has already been mentioned;
it is its unquestionable right to be called "the human level." Another of its
features also makes it very different from all other levels. The level of space (C)
already lives half in the brain cortex, although undoubtedly it felt quite comfortably in its old place, in the extrapyramidal system. Remember such outstanding masters of "controlling the space" as eagles, falcons, and albatrosses, although
birds do not have any traces of a pyramidal cortex. As far as the level of actions
(D) is concerned, it is absolutely inseparable from the cortex and, from all
indications, could not exist without it. The process of development of this level
is very closely coupled to the formation of new cortical areas, with a very special
structure, part of which does gradually emerge in the highest mammals, although
other parts are seen only in the human brain.

The excerpt from the famous work by F. Engels, which was used earlier to
describe this level, vividly describes one more of its characteristic features, its *close
relationship with the human hand*. This characteristic does not mean that its brain
centers or neural pathways are more closely related to the hand muscles than to
the muscles of the rest of the body. This is not so, and we know of many cases in
which someone who has lost both hands in an accident was able to learn how to
perform numerous, very accurate actions with the feet or mouth (gripping a tool
between the teeth). The point is that the human hand, as an instrument, is so rich
in mobility (see essay 2) and so wonderfully adjusted to very accurate labor
movements of all kinds, that, naturally, Level D prefers it over any other part of
the body as an executive organ. Undoubtedly, the development of the level of
actions (D) urged and directed with its requirements the development of the
human hand, while the hand developed, moved further and further from the paw,
and stimulated and encouraged the improvement of Level D. Such tangles of
interactions and mutual influences between two organs related by a common job
are seen frequently in the history of development.

Finally, several words must be said about another feature of the level of actions
that also makes Level D different from all other levels. Whereas many of the

internal body organs (such as the heart, liver, spleen, and stomach) that fill the thoracic and abdominal cavities are unpaired and asymmetrical lying sharply to the right or to the left of the middle body plane, *all the skeletal-muscular motor apparatus is strictly symmetrical.* Directly related to this symmetry, all the typical movements and coordinations thus far considered at Levels A, B, and C, are also bilateral and symmetrical. Let us consider movements typical for the level of space such as various locomotions and different gymnastic and acrobatic movements pertaining to the same level and movements from the level of muscular-articular links (B) such as facial expression, pantomime, and plastics. All these movements are perfectly symmetrical; their right side is equivalent to their left side. On the other hand, in movements controlled by the *level of actions* (D), due to absolutely unknown and until now inexplicable reasons, *the right hand leaves the left one far behind* and dramatically surpasses it in accuracy, adroitness in developing new coordinations, and even in force. In the relatively infrequent cases of so-called left-handedness, the left hand possesses similar advantages, but these are also cases of asymmetry, only of the opposite side. Cases of *full symmetry,* or two-handedness (*ambidexterousness*), that is, cases when both right and left arms are identically dexterous with respect to actions, are *very rare.*

It is very intriguing that this advantage of the right hand over the left one with respect to hand or object dexterity is reflected in the language: In most European languages, the word *dexterity* shares the same root as the word *right,* that is, sounds like "right-handedness."[3]

The essence of this asymmetry certainly does not lie in some peculiarities of the right hand itself. Indeed, it behaves in exactly the same way as the left hand in all simple movements pertaining to Levels B and C. The heart of the matter lies in the fact that the *left brain hemisphere,* where control of all the *right side of the body* is located (remember that all the neural pathways connecting the brain to the body parts, both sensory and motor, cross from the right side of the body into the left hemisphere, and vice versa) is *leading,* or dominant, in most people with respect to many functions, not only hand control. Paralysis of the right side of the body is frequently accompanied by a loss of the ability to speak, whereas left-side paralysis is not; this observation indicates that speech control also requires the soundness of the same left hemisphere. This soundness is also required for one to understand spoken words and for the ability to read and for many other things unrelated to the theme of our book. The dominance of the left hemisphere over the right one (in left-handed persons, it is certainly vice versa) starts only from those supreme, purely cortical areas that control movements at Level D. With respect to the pyramidal fields, described earlier as the brain motor equipment of the upper sublevel of space (C2), and with respect to

---

[3]In French, "right" is *droit,* "dexterous" is *adroit* (and vice versa; "clumsy" is *gauche* and "left" is also *gauche*). In Latin, "right" is *dexter* and "dexterity" is *dexteritas;* in English the word is nearly the same as in Latin, *dexterity.* In Italian, "right" is *destro* and "dexterity" is *destrezza.* In Spanish, "right" is *destro* and "dexterity" is *desteridad* or *destreza.*

the neural nuclei of Levels C1, B, and A, hidden in the depth of the hemispheres, both hemispheres are *quite symmetrical.*

As one might expect from the history of evolution, the brain hemispheres of mammals, which do not have the human Level D, are also symmetrical and equivalent to each other. The same is true with respect to a baby's brain until the age when the baby's central nervous structures of the level of actions mature, that is, until ages 1½–2 years.

One must certainly take into account that the superiority of the right hand over the left hand in the actions at Level D could not fail to be *secondarily* reflected in the general development of the hand itself and in the perfection of its coordination, already with respect to any of the levels.

The point is that during the growth and maturation of a person (immediately after adolescence), more and more of his movements represent chain, object, meaningful actions at Level D. We shall discuss this in more detail in the section "Types of Actions" later in this essay; now, let us note that a 5–7-year-old child usually barely exceeds the movements at the level of space (C): he walks, runs, jumps, and climbs, in the other words, "entertains" himself in all possible locomotor ways. Not without reason, he is also fond of playing "horses" or other, more contemporary means of transportation; not without reason, the essence of most of these games is in running. Finally, not without reason, he gets tired and bored quickly when forced to perform any activity at the level of objects (D). As movements of various motor skills and actions start to develop and force out the lower levels of construction, the lower levels, naturally, start to develop and accumulate more and more *background corrections* for these actions and skills. Clearly, there will be more of them for the right hand (or vice versa), whose load is greater, and will increase continuously. Eventually, because of this progressive domination of actions by the right hand, that hand is enriched with considerable coordination "funds" in all the background levels as well. The superior right-hand level, like a notable citizen, patronizes its more humble, provincial, opposite-sided relatives, helping them to find employment in the capital.

The more significant load of the right hand and its much higher level of training gradually lead to an increase even in the volume and strength of its muscles. As a result, for example, even in typical movements at the level of space (C) such as *striking* or *throwing,* the right hand of adults becomes not only more dexterous but also stronger than the left hand.

Corrections and Automatisms

Now I need to say a couple of words about some very peculiar features of the level of actions (D) related to its typical sensory corrections and motor skills that are built at this level.

We started the discussions of all the previous levels with questions: Where does this level get its sensory signals, which are necessary to control movements with sensory corrections? What are these signals? While discussing the level of space (C), we have already discovered that its controlling signals are far from raw, direct impressions created by the sensory organs. These impressions are replaced by an intricately organized and deeply processed mold, or synthesis, the space field. A very important feature of this synthesis, which we have already stressed, is that it includes many traces of earlier experience saved by *memory*. *The level of actions (D) controls actions* and their components, movements-links, as we have called them, by an even more complex *synthesis*, or blending. Level D has very few direct sensory impressions. Its leading corrections, the same important corrections that define whether the motor task will be solved or disrupted, are nearly completely based on general ideas and notions. As we will see in more detail in the next essay, the sources of the leading corrections pertaining to Level D are notions of an action plan, that is, of the order of and relations among its components, and so forth.

Therefore, its leading corrections themselves originate from a continuous, meaningful observation of whether a gradual solution of a motor task proceeds correctly, of whether a current movement-link does exactly what is required according to the essence and meaning of the task. All the rest, all the exact details about movements-links, are fully delegated to the lower, background levels. This creates very special relationships between the leading Level D and its background assistants. We need to understand them, since the features of the hand, or object, dexterity (discussed later) are completely dependent on these relationships.

Each *meaningful chain action* consists of elements, *actions-links*. Each action-link is a more or less independent motor act at one of the lower, background levels. Realization of such a meaningful chain represents a sequence of actions-links, some of which may be built at the upper sublevel of space, C2, and others at the level of muscular-articular links, B, and so on.

However, these movements-links have two prominent features that make them different from genuinely independent movements performed at the same lower levels.

First, the leading Level D, figuratively speaking, intently watches all the movement-links that take place under its supreme command and supervision. It gives them rather extensive leeway but, nevertheless, stamps its seal of approval

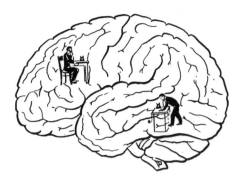

FIG. 25.

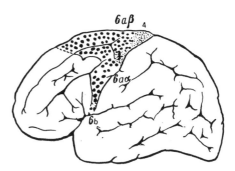

FIG. 26. The left human brain hemisphere showing the pyramidal (4) and premotor (6aα, 6aβ, and 6b) areas indicated.

on each of them; these may be just a couple of strokes of corrections typical for the leading level, which, however, introduce typical modifications into the flow of the whole movement-link, like a couple of strokes of a master artist that dramatically change the whole impression of a student's painting. Neither the lower, background levels nor movements-links produced by them can imagine, even for a second, that they are performing something independent, something that has its own meaning aside from the meaning of the whole chain. They must appropriately support the chain and take their step toward the solution of the general problem.

Second, these movements-links have a very special origin. Each level of construction of movements builds its own movements to meet the certain particular motor tasks that it is able to solve. Thus, the lower sublevel of space (C1) builds locomotions, transfers of objects, and so forth; the upper sublevel of space (C2) builds its accurate throws, strikes, hits, pointings, and so on. However, neither Level C, nor lower Levels B and A *can grasp the meaning of the object or chain problems*, which were the reasons for the development of the human level of actions, Level D. Indeed, the lower levels cannot have abilities or even reasons to form separate movements-links of such actions by themselves or for themselves.

The sublevel of C1, for example, is fully equipped with all the necessary corrections for the movement-link of striking a match on a matchbox. However, the list of motor problems whose meanings are accessible to this level does not include a problem that would consist of striking a match on a matchbox and nothing else. None of the animals, with the possible exception of a "monkeying around" monkey, could undertake such an action and be able to complete it successfully. The meaning and the objective of this movement are beyond the ceiling of this sublevel (C1) and are inaccessible to it.

Therefore, the lower, background levels develop movements-links for a chain action, not by themselves, by their own initiative, as they develop, for example, walking, running, or throwing, but only by following exact, direct *requests from the level of actions* (D). In essay 6, we are going to see how, during a process of a new skill elaboration, the central nervous system first tries to discover where to access the most appropriate corrections for a certain sequential link of the action and which background level should take the responsibility for it. Then, requests are sent to the lower levels to build certain movements-links. It looks as if Level D calls a lower level, B or C, by phone and commands it, "You must take full responsibility for a certain movement-link. You have all the necessary equipment. Moreover, the quality of your equipment is better and more appropriate for this particular link than that of any other background level. Please be advised to consult the drawings we are going to mail you."

Contemporary neurophysiology has absolutely no idea about how such fictitious phone calls between the levels take place and what the impulses are that Level D uses to inform a background level of what is required. Nevertheless, the *cortical organs*, which perform such controlling switching of the requests and their transfers to the lower levels, are *known with absolute confidence*. Our readers who are more interested in brain topography, may find these areas in Figure 5 under Number 6, immediately forward of the pyramidal motor field shown by Number 4. These controller's parts of the level of actions are called *premotor fields*. Comparative anatomy shows that cortical fields with such particular microscopic structure become defined and isolated *only in the highest mammals*, a fact nicely corresponding to everything we have said about the origin and development of Level D. Thus, the movements-links of the kind that usually composes a predominant part of the chain actions at Level D are fully controlled (with the exception of a couple of final, correcting touches from the leading level) by the lower, background levels but can be formed there only by request and detailed specification from Level D, which are, in turn, mediated by the premotor cortical fields. As we have already said in essay 4, all the background corrections usually take place automatically, without the participation of consciousness. Correspondingly, during movements-links of the type described here, only the supreme, corrective touches enter into consciousness, whereas all the rest take place automatically.

Sets of sensory corrections, which are developed by this mechanism at the lower levels (B and C) in order to provide special movements-links, are further referred to as "*higher automatisms*." In everyday speech, they may be described by different words in different cases: *motor skills, special skills, knacks*, and so on. In English, they are called "skills"; in German, "Handfertigkeiten," or simply "Fertigkeiten." The term *higher automatisms* is certainly more correct and precise than the others, albeit somewhat lengthy; however, you will not confuse it with anything else. We shall see, in essay 6, how these genuinely higher automatisms compose a group among automatisms in general; then, we shall give them a more precise definition.

Higher automatisms permeate all the everyday, common, practiced movements at Level D. They may emerge at all the levels without exception. Moreover, like the servants in the *bylina* (a traditional Russian fable) of the *boyarinia* (wife of a nobleman) Mamelfa Timofeevna, who themselves had full staffs of servants, these automatisms sometimes represent rather complicated structures with their own background levels.

ON THE KINDS OF DEXTERITY

Now, after we have briefly outlined all the levels of movement construction that take part in athletic and gymnastic movements and in most of the labor and defensive movements, it is appropriate and timely to suggest a classification of movements that require and display *dexterity*. Because our movements represent a number of layers that differ in origin, meaning, and many physiological properties, it is natural to expect that the *manifestations of dexterity* will also probably differ, depending on the level to which the movements exhibiting dexterity pertain. We shall see further that not only is this guess quite correct but also that people differ considerably in the degree of development of the different levels of movement construction and in the dexterity inherent to these levels. For example, you may meet people with a very good functioning of the upper space sublevel (C2) but a suboptimal functioning of their level of muscular-articular links (B). In others, Level B may work perfectly whereas Levels C and D are worse than average. A dexterous person does not necessarily need to possess dexterity of all kinds and at all the levels: Depending on which levels are inherently better developed, dexterity will manifest itself electively with respect to certain types of movements and actions, whereas during other actions, it will be quite mediocre.

These facts are evidence of how important it is to possess knowledge about the levels of movement construction in order to have a proper understanding of dexterity.

In order to carry out the proposed classification of the types of dexterity according to the hierarchical position of the level controlling the movements, let us, first of all, define the *basic* and most characteristic *feature of dexterous movements* with respect to their physiological construction.

None of the levels of control is able alone to provide dexterity for its movements. This statement is supported by the numerous, abundant examples in this volume. Each movement or action that we can consider, without hesitation, as *dexterous*, is always built at not less than two *levels*. The *leading level* of a dexterous movement or action displays outstanding *features of switchability, resourcefulness, and maneuverability*, whereas the supporting background level or levels display similarly outstanding features of *harmony, obedience, and precision* of work. We have earlier compared the leading and background levels to a rider and horse. Returning to this comparison, we might say that dexterity cannot be exhibited by the rider or by the horse alone; dexterity becomes possible only when the rider is inventive and quick-witted and the horse is obedient and accurate.

The level of muscular-articular links in humans leads to so few independent movements and movements that all are so insignificant and irresponsible that there is no place for dexterity to exhibit itself. We have already ridiculed it, in a friendly fashion, for the inapplicability of the notion of targeted accuracy (certainly, with all the respect that this highly esteemed and still irreplaceable veteran of our central nervous system deserves). Let us ask once again, trying not to offend it, where, other than in an anecdote, can the following expressions occur: "A man dexterously laughed" or "How dexterously she trembled with fear!"

So, real, perceptible manifestations of dexterity start in human beings from *the level of space* (C). Based on the basic feature of all dexterous actions just formulated, we can distinguish two kinds of dexterity. The first refers to movements performed at the level of space (C) and supported by the background activity of Level B (We do not mention here the background corrections from the level of tone (A), which are always present, without exception, in all the movements of healthy people). We shall call this type of dexterity *body dexterity*. The second type of dexterity reveals itself in the actions of the level considered last, the level of actions (D), with similarly obligatory background supporting activity of both sublevels of space (C) and sometimes also of Level B. We shall call this type of dexterity *hand or object dexterity*. Considering everything that has been said in the previous section about the highest automatisms, it will be easy to understand that the movements-links from Level C involved in a complex chain action may, by themselves, manifest the same features of body dexterity as any independent movements from Level C. In this case, supporting background corrections from Level B will be absolutely necessary. Thus, the group of manifestations of hand or object dexterity appears very complex in its composition, compared to the first group (body dexterity). Moreover, these manifestations will differ with respect to the background levels and sublevels that supply them with the obligatory supporting background corrections. On the other hand, in some cases, we shall see such actions at Level D possess *movements-links overloaded with body dexterity*; sometimes, the whole *action itself* demonstrates all the *signs of hand or object dexterity*. Examples will help us find our way in this diversity. The possibility of somehow classifying the numerous manifestations of dexterity is obviously more valuable than the necessity of lumping them all together.

FIG. 27.

FIG. 28.

Let us turn to some examples: Like a monkey, the ship's boy climbed up the mast dexterously. Before the market-woman collected her wits, the boy dexterously grabbed an apple and disappeared. The colonel dexterously rode the horse in front of the parade. The gymnast dexterously jumped over the table, leaning on his hand. The acrobat dexterously performed a double-somersault.

These are all examples of *body dexterity*, examples of movements controlled at the level of space, C, and supported by background corrections from the level of muscular-articular links, B. If the construction of a movement is expressed as a fraction, whose numerator denotes the leading level and the denominator denotes the background level(s), all these examples can be expressed with the formula $\frac{C}{B}$.

Here are two examples of *hand or object dexterity*, whose composition may be considerably more complex.

A soldier dexterously freed the machine gun stuck in the bushes and thick mud: $\frac{D}{C1}$.

With precise, dexterous movements of the tweezers, the jeweler placed a gear into a tiny watch: $\frac{D}{C2}$.

These are examples of the leading level being supported by more or less pure background activity at the level of space. The numbers 1 and 2 after the letter C in the denominators refer to the division of Level C into two sublevels, which were described earlier. Level C1 refers to the lower, more ancient sublevel related to the EMS and supported by the striatum. Level C2 refers to the upper, pyramidal, cortical level. The difference in the sensory signals that the two sublevels receive influences the details of the movements (or background corrections) that issue from each sublevel. Movements of *the lower sublevel (C1) are usually characterized by a fluid, continuous adjustment to space* and the external conditions in general, which is required, for example, during walking or running. Movements of *the upper sublevel (C2)*, which are related to the highly developed representation of sensory organs in the brain cortex, are more typically characterized by terminal, *targeted accuracy and precision* (as, for example, during a well-aimed throw or strike). Without delving too deeply into the details of these differences, which may frequently merge and disappear during simultaneous action of both sublevels, we deem it appropriate, however, to consider them briefly.

Consider a few more examples.

A nurse gently, quickly, and dexterously bandaged the piercingly painful wound: $\frac{D}{(C1)(B)}$.

With exceptional dexterity, the skier flew through the hard curves and the slalom gates: $\frac{D}{C1}$.

Hanging nearly to the ground and with his horse at full gallop, the rider used his teeth to pick up a dagger driven into the ground up to its handle: $\frac{D}{(C2)(B)}$.

The bull, blind with fury, rushed at the toreador, who stood motionless as a statue. Suddenly, with one quick move, the man delivered a precise, almost calm strike at the bull's medulla. The bull fell to the ground: $\frac{D}{(C2)(B)}$.

In this group of examples, the background activity at the level of space is clearly accompanied by background corrections from Level B. Here, we also can single-out cases of preferential activity at sublevels C1 and C2. The first examples of both Levels C1 and C2 (the nurse and the rider) demonstrate primarily *body dexterity* of movements-links; the second pair of examples (the skier and the toreador) demonstrate *hand or object dexterity* of the movement as a whole. Following is an example of dexterity manifestation with all the lower background corrections.

"Like a mad dog, Malyuta threw himself on Persten. But, with amazing dexterity, the ataman hit him with a fist in the solar plexus, kicked the window out with his foot, and jumped out into the garden" (A. K. Tolstoy, *Prince Serebryanny*, chapter 2).

The actions of a fencer or boxer among sportsmen and the actions of a surgeon or leather cutter among professionals may also serve as examples of dexterity with all the lower background levels activated and are represented by the formula, $\frac{D}{(C1)(C2)(B)}$.

TYPES OF ACTIONS

In the movements of an adult, actions at Level D occur in such abundance and in such prominent positions that their catalogue, were it possible to compile one, would be much longer than the list of movements belonging to the level of space. It would be extremely hard to apply order to them if it were not for the property of actions discussed in the section "Corrections and Automatisms." This is the custom of Level D to build its actions from movements-links controlled by what we called "higher automatisms." Each higher automatism is characterized by a movement controlled almost independently by one of the lower levels of construction. Within a complex chain of movements, where links built on various levels follow each other, it is always possible to define the more and less essential ones. One may reasonably speak of *leading and auxiliary, or background, successive links*, similarly to how we discussed leading and background corrections in each separate movement.

For example, for sharpening a pencil, the *leading* movements-links that directly participate in solving the problem are the forward movements of the knife blade that actually shave off the wood. Backward knife movements, movements of shaking the shavings off, blowing them off, adjusting the grip, and so on, play the role of *background* movements-links. In boxing, the leading movements obviously include those of delivering blows and the defensive movements to parry the opponent's blows. Backward arm movements following these and also the numerous intermediate movements familiar to anyone who has watched a boxing match are considered background links.

On this basis, we can classify actions according to which level or levels the most essential, leading movements-links of these chain actions pertain to. Let us outline such a classification. In each of the groups, we emphasize actions from everyday life, labor movements, and movements involved in physical exercise, sports, and other games. This is a very conventional classification, undertaken for the sake of clarity and higher resolution.

Remember that we have defined manifestations of hand or object dexterity as actions performed at Level D and supported by background activity at different lower levels. Within the proposed classification, we shall also consider examples of dexterous actions and peculiarities of their composition for each group.

A. Group 1

Let us assign to the first, introductory group, actions that lack any higher automatisms. This group includes movements of a "scouting" nature: watching, feeling, comparing objects, and so on. It also includes the simplest object actions that can be performed by a 3–4-year-old child: putting down an object, pouring something into a box, opening a latch, taking off a box cover, unlocking a suitcase, schematically drawing a house, and so on. Obviously, the movements of a novice can also be classified as being impoverished with respect to automatisms. These movements include those that have not yet developed special automatisms and that have failed to find appropriate automatisms among those developed earlier for other tasks. We mentioned earlier funds of background corrections, gradually accumulated by every person during the lifetime, and called them "brain libraries." Thus, the first group includes all movements that, forever or at least during initial stages, do not have appropriate supporting material in the lower libraries. Apparently, according to the definition of hand dexterity, dexterity has nothing to do with the first group of actions.

B. Group 2

The second group includes actions consisting of movements-links that are predominantly built at the *upper sublevel of space* (C2), at the cortical, pyramidal sublevel of long-range receptors of accuracy and precision. Here we meet actions from everyday life such as pulling a thread through a needle's eye, pouring out a dose of medicine, sharpening a pencil. (Obviously, for each of the groups and their subdivisions, we present only a few random examples as illustrations. To present a full list is certainly out of the question.) Professional and labor movements supported by background activity at Level C2 include, for example, movements of a watch repairer or engraver and the accurate assembling of machinery. The earlier example of the watchmaker who assembled tiny gears of a lady's watch with outstanding hand dexterity belongs to this group. In Zolya's novel *The Trap*, there is a very impressive description of the quick, highly automated work of a goldsmith, Lorillé, who made a chain from a golden wire whose links were nearly impossible to see with the naked eye. Group 2 also includes many operations performed with precision instruments (slide rule, micrometer, those thin wire hoops in precision chemical scales called "the riders," etc.). Here, also are many labor movements, such as those of the turner, the engraver, the optical grinder, the surgeon. In all these actions, dexterity is manifested in reserved, precise movements, unhurried but also without hestitation. In these movements, more than in any others, the pyramidal system demonstrates all its art of fine control, inducing contractions of all the muscles controlling involved arm joints to some intermediate level, then adding mion after mion with microscopic precision, and simultaneously turning off individual mions in resisting muscles. Visual control almost always plays the most vital role in achieving success during dexterous movements of this group. Their elaborated higher automatisms, as if without any involvement of consciousness, involve transformation of visual perception into barely noticeable movements of fingers or of a tool, which looks as though it were fused to the hand.

FIG. 29. Accurate actions with background corrections from Level C2.

FIG. 30. Actions with background corrections from Level C1.

Because this group of actions virtually represents the entire realm of small, fine finger movements, it naturally does not involve any athletic movements. There is, however, a whole area of games and puzzles in which success directly depends on the degree of hand dexterity and which belong to this group together with their leading automatisms. These include, for example, the well-known glass boxes for which the task is to maneuver small metal balls into tiny holes by rocking and shaking the box, or very unstable small figures that need to be balanced, or finally, card houses and spillikins.

C. Group 3

The third group unites actions whose leading components are mostly dependent on *the lower sublevel of space* (C1), a sublevel that, as the reader should remember, is based on the activity of *striatal* nuclei, the top EMS structures. Here are a few examples from everyday movements whose leading components make them belong to this group: tying shoe laces, ironing, rolling out dough, shaving, brushing hair, and turning pages. Among the examples that we have discussed earlier—a long chain of movements during lighting a cigarette—also belongs to this group of actions. Among professional actions, this group includes coupling cars into trains, driving a car or a steam engine, filing, polishing, laundering, and so on. Here we meet the large body movements that sometimes involve locomotions. The main feature of movements in this group is smooth, adaptive, and, one may even say, sensitive dexterity. In this area, there are already chances for the athletic and sports movements to reveal themselves. Appropriate examples include climbing a rope, a pole, a rope ladder, or a tree trunk and locomotions using complex devices like cycling or rowing. An example from an area close to acrobatics includes the balancing of objects (e.g., balancing a long pole on one's forehead or chin).

One should mention that it is virtually impossible to find examples that would not have a considerable amount of background activity at the lower level of muscular-articular links (B). In some cases, these background corrections par-

FIG. 31. Actions with background corrections from Level B.

FIG. 32. Actions with background
corrections from all the lower levels.

FIG. 33.

ticipate equally with striatal background activity from Level C1, for example,
during clambering (hand dexterity); in other cases, responsible background activity of Level C1 is complex by itself and includes its own background corrections
from Level B. Such are the movements of a person coupling cars into trains or
installing telephone lines (a combination of both hand and body dexterity).

D. Group 4

The fourth group includes actions in which *background activity at the level of
muscular-articular links (B) apparently dominates over spatial background corrections
from Level C.* Appropriate examples from everyday movements include tying and
untying knots, knitting, winding a clew, braiding hair, soaping and washing one's
body, and dressing. Among professional actions, let us name hammering, digging,
binding, and spinning and actions involving rotation of a handle (working with
a winch, drawing a bucket of water from a well with a windlass, pumping water,
etc.). Among athletic actions, very typical examples are represented by French
wrestling and particularly judo (earlier called jujitsu). This group includes many
of the magician's movements based on so-called sleight of hand and many thief's
and cheater's movements that are based on the same principle.

E. Group 5

The fifth group unites those actions that require participation of *both the level of
space (C) and the level of muscular-articular links (B).* It seems natural to classify
these movements into three subgroups, although the practical realization of such
a classification is very hard. Nevertheless, let us at least try to outline it because

this group of actions, with the most complex and richest structure, naturally includes the largest diversity of dexterous movements, including the most interesting and meaningful ones.

We imply combination of Level B, first, with *the lower sublevel of space (C1)*; second, with *the upper sublevel of space (C2)*; and finally, with both of them, that is, *the whole orchestra of background activity.*

In the first subgroup (combining Levels C1 and B), we are going to meet, in everyday actions such as hand sewing, sawing, winding a watch or a clock, and peeling vegetables or fruits. In the area of labor movements, we see mowing, using a sewing machine, tailor pleating, loading paper into a press and collating it in a printing house, applying a bandage, wrapping, tying, and so forth. In the area of physical culture and sports, the examples include slalom, acrobatics, and defense movements in fencing.

The second subgroup of actions is supported by a duo of the pyramidal sublevel of accuracy (C2) and the level of controlling one's own body (B). In everyday life, these include embroidering, darning, and making lace; blacksmith movements during precise, artistic forging and medical procedures like giving injections and applying cupping-glasses are examples of professional actions. In the area of athletic movements, offensive (striking) movements in fencing and boxing, archery, playing billiards, and throwing complex objects like boomerang, harpoon, or lasso. Two previous examples of high dexterity belong to this subgroup: with the horse at full gallop, the rider's plucking with his teeth the dagger driven into the ground and the conclusive actions of the toreador.

Finally, the third, most universal subgroup, in which the leading Level D is supported by all the lower levels, C1, C2, and B, I start with examples of such purely human actions as *speech and writing.* Accurate physiological analysis (which is not within the scope of this volume), shows that each of the levels of movement construction that exist in the central nervous system, from the bottom to the top, carries an important and vital load in these most complex and meaningful actions.[4]

For this subgroup, it is very hard to find examples among everyday movements. Quite naturally, these, the most complex of all the skills, require outstanding harmony and cooperation of all the levels of construction and are therefore observed only after considerable practice. For these reasons, they should be sought primarily in the professional areas of either labor or sports.

If one has ever witnessed the rolling of small iron pieces at a foundry, he is unlikely to have forgotten the scene. A seminaked worker, with just trousers and apron on, stands ready in front of a huge, towering wall of the mill, where large, wet shafts are quickly rotating with gritting. Then, a golden, fiery snake, the size of a thumb, jumps out of the slot between two shafts and rushes toward the worker. Before it passes two or three steps, the worker grabs it by the neck

---

[4]In this book, we shall not touch on those factors proving the existence of at least one more cortical level (E) in our brain, which is the actual leading level for these acts of human communication, because it is unrelated to the main topic, dexterity.

with large tongs hanging on a chain nearby. With amazing dexterity, he makes half a turn on the heels, like a dancer pirouetting, and puts the head of the fiery snake into another slot, between two other shafts rotating in the opposite direction. The shafts never cease to turn. If the worker delays for just a moment with pushing a fiery cable into the grinding slot, the inexorable shafts of the first pair will spew out a loop that would coil along the whole floor of the machine shop. If he does not catch the snake by its neck at the moment when it unexpectedly jumps out of the slot, it may pierce his body like an awl passing through a piece of butter. If he grabs it at a wrong place, not exactly half a meter from its tip, but a little bit farther or closer, he will never be able to push its soft body, breathing with fire, into the slot. Such things never happen. In a fraction of a second, the worker steps over a fiery loop, and it flies out of one mill into another at the same speed. And he is already standing again, like a hunter, light, agile, as flexible as a compressed spring, quiet as if he were not playing games with death—

Among professional labor movements, there are many examples of actions from this extremely complex subgroup. They all require immense, resourceful dexterity and almost always are connected to risk and danger to life. There are many such actions in the life of a firefighter, a sailor on a sailboat, a fisherman who defies the sea in a frail boat, or a diver who dives naked into the depths searching for pearl shells. All the magnificence of this kind of dexterity was displayed by the young hero of the ballad "The Cup" (by F. Schiller), but it failed him during the second dive. In this subgroup, each labor operation involves both athletic-acrobatic elements and elements of a dangerous combat. Each athletic or combat episode of this type represents extensive genuine professional training and experience. Such a movement is an interlacing of all the levels and, simultaneously, an unbreakable combination of all the most challenging types of human activity.

In the area of athletic or sports movements, which merges with the area of combat, we should first of all name bayonet combat, fencing, and boxing, taken as a whole. We have semiconventionally assigned the defensive actions of these types of combat to the lower sublevel (C1) and the offensive actions to the upper sublevel (C2), but in reality, they certainly always merge together so that it is very hard to separate them.

Here, we cannot overlook a whole list of actions within mountain climbing. As it is known to any mountaineer, this sport conceals many dangers and makes great demands on dexterity and motor resourcefulness. Similar situations leading to actions of similar structure are required from a hunter of dangerous animals, from a polar traveler crossing ice hummocks, from a paratrooper whose parachute does not open or who encounters problems at landing. However, in the area of sports, there are actions that definitely approach in their structure the actions of this highest subgroup, although they do not involve any element of danger. Sports games of this kind develop both versatile body and versatile hand dexterity. These include tennis, gorodki (a kind of skittles), and, to some extent, lapta (a Russian version of baseball). Not accidentally, these games have fascinated a number of outstanding philosophers, including the famous physiologist, I. P. Pavlov.

FORMATION OF MOVEMENTS IN A YOUNGSTER

In the third section of essay 4, while discussing movement development in the child we stopped at the age of 2. The point is, as we have mentioned, that at this age, the process of maturation of all the brain structures and conduction pathways is complete, and the slow and lengthy work of mutual adjustment of all the levels of construction and the development of their abilities start. It is certainly impossible to describe this mutual adjustment of the levels before the levels themselves have been characterized; therefore, it was necessary to delay the description of this so-called "second childhood."

Now, we can briefly compensate for the interruption by noting the most essential features of the motor development of a child between the ages of 2 and 14–15 years, the time of final maturation.

The development of the area of movements, called *motorics*, in a child does not proceed along a smooth, ascending line. In it, as in other areas of development, one may frequently observe stops or rapid leaps upward or, sometimes, even seeming retreats. This unevenness is particularly pronounced at ages just before puberty. At this time, preadolescents usually become very clumsy, awkward, and sluggish; bump everything; break dishes; drop everything on the floor; and wear quickly through their shoes. We shall soon see that these are, in essence, just temporary retreats.

At the end of the second year of life and during the whole third year, the higher motor systems are still in the process of final maturation. At this particular age, the number and success of *actions at Level D* start to grow considerably. This age is the time when the child ceases to be a "higher ape" and for the first time masters movements that are absolutely impossible for apes. From the area of object actions, the child learns some of the self-care procedures (undressing, washing, eating with a spoon), successfully plays with toys, builds bricks or sand pies, starts to draw something with a pencil. At the same time, and exactly in the described movements, the inequality between the two hands becomes obvious, and whether the child is right- or left-handed is defined. Also at the same time, coherent speech emerges, comprising complete, correctly assembled sentences and not simply separate words as it did earlier.

The next period, from ages 3–7 years, is predominantly a *period of quantitative strengthening and adjustment of all of the available levels*. Anatomically, they are all ready at the third year of life and start to fill with substance. We have already seen in the essay on the levels of construction, that higher and younger levels can control movements with more complex structure and require more background corrections prepared in advance. One may compare the levels of move-ment construction to bowls of larger and larger volume, which take more time to be filled.

Therefore, although a child is ready to put into action any of the human levels of construction, he actually uses mostly those easier ones that were the first to be filled with some content. These levels are mostly those of the EMS, ending with the sublevel of the striatum, that is, the lower sublevel of space (C1), the sublevel of locomotions and gymnastics-type movements.

In contrast to the way toddlers look—like clumsy bear cubs—children 3–7 years old are very agile and lively. They run quickly and adroitly, jump, and climb. They have a good sense of rhythm; they are, for example, very good at hopping over a rope revolved by their friends. They have very diverse and expressive facial expressions and gesticulate energetically and convincingly when telling something. They are also very good at mimicking the movements of others; when playing charades, one can very easily guess the activity from the movements of such a child; he is also able to achieve high and cruel virtuosity at cartoonish mimicking of the motor shortcomings of his friends.

However, if you try to place such a child in an occupation from the sublevel of accuracy (C2) or especially from the level of actions (D), you will immediately observe weakness and high fatigability. The proverbial restlessness of children during these years does not depend exclusively on his particularly high need in movements: While sitting, the child has only a very few things to occupy himself and quickly becomes bored. If the child is forced to do something that requires accuracy (for example, sewing or writing letters), he will take the first available opportunity to run away and play on the widely spread wings of his striatum. Prof. M. Gurevich very precisely pointed out that the apparent restlessness of a child is only superficial. Virtually all the child's movements are free, without burden, without any labor in its direct sense; they are movements that do not overcome any resistance and therefore do not require particularly high energy expenditure.

The predominance of the EMS in the movements of a child at this age is reflected in the natural coherence and grace of those movements. We have already spoken about the elegance of movement generally inherent to the level of muscular-articular links and about its causes. This is precisely the level that supplies most of the background corrections in children of this age.

The next period of motor development embraces approximately the ages from 7 to 10 years. At this time, the upper, pyramidal sublevel of space (C2) starts to accumulate background corrections. The motor repertoire of a child gradually acquires two new components: *force and accuracy*.

This development is reflected in both the games and the labor to which the child is gradually becoming accustomed. Without any knowledge about move-ment science, which has started to develop, as a science, only during the last few years, the wisdom of everyday life long ago, very wisely and accurately realized the age at which it makes sense to teach a child labor skills. This is exactly the age when the PMS becomes productive. Although children at this age are not ready for prolonged perseverance and concentration of attention, they start to develop small, precise movements and are able to occupy themselves while sitting at a table. Their handwriting, which at the beginning of education consisted of letters the size of walnuts, becomes smaller and more regular, their pencil draws lines that are not as thick as mostacciolli, and they break pencil points not more frequently than twice a day. The boys improve their throwing and hitting movements (not accidentally do the major fights and the maximum number of broken windows and bloodied noses occur at this particular age!) and develop accuracy in throwing. It is quite obvious that during these early school years, children start learning skills of the upper sublevel of space (C2): the just mentioned hitting and throwing movements requiring accuracy, accurate movements in the spatial field, and so on. Those who start teaching children to play musical instruments at this age are absolutely right.

After the age of 10–11 years, a period of a major and complex restructuring that involves all the aspects of a growing organism begins. This period lasts to the age of about 14–15 years, just prior to pubescence, and includes the period of pubescence itself. This stage is not easy to characterize.

On the one hand, the levels of movement construction methodically continue to accumulate skills and background corrections. Eventually, the level of actions, which during the first 10 years of life was forced to survive on the first group of actions according to our classification (i.e., actions without background corrections), starts to acquire the first higher automatisms, the basis of any kind of skill. At this time, it is possible and recommended to teach a child hand labor. At this age, it is easy to interest the child in actions and to stir his desire to build things. If one is lucky in detecting the child's interests and talents, much can be achieved at this age.

On the other hand, harmony and cooperation among the levels of coordination, which appeared to be reached at this age, once again fall apart in many aspects. This disruption happens, not because of any fault on the part of the levels, but because of profound shifts in the functioning of all the body glands, all its extremely complex internal chemistry. This basic restructuring of the metabolism and the switching of secretions and excretions of all the organs are perceived by the organism as an urgent task demanding the sacrifice of all the other bodily functions. This is the reason for the sluggish and awkward movement's looseness, the slowing down of motor reactions, and a temporary loss of dexterity and, sometimes, even of muscle force. It is well known that at this age, the personal life of teenagers also experiences a sudden change, one sometimes leading to actual nervous breakdown, which is, however, completely forgotten during the next stage of life. Because none of the temporary motor disturbances are related to disorders in the brain motor systems, one should not pay too much attention to the apparent motor clumsiness of teenagers and delay their training in labor or sports motor skills. Quite the opposite, if there are no direct medical counterindications, for example, recommendations by a physician, it is particularly important to continue the education of the levels of coordination, both low and high ones. Such systematic work will not lead to any detrimental effects and is likely to beneficially affect both the motor abilities and the general emotional life of the forming adult.

On Exercise and
Motor Skill

HOW WE SHOULD NOT THINK
ABOUT MOTOR SKILL

Since ancient times, one of the specific features of human beings (and some closely related animals) has attracted the attention of intelligent people. Machines and tools *deteriorate with use*; they wear out, loosen up, and generally become *worse*. The best machines are those that do not require repair for long periods of time. The situation with the "human machine" is the opposite. *The longer* a human participates in a certain activity, the *better* he or she performs it. A living organism not only does not deteriorate during work but, quite the opposite, becomes stronger, quicker, more enduring, more adroit and dexterous, particularly with respect to the type of activity that has been performed. This feature of living organisms has been termed *exercisability*.

Frequently, it is harder to explain a phenomenon than to notice it and to use it in practice. This is true for exercisability, which happens to be a widespread phenomenon. After discovering it in animals, humans started to tame them, that is, to train and exercise them in helpful skills. However, the nature and essence of this basic difference between living beings and machines was difficult to discover.

Since long ago, physicians held tenaciously to a superstition, one they have just now begun to give up—the idea that live nature differs from "dead" nature by the presence of a so-called "vital force." Many phenomena were in need of explanation, an explanation that required the introduction of the notion of a "vital force." Everywhere one could see how living organisms energetically struggled for their safety and well-being. A wound closed and healed, broken bones knitted by themselves, and the lower vertebrates "repaired" themselves so successfully that it was not a problem for a lizard to grow a new tail or for a starfish to grow a new leg to replace a lost, old one.

Because vital force already carried the burden of so many unexplained events, scientists deemed it possible to add one more—the phenomenon of exercisability. The situation was described like this: Labor by itself wears down a living organism just as it does a nonliving machine, but the vital force starts struggling against this deterioration and primarily strengthens the most worn parts, as a commander strengthens the points that are most vigorously attacked by the enemy. All kinds of work are detrimental but, fortunately, their effects are eliminated by the vital force, free of charge. This view deserved the attention only of those slave owners who despised labor and had enough leisure time to contemplate nature in those ancient times.

According to this view, the most exercisable organs should be those with the heaviest load during certain work. This idea is partly supported by direct observations. The thin skin of the palm gets covered with wear-protecting calluses. Muscles grow in an apparently selective pattern, depending on the type of load. Runners have stronger leg muscles, blacksmiths have stronger arm muscles, and load bearers have stronger body muscles. But here, we encounter the first problem.

If exercisability were confined to the improvement in the functioning of tendons, ligaments, and muscle growth, the consequences of exercising, for example, a right arm should benefit any kind of work performed by this arm. However, exercisability extends its benefit to only a few similar kinds of activity, whereas the arm remains at the same level of fitness with respect to all other activities. A person, who has trained for a long time in discus throwing, finds that his arm would be better able to throw a spear, a ball, a hammer, and a shot, but this training would not add anything to his ability to work with a saw or a winch. How can one explain why the same joints, muscles, and ligaments that, as a result of exercise, have been given endurance and dexterity by vital force have not improved at all with respect to unrelated activities?

The superstitions related to the idea of vital force were very harmful in medicine and in the practice of exercise and exercisability. First, according to this view, the ability of tissues to grow, heal, and knit clearly was greatest during tender childhood. Therefore, one needed to start practicing the most challenging movements during childhood as well. This conclusion justified the merciless crippling of children's bodies and the fabricating of numerous "gutta-percha boys" for entertainment of circus crowds.

Second, because the consequences of exercise were assumed to reside in the arm itself, in its muscles and ligaments, another idea emerged—that these muscles and ligaments could be corrected and improved with a direct surgical intervention. For example, numerous small bones and joints in the palm are ingrown into the soft tissues and tightly wrapped by ligaments. Because of this natural structure, the hands apparently were not useful enough. Practitioners believed it was easier to correct nature's mistake, not with warming up and release of the muscles, but with appropriate plastic surgery. For example, musicians playing the piano had plenty of trouble with the ligament connecting the tendons of the ring and middle fingers and submitted to "corrective" surgery. The consequences of surgery separating those fingers were certainly terrible and irreversible. A musician looked with sorrow at the ruined hand and probably thought that nature had taken revenge for the impertinent accusation.

These views changed dramatically in the 19th century with the onset of the energetic study of neurophysiology. The role of the brain became clearer. It was discovered that the control of movements and motor memory reside in the brain. Therefore, it also became clear that the exercise of body organs leads to changes in the brain and that motor skills are traces imprinted not on the arms, legs, or back, but somewhere above, deep in the brain's recesses.

What are these traces and how do they form in the brain? The answers to these questions were sought with the help of an analogy, one that had been considered very helpful but later turned out to be absolutely wrong. Nevertheless, it occupied the minds of physiologists and teacher-practitioners for 2–3 decades. Everything started with a dog.

It is well known that placing food in one's mouth leads to salivation, which is particularly strong if the food is dry. Food stimulates the mucous membrane of the mouth. This stimulation is transferred by sensory nerves to the so-called salivary brain center, which reacts to the stimulation with an order—an inflow of neural signals to the subordinate salivary glands. This phenomenon is observed in all animals who have saliva in their mouths and occurs with machinelike reproducibility, always and everywhere, even in the smallest cubs. Such inborn mechanisms are termed *reflexes*.

A famous Russian physiologist, I. P. Pavlov, who by that time had already been awarded the Nobel prize for his studies of digestion, discovered the following fact. If a hungry dog heard a bell or a whistle, saw a light of a certain color turned on, or experienced some other stimulation each day half a minute prior to feeding, repeatedly for many days, the animal gradually started to salivate, not when it received the food or not even when it saw the food, but when the stimulating signal was activated. It was found that this method could turn any signal into a salivation-reflex inducer. After a hundred presentations of the combined signal and feeding, one could force a dog to salivate by pricking certain parts of its body, by scratching, blinking, coughing, chirping, crackling, by anything. Certainly, only the stimulus that had been used during training could serve in this way, that is, became able to substitute for the simulation of the mouth by food. Novel signals do not induce salivation even in very hungry dogs. Not one of a thousand dogs taken from the street will react to chirping or light blinking, aside perhaps from pointing their ears. Moreover, only the laboratory's Bobik started to salivate at the chirping, Jack, at the light blinking, and Milka and Tobick, at any other conditional signal invented by the boundless imagination of the researcher.

It is clear that in each case, we witness the birth of a *new reflex* elaborated by artificial means. This is not an inborn, general reflex, like the salivation reflex, but a reflex reflecting the *enrichment of the personal experience* of a dog. I. P. Pavlov called these artificial reflexes "conditioned," in contrast with the inborn unconditioned reflexes.

The following proposal was advanced in order to explain how a neural pathway for a new reflex develops in the brain. It was known (as we have already told the reader) that auditory, visual, and tactile sensations have vast areas in the brain cortex where neural pathways from the corresponding sensory organs terminate. Let us *assume* that for each separate sensation, for each separate feeling delivered by the sensory organs to the brain, there are special, microscopically small "centers," for example, neural cells, where these impressions come and take their places next to each other, like honey in a honeycomb. When a chirping sound or light first reaches a dog's brain, the sensation finds a new, empty cell and settles there. Let us also assume that each of these cells has a neural connection to the salivary glands, but this connection, for some reason, cannot transmit neural signals. If you repeatedly combine an indifferent impression with feeding, as Pavlov did, the path between the two centers becomes "beaten" and gradually becomes able to conduct impulses. We have found an old rubber tube that is badly needed. We are taking a knitting needle to chisel out the dirt and debris. And, behold! The needle passes through the tube, and water starts to dribble from the other end, further cleans the tube by washing out the dirt, and eventually it runs happily pouring us with splashes. This scenario is approximately how physiologists imagined the beating of neural connective paths.[1] Experiments with dogs showed that such path beatings occurred with difficulty and very slowly, providing an explanation for the fact that one must practice long and hard to absorb a new experience or to acquire a new skill.

The discovery of conditioned reflexes in animals (first, salivatory, and later, motor reflexes) was actually a great success in the field of physiology and inspired much scientific thinking. The discovery made it possible to deliver the last hard blow to the idea of vital force. There were facts that begged interpretation in a very wide sense. The idea of beating neural paths in the brain was invoked to explain the ability to learn, to exercise, to acquire skills, and, in general, all types of personal experience accumulation.

However, equating human motor skill to a dog's conditioned reflex was fraught with serious errors, and caused medical practice as much harm as preachings of vital force theories. Fortunately, its active life was much shorter.

---

[1]The development of conditioned reflexes could not be ascribed to the growth of new neural paths in the brain, because it had been authentically established that after the intrauterine period, fibers in the central nervous system did not grow.

First, as it has been noted, acquiring experience in natural conditions and even absorbing external impressions are *active, not passive*, processes. A living being, from a worm or a snail to a human, does not passively submit itself to the flow of impressions but catches and grabs them. This process is not comparable to the situation of a dog tied to its laboratory stand and unable to react to what it hears or sees.

Besides this fact, serious questions are raised concerning the slowness and difficulty of the formation of these new brain connections, by all the months taken to form a conditioned reflex. In real, everyday life, neither a dog nor certainly a human requires dozens of repetitions of an impression to remember it and fix it in memory. An animal that required months to master each new impression would be very poorly equipped for the struggle of life. Harsh reality would not fiddle with such unimpressive species and would simply throw them overboard.

We know well enough from our experience that dogs and horses, not to mention monkeys, understand and remember many things from the first trial. Humans need repetition only in cases when something must be learned literally; if the task is to grasp the meaning, humans do not need repetition. Undoubtedly, this striking difference between single presentation in natural conditions and endless, repetitious presentations in experiments with conditioned reflexes derives mainly from the first, basic difference, namely, environment. In natural, normal life, an animal passes by those impressions that are unimportant to it and actively catches and grasps those that are of vital importance.[2] In a laboratory environment, the animal willy-nilly lets events happen around it, without taking any active part in them.

Motor skills do take time to develop. Consequently, they were easily comparable to conditioned reflexes. However, as we will see, each motor skill is complex, and because of this complexity, its development goes through a number of consecutive stages. One can readily observe some of these stages; for example, the ability to maintain equilibrium during bicycling or the ability to float on water comes in one step.

The practical harm caused by this erroneous analogy is obvious. First, the belief in total passivity, in the lack of vital, active interest, directly engendered the idea of passive learning by rote. Indeed, the semisleeping dogs fixed to their laboratory stands, showing absolutely no interest, were able to develop conditioned reflexes. Both thinking teachers and smart students know how ineffective such boring, repugnant repetition is.

Second, it is very wrong to identify the elaboration of a skill with the beating a neural path in the brain. The coefficient of efficacy of this method would be outrageously low, for example, to spend many hundreds of thousands of kilo-

---

[2]It is not accidental that the word *interest* has two meanings: "entertaining" ("What an interesting story!") and "gain," "income" ("What is my interest?" "I am not interested"). The harsh struggle for survival forces the living being to pay attention only to events that are vitally important.

gram-meters of work on numerous repetitions of a pole vault in order to move a few molecules in the brain that had been blocking the neural path. The actual importance of repetitions is quite different. *Repetitions* of a movement or action are necessary in order to *solve a motor problem* many times (better and better) and *to find the best ways* of solving it. Repetitive solutions of a problem are also necessary because, in natural conditions, external conditions never repeat themselves and the course of the movement is never ideally reproduced. Consequently, it is necessary *to gain experience relevant to all various modifications* of a task, primarily, to all the impressions that underlie the sensory corrections of a movement. This experience is necessary for the animal not to be confused by future modifications of the task and external conditions, no matter how small they are, and to be able to adapt rapidly.

HOW DID EXERCISABILITY EMERGE?

In essay 3, we have shown how the perpetually complicating and intensifying struggle for life required not only increasingly complex and accurate movements but, more importantly, an increased *ability to solve sudden, unexpected complications*. Primitive, underdeveloped ancient organisms required neither memory for acquiring life experience nor wits for getting out of an unexpected situation based on experience nor dexterity so that the muscles could adequately carry out a solution generated by the brain.

The increasing demands of life naturally led to the development of new brain structures, typical for the more highly developed animals, that were more and more *trainable*. The younger a new level of movement construction is, the more capable it is with respect to meaning and complexity of solvable problems, the more flexible, adaptive, "plastic" it is, and, thus, *the more exercisable it is*.

This notion is also supported by the comparative physiology of animals, which has served throughout this volume as a key to the ancient history of development. The primitive, soft-bodied animals, with their smooth muscles, are out of the question for training. It is very foolish to try to teach a jellyfish or snail or polyp anything. Even much more highly developed arthropods (insects, spiders, and crayfish) are absolutely untrainable and extremely stupid. It is interesting to consider that there are hundreds of thousands of insect species on Earth (many more than all the other animal species taken together), and humans have been able to use only two of them, the bee and the silkworm butterfly. (Unfortunately, humans have been used, during the same time, by many more species, including arthropods.) Even these two species are, in essence, not tamed in the same sense as are dogs or horses, and are not different from their wild forest siblings. The beekeeper may spend years working with beehives, but even the beekeeper is forced, at certain times, to don a protective net to avoid being stung by the bees. Once, trained fleas were very popular in circuses, but their trainer himself explained his secrets in the newspapers. He trained the fleas not to jump by keeping them for a long time in shallow boxes with glass covers. When the muscles of their powerful hind limbs weakened and the fleas could only crawl, the trainer had no problems in harnessing them into small carriages or in forcing them to pull a thin thread, whose other end was soaked in acid and induced a toy cannon to shoot. Most of the excitement was due to the finely constructed requisites, a carriage the size of a pea and a cannon half the size of a match, not to the training, which was absolutely lacking.

One cannot develop a conditioned reflex in insects, even in its simplest forms. These animals have not reached the level necessary for receptiveness or exercisability.

In vertebrates, there is a very direct relationship between position in the developmental hierarchy and receptiveness or exercisability. Fish and amphibia, with their highest brain structures being pallidums, are able to develop conditioned reflexes slowly and painfully, but they are impossible to train. Nearly the same can be said about reptiles. We have already mentioned in essay 3 that their lack of receptivity was probably the main cause of their extinction long ago. Birds, which have a striatum and a number of sensory cortical areas, can be tamed, trained, and exercised in many aspects. One can easily develop in them stable, conditioned reflexes (recall the typical conditioned reflex which forces all the inhabitants of a chicken house to rush to the learned voice of their owner calling "tsip–tsip–tsip"). Generally stupid parrots have a very good memory and a refined ability to imitate. The most highly developed carnivorous birds (for example, hunting falcons, which are able to learn numerous fine motor skills) can be trained almost as well as some dogs. Both the bird and its trainer were called *lovchiy* ("hunter" or "hunting," in English); no doubt, the word *dexterity* ("lovkost" in Russian) originates from this root. This etymology clearly shows that folk wisdom valued very highly the coordination skills of the hunting ("lovchiy") birds and the art of their trainers.

There is still one weak spot in all birds, including the most highly developed ones: They are not very well equipped for unexpected, unique movement combinations. In contrast to absolutely untrainable, cold-blooded creatures, however, birds are well suited for gradual learning and prolonged, monotonous skills, but these are the limit of their abilities.

The next developmental step was reserved only for the mammals.

Among mammals, there is a whole spectrum of species, from extremely stupid and untalented animals to the highly gifted apes. The more developed and differentiated the mammal brain cortex is, the closer it moves toward the formation of control centers for the higher levels of construction of movements and the higher the animal's *exercisability* and its *motor wits* in unexpected situations are.

Thus, exercisability is a relatively young phenomenon in the history of evolution. In essence, it is exactly the same age as the oldest areas of brain cortex. The primitive animal world did not possess exercisability; its representatives were born and died without learning anything during their sometimes quite lengthy life.

The next conclusion may be unexpected, but if considered deeply enough, it naturally follows the previous material: *Dexterity*, in the history of development, is a *younger sister of exercisability*. It was born later. Indeed, the ability to quickly find solutions to unexpected, new situations, to quickly create new motor combinations emerges only after plain, slow exercisability and requires more highly developed brain structures. This ability, in fact, forms the basis for dexterity. The conclusion about the relative youth of dexterity is directly confirmed by observations. Aside from clumsy crabs or lobsters, even the quick, agile, winged grasshopper strikes with its clumsiness. The movements of a crab turned on its back appear clumsy. A grasshopper creates the impression of a gracious and dexterous animal with its quick, long leaps, but Kozma Prutkov was correct to say,

> The grasshopper jumps
> without seeing where.

Indeed, the outcomes of most of a grasshopper's jumps are failures. I admonish my readers not to be lazy, to go and observe the behavior of any kind of insect; these observations will support the position better than any detailed argument.

We have already mentioned that dexterity should not be confused with quickness. The latter ability, quick mobility, we can find in abundance in many lower vertebrates, such as small fish, lizards, snakes, and so on. However, genuine dexterity that meets the high standards described here can be detected only in the higher representatives of birds and reaches its highest development only in mammals.

These observations provide for one more strong argument against relating exercisability and vital force. Indeed, we know that the clearest examples of what used to be called vital force—the ability to grow a new ray or a new tail to replace a lost one—occur at the lowest stages of development. A starfish can easily grow a replacement for a cut ray, whereas lizards or frogs cannot grow a new leg; a lizard can grow a new tail, whereas a fox terrier cannot. Exercisability, on the contrary, is a recent phenomenon, increasing from the lower to the higher animals.

It is very important to determine whether the increase in exercisability from the primitive to modern levels of movement construction holds true in humans as well. As we have shown in essays 4 and 5, humans have retained all the levels that ever existed in vertebrates, although not without shifts and modifications. Fish and frogs are virtually deprived of exercisability. Does this mean that the human level of muscular-articular links (B), whose structure corresponds to the upper nuclei of fish and frogs, is also not exercisable? The striate system controls human movements from the lower sublevel of space (C1), that is, locomotions and many of the athletic and gymnastic movements. Does this mean that it is as poorly exercisable in humans as it is in birds, in which it exerts supreme control?

This conclusion would be wrong. It is undoubtedly true that, in humans, the higher levels are more flexible and more susceptible to exercise and provide a better basis for displaying dexterity. This last point was revealed in the previous analysis of different levels. We see now how important it is for pedagogical practitioners to be able to analyze correctly a movement and to define which levels of construction it belongs to. Such an analysis can immediately show what level of exercisability can be expected from the movement, how easily or slowly it will develop.

However, despite the hierarchy of exercisability of different levels in humans, even the lower human levels are much more exercisable than their precursors in the lower vertebrates. This is directly related to the fact that, in humans, all the lower levels are controlled by the highly developed motor cortex. The participation of motor cortex in the development and formation of movements is a crucial factor. We have already explained how the cortex, at the level of actions, orders the necessary background corrections and how it uses the so-called premotor areas for this purpose. Undoubtedly, the level of space can also play the role of the customer who provides the lower levels with appropriate motivation and spur. One may say that the brain cortex has found an appropriate language for communicating with the more primitive, lower levels, and by using this language has managed to dramatically increase their exercisability in humans.

WHAT IS MOTOR SKILL?

During the last century, since the time when Helmholtz first measured the speed of impulse transmission along the nerves and found it to be close to 100 meters per second, numerous facts have been accumulated showing that the nervous system of humans and higher mammals is a very fast device. Although our ancestors contemptuously thought that ideas were faster than lightning, we humans now have to live with the fact that the speed of brain processes is much slower than the speed of electrical or light phenomena. Nevertheless, the human central nervous system counts its events in thousandths and ten thousandths of a second. Excitation waves run from a command cell in the spinal cord to a muscle in 3–4 *milliseconds* (this is term for one thousandth of a second, similar to *millimeter* and *milligram*). Travel time from one brain hemisphere to the other is less than one millisecond. Muscles are able to respond with contractions to impulses of electric current in less than one tenth of a millisecond. Approximately the same short time is required for a wave of neural excitation to jump from a branch of one neural cell onto another. As we see, according to all contemporary data, the human nervous system is a very fast organic device. It is difficult to understand how this quickness could quietly coexist with the idea that the nervous system needs months to "beat" in a single new connection path. What other explanation except carelessness can account for comparing this extremely fast device to a low-sensitivity photographic plate, which needs an unbearably long exposure to imprint a photo?

We are still confronted by the fact that our brain, which is able and is used to thinking and memorizing certain things virtually instantaneously, nevertheless requires rather long training to develop a motor skill. However, there is no contradiction here. If skill development were based on a monotonous (from the very first to the very last day) imprinting of a trace into the brain, its slowness would certainly be absurd. However, we know that a skill is actively built by the nervous system, and this process of building consists of several consecutive stages, similar to the stages of building a house or a factory, including a sequence of design, preparation of the area, construction of the foundation, brickwork of the walls, and so on—all of which take time.

Before moving to a brief description of all these stages of motor skill construction, let us very carefully consider again a basic fact mentioned in essay 2.

Because of a huge redundancy of the degrees of freedom in our effectors, *no motor impulses to the muscles, no matter how accurate they are, are able to assure a correct movement* corresponding to our intentions. The elasticity of muscles, which prevents them from transducing force as carefully and precisely as rigid rods, the enormous mobility of the long joint extremities, and finally, the numerous external forces that confront us from all sides lead to a situation where, in addressing a certain muscle, the brain cannot know in advance what the effects will be on the limb movement. As we have seen in essay 2, *there is only one way to make a limb controllable*: From the very onset, the brain must continuously and watchfully *check the movement based on reports of the sensory organs* and harness the movement with corresponding *corrections*. We have also mentioned that all the sensory organs, without exception, carry this additional load, which is called *proprioceptive functioning* of these organs.

Apparently, because the external conditions are so variable that the movement can be controlled only on the basis of sensory corrections, repetition of the same movement will be accompanied by *different motor impulses from the brain to the muscles*.

A trained athlete's consecutive running steps are as identical as coins of the same value, but this identity results, not from the brain's ability to send absolutely identical motor impulses to the muscles, *but only from the faultless work of sensory corrections*. Moreover, it has been established that even if the muscles received 10 absolutely identical motor impulses in a row, there would be, in the very best case, 10 ugly steps, each one different from the others and with a result quite different from running. In the worst case, the runner would stumble and fall during the second step. If it were necessary to urgently compensate for an unexpected external force caused by the unevenness of the track or a slippery spot, the brain, deprived of any adaptivity, would blindly and stubbornly produce its uniform commands.

Thus, and this is the most important note that we were going to make, the *motor skill* involved in even a very simple and monotonous movement *cannot be a motor formula or a motor cliché*, as it was wrongly thought by many, including those who equated motor skill and conditioned reflex. Therefore, it is wrong to consider a motor skill as an imprint or a trace somewhere in the brain motor areas.

On the other hand, the brain's sensory areas, which take care of sensory corrections, also do not elaborate some unchangeable clichés of corrections. External forces and perturbations are volatile, and so corrections, which reflect the influence of these factors, likewise cannot be permanent. Finally, the movements of a skill must also have in reserve a degree of adaptive variability, which increases from the lower to the higher levels. Therefore, the *brain sensory systems also accumulate and store*, not a permanent cliché, but a peculiar, specific *maneuverability*. The brain sensory systems gradually learn to be more and more skillful in making an instantaneous translation from the language of incoming sensations and perceptions reflecting the movement process into the language of corrective motor impulses that need to be sent to one or another muscle. We shall call this translation from the language of sensations to the language of corrections *reciphering of neural impulses*.

So, motor skill *is not a movement formula* and certainly not a formula of permanent *muscle forces* imprinted in some motor center. *Motor skill is an ability to solve one or another type of motor problem*. It becomes clear now, how tremendous the work of the nervous system is during the development of such a skill, how many deviations, variations, and special cases it must actually meet or consider. Here, we are not talking about beating one or two brain pathways for which one might hope, today or tomorrow, to invent a direct surgical procedure—to pick a fiber with micropincers and to brush it with a microbrush. The learned movement must *be actually performed many times* in order to *actually experience all the sensations* which form the basis for its sensory corrections. It must be performed *many times* to allow the brain sensory areas to become acquainted with all the variety of deviations and modifications and to combine a "vocabulary" for all future recipherings. Certainly, the most sensible and correct training would be organized in a way that combined a minimization of effort with a large variety of well-designed sensations and that created optimal conditions for meaningfully absorbing and memorizing all these sensations.

CONSTRUCTION OF MOTOR SKILL

The Leading Level and Motor Composition

We are going now to move to the history of the life of a motor skill. Among the variety of motor skills, it is impossible to find one that is representative of them all in all aspects of their development and being. We are going to use, as basic examples, a couple of motor skills but also invoke all other skills that may shed light on one or another side of the problem.

As we have already seen, there were two basic mistakes in the old understanding of motor skill. First, the skill was considered to enter, to root, into the central nervous system, whether the system liked it or not. On the contrary, the nervous system is not subjected to a skill but builds it inside itself: *Exercise is an active building process.* Second, the skill was considered to enter the nervous system gradually and slowly, like a nail being hammered into a wall or like a dye penetrating a cloth, first by 10%, then by 25%, then by 75%, and so on. Something is trodden and trodden until it is beaten. On the contrary, the construction of a skill, as any construction or any development, consists of separate stages qualitatively very different from each other. *Construction of a skill is a meaningful chain action* in which one cannot miss or misplace separate steps, just as one cannot button a coat without first putting it on or one cannot blow out a match before lighting a cigarette. The skill itself is not homogeneous: It includes a leading level and its background corrections, supreme and auxiliary structures, different automatisms, corrections, and recipherings, everything that we have discussed. The history of its conception, development, and life is similarly nonhomogeneous. Let us try to present this history in an orderly fashion, using two representative sports skills of different complexity, cycling and pole vault. We shall also borrow other examples from sports, labor, and everyday skills.

As soon as we encounter *a new motor task,* the first problem is certainly to define its guardian, the *leading level* that is supposed to take responsible care of it. However, in healthy adult humans, this problem may be considered solved even without any new motor task. One may say without hesitation that there is no such motor task, one that an adult man encounters for the first time in his life, and that would not require the leading control from the *level of actions* (D), at least the first time. There is at least some experience, accumulated during childhood and adolescence, with respect to virtually any human movement that can be independently led by the level of space (C). Because of this and also because in adult humans most of the movements are controlled by Level D, this level has become used to taking responsibility for building any new skills. This fact is certainly reflected in the differences between an adult's development of a motor skill and similar development in babies and animals who do not have anything higher than the upper sublevel of space (C2).

Let us note, in particular, that, because of this habit, the level of actions (D) always takes the leading role at the beginning of mastering a skill, even when that control will inevitably switch to the level of space (C). For example, this process occurs with a typical locomotion, such as swimming, if an adult starts learning it. The facts indicate that such *switching of the leading level* is a hard and painful process in contrast to the quick and easy switchings of background corrections. Thus, skills like swimming take much more time and more effort to become automated in adults than in children, because in children such skills are immediately put under the control of the level of space (C). Such spatial skills should be learned during childhood, just to save this effort.

The second stage of building a new skill is defined as the *composition of its motor structure*. Because the first stage (i.e., choosing the leading level) does not take much time, this is actually the starting stage of the process.

As far as simple movements, those controlled by the level of space, are concerned, motor composition includes everything referring to pattern and character of the movement, or, as it is frequently called, its construction. In athletic or gymnastic skills, motor composition largely coincides with what is called movement style. For example, there are Eastern and Western styles of the long jump, the breaststroke, the crawl, and the butterfly. A physiologist would call these different motor compositions for these locomotions.

The motor composition of the complex, chain actions of Level D includes both the structures of separate movements-links and the lists of these movements. For example, the motor composition of screwing a screw into a wall includes the movements of taking and handling a gimlet, starting a hole, grasping a screwdriver and a screw, turning the screwdriver and the screw, and so forth.

For most skills, there are no problems with defining motor composition. We have observed many movements or skills since childhood. A person who starts learning to ride a bicycle probably rode a tricycle in childhood, two skills for which many of the movements are the same. During athletic or gymnastic movements or labor movements, one usually has a coach or a teacher to demonstrate the movement, explain it, and discuss its separate elements. Nevertheless, we sometimes have to struggle with a number of complications when defining motor composition.

The complications arise most frequently when one tries to learn a skill by oneself. Sometimes, much of the time is spent directly on inventing the motor composition. Robinson Crusoe, on his desolate island, bitterly regretted that he had ignored simple professional skills during his youth. So, he spent much time learning the basic skills of a tailor, a joiner, and a potter. However, there are problems not only for the beginners. In particular, during a pole vault, there are many, extremely quick details that are indiscernible with the naked eye even after dozens of repetitions. Even when something has been noticed, it is not easy to adapt it to one's body, for example, turning an arm or the trunk in exactly the same way as the teacher does. Moreover, body complexion, musculature, and, particularly, structure and development of different brain levels are so different and unique that even after a skill has been generally acquired, each student must make many adjustments in the body's motor composition so that it better fits his particular abilities. Sometimes, the learner finds a particular twist of an arm that helps him vault over the plank, or specific ways of handling instruments or supporting material, and so on. There is much room here for inventiveness and rationalization, as has been demonstrated at the labor front by our brilliant Stakhanovites (the followers of Stakhanov, who started the drive toward "communist labor intensification" in the Union of Soviet Socialist Republics in the mid-1930s).

Identification and Distribution of Corrections

As everyone knows, to *see* how something is done thousands of times and to actually *perform* it are very different things. Frequently, when you watch the skillful performance of an experienced professional, it is hard to get rid of the feeling that you would do no worse at the first attempt. But it the artisan sees this mute thought in our eyes and lets us take the artisan's place, the novice experiences a peculiar feeling of awkward dismay that is impossible to forget. Our right hand, which is known to be an obedient and perfectly coordinated servant, becomes clumsy and untamed, as if it were numb or frozen. In adults, the "inhibiting centers," which prevent them from such awkward situations, are already strongly developed. Children, however, frequently get into such situations when something they see seems very simple and easy to repeat. This is the origin of cut noses and ears in boys who tried to shave after their fathers left for work and of pieces of cloth shredded by girls who attempted to sew when their mothers were absent. You can experience once again this feeling of awkwardness and make your hand as clumsy as a bug turned on its back: Place a mirror in front of you and block your right hand from your eyes with a piece of paper so that you can observe your hand only through the mirror. Then try to draw a rectangle with a pair of crossed diagonals inside, like an envelope, or something similar.

The reason for the unexpected disobedience is quite clear. From early childhood, we accumulate vast resources of motor skills at the level of actions and, particularly, at the level of space, each aspect of which was long ago accurately studied. We continuously act in the realm of these common and well-practiced movements. An exercise trains, *not the effector itself*, not its joints, bones, and muscles, but *a certain area of activity* of this organ controlled by the brain at one or another level. Each elaborated movement creates in the central nervous system a possibility of some "expanded interpretations," of transfer over other, similar skills, but does not lead to a general development. Our right hand, obedient in numerous elaborated skills, seems obedient in general, irrespective of the movement. However, this is not true.

After everything that was said in the previous essays, we are not going to be confused by the question of *why* is it so hard to perform a movement at the first stages although its motor composition is quite clear. If the relationships between muscle forces and movements were as simple as that between a steam engine's rigid rods and its wheels, reproducing with the hands a movement that we clearly "see" in our mind would be easy, just as easy as following the lines of a drawn rectangle. Actually, although we may see a clear image of a movement, we do not have the slightest idea either about the *corrections* that are necessary for its execution or about the *recipherings* that are necessary for explaining to the muscles what to do. We can observe how a craftsman performs seemingly clear and simple movements, but we cannot see from outside the concealed corrections and recipherings that take place in his brain. The difference between the second phase (motor composition) and the third phase (creation of correction) is exactly in that: During the second phase, a novice decides how the movements involved in a motor skill *look from the outside*; during the third phase, the novice learns how these movements and their sensory corrections *feel inside*. During this third phase of exercise, it is very important for one to repeat the task many times in order to feel as fully as possible all the changing external conditions and all the adaptive reactions of the movement itself to the changes in the environment. Prof. S. Gellerstein very aptly called this phase "playing the skill around" all imaginable changes of the task and of the environment.

We can take virtually any skill as an example: The phase of development of sensory corrections always reveals itself as a necessary and, usually, the most labor consuming of all the original, so to speak "planning" phases of constructing a motor skill. For example, during cycling, a beginner's legs start to feel the correct, circular pattern of the foot movement and the characteristic, alternating resistance from the pedals. The arms "study" the mobility of the handlebars and learn how to combine it with their support function. It takes much longer for one to develop and refine the feeling of bicycle's lateral inclines and how they are affected by turning the handlebars. An older instinct, based on a previous, space-related experience, may initially suggest turning the handlebars to the right when the bicycle inclines to the left. Slowly, this instinct is overcome, and the bicyclist learns independently or with the help of a teacher to turn the handlebars to the left so that the points of the bicycle's support are moved under the displaced center of gravity and the lost equilibrium is reestablished. All this and many other things *are not seen from outside*; they are accumulated by the learner only from his own experience, experience that is sometimes not quite painless. During this phase, if a beginner mounts a skateboard and falls many, many times, each new bump is a painful trace of sensory corrections that have started to develop. With each minute, the learner acquires new inflows of sensations, which he could not possibly have observed in anyone, and his central nervous system slowly starts to realize what kinds of corrections are required in this particular case.

Obviously, sometimes up to 75% of this work proceeds subconsciously, *but intelligent attention is able to accelerate it considerably.*

Simultaneously with this accumulation of experience related to sensory corrections, these corrections are being internally selected. A beginner may already realize *what* should be corrected but does not clearly know what kinds of sensations are best suited for these corrections. The central nervous system actively

FIG. 1.   Correct pedaling.

searches where, how, and what kind of sensory information is able to respond most effectively and quickly to a problem, to provide the most well-defined and precise correction. The next step is to define *which of the background levels* has an instrument that is best suited for leading the movement through a difficult, narrow passage.

At its first stages, skill development may take two different directions. When the basic, most important corrections have been defined, the leading level for the skill is either able or unable to provide these corrections with its own means. In the first case, the movement is first performed clumsily, as if "on crutches," and the sensory mechanisms available to the leading level play the role of wooden scaffolding used temporarily for building a brick house. And indeed, while the movement is performed on these surrogate props, the lower levels have time to elaborate actual appropriate background corrections or *automatisms* (discussed later). For example, when learning the skills of filing or mowing as well as the fine finger skill of playing the piano, during the first stages, the correctness of movements of the file, the mower, or one's own fingers is checked by vision, by one's staring intently at them. The ability to perform the movements more or less correctly under such surrogate control directs and accelerates the elaboration of genuine corrections for all these movements with the help of muscular-articular, proprioceptive *sensitivity*, which is skillfully controlled by the background level of muscular-articular links (B).

In other cases, the leading level ends up bankrupt with respect to background, auxiliary, but nevertheless vital corrections without which the movement cannot proceed. If, for example, we consider locomotion, its leading level (C1) is quite well equipped with all the meaningful corrections necessary to carry out the function of a movement "pilot." However, it may lack the necessary *synergies*, whose absence destroys the movement although they may be unrelated to the pilotage, final target, or movement objective. This is frequently the case with swimming and cycling locomotions. Beginners always initially fail to perform the movement; they either stubbornly submerge into the water or fall to the side with their bicycle. In both these cases (as well as in similar activities including skating, walking on a rope, flying a glider, etc.), an *absolutely universal rule* is being followed: First, at some time, these skills are mastered instantly as if due to a revelation. Second, once the skill has been learned, *it never vanishes*, regardless of how long ago the person performed it last or how poor his general fitness level is. The basic skill of being able to float on the water's surface or to maintain equilibrium on a bicycle or on a rope is impossible to forget, just as are the look of the sea even if seen just once or the taste of a food tried once.

The just mentioned sudden leap in understanding, characteristic of this group of skills, means that, at that instant a *background correction*, developed in the appropriate background level, was activated. Until this crucial moment, the movement was unsuccessful because the leading level did not have any appropriate corrections, even surrogate ones, which can save the situation in a number of other types of movements. The fact that the "secrets" of swimming or cycling *are not in some special body movements but in special sensations and corrections* explains why these secrets are impossible to teach by demonstration (*any movement can be demonstrated*) and why they are absolutely impossible to forget during one's lifetime.

Even aside from these special sensations and corrections, which are monopolized by Level B, neither the level of space (C) with its two sublevels nor the supreme level of complex actions (D) has appropriate means for adequate securing of all the corrections necessary for a certain motor skill. Therefore, there emerges the problem of *recruiting background levels as experts* in certain types of corrections. It is appropriate to compare the elaboration of a new motor skill to the building of a house. During the first stages of a project, an architect does not need anything except a set of drawing instruments and a piece of paper. However, when actual construction begins, the architect must recruit assistants, not because he has only one pair of hands and one pair of legs, but, more important, because those hands, skilled in drawing drafts and making calculations, are much worse at laying bricks or installing window frames than the hands of a bricklayer or a carpenter. Similarly, the phase of detection and identification of necessary corrections is followed by a phase of their *assignment to different background levels*. A person learning how to ride a bicycle or to pole vault or to figure skate or to do gymnastic exercises slowly develops proprioceptive signals, which are most skillfully captured and used by the level of muscular-articular links (B); signals from the organs of equilibrium, which induce the most refined and adequate responses in the level of tone (A); and so on. This is still the stage of *internal planning* of a skill, but we have moved closely to realization of these plans.

Assignment of Background Corrections

Now we move to the fourth, once again, qualitatively very different stage of construction of a motor skill. I ask my reader: Can you see any monotonous "beating" or "chiselling"?

Sometimes this stage takes a considerable part in all of the training and plays an exceptionally important role. This stage is *the one of actual readdressing down to background levels* those corrections that had been determined and assigned to these levels at the previous stage.

We have mentioned already that lowering of the background corrections down to the appropriate levels is the phenomenon of *automation* of a motor act. Let us, first, explain the reasons for this name.

During the first steps of building a motor skill, conscious attention may be distributed over all the numerous details of controlling the movement. Sometimes there are so many details and weak points that attention becomes confused and may disregard important, sometimes even vital, corrections. We have considered many examples of movements showing how much work is involved in various aspects of control and how rich with corrections each is, for example, locomotion of walking, running, swimming, or jumping. Obviously, even an exceptionally trained attention cannot grasp all this shower of corrections. The help comes from automatic switching down to lower, background levels.

The point is that for each human movement, whether complex or simple, full of deep meaning or feasible for any frog, *consciousness obtains only information relevant to what is being controlled by the leading level.* This is how our consciousness is built. Its spotlight, as a rule, cannot illuminate more than one level at a time, although it is able to illuminate them successively. Therefore, all the corrections that are transferred to the control of background levels, at the same time *go beyond the scope of the consciousness;* that is, the corrections start to proceed subconsciously, automatically. It would be a grave mistake, however, to think that movements or movement components controlled by *automatisms* are necessarily static and unchangeable, like a deep-rooted habit. Someone has very precisely noted the difference between habits and automated skills, saying, "We control the skill while habits control us." Sometimes, automatisms may be more flexible and adaptive than any conscious movement. Their distinctive feature is simply that they do not require conscious attention to proceed.

The importance of this feature of automatisms is quite clear. Besides the fact that during automatization each correction switches to the qualitatively most appropriate level, automatization of each correction means another step toward decreasing the load of attention, which then has a better chance of following the most important and essential aspects of the movement without being dissipated among the unimportant, minor details.

Automatization does not happen instantaneously but may sometimes take a large portion of all the time devoted to the construction of a motor skill. The reason is not only that the detection of necessary corrections and appropriate levels takes time. There is another, more important reason.

The necessary lower-level background corrections themselves are frequently far from being simple reactions that can be performed by a background level at the first attempt. Frequently, particularly in skills such as cycling and pole vaulting, the background corrections themselves are close to motor skills; they are far from being inborn or from waiting in a background level library, ready, like a toy hidden in a firecracker. They must be developed and exercised.

In some cases, the necessary background corrections are actually an integral, simpler independent skill, long ago elaborated by a novice and ready to be activated. Sometimes, such a background skill needs minor "polishing" to fit a required background role. There are, certainly, cases in which a skill must be developed from the very beginning.

An example of such independent background skills include the running start for a long jump, high jump, or pole vault. Running, to variable degrees of perfection, was elaborated in all humans long ago as an independent movement in the lower sublevel of space (C1). It must be modified to serve the general purpose of a jump, that is, *changed from running into running start*. These skills are certainly not the same, particularly running with a long pole in one's hands, but the leading level (D) needs only to modify it slightly and turn its leading position into a background position.

The locomotion of running acquires similar meaning of a background skill in soccer and tennis, walking in a moving train, walking while mowing grass, and so on.

In other cases, a movement or a submovement that will be controlled within a motor skill by a certain background level may not have any independent meaning because it is unable to solve any motor task when taken out of the context of the whole skill. Examples include the complex synergy of turning around with a discus in one's right hand prior to throwing it and the not-less-complex synergy of turning a pole while getting into a vertical handstand just prior to releasing the pole during a pole vault. Let us consider the moving of the bow with the right hand while playing violin and the complicated, fine movements of hands and fingers during knitting. All these movements and their components start making sense only when they are incorporated into an integral, meaningful movement or action and are subject to its corrections. An athlete must maneuver into a vertical handstand, not at any arbitrary time, but when the pole reaches a certain position, and in a particular way in order for the body to fly over the bar without touching it. A violinist must move the bow so that its direction, speed, and pressure on the strings create the required artistic impression, which is continuously controlled by the supreme, "musical" brain centers. Otherwise, neither an expert's eye nor a cinematographic recording will be able to distinguish this movement from a correct one, but the movement will not extract from the violin anything except squeaks. And so on.

These background corrections, which control movements but do not have independent meaning or which do not subserve separate movements by themselves, are termed automatisms. Sometimes they are further classified into higher automatisms (those subserving actions from Level D) and lower automatisms (those subserving actions of the lower level of space, C1), but this subdivision does not carry any additional meaning. Certainly, automatisms from the higher levels (also called special skills or knacks) are much more numerous, complex, and diverse than the lower ones. We have already met them in the description of the level of actions (D).

Similarly to the background corrections of the first type, automatisms may be either unknown to a novice, who must then develop them, or stored in a ready form by the novice's memory in a library of the lower levels. In the latter case, it is only necessary to take them out of the "cedar closet" and remodel and fit them to a new motor task. Obviously, automatisms of this kind were developed earlier as parts of some other skill, because *none of the automatisms can have independent meaning* or independent origin.

A beginner can probably find in his stock automatisms of pedaling and turning handlebars acquired when learning how to ride a tricycle. A student pilot will probably find in reserve quite a few automatisms acquired during cycling, driving a car, or perhaps some quite unexpected physical exercises that had developed in him automatisms of maintaining equilibrium, coordination of arm and leg movements, and so forth.

The usage of automatisms acquired at some time for a skill X in another, later skill Y is called *skill transfer* or *transfer of training*. This extremely important phenomenon requires deeper analysis, although it is still poorly understood.

For a long time, the nature of the ability of "wide interpretation" of acquired skills, or skill transfer, remained puzzling. This mysteriousness was deepened by the fact that two seemingly very similar types of movements could display a paltry degree of training transfer, whereas, in other cases, seemingly very different movements, like skating and cycling or sprinting and long jumping or even figure skating and shooting, displayed obvious and strong effects of transfer.

The mistake underlying all these confusions derived from the fact that the cause of *transfer was searched for in the external similarity of movements*, or in movement composition. There was a whole theory of so-called identical elements developed to explain the effects of transfer in motor and in elementary-school learning skills. Unfortunately, this theory was unable to correctly predict the phenomena, and therefore, was no good. The following analysis leads us much closer to the truth.

Training transfer is based on the use of earlier elaborated automatisms. Automatisms, however, are *not movements; they are corrections* that control movements and their components. Therefore, in cases in which movements appear very similar but are based on absolutely different corrections (for example, playing a violin and sawing or filing), there are no signs of transfer. On the other hand, in movements with established effects of transfer, it is easy to find identical or very similar *groups of corrections*. For example, cycling and skating have a very clear element in common: In both cases, one deals with the *maintenance of dynamic equilibrium over a support that has no width* (the line of support of a bicycle or a skate). Such seemingly very different skills as shooting at a target and figure skating also have a group of very important, similar corrections: good ability to judge by vision, postural control, equilibrated *stability* of accurate movements, and, finally, perfect *detection of a particular moment*.

Transfer of training is possible not only from one skill to another but also from one body organ to another, untrained organ. Such transfers occur, for example, when training is confined to the left arm, but its effects are seen in both left and right arms. This kind of transfer is very closely related to *switching*, to which we are going to return later.

Let us emphasize the importance of being able to analyze movements with respect to their level of composition and the structure of their automatisms in order to increase the expediency of efforts and the positive effects of an exercise.

FIG. 2. The power of habit.

One can reach exceptional success by selecting a "hierarchy of skills" so that each skill is able to make maximal use of the automatisms created for previous skills and simultaneously added to the library of accumulated automatisms.

There is a negative side to *transfer of skill*, which needs to be addressed here. This negative side is revealed when the process of elaboration of a new skill is affected by poorly suited or even detrimental old, rooted automatisms. For example, many of us have developed in childhood the automatism of turning the steering wheel to the right to turn the car to the right. Starting with a child's tricycle and "playing horses," this automatism was successfully transferred to bicycle, cars of all makes and models, and perhaps airplanes and gliders. The quantitative aspect, the differential between the angle of a steering-wheel turn and the actual turn of a vehicle plays a secondary role. In reality, the fact that one needs to turn a steering wheel of a heavy truck by 180° and the handlebars of a bicycle by 10° in order to achieve the same turn is immediately and subconsciously taken into account with the help of vision. We can see how a vehicle turns and immediately increase or decrease the angle of the steering-wheel turn based on the information from the eyes. But in steering a simple rowboat, the movements are opposite: In order to turn the boat to the *right*, our hands must make movements that would turn a bicycle or a car to the *left*. Everyone knows how hard it is to overcome the old, deeply rooted automatism. Because of this, the builders of all newer, better models of motorboats and speedboats have long ago switched to steering mechanism based on the automobile principle.

Examples of such *interferences* between old automatisms and new skills include the obsessive automatism of dipping a pen into an ink pot, exhibiting itself endlessly after one has switched to ballpoint pen; the automatic reaching for a light switch or door latch removed long ago; numerous skating automatisms that impede the correct skiing movements. The gradual overcoming and elimination of old automatisms sometimes add considerably to the fourth phase of skill construction.

Movement Automatization

Automatization—the elaboration of new background automatisms and the switching of movement corrections, one by one, to lower levels—is a continuous process. In the discussion of the level of actions in essay 5, we described how a customer level sends a request to a background level for an appropriate automatism. Because nearly all the new skills in adults are built under the control of the cortical level of actions (D), these orders for automatisms are, virtually in all cases, transferred through the premotor cortical areas. Initially, corrections at the leading level temporarily and imprecisely support a practiced movement component. Then, at some time, corrections in an appropriate background level mature and strengthen. The background level breaks free from the leading one, which has been supporting it (like the hand of an adult supporting a child who is trying to learn to swim), and takes entire responsibility for the new automatism. At this time, *automatization is complete.*

The previous discussion makes it clear that each motor skill may include several automatisms; that is, it may require the background corrections of a number of aspects. Therefore, during the process of skill acquisition, a number of moments of automatization may occur, independently of each other. For example, in cycling, these moments include the major, crucial step of mastering equilibrium; the automatism of correct, easy pedaling; the automatism that does not let the feet to slip off the pedals; the automatism of braking; the automatism of riding without using the handlebars; the automatism of very sharp turns.

These characteristics of automatization directly lead to the conclusion that it never occurs gradually but always appears as *an abrupt turning point, a crisis.* It does not look like "beating a trail" (expressed as a gradual increase in the amount of saliva in the experiments with conditioned reflexes) but rather like a "strike," a kind of exclamation—aha! Each athlete remembers the moment when he suddenly felt that water supported him or that his bicycle became as stable as if it had acquired a third wheel.

Another specific feature of automatization is also due to its essential aspect of *switching* part of the control of a movement to *another level,* of turning to *qualitatively different corrections.* Therefore, automatization is always a qualitative leap. Changes in the composition of the sensory organs subserving corrections of a specific aspect of a movement cannot fail to affect its essential features. Thus, each automating leap leads both to abrupt, dramatic improvement in the execution of a practiced movement and also to its qualitative changes in the movement.

For example, when, during filing metals or mowing, the control of the main working part of the movement shifts from the eyes to the muscular-articular sensory apparatus, which is the main tool of the level of synergies and muscular-articular links, the quality of the work improves dramatically. For example, the filing surface becomes smooth and shiny; the rows of mowed grass become precise, wide, and even. By observing how smoothly a tram stops and how precisely its door comes to the point of a stop pole, one can determine how automated the driver's skill in using the air brakes is.

There is another interesting, widespread characteristic of qualitative shifts related to automatization. If, as it frequently happens, automatization involves the delegating of corrections to the *level of muscular-articular links* (B), which does not use vision, it is accompanied by a well-known phenomenon, *turning off visual control.* Unexpectedly, a student finds out that he is able to perform a part of a task without looking, whereas before it was necessary to watch it intently. Everyone can easily remember many examples of such automated shifts from his or her own experience—tying and untying knots, tying a necktie, lacing a dress, playing a musical instrument, arm movements during rowing, and so on. Such liberation from visual control may serve as a good sign that an observed automatism has been developed at the level of muscular-articular links (B).

Achieving Harmony of Background Corrections

It is probably unnecessary to state that the classification of the process of training into separate phases, outlined in this essay, is conventional and oversimplifies the actual process. Actually, there may be very vague borders between these phases, and sometimes, successive phases may partially overlap. However, in general, this subdivision is correct, although it is not without exceptions.

It is necessary to state that the next phase that we are going to discuss does not actually happen abruptly after the previous one, as if the previous phase finished its job and went out slamming the door. Quite the opposite—automatization within a more or less complex skill happens, not in one, but in several successive steps. Events of the fifth phase very gradually merge into the general process of skill development, long before all the processes of automation are complete. This phase may be termed *the phase of achieving mutual harmony among the background corrections.* If one compares the development of a skill to staging a play, the previous phases were spent on assigning the roles to the players, rewriting the script, and learning lines by heart. Now, the time has come for rehearsals.

Although the process of skill construction has progressed considerably, it is still far from completion. There is still a great deal of work ahead on background corrections and automatisms until the man feels that he has successfully mastered them all. The first problem in mastering background corrections is that all these corrections and automatisms, controlled from different levels, are eventually realized by the same muscles, joints, and bone levers. So, they must adjust to each other to avoid mutual hampering. We have already discussed *interferences that occur because of a lack of correspondence among old automatisms and demands of a new, practiced movement.* Now, they are joined by interferences among *newly elaborated automatisms* until they start playing well together after a process of mutual adjustment. An example of such an adjustment occurs during the learning of how to ride a bicycle. At the beginning of the process, the level of tone (A), an expert in postures and grips, takes control over the gripping of the handlebars and adapts to a solid, conscientious grip. At the same time, the lower level of space (C1) needs to teach the arms to react sensitively to each starting heel of the bicycle with accurate changes in pressure on the handlebars. Some time is inevitably being spent on the struggle between the strong, tenacious grip of Level A and the quick, keen reactions of Level C1, which takes place within the same shoulder muscles. Sooner or later, both these automatisms not only find a common language but even elaborate a kind of sub-automatism at the level of tone (A), which starts to support the steering reactions with its economical tonic means. There may be similarly impressive collisions, at the first stages of practice, between the same equilibrating influences on the handlebars from the Level C1 and actual steering when making voluntary turns, which are controlled from the pyramidal Level C2. Similar interferences can be observed between the automatisms of pedaling and braking by reversing the movement of the pedals, between the common automatism of running and the automatism of carrying a clumsy, elastic pole, and so on.

Even in cases when we are unable to detect by observation the origin of an annoying obstacle and are unable to define which of the background corrections cannot agree on sharing the muscular-skeletal stallion on which they are forced to ride together, the presence of the obstacle itself is clearly seen. The point is, and this is well known, that there is not a single skill whose acquisition goes absolutely smoothly. These qualitative leaps and steps mentioned previously are frequently accompanied by more or less prolonged *delays*, or hesitations, and sometimes even seeming temporary deteriorations in skill. A student will sometimes complain in despair: "Everything was nearly perfect! Why has it again fallen apart to pieces?!"

An experienced teacher can always overcome such discouragement in the student. The teacher would be quite right to persuade the student that a temporary setback will be followed by a *qualitative leap to a better performance* if only the student does not give up and continues to work persistently, maybe allowing himself a short break in the training schedule or introducing some diversions into it. The teacher is right to make these statements because the fact is that such delays (sometimes explicitly called "creative pauses") *always precede a leap in automatization*, although, certainly, not each and every leap is preceded by a delay. Each delay or temporary deterioration suggests that there is an interference among essential background corrections which does not allow them to coexist peacefully. Eventually, the central nervous system will find a way out of this situation either by adjusting the background mechanisms to each other or, if this is impossible, by creating a new, more flexible, and more appropriate automatism. This creation of a new automatism takes time, comprising the creative pause that is so discouraging for the student.

Persistence in training when one feels an apparent interference delay and deterioration of a nearly perfect movement can even lead to visible harmful results. Let us conclude the section with this warning. If the central nervous system is not given enough time to analyze a complex situation and is forced to use both contradictory mechanisms of corrections simultaneously, it might haphazardly adjust to a *compromise in quality*. It will increase the range of acceptable errors with respect to both types of corrections and make them more tolerant of each other, thus allowing them to coexist. This compromise occurs, for example, when one is learning a complicated piano passage or practicing complex coordinated movements of all the extremities during some gymnastic or athletic exercises. If one very crudely divides corrections into two groups, during the early stages of training, the corrections of precision and accuracy cannot coexist with very quick movements, and corrections of speed do not allow high accuracy. As a result, the movements become smudged and imprecise, although quick enough to follow a required rhythm. In fact, teachers call such compromising "smudging." It is very harmful because after it has been developed, it is very hard to eliminate. Therefore, it is necessary to be very watchful of and attentive to interferences and delays. The teacher can decide whether it would be better to interject a complete pause into the training schedule, relying on a "creative pause" of the central nervous system or to radically change the training approach and exercises, allowing the brain systems to find a correct solution to the complex situation.

Standardization

Whereas researchers of the past saw only monotonous swotting, we have already witnessed so many various phases of the gradual process of skill elaboration that one wonders, not why this process requires time, but how it manages to fit into such a modest schedule. However, we have not yet considered all the phases. The complete development of a motor skill requires at least two more phases. These two phases are so important and time consuming that they take frequently more time than all the preceding phases. These two phases may be considered as the steps of making final adjustments, of applying final touches, and of polishing the skill. Although they do not follow each other but are rather tightly interweaved, we are going to consider them separately because their meanings and aims are different. These phases are called, respectively, *standardization and stabilization of motor skill*.

As discussed previously, many automated motor acts are characterized by a strikingly precise repetition of movement components (cycles). The consecutive steps during walking, the strokes during swimming or rowing, the vaults or salto-mortales performed by an experienced professional, are as similar to each other as guards in a formation. Similar identity can also be seen in the accurate movements controlled by the level of space, for example, in the terminal phases during grasping, pointing, hitting, or jabbing. However, this kind of identity cannot happen by itself, automatically, like the identical sounds produced by a record played several times. Moreover, such identity cannot be caused by some kind of cliché in the brain motor centers (we have already proven that such clichés cannot exist there). Quite the opposite is true: The central nervous system sometimes achieves this identity with great effort, and such identity is due only to the vigilant tracking of movements with sensory corrections. However, in nature, nothing is done without certain considerations of expediency, particularly if it requires hard work. If the brain strives in numerous types of skills toward such an identical repetition of movements despite its requiring substantial effort, the identity must be, in some aspects, helpful and important. We can observe how, at first, the nervous system struggles to reach this movement standardization when training a new skill. In a small child, who is just learning to walk and run, each step is different from the others. The same can happen in adults during first attempts at jumping or the first several strokes of rowing, and so on. The level of standardization of such movements may even serve as an indicator of the degree of skill development.

Why does the central nervous system strive for standardization despite multiple obstacles? It happens that the answers to this question are different for the different levels of movement construction.

Locomotor movements, such as walking, running, and jumping, are large synergies. They incorporate an orderly, coordinated activity of about a hundred muscles. The main difficulty in controlling such movements, however, is not in the number of muscles. Mobile links of the body are connected by many joints and are rich with degrees of freedom. Consequently, the movements of feet, shanks, thighs, shoulders, forearms, are accompanied by an enormous number of *forces of interaction*. The number and magnitude of these forces increase particularly *during* relatively *fast movements. An increase in the rate of such movements leads to an increase in the forces of interaction proportional to the square of the rate increase.* In other words, a two- or threefold increase in rate leads to a four- or ninefold increase in the forces of interaction. The forces of interaction, that is, the forces from some links acting on other links, are also called *reactive* forces.

Reactive forces during large synergies like running, jumping, or vaulting are so large and variable that they sometimes create virtually unsolvable problems for the coordination of such quick movements. These forces counteract muscular forces, push the links from each other, move the extremities in undesirable directions, and so forth. Their interaction is so complex that creating a motor composition for such a synergy, so that it becomes executable, is an exceptionally difficult task. It would seem that the enormous number of degrees of freedom in our organs would also create a similarly enormous freedom for choosing and combining movement paths (trajectories), but this is not the case. Considering, one by one, numerous combinations generously suggested by the mobility of the sets of moving links, the nervous system is forced to discard each combination one by one, because each of them is somehow destroyed by the reactive forces.

Now it becomes obvious that if it were possible to find such a pattern of movement in which the reactive forces did not exert their destructive abilities, the central nervous system would cling to it as to a life belt. Experience shows that only one or two and certainly not more than a few versions of such non-self-destructable movement patterns remain for large synergies of the type discussed here. These forms are qualitatively very different and are separated by wide intervals filled with impossible patterns. If one makes a movement slowly, as if reading haltingly, the wide joint mobility allows thousands of ways for its execution. If one tries to perform it quickly as a whole, however, so that it actually solves a real problem, the possibilities become mercilessly limited.

On the other hand, more careful observations reveal that biodynamics has given us an unexpected and very valuable gift. Among the small number of possible movement patterns there is an even smaller group that is characterized by a very important feature. In these forms, the movements are organized so that the *reactive forces* not only fail to disrupt the movement but *directly support it, providing it a particular kind of stability.* When a limb segment or a whole limb deviates from a prescribed trajectory, this deviation immediately gives rise to reactive forces that push the limb back onto the invisible rails. Such a movement can probably be compared to that of a ball rolling down a gutter. If the ball for some reason deviates from the bottom to the elevated edges of the gutter, the force of gravity pulls it back. Such movements can be called *dynamically stable.*

Now the reader probably understands why there is such a small number of different, so-called *styles* of athletic and gymnastic movements. These styles are, in fact, the motor compositions, found by pure chance, that possess, to varying degrees, *features of dynamic stability.* It is clear now why it is so hard to invent a new style of vaulting or swimming: There are very few possibilities, and certainly, a large proportion of them have already been discovered by the cooperative search of thousands of athletes all around the world.

Here, then, is a precise explanation for *movement standardization* in the types of skills discussed in this volume. This standardization does not occur by itself for any movement that we might like to practice. First, one must spend considerable effort in finding some executable patterns and in making these patterns stable with the help of sensory corrections, which guard and defend them against the destructive influence of the external forces (reactive forces in *executable* movements are already not that dangerous). After numerous repetitions of the movement, the central nervous system, which supervises this process of search and adjustment, will sooner or later, develop dynamically stable movement patterns. When such a form has been found, the protecting role of sensory corrections may be immediately weakened. Reactive forces take over the function of guarding the movement against the distorting influences of external forces and do so virtually automatically. The benefits of this process for all the sensory mechanisms, attention, and musculature are obvious. During the first stages, it was necessary to guard against the destructive effects of both external and reactive forces, with active muscle contractions, but with standardization, the conditions have changed dramatically. Starting from this moment, the reactive forces, which used to be in alliance with the external forces and cooperatively launched attacks on the movement, defect to our side. Now they attack the external forces and successfully counteract them, while sensory corrections take some rest and watch the battle being successfully won without their interference.

Humans always clearly feel this relief, although it is not easy to discover its actual roots. Such release of both the muscular system and all the central nervous systems is very highly valued by track-and-field athletes. They call it *relaxation*. Clearly, relaxation is not a kind of weakening of the muscles or loosening of the joints. The only thing that actually relaxes during acquisition of dynamic movement stability is the strong bridle of sensory corrections, which was necessary for keeping the movement on the tracks. Now, this effect is reached automatically and is accompanied by a premium of enormous economy along all the lines of the physiological enterprise.

The following should also be mentioned. *Even if it were possible*, at the cost of considerable effort, *to perform* an unstable, self-destructing movement pattern, *it is certainly, absolutely unrealistic* to repeat it consecutively several times. Therefore, such patterns do not become learned. On the other hand, stable forms have all the prerequisites for being easily reproducible and, therefore, should be easily memorized. The result is that *bad, unsuccessful movements are not fixed in memory*, whereas *successful solutions to motor problems* tend to be *firmly remembered*. This tendency is an example of the widely applicable "law of effect," formulated by the American psychologist Thorndike.

As far as the *accurate, aimed movements of the level of space* are concerned, their inherent standardization has a different, simpler explanation. As previously mentioned, the level of space has the ability to vary its movements extensively and skillfully uses their switchability and interchangeability when appropriate. However, in a number of cases, success directly depends on the *accuracy or precision* of the whole movement or of some of its parts. The highly developed sensory corrections of Level C are perfectly equipped for handling such situations. When a movement does not allow for even a 0.1 mm error (e.g., during an accurate jab, threading a needle, engraving, etc.), the movement is actually performed with the required precision. Consequently, a skilled person would not demonstrate any variability in successive trials.

Here, the standardization of movements or of their parts during skill development is a necessary prerequisite for their accuracy and precision.

Stabilization

Let us now turn to the last phase of skill elaboration, the phase of *stabilization*. During the development of a skill, this phase occurs simultaneously with the previous one, but it has a very different objective and a very different meaning.

Imagine two people, U and Y, who have developed a motor skill for the same movement. Both of them perform the learned movement, for example, a vault, a handstand on parallel bars, or mowing. The attentive observer is unable to detect a difference in the quality of their performance. They both perform the movement correctly, rationally, and expediently, with the same degree of ease and gracefulness. Which one is better?

Now, however, a complicating factor is introduced into the conditions of movement performance: If they learned to perform the task in bright light, the lights are turned off; the mowers are required to mow with shorter scythes or to mow an uneven meadow; the pole vaulter must perform on a windy day or on a wet track; the gymnasts must solve a mental arithmetic problem. An unexpected result is observed. U easily overcomes the obstacle presented; the obstacle does not affect the success of his movements. Y, however, becomes uncertain, confused, and clumsy; the movements apparently lose all their automaticity (they *deautomatize*), and the skill vanishes as if it were never there. The movements of both subjects proceed successfully as long as they are performed under a glass cover; however, a light wind is enough to reveal the depth of their difference.

Deautomation, that is, destruction of an already developed automation of a skill, is a major and dangerous enemy of motor skill. One needs to be sufficiently armed and prepared for it. When all the switching comprising automation of a motor skill is completed, *the skill has already been realized* in its major aspects. However, in terms borrowed from photography, the skill must be *fixed*. In order to adequately consider the process of fixation, or stabilization, it is necessary to realize the kinds of destructive forces that will confront the young skill and the kinds of self-defense that will be used by the different levels of movement construction.

Destructive influences may be crudely classified into three major groups. *The first and the second groups include secondary hindrances* of internal and external origin, which are not in any way related to the motor task itself, but which prevent it from being solved. Examples of internal disruptive causes include fatigue, headache or some other illness, suboptimal functioning of some of the sensory organs, or distracting anxiety (one more internal cause of deautomation is discussed somewhat later). Similarly incidental external examples include distracting noise, coldness, shocks, shakings, and so on. A stable, well-developed skill generally uses one and the same weapon of defense, general endurance and stability, against all these destructive influences. Persons with a more stable nervous system are less susceptible to nervousness, increased irritability, and so forth. They can better resist the destructive effects and prevent deautomation of the skill.

The *third group* involves destructive influences of a very different nature. It comprises *difficulties emerging within the motor task itself*. We already know that even the repetition of a required movement, without any changes or modifications, requires a significant preparatory work of sensory corrections, unless we are helped to some extent by a dynamically stable movement pattern. This means that *in order to keep the standard of a movement* we must accumulate plenty of experience relevant to movement corrections, which is acquired mostly during the last phases of skill elaboration. Therefore, one is likely to need much more of this kind of experience *to defend a skill against modifications and complications* of a task. None of these modifications and complications should be able to catch an experienced person by surprise, unprepared. Changes in the usual tool, material, style, shape, working place, environment are able to confuse a novice and to deautomatize the movements, even if the novice has already mastered the task in quiet, predictable conditions. In Russian literature, there is a beautiful example of mowing by two persons who nicely correspond to the conventional example of U and Y. The example is from the novel *Anna Karenina* by the great master of Russian literature, L. N. Tolstoy. The two mowers are an experienced old peasant, Tit, and a landowner, "nonprofessional," Levin. They both mow smoothly at an even part of a meadow:

> Levin did not think about anything, did not want anything except to keep up with the peasants and do his best. Somewhere in the middle of their work, there were minutes when he nearly forgot what he was doing, everything was easy, and his row was nearly as good and straight as that of Tit. The longer Levin mowed, the more frequently he felt minutes of oblivion when not his arms were moving the scythe, but rather the scythe moved along his full of life body, and as if miraculously, without thinking, the accurate and precise work was done by itself.

Here, we see an extremely clear picture of how a well-automated, smooth, and coherent movement feels from inside. Now we move towards destructive complications.

> It was difficult only when it was necessary to stop these unconscious movements, and to think: When it was necessary to mow around a hummock or a non-weeded sorrel. *The old man did it easily* [italics added]. When a hummock emerged, he changed the movement and, here with the front, and there with the back of his scythe cleaned it with brief strokes. While doing it, he looked ahead and watched what else was happening. Both Levin and a young guy just behind him *found these changes in the movements difficult* [italics added]. Both of them, *after arranging their intense movement* [italics added], were in a fervour of work, and were unable to modify the movement and simultaneously to watch what was lying ahead.

It is absolutely clear that the old man Tit can adapt to more modifications in the external conditions than can his younger partners. When the conditions are not complicated by any factors, it was nearly impossible to tell the difference between his work and that of the younger mowers. However, when there emerged a demand for adaptive changes, the difference immediately became obvious. Note how skillfully and beautifully L. Tolstoy emphasized that all these modifications did not change the automatization of Tit's movements. Tolstoy simply mentions that none of the changes prevented Tit from watching what was going around and ahead of him.

Each level of movement construction has its own general means and modes of activity; in particular, each of them acts differently in opposing disruptive influences. *The main weapons of the level of muscular-articular links (B) is standardization* and the elaboration of dynamically stable movement patterns. The predisposition of Level B toward stable, standard movement patterns was noticed by physiologists long ago, who however, interpreted it incorrectly, basing their interpretation on the assumption that motor centers of Level B contain templates, or formulas, of different automatisms. Now, we know how movement patterns actually emerge, and are able to understand how these stable patterns can successfully overcome difficulties and obstacles, in a certain range: a slippery or muddy track during running, waves during swimming, a thin crust of ice over snow during skiing, and so on. More significant complications cannot be resolved with such a passive self-defense, and it becomes necessary to seek help at the higher, more maneuverable levels. Here, the brain cortex must intercede.

The main weapon of the level of space, and particularly, of the level of actions against destructive influences is their characteristic high *switchability*. During the whole second half of skill development (certainly, this is a crude subdivision), there take place "simulations" of various modifications, complications, and variations. Obviously, during these phases of practice, it is very important for the novice to be *purposefully confronted* with as many such sensibly arranged modifications as possible. At the very beginning of skill elaboration, such intentional modifications might have been dangerous and able to totally confuse a novice; toward the end of the process, they become very appropriate. The major goal here is not to let the novice learn as many modifications as possible; the essence of this process of actual confrontation with various complications is the development of *resourcefulness*, the ability to avoid confusion in unpredictable situations and to find immediately solutions. Such resourcefulness of the leading levels is, as we have already established, *the main prerequisite for dexterity*. Similar to skills pertaining to the higher levels, it demonstrates an inclination toward wide interpretation, that is, to *transfer*. *Exercisability itself is exercisable*, as are virtually all the properties of brain cortical systems. *An even higher degree of exercisability is demonstrated by resourcefulness, or adaptive maneuverability*, which defends a developed skill against disruption and deautomatization and puts the final polishing touches—*the varnish of dexterity*—on the skill.

We must also mention another type of destructive influence, which can frequently occur during skill development and, even later, during its practical application. Such destructive, *deautomatizing influences are observed when a movement is being switched to another, unusual level of control*.

We know that consciousness always resides at the leading level for a given movement. All the processes taking place in background levels, all the automatisms and auxiliary corrections, proceed outside its boundaries. Therefore, *to fix conscious attention on one of the background mechanisms* virtually always means *temporarily turning a corresponding background level into the leading one,* that is, introducing a disruptive switching.

As we have mentioned earlier, switching the leading level is a hard and cumbersome process. If it takes place for serious, long-term objectives, as a part of relearning (e.g., in adults learning new ways of locomotion), switching requires considerable time and effort. If such a switching is temporary, short-term, as in the situation discussed, it virtually always leads to movement disruption and deautomatization, as happened with Levin in the presented example from *Anna Karenina:*

> When he relaxed and thought only about the final outcome of his movements, so that his row would be as nice and accurate as the row of Tit, the work proceeded smoothly and successfully. However, when he tried to think about his movements, they immediately started to break down.

There is a funny story about a toad and a centipede, which seems appropriate here:

> An old, ugly Toad was sitting on a hummock and watching with grumbling envy a glittering Centipede dancing happily under the bright sun. The Centipede lightheartedly and deftly drew on the sand the most intricate patterns. The bright sun was hurting Toad's eyes, while the glossy plates on the Centipede's back threw multicolored specks all around, like a diamond necklace.
>
> The Toad was overpowered by terrible envy. He crawled to the Centipede with an insidious and flattering smile and croaked:
>
> "Quack, how deft and beautiful you are! Quack, I would have given anything to learn it. Teach me the secrets of your art. While admiring your dance, I cannot find answers to many exciting questions. Answer some of them, please. Tell me, what do your 18th and 39th legs do, when the 23rd one is lifted up? And also, which of your legs move simultaneously with the 14th? And what helps the 31st leg, when the 7th makes it leap forward?
>
> And the Toad waited for the answer with an affectionate expression on his fat face.
>
> The Centipede started to think and could not remember what the legs, mentioned by the Toad, did. However, it did not bother her. She was flattered by the Toad's speech and decided to show him immediately the art of dance, and also to watch what actually the 20-somethingth and 30-somethingth legs were doing. She had never thought about them before.
>
> The Centipede was terrified to find out that she was unable to make a single step. The legs seemed paralyzed and refused to obey her orders. The more intently she thought about each of them and about the order in which they should move, the more they got confused and trembled helplessly without moving from the spot. Finally, the Centipede dropped on her back in exhaustion and fainted.
>
> The Toad panted gloatingly and crawled back on its hummock. His revenge was sweet.

FIG. 3.

Such things have probably happened to everyone. The role of the Toad is played by our desire to watch the details of the movements and to consciously control their automatisms. Doing so is always a mistake. Consciously watching the movements of a teacher and intent attention toward one's own movements make sense only at the beginning of the process of skill development, when the motor composition of the skill is being defined. After the automatisms have already been elaborated and switched out of consciousness, it is useless and even detrimental to chase them behind the movement curtain. One needs to trust the level of muscular-articular links (B); most of the time, our confidence is justified.

So, what should be in the focus of our attention during the final phases of skill development? There is a very definite answer. The attention should be focused on a level where consciousness resides and which takes the responsibility for movement success in its major and most important components. Therefore, one should concentrate on the *desire to solve a motor problem as accurately and expediently as possible*. This desire will lead to basic, meaningful corrections for the whole movement. For example, the attention of a person who has learned to ride a bicycle should be fixed not on his legs or arms but on the road in front of the bicycle; the attention of a tennis player should be directed at the ball, the top edge of the net, the movements of the opponent, but certainly not at his own legs or on the racket. Such *concentration on the problem* maximally mobilizes the leading level with all its abilities.

More undesirable consequences can be expected from another cause, which, in a sense, is the opposite of the one just discussed. If a movement has been learned at the correct, appropriate leading level, switching one's attention to its automatisms and background details may, at the very worst, temporarily deautomatize it. It is not very hard to eventually reconstruct it once again. Only centipedes, and only in fables, faint because of such temporary destabilizing influences. However, sometimes it happens that one *has developed a skill* related to a certain movement *at a wrong leading level*. In this case, when a teacher checks the student's achievements and asks him to perform the movement, whose requirements can be met only by the correct leading level, the student becomes struck with total confusion and deautomatization, which are very hard to correct. The learner cannot immediately switch to another level which is absolutely unusual for him, and an abrupt movement disruption occurs. This happens, for example, when a piano student learns a difficult musical passage as a kind of "finger locomotion," that is, at the lower level of space (C1). As far as accuracy and speed are concerned, the passage may be learned very well, but then the teacher reminds the student that he is actually performing a piece of art whose essence is not in finger acrobatics but in inducing sounds with a certain artistic impression and meaning. The teacher would formulate it more simply: "Listen to what you are playing." Then the student starts to behave like the Centipede from the fable, although due to a different reason: The student will *try to elevate the movement to a higher level* as compared to the one that was used for the skill construction. There is only one solution: to relearn the whole movement from scratch, and this is sometimes harder than learning something absolutely new.

Similar disruptions and deautomatizations happen in athletic or gymnastic exercises and during work movements. If a student has studied the movements of filing as a simple, rhythmical movement of a wooden dummy back and forth or has studied swimming movements by lying on his stomach on a bench and moving his extremities in the air, *the time and effort have been wasted to no purpose, and the only thing that can happen when he tries the "skill" in real conditions is deautomatization*.

This essay on skill and exercise might have been stopped here, but we would like to add a general, concluding comment.

Adherents to the view that exercise leads to beating a trail or imprinting a certain trace onto the central nervous system, somehow, have never paid attention to an important fact. A human starts learning a movement because he cannot do it. Therefore, at the very beginning of skill development, there is nothing to be beaten, or the only thing available for imprinting is wrong, clumsy movements that he is able to perform at the very beginning of skill acquisition.

In order to imprint something in the sense attached to this word by the advocates of the corresponding theory, this something must be repeated many times and as accurately and reproducibly as the conditioning signals in the experiments with conditioned reflexes. However, if a student is only repeating his unskilled, clumsy movements, the exercise does not result in any improvement. The essence and objective of exercise is *to improve the movements, that is, to change them*. Therefore, correct exercise is in fact a *repetition without repetition*.

How can one get out of this controversy, which, for unknown reasons, has not been noticed by the advocates of the theory of beating a trail?

Actually, the contradiction is superficial, and there are enough data to address it. The point is that during a correctly organized exercise, a student is repeating many times, *not the means for solving* a given motor problem, but *the process of its solution*, the changing and improving of the means. Obviously, the theory of beating the trail and imprinting is powerless to explain something whose essence and importance are in the fact that it does change. We think that views expressed in this book explain the elaboration and fixation of a motor skill much more correctly.

Dexterity and Its Features

WHAT DO WE ALREADY KNOW
ABOUT DEXTERITY?

Since the first essay, which was fully dedicated to discussing dexterity, it has remained in the background. We have become successively familiar with the problem of the control of the motor apparatus and with the history of the development of movements on Earth. We have analyzed the structure of our brain apparatus controlling our movements and the levels controlling movements of different purposes and complexity. Finally, we have outlined the process of construction of a motor skill. Throughout these essays, it appeared that we were not discussing dexterity itself.

On the contrary, if we think again about all the topics presented in the previous essays, it turns out that we have learned quite a bit about dexterity. Aside from the fact that knowledge of motor physiology has prepared us for a deeper analysis and characterization of dexterity, in this essay, as we are about to see just now, we are already much better acquainted with dexterity than is at first apparent. First let us summarize some of the important points.

First of all, we have come to the conclusion that our movement organs are very recalcitrant tools, which pose *serious problems for control*.

The problems arise both from their *passive* components, the skeletal-articular apparatus, because of its numerous degrees of freedom, and from the *engines*, the muscles, because of their complex and peculiar physiological and mechanical properties. An increase in the complexity of motor tasks leads to an increase in the requirements of accuracy and complexity of appropriate movements, to specification and individualization of the effectors, and to increased difficulties in control. These difficulties are aggravated further because development leads to an increase in the requirements for an ability to adjust quickly to new, changing environments; to solve unexpected, nonstandard motor tasks; to successfully overcome unforeseen circumstances. "Motor wits" are valued higher and higher. Prehistoric lizards, with their rigid, uneducable, cortexless brain became extinct and were replaced by a young, energetic race of mammals, who possessed a motor cortex and the pyramidal system and who started using their ability to exercise and to learn. Over the whole animal kingdom there looms the conquerer, the human brain, with a number of developed cortical systems, a brain that has mastered an immense number of new, unexpectedly emerging combinations of movements and actions.

The progress in mastering the motor apparatus and, by its means, the whole world of movements and actions, leads to an increasingly apparent role for the queen of motor control—dexterity.

Although exercisability is a relatively recent feature in the history of motor development, dexterity is even more recent.

Furthermore, we have seen that dexterity is not a skill or a combination of skills. *Dexterity is a capacity or an ability* defining the relationship between the nervous system and skills. The level of motor dexterity defines how quickly and successfully a person can develop a certain motor skill and what level of perfection he or she is able to reach. Although both *exercisability and dexterity* are certainly *exercisable capacities*, they both stay *above all the skills*, ruling them and defining their essential features.

Our further analysis of the psychophysical features of different levels of human motor control revealed that in both the general history of movement development and in each individual person, dexterity does not refer to all the possible movements but is typical for only the *uppermost, cortical levels* and uses the lower levels as an auxiliary background for its realization. Dexterity can be observed only in those upper levels, which are enriched with meaning, that possess, first, *exercisability* and, second, *switchability*, or *maneuverability*.

Based on the analysis of the construction of a whole variety of movements, we established a very important and general feature of dexterity, one which is probably typical for all its realizations. This analysis demonstrated that in order to exhibit dexterity one always needs the *simultaneous, cooperative functioning of at least two levels*, one of which controls the other. This cooperation was compared to a horse and rider. The rider, the leading level, must demonstrate very high maneuverability, resourcefulness, switchability, and flexibility. It is equally important for the horse, the rider's background, to be controllable and reliable in following the commands from the leading level characteristic for a given movement or skill.

Based on this inherent feature of dexterity, its realization through a duo of levels, we suggested *a classification of the manifestations of dexterity into two categories* or two kinds of dexterity. Those manifestations that occur at the *level of space* (C) and that are based on a solid background of the muscular-articular links (B), we decided to call *body dexterity*. With the leading level as a numerator and the background level as a denominator, body dexterity is expressed as $\frac{C}{B}$.

Dexterity which is manifested by the level of action (D) and that is based on backgrounds of various lower levels is *hand dexterity* or *object dexterity*.

Because the level of space in humans shows clear division into two sublevels, cortical and subcortical, and because the backgrounds for the hand or object dexterity are also provided by Level B, there appears to be a whole variety of subclasses defined by combinations of background levels controlling the major automatisms for a corresponding action. These subclasses were designated by different fractions with Level D as the numerator and were illustrated with a number of appropriate examples (see essay 5).

Finally, we mentioned one more factor important for understanding the notion of dexterity. Different levels of motor control are very differently developed in different people. In addition to the fact, that we meet many persons with very high or very low general development of motor coordination or at any interme-diate step, we frequently encounter people with very *different relations or propor-tions of development of different levels of motor control.*

As in the area of mental abilities, in which some people are gifted in mathe-matics but struggle with social sciences or languages, and vice versa, similar things happen in the area of coordination of movements. Some people easily master accurate, targeted movements from the upper sublevel of space (C2) but have problems with anything based on the level of muscular-articular links (B), that is, with any movement requiring large, high-amplitude synergies. Others are very strong in locomotions that are controlled from the lower sublevel of space (C1) based on a background from Level B but are not very apt with hand movements. In still others, everything that is above Level B may be retarded as compared to this level: They are graceful, elegant, and carry the body beautifully, based on Level A. One may expect from them quite impressive achievements in coordination, but they fail at virtually any motor enterprise.

Such qualitative differences in the motor abilities in different individuals were noticed long ago, and there were many attempts at classifying them. Moreover, one cannot argue that the best classification of such *motor types or profiles* should be based on a theory of levels, which the reader has only briefly encountered. *Whole levels* demonstrate different degrees of development in different persons. Therefore, if Mr. X and Mrs. Y are good at certain movements at the lower sublevel of space, we can predict on the basis of the analysis and descriptions presented in essay 5 at what kinds of other motor acts these persons are likely to succeed. A couple of movements characteristic for a certain sublevel will definitely be a predictor for a whole set of movements at that particular level for this particular person.

The same principle is true for dexterity. If Mr. X has shown that he is dexterous with respect to certain movements characterized by a certain symbolic formula (e.g., $\frac{D}{Cl}$), we may very confidently predict that he will also be dexterous in all other movements from the same group. Thus, we may speak about different *individual types or profiles of motor dexterity*.

These are the main conclusions concerning dexterity from the previous essays. Let us move into a more detailed analysis of this capacity.

WHERE AND HOW DOES DEXTERITY REVEAL ITSELF?

In the first introductory essay, we gave an initial, very general *definition of dexterity*: *a motor ability to quickly find a correct solution for a problem in any situation*, that is, to exhibit motor wits in any conditions. I ask my readers to set aside this definition for the time being and to rely on their feelings for the language and meaning of the words. Let us consider how appropriate or inappropriate it would be to describe the movements in the following examples as dexterous.

> A sprinter is running along a track. He has passed all the competitors, his strides are long, all the movements are impeccably beautiful, and deepest analysis proves their rationality and expediency.

Can this example, which exemplifies pure perfection, be described as dexterous? Probably everyone would agree that the answer is no. The word *dexterous* somehow sounds awkward. This beautiful movement lacks something that could be judged as dexterous.

Let us consider the next example:

> He needed to reach the forest edge faster than his enemies. The enemies tried to cut him off from the trees, shooting while they ran. It was hard to run. The field was full of shallow ditches. Once he nearly fell down after slipping on the wet grass. His boots were smeared all over with mud. But all his senses tightened up. Looking under his feet, he sometimes threw a glance at the enemies, guessing their next moves and simultaneously planning the next 10 meters of his run. At last, he flew like a bird over a ditch hidden behind the bushes and got beyond the edge of the forest.

No one would hesitate to say that the soldier's life was saved exclusively by his *dexterity*. What is the essential difference between this example and the first one?

In both cases, the movement was running. However, comparing these two cases, we come to a conclusion that *dexterity* apparently *is not in the motor act itself but is revealed by its interaction with the changing external conditions*, with uncontrolled and unpredicted influences from the environment. Running, by itself, is not dexterous, but the way the runner adjusted the movement for solving a certain externally posed problem is.

FIG. 1.

These examples were not chosen accidentally. Regardless of the kinds of movements we might consider, the capacity of dexterity appears to be, not in the movements themselves, but rather in their interaction with the environment. The more complex and unpredictable the interactions are, the more successfully a person overcomes them, the higher is the dexterity of those movements.

That's why we are fascinated by the dexterity of the labor movements of a skilled worker who is very efficient, and objects seem to be born by themselves under his hands. But no one would describe as dexterous very similar movements made by empty hands as, for example, when playing charades. For this reason, plain running along a track does not look dexterous whereas running with hurdles sometimes provides keen examples of dexterity. For this reason, simple walking turns into an act of superior dexterity when performed on a narrow ledge, for example, during a competition in mountain climbing. For this reason, running on hands and feet on a floor is not only far from being dexterous but rather resembles its antonym, clumsiness, whereas running on hands and feet up a rope ladder requires high dexterity. If a ship's boy climbs a bending mast in pounding rain, with the rope ladder swinging like a cobweb, one witnesses dexterity in its highest expression.

So, the first of the established essential features of dexterity is that it always refers to the external world.

Let us once again turn to examples. The following event occurred during an international competition in Paris. It is based on a story told by the late Dr. S. Znamensky.

During a long 10-kilometer cross-country race, when the Soviet team was represented by both of the famous brothers, Georgy and Serafim Znamensky, at the ninth kilometer, a member of the Finnish team purposefully stepped on Serafim's foot with a sharp cleated shoe, causing a painful, bleeding wound. The runner started to limp; there was not a chance to win the race. However, the tactical task was to finish at least fifth, in front of all the members of the Finnish team. So, Serafim Znamensky gathered all his strength, shouted to A. Petrovsky following just behind, to pass him, and started to follow the teammate, despite the unbearable pain. There were rainbow circles in front of his eyes. Someone was panting heavily behind, but Znamensky could not turn and look. The coach shouted: "Do everything you can!" Znamensky finished fifth and saved the team.

One cannot help but admire the rare self-control of the famous athlete, his endurance, and skill. But was it also an example of outstanding dexterity?

The following example is also based on a real event, which took place several years ago at one of the Moscow stadiums.

One of the best Soviet pole vaulters ran, placed the end of the pole in the middle of the support area, and flew into the air. He was already close to the bar, about 4 meters high, when the pole broke. The whole stadium gasped when the sportsman started to fall from the height of 4 meters. But the athlete did not panic. He quickly switched the movement, made a somersault, and landed on his feet.

Was the movement dexterous? The outcome speaks for itself: Here the word *dexterous* is as appropriate as the applause of the stadium for the quick-witted athlete.

Based on a comparison of these two examples, a new feature of dexterity can be formulated. In the first example, the athlete was faced with very challenging conditions, which required all his forces, endurance, and running skills. However, during the next 1.5 kilometers, there was *no element of the unexpected* and correspondingly *no demand* for quick, clever change. Quite the opposite occurs in the second case. Neither the first movement that started the jump nor the final movement (somersault) was difficult or unusual for the athlete. The heart of the problem was to quickly and correctly find a solution in conditions of an *unexpectedly changed environment*.

This feature of conditions for dexterity is not accidental. During a monotonous, unperturbed course of a movement, free of any unexpected events, there is no demand for dexterity. It emerges during various changes in the environment that require skilled adjustment and precise switching of an ongoing movement. More dexterity is required for adjusting to more unexpected, stronger changes.

When a boxer or a fencer practices with a passive training device, their moves and hits may be beautiful, quick, and strong, but the movements will never be dexterous. This capacity will be fully revealed only during boxing or fencing with a real opponent, when each instant is full of the unexpected and when being late by a hundredth of a second may well mean losing a match.

The same is true for soccer, tennis, hockey, and so on. One cannot say "He dexterously hit the ball with the racket," but the statement "He dexterously parried a fast ball" sounds quite appropriate. In the last case, the essence is in the impossibility to predict, even half a second prior to the hit, from where and how the ball will fly.

Similar quick and precise switches take place in different kinds of evasive actions, such as evading an overtaking partner in games or evading an approaching enemy in real life. They define the success of dexterous actions, for example, when a person hanging by his or her hands loses the grip and manages to grab another object to avoid falling or when one intercepts an object that was thrown to someone else. A cat held upside down in the air by its feet and then suddenly released manages to turn dexterously in the air and land on its feet, even if the height of its drop is just one meter, which corresponds to a flight time of under half a second. A trained dog can dexterously and accurately catch a thrown object no matter how and where the object is thrown. A seal is similarly good at catching balls with its nose. All these are related examples illustrating the feature of dexterity that has just been defined. This feature can be termed *extemporaneousness*.

In many movements and actions, there are no such absolutely unpredictable events as discussed earlier, but these movements nevertheless require quick and accurate *movement adaptation* to external events which cannot be predicted with certainty. If a juggler throws balls or plates into the air so that many of them hover over his head, the juggler cannot predict the movement of each and every item with absolute accuracy and must look at them all the time. The juggler exhibits a high degree of dexterity. If an acrobat balances a high pole on his forehead while a boy performs a gymnastic exercise on the top of the pole, the acrobat can predict either the forces acting on the pole or the direction of its possible tilt. The ability to keep the pole absolutely vertical and to immediately correct its deviations is certainly an expression of dexterity.

It is not easy to determine if all the cases of dexterous movements and actions must have an element of extemporaneousness. In a whole list of examples, this element is not at all obvious, although dexterity apparently is. A number of examples were provided by the well-known sportsman and scientist, N. G. Ozolin. How can unexpected things occur during a long jump? However, if during a competition, the mobilization of morale and physical resources allows an athlete to push more strongly than he used to during the training sessions, the unexpectedly strong push leads to a correspondingly longer jump requiring an adjustment during the aerial phase. During a high jump, an athlete sometimes finds out, when already in the air, that the bar is somewhat higher than expected. If the athlete is resourceful and dexterous, he can frequently modify his movements and clear the height without touching the bar. There is virtually no "real-life" movement that would not have an *element of adaptive switchability* to various, although perhaps minor, unexpected events. Thus, aside from the large golden nuggets of outstanding dexterity, gold specks are scattered all around the world of our everyday movements just like those in the gold-bearing sand on the river bed.

WHAT IS ACCOMPLISHED BY DEXTERITY?

So, we have supplemented our information on dexterity with two important properties: We have defined that dexterity always refers to the environment and that it always has an element of extemporaneousness. Let us now try to penetrate into its internal features and try to understand: *what it does and what is being accomplished by it.*

All the previously analyzed, numerous examples of body and hand dexterity show, first of all, that *dexterity is an ability to correctly solve a motor problem.* Dexterity is required when a motor task is complicated by a number of factors; however, it is always assumed that despite these complications we are able to solve the problem.

What does it mean "*to correctly solve a motor problem*"? This expression obviously has qualitative and quantitative aspects.

A correctly performed movement is a movement that leads to the goal, solves the posed problem. *Correct movement is a movement that does what is required.*

This is the *qualitative* aspect.

We do not consider as dexterous the bear in the fable who broke trees rather than bent them. We will not call a person dexterous who attempts to straighten a bent metal bar and leaves it damaged beyond recognition. We will not use this word for a figure skater who bravely and elegantly starts a complex figure and falls in the middle of it. A skilled professional deserves to be called dexterous,

FIG. 2. The Bear spoiled a lot of birch and elm trees, but all in vain!

FIG. 3. "Just hold it," said the Bear,
"I'll teach you quite a lesson!"

not because of speed, elegance, or other features of his movements, but, first of all, because of the quality of things made with his hands.

If this element is absent, all the other movement features are senseless. A movement is correct when it perfectly fits a motor problem just as a key easily opens a lock. Dexterity is the ability to create a perfect key for any emerging lock. This feature is well described by the word *adequacy. All movements of a dexterous person are certainly adequate for the posed problems.*

The *quantitative* aspect of movement correctness is in its *accuracy.* We have already seen that the scarce repertoire of movements at the level of muscular-articular links (B) does not allow the introduction of a measure of accuracy. This level also does not contain dexterous movements. On the other hand, as far as the upper control levels are concerned, it is impossible to imagine a dexterous movement pertaining to them which would not have an element of accuracy or precision. This element is so important that a whole class of movements, which are not distinguished by adaptation to unexpected events, can be called dexterous if they are brilliantly precise. Would you not call dexterous a precise, accurate needle prick or a precisely thrown ball into the middle of a small target? And what about the movements of an acrobat who guessed the precise moment of letting go the trapeze in order to be caught by the swinging partner's hands in the middle of the air? What besides the dexterity of the precise movements of conjurer's hands amazes the audience?

The precision of a movement is precision of its sensory corrections. During elaboration of a new skill, during its automatization, each movement element gradually finds its own level of control with the most adequate, qualitative corrections. However, an increase in sensitivity and accuracy of the sensory mechanisms underlying the corrections continues during the whole course of practice, even at the background level, where the final refinement takes place. The vestibular apparatus of an amateur cyclist starts to detect deviations from the vertical line and gives rise to corrective signals when these deviations are already rather large. This process is reflected in the general pattern of the movement, so that the track shows consecutive twists to the right and to the left. The sensitivity of the vestibular organs is much higher in an experienced cyclist so that he is able to show a nearly ideal, straight track even when riding slowly. An increase in the acuity of perception of the proprioceptive organs is reflected in runners who exhibit an increase in the standardization of their steps; in jumpers, who exhibit more and more accurate stepping on the take-off board; in tennis and soccer players, who exhibit an increase in the accuracy of angle at which the ball is hit.

An increase in the requirement for accuracy is particularly pronounced in *object skills*, for which hand or object dexterity dominates. We have already discussed a number of examples. Very high requirements for accuracy and a correspondingly high ability to match them are characteristic for the upper sublevel of space (C2), which we have also termed the sublevel of accuracy and precision. Consequently, all the skills from the level of actions (D), which are based on automatisms from the sublevel of accuracy, require outstanding accuracy to be considered dexterous. Many of the skills of a pharmacist, a precision mechanic, an engraver, a surgeon, a chemist, a marksman, a draftsman, and others refer to this level.

This ability of the sensory organs to increase their sensitivity during the practice of a skill is of high practical importance. In each motor skill, *accuracy is undergoing the influence of practice and has a high potential for improvement.* Accuracy also shows a clear example of the transfer of exercisability typical for the upper sublevel of space (C2). The development of accuracy from the practice of a number of different motor skills forms an important background for dexterity.

Let us now turn to another feature of dexterity, one that characterizes *what* dexterity does.

This feature is *quickness.*

Stating that quickness is a necessary feature of dexterity sounds obvious, even excessive. Is it similar to requiring that water be wet or that fire be hot?

This is not the case. The following discussion makes clear the necessity of explicating this feature. First, let us note that the notion of quickness also has both qualitative and quantitative aspects. Let us start with the qualitative aspect.

Quickness can refer to *how* something is done and *what* is actually done. In the former case, we deal with quickness in behavior, quickness of movements and actions, and so on. In the latter case, we deal with what can be called *quickness in achieving a result.* Imagine a person who develops quickness by rewriting repeatedly one and the same text or by making numerous identical nuts. No matter how quick he is, he will never be able to make more than a few copies or more than 100 nuts a day. Next to him, there are a couple of machines that leisurely spew out thousands of copies of the text and hundreds of thousands of nuts in an hour. Quickness of movements is certainly more obvious in the person whereas the machines are apparently quicker in achieving the result.

One may say that for dexterity quickness of achieving the result is vital. One can be an outstanding sprinter without being outstandingly dexterous. Certainly, all other conditions being equal, a person's quickness in achieving a result depends on quickness of movements, but quickness of movements by itself is not omnipotent.

There are a number of variations of a moralistic fable with the theme "Hurry up—make the people laugh" or "The slower you go—the further you get." In all these versions, an excessively hasty man is being beaten by a more methodic, calculating opponent, despite all the quickness of his movements. The indisputable wisdom contained in these fables poses another essential question: Why are all geniunely dexterous movements unhurried? Why do hastiness and fussiness in movements suggest poor dexterity?

I think that the explanation is rather simple. Poorly, unskillfully, clumsily performed work is always accompanied by many unnecessary movements. If one's goal is to keep a high pace of work, all the unnecessary movements need to be packed into short time intervals, and the person is forced to hurry! On the other hand, if the work is rational and methodic, it does not require any particular hastiness and nicely fits into a time frame, even when the results need to be achieved quickly.

In order to analyze more precisely the problem of quickness, one needs also to note the following. It is absolutely wrong to say that dexterity is always characterized by the greatest speed. Different kinds of activity can be performed with different degrees of quickness, and sometimes they themselves dictate the pace. This pace may be rather slow. For example, there are a number of precise, slow manipulations, such as chemical weighing or certain medical procedures, that do not simply require slow execution but in which the whole essence of dexterity is in performing them gently, smoothly, and *slowly*. On the other hand, there are special kinds of work (sometimes called *precision* work) that are impossible to perform other than slowly, for example, like the work movements of a jeweler handling a small watch the size of a pea. Movements of this kind sometimes show an inverse relationship: The smaller the movements are, the slower they become if one wants to maintain the same level of accuracy. Even in these cases, however, one can compare two persons and say that the one who does the job more quickly without sacrificing accuracy is more dexterous.

So, the quickness in achieving the result is required for and characteristic of dexterity. Note that relative, rather than absolute, quickness is of importance.

Quickness, as it is reflected in dexterity, has its own qualitative aspect, although it is not readily obvious. One can classify it along three lines.

First, dexterity requires *quickness of wits*. A good example is the previous case of a broken pole during a vault. The dexterity is not the pole vaulter's being confused by the unexpected event but rather in inventing a way out, and what is particularly important, in doing so quickly. It would not be of any satisfaction if the athlete found the solution (the somersault) when lying on the ground and massaging the bruised body. The value of such quick-wittedness is particularly clearly observed in fencing in which, in the fraction of a second, it is necessary to feel rather than to realize the opponent's maneuver, and to switch immediately to a unique, appropriate counterfeint that may save one's life.

The second aspect is probably *quickness of resolution*. The problem frequently is not only in quickly finding a correct action. Sometimes, our motor levels are so rich that they suggest not one but three ways out of a situation. Here, the excessive repertoire may harm rather than help if we are unable to choose quickly and without hesitation one of the plans of actions and to follow it. If we take into account that these movements are those that allow only fractions of a second for making the choice, the importance of quickness of resolution and the ability to follow steadily the chosen solution becomes quite obvious.

The third aspect of qualitative quickness that is important for dexterity can be called "rapid success" of the movements. This feature is hard to define precisely, but apparently it is not synonymous with merely quickness or speed. It is not accidental that people say "Quickly but not successfully." If quickness has already revealed itself in quick-wittedness and in immediate decision making, it must further provide smooth, undelayed realization of the decision. When movements smoothly and easily merge one into another, when muscle impulses do not oppose each other's actions and are in perfect balance with external forces, and when everything is performed at a high pace, we say that the work is "rapidly successful."

HOW DOES DEXTERITY WORK?

We have understood the requirements for the *outcome of dexterous movements and actions*. We may expect them to solve the problem correctly, that is, adequately and accurately, quickly and successfully. Now is the time to pose another question: *What are* dexterous movements and actions?

How does dexterity attain its results?

There is an old story about a huge boulder. It was sitting in the middle of the central square of a town for ages. The magistrate announced a competition on how to get rid of it. One bidder decided to build a huge platform on rollers and drive the boulder away and asked for 1,000 rubles. Another one suggested exploding it into pieces with dynamite and assessed the expenses at about 700 rubles. A peasant who happened to be nearby said:

"I will get rid of the boulder for 50 rubles."

"How???"

"I will dig a hole by its side and push it into the hole. Then I will level the ground all around the square."

That was what he did and got 50 rubles for the work and another 50 for a smart solution.

This short story presents a very good example. The boulder could have been removed by any of the suggested methods, and each method would also have taken approximately the same time. However, the advantages of the third project were simplicity and cheapness.

One can find many examples of a correct result obtained quickly but with an enormous expenditure of time, effort, tool wear, and so forth. All such actions are well decribed by the expression, "Shooting sparrows with a cannon." Baron Munchausen suggested the well-known project of plowing the fields by first burying truffles at even intervals and then by letting a herd of pigs into the field who would plow it by digging the truffles out.

If a woman asks her inexperienced husband to peel a potful of potatoes, she is likely to find a handful of perfectly clean potatoes the size of a walnut, a heap of peelings, and a destroyed pocketknife.

All these funny and not-so-funny examples reveal to us that, in order to be called dexterous, movements and actions must not only lead to a correct result but also do so rationally. This rationality is the first condition in answer to the question of how.

We have already decided that sprint running along a plain track does not have the prerequisites of dexterity. As shown by precise measurements, everything is sacrificed for the sake of speed during a sprint. The movements of even the best sprinters are not very rational. Experience shows that the body cannot squeeze reasonably well-constructed and economic movements into those fractions of a second, which are being spent for each step. According to scientific data, this is likely to be the main reason that it is so difficult to beat the world record (10.2 s for a 100 m race): At such super high speeds, the cost of movements increases at an outrageous rate. The situation is different for running over longer distances. Here, the task is not to show the highest possible speed but to maintain a certain speed for a considerable time. Therefore, rationality and expediency of movements become efficient. In fact, if someone describes the wide, easy, gracious steps of a middistance runner as dexterous, he would be close to the correct usage of the word.

It is easy to draw a distinction between the notions of movement *correctness* and movement *rationality*. Rationality refers to the movements themselves, whereas correctness refers to their result. A correct movement is the one that does *what is required*; a rational movement is the one that does it *how it is required*.

Rationality of movements has been thoroughly analyzed, particularly in the studies of professional and labor movements. However, even in these studies, rationality mostly referred to crude, general movement patterns, not their construction. As far as the fine rules of expediency and internal rationality are concerned, both labor and sports movements are still based on intuition and lucky guesses.

Rationality, similarly to other features that have been discussed previously, has both *qualitative and quantitative aspects*. The first one refers to everything dealing with *expediency* of movements and actions, whereas the second refers to their economy. Let us consider each of them.

In gymnastic and track-and-field automatic movements and skills, which are predominantly built at the level of space (C), practice long ago detected and developed the most rational movements. Their aspects concerning the *particular sequences of movements* are usually shown and explained to an athlete by the coach. Unfortunately, language is still too imperfect to explain the aspects concerning the internal area of sensory corrections and to define the *internal movement structure*. Here, especially at the beginning of skill acquisition, the athlete must thoughtfully and methodically work alone. It would be very smart of him to abandon swotting and attempts at imitating some great sportsmen whose body and nervous structure might well be quite different. Understanding his own movements and requiring the sensory organs to get information to his consciousness will eventually lead to the elaboration of motor acts that are best suited for the athlete and that are based on his own uniqueness. Do all people walk similarly? Yes, but each person has his own gait by which another can distinguish him from 100 paces after 10 years of separation. Gait is an individual, rational style of walking. The central nervous system of every human elaborates and constructs it subconsciously during childhood, as if foreseeing that there are tens of thousands of kilometers to be walked. Such habits are developed, instinctively or consciously, for all the important skills—gait, writing, horse riding, and so on. It is appropriate to say that each athlete should purposefully and methodically develop his own running, jumping, and putting styles.

In chain movements controlled from Level D, equally important are both expediency of the *motor act* and appropriateness of the *tool*. Here, the notion of dexterity is supplemented with a more conscious element. Apparently, successful resourcefulness with respect to an expedient movement and an appropriate tool is what is called *adroitness* and *deftness*. Let us once again turn to negative examples: It is hard to imagine anything that would look clumsier than extracting a splinter with pliers, pulling nails with wire cutters, sharpening a pencil with a table knife or teeth, and so on.

As far as economy of movements is concerned, the more dexterous of two movements is the one that accomplishes the task with less expenditure of effort. Observations show that such economy is usually developed during the later phases of polishing a motor skill and its standardization (see earlier discussions). The point is not only not to waste efforts during a smooth, quiet movement but also—the main difficulty—to produce a successful and economical way out of any unexpected situation with adaptive and switching actions. In a battle, for example, any speck of unnecessarily wasted effort can later lead to quite dramatic consequences. Youth spends generously its forces, which it does not know what to do with. Consequently, folk wisdom says that dexterity accumulates with years. It has an element of reasonable frugality, which sometimes helps an older, experienced fencer defeat with composure a younger, impulsive opponent.

THE HEART OF DEXTERITY

Now we are getting close to the analysis of the crucial feature of dexterity, which was included in the original definition—*resourcefulness*. A movement can be perfectly accurate and appropriate and it can lead to a required result quickly and rationally, but if the movement did not start, proceed, and terminate at the precise times when it is needed, its value is like that of rain over the sea.

What do the expressions "find a way out of any complication" or "display resourcefulness in any condition" from the original definition mean? These ex-pressions lead us to a wide area of phenomena related to the construction of movements and motor coordination.

First of all, let us note that there are both *passive* and *active* aspects of re-sourcefulness. The passive aspect refers to *stability* with respect to external, un-expected changes that are beyond our control. The active aspect concerns our own, active *interference* with the events.

The passive aspect can be termed steadiness or stability of movements (my readers already encountered the term *stabilization* in essay 6). This aspect of resourcefulness helps us to perform movements and to solve motor problems despite external, perturbing influences. It helps us find those adaptive switchings that save the motor act from destabilization and deautomatization, and the motor task from disruption when external changes and unexpected events occur.

When a person not only adapts to external changes in the environment but also *actively changes* the process of movement, searching for a route to an optimal result, the most important role is being played by the active aspect of resource-fulness. It may be termed motor *initiative*. Together, these two properties comprise the most important feature, the heart of dexterity.

In the description of the successive stages of constructing a motor skill (see essay 6), we considered the problem of developing movement stability, that is, movement resistance to perturbations, only insofar as it was necessary for drawing a general picture of skill development. Let us look more closely into what assures this stability. What kind of resources does the central nervous system have to ensure the movements against disruption?

Within the background Level B, providing stability is tightly coupled with another aspect—standardization of movements. This level has one general way of dealing with motor disruptions: to lead the movements along a uniform, dynamically stable trajectory with the help of all the richness of proprioceptive, muscular-articular information. This level is a skillful, cunning diplomat who prefers not to struggle with reactive and external forces. Rather, this level makes a pact with them so that the reactive (and sometimes also the external) forces themselves take part of the responsibility of guarding the movement against possible disruptions and tend it, like a sheepdog, by substituting for sensory corrections. Level B reciprocates by taking the responsibility of not violating movement standards and accepted borders.

Therefore, this level is deprived of any noticeable switchability and initiative.

Switchability and plasticity were born together with the brain cortex (see essay 3). The level of space (C) and particularly the level of actions (D) use this feature on an everyday basis, but this weapon becomes especially effective when it is guided by dexterity.

The level of space (C) possesses two major types of switchability, which it uses with comparable perfection and maneuverability. These may be called *motor-act switching* and *effector switching*. Both types are generally based on the same phenomenon called the *spatial field*. The level of muscular-articular links (B) has problems with substituting movements and particularly with substituting moving effectors because all its corrections are tightly coupled with the effector itself. All the abundant flows of sensory signals to its centers provide information about the behavior of one of the muscles, the position of one of the joints, the reactive forces in the center of gravity of one of the body links, and so forth. All these characteristics are inseparable from the effectors.

Corrections at the level of space are quite different. Although signals from proprioceptors take part in the construction of the spatial field, their role is very different. The leading role in the construction of spatial field is played by vision, which treats equally all visible body parts. As we have seen, the spatial field is an organized space spread in front of us, in which we are able to reach any visible or memorized point. The questions of which route will be taken to arrive at the point, which motor act will be used, or which of the extremities will play the role of rickshaw delivering us there, are secondary and easily solvable by the level of space. This is the origin of its switchability.

If a boy full of energy wants to cover 100 meters, he will walk part of it, hop another part, and maybe walk the rest on his hands. The same 100 meters in the mountains would require different locomotions—gaits, running, clambering, and hanging by one's hands.

It is not any more difficult for the level of space to switch the effector in use. This explains, in particular, the previously described transfer of a skill from one effector to another. Track-and-field athletes, for example, have noticed that if one stops the process of skill acquisition for the right arm and practices with the left arm for some time (making a mirror image of the movement), there is a visible improvement in performance of the untrained right arm. Such things happen with throwing movements. Similar temporary "mirror tranformation" of a movement is also beneficial with pole vaulters.

Movement switchability with respect to both motor act and effector is a powerful guard protecting the movements against disruption; that is, they provide

FIG. 4.

what we have called motor resourcefulness. The level of actions adds to this menu the switchability of chain motor composition and the switchability of the tool of action.

There is, however, one more class of movements that require other kinds of protection against disruption. As it frequently happens, the unique way, the one preferred by the brain for dealing with these movements, has not been forgotten by the thrifty nervous system. By understanding the major features of this type of coordination, we can easily detect its participation in the control of any movement.

Consider, for example, the throwing of a javelin at a target or the hitting of a ball while playing billiards. Both these movements are very brief, nearly instantaneous. Their important feature is that after the javelin has been thrown or when the ball has been hit, no corrections can be applied to adjust their movement. There are passionate billiard players who stretch over the table and groan and beckon the ball, but they themselves do not really believe in the effectiveness of these manipulations; they are simply giving in to the same instinct that forces the fans in a stadium to lift their legs when watching a high jump. In all these momentary movements of throwing or striking, every correction must be introduced prior to the impact, that is, before the projectile has actually started to move. Here, all the corrections must be introduced on the basis of *anticipation*, when the movement has not yet started and is not observable.

Generally speaking, jumping, which may be considered to be *throwing one's own body*, is a very similar situation. It is known that during the aerial phase of the jump, it is impossible to change the ongoing movement of the center of gravity of the body. It can be influenced only by an external force. An external force requires an external support, which is unavailable when flying. Therefore, in jumping, all the necessary corrections must also be introduced in advance, prior to the moment of

FIG. 5. The fans.

leaping from the ground. Therefore, everything here is also based on foresight. The difference between jumping and throwing is that during jumping you can change the configuration of your body (for example, by dexterously drawing in an arm or by pulling in the tummy in order not to touch the bar).

Such foresight, or *anticipation* as it is called in physiology, is based on a rich stock of previous experience. This experience lets you predict in advance the outcome of a throwing or striking movement. Moreover, in many everyday movements, which at a first glance have nothing to do with throwing or striking, an important role is played by anticipation. For example, during walking, the major muscle impulse that throws the leg forward occurs at the very beginning of this movement; however, it lets us make strides of uniform length. T. Popova showed that in children, who are without much experience, such anticipation is absent; they are forced to send a corrective impulse following the main one each time. This is a genuine sensory correction, clearly seen in photographs of children walking (so-called cyclograms). In the youngest children, even the corrective impulse is unable to assure strides of the same length.[1]

Anticipation, or the generation of corrections in advance, plays a very important role in motor coordination. For example, it helps us calculate the point where we would hit a car crossing one's way and to modify our route correspondingly. It allows us to estimate where a ball served by our opponent is going to

---

[1]If one looks carefully, the movement of leg transfer during walking, running, skating, skiing, and so on is in its essence a typical *ballistic* (of a throwing–striking type) movement. Consequently, it easily transforms into, for example, kicking (striking) a soccer ball. Anticipatory corrections play an important role in all ballistic movements.

land and to prepare the racket. It helps us take into account an obstacle in our way and change our walking pattern to avoid the obstacle with minimal deviation from the desired route. Finally, in many well-practiced movements, it lets us make most of the corrections in advance, at the very beginning of the movement, so that the movement requires little attention in the future, thereby leaving one time to prepare similarly for the next movement. All these examples make clear the importance of anticipation for dexterity.

Actually, what we have called motor resourcefulness is vitally dependent on the ability to predict the possible changes in the external conditions and to plan our movements correspondingly. *The value of anticipation is especially noticeable in different kinds of motor actions during wrestling.* It also plays a crucial role in the tactics of a long-distance runner. In the latter example, the dexterity of the master runner lies in anticipating the opponent's actions, of his own movements in the next few seconds, of the uneven sections of the track, of the turns, and so on. The role of the goalkeeper in soccer is all anticipation. At any given time, the goalkeeper simultaneously has several, equally possible actions ready to be initiated during the next second. One may say that a skilled goalkeeper fills the whole area of the goal: He is at the spot prior to the attempt by the opponents to score a goal.

The role of anticipation in fencing is not less obvious. Let us listen to Dr. F. Lagrange, an expert in hygiene of physical culture (From F. Lagrange. *L'hygiene de l'exercice chez les enfants et les jeunes gens.* Paris, 1896, p. 134):

> In fencing, a top-level master loses his physical fitness with years, but nevertheless, at the age of 45, many fencers are not worse than they were in earlier years. The reason is that, simultaneously with losing general physical abilities, there is a continuous development of an intellectual capacity termed "judgment." The fencer may not have the same power in his movements but has more quick-wittedness (d'à propos); his vision is not that acute, but his ability to judge by eye is better (de coup d'oeil); therefore, he is more able to predict his opponent's next movements. The ability to make judgments at lightning speed is based on experience. It helps him to firmly resist the opponent's sword (une parad ferme) not by following it from one spot to another but by unfailingly waiting for it at the very place where it is going to come. It is like some kind of an insight that tells him that the opponent will continue his attack in a quarter rather than in a sixth. A mature fencer has battled (a tâté) so many opponents that he has developed an accurate classification of different styles and tempers. After one or two "false attacks," he knows already not only the strength of the opponent but also his style. He can guess his opponent's plans by a kind of "calculating of probabilities," which is very close to certainty. Each day brings him new experience, as each opponent is a chance for expanding his knowledge. The importance of experience is exemplified by the advice given by all seasoned masters—to frequently change opponents. After one achieves a certain level, there is no possibility for further progress if one fences with one and the same, even a very good, master.

DEXTERITY AND INITIATIVE

Anticipation (i.e., guessing in advance) of the intentions of an opponent and consequences of one's own actions already builds a bridge for *moving further* to the most consummate types of dexterity. These most perfect, purely human types of dexterity fit the capacity that has been termed *initiative*.

There is an old temple with a high bell tower at the Peter Paul bastion in Leningrad, crowned with a 50-meter spire narrowing to its top. At the very top there is a sphere of about 2 meters in diameter, and on top of the sphere there is a statue of an angel about 3.5 meters high and a cross about 6.5 meters high. The whole spire is covered with gilded copper sheets.

More than 100 years ago (in 1830), there were recurrent problems with the angel and the cross threatening to fall.

A circus acrobat M. volunteered to reach the angel and the cross and to fix them, without any special constructions. The acrobat decided to climb, using small hooks on the spire, and relied on his general dexterity, strength, and bravery.

Early in the morning, M. took all the necessary tools and climbed out of a small window at the bottom of the spire, 50 meters above the ground. He grabbed the ledge closest to the window at the surface of the spire and somehow managed to get to the closest hook. Then he sat on it, aimed at the next hook, made a jump, and grabbed it with one hand. He mounted the hook, stood on it on one foot, spread his arms across the spire surface, and took a short rest. Then he made another jump to the next hook.

After 2 hours, the absolutely exhausted man climbed back into the window. He looked more like M.'s shadow than M. himself. During the 2 hours, he lost much weight and did not even notice the many bruises and bleeding cuts on his arms and legs, which had resulted from his reckless jumps. He, however, failed to get to the top of the spire. Thinking that he was hopelessly lost, he slid down to the window grabbing all possible uneven spots on the spire surface.

I have made up this acrobat, M. However, the next passage relates the actual events of that time, which are supported by historic documents.

A state peasant from Yaroslavl district, a roof maker, Petr Telushkin, heard the news about the plans to repair the angel and the cross on top of the spire of the Peter Paul Cathedral. He realized how much time and money would be spent for building the scaffolding and wrote a letter stating that he would do all the necessary repairs without any scaffolding. He asked also to be reimbursed for the materials and was willing to do all the work free, leaving it for the bosses to reward him as they liked.

Telushkin was an exceptionally strong person of average height. At first, he tied a rope around the spire and around his waist and started to ascend by grabbing the grooves on the spire surface and pulling himself up. Witnesses have said that his nails started to bleed because of the strain, but he ignored the strong pain and continued his ascent. He always kept the rope tight and it helped him to hang as the spire became thinner and thinner. Then he started to use the hooks on its surface and continued climbing with the help of small stirrups for the feet. Thus, he reached the sphere. Then it was necessary to climb on top of the sphere. Telushkin did it in the following way (as reported by the author):

> Telushkin tied two new ropes aroung the spire just under the sphere and made two new stirrups through which he put his feet. He tied another rope to the spire and around his waist and hung on it in a nearly horizontal position. In his hands he had yet another long coiled rope. With the help of a very strong wind, which was swinging the spire, Telushkin threw the rope around the base of the cross and caught the falling end. He made a loop at the end and pulled the rope so that the loop tightened around the cross. He made a number of smaller loops along the rope to use as stirrups, climbed the rope to the cross, and started to work. Sometimes we saw him climbing on the 5-arshin[2] angel, or sitting on the angel's wing and fixing it, or on the horizontal bar of the cross that was 9 arshin high, methodically fixing the torn sheets. On the third day of these aerial trips, Telushkin prepared a rope ladder about 26 sazhen high, took one of its ends to the sphere and tied it to the cross. Later, he used this ladder for bringing supplies and in 6 weeks fixed all the sheets torn by the wind and the angel's wing, and also pushed the angel up by 8 vershok along the cross.

The hero of the first example relied exclusively on his motor resourcefulness, with a firm belief in its omnipotence. It did help him to survive a situation in which 9 out of 10 men would have fallen and died. The hero of the second example did not want to follow the known proverb "The peasant will not cross himself until the thunder roars." He *anticipated* the difficulties and displayed *initiative* prior to actual action. He also needed strength, bravery, and dexterity, but the result was obtained because he multiplied them not by "maybe" but by an elaborate plan of actions. He differed from the first man generally in the same way that humans differ from apes.

Apparently, the ability to display initiative in movements and actions, as Telushkin did, is always based on foresight, that is, on anticipation. We may take risks only if we clearly realize the future events and can predict the impact of our actions on ourselves. In this way, we will not only be protected against harm from unexpected external events but may also be able to use these events to our advantage.

This is a new, unusual feature of dexterity, which directly follows on from resourcefulness and, in particular, initiative. Dexterity may turn to its advantage not only some potentially harmful external event but also a mistakes of the actors themselves.

Here are two examples.

A forward was ready to pass the ball with the right foot to his partner who was waiting on the right and ready to kick the goal. But the forward tripped or slipped.

---

[2]1 vershok = 45 mm = 0.045 m; 1 arshin = 711 mm = 0.711 m; 1 sazhen = 1.83 m.

His right foot went too far to the right, and the ball rolled to the left. Before the player could realize what was going on, his instinct and experience had already suggested a solution for the problem. As a result of slipping, his weight shifted on the right foot providing support for a straight kick into the goal, an action that was equally unexpected by both his partners and the goalkeeper. The goal was scored. The whole episode took less than 2 seconds.

A man needed to pull a heavy T-shaped pig of iron, which looked like an anchor, from a pit shaped like a well. He tried to throw a loop to catch the T-bar, but after several unsuccessful attempts, the loop was caught by a hook somewhere in the middle of the pit and became stuck. Then, the man lowered enough rope to reach the pig, slid it under the T-bar, and started to pull it up, against only half of its weight, because it worked like a pulley. Applying only half of the force, he pulled the pig half-way up the pit, where it was easy to grab.

In both examples, appeared a possible way to turn a misfortune into a very fortunate circumstance quickly, semiconsciously, and semiintuitively.

Such cases are not rare, at least in small details, for any person who considers himself dexterous in some form of activity. This ability is exhibited in the simplest forms of interaction with the environment up to the highest examples of art. There are well-known examples—when an accidental spot on a canvas suggested to the artist a new, much better version of a painting or when a vulgar song from the street or an accidental sound produced by a cat jumping on piano keys gave birth to new musical ideas in the composer's brain.

It is particularly hard to formulate rules and laws in an area in which initiative and inventiveness start playing their roles. Therefore, it makes sense to stop now, without going into the area of movement art, which is ruled by the highest forms of dexterity. There are no limits to human ingenuity.

Let us now summarize the detailed analysis of dexterity and its features. This summary will help us build an *expanded definition of dexterity* by including everything related to its essential, necessary aspects. This expanded definition can be stated in the following way:

Dexterity is the ability to find a motor solution for any external situation, that is, to adequately solve any emerging motor problem
    correctly (i.e., adequately and accurately),
    quickly (with respect to both decision making and achieving a correct result),
    rationally (i.e., expediently and economically), and
    resourcefully (i.e., quick-wittedly and initiatively).

We may just now move to some final comments on the possibilities of development and means of improving dexterity, but there are still some urgent questions concerning the completeness of this definition: Has everything been mentioned? Are there any apparent omissions?

DEXTERITY AND BEAUTY

During the initial stages of my work on this book, I asked many professionals in sports and physical culture how they defined dexterity. A minority—but a very sizable and insistent minority of experts—alleged that the definition of dexterity cannot exist without the notion of the beauty of the movements, their gracefulness, harmony, and so on. These experts noted that in many gymnastic exercises, beauty of the movement is one of the factors incorporated into the scores by the judges. They also pointed out that it was impossible to give an example of a dexterous movement that was not also beautiful and graceful.

Despite the rather insistent nature of these demands, I cannot agree with them. In defense of my view, I try to prove that the notion of *beauty should not be included in the expanded definition of dexterity.*

The first reason for its exclusion is that beauty is always subjective. Even if there are no arguments about the famous examples of beauty like the *Sistine Madonna* by Raphael, *Gioconda* by Leonardo da Vinci, and a dozen of paintings by Titian, Velazquez, Murillo, Botticelli, Brullov, Levitan, and so on, we speak here about the unattainable peaks of human genius, whereas for the purposes of this book a definition for everyday life is needed. Second, if you take a dozen art enthusiasts and give each of them a Paris' apple to be awarded to the best from this list, there would be no unanimous decision. Therefore, it seems very unreliable to include such an assessment into a scientific definition of an idea.

It is even more important that the element of beauty in dexterous movements is not primary or basic; that is, it is not an independent, equal aspect that is on a parity with the others. I am told: If you have a movement that is correct, quick, accurate, rational, and resourceful but not beautiful, you cannot call it dexterous. I answer: Give me an example of a movement that exhibits all the features of the expanded definition and yet simultaneously looks ugly and disharmonious, and then we shall continue our discussion. The point is that such examples are impossible to find.

There is an unavoidable element of artificiality in any definition. The words that we use are somewhat fussy and somewhat crude. Therefore, it is impossible to avoid in a definition some degree of overlap between separate aspects. Such an overlap has occurred in the previous section with the definition of dexterity. It was obvious even in the course of the analysis. Economy overlaps with quickness, resourcefulness with initiative, quick-wittedness with appropriateness and speed, and so forth. This is the way it is. However, all these aspects of dexterity are independent and are not consequences of each other.

Beauty is different. With regard not only to dexterity but also to any other form of pattern and movement beauty (so-called beauty of plasticity), one may say that *beauty is always a secondary feature,* a consequence of deeper and more essential features of the object. We consider harmonious and beautiful everything that combines economy and apprropriateness. Are not the brilliant constructions like the Eiffel Tower, the Crimean Bridge, the arm of a crane, a powerful steam engine, or a streamlined airplane beautiful? In the middle of the 1800s, a wrong idea was born which urged to "beautify" engineering constructions with ornaments and decorations. Steam engine mountings were built in the shapes of gothic arches, steam engines were painted with flowers (just as some sewing machines and clocks are still painted), and even Eiffel himself could not resist, sticking iron lacework onto his beautiful tower. Soon, this misunderstanding died and was replaced by the idea of modest, adequate simplicity which contains the highest degree of harmony. There is no question that our eyes appreciate these precisely calculated patterns, that we feel the harmony and beauty of the gracious curvature of the Crimean Bridge, of the aerial lightness of the stone arches of Moskvoretskiy Bridge, of the brave impetuousness of the Swiss mountain bridges, which look like high colonnades. This appreciation is not accidental. It is a result of the experience of many generations, who subconsciously imprinted it on their descendants.

It has been accepted for a long time that our ideals of male and female beauty reflect biological expediency. In men, beauty is force, a muscular body, and confidence in movements; in women, it is softness, grace, and the embodiment of ideal motherhood. What are the reasons for thinking that beauty of movements is different?

Beauty of human movements in general and of those most perfect movements we call dexterous is in the *combination of expediency and economy*. When all the requirements of dexterity are met, then movement beauty occurs as their inevitable companion. An ugly movement with all the objective features of dexterity is as difficult to imagine as a clumsy movement that is beautiful.

One more consideration shows that beauty is not a special, separate feature of dexterous movements but is born by the essential features of dexterity. If beauty were something additional that could be added to or eliminated from movements that have all other essential features of dexterity, then the athletes would naturally try to "decorate" their movements, that is, try something that was already compromised in technology. But what would we say about a long jumper who tried to add beauty to his movements by making an additional entrechat during the aerial phase or about a pole vaulter who blew graceful kisses to the audience? The absurdity of these examples is, perhaps, the most persuasive argument that all the beauty of dexterous movements is in their precise, economical, and effective expedience.

HOW HAS DEXTERITY DEVELOPED?

Sometimes, you might hear or read that dexterity is a purely inborn capacity and, moreover, that you can develop force, endurance, and speed but you must be born dexterous.

This view is totally wrong. It can be refuted by direct observation of the surrounding reality, but facts and observations can be interpreted differently. One might possibly say that Mr. X did not develop dexterity but rather that his movements allow him to demonstrate his inborn dexterity. Therefore, it makes sense to supplement the facts that can be seen by an unbiased observer with a number of more general reasons showing that *dexterity is exercisable*.

The first and major factor to be remembered is that motor dexterity is very closely *related to the functioning of the brain cortex*. These brain areas are the youngest in the history of brain development, and they are, so to speak, soaked with the ability to absorb one's individual life experience. The most characteristic feature of all the functions controlled by the brain cortex is their ability to develop, to exercise, and to strive for perfection. The highest forms of switch-ability, which do not require many repetitions but occur quickly and confidently at the first attempt, are related to the functioning of the brain cortex, which has made them possible.

Moreover, dexterity is a *complex activity*. We have seen that it requires the collaborative activity of at least two levels of motor control. Each level comprises sensory and motor brain devices. Furthermore, we have established that at least two types of dexterity must be distinguished—body and hand dexterity—which, in turn, are based on different brain systems.

The situation would be different if we were discussing a strictly confined, simple phenomenon, for example, a knee jerk (the thrusting of a leg that occurs when the leg is tapped under the patella). If the small area of the brain that controls this reflex is intact, the reflex is normal. If this area is underdeveloped, for some reason, the reflex will be absent. Reflexes of this kind are rightfully called inborn. However, when we are discussing a very complex capacity which is served by virtually all the brain, all its sensory, motor, and coordinating systems, an inborn deficit of this capacity would mean the underdevelopment of virtually all the brain systems. People with underdeveloped brains, so-called idiots or imbeciles, indeed have very low dexterity, but we are not speaking about them now. Each human with a normally developed brain has all the necessary pre-requisites for displaying natural dexterity, although different people may exhibit it to different degrees.

Thus, motor dexterity, as with all the complex types of brain activity, is indisputably a capacity that can be developed and trained, and the differences between people are simply quantitative.[3] One may say that some people have better abilities to develop dexterity, whereas others have worse abilities. This statement does not contradict the general statement that dexterity is exercisable. There is no question that any person can learn English. The fact that some

---

[3]One should note here, for comparison, another similarly complex psychophysical capacity, endurance, which has a high potential for development and training and which is not being questioned.

people can do so more easily and can reach higher levels of proficiency than others does not mean that one is born with knowledge of English.

As far as individual abilities of acquiring dexterity are concerned, remember that there are *different profiles or types* of these abilities. One person can more easily develop *body dexterity*, whereas another may be better suited for developing *hand dexterity*. These different profiles are inborn. Dexterity can be developed and trained in anybody, but it is not the case that *each type of dexterity can be trained to an equal degree* in all persons.

By approaching the question of how to develop and train dexterity, we shall see the value of our previous analysis of the main features of dexterity. Indeed, if you have only a vague idea about a subject, you do not know how to handle it. Now we know (in an expanded way) which features should be present in movements for them to be called dexterous, and it is much easier to approach the problem of their perfection.

The basic features of dexterity, which are reflected in its expanded definition, have very different psychophysiological bases and, therefore, should be trained differently. One approach is appropriate for developing movement precision and expediency; another one is good for training quickness. Moreover, it is always necessary to take into account the particular, individual characteristics of a trained person. Thus, one must be very cautious in forming general rules and recipes.

It is possible to say with certainty that each new, well-mastered skill adds to the general level of dexterity. *Dexterity accumulates with motor experience.* This experience enriches both the libraries of the lower levels of control and those funds of resourcefulness, versatility, and initiative, which form the nucleus of dexterity. It is especially fruitful to master different motor skills which complement each other.

Previously in this essay, we talked about two factors that were not included as basic features of dexterity but that indicate *conditions* that are necessary for exhibiting dexterity. Their general meaning is that dexterity is not confined within the movements or actions themselves but is revealed in *how these movements behave in their interaction with the environment*, with its unexpectednesses and surprises. Let us imagine that we had made a precise photographic recording of a movement from which all the images of surrounding objects have been removed so that there is just a person on an empty background. With such a photo, one could never say whether the movement was dexterous or not.

This fact alone makes important suggestions of how and where to look for dexterity. It is quite obvious that because dexterity is not a property of movements themselves, it will not develop if one exercises and attends only to movements, unrelated to the environment. Each movement that is supposed to enrich dexterity should *do something*. Dexterity will not gain anything from any movements that do not have an objective, although they may improve endurance, muscle force, and so on. One needs to do much to be able *to do it*; one needs *to be skilled* in many different things to be considered dexterous.

As far as *body dexterity* is concerned, one may expect its improvement from movements leading to a certain result or overcoming external obstacles or perturbations. I would not consider myself dexterous if I were afraid of gymnastic bars, rings, or hurdles; I would be dexterous when they started being afraid of me.

Movements that increase *hand or object dexterity* are always skills. It is impossible to name a skill controlled from Level D that would not be possible to train to very high levels of dexterity. It is possible to be dexterous in any sport; dexterity is required in all types of wrestling; one can be dexterous in any professional skill; finally, one can dexterously dress, button, brush hair, launder, and peel cucumbers. In each of these actions, from the most refined to the very common, dexterity is nurtured and better exercised when more deliberate variations and unexpected obstacles take place.

In all the exercises, it is certainly desirable and even necessary to stress separately each of the major features that we have decided to include in the expanded definition of dexterity.

For each motor skill, the *correctness of movements* (earlier described as movement adequacy and accuracy) must be developed *from the very first steps*. At this particular time, the motor composition of a skill is being created. At this particular time, the most appropriate sensory corrections are being chosen. At this particular time, conscious attention is still able to interfere with the detailing of movements that will later escape into the area of automatisms. Therefore, a careless attitude toward the quality of the movements during the first steps is the worst possible mistake. When a movement can barely be performed, one may be lenient toward speed and perhaps also toward force but never toward accuracy and adequacy. Otherwise, these qualitative errors become so deeply embedded that eliminating them is virtually impossible. If correct execution of a movement with respect to the desired result (see earlier in this essay) is very difficult at the first stages, this is not a problem. It is better to exhaust oneself in 10 minutes by an enormous strain of concentration and will that leads to the required result than to spend 2–3 hours practicing a less-than-correct execution, on "somehow" and "why not." Leave indifference to the dogs undergoing the elaboration of conditioned salivation reflexes.

Let us also take into account the following. Those corrections that control movement correctness belong mostly to the leading level because they are very closely related to movement success or failure with respect to the essence of a motor task. Automatization takes some of the corrections of accuracy and adequacy away from consciousness; those are corrections mainly dealing with the technical means of achieving the result. However, the most important, crucial corrections of this kind remain at the upper level. The responsibility for these corrections cannot be delegated to automatisms because they are required to provide the highest degree of adaptability and maneuverability.

Consequently, one must concentrate one's whole attention and will on the quality of the movement outcome not only at the beginning of training a skill but also during its later phases, when the skill is "perfect" (however, will it ever be possible to say that perfection has been reached?). One must think not only about the movements themselves (in order not to get into trouble like the centipede from the fable) but also about the essence of the task: to jump as far as possible, to draw a line as neatly as possible, to hit a tennis ball as close in a desired direction as possible, to cut something as accurately as possible, to wrap a chocolate bar or a dress shirt as accurately as possible, and so on. One must concentrate on the whats of the movements; the hows will come later by themselves.

Movement accuracy typically exhibits very wide areas of transfer typical for the level of accuracy (C2). Elaborating and improving the accuracy of one skill leads to the noticeable improvement with respect to a variety of other skills. Therefore, for developing dexterity, it is very important for one to exercise the ability to judge by eye, to practice muscular-articular judgement of dimensions and distances, and so forth. All these abilities later spread over various other skills and impart them with brilliance, like an oil film spreads on water.

Quickness, as an essential feature of dexterity, is somewhat different from all the others because it is not an independent feature. It can hardly be separated from *movement expediency*. However, out of two movements, more dexterity will be assigned to the quicker one. Although expedient movements, deprived of any nonessential elements, can always be unhurried, any expediency, certainly, becomes worthless if the work is being done listlessly.

Therefore, quickness is worth spending one's time on, and it may lead to considerable improvement.

Experience shows that one can decrease the time of even a very simple, semiautomatic motor reaction to an external stimulus (nearly a reflex). Apparently, the speed of more complex reactions can be increased as well. In such reactions, it is sometimes possible not just to increase speed quantitatively but to find a shortcut which requires less time. And there emerges even more potential for improving quickness.

Once again, we can make use of the ability *to anticipate*. The more experience we have, the higher is our ability *to feel in advance* the approach of an external event that might require reaction. In such conditions, reaction can become literally as quick as lightning. Our reactive action starts simultaneously with its cause or even *prior to the cause*. It is not necessary to explain the importance of such lightninglike, anticipatory reactions in a battle, for example, in hand-to-hand combat or in a jet fight. Such reactions may also predetermine victory in boxing or fencing.

The quickness of achieving the result, which is so important for dexterity, also heavily depends on the ability to make rapid, adroit movements; nevertheless, the best sprinters are frequently not the most dexterous persons in the world. For dexterity, it is much more important to possess what one might call *psychological dexterity*: quick-wittedness, resolution, reaction, and so on. Therefore, this aspect must be stressed in the development of dexterity. If an individual is typically inert, sluggish, or irresolute, that is, can be characterized as a dawdler or bumbler, no elaboration and practice of movements by themselves will be able to make that person dexterous. It is impossible to suggest a universal prescription for these negative features, but they are certainly, to a large extent, remediable. One must simply pay serious attention to them, and the sooner the better.

Movement *rationality* is a necessary condition for dexterity but, in contrast to the first two aspects, *it is not a general feature*. One can practice correctness, accuracy, and quickness in general, using their typical ability of generalized transfer; *movement rationality is inseparable from the movements themselves* and is not easily transferable. Consequently, one must develop it separately for each separate motor skill.

In contrast to correctness, the *rationality and expediency* of movements are perfected and polished mostly during the second part of skill development, *at the stages of the movement's standardization and stabilization*. Certainly in locomotor skills or, even more frequently, in object skills, much of their movement composition can be rationalized at the beginning of skill development. At this time, excessive movements can be reduced or eliminated, more appropriate and expedient motor acts can be found, and so on. However, the most important and deepest perfection of movements in this direction occurs after the stage of automatization, when all the corrections have already found their place and the movements are able to resist any changes or perturbing influences. At this time, it is hardly possible to interfere with the subconscious functioning of the lower levels; moreover, it hardly makes sense. On the other hand, pedagogical experience suggests that if the movements are performed carefully and appropriately and persistently perfected and polished during practice, the lower levels obtain the most favorable conditions for improving the rationality and expediency of the automatisms and, consequently, of the movements themselves.

Obviously, the importance of all these features fades when compared to the importance of *resourcefulness*—the nucleus of motor dexterity. Resourcefulness holds the record with regard to the number of superstitions concerning its inborn nature and the impossibility of exercising it. Undoubtedly there are people who are extremely quick-witted compared to others, whether this is an inborn feature or has been developed during the first years of life. However, even if one can speak about the different ability of different people with respect to resourcefulness, this difference does not mean that resourcefulness is not exercisable. On the contrary, we know (and this follows from all the previously discussed analyses) that *movement resourcefulness stands in a direct relation to accumulated motor experience*. Such experience in different kinds of skills and, more important, in different external conditions, directly affect the development of versatility and even of initiative. Teachers and coaches who purposefully force their students to encounter various deviations and complications during the second stage of a skill development act most optimally. Such exercises with the unexpected gradually transform for a student into exercises with anticipation and strengthen him or her more and more with respect to the most important core of movement dexterity.

From the Author

There is still much confusion in the understanding of dexterity in both its psychological and pedagogical aspects. None of the previously proposed definitions of this capacity has been able to win general acceptance. There is also an extreme shortage of facts from everyday observations and, even more so, from experiments.

During the past years, the general physiology and psychophysiology of movements have attained considerable success, which is due partly to the studies of athletic and gymnastic movements as the most perfect examples of healthy movements, and, on the other hand, to the studies of motor pathologies based on the abundant information on soldiers wounded during the Great Patriotic War (World War II). So, it seemed reasonable to try to move forward in the area of motor dexterity and its development based on the new concepts that have emerged in this area. As far as the general problems of motor coordination are concerned, we refer our readers to the book *On the Construction of Movements*, in which these problems have been carefully examined. Here, let us present only a brief summary from that work of the most important, basic ideas that are crucial for analyzing *dexterity*.

According to contemporary views, any mobile system, which is not forced to follow a fixed trajectory (like most existing machines), that is, which has more than one degree of freedom, needs a special organization that makes it *controllable*. The peripheral human skeletal-articular-muscular apparatus has numerous redundant degrees of freedom, numbering many dozens. The totality of the psychophysiological mechanisms of *motor coordination* represents the *organization of* control of this *peripheral apparatus* achieved by *overcoming its redundant degrees of freedom*.

Motor coordination is realized with the help of so-called *sensory corrections*, that is, the processes of continuous correction of movement based on information conveyed to the central nervous system from the sensory organs. In addition to perceiving impressions from the outside world (*exteroception*), all the receptor systems of the body carry the additional responsibility of perceiving the postures, movements, and efforts of the body and its parts, that is, *proprioception*, in its expanded or functional meaning. Certainly, the primary role in this complex receptor activity is played by proprioceptors in the narrow sense, that is, as the apparatus of articular-muscular sensitivity.

During the long millenia of animal evolution, there was a continuous complication and diversification of motor tasks, whose solution was vital in the struggle for survival. This complication of motor tasks was directed along three major lines: an increase in complexity of their meaning; an increase in complexity and accuracy of the required motor acts; and a continuous increase in the number of unexpected, unusual motor tasks, which had to be solved quickly and adequately.

The process of evolutionary adjustment to these requirements of life was expressed among the vertebrates as dialectical leaps, which occurred from time to time and which led to the anatomical complication of the central nervous system, namely, the emergence of new brain systems, which were more and more powerful in the emphasized directions. These younger structures, which had been born in this way, did not reject or eliminate the older ones but rather put them under control, thus forming a new, more productive and versatile synthesis. Each of these brain systems, which emerged during evolution, brought with it a new set or contingent of movements, or more precisely, a new set of motor tasks that could be mastered by the animal. We call these "coordination levels" or "levels of the construction of movements."

The motor-coordination organization of the human brain is the most complicated and perfect structure among living creatures. It has preserved the historically (evolutionary) evolved multilayered structure in which each of the levels of different ages assures the correct realization of its motor acts and, as we are going to see, essentially participates in the realization of movements controlled at the higher, younger levels by providing their coherency, quickness, and expediency. Each of these levels is characterized by its own particular anatomical brain substrate and by a specific composition and structure of its sensory systems, which provide sensory corrections (the so-called *sensory synthesis* or *sensory field*).

The increasing complexity of motor tasks, which were to be solved by the relatively slowly developing peripheral motor apparatus, naturally led to *an increase in the complexity and requirements of the purely coordinative abilities* of the controlling system. Motor acts that were more complex, accurate, quick, or that required precise force control required more and more diverse, precise, and adequate sensory corrections. None of the levels had enough resources in its own sensory synthesis to control all of the variety of the coordinative aspects of movements. As a result, more and more motor acts with a complex coordinational structure emerged. Control of such acts could not be concentrated at one level, so the higher levels were forced to solicit help from the lower, more ancient levels. The level that could embrace the essence of the motor problem in general took over supreme control of the corresponding motor acts and their most essential corrections. At the same time, more and more responsibility for auxiliary, technical corrections, which assured movement smoothness, quickness, and expediency, were delegated by the central nervous system to the lower levels that were best equipped for exactly these types of corrections. We use the term *leading level* to denote the supreme level for a motor act and the terms *background levels* and *background corrections* for the lower, subordinate levels and their corrections.

One should stress two major characteristics of background corrections: Background levels of coordination do not function independently, as when they play a leading role, but in a modified fashion, flexibly adjusting to the supreme leading level. Background corrections are not movements or parts of the movements but sensory corrections, playing an auxiliary role.

Clearly, motor acts with a background coordination represent *whole structures*, involving the highest levels and reaching, in highly organized beings, high levels of complexity. Consequently, they must be *gradually constructed*. Indeed, none of the background corrections are inborn, and, therefore, they must be developed by the organism. Moreover, perfect concordance in functioning of two or more levels requires a stage of mutual adjustment.

Directly related to this development is the phylogenetic emergence and parallel development of two features: two- and multilevel *coordinative structures* of motor acts; and individual exercisability, that is, the ability to develop new forms of movements during the lifetime, a feature totally absent at the earlier stages of development of vertebrates. Thus, one may say that each background motor structure represents a motor skill developed during the lifetime.[1]

We classify coordinative background corrections into two major categories: Background corrections of the first type represent whole complexes of corrections corresponding to an independent, meaningful movement at a given lower level. Background corrections of the second type are called *automatisms*. These are special corrections, at one of the lower levels, that *cannot control a whole movement at their level*, that do not have by themselves a meaning, and that are developed only in response to the particular requests of a higher level for technical support

---

[1]A kind of exception to this rule is a rather wide group of motor skills that can be observed in many animals and are called *motor instincts*. They are found at all the stages of evolution and range from very low instincts (building of honeycombs by bees, etc.) to rather high ones (e.g., a foal's ability to walk and run several minutes after its birth). These motor instincts are clearly different from the structures that we call motor skills, because of their inborn nature and their total lack of adaptive flexibility and variability. The physiological nature of these structures, which apparently have very complex background organization, is far from clear.

of a motor act. Such automatisms include, in particular, various technical knacks ("skills" in the English language), which are widely represented in professional skills in both labor and sports.

These background corrections are termed automatisms because of a very general and typical feature of the central nervous system: In each multilevel motor structure, human consciousness reaches only the subcomponents of the highest (leading) level, irrespective of its absololute position. Therefore, *all the automatisms are always carried out subconsciously.* Background corrections, which are consciously perceived when representing an independent movement, move out of consciousness when they start playing the role of background corrections.

At the beginning of the process of elaborating a new motor skill, the novice finds a solution for the problem using only one level, the leading level. In the course of practice, he either finds appropriate automatisms in the earlier accumulated funds or purposefully elaborates them and achieves a high level of control over them. Then, he gradually delegates the responsibility for executing various technical corrections, which were originally controlled in a surrogate manner by the leading level, to the corresponding lower levels. This process of gradual transfer of corrections to lower levels, which is accompanied by their removal from the scope of consciousness, is what we call *automatization of a motor act.*

This very important step in creating the background structure for a motor skill results in the following changes: The burden of purely technical work is taken from the leading level and consciousness. A sizable number of corrections are switched to the levels that are best equipped and most adequate for corrections of this particular type, a change leading to a qualitative shift toward movement improvement. These changes usually occur in several separate steps, with each step looking like a leap rather than like a gradual change.

The construction of a motor skill does not end with the completion of all the automated transfers. Then there is a more or less long period of the central nervous system activity whose purpose is to achieve the coordinated functioning of all the levels which participate in the motor task and its unavoidable variations and complications. Thus, this period can be characterized as the *organization of controllability of the background levels by the leading level for a given motor task.* Here, for the second time, we meet the notion of controllability, but now it refers to a different class of phenomena. Earlier, the basic precondition for coordination was the assurance of controllability of the peripheral motor apparatus; now a similar preconditon for real-life movements based on background motor structures is the absolute controllability of all the levels of coordination when they play auxiliary roles. This fact is very important for understanding the physiological mechanisms of motor dexterity.

Accordingly, we define *motor skill as a coordinative structure representing a developed ability to solve a definite type of motor task.*

Two principles are clear: The *construction of a motor skill is an active process* in both its external appearance and in its essence, not a passive submission to an external inflow of impressions and influences. The construction of a motor skill is a meaningful chain action consisting of a number of separate phases that logically follow each other; in other words, it is very far from a purely quantitative, monotonous, gradual "beating a trail."

It is also necessary to emphasize that certainly neither the automatisms providing for a motor skill nor the motor skill itself represent stereotypes, or once-and-forever-remembered templates. There is a typical increase in adaptivity, plasticity, and adequate versatility of the coordinative levels, from the older, lower levels to the higher, younger ones. Naturally, the transfer of a correction from the leading level to one of the lower levels in the course of its automatization leads to a decrease in its adaptive variability. Generally, each automatism and each motor skill are plastic and variable according to the resources of the level that carries them out. Therefore, one should not confuse the positive phenomenon of automatization with the negative phenomenon of forming stereotypic patterns.

This adaptive variability, typical to a different degree of all the automatisms and background corrections, forms the basis of the very important phenomenon of *transfer* of a motor skill; for example, transfer accounts for an improvement in the exercisability of a motor skill A due to the motor experience accumulated during practicing skills B and C. According to contemporary understanding, the mechanism of skill transfer uses memorized background corrections, elaborated earlier for other skills, with some modification or even without it. Apparently, the positive effects of the phenomenon of transfer are greater in cases of wider generalization of previously developed skills and when they are more numerous and diverse.

It is redundant to comment on the enrichment of psychomotor resources gained at the step in evolution when background coordinative structures emerged, bringing with them individual trainability and exercisability. However, the inevitable exacerbation of the struggle for survival posed new requirements, which were met by the formation of adequate motor responses at one of the next steps of evolution. We are here referring to the increasing need to have unique, unlearned motor reactions, in other words, of developing coordinative adaptability that would enable quick solutions to unexpected, nonroutine motor problems. Thus, one may schematically represent the general route of motor evolution as consisting of three consecutive phases. The first phase corresponds to the total absence of individual trainability and the limitation of the motor abilities of an animal by its inborn coordinative forms. At the second phase, these abilities are supplemented by background motor structures which are developed by the animal during its lifetime with gradual practice and construction. Finally, the third phase brings unique, extemporaneous, quickly formed motor reactions to unexpected and unusual problems, which, once again, expand the area of possibilities available for the animal in its struggle for life.

On the basis of these summarized facts and ideas on motor coordination, let us try to elaborate on the psychophysiological analysis of dexterity, which is the main subject of this book.

The basic, most important criterion for deciding whether dexterity is represented in a motor act is that dexterity is not contained in the movements themselves but in their degree of correspondence to the external conditions, in the degree of their success in solving a motor problem. If one makes a movie of a motor act and then erases all the environment, preserving only the body of the actor, no analysis of the remaining image can reveal whether the movement was dexterous or not. This basic feature of dexterity is called *extravertedness* (relation to the external world).

According to our expanded definition (essay 7), *dexterity is the ability to solve a motor problem correctly, quickly, rationally, and resourcefully.* This definition is likely to contain the most significant, characteristic features of dexterity that we are able to isolate now.

According to the existing information, motor acts that can be called dexterous always represent structures *with background levels.* A possible reason for this requirement is the fact that all single-level movements are primitive, and even a meaningfully complicated task can be solved by relatively simple coordinative acts which do not impose apparent requirements on motor dexterity. For example, the task of pointing the way through a maze from an entrance to an exit can be solved even by a person with ataxia; in other words, the task does not require well-developed background levels.

Anyway, in all, or nearly, all the cases, dexterous acts are subserved by at least two levels, a leading level and a background level, and the requirements imposed on the levels are very different. The leading level must have high marks for maneuverability, versatility, and motor resourcefulness; whereas the background level or levels must be, to a similar degree, compliant, flexible, and perfectly controllable. Returning to the basic definition of dexterity, one may say that the leading level provides for the first and last features, *correctness* and *resourcefulness,* whereas the background level or levels provide important conditions for the two middle features, *quickness* and *rationality.*

This structural specificity of dexterous motor acts—the presence of several levels—allows for the classification of all dexterous movements into two major classes, according to the levels of their structure: Dexterous motor acts which are led by the level of spatial field (C) with backgrounds from the lower levels belong to the class of *body dexterity.* Motor acts that are performed at the level of actions (D) with backgrounds from Levels C, B, and A belong to the class of *object or hand dexterity.*

In the monograph *On the Construction of Movements* the urgent problem of identifying individual *psychomotor profiles* is formulated: the problem of qualitative differences in motor control in different persons which depend on the differences in the relative development and perfection of one or more levels of the construction of movements. As far as the subject of this book is concerned, individuals possess very different relative and absolute degrees of development of the two classes of motor dexterity. The analysis of individual dexterity profiles and their definition with adequately developed methods would be of a great practical interest.

Among the enumerated features of dexterity, "first place" in relative importance should certainly be given to *resourcefulness*. The essence of motor dexterity is in the ability to find a solution in any situation, given the presence of the means in the central nervous system for a unique, improvised, and adequate solution to an unexpected or unusual problem. We have assigned this ability to the third, most recent phase of the evolution of motor functions. This feature of dexterity has been termed *extemporaneousness*.

If we now compare the fact that dexterous motor acts represent multilevel structures with the emphasized feature of extemporaneousness, we move more closely toward a complex of facts that expose probably the deepest psychophysiological core of dexterity. Apparently, the impromptu, unprepared creation of a complex, multilevel, and simultaneously adequate structure is possible only when it is based on a very high degree of controllability of the background levels by the leading level. Whereas mediocre psychomotorics requires long-lasting exercise, development, and elaboration of a new coordinative structure, high-level psychomotorics is able to immediately provide harmonious participation of all the levels at once, at the very time when it becomes urgent.

If Mr. A has average psychomotor abilities and is able to perform an automated operation successfully, quickly, and deftly only after prolonged training, whereas Mr. B is able to do the same at the first or second attempt, after only observing the movement, then it is difficult to find a better candidate than Mr. B for being called dexterous. Certainly, if one creates similar exercise conditions for Mr. A and Mr. B, Mr. B will exhibit higher indices of performance during a subsequent functional testing.

So, motor dexterity leads to the same results as exercise, that is, to the development of an adequately and successfully functioning structure. Dexterity can substitute for exercise or accelerate its effects. The opposite is generally not true: In all the numerous situations in which a motor act must be created quickly and unexpectedly, in which there is no time for the gradual development of a substitute, dexterity is indispensable.

The presented analysis of the nature of motor dexterity also leads to an interesting biological conclusion on the evolutionary youth of dexterity. This conclusion is corroborated by the deep and careful observations and analysis of comparative physiology of contemporary animals.

Our preliminary analysis of the psychophysiological structure of dexterity, even in all its incompleteness, allows for the formulation of a well-founded answer to important practical questions: Can dexterity be individually developed? Is it an exercisable capacity?

The answer is positive and multifaceted.

It is obvious that natural, inborn, and constitutional prerequisites for dexterity are and will be as different in different persons as their other psychophysical abilities. If this were not true, scientists would have no trouble in creating a new Znamensky, Ozolin, Novak, or Nina Dumbadze. The attainable individual peaks of development, the degrees of difficulty, and the necessary amount of time for achieving a certain result will inevitably cause great individual variations. It is much more important to state that all the natural prerequisites for dexterity *can be developed*. Both aspects of the structural complex, which give rise to dexterity, can be exercised and developed.

First, it is possible for an individual to considerably improve the controllability of the background levels by the leading levels, one of the most important physiological prerequisites of dexterity. It is easier to perform an extemporaneous multilevel motor act, no matter how unexpected and complex it is, when one has accumulated various background corrections that are diverse both quantitatively and qualitatively and generalized, in other words, when the depth of elaboration and the extent of range of the involved variables are greater.

Second, the purposeful introduction of unexpected and diverse motor problems into a training program requires adequate, quick, rational, and resourceful motor reactions. Such problems directly train and teach the upper, coordinative levels and, thereby, promote the elaboration of maneuverability, adaptability, versatility, and quick psychomotor inventiveness. At the same time, training at the upper level inevitably develops controllability of the background levels. It is not enough, certainly, to accumulate a wealth of background corrections at the lower levels if one cannot quickly and adequately use them. This ability to select appropriate background corrections at appropriate times and confidently control them can be substantially improved with practice.

This is the general material we have discussed in this book. Undoubtedly, the practical problem of developing and elaborating dexterity as well as the whole area of psychophysiology of movements and their control are at the very early stages of their development. This fascinating and extremely important area can move us closer to the deepest, concealed caches of knowledge about the human brain and its functioning. We are convinced that, in this area, Soviet science will one day take the first place in the world.

Part II

COMMENTARIES

N. A. Bernstein:
The Reformer of Neuroscience

I. M. Feigenberg
Jerusalem, Israel

L. P. Latash
Chicago, Illinois

Habent sua fata libelli ("Books have their own fate"), just like their authors. In both cases, an individual fate reflects the epoch, the social situation, and, in general, what is called the spirit of the times. The book by N. A. Bernstein *On Dexterity and Its Development* has its own fate, one resembling the fate of its author. Both were hard and dramatic, nearly driving the book and the author to the edge of annihilation, a fate similar to that of many people in Russia (Union of Soviet Socialist Republics) in the middle of this century. A great Russian writer, Mikhail Bulgakov, said, "Manuscripts do not burn." However, manuscripts and books did burn in the 20th century, both in Germany and in Russia. This book was lucky—it did not burn to ashes. More precisely, we are lucky to be able to read it.

We are going to describe briefly the biography of *On Dexterity*, the biography of its author, and the biography of some of his ideas. So, this chapter consists of three circles. There will certainly be intersections of the circles because some of the material is relevant to two or even to all three of the biographies. However, at each of these intersections, we try not to repeat the facts but to present their new meaning with respect to the book, its author, or his ideas.

N. A. BERNSTEIN IN POSTWAR RUSSIA

Let us move half a century back, to Moscow of the middle 1940s, when the manuscript of this book rested on the desk of its author. The time was just after the end of 4 years of exhausting war with Nazi Germany and its allies. Despite the hardships and heavy losses, the people were happy that the war had been won. There was a general feeling that a brighter period of life was starting.

The war had scattered the people all around the country. Nicholai Aleksandrovich Bernstein found himself torn from his prewar laboratories, far away in cold Siberia. The members of his family were starving. A witness (Prof. I. S. Kandror) recalled later that he had seen Nicholai Aleksandrovich collecting into a can for his family the leftovers off the plates in a communal dining room. At that time, there was not much left on the plates.

After some time, Bernstein's brother invited Nicholai Aleksandrovich and his family to stay with him in Middle Asia. There, the conditions were somewhat better. However, there were no chances to continue scientific work. In order to obtain at least some income and a ration card, Nicholai Aleksandrovich worked outside his area of expertise. And at home, he compiled a five-digit table of logarithms, just for fun.

After returning to Moscow, N. A. Bernstein became the head of the Biomechanics Laboratory in the Central Scientific Institute of Physical Culture. The members of the laboratory shared the general optimism in the country. The small group worked ardently, with energy and enthusiasm. While preparing for the 1946 New Year's party (the first postwar New Year!), Nicholai Aleksandrovich wrote the following verses for his colleagues:

Will you solve this problem under the forty-sixth star,
Or will you be scared of the ultimate fun:
Is the brain or the muscle the ruling Tzar
When you jump, walk, and run?

These four lines are characteristic of the upbeat, enthusiastic atmosphere in Bernstein's laboratory. They were running experiments. Nicholai Aleksandrovich was finishing his book, On the Construction of Movements (1947), which summarized his prewar studies. During the evenings and nights, at home, when the members of his family and their neighbors, sharing the communal apartment, quieted down, Nicholai Aleksandrovich was writing a new book targeted at a very wide audience—On Dexterity and Its Development.

The conditions of life and work were suboptimal, to say the least. Both laboratory and family budgets were meager. There was not enough paper, and Nicholai Aleksandrovich wrote on the back of old, expired photographic paper. This paper had spent the whole war in the abandoned laboratory. However, it soon became clear that there was not enough paper anyway, so Bernstein wrote on both sides. There were no margins—paper was too precious. At the top of each page, Nicholai Aleksandrovich wrote the date: We can see now that his work did not stop during the holidays.

On the Construction of Movements (1947) was finished first and sent to the publishing house Meditsina ("Medicine"). On Dexterity was prepared for the publishing house Fizkultura i Sport ("Physical Culture and Sport"), which had offered a contract for the book. An advance had already been paid to the author and was spent on a watch for Tanya, the stepdaughter of Nicholai Aleksandrovich, who was very proud of this first watch in her life, a rarity for a professor's daughter in Russia at that time.

Three thousand paperback copies of *On the Construction of Movements* (1947) were published on crude, yellowish paper. It had been eagerly expected by numerous physicians who were trying to correct motor deficits in the veterans wounded during the war. The book was a huge success. The Institute of Neurology of the U.S.S.R. Academy of Medical Sciences, headed at that time by Prof. Nicholai Ivanovich Propper–Grastchenkov, nominated the book for the Stalin Award, the highest award in science, literature, and art. Bernstein received the award.

The "Stateless Cosmopolite"

The book *On Dexterity* was finished and submitted to Fizkultura i Sport. The proofs were ready. At that time, the atmosphere within the country started to change rapidly. The postwar excitement was replaced by a national pseudopatriotism, and references to foreign authors in scientific books and dissertations were considered "adoration of the West." A wave of state anti-Semitism rose. The word *cosmopolite* ("citizen of the world") became a curse equivalent to the old Russian *zhid* ("kike"). The expression, "stateless cosmopolite," was usually used with respect to Jews. Jews had trouble trying to find jobs and entering a graduate school or a university. At the same time, everything Russian was praised above and beyond limits, both in art and in science. A graduate student could frequently hear the criticism, "Half of your references are to foreign authors!" In order to obtain a foreign scientific journal in a library, one had to bring a special request from a university explaining that the journal was necessary for scientific work and that the university guaranteed that the journal would be "properly" used by the reader.

Professor Bernstein also became a stateless cosmopolite. Prof. A. N. Krestovnikov wrote in an article entitled "On the Vicious Foundation" (the journal "Theory and Practice in Physical Culture," issue #5, 1949):

> Bernstein violated the principles of the [communist] party's approach and historical perspective. . . . vulgarized and perverted . . . displayed adoration of foreign scientists . . . neglected the importance of the works by I. P. Pavlov . . . pours water on the mill of foreign physiologists. . . . His works are . . . mechanistic and idealistic . . . characterize the antipatriotic essence of his scientific views.

The same journal (issue #4, 1949) published an editorial article against Bernstein entitled "Antipatriotic Statements," an article by S. G. Strashkevich (issue #6, 1950) entitled "The False Scientific Theory (A Critique of the 'Theory' by N. A.

Bernstein)," and another editorial article, "Idealistic Fabrications" (issue #12, 1950). This choir was joined by *Pravda*, the official paper of the U.S.S.R. communist party. Anything written in *Pravda* was supposed to be accepted by everyone not only as ultimate truth but also as an instruction for action. On August 21, 1950, P. Zhukov and A. Kozhin wrote in an article in *Pravda*,

> Bernstein bows in front of many bourgeois scientists. Using the names of the reactionary Sherrington and other foreign physiologists . . . Bernstein impudently slanders Pavlov. . . . Bernstein's "inventions" are examples of naked biologization and mechanicism. . . . The confused anti-Pavlovian preachings of Bernstein directly harm the physical culture.

A person attacked in *Pravda* could expect the worst, including an arrest. KGB (Komitet Gosudarstvennoy Bezopasnosti, Committee of State Security) representatives in the personnel departments were vigilant not to miss such an "instruction for action." Bernstein was fired; all of his laboratories were closed. The director of the Central Scientific Institute of Physical Culture himself smashed, with a hammer, the glass plates on the doors with the inscriptions "Biomechanics Laboratory" and "Professor N. A. Bernstein."

Bernstein was out of work. However, the last statement is not exactly correct. During those times, one of Bernstein's friends asked him, "Nicholai Aleksandrovich, you are not working, are you?" "On the contrary," answered Bernstein, "I always work. I am not employed." Actually, Bernstein was prevented from performing experimental studies (and he was a great experimenter!). He did not receive a salary, but he continued to work at his desk at home and created the "physiology of activity."

One of his friends once mentioned: "What terrible times we are living in!" Nicholai Aleksandrovich disagreed: "Oh no, the times are fantastic. All the people are as if they were dipped into a developing solution; you can immediately see who is who!" This was a very precise statement. Actually, after the article in *Pravda* was published, some of the closest colleagues were afraid to say hello when they met Bernstein in the streets of Moscow. On the other hand, a famous author of books for children, Korney Chukovsky, who had not met Bernstein before, visited Bernstein at his home just to shake his hand.

The Return of the Book

But let us return to the book *On Dexterity and Its Development*. The instructions "from above" were obligatory for the publishing house Fizkultura i Sport as well. The book was already far into production, the proofs were printed out, and Bernstein had received a part of the honorarium. However, the publishers could not risk publishing a book by such an ill-famed author. They preferred to lose money. Therefore, the first typesetting of the book was destroyed. It seemed as if the book were forgotten, even by those few who knew about its existence.

Even Nicholai Aleksandrovich himself never mentioned this book when talking to his colleagues, as if the book never existed.

Many years later, after Bernstein had died, I. M. Feigenberg (one of this chapter's authors) browsed through the dusty bookshelves in the room Nicholai Aleksandrovich had lived in. His stepdaughter, T. I. Pavlova, had given him permission to take and read whatever looked interesting. On the very top, just below the ceiling, I. M. Feigenberg found a dusty plastic bag containing sheets of exposed photographic paper covered with the familiar handwriting. The sheets were bound with a cardboard cover; the cardboard sheets were cut from the box that had originally contained the photographic paper. The same hand had written on the cover—"N. A. Bernstein. On Dexterity and Its Development." It was obvious that the cover had been made by the same hand. The discovery seemed impossible: In the libraries, we had never encountered bibliographic cards with this title. I. M. Feigenberg asked T. I. Pavlova what was in this bag.

"Some scratch paper."

"Is there a book in the apartment by the same name?"

"Yes, I remember it was somewhere around here. My watch was bought with the honorarium."

However, there was no such book on the shelves. T. I. Pavlova allowed I. M. Feigenberg to take the bag with its contents. She was planning to move into another apartment, and all the old papers were to be thrown out. Back at home, I. M. Feigenberg read the sheets and understood that it was imperative to publish the book.

I. M. Feigenberg recalled a past conversation with Nicholai Aleksandrovich. Both authors of this chapter frequently walked in the area of Zubov square in Moscow, where I. M. Feigenberg lived and L. P. Latash worked. On that day, Bernstein and Feigenberg had talked about different things. At some point, they started talking about the fact that Bernstein's works were hard to read and understand for the wide audience of physicians, teachers of physical culture, and even university professors of biology. I. M. Feigenberg suggested to Nicholai Aleksandrovich that it was necessary to write a popular book, understandable for the wide audience of specialists in different areas as well as for students, a book that would contain a description of Bernstein's studies and major conclusions in a clear and entertaining way. "I think you are right," replied Bernstein. "So, let us write such a book together."

Soon, Nicholai Aleksandrovich reviewed and approved the plan for the book and introduced some corrections, but he never mentioned that he had actually already written a popular book. Moreover, neither of us heard a word about this book from his friends and colleagues. It seemed as if the book had not existed at all! So, I. M. Feigenberg started to write a new book. Progress was slow, and at one point, the work on this project nearly stopped. It appeared that there was plenty of time ahead, and everyday problems forced I. M. Feigenberg to postpone the work on the book. At approximately the same time, Bernstein suggested to L. P. Latash that he write a syllabus on neurophysiology that would encompass all the contemporary findings based on the ideas of Bernstein.

Nicholai Aleksandrovich did not try to hurry us because he was busy creating the "physiology of activity." And he himself was in a hurry. Being a physician, he knew that the remaining years of his life were limited to a small number. We did not know this. The death of Nicholai Aleksandrovich Bernstein struck us like thunder in the midst of a seemingly sunny day. After his death, writing alone a book conceived together did not seem right or even possible to Feigenberg. Latash partially realized his plans in the book *Hypothalamus, Adaptive Activity, and the Electroencephalogram* published in 1968, 2 years after Bernstein had died. So, after finding the book *On Dexterity*, Feigenberg realized his obligation to have it published.

However, it was very hard to "push" the book through the bureaucracy of the publishing house. Note that it was a scientific book, written about 40 years earlier, by an author who had recently died as an "unrepentant anti-Pavlovian." Later, it became possible, with the support of an academician, Prof. O. G. Gazenko, to publish the main works by Bernstein in one of the most prestigious publications, the series *The Classics of Science* (Bernstein, 1990). Then, I. M. Feigenberg returned once again to the precious sheets of old photographic paper. The publication of Bernstein's works in *The Classics of Science* in effect made Bernstein one of the "classics." Now, the publishing house Fizkultura i Sport (the same one that many years ago had aborted the production of the book!) received, not an obsolete manuscript, but a never-before-published book by a classic of science. This was an entirely different matter!

By another turn of pure fate, one of the old employees of the publishing house had long ago saved a copy of the proofs of *On Dexterity*—with Bernstein's corrections on the margins. Now, it became possible to incorporate these corrections and, although this looked virtually unbelievable, to restore the original illustrations that Nicholai Aleksandrovich had wanted to see in the book. Not all the figures could be restored; the poor quality of the paper used for the proofs made many of the photographs impossible to reproduce. However, in the archives, we found other photographs of the same athletes, which could be used to replace the originals without losing the meaning. Only one photograph was added that had not been in the original manuscript—the photographic portrait of Nicholai Aleksandrovich Bernstein.

Eventually the book was published. The work on the manuscript was finished. Our own lives were on the verge of major changes (emigration) that could endanger the safety of the manuscript, and, in general, keeping this manuscript in private hands seemed too insecure. The manuscript could be important for someone in the future who would decide to study Bernstein's works. So, Feigenberg took the manuscript to the Department of Manuscripts of the U.S.S.R.

Lenin State Library. He explained to the librarians what the manuscript, its author, and its role in the history of science were. The librarians promised that the manuscript, among other materials, would be preserved, and that a Bernstein Foundation would be created. We hoped, despite all the troubles in Moscow, that this promise would be kept.

The biography of the book continued. While these words were being written by I. M. Feigenberg in Jerusalem and by L. P. Latash in Chicago, an English translation of the book was being prepared for publication.

One More Unpublished Book!

The previous section was a brief story about the fate of *On Dexterity*, which had balanced on the verge of annihilation and oblivion. Moreover, this was not the only book by Bernstein whose production was aborted after the proofs had been received by the author. The same happened with another Bernstein book, *Contemporary Studies in the Physiology of the Nervous Process*. However, the production of this book was aborted, not against Bernstein's will, but on his own command. In this book, Bernstein had strongly criticized Ivan Petrovich Pavlov's theory on higher nervous activity and conditioned reflexes. In 1936, while the manuscript was being prepared for publication, Pavlov died. At that very time, Bernstein had received the proofs. He considered it impossible to argue with a rival who had died and who could not reply to the criticisms. So, despite the fact that the publishing house would sustain considerable losses, Nicholai Aleksandrovich insisted that the production of the book be stopped.

Such a tactful and respectful attitude toward a scientific "adversary" was typical for Nicholai Aleksandrovich. On the other hand, the death of a scientist must not hinder the further development of science, so Bernstein always felt uneasy toward this book. Much later, in the mid-1960s, Nicholai Aleksandrovich was asked about the possibility of publishing the book. He refused. He said that during his remaining time, he had other, newer things to do. "And then," said Bernstein, "if you still want it, you may go ahead and publish that old book." Alas! Due to a number of factors, *Contemporary Studies in the Physiology of the Nervous Process* has not been published yet. We still hope that this book will find its publisher.

BRIEF BIOGRAPHICAL NOTES

The Early Years

Nicholai Aleksandrovich Bernstein was born in 1896 in Moscow, to the family of the famous psychiatrist, Alexander Nicholaevich Bernstein. This was a very gifted and hardworking family. Alexander Bernstein worked in the clinic of another outstanding psychiatrist, Prof. S. S. Korsakov. Bernstein's interests expanded far beyond narrow professional activity. In particular, he was interested in very different problems of natural history and cultural history. He liked music very much, and the home of young Nicholai Aleksandrovich was frequently visited by famous musicians of that time. As a child, Nicholai Aleksandrovich played the piano along with well-known professional musicians. The music of A. Skriabin was particularly popular in the Bernstein family.

Before having children, Bernstein's mother had worked as a nurse in a psychiatric clinic. Afterwards, she concentrated her attentions on the family and on the upbringing of her children. She did not know foreign languages but understood their importance and arranged a broad education for her sons. Her hands were quick and skillful. Perhaps, they gave the first impetus to her elder son to think about dexterity. His own hands were also very "smart": He built steam engines and trains out of tin cans and took photos with the primitive equipment of the beginning of the 20th century. When he became a scientist, he himself designed and assembled very sophisticated equipment for his studies.

His father's brother, Sergey Natanovich Bernstein, was a talented mathematician. He studied at the Sorbonne in Paris, as many Jews did because of the official 3% acceptance limit for Jews who wanted to study in Russian universities. Soon after graduation, he solved one of the famous Hilbert problems,[1] and after the revolution in 1917, became an academician, one of the leaders in Russian mathematics.

Thus, as a youngster, Nicholai Aleksandrovich Bernstein lived in an atmosphere of intellectual creativity and bubbling scientific activity. This style of life had deep roots in the family history. The paternal grandfather of Nicholai Aleksandrovich, Natan Osipovich Bernstein, was a famous physician in Odessa (a port city in the Ukraine). When Odessa University was founded, he became a *dozent* ("associate professor"), teaching human anatomy and physiology. This was during the short period in Russian history when a Jew could occupy a dozent position; in a few years, Natan Osipovich was fired from Odessa University. Natan Osipovich was also active in cultural life. He was one of the editors and authors of the magazine *Zion*, the goal of which was to educate the Russian Jews on Western European culture and the ideology of Zionism. Natan Osipovich died several years before Nicholai Aleksandrovich was born. However, his influence on the family and on the development of young Nicholai is obvious. Personality starts to develop well before physical birth, and all humans carry the seeds of the personalities of those who will live after them, whom they shall never meet. When I. M. Feigenberg was searching for documents in the Odessa University archives, he unexpectedly saw sheets of paper covered with very familiar handwriting. The handwritings of the grandfather and the grandson, who had never known each other, were hardly distinguishable.

If we moved even deeper into the past of the Bernstein family, our readers would meet many outstandingly active and creative persons, rabbis and traders

---

[1]David Hilbert (1862–1943) was a great German mathematician.

who left their marks on the history of culture. However, let us now move forward rather than backward.

The Researcher

Nicholai Aleksandrovich Bernstein graduated from one of the best Moscow gymnasia and entered the Medical Department of the Moscow Imperial University. After graduation in 1919, he worked as a physician in the Red Army, which, at that time, was fighting the Civil War.[2] In 1922, soon after demobilization, Bernstein became the head of the newly organized Biomechanics Laboratory in the Central Institute of Labor (CIL).

The CIL was organized by A. Gastev, a worker and an idealist-revolutionary who was inflamed with the idea of reorganizing physical labor, of making it exciting and productive rather than monotonous and exhausting. Gastev was one of those idealists who dreamed about such a reorganization of human life after the 1917 revolution and was ready to sacrifice anything, including his own life, for this dream. Unfortunately, people like Gastev did not last long. In the 1930s, they were exterminated by the Stalinist reign of terror. Gastev, too, perished. Even the date of his execution is unknown; most of those who entered Stalin's camps disappeared without a trace. However, in the beginning of the 1920s, when Bernstein joined the CIL, the Institute was basking in Utopian hopes.

When young Bernstein entered this upbeat atmosphere, he started to study the simplest element of labor movements: hitting a chisel with a hammer. This study delivered the first blow to the euphoria in Bernstein's soul. Gastev wanted quick results, direct recommendations for the workers on how to direct the hit to the chisel. Bernstein, however, realized that a serious study of the biomechanics of hitting was impossible until the knowledge of the basic principles of brain functioning was expanded. We remind the reader of Bernstein's words, written in the mid-1940s and quoted at the beginning of this chapter: "Is the brain or the muscle the ruling Czar, when you jump, walk, or run?"

Bernstein and Gastev took different routes. Bernstein left the CIL and organized laboratories of biomechanics in several scientific institutions. They all became parts of a wide front of movement studies directed toward understanding how the brain controls movements. In some places, movements of athletes were studied; at others, movements of people suffering from different motor pathologies; at still others, the developmental aspects of movements, biomechanics of playing the piano, and so on. All these studies originated from an observation made by Bernstein while he was at the CIL: Each time a hammer accurately hit the chisel, the trajectory of the tip of the hammer was different. This meant that the brain needed to send different commands to the muscles each time, depending on numerous factors. Thus, the worker needed to learn, not "the correct, optimal command," but the ability to find a new optimal solution each time.

---

[2]The Civil War (1918–1920) started soon after the October Revolution in 1917.

This period of work lasted until 1948. In 1947, *On the Construction of Movements*, was published, summarizing the progress in this direction. (The work would have been finished earlier but was delayed by the war.) The book starts with a dedication: "To the pure, eternal memory of my comrades who gave their lives in the struggle for the Soviet Motherland." In the introduction, Nicholai Aleksandrovich wrote, "In certain aspects, this book is more of a program for the future, urgent studies than a dogmatic report on firmly established findings" (p. 6).

However, in 1949, Bernstein was hit hard by the anti-Semitic campaign, against stateless cosmopolites, which established a dogmatic ultimate-truth attitude toward Pavlov's theory. We have already mentioned this period. Later, we discuss Bernstein's attitude toward the theoretical constructs of Pavlov and Bernstein's role in creating an alternative theory of brain activity.

In 1948, Russian biology in general and genetics in particular suffered a heavy blow as a result of the infamous session of the Union Academy of Agricultural Sciences. During this session, an ignorant person, though an academician, T. D. Lysenko, finished the job of exterminating Russian genetics. This process had been started much earlier and included the imprisonment and death of the leader of Russian geneticists, academician N. I. Vavilov and the elimination of the laboratories of his followers.

In 1950, a new blow was delivered by the joint session of the U.S.S.R. Academy of Sciences and the Academy of Medical Sciences. Everything that did not fit into the Pavlovian theory, as it was interpreted by ignorant administrators, was banned. The role of "hitmen" during this session was played by Profs. K. M. Bykov and A. G. Ivanov–Smolensky. Bernstein was among the victims. He was fired, and his laboratories were all eliminated. (We have already mentioned the effect of these events on the fate of his book, *On Dexterity*.) All of Bernstein's planned experimental studies were canceled; however, his research spirit survived. The scientific work of Bernstein during the ensuing time period took place at his home desk. This work did not have much of a visible outcome: The list of publications by Bernstein reveals a gap from 1949 until 1954, and during the next 6 years, he published only one or two small notes per year.

In 1961, the underground work of Bernstein produced its first significant result, reflected in the article "Problems and Approaches of the Physiology of Activity" published in the journal *Voprosy Filosofii* (*Problems of Philosophy*). During the same year, another major journal, *Problemy Kibernetiki* (*Problems of Cybernetics*), edited by the well-known Russian mathematician, A. A. Lyapunov, published another one of Bernstein's papers, "Urgent Problems of the Physiology of Activity." One more major paper, "New Trends in Contemporary Physiology," appeared in 1962 in the book *Proceedings of the Conference on the Methods of Human Physiological Studies*, edited by A. A. Letavet and V. S. Farfel.

This productive period lasted until Bernstein's death in 1966. It resulted in the creation of "physiology of activity," a new direction within general physiology, which was most fully described by Bernstein in his *Essays on the Physiology of Movements and Physiology of Activity*, published in 1966. Bernstein lived to see the proofs but not the book.

Scientists from around the world are becoming more and more interested in Bernstein's works, a trend reflected, in particular, by the publication of this volume, the first part of which is a translation of *On Dexterity* followed by commentaries by leading scientists from different countries. Bernstein's ideas in the area of physiology of activity, however, are still largely unknown to the world's scientific community. Physiology of activity was created long after *On Dexterity* had been written. Therefore, we recommend to our readers that they read the translation of *On Dexterity* first, before moving on to the last section of this chapter. In this section, "Bernstein and Pavlov: Changing the Paradigm," we discuss the evolution of Bernstein's theoretical views, from the relations between biomechanics and the processes of central control of movements to physiology of activity.

THE MODEL OF THE DESIRED FUTURE

The first movement studies performed by Bernstein led him to conclude that the elaboration of a motor skill cannot be equated with repetition of the same neural commands but rather with the development of an ability to solve the motor task differently each time. Bernstein suggested that movement is directed by a neural equivalent of its goal, *a model of the desired future*.

Bernstein was, in a sense, forced to introduce the notion of the model of the desired future by his studies of human movements. The central nervous system (CNS) creates an ideal goal of a planned movement based on its need, action objectives, and memory, and perceives information on the existing situation, that is, *what is*. It defines *what should be* as the outcome of the planned action. This means that, prior to a movement, the central nervous system encodes a model of the desired future, which is beyond the information about the current situation provided by the sensory systems. New and even unexpected changes in the environment give rise to stimuli that induce a reaction (an orienting reaction), which is not impartial, but is related, albeit hypothetically, to the model of the desired future. The process of comparing the information on the current situation with the model of the desired future defines *what should be done* in order to transform the current situation into another one that corresponds to the model of the desired future, and also *how this can be done* (i.e., which motor means are appropriate).

The model of the desired future is an image of something that does not yet exist but should materialize as a result of actions by the organism. It is created on the basis of past experience stored in memory, relevant information on the current state supplied by the sensory organs, extrapolation of the past into the future, and a comparison of the results of such an extrapolation with the needs and goals of the person, which provide the impetus for the whole process. *Goal* was understood by Bernstein as the model of the desired future encoded in the brain. It creates and organizes the processes, which may be termed *goal oriented*. The model of the present can be rigid and more or less defined, whereas the model of the future is more dynamic, based on what was later termed *probabilistic prognosis* (more details can be found in Feigenberg, 1972). Probabilistic prognosis affects the choice of behavior that, given the present situation, will have the highest probability of achieving the goal.

At the time of movement initiation, the brain creates a model of the expected outcome, which includes a model of the expected changes in the environment and of the position of the person in it, and a model of the effects of planned actions. According to Bernstein, the purpose of life and activity of a living organism is not the preserving of an equilibrium with the environment and with the flow of information generated by the environment (as I. P. Pavlov and his followers had thought) but the active mastering of the environment defined by the goal of an action as reflected in its model of the desired future. The model of the desired future is directed, not at a kind of passive adjustment of the organism to the environment, but at an active interaction with the environment corresponding to the organism's goals. Needs, goals, and current conditions define the choice of actions designed to achieve the desired future.

THE ROLE OF ACTIVITY

Activity was considered by Bernstein an essential feature of a living organism, a feature that defines its behavior. Physiology of activity was basically a new step in the development of neurophysiology, psychology, and biology in general; a step from viewing an organism as a reactive system to viewing it as an active system. Activity forms the basis of any action by a person and is particularly significant when a planned action requires overcoming the resistance of the environment. The organism spends its energy on overcoming this resistance until it wins in this struggle or perishes in the effort. The environment is ruled, similarly to all inanimate systems, by the second law of thermodynamics and moves toward increasing its entropy. An organism moves antientropically, decreasing its own entropy at the cost of an increase in the environmental entropy by means of metabolic processes, for example, the eating and digesting of food.

The principle of physiological and biological activity is in direct opposition to the reflex principle based on a simple reflex arc. A stimulus by itself never causes a response outside the context of the situation, which is determined by the significance of the stimulus—at least hypothetically. There are no "impartial" reflexes. So, to call any reaction to an external stimulus a *reflex* is misleading. It seems more reasonable to reserve this term for the automated components of an action that may take part in the realization of central commands. A theory that bases behavior on reflexes ignores the question *What is the purpose of a reaction by an organism?*

Classical physiologists, from Descartes to Pavlov, studied live organisms in quiet, inactive states. Such conditions were created artificially, for example, by surgical isolation of certain parts of the central nervous system, by the use of narcotic drugs, by fixation of an animal, or by the isolation of the organism from the environment. A living body was regarded as an organism sustaining a state of equilibrium with the environment provided by finely tuned reactions to external stimuli. Adherents of this physiology of equilibria and steady states did not study goal-oriented motor acts, the working states of an organism, its active exploration and changing of the environment. An animal was considered a reactive system whose behavior was defined and created by the environment with the help of stimuli.

Bernstein replaced this concept with an alternative one that considered activity a basic feature of the organism. He made the transition from studying an idle organism and its isolated functions to studying whole functions in natural conditions. According to Bernstein, in the process of evolution, advantage in the competition for survival is gained, not by the species who adapt to the environment best, but by those who manage to change the environment according to their needs best. For humans, this problem sometimes becomes ethical rather than biological.

A live system obeying the second law of thermodynamics would never have been able to move voluntarily or to change (particularly, in an adaptive fashion) if not for constant violations of its equilibrium with the environment. Note that the system, according to the physiology of equilibria, tries to minimize these perturbations, never being able to eliminate them completely until death. According to Bernstein, living systems themselves create violations of the equilibrium with the environment, and this characteristic gives rise to their major difference from inanimate systems.

N. A. BERNSTEIN AND I. P. PAVLOV:
CHANGING THE PARADIGM

This section of the chapter is dedicated to a comparative analysis of the theoretical conceptions of Bernstein and Pavlov, as those theories relate to integrative neuroscience. Because this analysis is inseparable from the situation in Russian science, which provided the scene for the struggle between the ideas, we describe this situation in more detail.

We remind the reader that the ideas of Pavlov have substantially influenced brain science and led, in 1935, to Pavlov's being pronounced the "*Princeps physiologorum mundi*" ("The Ruler of World Physiology"). At approximately the same time, Bernstein formulated his attitude toward these ideas.

There are two reasons to discuss Pavlov's ideas in this chapter. First, Pavlovian theoretical views have, for nearly 100 years, been considered by many scientists as the only rational, materialistic approach to brain mechanisms of mental events in humans and in higher animals. Even now, this theory of the purely reflexogenic nature of brain activity is accepted by many researchers, either based on reasoning or as religious dogma. The paradigm of conditioned reflexes has become the dominating approach in experimental studies of "higher nervous activity." Consequently, these studies are dominated by an emphasis on the senses, in which each and every action is initiated by perception. Without these perceptions, the brain of a newborn baby is considered a *tabula rasa* ("blank slate") somewhat scratched by inborn, unconditioned reflexes.

Pavlov and his colleagues conducted most of their studies using the "black box" approach by which input–output relations are investigated without taking into account possible effects of the internal organization of the black box. Based on such studies, the researchers generated conclusions about the laws, regularities, and mechanisms of the central nervous system in terms of "basic neural processes" (neuronal excitation and inhibition), conclusions that were originally flawed. Bernstein was one of the first to demonstrate the logical inconsistency of the theoretical conclusions based on these experiments. Moreover, Bernstein suggested an alternative to the theoretical views of Pavlov in the 1930s, that is, prior to the surge in cybernetic analysis and electrophysiological studies of the brain. At that time, only a very few colleagues were able to comprehend the importance of the theoretical innovations suggested by Bernstein. We should mention, however, that a number of outstanding scientists such as Sherrington, Lashley, Sperry, Anokhin, and later Pribram, Chomsky, Neisser, and Popper expressed views that were similar to the ideas of Bernstein with respect to certain aspects of brain functioning.

Second, the openly critical attitude of Bernstein toward many of the basic concepts and axioms underlying Pavlov's theory made him an "anti-Pavlovian" and, thus, a subject of political pressure and persecution. Pavlov's theory was declared by the leaders of the Communist regime in the U.S.S.R. an inherent part of the scientific foundation of the Marxism-Leninism ideology. Pavlov himself had nothing to do with all this. Actually, he had been dead for more than 10 years when the most violent persecution of anti-Pavlovians started. His students and followers, however, contributed significantly to this process. At approximately the same time, the foundations of Marxism-Leninism were also "strengthened" by the inclusion of T. D. Lysenko's "Michurin"[3] biology and by the destruction of genetics, the "bourgeois false science" of cybernetics, "idealism in physics" (i.e., quantum mechanics), and so forth. Bernstein's works at that time were considered "ideologically hostile" (see the aforementioned quotations from the articles published in the major journals, including the scientific ones).

---

[3]Ivan Michurin was a gifted, although uneducated, person who successfully selected and crossbred a number of plants, producing, in particular, fruit trees that could survive the harsh Russian winters.

The Joint Session of Two Academies

One of the most shameful episodes in the history of Russian science was the Joint Session of the Academy of Sciences and the Academy of Medical Sciences of the U.S.S.R. in 1950 (the so-called Pavlov Session). Among the immediate consequences of the session were the following: Bernstein was fired, the production of *On Dexterity and Its Development* was stopped, his earlier published books were not available to readers, and his papers were not accepted for publication.

A careful examination of the *Proceedings of the Joint Session of the U.S.S.R. Academy of Sciences and Academy of Medical Sciences* (1951) unveils an interesting fact. At that time, Bernstein was actually the only person whose views were radically, consistently, and unambiguously anti-Pavlovian. However, his name was not mentioned at all in the keynote addresses that pointed at the directions in science and the scientists who were declared according to the official ideology and "personally by comrade Stalin" (a typical expression of those times) as deviant or even (God forbid!) in opposition to Marxism-Leninism. Likewise, the name of Bernstein was not mentioned in the final declaration of the session. Only three secondary presentations mentioned the name of N. A. Bernstein as "one of those who do not appreciate and understand the theory of I. P. Pavlov" just prior to ending the phrase with "and others." The only person who dedicated more than one line to Bernstein was the obscure K. M. Smirnov. He started by praising Bernstein for the development of an "exceptionally refined method of cyclogrammetry," continued with saying that Bernstein "creates fantastic hypotheses on the origins of motor coordination and tries to disprove the theory of I. P. Pavlov by speculating that an automatic motor action may be performed without participation of the higher structures of the central nervous system" (p. 431), and ended by complaining that, unfortunately, the ideas of Bernstein had found their way into some contemporary textbooks. And that was it!

A list of the names of those who were extensively criticized by the Joint Session is also interesting. It turns out that the major blow was delivered to the most talented and independently thinking followers of I. P. Pavlov! They had, at the time of the session, created their own directions within the mainstream of Pavlov's ideas and only somewhat modified the traditional ways of performing experimental studies. Among them was the favorite student of I. P. Pavlov, academician L. A. Orbeli, as well as academicians A. D. Speransky and P. K. Anokhin. The most severe criticism was directed at academician I. S. Beritashvili (Beritov). Although Beritashvili studied behavior in the traditional reflexological way, he belonged to a different physiological school and was a student of Vvedenski, Sherrington, and Magnus. This difference had been reflected in his critical attitude toward Pavlov's ideas concerning the neural mechanisms of brain functioning and conditioned reflexes as the basis of mental activity. Other numerous unfortunate physiologists were criticized during the Joint Session on the basis of relatively minor issues and were, for the occasion, promoted to ideological enemies.

How can we explain the relative lack of attention of the Joint Session toward the theoretical position of Bernstein? We remind our readers that at the time of the Joint Session, 15 years had passed since the publication in 1935 of Bernstein's seminal article in the *Archives of Biological Sciences*, 4 years had passed since the publication of *On the Construction of Movements* (1947), and 3 years had passed since he had been awarded the Stalin Award. We suggest three nonexclusive explanations.

First, the organizers and most of the participants of the Joint Session simply did not understand the significance of Bernstein's works for Pavlov's theory. They thought that Bernstein's works had been mostly dedicated to particular, special problems of biomechanics and control of mostly athletic and labor movements. So, these works were considered irrelevant to the "basic" theory of brain activity and, therefore, unable to compete with Pavlov's theory. Those who were able to understand the importance of the works by Bernstein were themselves harshly criticized during the Joint Session and, therefore, were mostly preoccupied with problems of self-defense.

Second, the organizers of the Joint Session understood the importance of the works by Bernstein but were not sure of the possible outcome of a discussion, mostly because of the "shield" of the recent Stalin Award. The name of Stalin was taboo for any criticism.

Third, the Joint Session had nothing to do with objective analysis of the situation in science. The major goals of the organizers were to scare the "heretics," to strengthen the dictatorship of the Communist party in science (following the "pogroms" in genetics and linguistics that declared science an object and instrument of the "struggle of classes"), and, finally, to assure for themselves personally a comfortable place in the pseudoscientific, administrative hierarchy. With respect to all these issues, Bernstein was not considered a competitor.

It seems that, to some degree, all three explanations are valid. After the Joint Session ended, its results were officially declared a major ideological victory for Pavlov's views and a crushing defeat for its few rivals. Naturally, this outcome was also considered scientific proof of the Marxist-Leninist philosophy. At the same time, obviously, there was an explicit instruction from the party officials to complete the victory, accompanied by an explanation that the Stalin Award was not an obstacle. The instruction resulted in the creation of one of the worst pseudoscientific committees in the history of the U.S.S.R., the Pavlov Committee of the Academy of Sciences. So, after a short while, the "mistake" with respect to Bernstein was corrected. One month later, the party's official newspaper, *Pravda*, published the anti-Bernsteinian article mentioned earlier, and the process was initiated, the sole purpose of which was to make it impossible for one of the greatest scientists of the 20th century to do his work.

It is important to note that the critical attitude of Bernstein toward Pavlov's theory had always been well founded on the analysis of his own experimental observations. Personally, Bernstein's attitude toward Pavlov was one of high respect. Nicholai Aleksandrovich valued very highly the daring experimental genius of Pavlov, who had pioneered objective study of the physiological basis of mind. At the same time, Bernstein criticized the inadequate interpretation of the experimental findings and wrong theoretical constructions. We know that Bernstein and Pavlov met at least once, apparently at the beginning of the 1930s. Nothing is known about the issues discussed during the meeting. Pavlov never mentioned it. Apparently, the "Princeps physiologorum mundi" underestimated his young visitor and did not realize his potential. At the same time, after Pavlov had died, Bernstein refused to publish his book, *Contemporary Studies in the Physiology of the Nervous Process*, which contained a detailed criticism of Pavlov's theory.

Only after the death of Stalin (1953) did Bernstein find a job as a senior scientist, with one research assistant. However, after 1½ years he retired because of health problems and age (he was 60). After the ban on cybernetics was repealed, the role of Bernstein finally became acknowledged. (It is important to note that Bernstein expressed many of the basic ideas of cybernetics 10–15 years before its inauguration by N. Wiener.) At that time, the scientific activity of Bernstein increased. He wrote several papers (and they were published!) and also presented a number of talks and lectures.

Until the end of the 1950s, Bernstein mostly worked as a solitary researcher, which is rather typical for scientists who are much ahead of their colleagues. In the beginning of the 1960s, however, the situation started to change. Bernstein found himself surrounded by a small group of followers. After a long break, he resumed his participation in the national scientific conventions but no longer as a soloist. At the National Conference on the Philosophical Problems of Physiology of Higher Nervous Activity and of Psychology (Moscow, 1962), three papers out of thirteen were based on the theoretical views of Bernstein. They were presented by Bernstein himself (1963), by P. K. Anokhin (1963), and by N. I. Grastchenkov (Propper) together with L. P. Latash and I. M. Feigenberg (1963). At the Tenth National Congress of the Physiological Society, Bernstein presented a talk in collaboration with F. V. Bassin and L. P. Latash (Bassin, Bernstein, & Latash, 1966). In both cases, the presentations were followed by furious discussions with the adherents to Pavlov's views.

During the same time, a small group of mathematicians and neuroscientists led by academician I. M. Gelfand and his highly talented colleague, M. L. Tsetlin, began to congregate around the retired Bernstein. During the last years of Bernstein's life, and after his death, the members of this group contributed significantly to the elaboration and development of Bernstein's ideas (Gelfand, Gurfinkel, Fomin, & Tsetlin, 1971). The names of Gelfand, Tsetlin, and other members of this group are now well known in the scientific community. Here, we note the outstanding contribution of Mikhail L. Tsetlin, who unfortunately died at a rather young age, to the theory of nonlinear automata and its application to

Number of Citations

FIG. 1. The dynamics of the number of citations of Bernstein's works in papers published in the West and in Russia.

the problems of motor control. The world's scientific community is indebted to the members of this group for the preservation of Bernstein's ideas and for making them accessible for the members of the international neuroscience community.

We must emphasize that throughout his difficult scientific life, Bernstein had never denounced his ideas and had never issued a statement of "repentance" despite the pressure from the ideological administration. In contrast, such outstanding persons as Shostakovitch, Orbeli, many of Vygotskiy's followers, as well as many geneticists, psychiatrists, linguists, and so on, were forced to "repent" their uncommitted "crimes."

Eventually, Bernstein became an admitted scientific authority. His book *Essays on the Physiology of Movements and Physiology of Activity* (1966) was published in the U.S.S.R. (although the publishers were careful, starting the book with a preface which noted the "questionable theoretical conceptions of Bernstein"). Pergamon Press "discovered" Bernstein for the Western scientists. The graph in Figure 1 illustrates the influence of Bernstein on scientific research in the U.S.S.R. and in the West, showing the dynamics of the number of citations of Bernstein's works in papers published in the West and in Russia. We note the significant role of Peter Greene, Scott Kelso, and Michael Turvey in promoting the recognition of Bernstein's works among Western scientists, which has apparently been reflected in the dynamics of the citations in the West. The steady increase of citations in the West is contrasted with their stagnant, low level in Russia. Apparently, adherents to Pavlov's views are still dominant in the Russian physiological bureaucracy and are resisting the dissemination of Bernstein's ideas. However, to be fair, we note the apparent positive trend revealed, in particular, by Bernstein's admittance into the circle of *Classics of Science* and by the publication of *On Dexterity*.

Bernstein Versus Pavlov: David Against Goliath

We move now to an analysis of the substance of Bernstein's critique of Pavlov's ideas. This critique was based on the meticulous analysis of Bernstein's own data, which were collected with methods that were very sophisticated for that time and that were continuously refined. (Biological engineers of the 1990s are amazed by the existence of such methods as cyclogrammetry in the first third of the 20th century.) Bernstein formulated his critical remarks very slowly and carefully, although very steadily and consistently. First, he criticized how the theory of conditioned reflexes treated the problem of the generation and coordination of motor acts. Then, he moved to the creation of an alternative theory of the central neural control of movements, which currently forms the basis for virtually all the contemporary theories of motor control. His next step was to generalize the principles of motor control to other forms of control executed by the central nervous system. The main component of this step was the replacement of the keystone principle of reflexes with the principle of activity. In other words, the understanding of brain processes as reactions to external stimuli was replaced with the idea of the dominant active nature of these processes, which participate in the realization of many internal brain programs, including the genetically encoded ones.

In fact, the very first studies on the biomechanics of athletic and labor movements generated results that were impossible to explain according to the theory of conditioned reflexes. The basic finding was the variability of movement trajectories during repetitions of the same motor task, even when the movements became automated during the training process. On the basis of this finding, Bernstein generated a brilliant chain of deductions:

1. An unambiguous relation between a motor task and the outcome of a movement may occur in the absence of a similarly unambiguous relation between the task and the neural signals (both command and peripheral) as well as between the outcome and the neural signals.

2. Variability of movement trajectories cannot be avoided because of the unpredictable effects of external, uncontrolled forces (such as gravity, inertia, and friction) and reactive forces generated within the motor apparatus. In this situation, the variability of the efferent (command) signals is a prerequisite for achieving the desired outcome. The command signals must adjust to the effects of the external and reactive forces.

3. It is necessary for the brain to monitor the progress of a movement with the help of peripheral, afferent information. If this information signals a substantial deviation of the actual trajectory from the one generated by the model of the desired future, corrections must be introduced (the principle of sensory corrections). These corrections lead to a modification of the current command signals or even to the replacement of the whole ineffective motor program.

4. Any goal-oriented, purposive motor act is coordinated on the basis of a cyclic structure, a "closed reflex loop," according to Bernstein's terminology. (This term does not seem very appropriate now, but remember that it was introduced in the late 1920s.) The notion of a closed reflex loop was very different from the classical notion of the open reflex arc. Any part of the cyclic control structure was assumed to be able to initiate a movement. However, most frequently, movements were assumed to be generated from the central part of the loop, where needs formed the motor task and the goal based on the neural mechanisms of memory, which, in turn, were assumed to contain "exact formulae of movements," movement engrams.

This concept, as a whole, was originally published in 1935 in the famous paper by Bernstein, "The Problem of the Interrelation Between Coordination and Localization." In fact, the available data and their analysis had, at that time, created the foundation for Bernstein's theory, which represented an alternative to Pavlov's theory of brain functioning based on conditioned reflexes. However, in the 1935 paper, Bernstein avoided a direct confrontation between the ideas. Maybe he followed his favorite Latin proverb *Sapienti sat!* ("Sufficient for the wise!"), or he was waiting for a personal meeting with Pavlov, or he just thought that the concepts were not yet ripe. The paper still contained expressions like "conditioned motor reflex" or "closing the conditioned connection." These expressions would be purged later because of their semantic ambiguity. At the same time, much attention was paid to the structural complexity and integrity of voluntary movements. Some expressions sound like aphorisms. Here are a couple of examples:

"Movement never reacts to a detail with a detail." This statement means that a small change in the conditions leads to a reorganization of the whole movement. Therefore, each trajectory of an automated, repetitive movement is the result of a new movement organization. This view was later softened and replaced with the idea of "control matrices" for the lower control levels.

"Movement specificity is not in its object but in its manner." Organization of a movement is always based on an interaction of many brain structures, although the same structures are likely to interact during movement repetition. Movement is shaped mostly by the differences in the interaction (different organization of action), not by the differences in peripheral objects.

The theory of conditioned reflexes embraced the idea of rigid localization in the brain of the functions of interaction with the environment (so-called external brain functions). In particular, different perceptions, movements, and even single muscles supposedly had their own place in the brain. On the basis of the variability of automated movements, Bernstein argued that it was impossible to accept simultaneously the ideas of neuronal localization, control of single muscles, and conditioned reflexes. Probably, one or more of these notions had to be sacrificed.

In the paper published in 1935 in the *Archives of Biological Sciences*, Bernstein discussed directly the problems of interaction between the coordination of brain processes and localization of functions in the brain. Bernstein identified two types of localization: the geographical (topical) localization of functions on the cortex, and the interaction between the functional organization of an action and the brain substrate. In the second case, the important question is not *where* the process takes place but *what* happens with the function there and *how*. The geographical localization is usually not important for problems of movement coordination. A number of studies by such authorities in classical neurophysiology as Sherrington, Bethe, and Lashley have demonstrated that this kind of localization, at the very most, is related to brain inputs and outputs for special functions of interacting with the environment but not to the organization and coordination of functions during behavioral acts nor to movement in particular.

In the same paper, Bernstein stressed the importance of metric and topological characteristics of voluntary movements and introduced the notions of a motor image, which leads the actual motor acts; and of an abstract motor field, which is different from the external geometrical space and within which the topological organization of a movement is represented. This system of concepts and notions presented a viable alternative to the theory of conditioned reflexes.

The 1935 paper stands alone, like a skyscraper in a rural area. It presented many of the directions of the looming revolution in neuroscience. It also started the process of identifying the myths that needed to be replaced in order to make the revolution possible. The theory of conditioned reflexes is considered a set of such myths.

In his next major publication, *On the Construction of Movements* (1947), Bernstein moved to a direct confrontation with Pavlov's theory. The timing for such a confrontation was extremely poorly chosen. We have already mentioned that the U.S.S.R. Communist Party, at the time, had moved to a new stage of the struggle with "alien ideologies," and Bernstein was doomed to be one of the victims.

Here we review the criticisms of the theory of conditioned reflexes presented in the 1947 book. They still look rather local; that is, they deal with the central mechanisms of motor control, in particular, with the mechanisms of motor skill formation. However, the arguments are much more general than before and are directed at the heart of the theory of conditioned reflexes. Bernstein started by saying that the simplicity and appeal of the theory of conditioned reflexes, as well as its solid experimental basis, made it very popular. The theory has begun to be viewed as the foundation for a new materialistic psychology. Then, Bernstein stated that it was only natural to apply this theory to the problems of motor skill development and compared the fixation of conditioned reflexes in animals with the acquisition of a motor skill in humans, both achieved as the results of numerous repetitions.

Bernstein identified a number of problems within such a comparison. Elaboration of conditioned reflexes had always been based on the passive role of the animal. The experimenters tried to isolate the animal from "unrelated" external stimuli. As a result, the animal became sleepy. Pavlov noted that sleepiness was the worst problem in his experiments on the elaboration of conditioned reflexes. On the other hand, the elaboration of a motor skill is never passive. It involves the active psychomotor process of building the skill on the basis of the plans and needs of the person. As a result, acquisition of a motor skill and being sleepy are incompatible.

Another important critical point referred to the idea of "beating a path" as the basic mechanism of the conditioned reflex. Traditionally, numerous repetitions had been assumed to induce slow "memorizing" of a conditioned relation in a sequence of neurons. Recently, this process has been frequently associated with an increase in the effectiveness and number of synaptic links among the neurons. Bernstein presented a number of arguments, disproving the whole notion. They are related to the role of repetitions with respect to both command and perceptual components of a skill.

It has been known for a long time that perceptions that are highly significant for the organism may lead to a conditioned response even when they occur only once. This process has been proven to be a universal rule of the formation of conditioned reflexes. Particularly impressive evidence was obtained in the 1960s by Prof. J. Bures in his experiments with interhemispheric transfer of learning (Bures & Buresova, 1960). In this study, the so-called "spreading depression" was used to switch off temporarily one of the hemispheres of an animal with chemical agents. Then, a conditioned response was developed while apparently only one hemisphere was able to receive and process information. Later, the "off" hemisphere was turned on, and the conditioned response was elicited *only once*. Then, the other hemisphere was turned off. Now, the animal could process information only with the hemisphere that participated in the conditioned response only once. Such animals were able to demonstrate the conditioned response on the first trial. In other words, after the stimulus was established as significant during the first phase of the experiment, only one repetition was enough to establish a conditioned response. Apparently, no "path beating" occurred in this case.

Bernstein understood motor skill as a meaningful chain action with an inherent variability, a very complex internal structure, and qualitatively different mechanisms involved at different stages of skill development. Within this framework, beating a neural or synaptic path does not make much sense and may even be considered harmful. According to Bernstein, the purpose of repetition during motor-skill acquisition is not to accumulate identical stimuli but to find better tactical approaches to the motor task and more effective rules of coordination that are more flexible and that can adjust better to possible uncontrolled, random factors. Repetition of an exercise leads not "to repetition of a movement but to its construction . . . it is not the *means* for solving a given motor task, but the *process* of solving the task which improves the means from repetition to repetition" (Bernstein, 1947, p. 125). According to Bernstein, the essence of motor coordination is in overcoming the redundant degrees of freedom of the object of control (the effector). This redundancy leads to movement variability and to variable afferent (information from the peripheral receptors) and efferent (command) signals. In such conditions, stabilization of the relations among neurons within the brain may only be harmful. In general, the complex system of relations among the brain neurons and the dynamic, perpetually changing input signals to the brain make the idea of "beating a conditioned connection" quite unattractive.

The classification of the levels of movement construction suggested by Bernstein largely corresponds to the anatomical levels within the central nervous system. Apparently, Bernstein experienced difficulties in trying to identify the brain substrate for the highest level (E), which is above the neocortical level of actions (D). Level E incorporates symbolic, abstract actions such as speech, writing, playing music, painting, imitating movements without the object, and so forth. Bernstein wrote about these actions: "For this group of actions, we are presently unable to identify neither the leading afferent signals nor the cortical localization (with the exception of the areas within the frontal lobes, in particular Brodmann areas 9 and 10, that are apparently necessary for the generation of the efferent command)" (Bernstein, 1947, p. 147). In other words, the highest types of motor coordination seem to require a "supracortical" level, an idea that sounded blasphemous at a time when the prevailing theories were ones of progressive encephalization in the course of evolution and of conditioned reflexes. Now, these ideas fit well into the centroencephalic hypothesis of the highest level of brain integration.

The Final Years: Creating the Physiology of Activity

The last part of Bernstein's life coincided with the eventual appreciation of his outstanding contribution to integrative neuroscience and with the creation of the physiology of activity as an alternative to attempts at understanding brain integrative processes from the perspective of conditioned reflexes. The results of this work were published in a series of papers in the early 1960s, and were partly included in *Essays on the Physiology of Movements and Physiology of Activity*, published in 1966 after the death of Bernstein, and in *The Coordination and Regulation of Movements*, published in English in 1967 by Pergamon Press.

The basic ideas of the physiology of activity with respect to central neural control may be briefly described as follows:

1. The impetus for and the most important determinants of any action, not only movements, are intrinsic factors, which include needs and goals for a given action and programs for their realization (these may be genetically encoded or developed during the course of a lifetime). Extrinsic signals from outside are evaluated within the current program and play the role of triggers or sources of information on the progress of an action.

2. The purpose of an action (e.g., a motor task) leads to the creation in the brain of a neural equivalent, a model of the desired future. This model is based on the hierarchy of existing needs and motivations and the predictions of possible success of the action based on past experience (memory) and the current situation. Because of this, perception of external stimuli is selective; that is, it represents a *sensory action* whose purpose is to search for and select significant signals from the environment. In other words, the brain anticipates an outcome and creates a model of the desired future, which includes prediction of success and the dynamics of the environment. If the environment is organized probabilistically, this process is probabilistic as well.

3. The central nervous system organizes and coordinates actions whose goal is to solve the problem by overcoming possible resistance by the environment. This view is crucially different from the idea of equilibrating oneself with the environment, as postulated by the theory of conditioned reflexes.

4. The organization and coordination of actions within the central nervous system is based on circular control processes ("closed reflex loop," according to Bernstein), which may be activated or modified from any part of the controlling structure. This structure monitors continuously the progress of an action, detects unexpected external or reactive forces and deviations from the original plan, and generates corrective signals. As a result, this structure is able to assure an unambiguous relationship between the task and the outcome of an action in the absence of such a relationship with the efferent (command) or afferent (peripheral information) signals. Such an organization enables the organism to achieve reliable outcomes of irreproducible, singular actions based on a common coordinative structure. Automation of an action in the process of its repetition does not imply fixation of a neural organization, which eliminates variability. Results of experimental studies have demonstrated that variability remains after an action is automated. Rather, the process of construction of an optimal action, based on sensory corrections, transfers part of the control function to a lower control level.

These characteristics of the controlling, integrative function of the central nervous system are apparently incompatible with the theory of conditioned reflexes. The inadequacy of the theory of conditioned reflexes was also demonstrated by Bernstein, who used as examples some of its specific aspects. For example, the mechanism of establishing a conditioned link was assumed to involve the creation of a special path between the neocortical "centers" subserving an interaction between the environment (represented by a conditioning stimulus) and an unconditioned reflex. Assume, for the sake of discussion, that there is a special neuronal path beaten by numerous repetitions. Then, first, it is not clear how such a mechanism can emerge based on repetitions of *variable* movements characterized by different trajectories and different patterns of neuronal activity. Second, it is even less clear how this mechanism can form the basis for the observed variability of individual actions. If one assumes that each different version of an action leaves its own path in the neuronal substrate, the significance of action repetitions is lost, and the notion of a single, established neuronal link ceases to make sense.

The theory of conditioned reflexes was based on the notion of special brain topography, including the so-called "centers of functions," sometimes reduced to a single neuron. Bernstein called this approach "cellular mosaicism." One of the last papers by Bernstein (Bassin et al., 1966) was dedicated to the problem of the relationship between structure and function in the brain in light of the ideas of the physiology of activity. Specific brain areas (Brodmann areas) were considered as possible locations of functional operators participating in logical operations performed by certain neural networks. Such operators are "internal" brain functions, which are ambiguously related to "external" brain function; that is, one and the same operator can participate in various external brain functions, which are based on certain combinations of many operators.

All the available data about the topographic localization of the external brain functions, including cognition and speech, have been obtained either by studying the effects of local lesions of the brain tissue or by monitoring local changes in cellular metabolic processes (e.g., measures of blood flow, positron emission tomography, etc.). These methods are likely to reveal areas with a high density of neurons of the same type but do not reveal anything about the functional significance of such assemblies. It is quite possible that such high-density areas are related to inputs and outputs of the brain subsystems rather than to information processing. For example, a political demonstration could be detected by such a method and considered the place where major political decisions are made. We all know, however, that the decisions are made by smaller groups of people, although such decisions may be affected by a demonstration (an input) or result in a demonstration (an output). The processing of information within the brain is apparently the crucial component of brain functioning, and it is likely to proceed with participation of neurons scattered over vast brain areas. These processes apparently cannot be revealed with the mentioned methods.

Pavlov's theory considered behavior the result of a summation of elementary reactions, that is, of conditioned reflexes. Likewise, brain processes were viewed as the summation of the activity of single neurons unambiguously related to a certain function (neuronal mosaicism). Thus, within this theory, there was no place for the synthesis of a uniquely organized structure, a control system. As a result, Pavlov concluded that the emergence of speech in ontogenesis and the function of speech were based on conditioned reflexes. This concept of speech is known as the *second signal system*. Bernstein criticized this concept harshly: "Mosaicism quite logically represented the system of speech, with its inherently complex structure and deeply unique relationships between words and meanings, as one more collection of elements, a vocabulary distributed over the cortical cells" (Bernstein, 1963, p. 304). The function of speech was mostly reduced to its least important aspect, that of a signal, similar to signals used by animals. "Human speech is characterized by special features that elevate it above the signal level to a qualitatively new height" (Bernstein, 1963, p. 305). Later, the theory that learning human speech is based on the mechanism of conditioned reflexes was categorically rejected by Chomsky (1975). As an example of the inadequacy of the concept of the second signal system, Bernstein considered its impotence in trying to develop the principles of machine translation.

The failure of the theory of conditioned reflexes has also been apparent in other applied areas such as the elaboration of more efficient labor and athletic skills, the adaptation to limb prostheses, elementary school education, and the treatment of neurological and psychiatric disorders. The followers of this theory predicted therapeutic effects of sleep, including drug-induced sleep, based on its assumed function as a defensive inhibition. Attempts to follow these recommendations in the U.S.S.R. in the 1950s broke all the records in the number of complications and negative outcomes.

It was also predicted that conditioned reflexes would be most easily elaborated in the so-called "towers of silence" built in a suburb of St. Petersburg. It was assumed that the lack of external stimuli would eliminate distractions and increase the effectiveness of the only remaining conditioning stimulus, thus strengthening its connection with the reflex response. The result was the opposite: The elaboration of conditioned reflexes took more time, and the animals frequently became neurotic. Apparently, natural conditions with numerous random stimuli required active search, identification, and selection of the meaningful stimulus and were advantageous (or perhaps even necessary) for the development of a conditioned reflex.

Thus, besides solving fundamental problems of neuroscience related to the construction and control of movements, Bernstein played the key role in proving the inadequacy of the theory of conditioned reflexes and, moreover, suggested an alternative theory of the integrative function of the central nervous system. During the last 10 years of Bernstein's life, as well as during the following 30 years, much new evidence supporting Bernstein's theoretical positions has been accumulated. More and more neuroscientists have become Bernstein's followers, particularly in the West. Unfortunately, his Motherland still lags behind (see Figure 1).

Here we present a passage that expresses the attitude toward the theory of conditioned reflexes by one of the leading philosophers of the 20th century, Sir Karl Popper:

> As seen from our point of view, neither the conditioned reflex nor the uncon-
> ditioned reflex exist. From our point of view, Pavlov's dog, actively interested in
> the environment, *invents a theory*, consciously or unconsciously, and then tries it
> out. It invents a true and obvious theory, or expectation, that the food will arrive
> when the bell rings. Pavlov's interpretation sees the dog as a passive mechanism,
> while my interpretation attributes to the dog . . . interest . . . an exploratory instinct.
> Pavlov indeed noticed exploratory behavior. . . . But he did not see that this was

not a "reflex" in his sense: not a response to a stimulus but a general curiosity and activity.... From my point of view, for something to be a stimulus, it must relate to the action program of animal concerned.... Admittedly, the learning mechanism postulated by Pavlov is very simple.... But living organisms are not so very simple; nor are their adaptation to environment.... Organisms do not wait, passively, for repetitions of an event ... to impose upon their memory the existence of a regularity.... Rather, organisms actively try to impose guessed regularities (and ... similarities) ... upon the world.... It is this theory of actively proffered conjectures and their refutation ... which I propose to put in the place of the theory of the conditioned reflex....

The unconditioned reflex ... is part of the genetically determined functioning of an organ ... which solves, like a theory, certain problems of adaptation to a changing environment.... Our organs are problem solvers ... the reflex theory according to which all behavior is of the stimulus–response character is mistaken and should be abandoned. Organisms are problem solvers and explorers of their world. (Popper & Eccles, 1983, pp. 136–138)

It is hard to believe that these words were written, not by N. A. Bernstein, but by a person who, according to the list of references in the book, did not know that very similar ideas had been expressed and experimentally tested by Bernstein 30–40 years earlier.

CONCLUDING COMMENTS:
BERNSTEIN'S IDEAS MUST BE DEVELOPED

In conclusion, let us make a few brief notes on what we view as contemporary, urgent problems that follow the ideas of N. A. Bernstein and experimental material accumulated during the last few years. A whole list of established notions have turned out to be myths, which, similarly to phlogiston in chemistry and ether in physics, have hindered the progress in the area of integrative neuroscience by distracting investigators (and funds) and leading them into dead-end methodological and experimental directions.

Neuroscience is in urgent need of demythologization. Similarly to what has been happening in religion recently, the demythologization of neuroscience is likely to bring about heated arguments and resistance. However, neuroscience must get through this process, and the sooner, the better. It must rid itself of the following major myths:

1. The reflex nature of behavior and of the formation of controlling systems within the brain (the Reflexological Myth).
2. Anatomical localization of external brain functions (the Localization Myth).

3. The neocortex as the highest level of integration in the brain (the Cortical Myth).

4. Synaptic localization of the traces of long-term memory in the central nervous system (the Synaptomnemical Myth).

Although all these notions have been proven to be myths by many studies within different branches of neuroscience, the ideas of and studies by Bernstein were, to a large extent, crucial for these conclusions.

Similarly to all the existing theories of integrative brain functions, Bernstein's theory does not take into account the processes of consciousness (as a world of subjective experiences), their mechanisms, and their possible role in the organization of movements and behavior, including mental processes. This is a serious shortcoming. Both our own intuition and the analysis of evolution suggest a particular importance and uniqueness of the brain processes that take place with the participation of consciousness. However, the complexity of the problem is so immense that, currently, there are not any even tentatively promising hypotheses that could go beyond purely verbal constructions. During the last 20 years, researchers have witnessed the development of the ideas and methods in the area of nonlinear dynamics as applied to brain processes, with the emergence of such notions as deterministic chaos, strange attractors, fractals, and so forth. This whole area creates a vague feeling of a possible breakthrough if it were applied to the dynamics of the processes in complex brain systems, including the "wicked problem" of electrical wave processes in the brain that are reflected by the electroencephalogram. At least, there is no a priori feeling of an impasse or of inadequacy of this approach. We can only be astounded by the depth and power of the scientific intuition of Bernstein with respect to this modern area. In 1961, Bernstein wrote, "It would be very hard now to dispute the fact that the increase in the morphological, localizational differentiation of the brain substrate is a very strong factor favoring the development of non-local wave processes both inside and on the surface of the brain" (p. 296).

Thus, we see the current problems of integrative neuroscience as, first, the liberation of the minds of the researchers of the distracting and impeding ballast of obsolete theories, and, second, studies of the nonlinear dynamic processes in the brain in an attempt to attack the neurophysiological aspects of consciousness.

REFERENCES

Anokhin, P. K. (1963). Methodological analysis of key problems of conditioned reflexes. In *Philosophical problems of physiology of the higher nervous activity and psychology* (pp. 156–214). Moscow: Academy of Sciences.

Bassin, F. V., Bernstein, N. A., & Latash, L. P. (1966). On the problem of relation between brain structure and function in its contemporary understanding. In N. I. Grastchenkov (Ed.), *Physiology in clinical practice* (pp. 38–71). Moscow: Nauka.

Bernstein, N. A. (1935). The problem of interrelation between coordination and localization. *Archives of Biological Sciences, 38*, 1–34.

Bernstein, N. A. (1947). *On the construction of movements.* Moscow: Medgiz.

Bernstein, N. A. (1961). Problems and approaches of the physiology of activity. *Problems of Philosophy, 6*, 77–92.

Bernstein, N. A. (1961). Urgent problems of the physiology of activity. *Problems of Cybernetics, 6*, 101–160.

Bernstein, N. A. (1963). New directions of development of physiology and their relation to cybernetics. In *Philosophical problems of physiology of the higher nervous activity and psychology* (pp. 299–322). Moscow: Academy of Sciences.

Bernstein, N. A. (1966). *Essays on the physiology of movements and physiology of activity.* Moscow: Meditsina.

Bernstein, N. A. (1967). *The coordination and regulation of movements.* Oxford, England: Pergamon.

Bernstein, N. A. (1990). *Physiology of movements and of activity.* In O. G. Gazenko & I. M. Feigenberg (Eds.), *Classics of science.* Moscow: Nauka.

Bures, J., & Buresova, O. (1960). The use of Leao's spreading depression in the study of interhemispheric transfer of memory traces. *Journal of Comparative and Physiological Psychology, 53*, 558–563.

Chomsky, N. (1975). *Reflections on language.* New York: Pantheon.

Feigenberg, I. M. (1972). *Brain, mentality, and health.* Moscow: Nauka.

Gelfand, I. M., Gurfinkel, V. S., Fomin, S. V., & Tsetlin, M. L. (Eds.). (1971). *Models of the structural–functional organization of certain biological systems.* Cambridge, MA: MIT Press.

Grastchenkov, N. I., Latash, L. P., & Feigenberg, I. M. (1963). Dialectic materialism and some problems of contemporary neurophysiology. In *Philosophical problems of physiology of the higher nervous activity and psychology* (pp. 35–62). Moscow: Academy of Sciences.

Latash, L. P. (1968). *Hypothalamus, adaptive activity, and the electroencephalogram.* Moscow: Nauka.

Popper, K. R., & Eccles, J. C. (1983). *The self and its brain.* London: Routledge & Kegan Paul.

Proceedings of the Joint Session of the U.S.S.R. Academy of Sciences and Academy of Medical Sciences. (1951). Moscow: Medgiz.

The Bernstein Problem: How Does the Central Nervous System Make Its Choices?

Mark L. Latash
Pennsylvania State University

In the second quarter of the 20th century, two great physicists, Albert Einstein and Niels Bohr, discussed the basic principles of the physical foundation of our world. Recent progress in theoretical physics, at that time, had led to the formulation of the principle of uncertainty (the Heisenberg principle) according to which there are limits to the accuracy with which one can define position and impulse (the product of mass and velocity) of a particle. In a sense, this principle means that a particle is in a way spread over an area of space, and one can speak only about the probability of finding the particle in a certain point. This principle represented a huge leap from the determinism of the Newtonian classical mechanics. Einstein was very reluctant to accept this idea. He is attributed with saying that God does not play dice with nature. However, the later development in physics has proven that Heisenberg and Bohr were right: God does play dice!

Strong effects of the probabilistic properties of our world are commonly seen only at the level of elementary particles but not in the physics of everyday life. However, one is tempted to ask the following string of questions: Are the basic physical principles equally applicable to movements of inanimate objects and to the functioning of the human brain? Does the brain play dice with nature? How does it come to its wise solutions when it seems to have a virtually infinite number of choices? What does it mean to have a choice? Can one formally separate having a choice from being forced into a unique response? In this chapter, I move through this spectrum of questions, hoping that at the end I will be able to say something smart about whether the brain plays dice with nature.

CHOICE

There is choice in virtually each and every human action. One is free to choose different words to express the same meaning. One may choose different ways of handling a knife and fork when cutting a steak. One may choose a college to study in, a place to work in, a house to live in, and a person to live with. However, does one actually have a choice in each of these situations? Maybe, and perhaps the choice is only seeming whereas one is forced into accepting a unique solution by Fate, Nature, or God. Are we blind tools in the hands of the Creator or Fate or Nature? It is very tempting to speculate on these issues, but I am not going to venture deep into teleological discussions on free will versus the fatalistic approach to human behavior. Let us follow Bernstein's traditions and humbly restrict the analysis to something down-to-earth and measurable.

The example of picking up a matchbox discussed by Bernstein is probably one of the simplest ones. Remember that if a person is asked to pick up a matchbox from a table, the trajectories of the hand will differ substantially from trial to trial. So, the task, as the experimenter defines it, does not specify all the features of the solutions suggested by the central nervous system. One may suggest other examples of nonunique solutions: running during a punt return in football, picking apples in a grocery store, deciding whether to continue reading this chapter or to stop now, and many, many others.

Certainly in all these situations, one may argue that the initial conditions each time the task is presented are never the same, even if one tries his or her best to reproduce them. There is always some noise and some variability. So, the differences in the initial conditions make different trials of one task actually different tasks, and it is not surprising that the human problem-solving apparatus comes to different solutions. However, imagine an ideal experiment in which all the minute details are precisely reproduced in two successive trials (which is absolutely impossible). Will the outcomes be identical? This is a good question, and I argue later in this chapter that the answer is a definite no.

There are two qualitatively different bases of making a choice: first, if one cares about the outcome, and, second, if one does not care. In the second case, one can even speak not about making a choice but about allowing a choice to be made. An example of the first situation is choosing one's spouse. An example of the second situation is choosing 5 oranges from a box containing 100 identical fruits. So, when analyzing the behavior of a decision-making system that is supposed to make choices (e.g., the brain), one must first ask, Does the system care? If the system cares, the problem is in finding a set of its priorities that are used to make the choice possible. If the system does not care, one is confronted by a new set of questions: Is there a poorly predictable but measurable factor that makes the choice possible? Call such a factor *noise*. Is the noise external (coming from the environment) or internal (coming from some place within the body)?

The further one goes, the harder the questions. Is there a place for metaphors like *will*, *intention*, or *soul* in the decision-making system and, in particular, in the human system for control of voluntary movements? I would like to argue that the answer is a definite yes. In other words, I think that the functioning of the brain cannot be explained on the sole basis of its physical properties as a closed system, that is, without considering its interaction with some additional factors. These factors may actually originate from the brain (e.g., intention) but then affect the decisions the brain makes as an equal contributor.

Imagine the following experiment: A person is standing on a platform holding in front of him or her a cup filled with play dough (see Figure 1). The platform starts to move. There will be changes in the person's posture including the posture of the arm holding the cup. If one records the activity of muscles that maintain the vertical posture of the body and the posture of the arm, one will see changes in the levels of muscle activation. Some of these changes will happen very quickly, so quickly, that there is certainly no time for the person to feel the external perturbation to the balance, to think, and to pick a correct reaction. Such reactions are called *preprogrammed*. They are prepared by the central nervous system in anticipation of a perturbation and may be triggered by changes in the activity of the peripheral receptors (neural cells scattered all over the body and sensitive to different physical variables such as position, force, pressure, temperature, etc.) informing the central nervous system that there is a danger of losing the balance.

The same experiment can be repeated, this time with a cup filled with hot tea. The platform starts to move in exactly the same fashion. Imagine that all the forces, all the initial postures, and all the other conditions are the same. However, the preprogrammed changes in the person's posture and his or her arm movements will be quite different. This difference is due to the difference in the intentions of the person. In the first case, the major goal was not to fall; there were no major restrictions on arm movements. In the second case, not spilling the tea becomes comparably important to not falling. So, one's intentions appear to contribute to the decision-making process even if there is no time to make a decision consciously.

FIG. 1. A person is standing on a platform and holding a cup. If the platform starts to move unexpectedly, there will be quick changes in the activity of postural muscles. These changes will be different in two situations: when the cup is filled with play dough and when it is filled with hot tea.

Now, consider the next set of questions, which are more closely related to control of voluntary movements: Is the central nervous system finding exact solutions for certain equations of motion and prescribing movement patterns? Alternatively, are the patterns allowed to emerge whereas the central nervous system simply sets a general course of the movement, its goal, and only a few relevant conditions or constraints (e.g., not falling down, not spilling tea, not breaking glass, etc.)? So, the next step in analyzing the problem of choice is looking at the equations. The equations look very simple (although most of them do not have a unique solution!).

EQUATIONS

Recall that the current purpose is to understand how the brain makes its choices. The presence of choice means that the brain can manipulate more variables than the number of parameters used to define a task. In other words, the number of constraints imposed by the task and by the environment on the problem-solving apparatus is smaller than the number of variables that the brain can use to perform the task. The last two phrases sound very clumsy and cumbersome. Sometimes, it is easier to explain a concept by writing a couple of equations than by using many, many words. So, assume that the presence of choice is similar to solving n equations with k unknowns when $k > n$. A simple example is a system of two equations with three unknowns:

$$x + y + z = 10$$
$$x - 2y - 3z = 0$$

This system of equations has an infinite number of solutions; that is, it describes a hypothetical system that involves choice! One cannot solve this system without some additional information, which can be provided, for example, in the form of a third equation. Such problems are frequently called *ill-posed*. Finding additional equations (or, in other words, imposing additional constraints) is the heart of ill-posed problems.

The basic question turns out to be, Where does one find the missing equations? However, before asking this basic question, one needs to consider an even more basic one: Do these equations exist? Perhaps one is trying to solve the problem of choice, for the central nervous system, with a relatively well-developed but inadequate apparatus. Is this like looking for a lost coin under a street lamp rather than where it was actually lost?

DEGREES OF FREEDOM

Bernstein's most beloved notion in the area of control of voluntary movements was probably that of degrees of freedom. He showed how rich the motor system is in degrees of freedom as compared to the most sophisticated contemporary devices and machines. He also showed how a single, additional (redundant) degree of freedom can introduce an infinite flexibility, or, in other words, an infinite number of choices. Here it is—choice again! Apparently, the notion of degrees of freedom is extremely important for analyzing systems that have an ability to make choices. Let us spend some time defining, refining, and analyzing this notion.

Bernstein's definition of degrees of freedom relied heavily on the analysis of kinematic degrees of freedom of various systems. In particular, when analyzing the human upper limb, Bernstein considered all possible orthogonal axes of rotation in a joint as independent degrees of freedom, which were later summed over the joints. The apparent redundancy of the joints of the human arm in comparison to the three-dimensional space where we happen to live and where movements take place led Bernstein to his famous formulation that the essence of motor control is the elimination of the redundant degrees of freedom. The beauty and brevity of this formulation is stunning. A skeptic may want to decide whether control can always be reduced to the elimination of redundant degrees of freedom. In other words, I am suggesting that Bernstein's famous definition may not always be correct (blasphemy!!!).

First of all, the central nervous system probably uses its own means of communication with the muscles, which may not be analogous to the language of joint kinematics, that is, the specifying of trajectories in individual joints. If so, the number of variables that are accessible to the central nervous system for the purpose of control (call them independently controlled variables) may be different from the number of apparent kinematic degrees of freedom. Consider two simple examples.

A wheel of a car, generally speaking, has two degrees of freedom (rotation and its direction). Four wheels have the total of eight degrees of freedom. However, the car, as a whole, has only two degrees of freedom that allow it to move over a surface and two degrees of freedom at the control level, acceleration–deceleration (gas and brake pedals) and turns (steering wheel). So, here one is confronted with a typical problem of redundancy—how to force the four wheels to move over a surface. According to Bernstein, six redundant degrees of freedom should be eliminated. Apparently, this can be successfully accomplished with the structural constraints and design of the controls of the car, which are based on a number of engineering and ergonomic principles.

Now, imagine that there are two knobs that control the position of a dot along a straight line according to a simple rule:

$$P = x + y,$$

where P is the dot position and x and y are signals from the knobs. This is a case of typical redundancy at the level of control. Originally, there was no redundancy in the system; that is, it had only one degree of freedom for dot movements and only one variable that encoded the required dot position. However, the design of the controls introduced redundancy into this originally non-redundant system. This may be plainly stupid or it may serve a purpose. Next I show that such designs are not unusual for human joints.

So, the two examples demonstrate that controls may eliminate degrees of freedom or they may add them! Bernstein discussed only the elimination of degrees of freedom with controls, but actually both possibilities exist. It is already obvious that counting degrees of freedom at a kinematic level has its limitations. *Interest lies in how many independently controlled variables (degrees of freedom) are available for the controller. If this number is greater than the number of independent parameters describing a motor task, one confronts a genuine Bernstein problem—a problem of choice.*

During virtually all voluntary movements, the number of degrees of freedom (n) for a peripheral mechanical apparatus (e.g., a limb) is greater than the number of degrees of freedom (n_0) necessary to execute a motor task or to unambiguously describe its execution. The number of available independently controlled variables ("degrees of freedom") for the central controller, N, is commonly less than n due to a number of factors including, in particular, anatomical constraints and biomechanical links among the joints, for example, biarticular muscles (cf. the system of wheel suspension in a car). However, it is likely to be more than n_0 for most natural movements.

In other words, the central nervous system is presented with n_0 equations that contain N unknowns, $N > n_0$ (cf. the system of two equations with three unknowns previously mentioned). In order to unambiguously solve such a system, one needs to add ($N - n_0$) equations or, equivalently, impose ($N - n_0$) constraints on the system. One must keep in mind that N is the number of degrees of freedom (i.e., the number of independently controlled variables) for a hypothetical central controlling system but not for the peripheral system. Therefore, the Bernstein problem should be analyzed and solved in a central language but not in a language of motor performance. Unfortunately, motor control researchers have not been fortunate enough to find a viable central-control language for multijoint movements. This situation forces the researchers to reformulate the Bernstein problem with an inadequate language of performance, that is, to analyze the problem of finding patterns of changes in n *peripheral degrees of freedom* (e.g., individual joint angle rotations) that induce a required movement of the tip of a multijoint limb. Reformulation of the degrees-of-freedom problem in strictly peripheral terms can be called *the pseudo-Bernstein problem.*

It is obvious now that the question of which degrees of freedom to count is very important. Without a method of assessing the degrees of freedom for a hypothetical control system (a part of the central nervous system) one will never be able to define whether the control system makes a choice. The following examples will be more closely related to the problems of motor control than are controlling movements of a dot or designing car controls.

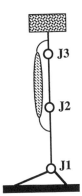

FIG. 2. A simple model of the human leg with three major joints (J1, J2, and J3). The number of peripheral degrees of freedom may depend on the state of the biarticular muscle.

HOW TO COUNT DEGREES OF FREEDOM

Figure 2 shows a stick figure of a standing person with three major leg joints—ankle, knee, and hip. Imagine, for simplicity, that each joint has only one degree of freedom. Then, the leg has three peripheral degrees of freedom. If one considers movements in the two-dimensional plane of the paper, a typical pseudo-Bernstein problem emerges. Now add just one biarticular muscle into this system. If this muscle is slack and does not exert any forces on the segments to which it is attached, it does not affect the movements in the joints, and the number of degrees of freedom remains three. On the other hand, if the muscle is absolutely rigid (i.e., its length is constant), it blocks movements in the knee and hip joints, thus eliminating two degrees of freedom, so that only one is left. But what happens, if a more realistic muscle affects both joints in an elastic fashion, like a spring with a moderate stiffness? How many peripheral degrees of freedom will there be?

Figure 3 shows a very simple system consisting of only one joint with only one degree of freedom. This system is nonredundant according to the pseudo-Bernstein formulation. But now imagine that there are two flexor muscles and two extensor muscles controlling the joint (it is quite typical for the major human limb joints to have more than one muscle acting in each direction). Imagine that each muscle can be controlled by the central nervous system independently. Then, there are at least four control variables at the level of control.

FIG. 3. There is no kinematic redundancy in this single-joint system; however, if the joint is controlled by many muscles (four in this case), there may be redundancy at the level of control.

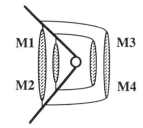

This is a typical Bernstein problem occurring in a system without any obvious kinematic redundancy.

So, depending on the situation, one may have a pseudo-Bernstein problem in the absence of a Bernstein problem or a Bernstein problem in the absence of a pseudo-Bernstein problem. So, which degrees of freedom should one count? The answer depends on what the basic task is.

Example 1

Imagine designing a machine (a limb of a robot) and planning to control its movements by telling each joint which torque it should develop. For this task, it is helpful to introduce the notion of an ideal actuator, that is, a torque generator that acts at a joint and can produce torques in either direction (flexion or extension). The exact mechanism by which the torque is produced is unimportant. It is important, however, that the joint torque produced by the actuator is independent of joint kinematics and external conditions (external forces). If each kinematic degree of freedom in each joint is subserved by one actuator and if torques produced by different actuators are independent of each other, then the number of degrees of freedom at a hypothetical control level is generally equal to the number of kinematic degrees of freedom of the limb.

In this example, if one considers only tasks of occupying different static positions in an external force field, and ignoring the time patterns by which the joints move from one position to another, Bernstein and pseudo-Bernstein problems become the same because the number of control variables is equal to the number of peripheral degrees of freedom. Note, however, that this type of control becomes rather unreliable if the task is to occupy a certain static position in a constant external force field, that is, when different positions may correspond to the same distribution of torques among the joints. All positions become unstable unless kinematic sensors whose output signals can control the torque actuators are added to the system. If time patterns of moving from an initial to a final position in a joint are considered, then immediately an infinite number of trajectories emerge, for each individual joint, that can successfully accomplish the task. Similarly, an infinite number of torque patterns may lead from the initial to the final position.

When the problem of redundancy is confronted in robotics design, additional equations are commonly added on the basis of some engineering considerations, for example, requirements to minimize energy expenditure, peak joint torques, joint wear, or something else. These considerations are frequently addressed as optimization principles. Adding these additional constraints may eventually solve the problem of redundancy and make the robotics limb controllable.

Example 2

One must take into account that muscles in the body are unidirectional; that is, they can only pull, not push. So, in order to control movements in a joint with only one degree of freedom, one needs at least two muscles, an *agonist* and an *antagonist*, or a *flexor* and an *extensor*. If one considers each muscle an ideal actuator, there are already two actuators for each peripheral degree of freedom. If each muscle can be controlled independently of any other muscle, in particular, independently of its antagonist, the number of control variables increases twofold; in other words, the genuine Bernstein problem emerges if it was absent or becomes worse if it was present in Example 1.

Example 3

I am not trying to design a humanlike moving machine but rather to understand how an existing machine (the human body) functions. There are huge differences between the design of the human peripheral apparatus and the design of a typical robotics arm. First, the muscles are not ideal actuators. They demonstrate a nonlinear, springlike dependence between their length, velocity, and generated force. This means, in particular, that any joint movement or any change in the external force field can lead to a change in the force generated by a muscle. As a result, forces in individual muscles and, correspondingly, positions in individual joints become dependent on the external conditions, and, therefore, rather unpredictable. There are also biarticular (or even polyarticular) muscles, which span two (or more) joints and which also demonstrate all the nonlinear, springlike properties typical of the more common, uniarticular muscles. Muscles do not immediately act on joints but pull compliant tendons, which, in turn, transfer muscle force to limb segments, inducing joint torque and rotation. Because of the tendon compliance, joint torque does not exactly follow the pattern of applied muscle forces but rather "feels" a smooth, filtered pattern of tendon forces.

All these features make the design of human limbs look much inferior to the design of a robot arm. Why did the Creator or Nature or Evolution introduce all these complications? Do they serve a purpose? Perhaps they are just boring atavisms.

I believe that the Creator or Nature or Evolution is smarter than the smartest of the engineers, and if it came up with a design that looks cumbersome and inefficient, this only means that we have not searched well enough to discover why the design of our bodies is much better than anything we can build. So, for me, the question is not Why are our limbs so poorly designed and hard to control? but What are the unique properties of the design of human limbs that make it incomparably better than any engineering construction?

So, let us accept the view that we should be proud of the design of our bodies rather than ashamed of it. Then, there are no reasons to assume that our bodies function according to the same principles as those that may be helpful for solving the problem of redundancy in Examples 1 and 2. Results of experimental studies of the patterns of joint motion during natural human limb movements suggest that control strategies used by the central nervous system look reasonable from different engineering standpoints. The system is not expending too much energy (although maybe not minimizing it), is not exerting extreme stress on the joints (although maybe not minimizing jerk in individual joints), is not going from New York to Philadelphia through San Francisco (although maybe not minimizing joint motion), and so on. Moreover, there are good reasons to think that the central nervous system is functioning according to very different principles, called *laws of coordination*. I turn once again to examples. This time, however, the examples are from actual experimental data.

I start with the classical experiment performed by Bernstein in the mid-1920s. Bernstein introduced into motor control research several ingenious approaches, in particular, a method for studying movement kinematics with high-speed photography. Bernstein attached small electric bulbs to points of interest on the subject's body (commonly, limb joints and endpoints), made a movie, and later analyzed it frame by frame, calculating joint angles and trajectories of the endpoints with the help of stick figures made of segments connecting the bulbs in each frame (see Figure 4). With this method, he analyzed various movements including the kinematics of running by the world record holder of that time, Ladoumegue; finger movements of pianists; and even locomotion in lions. But consider his studies of the movements in blacksmiths when they were hitting an anvil with a hammer (Figure 4).

Note that Bernstein's subjects had performed the same movements several thousand times a day, 6 days a week, for years. They were the best-trained individuals for this particular task. So probably, during their lives, they had elaborated an optimal, standardized pattern of control signals (call it *motor program*, following Bernstein) that was reproduced during successive hittings. Bernstein noticed that the repetition of this hypothetical motor program led to a highly reproducible trajectory of the tip of the hammer, although the trajectories of the individual joints of the arm might be quite variable.

How can this be? Apparently the central nervous system cannot send signals directly to the hammer. It sends signals to muscles acting at different joints. However, the joints move differently, following repetition of one and the same hypothetical motor program, which preserves the trajectory of the hammer. If one joint deviates from the track, other joints apparently compensate the induced error. So, what is encoded in the motor program? Certainly not a combination

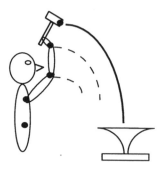

FIG. 4. An illustration of Bernstein's experiments with blacksmiths hitting an anvil with a hammer. Black dots show positions of the electric bulbs.

of joint trajectories, because they are poorly reproduced. Certainly not a combination of muscle forces or patterns of muscle activation, because, as Bernstein showed in later works, these are reproduced even more poorly. Only one candidate is left: the trajectory of the tip of the hammer. But it can be moved only through the action of muscles and movements of individual joints. This puzzle looks like a wicked circle; however, it is not as wicked as it appears, and I will shortly suggest a mechanism for the elimination of this wickedness.

I introduce the term *working point* for such "most important" points whose trajectory is vital for executing a motor task. This point need not even be in a permanent direct contact with the body. For example, when Michael Jordan (a famous basketball player on the Chicago Bulls) throws a basketball, the task is to get the working point (the basketball) into the basket. In this example, the working point is in direct contact with the player's hands only during the initial segment of its trajectory. Even the best players exhibit high variability of both velocity and direction of the basketball at the time of release; these two variables are, however, closely correlated, so the variability of the final position of the working point (at the time of contact with the basket) is relatively low. In most computer games, the working point is a fighter plane or ninja image or some other figure on the monitor screen, and one controls it by moving a joystick without any direct contact with the working point.

In the middle of the 19th century, it was very fashionable among physiologists to cut frogs into pieces and to observe the behavior of the pieces (so-called, "preparations"). A commonly studied preparation was the decapitated (beheaded) frog. Among others, the great German physiologist H. Pflüger studied the reflex behavior in decapitated frogs, in particular, the so-called "wiping reflex." If one places a small piece of paper soaked in a weak acid solution on the decapitated frog's back, the frog wipes it off the skin with a beautifully coordinated movement of the ipsilateral (same side) hindlimb (see Figure 5). More recently, such experiments were performed in Moscow by a group of motor control researchers (Berkenblit, Feldman, & Fukson, 1986). These experiments were performed on spinalized (a procedure in which the spinal cord is cut at an upper region and thus separated from the brain) rather than on decapitated frogs. Generally, the effects

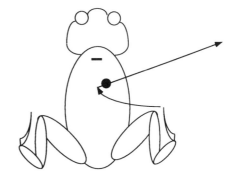

FIG. 5. An illustration of the experiments with the wiping reflex in spinalized frogs. A stimulus is indicated with the black dot. The level of the spinal cord transection is indicated with the black bar.

are the same (brain signals are unavailable for the spinal cord and body muscles), but the animal looks better. In particular, we tried to make the frog miss the irritating stimulus by applying mechanical constraints to the hindlimb. A loosely looped thread was placed on the hindlimb to prevent movements in the knee joint beyond a certain limit so that the maximal knee joint excursion was about 5° (in unrestrained conditions, changes in the knee joint angle are much greater). With the thread restraint, the frog was able to remove the stimulus from its back during the first attempt. Then, the knee was released, and a cast was applied to prevent movements in the next (more distal) joint. The frog once again wiped the stimulus on the first trial. Then, a lead bracelet was placed on the distal part of the hindlimb; the weight of the bracelet was nearly equal to the weight of the hindlimb itself. The frog still was able to wipe the stimulus accurately. In general, virtually all the attempts to fool the spinal frog failed if it was theoretically able to lift the hindlimb and reach the target.

So, what do the blacksmith, the basketball player, and the decapitated frog have in common? In all these examples, the central nervous system (or what is left of it in a spinalized frog) has a choice of solving the task differently. This choice is reflected in the variability of the trajectories and in the possibility of solving the same task when the loading conditions are changed. However, one can safely assume that each—the blacksmith, the player, the frog—was doing the same in different trials; that is, each was reproducing the same motor program, whatever it was. Therefore, the variability and flexibility of the peripheral motor patterns were due to the later steps in the processing of the hypothetical standard motor program.

With regard to the notion of degrees of freedom, in all these examples, one can think about degrees of freedom available to a hypothetical controller (independently controlled variables), even if this controller has not yet been discovered. On the other hand, apparently, there are peripheral degrees of freedom that may be drawn into play and contribute to the overall variability and flexibility of the observed, peripheral movement patterns.

INVERSE PROBLEMS

One of the pseudo-Bernstein problems deals with establishing a correspondence between working-point trajectories in the external three-dimensional space and movement trajectories in a space of joint angles. If one places the tip of the index finger on this page and tries to move the arm without losing the contact with the paper, there are an infinite number of combinations of joint angles corresponding to the fixed position of the working point (fingertip). The first question is, Does the system care about particular combinations of joint angles? The answer seems to be no. Nevertheless, an inadequate formulation of the Bernstein problem (or an adequate formulation of the pseudo-Bernstein problem) may be suggested in the following form: How does the system choose a particular combination of joint angles for a position of the working point in the external space, or How does the system choose a particular time sequence of such combinations in order to match a desired working point trajectory?

This problem is known as the problem of inverse kinematics. It belongs to the class of ill-posed problems because it cannot be solved without some additional information about the system or without additional constraints imposed on the system (compare it to the system of two equations with three unknowns discussed earlier).

Although robotics shares many common problems and approaches with human motor control, the ultimate quests are different. In human motor control the quest is to understand how voluntary movements are controlled. In robotics it is to design a method of controlling a humanlike (or "something-else-like") mechanical system (a robot). This difference makes some of the approaches, which are likely to have only a remote relation to motor control problems, quite useful for robotics. One of these is inverse kinematics. Another one is inverse dynamics.

If there is an ambiguity in relating movement trajectories in a joint space to working-point trajectories in the Cartesian space, it is even more apparent in attempts to draw such relations with patterns of muscle forces. Which time patterns of muscle forces are required to produce a desired working-point trajectory? This question is even more ill-posed (if this is possible) because the number of redundant degrees of freedom is likely to be even higher. However, this question, known as the problem of inverse dynamics, is one of the most frequently addressed in robotics.

Can one guess what happened at the level of joint positions and forces by looking only at a working-point trajectory? The answer is likely no, based on the observations of blacksmiths, basketball players, and spinal frogs described in the previous section. Can one define what pattern of footprints a fox will make, on the basis of the trajectory of the rabbit it chases? This inverse problem has no simple solution because different footprints may correspond to one and the same rabbit trajectory.

I will not analyze the problems of inverse kinematics and inverse dynamics here, but leave this area for the experts in robotics. Instead, I return to the problems of choice inherent in the production of voluntary movements in humans. Until now I have considered such problems during multijoint limb movements. However, is there anything special about multijoint movements that may require the hypothetical control mechanism to have special features that are absent in single-joint movements? At a first glance, the answer to this question is a definite yes. Multijoint movements have mechanical redundancy, which is absent in single-joint movements. Accordingly, the pseudo-Bernstein problem does not occur during single-joint movements, because position of the endpoint is unambiguously related to joint angle. However, I am interested in the processes of control, not in describing peripheral movement patterns. The example illustrated in Figure 3 suggests that control redundancy may occur without any obvious mechanical redundancy. Also recall the example of a dot controlled by a pair of knobs. The question is, therefore, whether the genuine Bernstein problem occurs at the level of control of single-joint movements.

THE BERNSTEIN PROBLEM
AT THE SINGLE-JOINT LEVEL

Quite frequently experimenters who study voluntary movements in humans try to confine the movements to a single joint, one degree of freedom, and, frequently, constant external load. Unfortunately for the experimenters, most of the commonly studied joints of human limbs (e.g., shoulder, wrist, and ankle) have more than one degree of freedom and are controlled by more than two muscles. Moreover, some of these muscles are biarticular; their contractions directly induce changes in joint torque and/or movements in two adjacent joints. These conditions complicate the description and analysis of the data from such experiments. For example, the presence of several degrees of freedom for a joint makes the classification of the muscles into agonists and antagonists or flexors and extensors quite artificial. Most human limb muscles are multifunctional; they can produce torque or movement or both in different directions. In addition, biarticular muscles provide mechanical, springlike links between the joints, which affect the movements. So, it seems that movements are never confined to a single joint. For the sake of discussion, however, assume that ideal single-joint movements exist. Following is an analysis of these fictitious phenomena.

How can one change the state of his or her joint if it is fixed by an external device, in other words, if it cannot move? Generally, there are two major possibilities. First, one can press on the external device with different force. Second, one can stiffen the joint without producing a visible net torque (summed moments of muscle forces). Therefore, at least two variables are needed to describe the state of a joint, for example, joint net torque and joint stiffness. Is an additional variable needed to specify joint position? The answer would be yes if joint torque and position were independent. Consider, however, the following experiment. If one produces a net torque in the joint and then the external fixing device is suddenly removed, the joint will move in the direction of torque and stop at a new position (try to perform this experiment with friends!). One can certainly correct this new position and even bring the joint back, but this movement will require a conscious change in the motor commands. If one does not try to correct for the induced joint displacement, the joint behaves like a spring with changing stiffness (a so-called nonlinear spring). Ignore the joint nonlinearity and consider its spring characteristic as a straight line on a torque–angle plane (see Figure 6). The dependence of joint torque on joint angle means that one and the same command may be used to produce changes in joint torque

Two Basic Commands for a Single Joint

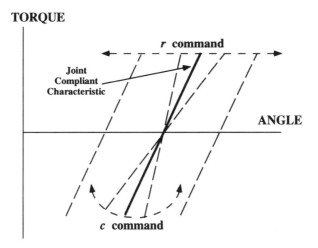

FIG. 6. Two basic commands for a single joint. The reciprocal command (r) shifts the joint torque–angle characteristic along the angle axis whereas the coactivation command (c) rotates the characteristic and changes its slope.

and joint displacement. The value of this command will define the position (zero length) of the joint spring characteristic. Another command will define its slope (Figure 6).

A pair of hypothetical central variables were suggested. These variables rather directly correspond to joint torque/position and stiffness and were termed *reciprocal command* (r) and *coactivation command* (c). Changes in the first command shift the joint characteristic along the angle axis whereas changes in the second command rotate the characteristic (see Figure 6). If the joint does not move, the reciprocal command leads to an increase in the activity of one muscle (e.g., a flexor) and a decrease in the activity of its antagonist (an extensor) so that it shifts the balance in favor of one of the muscles in the flexor–extensor pair controlling the joint. The coactivation command increases the levels of activation of both muscles and thus makes the joint stiffer, without affecting the relative balance of activity.

Remember that each joint is spanned by several muscles. Assume also that each muscle can be controlled by the central nervous system independently, that is, that there is one independently controlled central variable for each muscle; call this variable, λ. Apparently, one has as many variables at the control level as the number of muscles spanning the joint. If the joint is controlled by only two muscles, there are no problems, because the number of control variables, λ_1 and λ_2 equals the number of variables necessary to describe the joint behavior, r and c. Then, a simple relation between the {r, c} pair and λ's of the two muscles may be suggested (two equations with two unknowns!). This relation is true, however, only for a very simplified model of a joint with only one peripheral degree of freedom and only two muscles, a "pure agonist" and a "pure antagonist." Such joints do not exist.

The consideration of more realistic models, with multiple muscles whose action cannot be simply regarded as agonistic or antagonistic, leads to a typical Bernstein problem because the number of control variables (which, according to the assumption, is equal to the number of muscles) is greater than two. The central nervous system is again confronted with a problem of choice: How can it decide which combination of λ's to use in order to match required values for a pair $\{r, c\}$? This problem is as ill-posed as those dealing with the decomposition of a working-point trajectory into motions in individual joints or forces of individual muscles.

For example, the commonly studied elbow joint has three apparent major flexors and three heads of the apparent major extensor muscle (triceps), some of which are biarticular. Therefore, a complete description of the state of all the muscles requires six λ's, whereas the joint state can be described with only two variables, r and c. This is a typical Bernstein problem of redundancy. Because most of the muscles are polyfunctional, factors such as the necessity to provide stability in other joints, anatomical constraints, and perhaps other factors may lead to a deterministic solution of this problem. However, there is a possibility that some redundancy is impossible to eliminate, and the problem may be solved only probabilistically. Therefore, single-joint motor control appears to be a particular case of multijoint control with all its problems, including the Bernstein problem. Multiple muscles crossing a joint lead to a problem of choice. Does it matter which muscles carry out a motor task? Probably not. Does the central nervous system care? This is a good question!

Taking one more step "down" may show whether the Bernstein problem occurs at the level of control of a single muscle.

THE BERNSTEIN PROBLEM
AT THE SINGLE-MUSCLE LEVEL

The muscle may seem to be the smallest "sensible" unit involved in motor behavior; however, the muscle structure and the organization of its connections with neural cells in the spinal cord (called *motoneurons*) is rather complex. Each muscle consists of numerous muscular fibers, which are able to develop force (contract) in response to electrical signals from motoneurons. These fibers are controlled by motoneurons, whose number is considerably smaller. Each motoneuron sends signals to several muscular fibers, which always contract together, in unison, like a group of trumpeters in an orchestra playing the same score. Such groups of muscular fibers together with the motoneuron that controls them are commonly addressed as a *motor unit*. Each muscle consists of a wide variety of motor units, some of which are smaller and involve only a few muscular fibers, whereas others may be considerably larger. So, the orchestra of a human muscle consists of groups of instruments (motoneurons), with each group playing its own melody. Is there an order regulating which instruments start playing first and which support the symphony later?

In the 1960s and 1970s, much attention was drawn to the recruitment patterns of motor units during voluntary and reflex contractions, apparently stimulated by an impressive series of studies by Henneman (1968) and his colleagues. In these studies, it was shown that during a slow increase in muscle forces, the smallest motor units are recruited first, followed by larger and larger motor units. This regular behavior was termed the *size principle of motor unit recruitment*, or the *Henneman principle*.

One must also take into account that the contribution of a motor unit to muscle force depends not only on the motor unit size but also on the frequency of its contractions. Generally, the faster the motoneuron fires, the larger is the contribution to muscle contraction force given by its motor unit. Therefore, if the central nervous system wants to increase the force of contraction of a muscle, it can do so by recruiting more motor units or by increasing the frequency of firing of those already recruited, or both.

The following is a problem of choice: How does the central nervous system decide which motoneurons to recruit and at what frequencies in order to match a required level of muscle force? Currently, most researchers would agree that this problem has only a probabilistic solution, irrespective of the amount of available additional information about the system. If one maintains a level of muscle force for a certain time, the firing frequency of each of the recruited motor units fluctuates. Moreover, some motor units may stop firing and be substituted by other motor units. It seems that the central nervous system does not care much which motor units contribute to the overall level of muscle activation. Therefore, a more appropriate reformulation of the problem might be: Which rules are used by the central nervous system to define recruitment patterns corresponding to a given level of muscle activation (or force)? The size, or Henneman, principle may be considered an example of such a rule, which may be termed *coordinative*. Note that the Henneman principle does not prescribe precisely which motor units are recruited and at which frequencies; instead, it suggests an area where a solution may be sought.

Imagine that the conductor of an orchestra consisting of 100 drummers wants to produce noise at the level of 100 dB. If this level is not maximal, a typical Bernstein problem occurs: Whom should be chosen and how strongly should the chosen ones beat? Will the conductor care? Probably not, if the level of noise is the only thing that matters. You might simply instruct the drummers: "Listen to the level of noise. If it goes down, beat harder; if it goes up, beat lighter." The drummers themselves will control the level of noise, although probably not ideally—the noise will fluctuate noticeably.

The problem looks more and more bizarre: One can take one more step—to the single-cell level—and ask which channels should be open at each particular time or which electrons should move to ensure a certain level of current. There is no end. What is the problem? Why consider all these strange questions, which apparently do not have definitive answers? The problem is trying to attack a problem with wrong means, by analyzing the activity of a complex system with methods that are inapplicable to complex systems (i.e., trying to understand its function on the basis of the summed activity of its elements). This approach is sometimes labeled "reductionism." Apparently, this is a dead-end route.

COMPLEX-SYSTEM APPROACH

A group of scouts from one of the planets of Tau-Centaur visited Earth, stole a Ford Escort, and decided to find out how it works. On their planet, atomic and subatomic physics was very well developed, along with psychology (in particular, they could move things and travel by thinking, read minds, induce the growth of plants, control weather, etc.), but there was not such a thing as engineering or physics of complex systems.

Lt. Col. Dumb-Dumb submitted the following psycho-report: "Our minds hover over a beautiful, inhabited planet, the third planet of the solar system. We have completed the preliminary analysis of the psychic activity of most of the animals. The highest developed living beings with detectable psycho-activity possess the most primitive psycho-abilities, which are no match even for psycho-retarded Tau-citizens. However, we have encountered beings whose external activity is not matched by any discernible psycho-waves. Apparently they possess an extremely powerful psycho-shield. Their displacements in the physical world are meaningful and powerful. They are frequently serviced by the aforementioned "highest" psycho-active beings, although we have been unable to detect any commands initiating such service. Because of the lack of psycho-contact, I have decided to attempt physically kidnapping one of these creatures and bringing it to Tau for deeper analysis. I take full responsibility for this unprecedented move, but the situation that forced it is also unprecedented. Please be ready for deep psychic analysis or even physical analysis of the prisoner since all our attempts at psycho-contact have failed."

From a psycho-report of the Tau Academy of Science: "The psycho-blocked creature kidnapped from the Third-Solar planet resisted all available means of breaking through its psycho-shield. We have failed to establish contact and, consequently, to interrogate the prisoner. As a last resort, we have performed its physical analysis. All the components of its apparent body consist of subatomic particles well known to Tau-scientists. The particles are arranged in atoms and molecules similarly to those seen in nonliving structures on Tau. For the last three Tau-months, all the psycho-computers of Tau have been analyzing interactions at both subatomic and atomic levels, trying to understand the source of activity that induced the movements of the prisoner on its home planet and commanded its psycho-active servants to perform their duties."

Despite all their progress in physics of elementary particles and psychology, the Tau-scientists are unlikely to understand how the car works because they do not even have a language for approaching the problem. They are trying to solve the problem using an inappropriate language, even two inappropriate languages, that of physics of elementary particles and that of psychology. Their "psycho-computers" will die of old age before solving the problem. Just imagine a car manual that starts with the physics of elementary particles, then goes into molecular physics, spends hundreds of pages on deriving properties of materials from molecular interactions, then proceeds into the area of human psychology, and so on. Apparently, such a manual might be quite helpful in many aspects but not in explaining how to drive and service the car.

What would be the correct approach? First of all, it is necessary to realize that one is dealing with a *complex system*, that is, with *a system whose properties cannot be derived from and should not be searched for in the properties of its elements*. The first step in studying such a system is always *to define an appropriate level of analysis*, to choose correct words that meaningfully describe the functioning of the system. How can one obtain the correct words to start the analysis? There is only one way: by inventing a correct language based on intuition, basic knowledge, and common sense.

The human body is apparently a complex system. Even its subsystems (e.g., systems of circulation, breathing, and digestion, and certainly the motor system) are apparently complex. The ultimate controller of all the systems, the central nervous system, is also complex. Most textbooks, however, describe the central nervous system along the "Tau-route." They start by describing the properties of cell membranes and the processes of cell excitation, then explain simple reflexes, and then leap to a description of a function, with motor function a frequent example.

This kind of description creates the impression of a multimillion-piece puzzle, which is supposed to come out as a nice picture. However, the box cover, which showed the picture, has been lost, and so one must manipulate the pieces without any knowledge of whether they should come out as da Vinci's *La Gioconda*, as Sunflowers, or as the Westminster Abbey, in the futile hope that the pieces will somehow fit together and that the solution will emerge by itself. There is no chance for success unless one can intuitively imagine a possible picture and proceed according to this theoretical template (plan). Trying to fit the pieces together based solely on their properties (e.g., shape) is unlikely to be successful because each piece can be successfully attached to millions of others. The situation within any system that involves signal processing by the central nervous system is even more complicated, because the properties of any neuron (the way it processes incoming information and generates output signals) may change depending on numerous factors, including the activity of its neighbors. Imagine that pieces of the hypothetical multimillion-piece puzzle can change shape when one tries to fit them to each other!

As I have already suggested, a complex system should not be studied this way. First of all, one must realize its general properties and then introduce an appropriate, meaningful language (taxonomy). Systems of seemingly different complexity may be described with the same sets of notions. For example, our planetary system consists of zillions of atoms. However, the Bohr planetary model for just one atom is qualitatively very similar to the solar planetary system. The behavior of a motionless, heavy rock may be much simpler and more predictable than the behavior of an electron orbiting one of the atoms within the rock. This means that a complex system does not necessarily imply a complicated description of its behavior. Most of the objects surrounding us may be described with fewer parameters and simpler laws than an atomic nucleus. This simplicity of description is in fact the most important attribute of the complex-system approach.

For example, an officer can control hundreds of soldiers with a few, rather simple commands, such as "Forward" and "Stop." The officer does not know and does not care how each soldier controls the movements of his legs and arms or how individual muscles change their activity in response to the commands. The officer would probably be quite surprised to know that he or she is using the complex-system approach, but this is exactly what is happening. Apparently an attempt to use an inappropriate set of notions (an inappropriate language), for example, telling each soldier which muscle to contract and at which time, would be ridiculous and lead to catastrophic consequences for the army.

After an appropriate language has been established, the system has been studied as a complex system, and its general properties have been discovered, one may try to translate the properties of the system into its elements, if desirable and possible. This process is unlikely to be very fruitful: Nobody is seriously trying to interpret La Gioconda's face as a combination of the paint strokes that were originally used by Leonardo da Vinci.

Therefore, to understand the basic control principles for a complex system, one must start by observing the behavior of the system in various conditions. This approach will hopefully lead to a definition for certain general features of the system's behavior. Unfortunately, if the system is very complex and its behavior very flexible (the human body is a good example), one does not have a chance of gathering exhaustive information that would allow the assembly of a "Behavioral Encyclopedia" containing the behavioral patterns for all possible tasks and external conditions. The next step is impossible without intuition and good luck: On the basis of very limited information about the system's behavior and very limited information about the system's structure, one must create a reasonable model, that is, a model for the hypothetical central structure controlling the voluntary movements. The model should not only account for the known facts but also predict new facts, which can be tested experimentally.

Relying on intuition rather than on a foolproof, deductive approach is, for me, one of the most attractive features of the complex-system approach. One must guess right—and that is a real challenge!

ILL-POSED AND WORSE-THAN-ILL-POSED PROBLEMS

When dealing with the functioning of a complex system whose subsystems themselves represent complex systems, one frequently encounters problems that are commonly addressed as ill-posed. I suggest that there are actually two types of ill-posed problems—benign and malignant. Table 1 presents some of the general features of these two groups of problems.

Problems of the first type (benign ones) present researchers with too many degrees of freedom or too few constraints on the system; mathematically, they are akin to those of solving, for example, a system of two equations with three unknowns. Generally, however, these problems may be only temporarily ill-posed, and when more information about the system's functioning is acquired, one may obtain the missing equation(s) that will make the problem unambiguously solvable. When one encounters a benign ill-posed problem, the problem is to find the missing equations, which can be accomplished by performing a detailed study of the system's behavior. On the other hand, if the task is not to understand how an existing system works but rather to design a redundant system that would have certain properties, the missing equations may be invented rather than discovered. For example, as I have mentioned earlier, such equations may reflect certain optimization principles (saving energy, minimizing movement time, etc.) commonly used in robotics. The problems of inverse kinematics and inverse dynamics in robotics are examples of benign ill-posed problems.

Problems of the second type (malignant ones) may be labeled "worse than ill-posed." For these, one tries to solve a problem formulated at one level of complexity with a language pertaining to a different level. Frequently, this approach amounts to trying to find a deterministic solution for an inherently probabilistic system. These problems cannot be unambiguously solved, regardless

TABLE 1
General Properties of Ill-Posed and Worse-Than-Ill-Posed Problems

Ill-Posed Problems	Worse-Than-Ill-Posed Problems
Less equations than unknowns	A problem is formulated at one level of complexity but a solution is searched for at a different level
The lacking equations exist but have not been discovered yet	The lacking equations do not exist Looking for a deterministic solution for a probabilistic problem
Find the equations and solve the problem	Reformulate the problem
Example: Inverse problems in robotics	Examples: Inverse problems in motor control The Bernstein problem

of the quantity and quality of available information about the system's functioning. They should be either reformulated or totally abandoned.

As discussed previously, worse-than-ill-posed problems occur at each and every level of motor control, as the following list of problems shows:

Problem 1. Determine movements of each and every ion during the process of generation of action potential.

Problem 2. Find which motor units will be recruited and at what frequencies for a given level of muscle force.

Problem 3. Find the time patterns of muscle forces for a multijoint limb movement from a certain initial position to a certain final position.

Taking a risk of being accused of blasphemy (not for the first time!), I suggest that the famous Bernstein problem is also worse than ill-posed.

For Problem 1, probably even the hard-liners of classical neurophysiology would agree that there is no unique solution. One can talk only about the general characteristics of ion movements through the membrane, for example, the contribution of different ions to the transmembrane current. Therefore, Problem 1 has only a probabilistic solution; that is, one can define a probability curve representing the likelihood of observing, for example, a sodium ion crossing the membrane. Motor control researchers can only envy their colleagues working with membrane currents, who have at their disposal an elaborate physicomathematical apparatus that can be used to calculate the probabilities.

For Problem 2, the situation is similar, although some of the aforementioned hard-liners may argue that finding the patterns of motor unit recruitment constitutes the heart of motor control. However, most researchers would agree that one can define only the probability of firing at a certain frequency for each motor unit. For this problem, the probability curves have not been defined, and the only firmly established law is the previously mentioned size principle of Henneman. (Note that even this law is not without exceptions, for example, when the muscle is playing an auxiliary role rather than serving as a prime mover.)

Problem 3 is likely to engender a more diverse spectrum of opinions. There are quite a few models of human motor control based on the control of muscle forces or on the control of their direct precursors, such as muscle electrical activity (electromyogram), signals coming from all the motoneurons innervating the muscles, or all the signals coming to the motoneurons. Note that the signals coming to motoneurons (the so-called total presynaptic input) define unambiguously their output, which defines unambiguously the muscle electrical activity, which, for predictable external conditions, defines unambiguously muscle forces. Unfortunately, in principle one is unable to specify the total input to motoneurons because they receive mixed information not only from the brain but also from the peripheral receptors. Any change in the state of the peripheral apparatus (e.g., a movement in a joint, pressure on an area of skin, force generation by a muscle, etc.) leads to a change in the signals received by the motoneurons. Therefore, *when a control signal is issued, one cannot, in principle predict which force will actually be generated by each and every muscle.* Actually, this is obvious from the previously mentioned, classical experiments performed by Bernstein on blacksmiths in the 1920s!

Now for the "blasphemy" part. As I have mentioned a couple of times, there is a big difference between controlling something and allowing something to happen. This difference is analogous to the difference between caring and indifference. Therefore, does the brain care which joints do what, when the task is to take a matchbox from the table or to hit the anvil with the hammer or to wipe a stimulus off one's back or to put a basketball into the basket?

All the available information indicates that the answer to the last question is a definite no. The brain apparently allows the joints to move along different trajectories as long as the task is successfully accomplished. Joint trajectories are allowed to occur rather than being prescribed by the brain.

Driving to a store that is four blocks east and four blocks north of one's house requires as few as one turn or as many as seven (see Figure 7). Usually, there are preferred routes, which may correspond to a minimal amount of time, a minimal number of turns, a minimal number of stop signals, or a minimal number of potholes. Actual choice of the route may depend on such poorly quantifiable

A Problem of Choice:
How to Get from the Home to the Store?

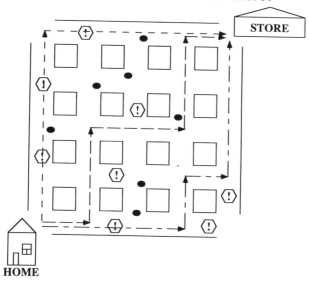

FIG. 7. An illustration of a typical problem of choice that does not have a unique solution.

parameters as traffic, weather, or even one's mood. Occasionally one may find out that he or she has missed a turn on the preferred route. Instead of making a U-turn and returning to the original route, one can make an "on-line" adjustment and switch to an alternative route so that the ultimate goal (reaching the store) is achieved. So, even "optimization principles" affecting the choice of route, do not work in 100% of the cases. Rather, they define a probability distribution for different routes, making some routes more preferable than others.

Many observations, starting with those from classical Bernstein experiments, suggest that the actual patterns of joint involvement during multijoint movements also vary according to a certain probabilistic distribution. This distribution may be affected by a number of factors including, in particular, the following factors:

1. Anatomy of the limb and physiology of the neuromuscular apparatus. One might call these factors "hardwired," even though practice may change them.

2. External task parameters.

3. Internal task parameters, which may involve such poorly quantifiable factors as mood, will, and intention. Remember the example of moving a cup filled with play dough and one filled with hot tea?

4. Coordination laws elaborated during the lifetime. For example, when babies start moving, they make many flapping, poorly controlled hand movements. After some time, these movements are transformed into coordinated reaching.

5. Inherent, irreducible noise within the central nervous system. Because all the elements (neurons) are supposed to work according to certain probabilistic laws, their firing patterns are not 100% predictable. Peripheral receptors may also contribute to the internal noise because of unpredictable variations in the external conditions (e.g., wind, friction between one's skin and clothes, etc.). Actually, noise may play an important role in the processes of pattern generation, but this theme is certainly beyond the goals of this chapter.

Therefore, what remains is an unexpected answer to the title statement of this chapter: *The central nervous system does not make all the choices but allows some of them to be made.* It states a general goal and imposes certain limitations on the motor system (call these *coordination laws*). These limitations make not all possible ways of solving the problem equivalent. In other words, the central nervous system imposes certain specific patterns of probability distribution, but the actual solution emerges mostly by itself. The brain does play dice!

One more example follows. When a river defines it route of flow (its river bed), it follows the major coordination law, Go down! However, this law by itself does not define unambiguously where the river bed will be. It may even change from season to season, following possible changes in wind patterns, soil properties, vegetation, and so on; as water eventually flows to the ocean, the hammer of a blacksmith eventually hits the anvil, the frog's hindlimb eventually wipes the stimulus off the skin, and the basketball eventually gets into the basket.

WHERE DO WE STAND NOW? (AND IN WHICH DIRECTION DO WE GO, BY THE WAY?)

So, I have arrived at a seemingly pessimistic conclusion that the exact patterns of changes in muscle force or muscle activation patterns for a goal-directed, multijoint limb movement will never be defined. But why call it "pessimistic"? Physicists are not driven into depression by the fact that they are unable to define the position of an electron with infinite precision. They are rather happy to have a whole new area of study that requires new, specific ways of analysis and that promises new insights into the physical foundation of our world (not to mention the exciting possibility of receiving grants in new, virgin areas!). Let us follow their example and try to formulate promising directions of research in the area of control of voluntary movements. Following Bernstein, this area can be used as a tool for studying the basic principles of brain functioning.

On the basis of what was discussed earlier, one can say that the system for the production of voluntary movements is a complex, nonequilibrium system that involves the neural structures, the muscles, and the peripheral motor apparatus, and that is in constant interaction with the environment. In characterizing such systems, it is helpful to use certain parameters that define the general mode of the system's functioning. These are called *order parameters* or *collective variables*. For example, if one is tapping a rhythm with two hands, only two stable regimes exist, in-phase and out-of-phase. The relative phase of the tapping may be considered a collective variable. The value of this variable tells one how different parts of the complex system are coordinated, without delving into "minor details," such as the amplitude of tapping.

Collective variables are extremely important for defining the general coordination mode of the system's functioning; however, they apparently are not enough. Another group of contributors to the process of motor control can be called *control variables*. The patterns of these variables are generated by the central nervous system according to numerous factors reflecting task, environment, and intention. These patterns may, in particular, lead to changes in collective variables; that is, they can induce qualitative changes in the system's behavior. For example, if one voluntarily increases the frequency of an out-of-phase two-hand tapping with the help of hypothetical control variables, the original pattern will eventually turn into in-phase; in other words, a jump in the collective variable will occur.

Control variables may be considered as a kind of internal language used by the central nervous system to communicate its motor needs to the executive apparatus (muscles with their central reflex connections). This apparatus is unlikely to understand the language of Cartesian coordinates and may be expected to be more comfortable with the language of levels of neuron excitation, reflex gains and thresholds, and so on. Apparently, it would be advantageous for the system to have a language that is independent of possible, and frequently unpredictable, changes in the environment. This hypothetical language is based on variables that may be termed *independently controlled*. Identifying independently controlled variables is a necessary step when one deals with a complex system. Currently, researchers in motor control have at least a hypothetical language for single-joint motor control. They may not be far from discovering an appropriate language for multijoint motor control, but it does not yet exist.

Figure 8 illustrates the organization of a hypothetical sequence of the steps involved in the generation of voluntary movements. Note that at each step, the output defines the input according to a certain nondeterministic law (a probability curve), so that the uppermost controller does not know exactly what happens at the periphery. It certainly may update its knowledge on the basis of the information from the peripheral receptors, but this process takes time, and such knowledge may frequently be outdated, particularly during very fast movements. This knowledge is certainly necessary for planning motor actions but may not be very helpful for on-line corrections of an ongoing fast movement. It does not matter how many steps are involved in the process illustrated in Figure 8; there may be only one step or a hierarchy of several steps. I think that some kind of hierarchy exists, although this view is not shared by some of my most respected friends-colleagues. For the first step, the input is task parameters and intentions or will of the person. (To me, will or intentions are external input parameters similar to task parameters.) The input defines, in particular, values

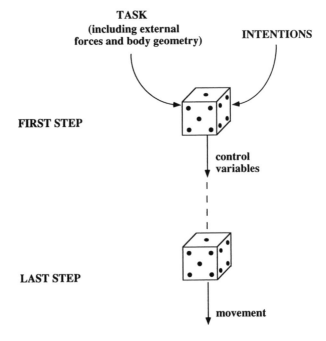

FIG. 8. The brain does play dice!

of the collective variables at this level. The processing of the input information within the first black box involves nondeterministic mechanisms so that the output is unpredictable or, better said, predictable only in terms of probabilities. The output of this step is patterns of control variables that will define values of the collective variables for the next step. And so on . . .

How can such a system be studied? Two lines of research seem equally important. First, one should define the appropriate collective variables at each step of the hypothetical system illustrated in Figure 8. Second, one should define the independently controlled variables used as the output at each step. The word *define* in the previous two phrases may rather be substituted with *guess*. Guessing is actually the most exciting part of research in this area! After guessing right, the probability curves and/or the mechanisms defining them should be searched for. Scientists are only at the first stages of this exciting, adventurous trip into the realm of the gambling processes within the human brain. There are enough unsolved and even unformulated problems for all to have their share of fun.

REFERENCES

Berkinblit, M. B., Feldman, A. G., & Fukson, O. I. (1986). Adaptability of innate motor patterns and motor control mechanisms. *Behavioral and Brain Sciences*, 9, 585–638.

Henneman, E. (1968). Peripheral mechanisms in the control of muscle. In V. B. Mountcastle (Ed.), *Medical physiology* (Vol. 2, pp. 1697–1716). St. Louis, MO: C. V. Mosby.

On the Biomechanical Basis of Dexterity

Gerrit Jan van Ingen Schenau
Arthur J. van Soest
Vrije Universiteit, Amsterdam

It has often been stated that the ideas of Bernstein, relevant to many disciplines that constitute the human movement sciences, placed him ahead of his time by 20–50 years. Many physiologists, psychologists, anatomists, biomechanists, and even philosophers have been inspired by his impressive work.

The recently rediscovered book by Bernstein, *On Dexterity and Its Development* again summarizes his strong arguments and his creative perspectives. Moreover, it demonstrates another quality of Bernstein: his capacity to write for a broad audience and to illustrate his reasoning with numerous nice examples and anecdotes.

Now, about 100,000 scientific papers on subjects relevant to motor control later, it would be amazing (and a pity for those papers) if one were not able to dispute any of his arguments. In this chapter we indeed dispute some of his arguments. Yet, we are really amazed by the fact that the major perspectives Bernstein offered again in this book are still highly up-to-date and exceptionally useful in continuing to guide contemporary research. Though many will dispute some of our arguments, we believe that Bernstein's approach and ideas can still serve as a model in many respects, including the following examples:

His emphasis on the active sometimes even creative nature of motor behavior; his deep insight in the nature of motor control; his warning against reductionism ("the whole is more than the sum of parts"); and his demonstration of a successful top–down approach.

The integration of knowledge from various sources (physiology, anatomy, psychology, cybernetics, biomechanics, mathematics, medicine, and training practice), which appears to be a prerequisite for sound and testable theories on motor control and human movement science in general.

His strong focus on perception and the role of sensory information in guiding actions, as well as his reservations toward cybernetic models, a reservation associated with his emphasis on the necessity for anticipation in most actions.

His ideas about functional implications of the brain as a multistory building with relatively autonomous subsystems, which allows the parallel processing of different aspects and the generation of, for example, (muscle) synergies. This approach has been successfully applied to other aspects of human and animal behavior as well.

The strong emphasis on development and learning as processes necessary as a basis for dexterity, two aspects that, in part, solve Bernstein's problem with respect to the controllability of the extremely complex human movement organs.

These perspectives lead us to the conclusion that this book may still, 40 years after its genesis, serve as an excellent introduction into the major issues of motor control.

Our aim in this chapter is to discuss the biomechanical basis of dexterity. Because biomechanics, indeed, does not have much to contribute to the intellectual aspects of dexterity, we mainly focus our discussion on what is usually loosely referred to as "Bernstein's problem," with examples of movements up to Levels B and C only (related to body and object dexterity). Although mathematics is the major language of mechanics, we attempt to follow the easy reading style of Bernstein's book as much as possible. After providing a short description of Bernstein's view in the light of recent advances, we present an overview of (the limitations of) a number of ideas, models, and theories forwarded as solutions to the motor control problem. The final part of our contribution contains our observations and ideas about coordination between muscles spanning one joint (monoarticular muscles) and those spanning two joints (biarticular muscles), as far as they are relevant to this topic, and finally a discussion of a few more general perspectives on movement organization triggered by Bernstein and supported by recent publications. As requested by the editors we limit the references to a few key publications only.

PROBLEMS IN MOTOR COORDINATION: BERNSTEIN'S VIEW IN THE LIGHT OF RECENT ADVANCES

In Bernstein's discussion of the motor coordination problem, two central themes can be discerned, the first referred to as the degrees-of-freedom problem and the second that may be referred to as the controllability problem. Although the ensemble of these problems is usually referred to as "Bernstein's problem" (see also chapter by M. L. Latash, this volume), we prefer to discuss the degrees-of-freedom problem and the controllability problem separately.

The Degrees-of-Freedom Problem

In Figures 1 and 2, two examples are presented which demonstrate aspects of the kinematic degrees-of-freedom problem and which are used to illustrate other aspects later in this chapter as well. The subject in Figure 1 is an experienced cabinetmaker, who pushes the saw along one distinct trajectory with high accuracy. Figure 1 illustrates the point made by Bernstein that because the number of kinematic degrees of freedom of the carpenter's skeletal system outnumbers the degrees of freedom of the task goal (the saw's trajectory), the required saw trajectory can be realized through a myriad of combinations of joint movements. Similarly, as illustrated in Figure 2, an explosive movement such as the vertical jump can be performed in many different ways. Despite the freedom of choice, experienced cabinetmakers will not exhibit essential differences while performing this action although some individual styles may be distinguished. Experienced vertical jumpers, such as volleyball players, show even less variation in the kinematics during their push-off.

Interestingly, the degrees-of-freedom problem does not occur solely at the level of kinematics. As noted by Bernstein, a similar problem occurs at the level of joints that are spanned by more than one muscle: To achieve a certain movement, the sum of the muscle forces must have a specific value; however, due to the fact that humans have an abundance of muscles spanning each joint, there is an infinite number of combinations of individual muscle forces that result in the required summed force, or more precisely, in the net joint torque. Yet again, it has been shown that for those who are well trained in the tasks the variation in activation patterns of different muscles is remarkably small.

The nature of the degrees-of-freedom problem can be stated summarily: To achieve a certain goal, an infinite number of possible solutions is available, yet humans appear to use only a very small subset of these possible solutions. On the one hand, this leads to the important question raised by Bernstein: Which

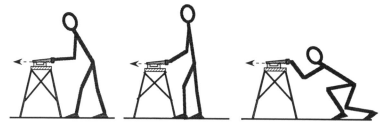

FIG. 1. The degrees-of-freedom problem: A cabinetmaker can realize the saw's trajectory by various joint movements.

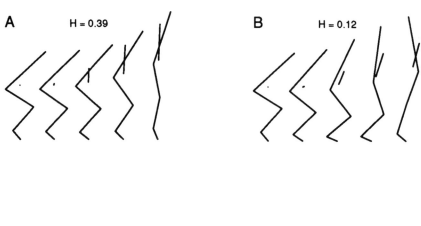

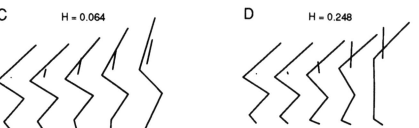

FIG. 2. Stick-figure representations of the push-off of simulated vertical jumps. Leftmost figure in each sequence is the starting position; rightmost figure, position at take-off. Individual figures are linearly spaced in time. Vector, which originates from the body center of gravity, represents velocity of the body's center of gravity. H is jump height, relative to upright standing. A–Push-off resulting from applying the *optimal* muscle activation pattern as obtained through numerical optimization. B–Movement that results when the hamstrings are activated 100 ms earlier than in A. C–Movement that results when all muscles are maximally activated throughout the push-off phase. D–Movement that results when the activation pattern of A is applied to a model in which maximal knee extensor force is increased by 50%.

constraints lead the central nervous system to these rather stereotyped solutions? On the other hand, one should bear in mind what Galen (A.D. 131–201) postulated: "Nature, just in everything has made the size of the muscles to accord with the usefulness of the actions they must perform" (*De usu partium*, I, p. 171). We paraphrase slightly: Although the muscular-skeletal system may seem highly redundant according to contemporary mathematical models, possibly it is not at all redundant in a functional sense: A system with fewer muscles would be less flexible. As noted by Bernstein, the enormous number of muscles (700–800) in the human action system enables humans to stray away from stereotypical solutions to movement problems (if necessary) and therefore forms the basis for dexterity.

The Controllability Problem

Quite aside from the degrees-of-freedom problem, there are a number of characteristics of the motor system that make the control of complex movements far from simple.

Tendon Elasticity. Muscles consist of two parts connected in series: the muscle fibers and the tendon. It is now well established that most of what has been known as the "series elastic component" since the English physiologist A. V. Hill published his work on muscle physiology in the 1930s, is not located in the muscle fibers but rather in the passive tendons and tendon plates. There is now concluding evidence that the stretch of the tendon is less than 5% of its own length when the muscle fibers attached to it exert maximal force. The mechanical significance of this elastic property with respect to its role in both shock absorption and storage and release of elastic energy (when properly timed) is undisputed. Irrespective of its mechanical significance, tendon elasticity has serious consequences for motor control. To clarify this problem, we first introduce the term *muscle–tendon complex* to refer to the ensemble of a muscle belly, containing the muscle fibers, and a tendon. As these elements are connected in series, the length of the muscle–tendon complex is the sum of the lengths of belly and tendon. Because the muscle–tendon complex is rigidly connected to the skeleton at its endings, its length directly indicates the angle of the joint it spans. Thus, if humans were able to control the length of the muscle–tendon complex, they would have control over the movement of the joint. Unfortunately, the tendon is a purely passive structure with a length that depends on the force exerted on it. Thus, as rightly observed by Bernstein, even if humans were able to control the length of the muscle fibers, this control still would not imply control over joint angles.

A theoretically possible solution for this problem may be found in the Golgi tendon organs, small sensors that produce a neural signal that codes for tendon force. As we mentioned earlier, tendon stretch is largely a nonlinear function of tendon force. Thus, the signal produced by the Golgi tendon organs may be used in the central nervous system to estimate the length of the tendon. The combination of direct control over muscle fiber length with this estimated tendon length would, in theory, result in direct control over joint angle.

Muscle Fiber Characteristics. The force exerted by muscle fibers does not depend solely on their neural activation; even in the simplest model, the dependency of this force on fiber length and fiber velocity must be taken into account. Motor control is further complicated by the fact that preceding contractions may affect the force-length and force-velocity characteristics; as a result, both improvement (potentiation) or reduction (fatigue) of the muscle's force-generating capacity may occur (*history effects*). Furthermore, during fast stretching of an active muscle, its force-generating capacity is dramatically affected, due to a process referred to as "cross-bridge yielding" in muscle physiology. In short, the force produced by a muscle does not depend solely on its neural activation but also on its length, velocity, and contraction history, to name but the most important variables. What is the consequence for motor control? That a one-to-one correspondence between neural activation and muscle force definitely does not exist.

Interaction Between Body Segments. As noted by Bernstein (essay 6), the movements of different segments influence each other through joint reaction forces. As a consequence, the effect of a particular muscle is not limited to moving the joint or joints that are crossed by that muscle. Zajac and his colleagues (e.g., Zajac, 1993) provided convincing evidence that in multijoint movements each muscle has its own unique function, a function which depends largely on internal and external conditions. For example, when one stands up from a chair, extension of the knee is partly achieved by the plantarflexors of the ankle! Clearly this feature magnifies the problem of motor control: When one attempts to correct the movement at one joint by adapting the force produced by the muscles spanning that joint, this maneuver will lead to new disturbances of the movement of many other joints!

Interaction With the Environment. Virtually all human movements are aimed at achieving something in the environment. In any case, each and every movement takes place in an environment. Mechanically, the environment influences movements through the forces from the environment that act on the body. Examples of such forces are gravity and friction. One might wonder to what extent motor coordination is affected by variation in these external forces. Suppose the cabinetmaker (Figure 1) needs to saw a miter joint without using a miter box. To this aim, he or she would have to keep the saw at an angle of 45° from the vertical. By bending his or her trunk *sideways* by the same angle, the cabinetmaker would be able to produce the desired saw trajectory by exactly the same shoulder, elbow, and wrist movements as used for the vertical sawing situation. However, the effect of gravity on each of the segments involved clearly differs between both situations. Thus, to produce the same joint movement, the cabinetmaker needs quite different muscle-force profiles for both situations described. In a less extreme formulation, when one starts a movement, the situation is unlikely to be exactly the same every time, even in stereotyped movements. Even a small deviation in initial position will lead to an unsuccessful movement if the muscle forces are not attuned to the external forces. We therefore draw the following conclusion: The muscle forces needed to produce a certain joint movement depend strongly on external conditions.

Disturbances Are Everywhere! One might think that as long as a movement unfolds according to plan, the complicating factors mentioned are not that important. With the following list of disturbances and uncertainties, we hope to convince the reader that he or she is unlikely to have ever completed a movement about which everything was certain at the start: In sawing, the resistance offered by the wood will vary continuously; in picking up a cup of coffee, the weight is not exactly known; in turning a key, the amount of force required is unknown; in pole vaulting, there is often a disturbing effect of wind; in cycling, the friction between tires and road varies with weather conditions; after a meal, gravitational forces are larger.

All these (and other) factors led Bernstein to the conclusion that there does not and cannot exist an unequivocal relation between central commands and muscle force. As a consequence, net joint torques cannot be represented either, and, thus, no fixed relation can exist between central commands and the kinematics of movements (see also Bernstein, 1967). With that established, how *does* one control movements? In the following discussion, we consider one option: motor control on the basis of extensive use of feedback.

SOME NEW INSIGHTS RELEVANT TO BERNSTEIN'S VIEW

Feedback-Based Motor Control?

Feedback plays an essential role in the control of many processes. Consider a game of chess as an example. After making a move, one observes what the effect of that move is (i.e., what move the opponent makes), and on the basis of that effect, one adjusts the plans for the next move. If the reader is not convinced that feedback is essential here, he or she should try playing a game in which the opponent's moves are hidden from view; we guarantee that both the game and the reader's doubts will soon be over!

The possibility of basing the control of one's movements on feedback of course presupposes the presence of sensors in the body. In that respect humans are well equipped. First of all, humans are able to sense important aspects of their relationship to the environment (vision, hearing, touch); furthermore, they have sensors that provide information about aspects of the state the body itself is in, such as joint receptors, Golgi tendon receptors (see previous discussion), and muscle spindles, which provide information on both length and velocity of the muscle fibers. Is the presence of sensors sufficient for concluding that feedback-based motor control is feasible? In Bernstein's and our view, not necessarily. First, the mechanical interaction between body segments complicates feedback-based control: As we discussed earlier, the effect of muscle forces is not limited to the joint spanned by the muscle. If feedback-based control is to take these interactions into account, the control of each individual muscle will have to be based on feedback from numerous other muscles. More important, motor control differs from a chess game in that the duration of many movements is just a fraction of that of even a single move in chess! Consequently, the process of sensing something, transferring the information, translating it into the proper activation level of a number of muscles, transferring this information to the muscles, and finally converting this "command" into muscle force may just take too much time to be useful in fast movements. In fact, the fastest neural feedback loops (termed the short- and medium-latency responses) have latency times between 30 and 70 ms. What must be added to that is the time shift between muscle activation and muscle force: Due to various physiological and biochemical processes, it takes some time for neural activation to result in muscle force. In order to estimate the magnitude of this time shift, one would have to measure simultaneously the muscle's neural activation and the force it produces. Instead of measuring the neural activation directly, which is difficult in humans, one can measure the potential differences that result from depolarization of the muscle fibers. This signal, which is termed the *electromyogram* (EMG), is thought to be proportional to the neural activation of the muscle. Direct measurement of muscle force is also difficult in humans. Instead, one measures the torque that the muscle produces relative to the axis of the joint it spans, using a dynamometer. In case of static contraction, this torque is directly proportional to the muscle force. Figure 3 shows an example of the electromyographic activity of the vastus lateralis muscle, a thigh muscle that extends the knee joint, together with the knee extensor torque as measured during a static dynamometer experiment in which the person was instructed to generate a knee extensor torque that varied

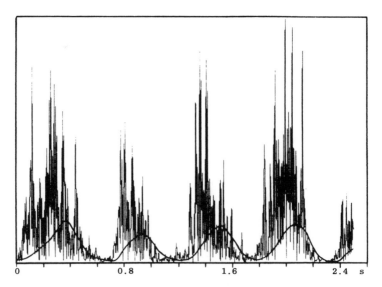

FIG. 3. Intensity of EMG (rugged curve), representing neural activation of the vastus lateralis, a major knee extensor muscle, and simultaneously measured knee extension torque (smooth curve), representing the force exerted by the knee extensors. Note that the torque curve is shifted to the right relative to the EMG curve. The magnitude of this shift (determined by a cross-correlation technique) is approximately 90–100 ms.

sinusoidally with time. The force response is clearly delayed, relative to the electromyographic signal. The time shift between muscle activation and muscle force has been measured for various static as well as dynamic movements and appears to have a magnitude of about 90–100 ms for human leg muscles. Thus, the total delay between sensing anything and adapting muscle force amounts to 120–170 ms. As the duration of many leg extensions, for example, is less than 300 ms (see, for example, the sprint push-off outlined in Figure 7), this delay is quite substantial. Motor control on the basis of such delayed feedback would be comparable to a chess game in which one must base the nth move on the opponent's position after $n - 3$ moves. We conclude that for all (medium) fast human leg actions, the feedback delay is too large to adjust an ongoing movement on the basis of sensory feedback as part of the organization of undisturbed movements. This conclusion severely restricts the applicability of closed-loop control theories. It supports Bernstein's statements (essay 7) that in actions like throwing and jumping, all sensory corrections must be introduced on the basis anticipation when the movement has not yet started. The same holds for actions like sprinting and speed skating. We also support Bernstein's view that with experience, anticipation becomes increasingly important in less explosive actions such as walking, running, and skiing. Though the total delay for arm muscles seems to be somewhat smaller than these, for fast and medium-fast arm movements, this necessity for anticipation will be true as well.

Counteracting Disturbances

In the previous section, we concluded that it is impossible to control (medium) fast movements on the basis of feedback; anticipation, or in terms of control theory, open-loop control is predominant. Yet, this principle cannot be the whole story, because it cannot explain how unexpected disturbances that occur during execution of the movement and that were thus not incorporated into the open-loop plan are handled. Of course, this is a serious issue only if these unanticipated disturbances have a large influence on the movement that follows. Systems for which a small disturbance has serious consequences are usually referred to as *unstable* systems. A prime example of a *stable* system is the pendulum of a clock: No matter how one disturbs the pendulum's movement, in due time, it will return to its original movement, with no need for any corrective action whatsoever. In contrast, a stick balancing on one's finger is a prime example of an unstable system: If someone applies even the smallest of forces to the top end, the stick's motion will change dramatically and result in its fall, unless corrective action is taken. For obvious reasons, such a balancing stick is referred to as an "inverted pendulum." The skeletal system is mechanically analogous to multiple inverted pendulums in tasks such as walking, jumping, and throwing, and is thus inherently unstable. This instability results in amplification of disturbances, no matter how small they were initially. Thus, just as in the case of the balancing stick, humans need a mechanism for corrective action if they are to prevent falling because of small unexpected disturbances. Bernstein indicated the direction in which to look for such a mechanism by stating in essay 6 that the general structural principle is to delegate any task to as low a level in the nervous system as possible: By solving basic problems at a low level (e.g., the spinal cord), the higher levels (e.g., neocortex) can be involved in more global (e.g., planning) activities. Bernstein was right to look low in the hierarchy; recent findings have shown that it is, in fact, not even in the nervous system but rather in the muscles themselves where small disturbances are annihilated: Small disturbances may be handled by the muscles without any involvement of the nervous system, as we explain later.

Earlier in this chapter, we pointed out that at a given neural activation level, the force exerted by a muscle depends on, among other things, fiber length and fiber contraction velocity. We noted that the underlying force-length and force-velocity characteristics complicate motor control because they preclude a one-to-one correspondence between muscle activation and muscle force. Recently, the other side of the coin was emphasized by van Soest and colleagues (van Soest & Bobbert, 1993; van Soest, Bobbert, & van Ingen Schenau, 1994), who demonstrated that these characteristics have a pronounced positive effect on the stability of human movements. To explain this phenomenon, we must first go into some detail concerning the force-length and force-velocity characteristics.

The force-length characteristic describes how the force that a muscle exerts depends on its length if all other variables (e.g., neural activation, velocity) are constant. Physiological experiments have shown that muscle fibers can actively generate force over a limited range of lengths; outside this range, active force production is zero. Furthermore, active force has a peak near the middle of the range, at a length referred to as *optimal length*. In the large majority of cases, muscles operate below optimal length. In this region, stretching the muscle results in increasing force and vice versa, just as in any type of spring: *The force-length characteristic results in springlike behavior.*

Similarly to the force-length characteristic, the force-velocity characteristic describes how active force depends on contraction velocity, all other things being constant. It has long been known that force decreases monotonously with contraction velocity: The faster the muscle shortens, the lower the force. This behavior reminds us of a dashpot, which, in physics is an object that opposes movement with a force proportional to the velocity of movement. Thus, *the force-velocity characteristic results in dashpot-like behavior.*

With this insight into the workings of the force-length and force-velocity characteristics, we can explain how these properties reduce the effect of disturbances. Consider the following example. Imagine a person instructed to stand motionless with the knees bent. To achieve this, the person must set the neural activation of the knee extensor muscles to a level that is just sufficient to counteract gravity. Now suppose that we are able to push the person's knees into further flexion without the person's noticing this, and, consequently, without any adaptation of the neural activation occurring. The question is What would happen? Clearly, due to the increased knee flexion, the knee extensor muscles are stretched, and according to the previous description of the force-length characteristic, as a result, the force produced by these muscles will increase. This increased extensor force will drive the knee in the direction of extension, until equilibrium is reached exactly at the knee angle from which this mental experiment started! In accordance with the concept of stability, clearly the force-length characteristic is responsible for stability against positional disturbances. We leave it to the reader to assess that, similarly, the force-velocity characteristic results in stability against velocity disturbances.

Interestingly, this stabilization against disturbances resulting from the muscle's force-length-velocity characteristic is not at all limited to static situations, such as the one described, but applies equally well to highly dynamic tasks, as was shown by van Soest and coauthors (van Soest & Bobbert, 1993; van Soest et al., 1994), who studied maximum-height jumping. In their studies, the following steps were taken. First, a model of the muscular-skeletal system was devised, in which muscle activation was its input and the resulting movement its output. Next, a static starting position from which the model had to jump was defined. By systematically varying the activation pattern of each of the muscles, van Soest and colleagues identified the set of muscle activation patterns that resulted in the highest jump possible. The resulting optimal movement is depicted in Figure 4(A), in the form of stick-figure diagrams of the push-off phase, in which the leftmost figure represents the static starting position and the rightmost represents the instant of take-off. Next, van Soest and colleagues turned to the interesting part: They perturbed the initial static position and watched the effect on the following movement, not allowing the activation pattern to be changed. In fact, they perturbed the initial foot angle by as little as 0.01 radians (i.e., by less than 1°). In order to evaluate how well the force-length-velocity characteristic succeeded in counteracting such disturbances, they also prepared a model in which these characteristics were absent. That the force-length-velocity characteristic indeed acts to stabilize against disturbances is obvious from a comparison of the pattern in A to the patterns in B and C, in which the disturbance was applied. The B pattern illustrates the "handicapped" model (no force-length-velocity characteristic but otherwise identical). In that case, jump height was reduced to 23% of its undisturbed value as a result of a seemingly negligible disturbance, a result indicating the inherent instability of the system. In contrast, in the C pattern, jump height was hardly affected.

What is the conclusion from all this? In fact, it is quite straightforward: First, in explosive movements, such as vertical jumping, neural feedback cannot be used to counteract disturbances because the feedback loop is just too s–l–o–w. Second, in such movements, it is the force-length-velocity characteristic of the muscle itself that reduces the influence of unexpected disturbances. Third, this peripheral control system has the important advantage that correction occurs instantaneously: *The muscle's force-length-velocity characteristic forms a zero-lag peripheral feedback system.* In hindsight, Bernstein was right to look for stabilizing mechanisms low in the hierarchy (e.g., low-level neural mechanisms like the short- and

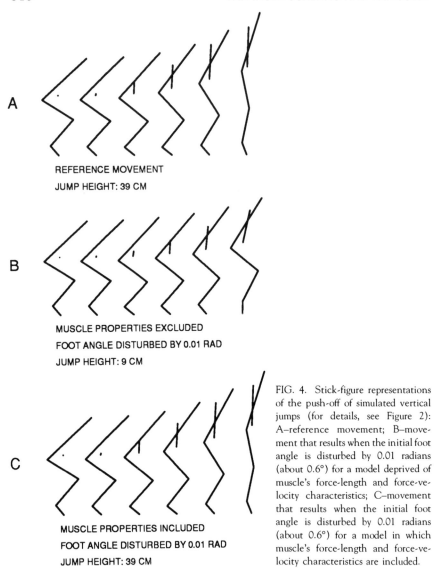

A

REFERENCE MOVEMENT
JUMP HEIGHT: 39 CM

B

MUSCLE PROPERTIES EXCLUDED
FOOT ANGLE DISTURBED BY 0.01 RAD
JUMP HEIGHT: 9 CM

C

MUSCLE PROPERTIES INCLUDED
FOOT ANGLE DISTURBED BY 0.01 RAD
JUMP HEIGHT: 39 CM

FIG. 4. Stick-figure representations of the push-off of simulated vertical jumps (for details, see Figure 2): A–reference movement; B–movement that results when the initial foot angle is disturbed by 0.01 radians (about 0.6°) for a model deprived of muscle's force-length and force-velocity characteristics; C–movement that results when the initial foot angle is disturbed by 0.01 radians (about 0.6°) for a model in which muscle's force-length and force-velocity characteristics are included.

medium-latency responses); he might have been surprised that the lowest-level mechanism is located in the muscular rather than in the neural system!

From Rotation to Translation

A phenomenon that was not explicitly incorporated in Bernstein's arguments (although it may well be in his equations in his previous work) concerns the fact that although the aim of human actions is usually a *translatory* movement, the only

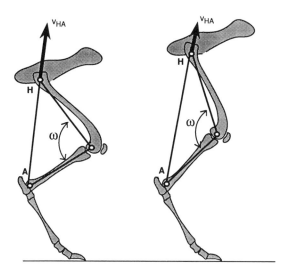

FIG. 5. The transfer of the joint extension velocity ω to the translational velocity difference v_{HA} between hip (H) and ankle (A) in the direction indicated is dependent on the knee angle. The more the knee approaches extension, the worse this transfer is.

means available are joints that only allow significant *rotations* to occur. Therefore, if one plotted joint angle (or, alternatively, muscle length) against displacement of the body's center of gravity (or displacement of an object to be moved), one would not obtain a straight-line plot. This phenomenon is usually referred to as a nonlinearity in the transfer between joint angle and the position of the body's center of gravity or an object. Although such a nonlinear transfer in itself complicates control to a certain extent, it may not cause too many problems in slowly executed movements; in explosive actions in throwing, sprinting, and jumping, however, this nonlinear transfer is a serious problem indeed. Imagine that the animal whose leg is illustrated in Figure 5 is trying to jump as high as possible by extending its knee while the trunk and foot remain in about the same position (this is how speed skaters push off). As long as the knee is far from extension, there is a good transfer of joint angular velocity to the translational velocity of the distance between hip and ankle joints. (The same holds true for the transfer between rotational and translational accelerations.) However, the more the knee approaches extension, the worse this transfer will become. In fact, velocity difference will decrease to zero at full extension, irrespective of the joint extension velocity. In other words, the maximal velocity difference between hip and ankle occurs at a knee angle far in advance of full extension. If no other movements were incorporated, the animal would lose contact with the ground at this instant (this is indeed what occurs in the speed-skating push-off, in which ankle extension must be avoided during the gliding push-off). Experienced sprinters and jumpers appear to solve this problem by a distinct timing of the onset of joint extensions. They begin with hip extension; then knee extension starts; and, finally, a powerful ankle extension follows (see van Ingen Schenau, 1989, for a detailed discussion). This order in the onset of joint extension is also reflected by a distinct proximal–distal sequence of muscle activations in all these movements. Studies based on modeling of the human muscular-skeletal system have demonstrated that this proximal–distal sequence in timing is crucial for achieving an optimal jumping height. These studies also revealed that the muscular-skeletal system is extremely sensitive for the correct timing of muscle activation and for changes in muscle properties. The A sequence in Figure 2 shows the optimal jumping performance of the standard model. The B sequence shows what would happen if the hamstrings were turned on only 0.1 s earlier and all other muscles were activated as in the optimal sequence (A). This small difference in timing appears to lead to a complete disintegration of the movement. The result shown in the C sequence demonstrates the performance if the jumper activated all extensors at the same time.

Now imagine that a coach or a physical therapist working with athletes or patients trains the person's quadriceps with powerful knee extensions in a monoarticular dynamometer, or strength-training apparatus. Imagine further that the training increases the quadriceps strength by 50% (at all contraction velocities!). As shown in the D sequence, the result is highly disappointing. The person jumps considerably lower than before this intervention.

The message is clear: The change in muscle property of the quadriceps requires a change in the overall timing pattern before it will result in a higher jump. Indeed, the computer appeared to find a distinctly different pattern (even when expressed as a relative timing), which leads to a jump that is almost 20% higher than that achieved by the standard model. Even if all muscles are strengthened by the same percentage, a new timing pattern still has to be found (due to the fact that gravity does not change). These and other arguments discussed later lead to the conclusion that the ability to change one's timing with respect to both the magnitude and the sequence of muscle activation must be judged as an important prerequisite for dexterity.

A Forceful Attack on Bernstein's "Enemies"

As biomechanists, we feel obliged to take a critical look at Bernstein's discussion of the role of different kinds of forces, before turning to recent advances concerning the control of external reaction forces.

Reactive Forces Are No Enemies. We believe that Bernstein's view on the nature of reactive forces does not help in understanding the mechanical backgrounds of multijoint movements in the light of motor control issues. On the other hand, we realize that a formal application of the Newtonian mechanics (other than in quantitative analyses and simulations) does not help much either. This problem has to do with what is actually to be judged as the cause of a movement and what as the desired effect. A straightforward application of Newton's second law to a vertical jumper as a system, for example, would correctly lead to the conclusion that jumping height is entirely determined by the ground reaction force and gravity (given the position of the center of gravity at the onset of the jump). This conclusion, however, should not lead to the idea that it is the ground reaction force that is to be qualified as the actual cause of this movement. Clearly, the forces generated by the muscles must be seen as the ultimate mechanical causes of human movements. An application of Newton's second law may lead to a perfectly correct statement about the significance of the ground reaction force, but this statement per se does not further the understanding of the significance of, for example, the proximal-distal sequence in the timing of muscle activation discussed earlier.

Because mechanics does not offer an unambiguous solution for this problem, especially for systems with more than one segment, various approaches can be found in the biomechanics and motor control literature when an author attempts to explain the backgrounds of a movement to a broad audience. A simple example may illustrate some further aspects of this largely didactic problem. Imagine a task in which one must whip a ball with a relatively heavy stick into a target. For simplicity, assume that the force that the hand exerts on the stick, F_{hs}, is directly controlled by the central nervous system, setting aside considerations of torques and rotations. The problem in applying Newtonian mechanics in order to understand causes and effect of this action is associated with the choice of the system (in mechanics referred to as "free body diagram") on which to apply Newton's laws. It is simply not possible to apply Newton's laws in such a way that one can directly relate the control force F_{hs} to the desired acceleration of the ball, because two separate bodies (stick and ball) are to be accelerated. If one assigns the stick as the free body diagram, the effect is the stick's acceleration and the causes are the force F_{hs} exerted by the subject, the reaction force F_{bs} from the ball on the stick, and the gravitational force G_s on the stick. From a perspective of trying to understand what has to be controlled by the central nervous system, this analysis does not really help. With respect to the causes of this movement, clearly one cannot directly influence F_{bs} (which from the point of view of Newtonian mechanics is as equally important a cause as F_{hs}), because it is a reaction force that is dependent on F_{hs} as well as on the entire dynamics of the stick and ball and their interaction. Moreover, most readers will agree that the real interest is not in the acceleration of the stick as the effect of the action. The actual result of this action is related to the acceleration of the ball, not that of the stick. By applying Newton's second law to the ball, one sees that the cause of this acceleration is the sum of the force of the stick on the ball F_{sb} $(= -F_{bs})$ and the gravitational force on the ball G_b. In this approach, however, F_{hs} (which is the only force which is in some way controlled by the central nervous system) is no longer present. So, now the question of the effect is rather clear, but the causes can no longer be understood on the basis of what is controlled by the central nervous system. With both systems taken together, these problems are not solved either, because in that case, the external forces (F_{hs} and gravity) cause the acceleration of the center of gravity of stick and ball together, which is not a really interesting parameter. We chose this example in order to separate the actor from the stick and ball, but, in fact, the same situation exists when one throws a ball by moving the arm segments. As before, the forces acting directly on the ball, that is, the forces of the hand and of gravity, can be seen as the causes of the ball acceleration. However, the central nervous system has no direct control over the force exerted on the ball, because the acceleration of the arm segments influences this force as well.

In essay 6, Bernstein qualified external forces—internal joint reaction forces and inertial forces—as "destructive enemies," which one had to learn to exploit and "to defect to one's camp." We believe that a point of criticism is in place here, although we realize that our approach will prove to be open to discussion. As noted, in a strict Newtonian view, all forces are equal (i.e., equally important determinants of acceleration). Yet, we advocate trying to identify some forces as "more equal than others," and doing so in a task-specific way. For example, in explaining the mechanical backgrounds of the stick–ball example, we agree with Bernstein in qualifying the inertial force on the stick (equal to the mass of the stick times its acceleration) as a disturbing factor (and thus not as an effect according to Newton's second law). However, we would certainly not qualify the reaction force F_{sb} as a destructive enemy that one must learn to exploit. On the contrary, what one must learn is to let the adequate F_{bs} ($= -F_{sb}$) emerge, despite the disturbing inertia of the stick. In other words, we advocate that F_{hs} must be considered the cause of the movement and F_{bs} (and as a consequence the adequate acceleration of the ball) the required mechanical effect of this action. In a way, one might say that it is F_{sb} that ultimately has to be controlled by the central nervous system. In other situations, the concept of inertial forces and its qualification as a disturbing factor, however, may be completely meaningless. For example, in the vertical jump mentioned earlier, the acceleration of the body's center of gravity as a function of time constitutes an important determinant of jumping height. In this case, the product of body mass and body acceleration is not an enemy but rather the effect of the action. According to Newton's second law, because this acceleration is entirely determined by ground reaction force and gravity, it is difficult to view this ground reaction force as an enemy either. As we explain next, there are strong arguments for judging this force as an important parameter to be (indirectly) controlled.

With respect to joint reaction forces, we again advocate not qualifying these as enemies. Joint reaction forces, as well as reaction forces from the environment, are not out there in their own right, with the muscle forces counteracting or exploiting them. Rather, reaction forces should be judged as "offspring" of the muscle forces and not as independent enemies. In fact, the contribution of joint reaction forces to motor control issues is limited to their generating the intersegmental coupling described earlier.

Because these problems (not only the didactic aspects) are, at least in part, associated with difficulties in applying Newtonian mechanics to complex systems of linked segments, it seems likely that this is an area in which biomechanics and dynamic system theory might make a productive match in the near future.

Dissipative Forces Are Enemies. Finally we do support Bernstein in considering external dissipative forces (e.g., air friction) enemies. First of all, in contrast to the reaction forces just discussed, these forces *do* exist independently from the muscle forces and, thus, must be counteracted. Perhaps more important, dissipative forces are the main enemies from an energetical point of view: Without these forces, there would hardly be an environmental problem in this world. At the level of the individual, all energy dissipated by frictional forces, in the end, must be produced by the muscles.

Joint Reaction Forces as Stabilizers? Bernstein further stated in essay 6 that the low variability in the execution of skilled movements, both between and within persons, results from the *joint reaction forces* pushing the limbs into the stable pattern. On the basis of the arguments previously mentioned, the reader will rightly guess that we cannot agree with this point of view. Once again, joint reaction forces are dependent forces, and, as indicated by their name, their value depends on other variables, in particular, the muscular forces. If any forces are to be identified as the stabilizing ones, one must look for them within the category of independent forces, where muscle forces are the favored candidates.

A related issue concerns Bernstein's claim that the number of preferred movements within an otherwise chaotic world is small because only these movements are intrinsically stable. In fact, his claim finds substantial support in various rhythmic (e.g., tapping, pendulum, juggling) movements studied from the perspective of dynamic system theory (e.g., Beek & van Santvoord, this volume; Turvey, 1990). However, for the class of movements discussed here, no support exists for his assertion that these are the only stable movements. On the contrary, one can jump in various ways; one can learn "wrong" movements, especially in cultural skills; and so forth. Thus, we think that the reason athletes show little variation in their movements is because they have learned that this movement results in optimal achievement, not because this is the only stable movement available. This principle is especially true for discrete movements and also for rhythmic movements such as swimming, skating, and skiing. Knowledge of results and performance and imitation and instructions will certainly influence this learning process. As we discuss later, we further sympathize strongly with Bernstein's later ideas (see the last chapter in Bernstein, 1967) concerning directive properties of the brain, which might help to guide the organization of (aspects of) human movements. This idea might also help explain why humans perform even relatively simple pointing and reaching movements in a rather stereotyped way.

External Reaction Force as a Parameter to Be Controlled

Notwithstanding our criticism of the role that Bernstein attributed to various kinds of forces, he was completely aware that changing external forces require completely different muscle activation patterns. In this respect, he was far ahead of his time: Usually, muscle functions were (and still are) erroneously explained by the degree of freedom that they are supposed to control in the joint crossed. Such explanations seem to refer to a weightless subject hanging in space without any contact with the environment, whose muscles are stimulated one by one with all other muscles relaxed. This scenario more or less represents how Duchenne, in the 19th century, established the function of muscles (albeit in the presence of gravity), using electrostimulation. In contrast, almost two millennia ago, Galen (A.D. 131–201) had already stated that one cannot identify the function of a muscle if it is not studied in its normal context of a complete action. From a biomechanical point of view, one might even state that external forces should frequently be judged as the major determinants of success or at least as important collective variables in the dynamics of the entire action including the actor and the environment. Two examples may support this view.

Imagine a person sitting at a table, pushing an object in the direction indicated (see Figure 6). This task requires an elbow extension combined with a movement in the shoulder joint, defined by anatomists as a horizontal adduction. According to textbook explanations, one would simply need to activate the elbow extensors and the horizontal adductors to perform this task. If one tries this movement with a two-joint robot arm, one soon finds that this does not work. The reason is that the displacement of the object requires that a force be exerted by the hand on the object in order to overcome the friction between the object and

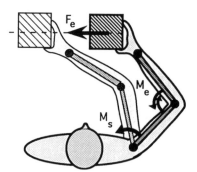

FIG. 6. An example of a contact control task with conflicting requirements with respect to joint torque and joint displacement. Imagine that the subject is seated at a table and tries to displace a heavy object to the left. This requires an external force F_e to be exerted by the hand, which can only be realized through the control of a specific combination of net torques about the arm joints, in this case, a horizontal adduction torque about the shoulder and a flexing torque about the elbow. Note, however, that the movement requires an extension of the elbow joint.

the table or to accelerate the object or both. Such an external force can be realized only through one particular combination of a net flexing torque in the elbow joint and a horizontal adduction torque in the shoulder joint. These net joint torques can be calculated for any movement (including ballistic movements in which the object and the arm segments must be accelerated) by a technique known as *inverse dynamics*. Even without a background in mechanics, the reader may understand this situation by imagining what would happen if one tried to push the object to the left with a simple two-link construction with a frictionless hinge joint at the elbow. If the elbow joint did not contain an element preventing extension (e.g., a spring as flexor), it would be impossible to exert any force on the object in the required direction. Thus, this is a simple example of a task in which one must activate a flexor muscle whereas the task requires a (controlled) extension of the joint. The type of tasks in which external forces have to be controlled are called *contact control tasks* and are quite common in the human movement repertoire. Each direction of the external force requires a particular combination of net torques in all joints involved. If other forces, such as gravity, become involved (e.g., the same task on a nonhorizontal table or a throwing task), tasks that are identical in terms of desired kinematics require totally different combinations of net joint torques.

The same is true for leg movements, which are almost always contact control tasks, and is illustrated in Figure 7, in which the ground reaction force is shown during the second step in a sprint. Despite the fact that the horizontal accelera-

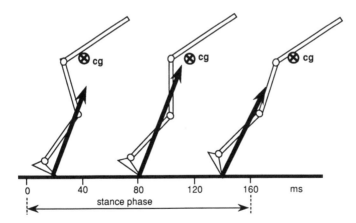

FIG. 7. During the second step of a sprint start after leaving the blocks, one would expect a largely horizontally directed ground reaction force because this force must accelerate the sprinter's center of gravity. What is actually observed is a reaction force that points mainly in the direction of the center of gravity, because a more horizontally directed force would cause the sprinter to fall on his or her back. This constraint with respect to the direction of the ground reaction force is present in most human leg actions. Note that the stance phase in such an explosive movement lasts only about 160 ms.

tion of the sprinter relies almost entirely on the horizontal component of this ground reaction force (air friction being low in this phase), this force is largely upward in the direction of the person's center of gravity. From a mechanical point of view, this upward force is necessary in order to maintain the upright position. Because gravity has its point of application in the body's center of gravity, the rotation of the entire system (in mechanics, *angular momentum*) is largely determined by the torque of the ground reaction force relative to the body's center of gravity. In other words, as long as no somersaults are intended (and other external forces can be ignored), the mean value of this torque averaged over a movement cycle must be zero. This, again, requires the control of a distinct combination of net torques in all joints involved. Because the ground reaction force (together with constant gravity) also determines the acceleration of the center of gravity of the person, many of the elements that determine the stability and success (high acceleration) of this movement seem to be summarized in this force. Clearly this principle is entirely true as well for most other leg movements that occur in standing, walking, climbing stairs, standing from a chair, and so on. Inspired by our colleagues experienced in nonlinear dynamics, we hypothesize that the ground reaction force and its point of application might prove to be one of the most important and low dimensional collective variables in these movements.

This hypothesis, however, does not contribute much to a solution of Bernstein's controllability problem. The fact that humans must not only control the displacements of the body and body segments but also control the direction and magnitude of external forces further complicates the problem. Only one particular combination of net joint torques as a function of time can lead to the desired kinematics and external forces. A task like the one illustrated in Figure 1 often requires not only the realization of a highly accurate saw trajectory but also a precisely controlled external force on the saw. A combination of several hundreds of coupled mechanical equations would have to be solved in order to calculate the net joint torques as a function of time necessary to realize such a task (the same of course is true for an accurate throw of an object to a target). We agree with Bernstein that the central nervous system does not and cannot solve this inverse problem through calculation of all these torque–time functions in advance. However, as we explain later, the major theories on movement control, developed since Bernstein's previous publications, that claim to eliminate the necessity of specifying the net joint torques beforehand are based on point-to-point movements only. They are not suitable for explaining the combination of required joint displacements with, for example, the realization of a distinct external force exerted by the hand which depends on the environmental conditions. On the other hand, one should realize that the fact that humans can learn to saw, sprint, or throw with high accuracy means that obviously humans do manage to generate the correct torque–time functions necessary to meet all these task demands, in spite of the redundancy in the number of muscles, the unequivocal relationship between central commands and net joint torques, the time shift between activation and force, the muscle elasticity, and so forth. The necessity of controlling the direction and magnitude of external forces enlarges enormously Bernstein's controllability problem about how the central nervous system might manage this extremely complicated job.

Even for relatively simple systems, such as robotic manipulators with only a few degrees of freedom, it appears extremely difficult to control both position and external force. This is still a major problem in robotics. The human capacity to (learn to) let the adequate time varying joint torques emerge in tasks with more than 100 degrees of freedom and hundreds of muscles involved certainly is one of the most important prerequisites for dexterity. But, how do humans manage this?

TO WHAT EXTENT IS BERNSTEIN'S PROBLEM SOLVED?

Bernstein proposed the following strategies in mastering the problems of motor control:

The formation of synergies and sensory corrections (tunable automatisms) at different, low hierarchical levels during development or learning or both.

An internal representation of actions on a rather abstract level; related to possible solutions of a motor problem and not to specific motor commands.

In the light of the thousands of papers published in the past 40 years, it is remarkable that these issues have received considerable support. It is now beyond dispute that innate or learned movements are not organized in a sequential way of perception–cognition–action but that various processes run in parallel (in part reflected by the different descending tracts in the spinal cord) at various levels of the central nervous system without any cognitive intervention. It should be noted, however, that the spinal cord has been rehabilitated in the past decennia from Bernstein's "simple impulse transducer" back to what it originally was in our ancestors—a rather sophisticated system capable of generating various task- and context-specific muscle synergies, triggered, modulated, and tuned by descending as well as by peripheral information. Even the so-called spinal short-latency responses appear not to be simple, rigid stretch reflexes but part of a tunable muscle synergy with variable gain, even in muscles that are not stretched at all. Though such responses are now believed to play a major role in correcting relatively large unexpected disturbances, it seems likely that propriospinal networks may play a role in the organization of the undisturbed movement as well, and not only in animals.

In addition to muscle synergies, the existence of functional synergies (i.e., synergies that can be executed with different groups of muscles) has been demonstrated rather convincingly as well. A nice example was described by Green

(1982). It concerns a writing task with the right and left hands, which can easily be tested by the reader. If you are right-handed, you will experience extreme difficulty in writing a sentence (or your signature) *upside down and from right to left* with the left hand. When paper is turned, the text (and certainly the signature) will hardly be readable. Now, you take a stout piece of paper in your left hand and fix your right hand with the pencil (or fasten the pencil in a bench vise) and move the paper with your left hand to write the same sentence or signature, the task is now considerably easier. As a third experiment, repeat this second task but with a second pencil fixed in your left hand in such a way that the movements of your left hand are registered during this task. You will notice that your left hand is making exactly the movement that was required in the first task, but now considerably more accurately. What is the conclusion? The difficulty of the task is determined, not by the muscle actions required, but rather by the way in which sensory (in this case mainly visual) information guides the movement of the pencil. This coupling between perception and action apparently occurs at a level that has little to do with the muscle activation patterns.

In regard to the class of leg movements discussed in this chapter, Bernstein appears correct in his statement that sensory corrections do not often play a significant role during ongoing leg movements, other than correcting relatively large, unexpected disturbances. Even the relatively autonomously operating (and phylogenetically older) posture-preserving system appears to anticipate unexpected balance problems, rather than providing corrections during these relatively fast leg movements.

Convincing evidence for these statements can be deduced from studies of movements in deafferented animals or humans, which shows that humans can move their legs reasonably well without any peripheral feedback. Obviously all information concerning the environment and the initial states of the limb necessary to deal with the context-conditioned variability is already processed in advance with intact afferent information. It should be noted, however, that many longer lasting actions of Bernstein's Level C do require a response during the ongoing action. There is now substantial evidence that even changes in the visual flow field can indeed cause rather fast adaptations in the ongoing movement, possibly due to an automized process that uses relatively fast, subcortical pathways.

That synergies appear highly tunable and adaptable to various task demands may possibly be a major reason that the search for invariants in the kinematics or dynamics of multijoint movements has not led to convincing evidence of the existence of principles that hold for a variety of movements. As we discussed previously, any invariant in the magnitude or sequence of the timing of muscle activation severely limits dexterity, and much evidence has emerged showing that such invariants do not exist in general. In cycling, for example, an increase in pedal frequency at constant power output from 50 to 110 revolutions per minute activates all muscles earlier relative to the position of the crank, an adaptation obviously meant to deal with the constant time shift between activation and force through anticipation. More important, the rectus femoris as well as the hamstring muscle activity show distinct changes in timing as well as in magnitude, whereas the magnitude of the monoarticular hip and knee extensors remains the same. These changes in muscle activation patterns can be remarkably well explained by what Bernstein stated about the "exploiting of nonmuscular forces," because the system clearly adapts itself to the increasing inertial forces of the leg segments.

Equilibrium-Point Hypotheses

Though Bernstein treats muscle elasticity as a passive and complicating property (comparable to the series elastic element in Hill's muscle model), many advocates of equilibrium-point models apparently refer to Bernstein as their source of inspiration. However, we must stress that in these hypotheses, the muscles are supposed to behave in a springlike manner on the basis of their *active* (intrinsic) properties. Nevertheless, these hypotheses appear to address explicitly much of Bernstein's problems concerning the way in which the central nervous system might deal with all those complicating, nonlinear properties of the muscular-skeletal system, initial conditions, disturbances, and so on. For a simple monoarticular system, the idea can easily be explained. Imagine a joint controlled by two "muscles," one flexor and one extensor, which behave like simple springs: The force they exert increases as they are stretched. How would such a system behave? Suppose that one starts from a fully flexed position and then releases the joint. Clearly, in the fully flexed position, the extensor spring will be stretched considerably and the flexor spring will be maximally shortened. Thus, the extensor-spring force, trying to extend the joint, will be greater than the flexor-spring force, trying to flex it. As a result, the joint will move in the direction of extension. As the joint extends, however, the flexor spring will be lengthened whereas the extensor spring shortens. As a result, the extensor force, which was the greater force at the start, will decrease whereas the flexor force will increase. At some joint angle, the two forces will exactly cancel each other, and due to friction, the arm will ultimately come to rest in this position. No matter in what way the arm is subsequently perturbed, it will automatically return to this equilibrium position after the perturbation. Thus, together these two springs define one particular equilibrium position for the arm. The equilibrium position, as well as the stiffness of the joint, depends on the rest length and stiffness of the springs. The central idea of equilibrium-point models is that one can move an extremity to a desired position just by setting the rest length and the stiffness of the springs. The charm of this idea is that the central nervous system has only to specify these rest lengths and stiffnesses. No knowledge about all the properties of the muscular-skeletal system is required. Neither is it necessary to solve the inverse problem: *The link is attracted toward the equilibrium position irrespective of initial position, disturbances, and its own inertia.* In multijoint reaching movements, the situation is slightly more complex:

Here, the job for the central nervous system is, first, to specify the equilibrium position of the endpoint (hand, foot) and, next, to "translate" this into rest lengths and stiffnesses of all muscles involved.

The viability of equilibrium-point theories has been addressed in a significant number of experimental studies over the past 30 years (see Bizzi, Hogan, Mussa-Ivaldi, & Giszter, 1992, and Feldman, 1986, for details and references). One of the experimental findings was that in reaching movements, the equilibrium point is not set at the desired endpoint but rather follows its own trajectory, which can be quite complex and, in any case, does not necessarily coincide with the actual desired trajectory. Clearly, control of reaching on the basis of such a virtual equilibrium-point trajectory presupposes the generation of an equilibrium-point trajectory rather than of a single equilibrium point. A further complication arises in situations in which the arm is subject to external forces like gravity; in these cases, not even the final equilibrium point coincides with the desired final position of the arm. Clearly, the charm of these hypotheses would be entirely lost if one assumed that all aspects of the controllability problem could be incorporated in the calculation or representation of such virtual trajectories.

An essential property of these models is that the trajectories are planned on the basis of kinematic information only. This statement is largely in agreement with Bernstein's ideas about the construction of movements at Level C and seems to be supported by various studies, with respect to activity of neurons measured in the neocortex and on the basis of actual hand trajectories in point-to-point reaching movements. According to these studies, there appears quite a consensus that especially the direction of the movement of an endpoint is an important variable that guides the organization of multijoint movements.

There has emerged also quite serious criticism against these hypotheses, however. First of all, as discussed by Soechting (1989), one would expect that if a fixed equilibrium-point trajectory is used, actual hand (or foot) trajectories are influenced by velocity and by additional inertial loads, which appears not to be the case generally.

Comparable arguments can be deduced from studies of slow reaching movements of the arm and from the earlier discussions of contact control tasks. Recent experiments have demonstrated that distinct deviations of the actual hand trajectories from a straight path occur. These deviations were highly systematic and appeared not to be influenced by gravity (arm horizontal or vertical) or the use of a stick. As we noted earlier in the context of contact control tasks, changing the direction of the force to be applied to the object while requiring the same changes in joint positions requires the generation of completely different net torques in the joints.

For types of movements other than reaching, additional problems emerge. Studies of jumping in cats and in humans have demonstrated that some muscles may show more than one burst of activity during one simple leg extension, which appear not to be related to its length change, as one would expect from a springlike behavior.

Within the framework of equilibrium-point theories, all these findings can be explained only by either assuming that in the "calculation" of the virtual equilibrium-point trajectory all such complicating factors are taken into account or assuming that at a lower hierarchical level (e.g., Bernstein's Level B), a second transformation occurs in which these changing conditions are dealt with. In their discussion Bizzi et al. (1992) mention the first option along with another possible solution (pp. 814–815):

> Information on all complicating factors is included in the calculation of virtual trajectory in such a way that the actual trajectory follows the desired path, or a relatively simple virtual trajectory (e.g., straight line from starting point to virtual endpoint) is generated that results in an actual trajectory that deviates from the desired trajectory, the deviation depending on the complicating factors mentioned as well as on the stiffness of the hand.

As we have argued, in the first option very little is left of the charming simplicity of the original equilibrium-point hypothesis because it would require a complete internal representation of all aspects of Bernstein's controllability problem. The second option would preserve the solution of this problem but would lead to deviating trajectories. On the basis of hand-stiffness measures presented by Shadmehr, Mussa-Ivaldi, and Bizzi (1993), one could predict, for example, that an external force of 60 N in the task illustrated in Figure 6 would cause a deviation from a straight-line path as large as 10–20 cm! This prediction is refuted by experimental data showing that deviations are in fact quite small. Apparently, humans can learn to perform contact control tasks with remarkable accuracy. Of course we cannot at present preclude the possibility that hand stiffness in contact control tasks is substantially greater than that reported by Shadmehr et al. However, one should realize that the high degree of coactivation between antagonists necessary to produce sufficiently high stiffness is inefficient due to the lengthening of active muscles. In tasks such as skating, running, cycling, and jumping, such a waste of energy is not observed. The performance of those tasks in well-trained persons is highly accurate, without any apparent concession to efficiency. These arguments lead us to conclude that the equilibrium-point theories do not offer an attractive explanation of the control of both contact control tasks and explosive tasks. We rather support Bernstein's arguments that humans have dexterity in their capacity to master all these complicated problems during development and skill acquisition.

Can Biarticular Muscles Help?

The extremities of mammals contain not only muscles that span one joint but also muscles that cross over two or more joints (called *biarticular* and *polyarticular* muscles, respectively). Although some important unique actions of biarticular muscles had already been illustrated in the previous century (e.g., Cleland, 1867), contemporary textbooks describe the function of these muscles as though they behave as two independent monoarticular muscles (e.g., the hamstrings are described as hip extensors *and* knee flexors). Our own recent observations have led us to conclude that the biarticular antagonists of the upper leg and the upper arm especially can be judged as important actuators in the regulation of the distribution of net joint torques necessary in contact control tasks. Moreover, all biarticular muscle actions result in a type of coupling of movements in the joints crossed, which in some cases results in an actual reduction of the number of degrees of freedom in an extremity. This phenomenon occurs particularly in animals in which these synergies are realized through a fixed construction. In hoofed animals, the lower leg muscles are largely tendinous in nature. The functional significance of such a design is illustrated in Figure 8(A). As a result of the two antagonistic biarticular tendons at both sides of the lower leg, knee movements are coupled to the ankle movements. Apart from small effects due to stretch of these elastic tendons, knee extension is directly coupled to plantar flexion, and knee flexion to dorsal flexion. Consequently, the number of degrees of freedom in these two joints in the sagittal plane is reduced from two to one. An important advantage of this design is that the bulk of active muscle mass can be located close to the trunk, a feature that sharply reduces the moments of inertia of these animals. This effect is reinforced by their long, slender metatarsi and is an important reason for their high

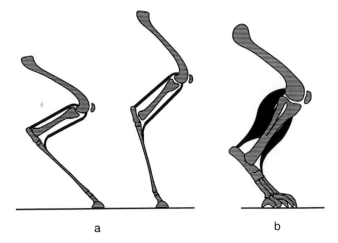

a   b

FIG. 8. Hoofed animals (a) possess bi- and polyarticular lower leg muscles that are largely tendinous. This leads to stereotyped couplings of the movements in the knee and ankle joints and thus to a decrease of the number of degrees of freedom. Other animals such as predators (b) and humans have active lower leg muscles, which allow the animal to move its knee and ankle independently. This is a prerequisite for a richer movement repertoire, but a disadvantage is a much larger moment of inertia, which reduces the animal's economy in long-distance running.

economy in long-distance running. However, if one remembers the clumsy way in which these animals scratch themselves, the disadvantage is immediately clear: The fixed synergy strongly reduces the animal's flexibility. The construction allows only stereotyped, combined knee and ankle movements. Figure 8(B) is a schematic of a predator's leg with an active biarticular gastrocnemius, which can perform the same action but which allows the animal to choose when and how strongly knee and ankle movements are to be coupled. Cleland (1867) defined this property of active biarticular muscles to couple joint movements as the "tendinous action" of these muscles. Clearly due to the hamstrings and rectus femoris in the upper leg (present in all quadrupeds and in humans), a coupling between hip and knee movements can also be effected if necessary.

Of course, these are not the only means of realizing synergies. Patterns of muscle activation can also be coupled by the central nervous system, for example, by tuning the connectivity of pathways within propriospinal networks.

The role of the upper leg biarticular muscles in the regulation of the distribution of the net torques about the hip and knee joints has been identified in a number of different leg movements. An analysis of cycling revealed that cyclists continuously change the direction of the force on the pedal during leg extension from slightly forward around top dead center to slightly backward around bottom dead center (obviously meant to push the pedal in its fixed movement direction). Cyclists achieve this change in force direction by a continuous increase of the net hip-extending joint torque combined with a decrease of the knee-extending joint torque, even to negative (i.e., flexing) values while the knee is still extending. Remarkably this phenomenon is not reflected by a change of activity of the monoarticular hip and knee extensors but entirely by an increase of hamstring activity and a simultaneous decrease of rectus femoris activity (van Ingen Schenau, Boots, de Groot, Snackers, & Woensel, 1992). Additional experiments of static leg extensions from various positions completely confirmed this unique role of these biarticular muscles (Jacobs & van Ingen Schenau, 1992). Comparable differences in the action of mono- and biarticular muscles were also found in analyses of speed skating, running, and standing from a chair. In all these movements, monoarticular muscles showed rather stereotyped patterns of activation closely related (and anticipated) to the periods of muscle shortening. Thus, in this energy-consuming class of tasks, monoarticular muscles appear to behave as ideal work generators whereas the activity of the biarticular muscles does not show any relationship to muscle shortening (or lengthening) but a remarkably high correlation with the direction of the external force. Comparable observations have been reported for various hindlimb movements in the cat, that is, monoarticular muscles showing stereotyped flexor or extensor synergies and biarticular muscles showing a task-specific, complex behavior.

Clearly, if mono- and biarticular muscles have different roles, the organization of their excitation patterns must be based on different processes and guided by different sources of information.

Remarkably, the observation that monoarticular muscles behave in these tasks as ideal work generators is not in conflict with equilibrium-point control hypotheses in the sense that their activation is a function of expected muscle-length changes, irrespective of the required net joint torques. The organization of the activation patterns might therefore be based on kinematic information (e.g., the desired direction of movement) but only as advocated more generally in the studies mentioned. A parallel process, however, would have to be hypothesized for the generation of the activity patterns for the biarticular muscles. As we have stated, the generation of net joint torques must be based on multimodal sources of information, proprioceptive as well as exteroceptive. Expressed in terms of Bernstein's levels, this generation can be organized only in part at Level B, although the organization of ground reaction forces related to posture control is likely to be based on already rather old and well-established brain structures. Cultural tasks, however, will certainly require the involvement of Level C.

The hypothesis proposed here concerning different types of organization of the control of mono- and biarticular muscles can prove to be only a small step in reducing the complexity of contact control tasks and is certainly not a solution to Bernstein's problem in general. Moreover, we stress that net torques cannot be tuned by the biarticular muscles without information on the contribution of the monoarticular muscles to these torques.

From a mechanical point of view, the proposed difference in muscle action enormously improves the efficiency of the muscular-skeletal system, because situations in which active muscles are lengthened, in which mechanical energy is transformed into heat, can largely be avoided, compared to a system without biarticular actuators. Moreover, the biarticular muscles allow the monoarticular muscles to contribute to the work, even in situations that require a net joint torque opposite to the joint angular displacement. However, the human movement repertoire contains many actions that do not rely on efficiency and these movements will possibly prove to be based on completely different strategies from the one outlined here.

SOME VITAL NOTES ON MOVEMENT ORGANIZATION

From On Dexterity as well as from earlier publications (e.g., Bernstein, 1967), it seems beyond dispute that Bernstein emphasized development, motor learning (including perception), and training as the major means to turn the extremely complicated movement organs into a goal-oriented, controllable system. This conclusion is in complete agreement with our own experience and has been stressed by many others before. Three centuries ago Borelli (1680–1681/1989) stated that "such a habit is acquired only after many and frequent actions ordered by the will have been carried out. This repetition by training the spirit, develops a certain ability and trains the organic instruments by making them quicker to react." If "will" is replaced by "neocortex" and "spirit" by "older brain structures," this statement appears in close harmony with Bernstein's ideas and with recent publications on the possible role of the neocortex and on, for example, the cerebellum during learning. We shortly discuss the latter to provide a conceptual framework that might shed some light on a few remaining questions of Bernstein's problem and on the organization of the higher levels of dexterity.

What Is Learning?

Though we sympathize strongly with Bernstein's arguments against learning as only a process of "beating" a conditioning reflex in the brain, his alternative description is as abstract as what has been stated on this subject by contemporary theorists who deny any relation between specific brain structures and function.

   The applicability of any theory to motor control with respect to interventions in sport, rehabilitation, and labor depends heavily on the extent to which one can find answers to questions about the nature and locations of changes within the central nervous system that are realized during development, learning, and training. At the present time, it seems beyond dispute that these changes are related to gradual (sometimes rather fast) adaptations of the connectivity between neurons within networks of neurons and between different networks, and so on. An important learning rule, which has been identified in neurophysiological studies, appears to be the strengthening of synapses between neurons that often fire simultaneously and the weakening of the synapses between neurons in which this is not the case (often referred to as "Hebbian learning"). After development or learning, the acquired knowledge or skill is represented in the changed strengths of the network connections. With computer simulations of such processes, researchers have demonstrated that large numbers of neurons can thus become remarkably organized in producing low-dimensional outputs related to inputs with a large number of degrees of freedom. This collective property thus serves as an important tool in solving a part of the degrees-of-freedom problem.

   Due to the enormous complexity of the human central nervous system (some call it the most complex system of the universe) and due to the rather early phase of development of this field, the how, where, and when questions are still subject to considerable debate. This, however, does not prevent us from presenting a simplified conceptual framework that might help the reader to imagine how skill acquisition might work.

How Learning Might Work

The anatomy of the cerebellum has been a source of inspiration for many theories on the learning of motor skills. This statement is especially true with respect to its large Purkinje cells, which receive an enormous amount of information from different so-called *mossy fibers* (from 500,000 to 1 million fibers per Purkinje cell) from various sensors (proprioceptive, exteroceptive) and other brain structures. The actual function of the cerebellum, however, is still subject to considerable debate: For example, it has been said to function as a comparator (in many respects), a controller of stability, a generator of parameters (anticipatory, for tuning other networks such as the red nucleus or reticular nucleus etc.), a pattern generator, and a device for automatic perception of multimodal sources of information. What seems beyond dispute, however, is that the strength of the many synapses on the dendrites of the Purkinje cells is adapted under the supervision of only one other fiber, the so-called *climbing fiber*. Because our example of how learning in the cerebellum might work is certainly not beyond dispute, we refer, in this case, to the three original papers on which it is based. These are an overview of possible functions of the cerebellum by Stein (1986), experimental work on this type of learning in monkeys by Kennedy (1990), and evidence for the capacity of the primary motor cortex in primates to form and adjust muscle synergies within very short time intervals (Sanes & Donoghue, 1993).

Kennedy (1990) found that the climbing fibers obviously teach the Purkinje cells to fire at a particular combination of information. At the onset of the learning process, the Purkinje cell does not react to any combination of activity of the mossy fibers on its dendrites. However, on command from the climbing fiber, it always fires, and, consequently, the strength of the synapses of only those mossy fibers that are simultaneously active is increased. After sufficient repetitions, the specific combinations of mossy fibers can excite the Purkinje cell without any further supervision of the climbing fiber. Because the Purkinje cell does not know where that particular combination of information stems from, this process is an illustrative example of how sensory information might be directly coupled to action without any cognitive intervention of higher brain centers. The type of action may be subject to debate, but it most likely has to do with Bernstein's sensory corrections. Because visual information is available in the cerebellum via subcortical pathways, this example might also give some idea on other phenomena: how the automatic and fast identification of the well-known "time to contact" might work; why the accuracy of kicking in soccer apparently sharply decreases at the instant that the advertisement boards in the stadium are replaced; or any other remarkable automatic response to changes in visual information that most readers will have experienced themselves. Lower systems can thus become rather autonomous in the perception–action coupling, a phenomenon that nicely supports Aristotle (384–322 B.C.), who stated more than 2,000 years ago with respect to motor control: "as in a common wealth; when order is once established in it, there is no need for a separate monarch to preside over each separate task" (De motu animalium, p. 703). The capacity to react, anticipate, adapt, inhibit, tune, or whatever the output of the Purkinje cells may do, it cannot emerge spontaneously but needs a supervisor during learning that allows the climbing fibers to fire at the right instants. Kennedy (1990) observed that these climbing fibers are supervised by the cerebral motor cortex (via the inferior olive) and that the animal learns to perform the task without intervention of this supervisor. Because in humans consciousness is supposed to be primarily related to its youngest brain structures (neocortex), such a process of learning might prove to be in close harmony with the cognitive, associative, and automatic phases of learning, as has often been described in psychological textbooks on motor learning. Sanes and Donoghue (1993) showed that Bernstein's statement that the beating of connections in brain structures takes considerable time is wrong. In part, Bernstein's statement may be true for the oldest structures, but in the neocortex, even complete muscle synergies appear to be formed (and tried out) and adapted within minutes (also associated with synaptic adaptations). This younger structure thus appears an important tool in supervising the older brain structures, much in the way Bernstein advocated. However, as we have emphasized, this example should be taken only as a conceptual framework of Bernstein's notion that higher centers are the supervisors of older structures. The actual function of the described process is still subject to debate, and many other structures are involved as well.

Albeit only a conceptual framework, it may be argued that this example displaces an important question in any theory on motor control: Who is supervising the supervisor or who is that homunculus in the system (the "ghost in the machine") or who decides what is necessary to solve the motor problem? Expressed in terms of the problems raised by Bernstein, how is it possible that there is so little variation in the kinematics and kinetics between and within individuals (especially in skilled movements but also in various movements in daily life), compared to the often infinite number of possible patterns? Because the origin of dexterity is largely associated with this question, even biomechanists cannot ignore this issue, which is therefore the subject of the remainder of this chapter.

Who Is the Supervisor of Dexterity?

For skilled movements, we have already argued against Bernstein's idea that nonmuscular forces allow only a few solutions to be stable. Apart from this reactive force hypothesis, we agree that there will exist only few solutions or possibly even only one solution that leads to a skilled movement, for example, an optimal vertical jump when expressed in jumping height. The question then remains, Is there a homunculus or some other supervisor or attractor that guides humans in finding this optimal solution? Because it is beyond dispute that one can perceive the result of a jump, one may argue (and Bernstein does so on various occasions) that the optimal solution is discovered in a process of trial and error guided by this knowledge of results. Our colleagues in nonlinear dynamics might argue that not only the reactive forces but also the entire dynamics (including aspects of the mechanics of the process, neural substrates, and information between actor and environment) of the system attracts the actor to only a few possible stable solutions. They have demonstrated that this is certainly true for particular phase relations between limbs or even between subjects. However, they will agree that humans do not possess intrinsic, predetermined attractors that automatically lead them to the optimal solution for the discrete skilled movements described in this chapter. So, the questions of what, where, when, and how changes in the central nervous system are realized are still to be answered.

In his later work (see the last two chapters of Bernstein, 1967), Bernstein dissociated himself to some extent from the idea of trial-and-error learning on the basis of the limited success of the random trials. Although one of his arguments (the overly long time it would take to beat new connections in the brain) is now proven not to be strong, we sympathize with his other arguments.

As indicated in *On Dexterity* and further substantiated in his later work, Bernstein argues that dexterity cannot be explained entirely by the interaction of an actor and the environment. Living organisms are more than reactive machines "but act as determinants of action and behavior." For the highest levels of dexterity the brain must have created a directive in order to anticipate future requirements. In chapters 5 and 6 of his 1967 book (written in 1961 and 1962, respectively) Bernstein further states that the life process is not aimed at a balance with the environment but at "an advance towards fulfilment of the developmental and self-preservational program of the genus." This requires more than the pure luck he mentions in *On Dexterity*. He argues that the increase of the probability in discovering solutions for complex and new motor problems might be guided by the evolutionarily determined needs of the organism. Because genetically influenced components in various aspects of human behavior are now beyond dispute (remember, for example, the popular twins studies and also aspects of behaviors common in various cultures), we would really be amazed if Bernstein were not proven to be right in this respect.

Expressed in contemporary terminology, not only the stories of the human brain building (spinal cord, limbic system, pyramidal system, etc.) but also some aspects of the architecture of networks and strength of connections within networks are genetically predetermined at least in some crude form. This explanation would certainly help solve part of Bernstein's problem. In the light of the discussed problems with respect to explosive movements, such as jumping and running, we indicated that we humans needed a distinct proximal–distal sequence in the timing of the hip, knee, and ankle extensors. Because this type of leg movement would certainly have influenced the chance of our human ancestors to escape from enemies, the basic layout of the control requirements would have been a serious candidate to be encoded into our genes, preferably in such a way that it could be adapted to changing body dimensions, muscle properties, and external circumstances.

We were very pleased to discover that indeed this property was recently successfully incorporated as a "value system" in a model including adaptive neural networks used in the study of the emergence of coordinated movement (Sporns & Edelman, 1993). This study represents the very onset of the application of

Bernstein's idea. Moreover, it seems likely that many such studies will follow, because the alternative idea that, unlike all other animals, every generation of humans must start all over again from scratch has lost many of its advocates in the last decade. Clearly, the credibility of dynamics system theory is also improved for discrete movements, because it is assumed that some optimizations can spontaneously emerge on the basis of genetically coded attractors (see, e.g., Zanone & Kelso, 1992).

These developments are examples of how Bernstein still helps dynamic system theory. On the other hand, we believe that the reverse is true with respect to his last questions about how humans are able to solve motor problems that are completely new to them or to invent new patterns or even to start a movement completely independently from any trigger. Because these questions are related to philosophical issues, such as existentialism and free will, far from our own expertise, we limit ourselves to one short statement: What dynamics system theory has demonstrated is that large numbers of interconnected subsystems, such as the human's billions of interconnected brain neurons, can produce a collective behavior that cannot be predicted from the properties of the subsystems. With respect to the highest levels of organization in the brain, which can—by definition—no longer be subject to scientific research (because we humans cannot place ourselves at a distance from ourselves), new behavior can emerge that cannot be predicted as long as we are unable to simulate the entire brain (with all its initial conditions!!). We believe that this knowledge of the possibility of the emergence of undetermined behavior might help in understanding what Bernstein might have meant when he suggested about the supervisor in the brain that "the very dynamic form of its organization and connections" determines the operator (chapter 5, Bernstein, 1967).

This was truly an astonishing (and dexterous) man!

REFERENCES

Bernstein, N. A. (1967). *The coordination and regulation of movements.* London: Pergamon.

Bizzi, E., Hogan, N., Mussa-Ivaldi, F. A., & Giszter, S. (1992). Does the nervous system use equilibrium point control to guide single and multiple joint movements? *Behavioral Brain Sciences, 15,* 603–613.

Borelli, G. A. (1989). *On the movement of animals* (P. Maquet, Trans.). Heidelberg, Germany: Springer–Verlag. (Original work published 1680–1681)

Cleland, J. (1867). On the actions of muscles passing over more than one joint. *Journal of Anatomy and Physiology, 1,* 85–93.

Feldman, A. G. (1986). Once more on the equilibrium-point hypothesis (λ-model) for motor control. *Journal of Motor Behavior, 18,* 17–54.

Green, P. H. (1982). Why it is easy to control your arms. *Journal of Motor Behavior, 14,* 260–286.

Jacobs, R., & van Ingen Schenau, G. J. (1992). Control of an external force in leg extensions in humans. *Journal of Physiology, 457,* 611–626.

Kennedy, P. R. (1990). Corticospinal, rubrospinal and rubro-olivary projections: A unifying hypothesis. *Trends in Neuroscience, 13*, 474–479.

Sanes, J. N., & Donoghue, J. P. (1993). Organization and adaptability of muscle representations in primary motor cortex. In R. Caminiti, P. B. Johnson, & Y. Burnod (Eds.), *Experimental brain research series: Vol. 22. Control of arm movement in space: Neurophysiological and computational approaches* (pp. 103–127). Berlin: Springer–Verlag.

Shadmehr, R., Mussa-Ivaldi, F. A., & Bizzi, E. (1993). Postural force fields of the human arm and their role in generating multijoint movements. *Journal of Neuroscience, 13*, 45–62.

Soechting, J. F. (1989). Elements of coordinated arm movements in three dimensional space. In S. A. Wallace (Ed.), *Perspectives on the coordination of movement* (pp. 47–83). Amsterdam: Elsevier.

Sporns, O., & Edelman, G. M. (1993). Solving Bernstein's problem: A proposal for the development of coordinated movement by selection. *Child Development, 64*, 960–981.

Stein, J. F. (1986). Role of the cerebellum in the visual guidance of movement. *Nature, 323*, 217–221.

Turvey, M. T. (1990). Coordination. *American Psychologist, 45*, 938–953.

van Ingen Schenau, G. J. (1989). From rotation to translation: Constraints on multi-joint movements and the unique action of bi-articular muscles. *Human Movement Science, 8*, 301–337.

van Ingen Schenau, G. J., Boots, P. J. M., de Groot, G., Snackers, R. J., & van Woensel, W. W. L. M. (1992). The constrained control of force and position in multi-joint movements. *Neuroscience, 46*, 197–207.

van Soest, A. J., & Bobbert, M. F. (1993). The contribution of muscle properties in the control of explosive movements. *Biological Cybernetics, 69*, 195–204.

van Soest, A. J., Bobbert, M. F., & van Ingen Schenau, G. J. (1994). A control strategy for the execution of explosive movements from varying starting positions. *Journal of Neurophysiology, 71*, 1390–1402.

Zajac, F. E. (1993). Muscle coordination of movement: A perspective. *Journal of Biomechanics, 26*, 109–124.

Zanone, P. G., & Kelso, J. A. S. (1992). Evolution of behavioral attractors with learning: Nonequilibrium phase transitions. *Journal of Experimental Psychology, 18*, 403–421.

Dynamics of Bernstein's Level of Synergies

Michael T. Turvey
Claudia Carello
University of Connecticut
Haskins Laboratories

It has been suggested frequently that the human movement system is hierarchical, with each level solving a particular class of motor problems in the assembling of an act. In Bernstein's hierarchy, the tasks of forming synergies of large muscle groups and different patterns of locomotion are solved by Level B—*the level of muscular-articular links or the level of synergies*. Bernstein suggested that this level developed in evolution to subserve all the locomotion forms made possible by articulated bodies and their articulated appendages. The achievements of the level of synergies are both remarkable and insular. They are remarkable because they have to do with the formation of patterns among limbs and limb segments that are stable against fluctuations and perturbations and reproducible in their basic details, even though they involve very many components of different sizes (e.g., muscles, cells) interacting in many different ways and at many different rates. They are insular because the patterns produced by the level of synergies are independent of environmental requirements. To be sure, they are exploited by higher levels in meeting such requirements, but they are purely patterns.

How patterns are formed and selected has been a topic high on the agenda of science in the nearly five decades that have passed since Bernstein wrote *On Dexterity and Its Development*. Physicists, mathematicians, physiologists, biologists, and psychologists have been engaged in shaping theory and conducting experiments toward an understanding of how the many different parts of a thing (a liquid, an organism) can cooperate to produce spatial, temporal, and functional order. They have been busily trying to understand *synergies* in the broadest sense. We suspect that Bernstein would have liked this interdisciplinary enterprise, especially its careful crafting of mathematical tools to reveal the essential qualities of synergistic behavior. In this chapter, we attempt to portray aspects of this enterprise as they bear most directly on understanding the level of synergies.

THE LEVEL OF SYNERGIES AND ITS RELATION
TO HIGHER LEVELS

Included in the neural substrate of the level of synergies are mechanisms for handling—directly and swiftly—the full array of signals from the sensory endings in muscles, tendons, and joint capsules. As Bernstein contended, this possession of universal and direct sensory connections with muscular and articular states renders the level of synergies unique among the levels of a biological movement system. No other level, lower or higher, is able to control the large-scale, all-encompassing synergies—such as running, jumping, swimming—controlled by Level B. Higher levels are considerably more" "frugal" with respect to the number of muscles engaged simultaneously. They rely on the level of synergies' ability when many muscles are involved. Because of the special relation between motor and sensory processes characterizing the level of synergies, the movements it controls are always coherent and harmonious. Rhythmic movements typify the level's special expertise. It exhibits the remarkable facility to produce successions of cycles that are "as similar as minted coins; consecutive cycles during sawing, filing, mowing, hammering, etc., are more alike than two drops of water" (Bernstein, essay 5). This facility is of particular significance for the formation of motor skills and for the automation of movements. At the same time, because it has few direct connections with vision and hearing (the nervous pathways go to higher levels), the level of synergies' facility in guaranteeing the internal coherency of a movement contrasts with its inability to adjust the complex and harmonious movements it produces to changes in the environment. In respect to legged locomotion, the level of synergies can generate the intra- and interlimb patterns but not actual, functional locomotion, which requires continuous and meaningful adjustments in anticipation of upcoming circumstances (so-called, *prospective control*).

The level of synergies is at all times primarily concerned with the body. The information it has is about the states of the muscular-articular links. In the construction of movements from this level, the focus is on the dynamical criteria of pattern stability and reliability. Real legged locomotion must satisfy very different expediencies, those associated with steering among clutter (e.g., trees, rocks, other animals) and over uneven terrain for particular purposes. The latter achievements require the contribution of higher levels. In Bernstein's hierarchy, the higher levels are Levels C and D, the *level of space* and the *level of actions*, respectively. Moving the body in space (as in walking to a particular location) and moving objects (as in transferring a cup from table to mouth to table or throwing a baseball to home plate) are unique achievements of the level of space under the supervision of the level of actions. The class of motor problems solved by the level of space is the translation of an object's spatial coordinates into a sequence of muscle activation. The movements unique to this level are not harmonious like those of the level of synergies; relatedly, they tend to be frugal in the number of muscles involved and to be brief. Typical of Level C are aimed, transferring movements characterized by the criteria of accuracy and precision. The task of the level of actions (D) is to systematically sequence different movements that succeed each other and that lead to the solution of a problem whose meaning (function, purpose) dictates the relation among the components. Whereas the primary sources of corrections and adjustments at the levels of synergies and space are perceptual, those at the level of actions are plans and intentions. The facility of constructing interleaved and nested structures and of adapting them, componentially, to changing goals and circumstances characterizes the expertise of the level of actions.

CHALLENGES FOR THE LEVEL OF SYNERGIES

What is required of the level of synergies? One problem to be resolved is nicely illustrated by the everyday task of reaching for a nearby object, much as people do when they are at the dinner table. Here, the level of synergies is under the guidance of the level of space. The question is, What are the difficulties that must be resolved by the level of synergies? To move the whole arm in a particular direction, the muscles at the shoulder must provide, through their respective contractions, a particular pattern of forces. Figure 1 is adapted from a classic paper written in 1941 by Paul Weiss (a pioneer in developmental biology and in an area that would be referred to today as the "theory of complexity"). It shows the arm at the shoulder and the controlling muscles. There are 10 or 12 muscles, depending on how they are counted. For simplicity, Weiss parsed them into four functional groups. Figure 1 is compelling in its portrayal of the flexibility of muscular activity. It is commonplace in textbooks for the muscles at a joint to be described as *agonists* and *antagonists*, as if those roles were permanently assigned. What Figure 1 makes clear is that any two muscles can work together (as agonists) or in opposition (as antagonists), depending on the specific way in which the arm is to move. A challenge for the level of synergies is therefore defined: *how to select the pattern of agonist and antagonist muscles that will produce a given movement trajectory.*

The example of reaching for a utensil or a dish at the dinner table reveals another challenge. Casual observation suggests that such movements are close to linear: The hand moves on an approximately straight line from its initial position to the desired object. In order to see what this linearity implies about a group of muscles acting synergistically, consider a simple reaching movement executed by

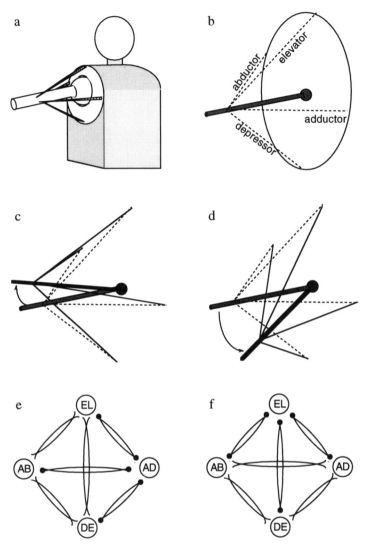

FIG. 1. A schematic (a) of the shoulder joint as a ball and socket with the four main groups of muscles attached to the humerus that (b) pull it upward (the elevator group), forward (the adductor group), downward (the depressor group), and backward (the abductor group). Two directions of motion (indicated by arrows in c and d) from the same starting posture (the shaded cylinder), for which all muscles are evenly contracted (dotted lines). The motion in c is produced by the elevator, abductor, and depressor groups; the motion in d is produced by the abductor, depressor, and adductor groups. Illustrations e and f depict the changing agonistic (v) and antagonistic (•) relations between any two muscles in the course of producing those motions of the humerus. From Weiss (1941). © 1941 by Johns Hopkins University Press. Adapted by permission.

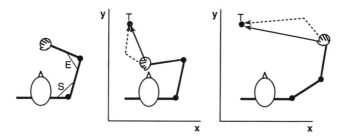

FIG. 2. Schematic of an arm governed by two different synergetic strategies. The muscles at the elbow (E) and those at the shoulder (S) can begin their contractions together, contract at the same rate, and stop contracting when their respective contributions to the movement are complete (dotted trajectories); or the muscles can begin and end contracting at the same time by contracting individually at rates adjusted for the difference in the lengths of their individual contributions to the movement (solid trajectories).

a very simple "arm" with one muscle S at the shoulder and one muscle E at the elbow as depicted by the left illustration in Figure 2. (The example was suggested in 1988 by Bullock and Grossberg, leading modelers of the neural networks underlying synergies.) The hand moves to a target T in an XY plane parallel to the ground. It is drawn across the midline of the body (in the X direction) by S and away from the body (in the Y direction) by E, with the two motions occurring simultaneously. The center and right illustrations show how the hand would move under two contrasting strategies. In one strategy, the two muscles start contracting together and continue at the same rate, with each stopping when its particular contribution to the reach is complete. Their contractions, therefore, are asynchronous. In the other strategy, the two muscles start contracting together but contract at different rates, which are adjusted according to the difference in the movement lengths that each is responsible for, that is, the $X - Y$ difference. In this second strategy, the muscles stop contracting at the same time. Their contractions, therefore, are synchronous. The major difference between the two strategies is that the asynchronous strategy produces reaching movements that involve changes in the direction of motion of the hand, whereas the synchronous strategy produces the sought after straight paths from the starting positions to T. Straight paths have a number of advantages over the bent variety. For example, they facilitate the transport of objects (as when a cup of coffee is brought to the mouth) in two ways: First, straight-line trajectories minimize unexpected directional changes, which create momentary imbalances. Second, moving an object from one specific point to another requires that a force be applied in a specific direction; achieving this specificity is simpler if trajectories are straight lines. Additionally, the synchronization of component movements, which straight paths imply, facilitates the achievement of smooth transitions between the parts of a sequentially organized behavior. At all events, a second challenge for the level of synergies is therefore defined: *how to bring about muscular synchronization in which different muscles must contract by different amounts in equal time.*

The extremities of animals are built, as nearly as matters, from cylinders. In humans, the hinged cylinders that compose an arm differ in size from those that compose a leg. In four-legged animals, the cylinder-like hind legs tend to be larger, especially closer to the hip joint, than the cylinder-like forelegs. These differences between arms and legs, and between front and back limbs, have some simple but important consequences. If an arm and a leg were detached from the body (as might be done in a course on gross anatomy) and each was allowed to swing freely from an axis at its topmost point, the larger leg would tend to swing more slowly than the smaller arm. This difference in the frequencies at which a detached arm and a detached leg oscillate freely in gravity, that is, their natural frequencies, might translate into a difference in muscular and neural activity when the arm and leg are attached. Physically but simply speaking, it is much easier to move a cylindrical pendulum at the frequency it likes to move than at some other frequency. Moreover, the motions at the preferred tempo tend to be more graceful and harmonious to the eye. In general terms, one can say that an extremity has a preference for how it should move. When all extremities must be in cyclic motion, as in walking, the cyclic preferences of all of them cannot be satisfied simultaneously. There will necessarily be a kind of competition due to the different likes and dislikes. Nonetheless, an agreement must be reached among the extremities. They must cooperate with each other and, to do so, each must be prepared to compromise its preference. Thus, a third challenge for the level of synergies has been defined: *how to bring about segmental synchronization, so that limbs and limb segments with different frequency preferences move at the same frequency.*

As we have noted, the level of synergies is very much the product of locomotion's demands. Included among these demands is the ability to produce the same pattern among the limbs and limb segments at different speeds. A cat might walk, trot, or gallop, and it might do so comparatively slowly or comparatively quickly. The phase relations among the four limbs for the walk, trot, and gallop are shown in Figure 3. In each gait, of course, the four limbs must go

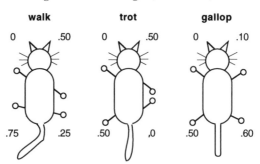

FIG. 3. Schematic of three quadruped gaits as exhibited by a cat. Numbers identify where each limb is in its cycle relative to the front left leg. Thus, in the walk, the front right leg is halfway through its cycle, the right hind leg is one fourth of the way through, and the left hind leg is three fourths of the way through, when the left front leg is at the start (or finish) of its cycle.

through their cycles in equal time (Challenge 3). The motions of the limbs and limb segments must be "in lock" with respect to frequency; otherwise, the simple fact of locomotion (to move from place to place) by walking, trotting, and galloping will not occur. As the cat scales up or scales down its speed of loco-moting in any one of the three gaits—that is, as it increases the power of its movements—the phase relations characterizing the gait and the essential syn-chrony of limb motions are preserved. A fourth challenge for the level of synergies is thereby defined: *how to separate timing from power, pattern from energy*.

There is an implicit contrast between Bernstein's Level B and the higher levels of C and D. For many actions, Levels C and D will lead Level B, provid-ing corrections according to their specialized environmentally based and goal-based criteria but leaving the major internal corrections to Level B. Those corrections germane to Level B seem to be directed at preserving the func-tional form of a movement pattern, that is, at keeping the essential variables of the pattern stable, whatever they might be. Bernstein commented, "Each level of movement construction has its own general means and modes of activity; in particular, each of them acts differently in opposing disruptive influences. The main weapon of the level of muscular-articular links (B) is standardization and elaboration of dynamically stable movement patterns" (essay 5). The level of synergies is oriented to the stability of patterns, and its corrections are aimed at restoring patterns when they are disturbed by fluctuations and external factors. Bernstein was particularly taken by the correlations he frequently observed among component motions that were often separated substantially in space and time. In hammering, a slight change in the elbow's trajectory meant a change in the hammer's inclination to the horizontal in raising, a change in the relation be-tween swing speed and impact, a change in the relation between the velocities of the wrist and hammer head, and so on. Similar long-range correlations were seen in other multisegmental rhythmic activities, such as chiseling, sawing, and walking. These observations led Bernstein (1967) to note that a synergy "never responds to detailed changes by a change in its detail; it responds as a whole to changes in each small part" (p. 23). Modern experimentalists have been similarly impressed by the remote compensatory reactions observed among the articulators of speech and among ipsilateral and contralateral muscles during simple manual acts. It would not serve a biological movement system well if the stability-pre-serving, long-range corrections expressed by a synergy were not its responsibility; the effects are caricatured in Figure 4 (a). A synergy must be a self-organizing system that takes care of its own degrees of freedom through some kind of mutual understanding among them, as implied in Figure 4 (b). A fifth challenge for the level of synergies is therefore identified: *how to make the component degrees of freedom correct themselves to ensure pattern retention*.

In the following discussion, the third, fourth, and fifth challenges are of major concern.

a

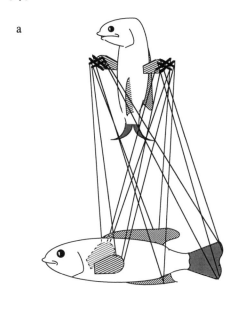

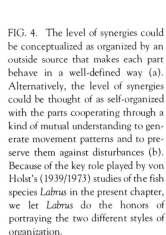

FIG. 4. The level of synergies could be conceptualized as organized by an outside source that makes each part behave in a well-defined way (a). Alternatively, the level of synergies could be thought of as self-organized with the parts cooperating through a kind of mutual understanding to generate movement patterns and to preserve them against disturbances (b). Because of the key role played by von Holst's (1939/1973) studies of the fish species *Labrus* in the present chapter, we let *Labrus* do the honors of portraying the two different styles of organization.

b

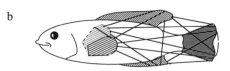

NEARLY DECOMPOSABLE SYSTEMS

Not surprisingly, the experimental analysis and theoretical treatment of synergies are themselves challenging problems. Viewed from the perspective of Bernstein's Level B, synergies are elementary. It is painfully clear, however, that they are exceedingly complex. One can hardly imagine all the activity that is going on, both neurally and muscularly, both up and down the central nervous system and back and forth in the peripheral nervous system, to produce the trotting cat. Yet, at the same time, the visual impression of trotting is that the movement has a large-scale simplicity; as students of movement, we feel the need to be able to address synergies as elementary. What might permit us to do so?

As noted previously, Bernstein saw the mammalian movement system as stratified, consisting of layers distinguished by what they do. Within any layer, a similar stratification can be expected. This is the nature of hierarchies. Subsystems making up a level have their own subsystems. A subsystem and its constituents are distinguished from each other in important ways. Clearly, the constituents are smaller and faster; that is, they go about their business on length scales that are shorter and on time scales that are briefer than the corresponding length and time scales at which things are done by the subsystem. As illustrated in Figure 2, the contractions of the fibers comprising S and E are processes occurring over small regions of space and at a high frequency relative to the spatial extent and frequency of the process in which S and E cooperate to move the hand to a specific place.

It is also the nature of hierarchies to exhibit interactions—both among and within subsystems. As highlighted in 1962 by Herbert Simon, a Nobel Laureate and leading figure in the sciences of artificial and complex systems, the interactions within a subsystem tend to be strong, but the interactions between subsystems tend to be weak. The subsystems are *almost* independent of each other. Now, if this difference in strength of interaction and the difference in time scales are considered collectively, a very helpful proposition or postulate emerges, as noted by Simon: A hierarchic system is *"nearly decomposable."* This means two things. First, the short-run (high-frequency) behavior of a subsystem is approximately independent of the short-run behavior of the other subsystems. That is, given interacting subsystems, the internal processes of one subsystem have little concern for and are little affected by the details of the internal processes of the others. Second, in the long run, the behavior of a subsystem depends, in only an aggregate way, on the behavior of the other subsystems with which it interacts. The summed effect of the other subsystems is what matters, not their individual effects. Applying both the second and first features of a nearly decomposable system to the trotting cat leads to the following conclusion: The behavior of an individual limb is significantly affected by the relatively slowly changing spatial and temporal relations among the other limbs but is mostly impervious to the relatively quickly changing, internal (neuromuscular) details of the other limbs. We state this conclusion in terms more useful for the purposes of the subsequent discussions: The behavior of a collection of rhythmic units, their collective dynamics, is relatively independent of the specific mechanisms that generate the rhythms in the individual units.

THE PRIMACY OF RHYTHM

Bernstein highlighted the special facility of the level of synergies to produce rhythmic behavior. As he remarked, the successive cycles of a repeated act are like "minted coins." The rhythmic capabilities of the level of synergies are compelling for five major reasons.

1. Rhythmic phenomena are ubiquitous in living systems, a fact therefore compelling their careful study as a source of insight into foundational concepts.

2. Rhythmic behavior is a primary expression of how the nervous system organizes movements in space and time, how it achieves highly precise and reproducible patterns, and how it resolves issues of efficiency of motion.

3. Rhythmic behavior seems to obey simple, elegant rules despite the great complexity of the parts and subparts that are involved. It is one of the nervous system's original models of how to generate simple, large-scale behavior from functionally rich and structurally intricate underpinnings.

4. Generally characterized, movements are patterns that evolve "nonmonotonically" in time, that is, with different levels of variation. In principle, therefore, they can be understood as a sum of periodic components.

5. Oscillations, both regular and irregular, have been the foremost topic of interest in contemporary efforts to develop dynamics in ways that might address complicated systems, such as biological movement systems. Traditionally, by *dynamics*, one means the "laws of motion and change." This meaning is preserved in contemporary developments, but it is often expressed in the following (and, as we show, useful) methodological paraphrase: "Dynamics is the study of the time dependency of observable quantities." The special importance of this fifth reason lies in its relation to the third. Dynamical analysis promises to reveal the simple, elegant rules characterizing the level of synergies.

For the five reasons cited, if one could identify and interpret the major qualitative and quantitative features of rhythmic movements, then the reward ought to be a deep understanding of Bernstein's level of synergies. An appropriate beginning is the work of a contemporary of Bernstein's, whose innovative methodology and astute observations inspired the study of rhythmic synergies in dynamical terms.

VON HOLST'S FISH

In the 1930s, the German behavioral physiologist von Holst (1939/1973) observed fish that swim strictly by the oscillations of their fins (the main body axis is immobile). Sometimes these fins oscillate at the same frequency and at a phase relation that is very nearly the same from cycle to cycle, as Figure 5 (left) shows for the pectoral and dorsal fins of *Labrus*. Von Holst referred to this frequency-locked, phase-locked interfin coordination as *absolute coordination*. On other occasions, however, the fins did not preserve a fixed frequency or phase relation. Rather, each fin oscillated at its own rhythm. The circumstance, however, tended not to be one of *no coordination*. It was not the exact opposite of absolute coordination, as depicted in the contrast between the left and right illustrations in Figure 5. Even though the fins moved at different tempos, they still showed an attraction to some phase relations more than to others. Thus, two fins would maintain a relatively constant phase relation for a number of cycles, then would begin to wander in phase—changing their phase relation on each successive cycle—eventually returning to the original, relatively constant relation. Throughout, reciprocal quantitative modulation of the behavior of one fin by

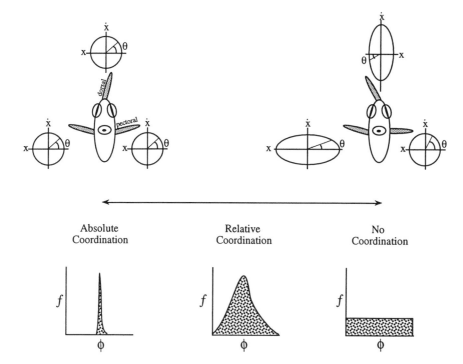

FIG. 5. In *absolute coordination*, the fins of *Labrus* oscillate at the same frequency, and their phase angles θ maintain a constant relation. The space defined by $\dot{x}$ (velocity of fin) and x (displacement of fin) is referred to as a *phase space*. The closed orbit in the phase space represents the limit cycle, a trajectory of points (with each point identifying a particular velocity at a particular displacement) to which the fin returns following a mild disturbance. For illustration, in absolute coordination, the fins' limit cycles are depicted as identical as are their phase angles at any point in time. The distribution of relative phase, the plot of f (frequency of occurrence) against ϕ, concentrates at a single value of relative phase ϕ. When there is *no coordination*, the limit cycles are very different. There is neither a common frequency nor a prominent relation among the phase angles; all relative phases occur equally often. *Relative coordination* lies between these extremes. There is no enduring frequency locking or phase locking; so as in no coordination, all relative phases are "visited." But unlike no coordination and like absolute coordination, relative coordination exhibits a preference. There is a tendency to stay in the vicinity of one relative phase value more than in the vicinity of others.

the other was in evidence. This form of coordination, in which there is no frequency locking but in which there are mutual influence and phase attraction, was referred to by von Holst as *relative coordination*.

In order to bring these interfin coordination patterns under experimental control, von Holst (1939/1973) made a transversal cut through the central nervous system of *Labrus* at the level immediately above the medulla (a simplification that essentially insulated the spinal cord and the lowest section of the brain from the levels of space and action). These surgically prepared fish were then placed in a tank of water, rested on supports that held the body in place without impeding the fins, and a glass tube was inserted in the mouth to provide a steady flow of water (air) into the fish (the surgery disabled respiration). Within a couple of hours of surgery the fins began to oscillate and do so regularly (until the fish's death) as long as the internal and external conditions were maintained constant. Through his studies of the "fish in a tank," von Holst identified three fundamental processes in the formation of rhythmic synergies: The components of a synergy compete (*the maintenance tendency*), combine (*superimposition*), and cooperate (*the magnet effect*).

Each fin had a preferred frequency at which it would oscillate if left to itself. A variety of observations suggested to von Holst (1939/1973) that this preference of an individual fin did not go away in the face of the demands of coordination. Two major observations are represented in Figure 6. In absolute coordination of two fins with different preferred frequencies, the fin of intrinsically higher frequency would be further ahead in its cycle than the fin with intrinsically lower frequency. That is, there would be a deviation from a perfect in-phase coordination (0° or 0 radians) or a perfect antiphase coordination (180° or π radians). Further, if during absolute coordination, one of the fins was stopped abruptly, the other fin would return immediately to its preferred pace. Von Holst referred to the continued manifestation of the preferred, or uncoupled, frequency during a bout of interfin coordination as the *maintenance tendency*. The special significance of the maintenance tendency becomes apparent when two fins with different uncoupled frequencies must

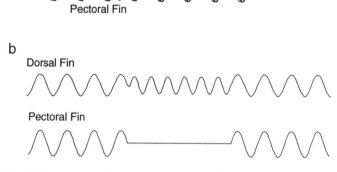

FIG. 6. Experimental phenomena demonstrating the maintenance tendency. In absolute coordination (a), the dorsal fin, which oscillates at a higher frequency in the uncoupled state than does the pectoral fin, leads the pectoral fin in phase. In absolute coordination (b), the dorsal fin oscillates at a frequency tailored to the frequency of its partner. However, as soon as the pectoral fin's motion is arrested, the dorsal fin returns immediately to its higher natural frequency.

oscillate at the same tempo. Because of their respective and different maintenance tendencies, the fins are in competition. Each wants the common frequency to be its preferred frequency. Clearly, if two or more fins must beat in time, then a process is required that can overcome this competition.

The maintenance tendency is evidence that component synergies (components, e.g., of the swimming synergy) are basically independent, autonomous entities. When fins are active together, however, influences of one fin on another can be observed. Von Holst's (1939/1973) investigations revealed that these influences were of two distinct kinds. Figure 7 shows one kind of influence revealed in *relative coordination*, when fins beat at their own preferred frequencies. The dorsal fin oscillates at twice the frequency of a pectoral fin. When a pectoral fin oscillates when the dorsal fin is oscillating, the regularity of the dorsal fin's rhythm is disrupted. What emerges is a waveform that would be expected if there were a mechanism that simply added the nearly sinusoidal pectoral pattern to the nearly sinusoidal dorsal pattern, as depicted in Figure 7. Von Holst referred to this process as *superimposition*. Its additive nature was most fully revealed in experiments in which mirror waveforms for the two pectoral fins were created. In consequence, whatever was added to the dorsal fin by one pectoral fin was subtracted by the other pectoral fin. The upshot was a dorsal fin that beat in regular sinusoidal fashion.

Superimposition means that when a number of rhythmic synergies are active, the behavior of any one synergy is quantitatively dependent on that of the others. This important principle can be stated more positively. With respect to the capabilities of the level of synergies, superimposition identifies, first, a mechanism through which quantitative, reciprocal adjustments can be made automatically among the subsystems composing any large-scale, all encompassing synergy; and, second, a means of producing more elaborate rhythmic synergies by combining simple rhythmic synergies. Here, the works of the two most remarkable behavioral physiologists of the 20th century, von Holst and Bernstein, converge. The major finding of Bernstein's dedicated studies in the 1920s and 1930s of walking, hammering, sawing, and so on, was that the courses of these rhythmical movements could be represented with an accuracy of 1–3 mm by the sum of three or

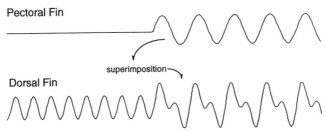

FIG. 7. The phenomenon of superimposition. In relative coordination, the oscillations of the dorsal fin can be understood as the sum of the pectoral fin's oscillations and the oscillations of the dorsal fin when uncoupled.

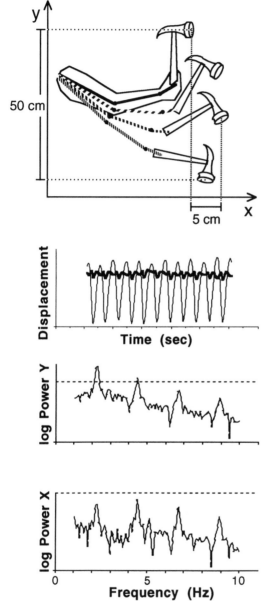

FIG. 8. The top two panels show a particular act of hammering and the time series of its X (smaller, dark oscillations) and Y coordinates. The two power spectra show that each time series is composed of the respective fundamental frequency and its three (at most) harmonics.

four sinusoidal functions. Figure 8 is a specific example from our own laboratory. The time series of a particular bout of hammering is shown for both the vertical and horizontal motions of the hammer head. The corresponding power spectral analyses (which decompose the two time series into their component sinusoids and their squared amplitudes) reveal the prominence of component oscillations at a fundamental frequency, $f \approx 2.2$ cycles per second, and its harmonics, $2f$, $3f$, and $4f$.

The discoveries of von Holst and Bernstein dovetail and thus provide an important insight into how more complicated rhythmic patterns are created at the level of synergies, namely, by *superimposing very elementary rhythmic patterns in particular phase relations*. The second influence between fins observed by von Holst (1939/1973) is of special relevance in completing the picture just painted. This influence concerns how the fins interact to bring about particular *qualitative* effects—one particular rhythmic pattern rather than another, two fins oscillating together at the same frequency rather than separately at different frequencies. Whereas superimposition combines rhythmic patterns and provides a means of achieving *quantitative* reciprocal adjustments among the components of a synergy, the second influence *determines and maintains the frequency and phase relations among the components*. Hammering is a rhythmic pattern (as Figure 8 depicts) that is achieved through frequency- and phase-locked oscillations about the shoulder, the elbow, and the wrist. The sinusoids that sum to produce its trajectory are in-phase.

Whereas superimposition is seen most obviously in the amplitudes, this second influence is seen most obviously in the frequencies. Von Holst (1939/1973) observed that as two fins beating at different frequencies and with different amplitudes became phase locked, the frequencies changed to become one and the same, but the amplitudes remained relatively unaltered. Von Holst referred to this achievement of a common frequency and a constant relative phase as *the magnet effect*. How do the two different sources of interfin influences relate? When fins are coordinated, superimposition and the magnet effect act together in a highly specific way, as depicted in Figure 9. The phase relation into which the magnet effect attempts to draw the fins is the phase relation in which superimposition results in a magnification rather than in a reduction of amplitude.

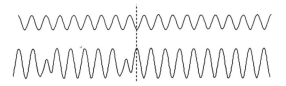

FIG. 9. Absolute coordination occurs at the relative phase at which superimposition is additive.

A FIRST STEP TOWARD THE DYNAMICS
OF SYNERGIES

Implicit in the fish-in-a-tank studies are a number of dynamical concepts. Making them explicit is the task that follows. We discuss in dynamical terms what it means to achieve a common tempo for two rhythmically moving body segments. Specifically, this discussion concerns the identification of the dynamical principles governing the relative phase between the fins of *Labrus*. As this discussion makes apparent, this variable is a particularly useful one through which to view the achievements of the level of synergies—it reflects, in the most simple quantitative way, the spatiotemporal structure of rhythmic synergistic patterns. In the initial foray into the dynamics of interfin coordination, we adopt a formal analysis that was inspired by experimental work on another kind of fish, the lamprey eel. (The study of the lamprey has a long and distinguished history; even Sigmund Freud can be included among earlier investigators who sought general insights into the nervous system through the primitive circuitry of the lamprey spine.) The formal analysis in question was developed in the 1970s and 1980s by American biologists, mathematicians, and physicists, most notably Avis Cohen, Nancy Kopell, Richard Rand, and Philip Holmes (e.g., Cohen, Holmes, & Rand, 1982; Kopell, 1988a, 1988b). Consonant with the postulate of "nearly decomposable," the strategy for modeling the interfin dynamics makes no assumptions about the internal details of individual fins and their means of interacting. The modeling refers only to the observables (measurable variables) of the fins in oscillation. Because we will make much of this strategy in developing the dynamics of the level of synergies, we must here state its precise purpose: The scope of a dynamical study of a rhythmic synergy is the specification of the observables that describe the synergy and a characterization of the manner in which these observables are linked.

The initial questions are how to characterize the individual fin and how to characterize the interfin interaction that von Holst called the magnet effect. Any individual rhythmic synergy—such as the dorsal fin of *Labrus*—is assumed to conform to a *steady-state limit cycle* at all times. This is a closed orbit in the phase space of velocity and displacement (such as those shown in Figure 5) to which the synergy returns following a perturbation. It is further assumed that the fin's state can be specified by a single variable θ representing the phase of the limit cycle (again, see Figure 5), where θ passes from 0 radians to 2π radians in one cycle and where θ can be made proportional to the fraction of the cycle period that has elapsed. Hence, for the dorsal fin oscillating free of the influences of the other fins, the rate of change of phase can be expressed as

$$\dot{\theta}_{dorsal} = \omega_{dorsal} . \qquad (1)$$

That is, its rate of change of phase (the dot over θ designates the time derivative) is equal to the fin's eigenfrequency ω (roughly, the frequency at which the dorsal fin prefers to run if left alone). By integration of Equation 1 and the recognition that each dorsal fin cycle is very much the same as the ones preceding and succeeding it (the so-called mod-2π convention), phase angle at time t can be expressed as

$$\theta_{dorsal}(t) = \omega_{dorsal} + \theta_{dorsal}(0) \ mod \ 2\pi. \tag{2}$$

That is, at any point in time (t), the fin's phase angle is determined by its eigenfrequency and the phase angle at which the oscillations began. A lesson from the fish-in-a-tank studies is that the coupling between fins is never overly strong (recall the features of relative coordination). If the dorsal fin is weakly coupled to a pectoral fin and if the effects of superimposition are slight, then the dorsal fin will remain, when coupled, close to its limit-cycle orbit at all times, and θ_{dorsal} will retain its status as the essential variable. What the coupling will do is simply speed up or slow down the change in θ_{dorsal}. It will act as an influence on θ_{dorsal} in addition to the influences identified in Equation 2. Von Holst (1939/1973) intuited that the magnet effect was the endeavor of, say, the pectoral fin to make the dorsal fin behave like it, that is, to make the dorsal fin's phase angle conform to its own phase angle. This intuition suggests that the magnet effect, or coupling, can be thought of as an added influence that depends, somehow, on the phase angles of the two fins. Accordingly, Equation 1 can be expanded to

$$\dot{\theta}_{dorsal} = \omega_{dorsal} + M_{[pectoral \rightarrow dorsal]} \ (\theta_{dorsal}, \theta_{pectoral}). \tag{3}$$

An immediately important feature of Equation 3 is that it expresses the coexistence of the maintenance tendency ω_{dorsal} and the magnet effect $M_{[pectoral \rightarrow dorsal]}$. By the assumptions made thus far, the magnet effect, or coupling function, $M_{[pectoral \rightarrow dorsal]}$ depends only on θ_{dorsal} and $\theta_{pectoral}$. Note that this phase-dependent coupling is constrained by the requirement that, in order for the motion expressed by Equation 3 to be that of frequency-locked fins, the M effect of the pectoral fin on the same phase point of the dorsal fin must always be the same. Moreover, $M_{[pectoral \rightarrow dorsal]}$ must be a function of the two phase angles, repeating itself every 2π radians (or every cycle of the dorsal and pectoral fins). The simplest form of $M_{[pectoral \rightarrow dorsal]}$ is so-called *diffusive* coupling, a term borrowed from the study of chemical oscillations. Given two unequal chemical concentrations, a flow from the greater to the lesser concentration will occur and stop once the difference no longer exists. With respect to Equation 3, diffusive coupling is the assumption that coupling increases with the size of the difference $\theta_{dorsal} - \theta_{pectoral}$ between the two phase angles and that it desists (that is, no coupling, no magnet effect) when the two phase angles are equal, $\theta_{dorsal} = \theta_{pectoral}$. Von Holst's (1939/1973) observations suggested to him that the magnet effect was a diffusive coupling. He wrote, "As soon as the two rhythms maintain the mutual phase relation which is appropriate to absolute coordination, the influence of one rhythm on the other is zero" (p. 62). His fish-in-a-tank observations also suggested the general form of M: *It is a negative sine*

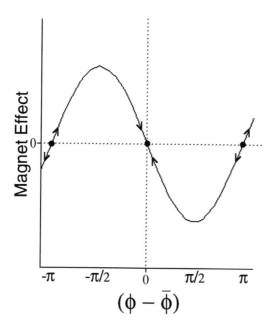

FIG. 10. Von Holst's (1939/1973) discovery of the relation between the strength of the magnet effect (coupling) and the deviation of current relative phase ϕ from the relative phase of absolute coordination $\bar{\phi}$. The inward pointing arrows denote attraction and the outward pointing arrows denote repulsion.

function. As Figure 10 reveals, if absolute coordination occurs at a relative phase of $\bar{\phi}$, then, as the current relative phase $\phi = (\theta_{dorsal} - \theta_{pectoral})$ deviates from $\bar{\phi}$, the strength of the magnet effect increases to a maximum at $\pm\pi/2$, then decreases to zero again at $\pm\pi$. Astutely, von Holst identified $(\phi - \bar{\phi}) = 0$ as an attractor and $(\phi - \bar{\phi}) = \pm\pi$ as a repeller. Because of von Holst's perspicacity, a particular interpretation can be applied to M and to the relation between the phase angles. That is,

$$M_{[pectoral \rightarrow dorsal]}(\theta_{dorsal}, \theta_{pectoral}) = m_{[pectoral \rightarrow dorsal]}\sin(\theta_{pectoral} - \theta_{dorsal}), \qquad (4)$$

where m, the coefficient of the sine function, represents the strength of the magnet effect or coupling.

Von Holst's (1939/1973) magnet effect is most often mutual. While the pectoral fin is endeavoring to capture the dorsal fin, the dorsal fin may well be attempting to do likewise with the pectoral fin. Consequently, the motion equations for the two fins take the following forms:

$$\dot{\theta}_{dorsal} = \omega_{dorsal} + m_{[pectoral \rightarrow dorsal]}\sin(\theta_{pectoral} - \theta_{dorsal}) \qquad (5)$$

and

$$\dot{\theta}_{pectoral} = \omega_{pectoral} + m_{[dorsal \rightarrow pectoral]}\sin(\theta_{dorsal} - \theta_{pectoral}). \qquad (6)$$

When the motion equation for the pectoral fin is subtracted from that of the dorsal fin and the identity $\sin(\theta_{dorsal} - \theta_{pectoral}) = -\sin(\theta_{pectoral} - \theta_{dorsal})$ is used, the motion equation for the phase relation can be expressed as

$$\dot{\phi} = \Delta\omega - m \sin\phi, \tag{7}$$

where ϕ is the phase difference $(\theta_{dorsal} - \theta_{pectoral})$, $\Delta\omega = (\omega_{dorsal} - \omega_{pectoral})$, and $m = (m_{[pectoral \rightarrow dorsal]} + m_{[dorsal \rightarrow pectoral]})$. Equation 7 signifies that the phase relation between the dorsal and pectoral fins changes at a rate dependent on the size of the competition between the fins $(\Delta\omega)$ and the current strength of the cooperation between the fins $(m \sin\phi)$. Because of the nearly decomposable nature of the movement system, changes in ϕ represent the collective behavior of all the underlying subsystems. Consequently, Equation 7 can be described in more general terms as an approximation of the dynamical law that *generates the time-evolution of the collective states of the central nervous system at the level of synergies*. In Equation 7 lie the answers to the third and fourth challenges for the level of synergies identified previously.

According to Equation 7, the interfin coordination pattern will be constant when $\dot{\phi} = 0$. This constant phase relation, designated $\bar{\phi}$, can be referred to as a *fixed point*, a *stable point*, an *equilibrium point*, or an *attractor* and is expressed as

$$\bar{\phi} = \arcsin(\Delta\omega/m). \tag{8}$$

Because of the nature of the arcsine function [it takes numbers satisfying $-1 \le x \le 1$ and maps them onto numbers satisfying $-\pi/2 \le \arcsin(x) \le \pi/2$], it follows from Equation 8 that there will be an equilibrium point (meaning there will be absolute coordination or frequency locking) only when $\Delta\omega < m$, as von Holst (1939/1973) most clearly realized. If the coupling strength m in the medulla-transected *Labrus* vacillates, then the value of $\Delta\omega/m$ will vary with the possibility of a drifting back and forth between $\Delta\omega/m > 1$ and $\Delta\omega/m < 1$. The consequence would be an interfin behavior of frequency wandering (relative coordination) and frequency locking (absolute coordination), much like that which so intrigued von Holst.

THE SIMPLE BIFURCATIONS OF INTERSEGMENTAL COORDINATION

The last remarks are a starting point for a deeper understanding of the level of synergies. Specifically, they open the door on the important concepts of *control parameter*, *broken symmetry*, and *bifurcation*. In the von Holst (1939/1973) dynamics that we have just developed, and expressed through Equation 7, m is the control parameter, and the symmetry of the dynamics is broken when $\Delta\omega$ does not equal zero. The situations studied by von Holst were mainly situations of broken symmetry: The dorsal, pectoral, and tail fins all differed in their maintenance tendencies and, therefore, could not play identical roles in the coordination pattern. When the symmetry is broken, mere increases and decreases in m can promote richly varied changes in the behavior of a synergy. These behavioral changes arise from increases in the number of equilibria (fixed points, stable points, attractors) and from changes in the stability (e.g., from stable to unstable) of these equilibria. A change in the number or stability of equilibrium points is called a *bifurcation*.

Consider the left column of the graphs in Figure 11. Each graph is simply a plot of $\dot{\phi}$ versus ϕ from Equation 7 with $\Delta\omega = 0.25$ (imagine that the dorsal fin's preferred frequency is 0.25 Hz greater than that of the right pectoral fin) and with positive m decreasing in each succeeding graph down the column. As in Figure 10, where the curve crosses at $\dot{\phi}$ = zero with a negative slope, a stable equilibrium point is defined. The pattern is like a negative correlation: As one number increases, the other number decreases; as the relative phase deviates from the point of the zero crossing, the change in relative phase lessens. A zero crossing with negative slope, therefore, attracts the relative phase toward it. Conversely, where the zero crossing has a positive slope, an unstable equilibrium is defined; relative phase is repelled. Because of the broken symmetry, the stable equilibrium point in the top graph is not at $\phi = 0$ but has been shifted to a value greater than zero. This pattern means that although the two fins are close to in-phase the phase of the dorsal fin leads that of the pectoral fin by a particular amount (as was shown in Figure 6a). Downward from graph to graph, as m decreases (the magnet effect becomes weaker), the stable equilibrium point drifts farther from $\phi = 0$ and approaches closer to the unstable equilibrium point. Eventually, there is no stable equilibrium: The two equilibria have come together and annihilated one another in a variant of what is called a *saddle-node bifurcation* (see Figure 16). An inspection of the last two graphs in the column suggests, however, that some hint of an equilibrium point remains. There exists an *attraction* to a certain phase, even though there is no longer an attractor and no longer any basis for frequency locking and phase locking. Kelso and Ding (1993) suggested that such ghostly attractors could be the source of the relative-phase distribution characterizing relative coordination (see Figure 5), that is, the tendency of the interfin coordination pattern to visit a wide range of values accompanied by a tendency to hover in the vicinity of one preferred value.

Consider now the right column of Figure 11. Here the value of m decreases to zero and then becomes increasingly negative. As m changes in this manner, the stable equilibrium point near $0°$ and the unstable equilibrium point near $180°$ disappear when m approaches and passes through zero. As m grows in negativity, stability returns, with the previously stable equilibrium near $0°$ now an unstable equilibrium and the previously unstable equilibrium near $180°$ (or π) now a stable equilibrium. The fish-in-a-tank experiment often exhibited a bifurcation of the kind just described. One interfin pattern shifted spontaneously and abruptly to the opposite interfin pattern.

A MODEL EXPERIMENTAL SYSTEM
FOR INVESTIGATING INTERLIMB
RHYTHMIC SYNERGIES

Equations 7 and 8 provide useful insights into the conditions that govern the basic coupled state in biological movement systems—the 1:1 frequency locking between any two body segments (limbs, fins, wings, spinal sections). The con-

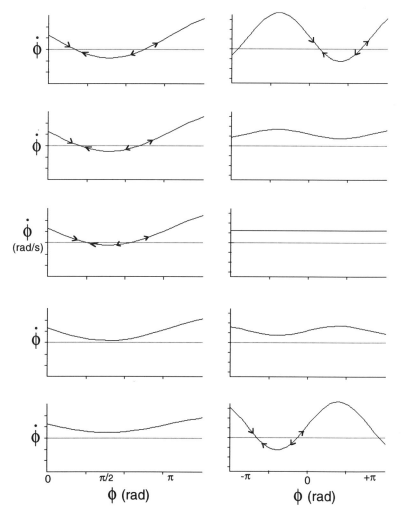

FIG. 11. *Left*–The *m* parameter of Equation 7 is decreasing from the top plot to the bottom plot for two dissimilar rhythmic units, like the dorsal and pectoral fins ($\Delta\omega = 0.25$). The stable equilibrium (arrows pointing in) and the unstable equilibrium (arrows pointing out) become closer together as *m* decreases. At some value they "collide" and there are no definite equilibria—a saddle-node bifurcation results. But a suggestion of an equilibrium point remains. *Right*–The same conditions are repeated, but *m* passes from positive to negative. The unstable equilibrium point in the vicinity of π when *m* is a (relatively) large positive value becomes a stable equilibrium point when *m* is a (relatively) large negative value.

ditions depicted in Figure 11 can be elaborated: the constant-phase difference $\bar{\phi}$ becomes larger as $\Delta\omega$ (the size of the difference between the maintenance tendencies) increases and smaller as m (the strength of the magnet effect) increases. Further, if $\Delta\omega \neq 0$, then variations in m will further affect $\bar{\phi}$, but if $\Delta\omega = 0$, then variations in m will be inconsequential for $\bar{\phi}$. These predictions, and others, can be seen by plotting the "vector field" of the dynamics $\dot{\phi}$ versus ϕ for different values of $\Delta\omega$ and m, as was done in Figure 11. A way of examining these more specific predictions concerning the elementary synergy of intersegmental coordination is needed. Oddly enough, the sought-after way can be provided by procedures involving intact human participants. Probing the level of synergies proves to be easiest and most revealing with the biological movement system that is governed, more than any other, by the level of actions.

In order to study the presence of both absolute and relative coordination in human interlimb coordination, von Holst (1939/1973) had individuals move two levers (one for each arm) at different frequencies. For example, the individual attempted to produce a rhythm with one lever that was twice that produced with the other. A better procedure, that is, one that is more manipulable and that is modeled more closely on the specifics of von Holst's experiments with *Labrus*, can be devised.

Von Holst's (1939/1973) fish-in-a-tank studies suggest four major requirements for a general experimental method directed at the dynamics of interappendage rhythmic synergies:

1. The eigenvalues of the individual rhythmic movement units must be manipulable and easily quantified.
2. The frequency at which the two rhythmic units move when coupled must be manipulable.
3. The interlimb system must be easily prepared in one of the two basic patterns of in-phase (homologous muscles contracting at the same time) and antiphase (homologous muscles contracting alternately).
4. The focus of measurement and dynamical modeling must be on the interactions of phase.

Requirement 4 can be met by Equation 7. Requirements 1–3 are satisfied by the experimental procedure depicted in Figure 12 and described in a monograph published by Kugler and Turvey in 1987. In the upper left quadrant of the figure is an illustration of a person seated and holding a pendulum in each hand. The pendulums can vary physically in shaft length, the mass of the attached mass bob, or both. Each of the two pendulums is swung parallel to the sagittal plane about an axis in the wrist (with other joints essentially immobile). The eigenfrequency of such an individual wrist–pendulum system can be approximated on the basis of the eigenfrequency of the equivalent simple pendulum, $\omega = (g/L)^{1/2}$, where L is the simple pendulum length and g is the constant

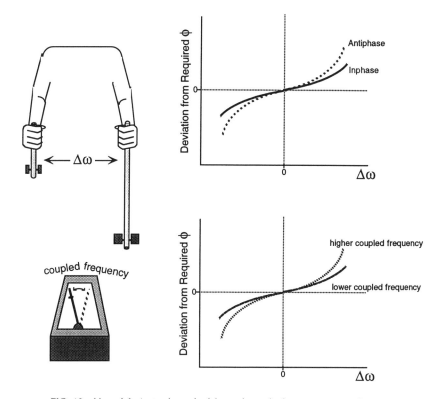

FIG. 12. *Upper left*–A simple method for studying rhythmic synergies in humans is diagrammed. Differences in pendulums control the contrasting maintenance tendencies, and a metronome (*lower left*) controls the magnet effect through the coupled frequency. *Right*–Typical data, showing the significance of frequency competition (Δω), required phase (in-phase vs. antiphase), and coupled frequency.

acceleration due to gravity. The quantity L can be calculated from the magnitudes of shaft length, added mass, and hand mass, according to the standard methods for representing any arbitrary rigid body oscillating about a fixed point as a simple pendulum.

Frequency competition between the component rhythmic synergies can be brought about by left and right pendulums that differ in L (see Figure 12). Further, a metronome can be used to pace the frequency at which absolute coordination is performed (see lower left quadrant of Figure 12). Preparing the interlimb coordination in either in-phase or antiphase is a relatively simple matter of instructing the participants to maintain one or the other basic pattern in the course of a trial.

In Figure 12 (right quadrants), we also present a generic picture of the kinds of results that are typically found in experiments in which Δω is fixed on a particular trial and the participant produces 1:1 frequency locking in either in-phase or antiphase. The typical results exhibit a feature that is not expected from von Holst's (1939/1973) dynamics; namely, the shift of equilibria (from 0° or from 180°) due to symmetry breaking is greater for antiphase than for in-phase. They also exhibit a feature that is of both great theoretical and practical significance. With an increase in the coupled frequency, the equilibrium shift becomes greater at each $\Delta\omega$, exactly what would be expected from Equations 7 and 8 if the magnet effect, or coupling, weakened. Apparently, the higher the frequency at which an intersegmental coordination operates, the weaker is the coupling between components. In an experiment with human participants, metronomic regulation of the coupled frequency *is* regulation of *m*; that is, coupled frequency is the control parameter. Later, we make much of these two features brought to light in Figure 12.

THE LEVEL OF SYNERGIES IS SELF-ORGANIZING

One's efforts to grasp the dynamics of the level of synergies can be advanced considerably by recognizing a simple contrast between the two major intersegmental organizations, which somehow escaped von Holst's (1939/1973) critical eye. It is fairly obvious that 1:1 frequency locking occurs primarily in two patterns, in-phase ($\phi = 0$) and antiphase ($\phi = \pi$). The simple (but theoretically penetrating) contrast in question is that in-phase is more attractive than antiphase. This contrast was made particularly evident in an experiment in which a person had to oscillate the two index fingers (or two hands) at a coupled frequency that was varied by a metronome, which the person tracked. This experiment was conducted in the United States in the early 1980s by Kelso and reported in 1984. It proved to be the springboard for the contemporary study of coordination dynamics. In Kelso's experiment, if the person's fingers began in antiphase, with increasing coupled frequency and instructions not to resist any change when it occurred, the fingers then switched suddenly to in-phase. Simply, the participant could not keep the antiphase organization at the higher rates of behavior, much as a four-legged animal (like the cat of Figure 3) seems forced to switch from an antiphase gait (e.g., the trot) to an in-phase gait (the gallop) at faster running speeds. In Kelso's coupled-fingers experiment, the transition from antiphase to in-phase was not reversed, however, by a reduction in the coupled frequency, and if the fingers began in in-phase, the increase in coupled frequency did not bring about a switch to antiphase. This simple experiment and its simple results clarify how the level of synergies meets the fifth challenge identified previously.

Typical of self-organizing systems is the acquisition of a new state—a new dynamic pattern in space–time—that arises at critical values of one or a few control parameters. The precise nature of the new state is specified from within the system, not by the control parameters; the control parameters merely force the system indirectly to acquire its new state and prescribe none of its details (as was illustrated with manipulations of *m* in Figure 11). Hallmark behavioral features of a self-organizing system that approximate a pattern transition are *critical fluctuations* and *critical slowing down*, with the former referring to large fluctuations in the macroscopic observables and the latter referring to a marked increase in the time taken by the system to recover from perturbations. In the vicinity of the transition, the dynamics is dominated by one or a few *order parameters*. These macroscopic quantities capture the spatiotemporal details of the system and change more slowly than the variables characterizing the states (e.g., velocity, amplitude) of the component subsystems. In the simple experiment just described, coupled frequency was a control parameter that forced the system of coupled index fingers to acquire a new pattern, and relative phase ϕ was the system's order parameter. These conjectures have been proven by experiments that demonstrated an increase in the standard deviation of ϕ ($SD\phi$) and an increase in the relaxation, or recovery, time (τ_{rel}) following a perturbation as the coupled frequency attained values close to the transition point. These properties, together with the experimentally observed *hysteresis* (in-phase does not return to antiphase as the coupled frequency is reduced), are the defining qualities of what are referred to as *nonequilibrium phase transitions*. Such transitions are characteristic of systems that organize themselves (rather than receiving specific instructions from an external organizer). With respect to the level of synergies, these experimental results offer a most significant insight: *Processes at the level of synergies are self-organizing.*

THE LEVEL OF SYNERGIES DEALS IN POTENTIAL FUNCTIONS

Equation 7 is a first-order differential equation. That is, it models the rhythmic synergy exhibited by *Labrus* simply by accounting for changes in relative phase as a function of time; no higher order time rates of change are needed. Characteristic of first-order differential equations is their capacity to be put into an especially useful form, namely,

$$\dot{\phi} = -\frac{dV(\phi)}{d\phi}, \qquad (9)$$

where $V(\phi)$ is a so-called potential function. The inspiration comes from the common observation in mechanics that any object free to move on a curved surface, like a marble in a salad bowl, will move in the direction of the curve's nearest lowest point. Functions like Equation 7 have the nice feature, shown in Figure 11, of the vectors "flowing" toward stable points and away from unstable points. In the concrete case of a marble in a salad bowl, to think about the marble's behavior in terms of a potential function one must focus on the bowl's curvature and see the marble's behavior as determined by that curvature. Any point on the inner surface of the bowl has a height value H (relative to the bottom of the bowl) and a position value p (the point's perpendicular distance from the bowl's central vertical axis). Given a location of the marble on the bowl's inner surface, one can determine with simple mechanical calculations, in what direction and at what rate its p value will change. In the abstract case of a system like a rhythmic synergy, one is attempting to identify a heightlike quantity V, which is a function of a position-like quantity ϕ, such that a particular V at a particular ϕ determines the synergy's behavior; $V(\phi)$ indicates in what direction and at what rate ϕ will change.

In 1985, Haken (a German physicist who developed a major interdisciplinary approach to self-organizing systems referred to as *synergetics*) published with Kelso and Bunz an account of Kelso's phase-transition data based on the following potential function:

$$V(\phi) = -a\cos(\phi) - b\cos(2\phi). \tag{10}$$

Figure 13 illustrates how Equation 10 defines a surface, or an "energy landscape," with valleys centered at $\phi = 0$ and $\phi = \pm\pi$ when the ratio of the b coefficient to the a coefficient is high (e.g., 1.5). The deepest valley is at $\phi = 0$, but for larger b/a values, a marble on the surface could settle quite comfortably (be perfectly stable) at either the deep or the shallower valleys. As an inspection of Figure 13 reveals, the shape of the surface changes fairly dramatically with a reduction in b/a. Most notably, the valleys at $\pm\pi$ disappear; indeed, they turn into hills. Think of a marble that has been "hanging out" in one of the shallower valleys. At the value of b/a at which the shallower valleys disappear, the marble

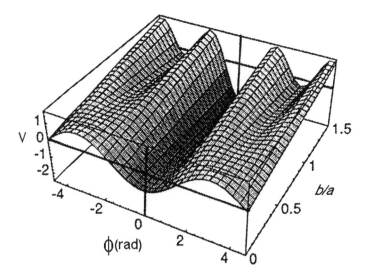

FIG. 13. The potential function defined by Equation 10.

would have no option but to roll into the deeper valley. Its position at π becomes unstable and it moves to a new location at 0, which is stable. It is apparent that reversing b/a would not dislodge the marble from its newfound stability at 0. It is also apparent from an inspection of Figure 13 that if the marble started out in the deeper valley it would have no impetus to move to the shallower ones as the value of b/a increased. Each of the preceding scenarios concerning the marble on the surface of Figure 13 was witnessed by Kelso (1984) in his coupled-fingers coordination experiment.

Continuing the ideas used to discuss Figure 11, we call the critical value of b/a "a bifurcation point" and the qualitative change in the landscape a "bifurcation." The type of bifurcation that occurs is called a *subcritical pitchfork bifurcation*. As the marble moves along the valley at +π from b/a = 1.5 (see Figure 13), there are two ridges of identical convexity to its right and left. Any point in the valley is an attractor; any point on a ridge is a repeller, or saddle point. At some value of b/a (it happens to be 0.25), the repellers and attractor come together, and the attractor disappears, as schematized in Figure 14. From the marble's perspective, when the stable point at π is annihilated, the stable point at 0 suddenly appears. Von Holst (1939/1973) noted that pattern transitions in *Labrus* were abrupt, as were the transitions in interfinger coordination observed by Kelso (1984). This abruptness, however, is not seen in the right column of Figure 11. There, when a stable equilibrium was lost, no other stable equilibrium was available. Another stable equilibrium does not appear until the control parameter has gone through a substantial range of values and relative phase has wandered through its many possible magnitudes. In sum, the dynamics underlying Figure 11 could not give rise to an abrupt transition. Like Kelso, von Holst could have been watching an organization at the level of synergies that was bistable.

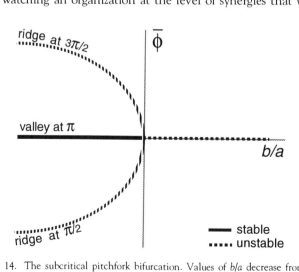

FIG. 14. The subcritical pitchfork bifurcation. Values of b/a decrease from left to right.

Perhaps Equation 7, describing a monostable system, is not really the dynamics of the interfin rhythmic synergy.

NOISE CONTRIBUTES TO PATTERN CHANGES AT THE LEVEL OF SYNERGIES

The marble on the surface depicted in Figure 13, whose adventures have been followed in some detail, is our simple way of representing the rhythmic synergy. More correctly, it has been our way of representing a certain macroscopic property of the synergy, namely ϕ. The postulate of "nearly decomposable" has allowed us to take such liberties. Relative phase is a projection, on a fairly big scale, of the internal states of the synergy, which are operating on very much smaller scales. The relative phase is the macroscopic mode (way of behaving) of a large collection of relatively microscopic subsystems, such as muscle fibers, interneurons, reflexes, and so on. Figure 15 (top) provides a simple depiction; it also conveys the image

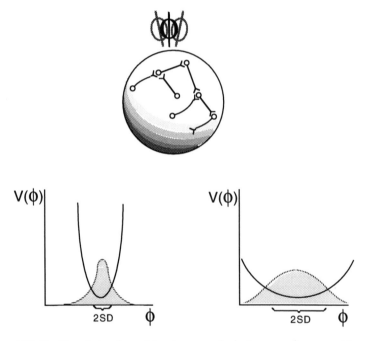

FIG. 15. The relative phase of the elementary rhythmic synergy (represented by a marble rolling around on the surface depicted in Figure 13) fluctuates because of the interacting degrees of freedom in its interior. If a potential well is steep, the random force pushing the marble will not push it too far—the standard deviation of relative phase will be small (*lower left*). In contrast, if the potential well is shallow, then these random pushes will produce large variability in relative phase (*lower right*).

of a macroscopic mode that wobbles. The wobbling of relative phase comes from the noise generated by the interacting subsystems. This noise functions as a fluctuating, random force, which affects the moment-to-moment state of relative phase.

For the marble on the surface depicted in Figure 13, the fluctuating force can be represented as kicks that cause the marble to move randomly in the vicinity of a fixed point. If the marble is resting at a particular location of the π valley, then the kicks will cause it to move up the walls of the valley. Suppose that the fluctuating force has a particular average strength. The marble's movements will then be captured by a distribution function—a plot of the frequency with which it is found at the fixed point and at points nearby. As Figure 15 shows, this distribution function can be narrow when the valley is steep (higher b/a) and broad when the valley is shallow (lower b/a). A magnification in the standard deviation of relative phase was observed in the coupled-fingers coordination experiment (as noted) with proximity to the bifurcation point where the valleys at $\pm\pi$ flatten (see Figure 13). It is evident that armed with fluctuations, the marble need not wait for the annihilation of the valley at π. Its random motions within the flattening valley are like explorations of the lie of the land. It can discover, via its fluctuations, that the valley on the other side of the ridge is indeed greener or more stable. That is to say, the noise welling up from the interior of rhythmic synergies provides a mechanism that facilitates the switching of synergistic patterns.

THE BISTABLE DYNAMICS OF THE RHYTHMIC SYNERGY

Needed now is an equation for the time–evolution of collective neural and muscular states at the level of synergies that recognizes their multistability. It follows from Equation 9 that the differentiation of Equation 10 should lead the way to an appropriate motion equation:

$$\dot{\phi} = -a\sin(\phi) - 2b\sin(2\phi). \tag{11}$$

Equation 11, however, does not include the source of fluctuations and is limited to cases in which the segments are symmetric. As we have noted, for the more general case, symmetry is broken. To accommodate broken symmetry, $\Delta\omega$ must be introduced as a quantity to express the different symmetrical states. To accommodate the random kicks from the interior of the rhythmic synergy, a term that expresses both the strength and the distribution of these kicks must be added. For simplicity, we will just identify it with N (for noise). With these additions, introduced in papers by Schöner, Haken, and Kelso (1986) and Kelso, DelColle, and Schöner (1990), Equation 11 becomes

$$\dot{\phi} = \Delta\omega - a\sin(\phi) - 2b\sin(2\phi) + N. \tag{12}$$

Equation 12 can be considered the motion equation for 1:1 frequency locking in biological movement systems. It is a *dynamical law of intersegmental rhythmic coordination*. Equation 12 makes a host of predictions about both the transitory and stable behavior of the synergy, and like any good law, makes predictions that are unintuitive but correct.

The best way one can tease out the predictions is to plot $\dot{\phi}$ versus ϕ for various magnitudes of $\Delta\omega$ and b/a. Two plots are shown in Figure 16, for $\Delta\omega = 0$ (top) and $\Delta\omega = 1$ (bottom). Just as was done, with respect to Figure 11, one scouts for zero crossings and, having found them, inspects the slope of the surface at the crossing. A negative slope means a stable equilibrium. Figure 16 (top) reminds one that when the dynamics are symmetrical, the stable equilibrium remains at 0 across decreasing b/a (increasing coupled frequency) and remains at $\pm\pi$ until the (subcritical pitchfork) bifurcation. What can now be developed are the expectations for the dynamics based on the *degree* of slope through the zero crossing. Because ϕ is the ratio of one line segment length to another expressed in radians, it is a dimensionless quantity; $\dot{\phi}$ is radians per second, an obviously dimensional quantity (1/time). If the rate at which $\dot{\phi}$ changes with ϕ (the slope at the zero crossing) is calculated, its inverse is a quantity measured in seconds. It quantifies how much time the rhythmic coordination takes to return to the stable equilibrium point following a small kick. The quantity given by the inverse of the slope through the zero crossing is the relaxation time τ_{rel} that was briefly mentioned in reference to the behavior of interfinger coordination. Basically, it indicates just how stable or attractive a stable equilibrium point happens to be. Now it is clear that in the symmetrical dynamics illustrated in Figure 16 (top), although neither the 0 nor the π attractor is budged by the control parameter (as confirmed by experimental data, see Figure 12), their attractiveness is altered. The smaller b/a is, the less attractive $\phi = 0$ and $\phi = \pi$ are and the more variable the relative phase becomes. It is also evident from an inspection of the slopes shown in Figure 16 (top) that the degree of stability is always greater for 0 than for π.

When the symmetry is broken, as is the case represented by the bottom part in Figure 16, the dynamics are changed. First, the equilibria are displaced systematically from 0 and $\pm\pi$ by the reduction in b/a. Second, for the same values of b/a the slopes through the stable equilibria are more shallow for broken symmetry than for symmetry; that is, the equilibria are less stable. Third, the bifurcation point at which equilibria at $\pm\pi$ disappear is at a higher value of b/a for broken symmetry than for symmetry; that is, antiphase coordination can be preserved over a smaller range of coupled frequencies. Fourth, a further bifurcation point exists at which the equilibrium in the vicinity of 0 is annihilated, an occurrence leaving no equilibria. Fifth, the bifurcation in the broken symmetry condition is a different type from that in the symmetry condition; it is the

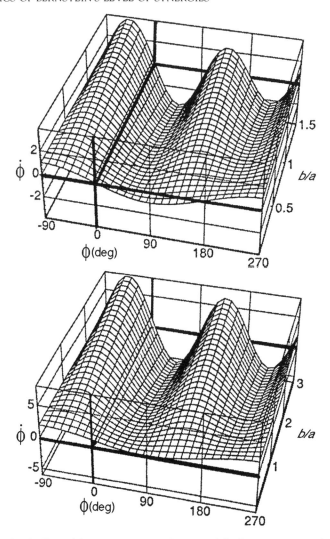

FIG. 16. Plots of the motion equation, Equation 12 for the symmetric case (*top*) and the asymmetric case (*bottom*). Note where the two landscapes sit in relation to $\dot{\phi} = 0$.

so-called saddle-node bifurcation, discussed earlier in reference to Figure 11. This bifurcation is depicted in Figure 17. These expectations about the equilibria and their degrees of stability for symmetric and asymmetric dynamics have been confirmed by a number of experiments conducted in the last 2 years, most notably those by American psychologist Richard C. Schmidt and his colleagues, using the pendulum method depicted in Figure 12 (see summary in Schmidt & Turvey, 1995).

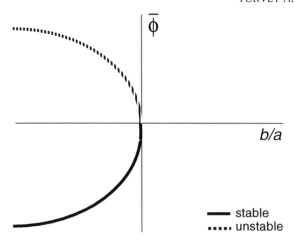

FIG. 17. The saddle-node bifurcation. Saddles are points that attract in one direction and repel in the other direction. Nodes are simply stable equilibria. Read the bifurcation diagram from left to right with larger *b/a* values on the left. When the saddles and nodes "collide" at the critical point, at a critical *b/a*, no equilibria remain.

RESONANCE CONSTRAINTS ON THE LEVEL OF SYNERGIES

We now turn to issues of dexterity and discuss in what particular ways the level of synergies contributes to dexterous movements. In Bernstein's view, dexterity requires minimally two levels of the movement hierarchy. The leading level is characterized by the facility to switch among patterns and to adjust them as needed. The background level is characterized by harmony, precision, and obedience. His favorite metaphor is of the rider (the leading level) and the rider's horse (the background level). Dexterity cannot be achieved by either alone, but only by an "inventive and quick witted" rider and an "obedient and accurate" horse.

A major achievement of the human movement system, particularly evident in the playing of musical instruments, is multifrequency behavior in which different limb segments move at different frequencies. Based on Bernstein's theory, a reasonable hypothesis is that these musical skills involve the level of actions in the leading role and the level of synergies as background. If this hypothesis is the case, then some inroads on the acquisition of musical skills can be made by developing further an understanding of the dynamics of the level of synergies. Thus far, only the dynamics of the rhythmic synergy underlying body segments moving at the same tempo have been considered. What can be said about more complicated temporal relations? If the "horse" in musical performance is the level of synergies, then what can it do obediently and accurately?

The answer requires the consideration of some fundamental facts about multifrequency in systems of two coupled oscillators. Suppose that there are two different oscillators with frequencies of P and Q, where P and Q are integers, for example, 2 and 3. Suppose now that the oscillators are coupled so that their oscillations become locked together in a fixed ratio M:N, which is the same as their uncoupled ratio; that is, every third cycle of one oscillator is completed at the point in time that the other completes its second cycle. Focusing on the frequency of the faster oscillator, one can say that the same physical situation, for example, both oscillators at zero-phase angles, occurs only once every three cycles. At all intermediate points, the states (that is, the phase angles) of the two oscillators are different. The repeated physical situation allows mutual influences to build up in a resonance-like manner. As a general rule, oscillators with smaller frequencies composing the multifrequency ratio means stronger resonance and easier mode locking. It is rather like trying to keep a child's swing going. If one pushes at the right time every swing (1:1), then there is no problem. If, however, one pushes every second (1:2), third (1:3), or fourth swing (1:4), the swinging motion is weakened (one's contribution is dissipated) during the lapse, and more effort will be required, when one does push, to ensure its perseverance. The prominence of 1:1 frequency locking witnessed in the fish-in-a-tank studies and in everyday behavior of the person on the street is not, therefore, surprising. It is the resonance that can build up most easily.

There are useful conceptual tools for representing resonances (as one may now call the multifrequency ratios). One is known as the *Farey tree* and it is shown in Figure 18 (top). It orders the rational fractions (those assembled from real numbers, like ⅔, ¼, ⅝) that lie between 0 and 1, according to their increasing denominators. Another representation (see Figure 18, bottom) is the *Arnold's tongues* representation, so-named in deference to the Russian mathematician who first provided this particular formulation (Arnold, 1965). An Arnold's tongue defines a region within which a particular ratio of frequencies W is achieved when the two oscillators are coupled, given the ratio of uncoupled frequencies Ω and the strength of the coupling K. An examination of Figure 18 (bottom) reveals that if the required W equals 1:2, then when K is very small Ω must be precisely ½ if the requirement is to be satisfied. In contrast, when K is large, the requirement of $W = 1:2$ can be satisfied for a range of Ω values around ½. The widest frequency-locked regions (e.g., $W = 1:1$, 1:2, 2:3, 1:3) in the Arnold's tongues representation, corresponding to the lower levels of the Farey tree, are the most stable and attractive. Suppose the level of synergies has the capacity to generate any rhythm but is governed by the resonance constraints; then the process of acquiring any polyrhythmic skill—like playing the piano— would require that the leading level, the level of actions, determines how to insulate required polyrhythms, such as 3:5, from more attractive resonances, such as 1:2 or 2:3 and, in particular, 1:1. Accordingly, a basic question is, Does the level of synergies obey resonance constraints?

In one method of studying this question, reported by Treffner and Turvey in 1993, the person swings a pendulum in the right hand close to its characteristic frequency, and a metronome is then set at a frequency that forms a particular integer ratio with the pendular rhythm. The metronome is tracked with pendular motions of another, much smaller, pendulum. The person is thereby "prepared"

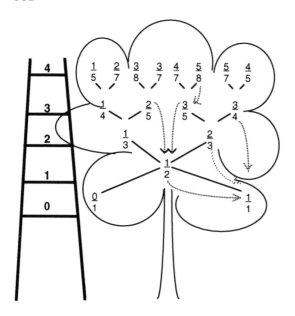

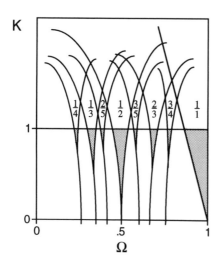

FIG. 18. The Farey tree (*top*) and the Arnold's (1965) tongues (*bottom*) representations of the resonances.

in an integer ratio with neither explicit knowledge of nor responsibility for the ratio; the idea is to impose a complex rhythm without involving the level of actions. Results show that the two limbs can be so prepared at any ratio. Of importance, prepared ratios are not always maintained, and transitions from the prepared ratio to other ratios occur. The resonance constraints captured in Figure 18 suggest that transitions should be in the direction of the most attractive neighbor. The 3:5 coordination in the Arnold's tongues representation has two reasonably sized neighbors, 1:2 and 2:3. Because 1:2 is more easily accessed than 2:3 (the width of the 1:2 tongue is wider), a 3:5 coordination is most likely to change to a 1:2 coordination. Similarly, because 1:1 is larger than 2:3, a 3:4 coordination is most likely to change to a 1:1 coordination. These bifurcation routes can be determined formally. In the Farey tree diagram, they are shown as dotted lines. In their experiments, Treffner and Turvey observed that the participants tended to change the frequency of the nonmetronome pendulum (without knowing that they had done so) to stabilize the interlimb coordination at the largest neighboring resonance. That is, the spontaneous changes in the interlimb rhythmic synergy were along the routes one would expect if Bernstein's level of synergies is shaped by resonance constraints.

In terms of Bernstein's favored metaphor, the horse might not be very obedient to the wishes of the rider. The rider has definite goals in mind and clearly identified paths to travel, but the horse, in this case, has another master—resonance constraints—that must also be satisfied. As anyone who has attempted to acquire multifrequency behavior will readily attest, the body seems unwilling to participate. To perform successfully, resonance constraints on the level of synergies must be countenanced.

FUNCTIONAL ASYMMETRY AT THE LEVEL OF SYNERGIES

Bernstein highlighted the significance of manual asymmetry to the dexterity of humans. In movements that are characteristic of the level of actions, the two hands contribute to the performances of bimanual tasks in different ways. Further, for a particular task, the roles assumed by the right and left hands depend (oftentimes) on the handedness of the person. For the majority of people, the right hand tends to surpass the left in precision of control and facility in developing new coordinations and usually assumes a leading role in bimanual sequences. For Bernstein, this functional asymmetry was not manifestly evident in the movements that characterize the level of synergies or, for that matter, any level below Level D.

In agreement with Bernstein's surmise, the motion equation, Equation 12, developed for the collective states of the level of synergies, has no left–right asymmetry. The coupling is symmetrical (the two rhythmically moving limb segments affect each other identically), and any right lead or right-lag pattern (of the type shown in Figure 6) is dictated strictly by the sign of $\Delta\omega$. If this elementary rhythmic synergy is truly left–right symmetric, however, then the question arises of how needed biases to a left or right limb might be imposed (by the levels of space and actions) in tailoring locomotion patterns, for example, to environmental conditions. Michael Peters, a Canadian psychologist and an authority on handedness, noted recently, "The ability to interrupt the flow of bilateral coordinations, essential to locomotion in a world that offers obstacles and requires sudden changes in direction, forms the evolutionary basis for skilled bimanual coordination in humans" (1994, p. 596). Perhaps the left–right asymmetry is manifest at the level of synergies, albeit subtly.

In principle, one can conduct a simple evaluation of functional asymmetry at the level of synergies. All one needs to do is watch people who are right-handed and people who are left-handed execute the simple task of 1:1 frequency locking in the experimental procedure shown in Figure 12. Treffner and Turvey (1995) conducted such an experiment. They found that when the dynamics of the task was symmetrical, that is $\Delta\omega = 0$, right-handed participants exhibited a small but reliable right lead, and left-handed participants exhibited a small but reliable left lead. Based on the definition $\phi = (\theta_{left} - \theta_{right})$, ϕ was less than 0 (when the required coordination was in-phase) and ϕ was less than π (when the required coordination was antiphase) for the right-handed participants; for the left-handed participants, the pattern was $\phi > 0$, $\phi > \pi$. Handedness, it seems, broke the symmetry of the swinging pendulums. A second result was that for right-handed participants, the shifts of equilibria from 0 and π were greater under $\Delta\omega < 0$ (right oscillator was of higher frequency) than under $\Delta\omega > 0$, whereas for left-handed participants, the equilibria were displaced more by $\Delta\omega > 0$ than by $\Delta\omega < 0$. It seems, therefore, that there is an asymmetry at the level of synergies and that there are attractors in addition to 0 and π shaping the dynamics of the fundamental form of interlimb rhythmic synergies.

Interestingly enough, any discussion of a functional asymmetry in rhythmic synergies leads one back to fish, especially the lamprey eel, which inspired the formalism with which we addressed the results of von Holst (1939/1973). The spine of this very primitive fish exhibits two important phase relations. Within any cross section of the spine, the neural oscillators on either side are in antiphase, and across two adjacent cross sections of the spine, the neural oscillators maintain a constant phase difference ($0 < \phi < \pi$). The lamprey swims by undulation; that is, it produces waves with its body. The lengths of these waves are equal to the length of the lamprey's body—a new wave starts at the head just as the previous wave has reached the tail.

The theoretical fun begins when one notes that, regardless of how fast the lamprey swims, the wavelength is always the same. A uniform, traveling wave means that the nonzero relative phase between neighbors on the same side is of exactly the same value all the way along the entire chain of neural oscillators. If one attempts to use Equation 12 to address this fact, a rather special difficulty arises. A constant, nonzero relative phase requires something that breaks the symmetry of the dynamics, and the only element in Equation 12 capable of symmetry breaking is $\Delta\omega$. The reader is reminded that symmetry is broken when $\Delta\omega$ is not equal to zero. Translating this requirement to the needs of the lamprey eel means that there must be a gradient of natural frequencies. If the natural frequency of the oscillator at the tail is 2 ("whatevers"), and the next oscillator up the chain is 1.75 (whatevers), then its immediate same-side neighbor must be 1.5 (whatevers), and

$$\dot{\phi} \quad = \quad \Delta\omega \ - \ [a\sin(\phi) + 2b\sin(2\phi)] \ - \ [c\cos(\phi) + 2d\cos(2\phi)] \ + \ \sqrt{Q}\xi_t$$

coordination   frequency   symmetric coupling   asymmetric coupling   stochastic

change   competition   attractors: $0, \pm\pi$ force

attractors: $\frac{-\pi}{4}, \frac{-5\pi}{4}, \frac{3\pi}{4}$ attractors: $\frac{\pi}{4}, \frac{5\pi}{4}, \frac{-3\pi}{4}$

(for c and d > 0)   (for c and d < 0)

FIG. 19. The larger dynamics of the interlimb rhythmic synergy.

so on. Unfortunately for this interpretation, inspired by Equation 12, the natural frequencies of the neural oscillators making up the spine of the lamprey are all identical. Where, then, is the source of the symmetry breaking? The answer must be, "In the coupling." Mathematical biologists, such as Nancy Kopell (1988a, 1988b), have argued that the 2π periodic coupling function (such as that discovered by von Holst, 1939/1973, and shown in Figure 10) must include a periodic term that shifts the stable equilibria slightly from relative phases of 0 and π when the coupled oscillators are of identical preferred frequency. This seems to be the clue to understanding handedness effects at the level of synergies. The sine terms of Equation 12 must be complemented by cosine terms, as detailed in Figure 19. The dynamics described in Figure 19 may be considered the full form of the elementary synergy. When c and d are positive, the synergy is biased to the right hand; when c and d are negative, the synergy's bias is to the left. One can see from Figure 19 that the synergy's behavior depends on the strength of the symmetric coupling relative to the asymmetric coupling. One can also catch a glimpse of how Bernstein's levels of space and actions harness the level of synergies: They can particularize the interlimb rhythmic synergy by adjusting the signs of c and d and the ratio d/c relative to b/a.

CONCLUSION

Components of a system cooperate to produce spatial, temporal, and functional patterns at a variety of levels. Bernstein is not alone in noting that an examination of behavior within these different levels reveals distinctive qualities about how behavior is initiated, organized, and modified. But with his recognition that synergies are exploited in the execution of higher-level behaviors and with his focus on the level at which behavior can be said in a very real sense to "run itself," Bernstein was ahead of his time. As we have tried to show in this chapter, modern developments on both the conceptual and technological sides are verifying insights that Bernstein had decades ago.

ACKNOWLEDGMENTS

Preparation of this manuscript was supported by National Science Foundation Grant BNS 91–09880. We thank Eric Amazeen and Dave Collins for conducting the hammering experiment.

REFERENCES

Arnold, V. I. (1965). Small denominators. 1. Mapping of the circumference onto itself. *American Mathematical Society Translations, 46*, 213–284.

Bernstein, N. A. (1967). *The control and regulation of movements.* London: Pergamon.

Bullock, D., & Grossberg, S. (1988). Neural dynamics of planned arm movements: Emergent invariants and speed accuracy properties during trajectory formation. *Psychological Review, 95*, 45–90.

Cohen, A. H., Holmes, P. J., & Rand, R. R. (1982). The nature of the coupling between segmental oscillators and the lamprey spinal generator for locomotion: A mathematical model. *Journal of Mathematical Biology, 13*, 345–369.

Haken, H., Kelso, J. A. S., & Bunz, H. (1985). A theoretical model of phase transitions in human hand movements. *Biological Cybernetics, 51*, 347–356.

Kelso, J. A. S. (1984). Phase transitions and critical behavior in human bimanual coordination. *American Journal of Physiology: Regulatory, Integrative, and Comparative Physiology, 15*, R1000–R1004.

Kelso, J. A. S., DelColle, J. D., & Schöner, G. (1990). Action-perception as a pattern formation process. In M. Jeannerod (Ed.), *Attention and performance* (Vol. 13, pp. 139–169). Hillsdale, NJ: Lawrence Erlbaum Associates.

Kelso, J. A. S., & Ding, M. (1993). Fluctuations, intermittency, and controllable chaos in biological coordination. In K. M. Newell & D. M. Corcos (Eds.), *Variability and motor control* (pp. 291–316). Champaign, IL: Human Kinetics.

Kopell, N. (1988a). Chains of oscillators and the effects of multiple couplings. In J. A. S. Kelso, A. J. Mandell, & M. F. Schlesinger (Eds.), *Dynamic patterns in complex systems* (pp. 156–161). Singapore: World Scientific.

Kopell, N. (1988b). Toward a theory of modeling central pattern generators. In A. H. Cohen, S. Rossignol, & S. Grillner (Eds.), *Neural control of rhythmic movements in invertebrates* (pp. 369–413). New York: Wiley.

Kugler, P. N., & Turvey, M. T. (1987). *Information, natural law, and the self-assembly of rhythmic movement.* Hillsdale, NJ: Lawrence Erlbaum Associates.

Peters, M. (1994). Does handedness play a role in the coordination of bimanual movement? In S. Swinnen, H. Heuer, J. Massion, & P. Casaer (Eds.), *Interlimb coordination: Neural, dynamical, and cognitive constraints* (pp. 595–615). New York: Academic Press.

Schmidt, R. C., & Turvey, M. T. (1995). Models of interlimb coordination—Equilibria, local analyses, and spectral patterning: Comment on Fuchs and Kelso (1994). *Journal of Experimental Psychology: Human Perception and Performance, 21*, 432–443.

Schöner, G., Haken, H., & Kelso, J. A. S. (1986). A stochastic theory of phase transitions in human hand movement. *Biological Cybernetics, 53*, 247–257.

Simon, H. (1962). *The sciences of the artificial.* Cambridge, MA: MIT Press.

Treffner, P. J., & Turvey, M. T. (1993). Resonance constraints on rhythmic movement. *Journal of Experimental Psychology: Human Perception and Performance, 19*, 1221–1237.

Treffner, P. J., & Turvey, M. T. (1995). Handedness and the asymmetric dynamics of bimanual rhythmic coordination. *Journal of Experimental Psychology: Human Perception and Performance, 21*, 318–333.

von Holst, E. (1973). *The collected papers of Erich von Holst: Vol. 1. The behavioral physiology of animal and man* (R. Martin, Ed. & Trans.). Coral Gables, FL: University of Miami Press. (Original work published 1939)

Weiss, P. (1941). Self-differentiation of the basic patterns of coordination. *Comparative Physiology Monographs, 17*, (4).

Dexterity in Cascade Juggling

Peter J. Beek
A. (Tony) A. M. van Santvoord
Vrije Universiteit, Amsterdam

In contrast to Bernstein, who approached the problem of dexterity by developing a number of hierarchical levels under which different skills with different phylogenetic ages are subsumed, we examine the problem of dexterity in the context of a single, specific skill, cascade juggling. The two approaches are, of course, complementary, and we are interested in seeing how our theoretical and empirical findings about juggling compare to the more general theoretical framework proposed by Bernstein.

There are many reasons why cascade juggling provides an appropriate context for an examination of dexterity. We mention five. The first and foremost reason is that juggling, as was recognized by Bernstein (essay 7), requires a high degree of dexterity. The "sleight of hand" demonstrated in juggling has captured the attention and imagination of people for thousands of years and continues to do so. The old French word for juggler, *prestidigitateur* ("he who is nimble and swift with his fingers"), nicely illustrates the primary attraction of juggling as a performing art. It is further intriguing to read that the root of the Russian word for dexterity (*lovkost*) is *lov* ("catch"). Doesn't it follow then that a game of catch should be the basis of a scientific study of dexterity?

A second reason is, given the occasion of the publication of Bernstein's book on dexterity, we deem it an apt tribute to Russian culture to examine the ideas of one (if not *the*) founder of modern movement science in the context of a motor skill at which the great Russian performers of the celebrated Russian circus schools, most notably Ewgenji Biljauer, Serge Ignatov, and Gregor Popovich, made a lasting impact. Ewgenij Biljauer was known for his extraordinary ball

377

manipulation and his ability to perform a full pirouette with five clubs. Serge
Ignatov long held the world record with 11 rings until he lost that to Albert
Lucas of the United States, who succeeded in adding one. Gregor Popovich is famous for juggling five clubs from behind his back, while standing on top of an
unsupported ladder, a body-and-hand-dexterity trick he now performs for money
in the gambling temples of Las Vegas, not quite unlike his fellow countrymen
who are hired for their academic acumen by large American universities.

A third reason is that juggling constitutes an exemplary motor problem, in
the sense implied by Bernstein: What the problem is about can be described
with great precision thanks to its rather severe physical, spatial, and temporal
constraints. A precise description of a particular motor problem is a prerequisite
for studying how that problem is solved and for understanding what it means
to do so with dexterity. Because the task constraints on juggling are not primarily
energetic, as in speed skating or swimming, juggling has the additional advantage
that its limits on performance have to do with the principles of coordination
and the degree of dexterity rather than with the power-supplying machinery.

A fourth reason is that juggling must be exercised for one to be able to
perform even the most basic three-ball patterns. Only very few people can perform a basic juggle without any practice, but almost everybody can learn to
juggle, regardless of age and strength. In principle, and as for most other things
in life, there are no limits to learning. The difficulty of juggling increases dramatically with the number of objects juggled. Typical learning times are measured
in hours or days for three balls, weeks or months for four balls, and months or
years for five. We can safely say that each added object over five requires more
than a year of practice before the performance is perfected. As a result, there is
a wide range of expertise from which a study of dexterity can benefit.

A final, pragmatic reason is that, after many years of analytical and empirical
study of juggling, it does not seem at all premature to attempt to identify some
of the main features of dexterity in cascade juggling.

The way in which this chapter is organized follows directly from what we
are trying to accomplish. First, we characterize the motor problem of cascade juggling by identifying the primary physical, spatial, and temporal constraints on the activity and by analyzing how these constraints become more
severe as the number of juggled objects increases. Second, we examine the
spatiotemporal properties of juggling patterns produced by jugglers of different
skill levels, with the goal of discovering how these jugglers confront the constraints defining the motor problem of juggling. We are particularly interested
in how these solutions evolve as a function of expertise. Third, we focus on the
relative role of optic and haptic information in cascade juggling, with the aim
of finding differences in the perceptual basis of dexterity between jugglers of
different skill levels. Finally, we conclude by summarizing the main properties
of dexterity in cascade juggling and by comparing our insights with those put
forward by Bernstein.

THE MOTOR PROBLEM OF CASCADE JUGGLING

It is not easy to provide a satisfactory definition of juggling, certainly not one that includes the broad spectrum of object manipulations that can be argued to comprise juggling: contact juggling in which balls or hoops are rolled along parts of the body, bounce juggling, ball or plate spinning, devil sticking, and so on. The narrow definition of toss juggling, however, is rather straightforward: to keep (two or) more objects in the air at one time by alternately tossing and catching them. By definition, toss juggling requires that the number of juggled objects be greater than the number of hands that juggle; for example, two balls may be juggled by one hand, or six balls may be juggled between two persons.

The simplest juggling pattern is a cascade with three objects. In the cascade, an object is always thrown from a position near the body's midline in an arc passing underneath the preceding throw and toward the other side of the body, where it is caught and transported again toward the body's midline for the next throw. As a result, the balls travel along the figure-eight path that is characteristic of the cascade. The hands alternate catching and throwing and travel along elongated ellipses angled slightly inward from vertical. The movements of the hands mirror one another: One is cycling clockwise and the other counterclockwise, with an average phase difference of about 180°. Figure 1 provides a schematic representation of a three-ball cascade and defines the essential spatial variables of juggling, namely the height (h) to which the balls are thrown relative to the hands, the angle of release (ϕ_r), the base width of the parabolic flight trajectories (F), and the horizontal distance over which the hands transport a ball from catching to throwing (D). The cascade is the standard for juggling any odd number of objects (3, 5, 7, and 9) with two hands.

The basic constraint of a standard toss juggle, such as a cascade, is that each ball must be thrown sufficiently high to allow the juggler time to deal with the other balls. The higher the balls are thrown, the more time the juggler has available for throwing and catching the other balls and for avoiding and correcting mistakes. Moreover, the probability of a collision of the balls in the air is smaller in a high pattern than in a low pattern. Unfortunately, because the time that a ball spends in flight between being thrown and being caught is proportional to the square root of the height of the throw, a great increase in height (and thus of the energy imparted to the balls during the throws) results in only a small increase in time. Even worse, throwing the objects higher has the effect of increasing the size of the error in the flight and landing location, which results from an error in the location and angle of the throws. For juggling throws only a few meters high, an error in the throwing angle of only 2° or 3° can cause an error in landing location of 30 cm or more. Thus, there is a conflict between the speed and accuracy requirements of juggling: On the one hand, juggling speed should be slow enough to allow sufficient time for accurate throwing and catching; on the other hand, the juggling speed should not be too slow because of the severe accuracy constraints on high throws.

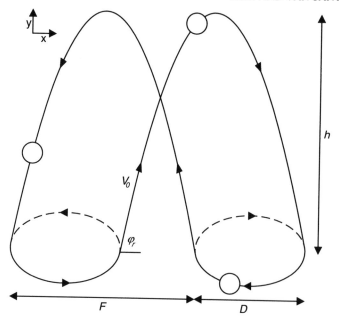

FIG. 1. Schematic representation of juggling three balls with two hands in a cascade pattern, momentary situation: ϕ_r is the angle of release, V_0 is the velocity of the ball at the moment of release, h is the height to which the balls are thrown relative to the point of release, F is the base width of the flight parabola, and D is the width of the elliptical hand movement. From "Spatiotemporal Variability in Cascade Juggling," by A. A. M. van Santvoord and P. J. Beek, in press, *Acta Psychologica*.

Both the severity of the speed and the accuracy demands (and, hence, the difficulty of the patterns) increase rapidly with the number of objects juggled. Given a certain throwing height, for example, juggling five balls is faster than juggling three, because two more balls must be manipulated in the same time frame. At the same time, the throws must be more accurate both in terms of their heights and their timing. Because there can be two balls traveling from one hand to the other at the same time, which is never the case in a three-ball cascade, a high throw followed by a low throw will decrease the time interval in which two successive catches must be made by the same hand, which still must throw a ball between the two catches. The same problem occurs when two balls are thrown from one hand to the other without sufficient time between the throws. This mistake may also result in a collision between the ascending ball and the descending ball. The need to simultaneously satisfy both the speed and accuracy requirements makes juggling patterns quite difficult to perform: The speed of the pattern makes it difficult to make accurate throws, whereas accurate throws are needed to control the speed. It is, therefore, quite apparent why the difficulty of juggling increases so rapidly with the number of objects juggled.

At a more formal level, the increase of the severity of the temporal constraints on juggling with an increasing number of balls is elegantly described by Claude Shannon's juggling theorem (see Shannon, 1993). Shannon, whose fame is usually associated with information theory, was the first to realize that for any periodic juggling pattern, such as the cascade, in which no hand is filled with more than one ball at any one time, there is a logical relationship between the component times of juggling, the number of balls juggled (N), and the number of hands that juggle (H). The component times of juggling are the length of time that a ball is in a hand between a catch and a throw (time loaded, T_L), the length of time that a hand is empty between a throw and catch (time unloaded, T_U), and the length of time that a ball is in flight between a throw and a catch (flight time, T_F). Now, for a periodic juggling pattern, let T denote the duration of a complete N-ball–H-hand juggling cycle that begins and ends with the same event, for example, catching ball i in hand j. Assuming that T, T_L, T_U, and T_F are constant, the total loop time for hand j during T has to be equal to $N(T_L + T_U)$ because hand j manipulates N balls during T (see Figure 2, top); whereas the total loop time for ball i has to be equal to $H(T_L + T_F)$ because ball i passes H hands during T (see Figure 2, bottom). Hence, $N(T_L + T_U) = T = H(T_L + T_F)$. In other words, the ratio of the loop time of the hand to the loop time of a ball defines an integer ratio equal to the number of hands (H) divided by the number of balls (N).

The significance of Shannon's (1993) juggling theorem lies in its showing how each of the component times is constrained by the other two, with N and H given. For example, if T_F is fixed, two options for temporal flexibility are left: The juggler can slow down the pattern slightly by holding each ball longer

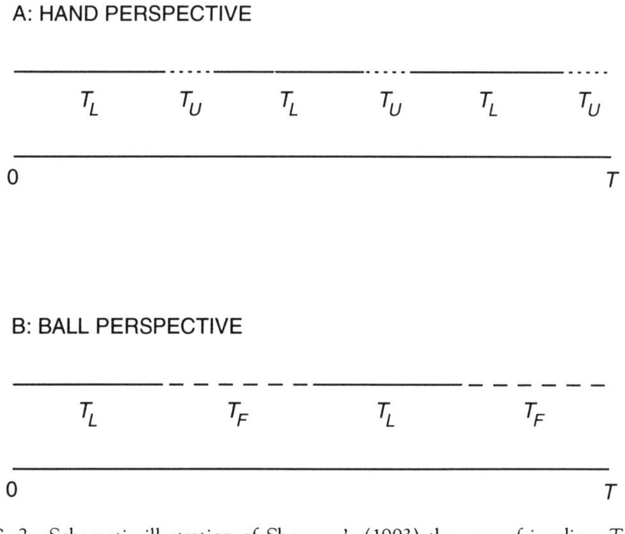

A: HAND PERSPECTIVE

| T_L | T_U | T_L | T_U | T_L | T_U |

0   T

B: BALL PERSPECTIVE

| T_L | T_F | T_L | T_F |

0   T

FIG. 2. Schematic illustration of Shannon's (1993) theorem of juggling. T_L is the time a hand is filled with a ball; T_U is the time a hand is empty; T_F is the flight time of the ball.

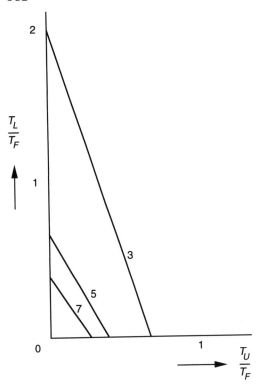

FIG. 3. The implications of Shannon's (1993) juggling theorem for the severity of the temporal constraints on increasing number of objects (3, 5, and 7 balls). From "Temporal Patterning in Cascade Juggling," by P. J. Beek and M. T. Turvey, 1992, *Journal of Experimental Psychology: Human Perception and Performance*, 18, 934–947.

(increasing T_L) or speed up the pattern by releasing each ball faster (increasing T_U). As the number of juggled objects increases relative to the number of hands, the juggler's freedom to vary T_L and T_U decreases. This principle is illustrated by Figure 3. The intersections with the abscissa in this figure ($T_L = 0$; $T_U/T_F = H/N$) represent "hot potatoes juggling," whereas the intersections with the ordinate [$T_U = 0$; $T_L/T_F = H/(N - H)$] represent "delayed juggling." The ratio of these two extremes, [$H/(N - H)$]/[H/N] = $N/(N - H)$, expresses the juggler's freedom to vary his or her speed between the slowest and the fastest juggling times and decreases with N and increases with H. Hence, as N increases, the need for exact reproducibility of the time components of juggling becomes more severe. The size of the pattern has to increase with increasing N to create sufficient room for the balls to travel and to reduce the probability of collisions in the air, all of which can be achieved only by throwing very consistently to a specific height and with a minimum of variation in the angle of release.

SPATIOTEMPORAL REGULARITIES

Given the preceding description of the motor problem of cascade juggling, we believe it would be useful to examine how performers of different skill levels accommodate to the physical, spatial, and temporal constraints on juggling. Such an analysis requires a precise analysis of the spatiotemporal patterns that are produced. An example of such a pattern in two dimensions is provided by Figure 4. As this figure shows, the trajectories of the balls in a bout of cascade juggling are highly regular and reproducible, but no two trajectories are perfectly identical. In the words of Bernstein, they repeat themselves without repetition.

Coordinated movements, even when performed by the most skilled, are intrinsically variable, and much can be learned from the pattern of variance that is present in multiple cycles of a rhythmic motor act. Analyses of the variability of the relevant spatial and temporal variables of juggling have revealed some important facts about the manner in which jugglers solve the motor problem of juggling (van Santvoord & Beek, in press). The spatial variability of the points of throwing, defined as the mean absolute distance relative to their mean left and right locations, was found to be smaller than that of the zeniths of the ball flights, which, in turn, was smaller than that of the points of catching. One can appreciate these relationships by comparing the size of the circles, which index

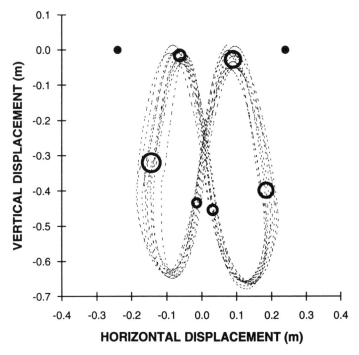

FIG. 4. An example of the ball trajectories in a three-ball cascade (position data filtered at 10 Hz) in which the balls are thrown to two externally specified target heights (filled circles). The open circles represent the mean absolute distance of the events to their mean spatial location for the zeniths (top two open circles), the throws (bottom two open circles) and the catches (middle two open circles). From "Spatiotemporal Variability in Cascade Juggling," by A. A. M. van Santvoord and P. J. Beek, in press, *Acta Psychologica.*

the degree of spatial variability, in Figure 4. Whereas this finding might have been due, in part, to the chain of causation from throwing to catching, the variability of time flight was smaller than that of time loaded, which, in turn, was smaller than that of time unloaded. Furthermore, the variability of ball cycle time $(T_L + T_F)$ was smaller than that of hand cycle time $(T_L + T_U)$. This finding suggests that the focus of control is the temporal component of Shannon's (1993) equation related to the events associated with the balls rather than that related to the events associated with the hands. In addition, an analysis of the variability of the horizontal and vertical components of the velocity of release suggested that the height to which the balls are thrown is more tightly controlled than the horizontal distance over which the balls are thrown. Finally, the variability of the horizontal distance between throwing and catching by different hands proved to be less than that of the horizontal distance between throwing and catching by the same hand. Interestingly, differences between the juggling by expert and that of intermediate three-ball jugglers resided predominantly in the variability of spatial variables, such as the angle of release, the base width of the flight parabolas, and the width of the elliptical hand loops, and not in the temporal variables and variables associated with timing, such as the height and the velocity of release.

Collectively, these findings show, as would be expected from our analysis of the motor problem of juggling, that jugglers attempt to throw the balls as consistently as possible, both in space and in time. Their focus of control is on reducing the spatiotemporal variability of the ball trajectories rather than the variability of the hand trajectories. The balls are thrown from a stable spatial projection point to a relatively fixed height and caught in such a way that, of all relevant time components, variations in flight time are minimal. In this sense, juggling may be considered a creating and sustaining of a spatial clock. By throwing the balls accurately to a specific height, jugglers conveniently exploit the extrinsic timekeeper provided by the gravitational field, for cycling the hands and for the adequate timing of throwing and catching.

Given that jugglers control the flight times of the balls by throwing them consistently to an intentionally selected height relative to their hands, one must next consider how jugglers handle the remaining degree of freedom of Shannon's theorem: the magnitude of the time that a hand holds a ball, T_L, relative to the time that the hand moves empty, T_U. This relationship is expressed by the relative timing ratio, $k = T_L/(T_L + T_U)$. This "dwell ratio" is of essential importance in the organization of juggling because it directly determines the time-averaged number of balls in the air N^*, according to $N^* = N - Hk$, which may be considered an index of the task goal of keeping as may balls aloft as possible. With regard to the value of k, there are conflicting demands. If k is large, the probability of collisions in the air will be small, and conditions will be favorable for accurate throwing because the hand is filled with a ball for a relatively long time. On the other hand, if k is small, N^* will be large, and conditions will be

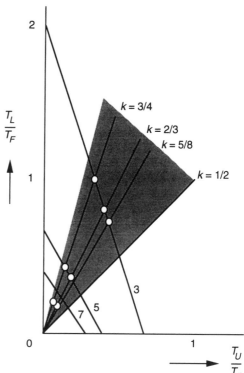

FIG. 5. The range of empirically observed values of the dwell ratio $k = T_L/(T_L + T_U)$ (shaded area) and the most commonly observed solutions (white circles) to Shannon's (1993) constraint.

favorable for making corrections because the hand is empty for a relatively long time. A key question, therefore, is, What values of k do jugglers assume, and how do these values depend on the number of objects juggled and on skill?

In principle, there is an infinite number of possible values that k can assume in order to accommodate Shannon's theorem, with T_F, N, and H given. Analyses of the juggling performance of experts (Beek, 1989; Beek & Turvey, 1992) and novices (Beek & van Santvoord, 1992) suggest that the dynamical constraints on juggling restrict the k values assumed by human jugglers to those in the shaded area in Figure 5. The rays corresponding to $k = \frac{1}{4}$, $\frac{2}{3}$, and $\frac{5}{8}$ (the circled points in the figure) are the preferred ratios. The observed range of variation of k was largest for skilled jugglers performing a three-ball cascade. Whereas novice jugglers always operated in the vicinity of $k = \frac{1}{4}$, the intermediate and expert jugglers attained much smaller values, seemingly with $k = \frac{1}{2}$ a boundary of performance. For these more proficient jugglers, the k values of $\frac{2}{3}$ and $\frac{5}{8}$ appeared to be preferred solutions at higher juggling speeds. In the five- and seven-ball cascades the observed values of k clustered more around $\frac{1}{4}$. Only when these versions of the cascade are very well mastered do the most proficient jugglers seem to be able to attain lower dwell ratios, among which $\frac{2}{3}$ again appears to dominate. This last finding was corroborated by a new set of observations in our laboratories. Using a simple video analysis also Jack Kalvan, an outstanding juggler from the United States, measured dwell ratios in the five- and seven-ball cascades of around ⅔ for himself and around ⅔ and even ⅝ for Anthony Gatto, one of the best jugglers in the world.

The predominantly observed ratios between small integers—¼, ⅔, and ⅝— were interpreted by Beek and Turvey (1992) from the perspective of nonlinear oscillation theory. By interpreting the juggling hands as a system of coupled oscillators with loaded and unloaded regimes, a tentative account of the observed ratios was derived in terms of mode locks, that is, as locked-in solutions of the underlying frequencies. In a system of coupled oscillators, when the component (sub)frequencies stand in integer relation to one another, the behavior of the system is stable and reproducible and said to be mode locked. On this account, the theoretically interesting observation from the obtained findings is that in the case of a three-ball cascade, in which the task constraints are less severe than in five-ball and seven-ball cascades, expert jugglers exploit multiple solutions that they can switch between. They lean toward these solutions to ensure sufficient stability, but they are never completely locked in and thus stay adaptive and flexible. By living on the border of the mode-locked regimes of k, the jugglers are in a better position to correct for the external perturbations and self-inflicted minor mistakes that occur time and again in juggling. Particularly, the smaller mode-locked values of k provide an ideal basis for this, because the larger the proportion that the hand is empty during its cycle, the more room there is for the hand to adjust the timing of the pattern by changing the moment of catching (which explains why T_U and T_L are always more variable than T_F). Juggling with smaller k values, however, requires very accurate throws in a proportionally smaller time span. When jugglers are less skilled or the number of balls is high, emphasis will typically be placed more on the accuracy of the throws and the stability of performance, and, hence, on attaining higher mode-locked values of k, than on adaptability. As a result, the performance will be more vulnerable to external perturbations and self-inflicted mistakes.

These considerations nicely illustrate two of Bernstein's interpretations of dexterity in the context of juggling. In juggling, one can either be dexterous in the sense of being flexible and able "to switch" fluently from one style of juggling to another or be dexterous in the sense of being "brilliantly precise" (see Bernstein, essay 7). In fact, in the world of juggling, these two types of dexterity correspond to two different styles of juggling. In one style, showmanship is achieved by using as few props as possible (mostly three). In the past, the Kremos, father Bela and his son Kris, explicitly advocated this idea of minimalization, which makes perfect sense from our analysis of juggling. When juggling three objects, the identified physical, spatial, and temporal constraints on performance are sufficiently severe to be reckoned with but otherwise allow for ample opportunity for variation, adaptation, tricks, and gimmicks that can be blended together into a continuously mesmerizing act. In the other style of juggling, called number juggling, showmanship and perfection are achieved by keeping as many objects aloft as possibly. Number juggling requires extreme precision of throwing and can, indeed, also be very impressive to watch. We vividly remember watching Michiel Hesseling, a Dutch juggler, who participated in many of our experiments, juggle seven balls in a rather low room: All throws reached their zeniths just a centimeter short of the ceiling without once touching it, ticking with the precision of a Swiss clock. It needs no elaboration that the identified types of dexterity in juggling are entertaining in rather different ways. Somehow, the element of the unexpected in the three-ball routine has the more lasting impression, although this is probably less true when the spectator happens to be a movement scientist.

THE PERCEPTUAL BASIS OF JUGGLING

As we have shown, the motor problem of juggling might be portrayed as achieving a proper phasing between the events associated with the hands and the events associated with the balls. Hence, the actor must have information not only about the future location of an airborne object to be able to catch it on arrival but also about when and to what height the next ball must be thrown in order to achieve a proper phasing. There are few contexts in which the conventional coaching advice "to keep one's eye on the ball" makes as little sense as in juggling. Bernstein's suggestion that a juggler must look at the balls at all times (see essay 7) should not be taken too literally. During a cascade there are minimally $N - 2$ and often $N - 1$ balls in the air. Visual attention must be shifted at regular intervals, corresponding to the phasing of the balls in the air. This necessity implies that optical information must be picked up from only certain segments of the ball flights during brief viewing times. Two important questions are which segments of the ball flights are visually attended to and do these segments provide more valuable optical information than others. A possible answer to the latter question is suggested by the observation that jugglers will typically look at the topmost part of the ball trajectories. "Look at the highest point" and "Throw the next ball when the previous one reaches the top" are instructions commonly used in teaching. At the same time, however, proficient jugglers appear to rely little on optical information when performing a simple pattern such as the three-ball cascade. In fact, many skilled jugglers are able to juggle blindfolded for several minutes.

Austin (1976) investigated how large a region around the zenith had to be seen by jugglers of intermediate skill to be able to sustain juggling. He partially occluded the ball flights by placing a fanlike screen containing a wedge-shaped notch in the frontal plane between the hands and the eyes of the juggler. The notch in the screen could be gradually closed in such a way that the topmost part of the ball flights could be observed through apertures of increasingly smaller widths (see Figure 6). Failing to catch a ball occurred when as little as 1 inch

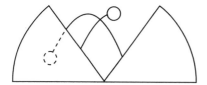

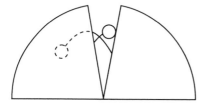

FIG. 6. The experimental restriction
of vision used by Austin to examine
the optical basis for cascade juggling
(adapted from Austin, 1976).

of the top of the ball flight was visible, a span which roughly corresponds to a
viewing time of 80 ms or less. This result implies that viewing the zeniths of
the ball flights for a very brief time provides the juggler sufficient optical information to sustain juggling. The result does not, however, imply that the juggler
must necessarily see the zeniths to sustain juggling nor that the zeniths provide
the most valuable optical information for juggling.

We (van Santvoord & Beek, 1994) investigated the optical basis for cascade
juggling by examining the relationship between the phasing of the hand movements and the pickup of optical information. Three jugglers of intermediate skill
performed a three-ball cascade while wearing liquid-crystal glasses that opened
and closed at preset intervals and that thus permitted intermittent viewing of
the ball flights (see Figure 7, top). In principle, under these adopted task constraints, jugglers would be able to control what they saw by adjusting their cycling
rate and the phasing of juggling relative to the cycle of the opening and closing
of the glasses. From the relationship between the phasing of the balls in the air
and the rhythm defined by the glasses, we could deduce where the balls were
located when the glasses were open, whether certain segments were preferred,
and if and how the phasing of the hand movements supported the pickup of
information contained in these segments. Interestingly, one of our participants
exactly matched the frequency of juggling to the frequency of the opening and
closing of the glasses so that he always saw the segment of the ball flight following
the zenith. This preference for seeing that segment was also hinted at by the
performance of the two other participants. By gradually reducing the viewing
time to zero, in steps of 8 ms each (see Figure 7, bottom), we established the
minimal viewing times at which the participants, who were jugglers of interme-

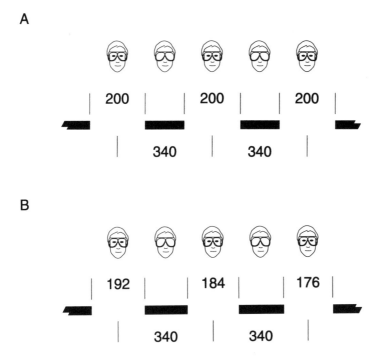

FIG. 7. The experimental restriction of vision for examining the optical basis for cascade juggling: A–Viewing window of fixed duration; B–Viewing window of gradually decreasing duration (numbers in milliseconds).

diate skill, were able to sustain the task. The minimal viewing times varied between 24 ms and 150 ms; the shortest minimal viewing times were achieved when the frequency of juggling matched that of the glasses. In a small pilot experiment, however, we found that expert jugglers had no problems in sustaining a three-ball cascade under the imposed task conditions until the glasses remained closed. An extremely skilled juggler from the United Kingdom, Haggis McLeod, succeeded in sustaining a five-ball cascade up to minimal viewing times varying between 24 ms and 40 ms.

These findings imply that the juggler's vision of the balls becomes less and less important when the level of skill increases. Whereas novice and intermediate jugglers seem to rely predominantly on optical information, haptic information is apparently more important for expert performers. The hypothesis that optical information about the ball flights gradually calibrates the haptic system in the course of learning seems to be at least plausible. Once this process has been accomplished, the juggler no longer needs to rely heavily on optical information. William James (1890/1950) reported that the juggler Robert Houdin practiced juggling four balls while reading a book. This difference in the relative importance of the optic and the haptic systems also has implications for the manner in which the intrinsic variability of juggling performance is dealt with. An expert juggler immediately feels a slight deviation in the desired angle of release or in the energy imparted to the ball, whereas a less skilled juggler must wait to see the effect of these mistakes in the flight trajectories of the balls. As a consequence, the corrections made by an expert juggler are often dealt with locally, without disturbing the integrity of the pattern, whereas the corrections made by less skilled jugglers often disrupt the global stability of performance. This observation implies that there might be two sensory mechanisms for corrections in juggling: one relatively late correction mechanism based on optical information and one relatively early correction mechanism based on haptic information. The late-correction mechanism is established early, and the early-correction mechanism late in learning. Only when the latter type of correction mechanism is established in the "background" does juggling become truly stable and automatic. If these speculations are true, they would surely support Bernstein's distinction between the identification and distribution of corrections and the assignment of background corrections as two separate stages of learning.

CONCLUDING REMARKS

In this chapter, we have identified some aspects of dexterity in cascade juggling that correspond remarkably with elements from Bernstein's more encompassing conceptual framework. By analyzing the motor problem of juggling and the manner in which jugglers of different skill levels confront this problem, we have encountered two different types of dexterity identified by Bernstein—those captured by the terms *switchability* (adaptability) and *accuracy* (stability). To us, this polarity is at the heart of Bernstein's analysis of the problem of movement coordination in general. Bernstein, after all, understood movement coordination as the transformation of an uncontrollable system into a controllable system without, however, losing the ability to respond to expected and unexpected, self-inflicted and external disturbances. An efficient coordination, therefore, requires that a balance be struck between reducing the relevant number of degrees of freedom to a conveniently small number and maintaining a sufficient number so that the motor organization can remain flexible. The take-home message from our analysis of cascade juggling is that the manner in which a particular actor strikes this balance is a function of his or her goals as a performer, the task constraints, and the abilities he or she has developed to deal with these constraints.

ACKNOWLEDGMENTS

The writing of this chapter was supported in part by National Science Foundation Grant SBR 94-22650 awarded to M. T. Turvey and R. C. Schmidt. Thanks are due to Wiero Beek, Piet van Wieringen, and Claire Michaels for their very helpful comments.

REFERENCES

Austin, H. A. (1976). *A computational theory of physical skill*. Unpublished doctoral dissertation. Massachusetts Institute of Technology, Boston.

Beek, P. J. (1989). Timing and phase locking in cascade juggling. *Ecological Psychology, 1*, 55–96.

Beek, P. J., & Turvey, M. T. (1992). Temporal patterning in cascade juggling. *Journal of Experimental Psychology: Human Perception and Performance, 18*, 934–947.

Beek, P. J., & Van Santvoord, A. A. M. (1992). Learning the cascade juggle: A dynamical systems analysis. *Journal of Motor Behavior, 24*, 448–453.

James, W. (1950). *The principles of psychology*. New York: Holt, Rinehart & Winston. (Original work published 1890)

Shannon, C. E. (1993). Scientific aspects of juggling. In N. J. A. Sloane & A. D. Wyner (Eds.), *Claude Elwood Shannon, collected papers* (pp. 850–864). New York: IEEE Press.

van Santvoord, A. A. M., & Beek, P. J. (in press). Spatiotemporal variability in cascade juggling. *Acta Psychologica*.

van Santvoord, A. A. M., & Beek, P. J. (1994). Phasing and the pick-up of optical information in cascade juggling. *Ecological Psychology, 6*, 239–263.

Change in Movement and Skill: Learning, Retention, and Transfer

Karl M. Newell
Pennsylvania State University

Observing individuals engage in action through the life span leads inevitably to the realization that certain properties of movement forms and their outcomes persist over time whereas others tend to change. Persistence is evident in that some properties of movement sequences remain essentially invariant to a given action, whereas other properties vary either systematically or unsystematically. Furthermore, the fact that similar properties of movement sequences are evident in different actions suggests that the persistence of movement organization is present across activity categories. Bernstein, in his lifetime collection of writings on the physiology and mechanics of human movement, sketched out the significance of change and persistence for a theory of movement coordination, control, and skill. Some new elements of his theoretical framework for the learning and performance of movement skills have been introduced here, in this volume on dexterity and its development.

Bernstein did not use the labels *persistence* and *change* in his theorizing, but these terms capture issues central to his theoretical framework of human movement—a perspective that has gained in recognition as his writings have become increasingly available to a broader audience. A measure of Bernstein's significant but delayed impact on the field of motor control may be deduced from the fact that the issue of movement coordination is often articulated today as "Bernstein's problem." It should be noted, however, that he has received less recognition for his ideas on the focus of this chapter—the learning, retention, and transfer of movement skill—than for his other ideas. The publication of this volume may help compensate for this imbalance of perspective, given the centrality of the construct of dexterity to the preceding chapters—a construct that Bernstein used to capture many of the same movement qualities often identified under the label of *skill*.

In this chapter I consider, in some detail, the issues of persistence and change in the coordination and control of movement. My focus is to highlight the line of theorizing that is central to Bernstein's perspective on the learning, retention, and transfer of movement skill. This theoretical framework is buttressed with some principles from the ecological approach to perception and action, a theoretical perspective that incorporates many of Bernstein's (1967) ideas on motor control but that is also driven by the direct perception theory of Gibson (1979) in regard to the role of information in action. The ecological approach to perception and action also draws on the developing science of nonlinear dynamics to formally characterize the persistence and change of movement organization.

The ensuing discussion in this chapter captures some of the elements essential to the acquisition of movement skill both within Bernstein's line of theorizing and within that of the ecological approach to perception and action. To begin I focus, albeit briefly, on some background issues of motor-skill acquisition: the degrees-of-freedom problem; a framework for the definition of coordination, control, and skill; observation of movement dynamics; levels of movement construction; and the influence of task constraints. All these issues may be seen as standard motor control problems. These issues are introduced here to ensure the necessary background for considering the central matter of this chapter, which is the changes in movement coordination, control, and skill that are reflected in the learning, retention, and transfer of action. There are many changes in movement organization and other manifestations of skill that occur across the life span of an individual and even on the short-term time scale of trial-to-trial variation. Unraveling the theory and practice of the different types of change in movement and skill for learning, retention, and transfer is the focus of this chapter.

PRELIMINARY ISSUES FOR A THEORY OF LEARNING, RETENTION, AND TRANSFER OF MOVEMENT SKILL

The Degrees-of-Freedom Problem

Bernstein identified the degrees-of-freedom problem as a central issue in the coordination and regulation of movement. This problem for movement coordination can be restated in the form of a question: How are the many degrees of freedom at each level of analysis harnessed together to produce the movement form, variability, and outcome of action? Bernstein emphasized initially those degrees of freedom associated with joint space, that is, the number of independent planes of motion at the joints that can be coordinated and controlled by an individual. The concept of degrees of freedom is not, however, specific to a particular level of analysis of the body, such as joint space, but can also be applied to other levels, such as muscles, motor units, neurons, and so forth. Indeed, the general definition of degrees of freedom usually refers to it as the number of independent dimensions (coordinates) required to specify uniquely the position in space of the element under consideration, without violating the geometry of the element. Bernstein provided a more detailed theoretical outline than he had before of how the structure and function of the skeletal-articular-muscular system is related to the degrees of freedom to be controlled in movement and action.

The number of degrees of freedom of biological systems increases rapidly as the level of analysis becomes more microscopic. For example, the number of degrees of freedom in joint space is $>10^2$, in muscle space $<10^3$, and in neuronal space approximately 10^{14}. Thus, coordinated biological motion is the product of the harnessing of many millions of degrees of freedom across several levels of biological analysis. The adept facility of the biological system to solve this problem in the face of a myriad of contextual circumstances is perhaps, as suggested by Bernstein, most readily illustrated by robotic systems. Even in this computer age of the late 20th century, robotic systems have difficulty controlling six or more degrees of freedom. It is also important to note that the high dimensional control evident in biological systems is realized in the face of continually changing demands, both internal and external, on the organism. For example, the everyday fundamental activity of upright postural stance is the product of a movement solution to coordination and control over a continuously changing internal milieu of the organism and, often, varying and uncertain external demands.

Bernstein considered the degrees-of-freedom issue primarily in relation to the physical components of the biological system and how they are harnessed in the realization of the coordination of movement. The ecological approach to perception and action also considers the degrees-of-freedom issue in relation to the information that may be picked up in support of action, namely, that information that specifies what the environment affords for action and its accompanying movement-related information. Gibson proposed that there are informational invariants that organize humans' perceptions of the world around them and contribute to the coordination of their accompanying motions of the torso and limbs in support of action. These invariants are hypothesized to have few degrees of freedom, because they provide global informational properties, which are used to initiate and regulate action. In this view, perception and action are both organized on the basis of a low-dimensional (few-degrees-of-freedom) solution, and the mapping of perception and action is seen as the heart of the movement coordination and control problem.

Observations of an individual learning a motor skill suggest that the solution to the coordination problem *changes* over time. That is, the qualitative and quantitative properties of coordination and control in the early stages of learning a movement skill tend to differ from those apparent in highly skilled performers. Such changes in the properties that constitute the movement *form* tend to be related to the changes evident in the outcome of action that accompany practice. This change in the coordination solution and its outcome occurs in the performance progressions over time and are evident in both phylogenetic and ontogenetic activities. Phylogenetic activities are viewed as those indigenous to the species, such as walking, running, and standing, in the sense that all members of the species engage in these activities. Ontogenetic activities are those that appear to be peculiar to the short-term and variable influences on the individual by family, society, and culture, influences that lead through ontogeny to the development of skills, such as piano playing, pole vaulting, and so on. The categorization of phylogenetic and ontogenetic activities is based on a relative rather than on an absolute distinction, because over the long-term time scale of evolution, the activities indigenous to a species can and do change.

Traditionally, different theories have been advanced to account for the changes in movement coordination, control, and skill evident over time in phylogenetic and ontogenetic activities. For example, maturation theory has dominated much of the thinking about the development of coordination in phylogenetic activities in the fetal period and through infancy and early childhood. In contrast, the study of the acquisition of ontogenetic activities has been dominated by the early 20th-century traditions of learning theory and the more recent theoretical frameworks of information processing and cognitive science. In the theoretical framework developed here, the principles that organize the processes of change in movement organization are viewed as common to all actions, not as activity or age specific. Thus, the issues of persistence and change are seen as central to both phylogenetic and ontogenetic activities, although, as Bernstein showed with many examples, the constraints to action change considerably over the life span of the individual.

Coordination, Control, and Skill

In the preceding chapters by Bernstein, he distinguished, albeit briefly, between the constructs of coordination and dexterity. In this section, I elaborate on this distinction through a consideration of the constructs of coordination, control, and skill. These are terms that are used quite frequently in the motor learning and control literature, often with an uneveness of application. This also seems the opportunity to contrast Bernstein's use of the term *dexterity* with the term more frequently used in Western literature, *skill*. Indeed, there are very many ways in which the term *dexterity*, as used by Bernstein, is synonomous with the Western use of the term *skill*. There is some sense from his text that Bernstein wished *dexterity* to hold a more general meaning than the common use of the term *skill*, but he does not develop this position.

In other writings, Bernstein outlined the view that coordination is an activity that guarantees that a movement sequence has homogeneity, integration, and structural unity. He proposed that coordination is the *process* of mastering redundant degrees of freedom of the moving organism, in other words, its conversion to a controllable system (Bernstein, 1967, p. 127). There are a few key words from this definition that can be usefully elaborated to drive home the significance of Bernstein's view of coordination. The first is the proposal that coordination describes an active process involving both persistence and change in movement relations over time. In this volume, Bernstein elaborated on this point and indicated that the construction of a motor skill is a meaningful chain action consisting of a number of separate phases that logically follow each other. A second proposal involves the recognition that the degrees of freedom that require constraint in action are usually greater in number than the number required to solve the motor task itself. In other words, there are redundant as well as multiple degrees of freedom to be coordinated and regulated. This redundancy in degrees of freedom resides, for most task conditions, at all levels of analysis—joints, muscles, motor units, neurons, and so forth. It is, of course, the redundancy of the system that affords the large and flexible repetoire of behavior and the movement-form qualities of complex dynamic patterns—adaptability and aesthetics.

Coordination can be viewed, then, as the function that constrains the potentially free variables (degrees of freedom) of the system into a behavioral unit. The term *coordination* implies a bringing into relation (coordinating) of the parts of the system, and leading operationally to an emphasis on the structural or qualitative movement-form properties. Implied is the assumption that the topological properties (those that remain invariant in the face of transformations of scale) of the coordination function provide the structure, or as it is more commonly referred to, the *form* of the observable movement properties. The parameterizing, or scaling, of the topological relations of the coordination function is the control problem. Therefore, coordination and control play complementary roles in the regulation of movement. In this view, coordination and control are embedded constructs—one cannot have one without the other.

In a model of coordination dynamics based on Haken's concept of synergetics, the parameter or parameters identified as defining the qualitative feature of the movement dynamics have been called the *order parameters*. The order parameter or parameters identified as defining the form of the movement pattern are assumed to be more readily achievable if a transition is induced in the pattern of the movement dynamics. A transition can be induced into the qualitative properties of the movement dynamics by scaling a variable (here called a *control parameter*) that leads the system through its transitions of state and the emergent movement patterns. An interesting feature of this approach is that the control parameter may have no obvious informational link to the resultant movement pattern.

Skill is an emergent property manifested according to the degree of probability of realizing the task demands and the optimality of scaling the coordination function. Optimization may be determined on several dimensions, including energy expenditure, veridicality of information input, and so on. Skill is determined by *what* movement form and outcome is realized, and one can analyze how various constituent dimensions are optimized to bring about this realization.

Bernstein recognized that the term *dexterity* is used primarily with some physical activities and not others; the same holds true for the term *skill*. For example, in everyday language, one tends not to speak of a skilled walker or the skill of walking. In its adjectival form *skill* tends to characterize performance capabilities and qualities in ontogenetic activities, in which the adaptive component to the skilled performance is presumed to be significant. As a noun, *skill* implies that the individual is adaptive to the changing internal and external demands. That is, the individual adjusts the movement coordination and control solution according to the changing constraints inherent in the action. The time scales of the changing constraints to action can vary considerably from the unpredictable and immediate to the expected and more permanent.

A skilled performer changes the solution to the movement coordination and control problem according to the various changing demands of the organism–environment interaction and to the pursuit of the task goal. In general, a skilled performance may also be characterized by an anticipation of the consequences of future events including one's own action. This anticipation, or *prospective control*, is based on the pickup and utilization of task-relevant information and is a factor that underscores the tight link between movement information and movement dynamics in action. In short, skill, or as Bernstein would say, dexterity, is an ability to solve a motor problem—correctly, quickly, rationally, and resourcefully. Dexterity is finding a motor solution for any situation and in any condition, and it becomes a more dominant feature of action the higher up the phylogenetic scale the animal resides and the more the higher brain centers are developed.

This kind of analysis naturally leads to the question, *What* is the language of the motor system? To put it another way, What is the nature of the variables that are organized in the coordination function? Over the years, many solutions have been advanced in relation to this question, solutions incorporating variables from different levels of biological analysis, including cells, neurons, motor units, muscles, limbs, the dynamics of limb trajectories, and so on. The solution to the coordination function that harnesses the degrees of freedom, both within and between levels of analysis, remains perhaps the central issue to be resolved in the theory of movement coordination, as it was when Bernstein originally wrote his text.

Observation of Movement Dynamics

The aforementioned framework of movement coordination and control needs to be interpreted operationally within a common measurement scheme for biological motion. Usually the qualitative and quantitative properties of a movement sequence are measured in terms of their kinematic or their kinetic features. The measurement category of kinematics considers the space–time properties (and their derivatives such as velocity, acceleration, etc.) of the motion of a body without respect to the causal forces involved. The measurement category of kinetics refers to the force and mass–time properties of the motion, or statics, of the body. The categories of kinematics and kinetics are usually characterized as belonging to the field of dynamics.

Observers of biological motion naturally perceive the space–time properties of movement, and there is some evidence that kinematics can directly provide information about the kinetic properties of movement. The question arises as to which kinematic properties of human movement observers perceive, given the large number that arises from the changes in position over time of the many joint–space degrees of freedom? For example, What properties of the motion of the torso and limbs specify to an observer that an individual is walking rather than running, or throwing rather than bowling?

It is useful to distinguish the motion of a body in terms of its absolute, relative, and common motion components (see examples in Figure 1). *Absolute motion* refers to the spatial–temporal motion of each individual degree of freedom relative to a common external frame of reference, such as Euclidean space. *Relative motion* refers to the motion of a given body segment (degree of freedom) with respect to the motion of another body segment(s). *Common motion* refers to the direction of motion that is common through the event time of the action to all degrees of freedom in Euclidean space. Within this analytical framework, the literature on perception of motion suggests that human observers strongly emphasize the relative

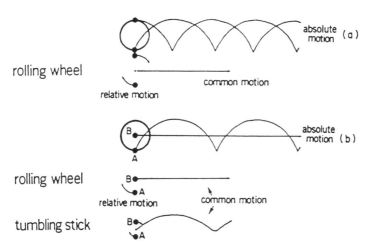

FIG. 1. Examples showing the frames of reference for the measurement of absolute, relative, and common motion. Example (a) has a two-light stimulus with lights mounted 180° opposite one another on an unseen wheel rim. Example (b) has a two-light stimulus with one light on the perimeter and one at the center. In (a), the absolute motion paths are two cycloids, 180° out of phase. The relative motion paths (b) are circular and 180° out of phase around their midpoint. Common motion is the path of this midpoint, which is linear. Example (b) from J. E. Cutting & D. R. Proffitt (1982). Copyright 1982 by Academic Press. Adapted with permission.

motion in a dynamic display as opposed to the absolute motion of the degrees of freedom. Furthermore, it is apparently the *discontinuous* properties in the relative motion of the degrees of freedom that specify many types of perceptual events. Elaborating from these findings, one may propose that each physical activity is defined by a unique set of topological properties of relative motions of the body in the context of the environment. In other words, the natural nominal categorization of activities is based on the topological kinematic relations that are preserved in the transformations of scale of the torso and limb motions across a range of environmental, organismic, and task conditions.

It also appears that unique nominal categories of motion are perceptually judged on the basis of the crossing by a relative motion variable over a threshold region on the *continuous* scaling. For example, it has been suggested that it is the relative time that the lower leg limb spends moving forward as opposed to moving backward within a step cycle that primarily determines the perceptual judgement of the locomotory activity category, such as limping, walking, jogging, and running. In other words, critical regions on the continuous scaling of this relative motion property impose boundary conditions on the perception of different locomotory activities, as they do in the perception of environmental properties, such as color. Presumably these critical kinematic boundaries to styles of locomotion hold some common properties across individuals and contextual circumstances.

Bernstein (1967) suggested that a considerable change in the absolute motions of the individual degrees of freedom can be tolerated and individuals still judge the qualitative topological properties of a given activity to be preserved. This perceptual preservation of the activity category is a reflection of the phenomenon known as *perceptual constancy*, a feature that has been extensively studied with regard to many types of perceptual events, although less so in the perception of action categories. Currently not enough is known about the information in movement forms that supports the perceptual constancy that defines physical activities. The perception of the persistence and change of the kinematics of biological motion is an underresearched area in the study of movement and skill.

Establishing a framework for operationalizing movement coordination and control not only is important from a motor-control standpoint but also has significant ramifications for the consideration of *change* in movement coordination over time and the related constructs of learning, retention, and transfer. In all theoretical frameworks, both the persistence and the change in the topological and quantitative kinematic properties over time may provide a window into the changing nature of the coordination solution with increments of skill. A major problem is that there is *always* change in the movement kinematics between repeated attempts of a given action, even in those of a skilled performer. To put it another way, there is always between-trial variability in the kinematics of the movement sequence and in properties at other levels of analysis of the biological system. Thus, an understanding of *which* changes in the movement kinematics are persistent and *which* changes are temporary is critical in the assessment of movement coordination and control and to the resultant inferences about the change over time in learning, retention, transfer, and skill.

Levels of Construction of Movements

Bernstein introduced the idea that coordination and skill are dependent on the organization of the levels of construction of movements. This scheme is built very directly on an evolutionary perspective of structural and functional development and progressive change in the action capabilities of the different species that have evolved over the phylogenetic scale. Bernstein used this scheme to explain how new classes of motor tasks developed in different species and how different human actions are coordinated and controlled by these levels of movement construction. Here, I briefly reiterate some of the key ideas of Bernstein's scheme before discussing its significance for the concepts of learning, retention, transfer, and skill.

Level A is the level of postural tone and is based on the early phylogeny of the preextremity era. Accordingly, this level specializes in the tone of the trunk and neck muscles and is most readily observed in environments in which the organism is in equilibrium without the apparent action of gravity, such as water. In general, Level A provides the background postural support for action rather than serving as a leading level in the organization of movement in action. Level A can also inhibit or block descending motor impulses and thus provide some constraint over muscular organization, as seen, for example, in the movement disorder of rigidity.

Level B is the level of muscular-articular links, which were developed in phylogeny in order to subserve all possible locomotions on the ground and, later, in the air. This level provides the control of the musculature at the extremities and organizes the basic synergies between the limb segments. A key feature of this level is the standardization and elaboration of the dynamically stable movement patterns, that is, those that are resistant to perturbation. The influence of this level of movement construction changed over the evolutionary time scale, and some of its original functions were subsumed by other levels of construction, which emerged with the development of the higher cortical centers. A major reason for this development is that a synergistic activity, even an elementary one such as walking, is not conducted in a vacuum: Changing environmental demands during action require accommodation to the solution of movement coordination and control.

Bernstein viewed Level B as functioning from the ongoing development of a set of memory representations for these coordinative structures, without the participation of consciousness. In Bernstein's terms, the better the collection of memory representations for action is, the more quickly the organism can find a motor solution for any situation and the more dexterous the organism is. Bernstein did not elaborate the details of the nature of this representation scheme for memory of the synergies that provides what he called the movement automatisms. Thus, it is not clear how he viewed the important issue in movement coordination and control of the relation between the degrees of freedom to be controlled and the degrees of freedom to be represented in memory. The development of a theoretical framework for the persistence of the movement form that emerges from the history of experiences of the individual is a central and difficult challenge for theorists of motor learning.

Level C is the level of space and embraces the higher cortical centers, which, according to Bernstein, are still developing structurally to handle the functional demands of interacting with the environment. The movement construction level of space emerged as the types of sensory receptors developed to deal with the organism's ever-increasing range of interactions with and manipulations of the environment. Level C provides the facility of switching coordination solutions to meet environmental demands. Accordingly, and parallel with ideas expressed earlier in relation to the effector synergies of Level B, Level C also has a sensory memory representation scheme. This sensory representation scheme provides the basis for corrections to movement, which Bernstein articulated in a variety of ways as the most significant factor in the acquisition of movement dexterity. As with the scheme for memory of musculature synergies, Bernstein did not elaborate on the nature of the memory system for information from the senses nor on its theoretical links to forming effective corrections to movements.

This level of movement construction provides the basis of what Bernstein called the perception of space field and includes the perception of distance, object size and shape, angles, directions, and so on. Level C of movement construction leads to a different type of movement organization than that produced from Level B. Level C leads the organization of the levels of construction in movements that emphasize transfer of the body from location to location, aiming movements, and switching action solutions to task demands. The movement corrections undertaken by Level C tend to be environment relative, whereas the corrections undertaken by Level B tend to be body relative.

The final level of movement construction in Bernstein's scheme is Level D—the level of actions. Level D is intimately related to the development of higher cortical centers, a number of which are present only in the human brain. This level of construction is consistent with the generally accepted view that movements are a necessary but not sufficient condition for action. The goal and meaning of the action to the organism provide boundary conditions to the coordination of the degrees of freedom at each level of movement construction. Level D leads in the organization of actions, giving them order and relations among components. Bernstein outlined a range of action categories in Level D, including locomotions, whole-body movements in space that are not locomotions, accurate targeted movements of arms, movements that overcome resistance, and ballistic movements. Specific to actions led by Level D are those that have a chain of sequential motor structures and that require adaptation to the environment.

This basic scheme of the levels of movement construction provides the background for considering and reconsidering many aspects of coordination, control, and skill in action, along with the learning, retention, and transfer of movement and skill. Here I consider only a few points from Bernstein's framework. A key assumption in this framework is that dexterity requires the coordination of at least two levels of movement construction in the realization of action goals. How this coordination between levels of movement construction takes place was a mystery to Bernstein, as it remains so today. Nevertheless, Bernstein outlined functional, directional relations between levels of movement construction in action and the limits of different levels to produce movement consequences and corrections in certain activities. Each level of construction builds its own movements to realize those particular motor tasks it is able to solve, but only Level A directly relates to the meaning of the action. Actions, too, may be classified according to the level (or levels) of movement construction that leads the organization of the movement links, and, in this regard, Bernstein distinguished actions of everyday life, labor movements, and movements in exercise and sport.

Bernstein proposed that, in the acquisition of movement skill, individuals develop each level of movement construction to differing degrees together with different facilities to coordinate between levels. These different degrees of development of the movement levels lead to different degrees or types of dexterity. This position is well captured by Bernstein's perspective that the development of children's movement skills parallels the development of the neurophysiological levels of construction that support action. Indeed, Bernstein tended to promote a traditional structure-to-function perspective on the development of action. The relative contributions of the movement levels to movement skill are captured in Bernstein's statement that the leading level of dexterous action exhibits resourcefulness, switchability, and maneuverability, whereas the supporting background levels feature harmony, obedience, and precision of work.

In this action-oriented framework, Bernstein emphasizes, more than he did in most of his other writings, the role of information and the individual's conscious attention in the coordination, control, and skill of physical activity. Bernstein proposed no theoretical principles with respect to the role of information in action or the changing role of information in the acquisition of skill, but this is a central theoretical issue in the contemporary ecological approach to perception and action. Nevertheless, Bernstein's evolutionary-based, neuromuscular-skeletal scheme provides a neurophysiological framework for examining the coordination problem of degrees of freedom and the changes that occur with learning, retention, and transfer.

Coordination Solution to the Task Demands

The coordination solution realized to meet a particular action goal depends on the conditions under which the movement sequence is to occur. It follows from this perspective that skill, an emergent feature of action, is specific. Of course, individuals can be and are skilled at many activities, but the notion of task or skill specificity suggests that a person skilled at one activity may not be skilled at another apparently similar or related activity. In his elaboration of dexterity, Bernstein implied that dexterity as a broader construct than that of skill, in effect, referring to the adeptness of the individual to deal skillfully with all actions. In this sense, dexterity takes on the meaning of general adaptiveness of the individual to all task-relevant demands.

It has long been recognized that one must consider properties of the organism *and* the environment in constructing a theory of action or motor learning. Over the years, different theories have given different degrees of emphasis to the relative contributions of the organism and the environment to action. For example, maturation theory emphasizes the endogenous genetic contributions of phylogeny to the development of action. In contrast, the traditional general theories of learning emphasize the effects of exogenous environmental features on the change in performance over time. The strong polemical debate on the contribution of environment and organism to action and the change in features of action over time has waned to some degree in most contemporary theorizing of action. Some background consideration of the way in which the conditions of action influence movement and its outcome is the focus of this section.

In the viewpoint developed here, there are three general sources of constraint to action—the organism, the environment, and the task (see Figure 2). The organism has many structural and functional constraints that channel the emerging dynamics of biological motion. As Bernstein explained, these constraints reside at all levels of analysis to the system, from the very microscopic to the macroscopic degrees of freedom (biochemical, neurological, morphological, biomechanical, etc.). Similarly, the environment has many sources of constraint to action that influence the resulting movement form and its outcome. Some environmental constraints are ambient or global to action (e.g., gravity, temperature), whereas others are local and focal to action (e.g., tools). Task constraints include the goal of the action and the rules that may be present to channel or specify the movement dynamics in the execution of the movement sequence. For example, certain sports tasks, such as shot put and pole vault, not only have a clearly defined action goal but also rules that limit or specify the organization of the torso or limbs in the execution of the action. Indeed, in some activities such as gymnastics and highboard diving, the goal of the action is arguably the production of a particular solution of coordination and control.

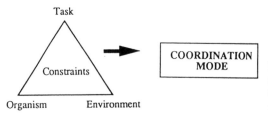

FIG. 2. A schematic of the three general sources of constraint to action—organism, environment, and task.

In summary, three sources of constraint to action, namely the organism, environment, and task, coalesce to provide a dynamic framework of boundary conditions to the emerging movement coordination modes of action and to the resultant expressions of skill.

The task constraints to action may be perceived by the individual as a consequence of the natural interaction of the organism and the environment, or they may be specified directly by some external source, such as a teacher or friend or other environmental property. Gibson's ecological approach to perception and action emphasized that environments afford certain actions for the individual. In this viewpoint, it is the mutuality of the organism–environment fit that specifies *what* the environment affords the individual for action together with the information to initiate and regulate the resultant movement sequence. Thus, information present in the environment is specific to the individual and the actions of that individual, although there are informational invariants that hold similar relevance for groups or populations of individuals.

Constraints may be viewed as boundary conditions to action that have spatial or temporal components or both. What one usually labels as structural constraints tend to have relatively slow rates of change, whereas functional constraints tend to have more rapid rates of change. For example, the structures of the many body components (degrees of freedom) are always changing over time, but the rate of change in a particular component may be so slow that it is perceived as not varying over a given portion of the life span. Individuals are not generally perceived as having grown or aged over a span of 24 hours, although changes in the relevant parameters of growth and aging may well have occurred (in fact, recent data show saltatory change in infant growth). The coordination solution accommodates these time-varying constraints, both in the short term of moment-to-moment movement control and in the longer term of qualitative and quantitative change in the coordination solution.

Small quantitative changes of a given parameter in any one source of constraint can lead to both qualitative and quantitative changes in the movement form produced and in the outcome realized in action. For example, a small change in the environmental variable of gravity or altitude would probably change the performance outcome for an individual in a given activity (such changes explain why certain track-and-field records are easier to break in particular regions of the world). Consider also that a small change in the length of a limb can lead to significant changes in both the movement organization (coordination solution) and the outcome of action. Furthermore, a small task change in the distance required to throw a ball can lead to a change in the qualitative properties of the coordination solution used to realize the task goal. There are, therefore, many potential changes in the constraints to action that can and do occur over time. The dynamic properties of these constraints coalesce to provide changes in movement and its outcome that are both persistent and fluctuating in nature.

In summary, organization in biological motion is bounded by three general sources of constraint to action, all of which have a variety of spatial and temporal conditions. These sources of constraint channel the emerging movement dynamics into a motor solution with qualitative and quantitative properties, which demonstrate both persistent and fluctuating features. The facility of the system to systematically accommodate the motor solution to the changing demands on action in both the short and long term is an hallmark feature of learning, retention, and transfer.

CHANGE IN MOVEMENT OUTCOME AND COORDINATION

A number of systematic ways in which the change in movement sequences and outcomes occur over time have been identified. Usually, the change in movement organization and outcome occurs as a consequence of practice in the particular action, although change can also occur in the apparent absence of practice specific to a particular task goal. For example, people can improve their performance of an activity or task over a period of time during which no practice of that given activity or task occurs. Similarly, performance decrement on a given task can occur over periods of time with or without practice on the task in question. A characterization of the types of change in movement and its outcome as a function of practice is now provided under the sections of movement outcome, coordination mode changes, and other changes. The focus of this section is the identification of those changes in movement organization and its outcome that persist and those that fluctuate over time.

Here I should formalize the traditional definitions of learning, retention, and transfer so that these constructs and the issues surrounding the change of movement and its outcome over time can be considered simultaneously. *Learning* is classically viewed as a relatively permanent change in behavior over time. This traditional definition does not take into account the nature of the goal that is being approached by the learner. More recent definitions add the qualifier that the relatively permanent behavioral change occur toward a specific goal. Thus, learning is very much concerned with how and what movement changes persist over time, with the proviso that they are not due to maturation or temporary states of the organism (e.g., drug-induced states). *Retention* is concerned with the degree to which the current movement performance by the organism can be reproduced after some time interval (usually an interval of more than 24 hours). Any decrement in movement organization or outcome is usually considered a retention loss or a reflection of forgetting. Forgetting implies that there is some loss of the representation in memory for the action, but note that a retention loss can occur without forgetting in this traditional sense. *Transfer* is the degree to which the practice on one task can influence the performance on another. The concepts of learning, retention, and transfer are intimately related due to their common concern with and interpretation of the change in movement organization and its outcome, a feature that becomes more apparent in the following discussion of the types of action-related changes that occur over time.

Movement Outcome

Actions have goals, and the outcome of action is usually measured in the same terms (that is, in the same dimensions) as the goal of the action. There are a number of different types of action outcomes, each of which makes important contributions to characterizing movement and the change of movement over time. An outcome of an action is usually measured either directly or indirectly with regard to the dimensions of space and time.

The goals in sporting events provides many examples of the space–time criteria of an action. For example, if the goal of the act is to throw a javelin as far as possible according to the rules of the event, the action outcome is the distance thrown. In a number of sporting events (running, swimming, cycling), the outcome is the minimization of the time required to travel a particular distance. The space–time criteria of actions may have varying degrees of precision and may occur at varying points toward the maximal outcome that an individual can achieve on that dimension, given a particular set of task constraints. Many sporting events are concerned with maximal performance, whereas activities of daily living (such as getting out of a chair, washing up, reaching for an object on a shelf) tend to require outcomes that are less demanding relative to the potential of the individual.

Some activities, such as pistol shooting, have the variability of the space–time outcome as the primary measure. That is, the degree of fluctuation in a certain element of the movement organization and its outcome is directly reflected in the outcome of action. For some activities, the outcome is the percentage of times that a particular criterion is met. In other activities, the precision with which a movement outcome is measured can influence the nature of the observed change in movement over time, and the resultant inferences about learning. It is evident, therefore, that there are a variety of ways to categorize and measure movement outcomes in action.

Learning is an inference drawn from repeated observations of the person's engagement in the action at hand over time. The primary measure of learning has been based on the degree of systematic change in the movement outcome over time. This approach leads directly to the plotting of performance outcome over time and to inferring the principles by which learning occurs from the nature and degree of the changes in performance. In fact, plots of performance outcome over time are generally considered to be *learning* curves.

Figure 3 depicts four hypothetical learning curves for individuals engaged in practice over time. These examples show that there can be considerable variability

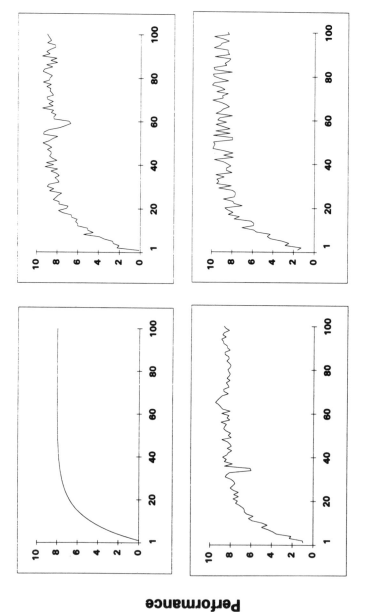

Performance

Trials

FIG. 3. Examples of hypothetical learning curves.

between individuals in the way they change performance outcome over time and that even in intraindividual performance there are systematic and less systematic (even random) changes. The less systematic changes occur in the short term, from trial to trial, whereas the more systematic changes occur in the long term, appearing as a persisting trend of the change in movement outcome over time.

It is generally recognized that a power law best fits the systematic changes in movement outcome over time as measured in the study of motor learning (see Figure 3, top left). A power law for a learning curve is generally of the form $T = BN^{-a}$, where T is the time of the trial (the outcome measure), B is the performance time on the first trial $(N = 1)$, and a is the slope of the performance curve. This function reveals that the systematic change in the performance outcome improvement over time becomes smaller as the level of practice increases, in a fashion consistent with a power function. The plots of the change in movement outcome over extended time periods also suggest that the limits to learning are rarely if ever reached by an individual in a particular task. Long-term studies of motor learning are needed so that the veridical nature of the movement outcome changes that occur over time, particularly at the more advanced levels of learning, can be adequately characterized.

The ubiquity of the power law of learning in motor and cognitive tasks provides powerful evidence for a common set of principles of learning over a range of tasks. However, in the motor domain, the study of learning phenomena has been narrowed by the choice of task to be studied. Often the task chosen is one in which the biomechanical degrees of freedom to be coordinated are reduced to unidimensional, discrete, single-link-segment activity (finger key press, single-joint arm motion). Even for tasks that require more apparent coordinated activity, the chosen task has been minimized by requiring study participants to scale an already producible coordination mode to satisfy the particular quantitative task demands. The net result is that the study of learning has not focused sufficiently on the qualitative changes in the coordination mode that occur with learning (particularly those in the early phases), a focus that could also reveal potential qualitative changes in the performance outcome. Thus, it is possible that the continuous power-law function may apply to a special case of learning and that its omnipresence is only a consequence of the narrow range of tasks selected for study at particular stages of an individual's development. Systematic, discontinuous changes in performance outcome over time may occur in response to particular instances of organismic, environmental, and task constraints. Bernstein gave several brief descriptions of motor learning that are consistent with the idea that discontinuous changes in motor performance over time do indeed occur.

The issue of whether learning is continuous or discontinuous is still, therefore, a contentious issue, although the current dominance of a power-law interpretation emphasizes the notion of continuous change in motor learning. Apparently, empirical work to date has primarily characterized limited segments of what one might consider the middle phase of motor learning. Insufficient attention has been given to both the early phase, which involves the construction of a task-relevant coordination mode, and the later stage of learning, in which the optimization of performance is quite evident. The change in performance outcome must also be considered in relation to the change in the coordination and control of the movement sequence producing the outcome, and this is the focus of the next section.

Movement Coordination

A hallmark feature of motor learning is that individuals change the *form* of movement organization as well as the outcome. The study of the qualitative changes in movement form has its origins in biomechanics and motor development and in the characterization of the changes that occur in the development of the fundamental movement patterns of posture, locomotion, and prehension. This early work has been buttressed lately by an increasing number of studies in which were examined the changes in coordination mode or movement form that accompany adults' learning of a particular task. The study of the change in the dynamics of movement forms has been facilitated by computerized movement-recording systems, which afford the facility of measuring and visualizing the motion of many biomechanical degrees of freedom simultaneously. Figure 4 illustrates some qualitative and quantitative changes in the movement kinematics that accompany several weeks of practice on a ski-simulator task. Even from this static display of a dynamic event, it is clear that a considerable number of persistent and fluctuating changes occur in the organization of the torso and limb kinematics as a function of practice and learning.

It has been shown that there is a strong trend for the change in the pattern of coordination effected by practice to follow directional trends in the organization

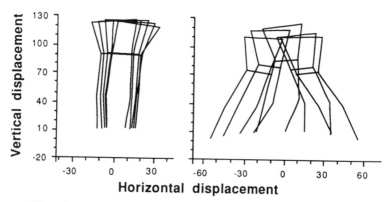

FIG. 4. Stick-figure example, from the frontal plane, of the changes in kinematics as a function of practice on a ski-simulator task: *left*–novice; *right*–expert. From B. Vereijken, R. E. A. van Emmerik, W. J. Beek, & K. M. Newell (1992). Unpublished data.

of the torso and limb degrees of freedom. This trend was first noted by Gesell some 50 years ago in his groundbreaking studies describing the development of the fundamental movement patterns. He observed that infants tended to change the organization of the movement coordination pattern of the fundamental physical activities in a cephalic–caudal, proximal–distal, or ulnar–radial direction. Bernstein also showed that these same directional trends occur in the development of locomotion over the broader time span of birth to maturity. These directional and functional changes in movement organization paralleled the directional changes in the structural features of the morpological development of organisms. Gesell interpreted these directional trends in the development of movement organization as reflecting one of the important principles of development.

These directional trends in the change in movement organization are also evident in adults learning motor skills. In tasks involving predominantly the arm and hand complex, such as handwriting, dart throwing, and hitting, initially in practice the learner freezes the more distal limb joints and operates the arm–hand complex more or less as a single degree-of-freedom system from the shoulder joint. With practice, more distal segments of the system are released, a change reflecting the directional shift in order with which the control of the system is changing over time. The amount of practice required to produce these directional changes in the qualitative properties of the limb organization appears to be specific to the individual and to the task.

There are common principles governing the way in which the changes in the coordination mode occur with practice in both phylogenetic and ontogenetic activities. Note that the existence of common directional changes in the coordination mode dynamics does not mean or require that the changes are genetically programmed to occur in this fashion, as was implied by the developmental maturational view of Gesell. Rather, these trends exist because of the common confluence of constraints evident in a broad range of task situations. In this view, then, departures from or reversals of these predominant directional trends can occur, based on the particular set of constraints in the learning situation.

A broader range of task constraints is required for a fuller examination of the principles governing the directional coordination mode changes with learning. In future studies researchers must also tease out the theoretical rationale for these directional changes in the coordination mode. Bernstein (1967) suggested several hypotheses for these trends (anatomical, physiological, mechanical), but he clearly viewed the relative mechanical constraints of the differently sized limb segments as a major factor in determining the directional limb-order effects evident in motor learning and development.

In addition to the changes in the qualitative properties of the relative motions of limbs that accompany learning and development, practice leads to quantitative changes in the trajectory of a given limb segment. Generally the trajectory of a limb segment tends to follow a more efficient pathway as a consequence of practice under a particular set of task constraints. Efficiency is characterized by the ratio of mechanical work produced to the energy expended. One can view these changes as additional modifications to the movement form, albeit ones that are often less noticeable to the observer than the qualitative changes discussed earlier.

Finally, changes with practice also occur with respect to the relation of the movements of the body to the environment, even in tasks in which the organism–environment relations are not directly a feature of the task constraints. Many tasks, however, require direct spatial and temporal coincidence with environmental constraints, and sometimes those constraints change, with varying degrees of predictability, from moment to moment. Tasks in which the environment may change in an unpredictable way have been labeled *open skills*, and the constraints evident in these tasks place enhanced emphasis on vision and the learning of prospective control.

Other Changes

Many other changes in the organization of the motor system occur concomitantly with the previously discussed movement and outcome changes and the resultant acquisition of skill. In general, one might anticipate that changes occur at every level of analysis of the system, even if they are typically not observed or measured. For example, many changes in the various physiological systems are consistent with the hypothesis of reduction of energy expended for the given task constraints. Similarly, changes associated with practice in motor skills have been observed in certain muscular, neurological, and biochemical subsystems, although their direct linkage to the changes in the dynamics of motion is not well established. The relation between change at one level of the system and change at another level of the system as a function of practice has been insufficiently studied, but one can expect to see more multidimensional analyses of learning, considering the continued advances in biological instrumentation, and the development of more general and encompassing theories of motor learning.

STAGES OF LEARNING

Observations of the systematic changes in movement outcome and coordination mode organization that constitute or accompany motor learning and development have provided the fundamental backdrop to theoretical interpretations of the principles of learning. One particular principle commonly advanced is that in learning a skill individuals pass through what have been called "stages of learning." The notion of stages in learning and development has proved a slippery construct, often having more intuitive appeal than rigorous scientific relevance. For example, the terms "beginner" or "advanced performer" are often used to describe the skill level of an individual as intuitive categories or as stages of learning. It is generally agreed that for the stage idea to be theoretically useful it must be at the construct level and divorced from restating (in different terms) the observation of a particular qualitative change in behavior. The concept of stage should hold some general relevance across individuals to the group or population level. There have been several attempts to characterize stages in motor learning and development, but consistent with the theme of this volume, I emphasize Bernstein's account of the qualitative change in movement organization.

Bernstein (1967) developed his own formulation of the stages of motor learning and development. He based this formulation on his observations of the systematic change in organization of the dynamics of the torso and limbs that accompanied the learning and development of a wide range of physical activities. In essence, Bernstein proposed three stages of learning. These stages capture the change in the major qualitative categories of movement dynamics in motor learning and development. I briefly outline this framework before linking it to the scheme that Bernstein advanced in relation to changes in motor learning based on his levels of movement construction.

Stage 1: Freezing of Degrees of Freedom

Because the basic problem of coordination is the harnessing of the extreme abundance of degrees of freedom of the system, the first stage in learning is characterized by coordination solutions that reduce the number of degrees of freedom at the periphery to a minimum. This freezing strategy effectively reduces the number of biomechanical degrees of freedom that need to be coordinated and controlled.

Stage 2: Release of Degrees of Freedom

The second stage is characterized by the release of the ban on the degrees of freedom, that is, releasing the freeze on the constrained degrees of freedom. Eventually, the coordination solution of a skilled performance will incorporate all possible degrees of freedom at the periphery.

Stage 3: Use of Reactive Phenomena

The most advanced stage of motor learning corresponds to the system's utilizing entirely the reactive phenomena that arise from the interaction of the organism with the environment. In this stage, the coordination solution exploits, rather than resists, for example, the reactive torques of intersegmental coupling. This acquired functional use of the reactive torques also reduces the perceived and actual effort of movement production.

A number of studies have provided evidence for one or even two stages of this three-stage scenerio for motor learning and development, but no data sets reflect all of these hypothesized stages in the intraindividual acquisition of a particular skill. Nevertheless, there is some evidence for each of these individual stages across a variety of motor tasks and types of individuals, including young babies. There are also, however, a number of aspects of this rather general three-stage concept of the stages of learning that require further examination.

It would seem that the extent of freezing of the degrees of freedom in the initial practice of a given task would be individual specific. That is, different individuals may need to freeze a different number and different types of the degrees of freedom in order to be coordinated and controlled in a given action. Thus, the principle of freezing to a minimum is based on what can be minimally controlled by a given individual in attempting safely to find a motor solution to the task goal, not on what is minimally available generally to humans. The caveat of "safely" is introduced because the search for a coordination solution is also conducted within a context of preserving to some relative degree the overall stability and physical integrity of the individual (Level A tone)—a matter that I elaborate in a subsequent section.

The order to the release the degrees of freedom may also afford more individual and task variability than has been shown to date in the aforementioned studies on change in coordination mode. The reason for this variability is the often numerous solutions to a particular set of task constraints. Some solutions may be more appropriate for a given set of organismic constraints, giving rise to individual variability in the strategy of changing the solution of coordination and control over time. It has also been hypothesized that under a certain set of task constraints, the directional order of change, for example, the proximal–distal order, may become reversed, because the observed order effects are due to the confluence of constraints on action, not merely the organismic structural and functional limitations. There appear to be many subtle individual and task influences on the pattern of qualitative changes in movement organization arising from practice.

The three-stage concept of change in coordination and control proposed by Bernstein offers some useful qualitative dynamic categories of change evident in motor learning and control. Indeed, one of the strengths of this formulation is its broad generalization to movement-skill acquisition; it is not bound by task type or age of the organism. This stage formulation of motor learning and development, however, like many of the extant stage conceptions of change of behavior, is largely descriptive. The stages of learning outlined here do not constitute a theory of change in movement coordination and control; rather, they reveal observations of systematic change that a theory of motor learning must be able to accommodate.

Bernstein's theory of the levels of movement construction provides a conceptual framework at different levels of analysis for the behavioral phenomena of the three-stage scheme of motor learning. Passage through the three stages of motor learning is accompanied by changes in the coordination of the four levels (A–D) of movement construction. Bernstein viewed the construction of skill as a sequential process, but the process is nonhomogeneous because it depends on the particular interaction of the environmental, organismic, and task constraints on the action.

Bernstein proposed some key elements in system organization that drive this sequential learning process: identification of leading level (nearly always Level D, even when it is not appropriate for the task); composition of the motor structure; creation of the appropriate corrections; assignment of the appropriate background corrections; development of movement automation; and standardization and stablization of the motor solution. The continued improvement of the movement outcome and the refinement of the movement organization arise from the more task-relevant coordination of the levels of movement construction, the adoption of the appropriate level as the leading level in system control, and the development of automatic correction processes. Bernstein's scheme of the levels of movement construction and its change in organization effected by learning both provide a new set of hypotheses for the three-stage process of coordination, control, and skill of physical activity.

FOUNDATION ISSUES FOR A THEORY OF CHANGE IN MOVEMENT AND SKILL

The description of the change in movement and its outcome previously outlined refers primarily to the behavioral level. It reflects the behavioral product of the harnessing of the many degrees of freedom of the system over the many levels of analysis in the organism–environment interaction in light of the task constraints of the action. What clues as to the organization of the system, the motor solution to use Bernstein's terms, are forthcoming from this description?

Traditionally, theories of motor learning were based on the observations of the systematic change in movement outcome over time, with little or no reference to the accompanying changes in the coordination mode that also occurred with practice. However, the previously reported observations of the changes in the dynamics of the coordination mode clearly suggest ways as to *how* the outcome changes over time. I am not implying here a one-to-one relation between movement outcome and the coordination mode dynamics, because the redundancy in the system degrees of freedom often provides, as Bernstein noted, a small set of stable solutions to the same task demand. This facility of the system to realize the same goals through different means is referred to as *motor equivalency*.

There do appear, however, to be *preferred* coordination mode solutions to particular task demands. Although these preferred coordination solutions exist within individuals, the emerging patterns of the changes in movement organization appear evident across relatively homogenous groups of individuals. The probability of a particular coordination solution emerging for a particular task demand also tends to vary as a function of the stage of learning. However, it is also evident that there are *preferred* pathways or strategies to the ways in which the changes in the coordination modes and their outcomes occur with practice. This trend is evident both within individuals and across groups of individuals learning the same movement skill. These preferred coordination mode solutions to task demands, together with their preferred patterns of change over time, suggest principles about the nature of movement coordination and control and principles about the resultant constructs of learning, retention, transfer, and skill.

In this section I discuss some foundation issues key to the development and elaboration of a dynamical theory of motor-skill learning. These issues include attractor dynamics and coordination modes, search strategies and the construction of attractor dynamics, and, finally, augmented information and the facilitation of the search for task-relevant attractor dynamics. These are interdependent foundation issues that are central to the development of a theory of change in motor learning and development.

Formation of Attractor Dynamics and the Perceptual–Motor Work Space

Movement dynamics are emergent properties of the constraints on action and arise from three interacting sources, namely, the organism, the environment, and the task. The movement patterns and the changes in movement patterns observed parallel other patterns of organization and change of the available degrees of freedom in numerous levels of analysis of the system. The organization of the movement patterns tends to be task specific, a feature which reflects the flexibility of the system to adaptively harness the degrees of freedom according to the task demands. This special-purpose capacity of the system also underscores the importance of the intention of the organism and the information in the action available to the organization of the resultant movement dynamics.

The persistence of movement patterns over time has traditionally been accommodated by the postulation of some accompanying representation in memory of that movement sequence. The level of detail in the representation of the movement sequence stored in memory has differed within the various theories of motor learning and control advanced over the years. Some theorists have postulated, in effect, a one-to-one relation between what is stored in memory and the details of the unfolding movement sequence, whereas other theorists have postulated a one-to-many relation between the memory representation and the movement produced. In this latter scheme, a generic movement plan can be modified to produce a variety of movement sequences and task demands. Bernstein's account of levels of movement contruction includes memory representation systems for both the development of muscle synergies and the process of movement corrections, but Bernstein did not provide details of his theorizing about memory representation. A major issue within the ecological approach to perception and action is the construction of representation schemes for movement and action that require fewer degrees of freedom than are being regulated in the action and that are consistent with a lawful approach to the coordination of information and movement dynamics.

In the ecological approach to perception and action, the coordination modes are emergent properties of the mapping of perception and action at a hypothetical–dynamical interface called the *perceptual–motor work space*. Figure 5 depicts this hypothesized relation in an extension of the schematic of the sources of constraint on action previously illustrated in Figure 2. In this view, movement coordination and control in action emerge from the interface of the information available in the perceptual kinematic flow-field and the dynamics of the kinetic flow-field arising from movement. As used here, the term *field* is a region of a state space characterized by a physical property, and *flow-field* refers to the iterations of this set of properties over time with respect to the perceiver.

This formulation of perception and action is built in part on Gibson's (1979) proposal that the invariant properties of a perceptual field, for example, the optical flow-field, provide information based on the gradient and distinctive qualitative boundary properties of the kinematics of that flow-field. In other words, information is in the structured energy arrays that contact the sensory receptor systems, and this information specifies to the individual what actions the environment affords. Thus, perception of the qualitative and quantitative properties of the flow-fields of the perceptual–motor work space provide a dynamical, organizing structure for the conduct of action. The informational input specifies the nature of goal states that can be achieved and the movement sequences for realizing those goals. Motor learning is, in part, based on the education of attention to the task-relevant informational cues that are available in the interaction with the environment. This theoretical view of Gibson's is not restricted to the sense of vision, although visual perception is the area in which he did the majority of his empirical work. Rather, this account of the significance of the qualitative properties of the dynamical interface of the perception–action cycle is generic to the senses as information-detecting systems.

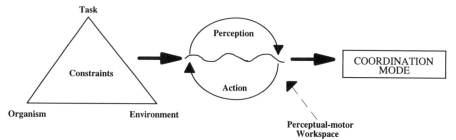

FIG. 5. A schematic showing the projected relation between the constraints on action, the perceptual–motor work space, and coordination modes. From K. M. Newell & P. V. MacDonald (1992). Copyright 1992 by Human Kinetics. Adapted with permission.

The perceptual–motor work space can be modeled as a dynamical system, with a consideration of the construction and destruction of different attractor types and their evolving spatial–temporal patterns. A dynamical system is a mathematical model (usually simplified) of the time–evolutionary states of an actual system. This approach to modeling has become popular for the examination of complex systems that have many degrees of freedom. The concept of self-organization is central to the dynamical organization of these systems in that their emergent properties, expressed in spatial–temporal patterns or functional structures, are due to the intrinsic and extrinsic forces that shape the stable and unstable states of the system. An attractor is a particular qualitative spatial–temporal organization toward which trajectories in a state space gravitate, independent of their initial conditions. There is a small group of attractor types that vary in the number of dimensions required to describe them. These include the point attractor (dimension is zero), limit-cycle attractor (dimension is 1), and strange attractor (dimension is a noninteger). The abstract mathematical relations of attractors are apparently manifested in a wide range of physical and biological systems.

The concept of attractors provides a formal basis from which to consider the stability and instability of the system at hand—the stability of the movement dynamics. It is clear that certain movement patterns are more stable and repeatable than others. By the same token, certain movement patterns are very difficult to learn, even with considerable practice. The confluence of constraints on action provide natural boundary conditions to the construction of the attractor layout of the perceptual–motor work space and to the resultant stability and instability of movement patterns. The nature of the constraints on action and the dynamics that provide different degrees of movement stability are currently major research questions. One particular theoretical strategy is to focus on the transitions between movement forms or coordination modes as a useful window into the organization of the motor system. In this experimental and theoretical framework, it is assumed that the boundary conditions of movement instability for a given task goal are most significant in specifying the stability of the attractor dynamic supporting the action. Another complementary strategy is to focus on the dynamics of the steady state conditions in movement coordination. The principles of nonlinear dynamics and stability theory provide formal means for considering the stability and instability of movement coordination and control.

There appear to be several formal advantages for using dynamical systems to model movement, aside from their intuitive appeal. One advantage is the availability of established formalisms and a common language of nonlinear dynamics, which are now extensively used to model physical, biological, and social systems. This potential linkage squarely places the study of movement coordination on the same basis and terms as the study of other phenomena. A second potential advantage is that it is a principled way to approach Bernstein's degrees-of-freedom problem, because the number of degrees of freedom required to define the dynamics of the attractor layout in the perceptual–motor work space will typically be less than that required to describe the degrees of freedom in joint space. This condensing of the degrees of freedom in the perceptual–motor work space and its relation to the dynamics of joint space is consistent with the broader theoretical notion that complex dynamics can emerge from relatively simple nonlinear relations of the components of a system.

To date, most of the dynamical modeling of movement has been confined to the regulation of two biomechanical degrees of freedom (e.g., two-finger- or wrist-coordination tasks), in which there is no redundancy available in joint space to satisfy the task demands. Nevertheless, there are increasing empirical data suggesting that many of the dynamic movement phenomena evident in the coordination of two limbs can be accommodated by relatively simple dynamical models. Furthermore, the fundamental dynamic properties of stability—loss of stability, bifurcations, fluctuations, and hysterisis—all seem to be present in the coordination of two biomechanical degrees of freedom under different task constraints.

The natural ongoing interaction of the individual with the environment in the pursuit of various daily task goals gives rise to continual change in the attractor dynamics supporting action. In other words, the attractor dynamics supporting action are typically nonstationary over the extended time scales of practice sessions. The degree to which the attractor layout of the perceptual–motor work space changes over time will be due to the specific organism–environment interactions occurring over time, along with the effects of the mere passage of time itself. Thus, what are typically called learning, retention, and transfer of movement skills, will be driven by the systematic and fluctuating changes in the ever-ongoing construction of the task-relevant, perceptual–motor work space.

A focus of motor learning is the facility to construct new attractor dynamics in the perceptual–motor work space. This process requires the move away from the stable regions of a readily constructed attractor dynamic to the more unstable regions associated with the initial formation of a new attractor dynamic. This change in the dynamical properties of the perceptual–motor work space and its accompanying change in the dynamics of the movement form are influenced by both chance and choice: chance, in the sense that qualitative changes in coordination mode dynamics may arise from the random fluctuations in the spatial–temporal organization of the attractor dynamic of the perceptual–motor work space; choice, in the sense that intentional, systematic search strategies through the work space may be used to change coordination modes and the qualitative progressions observed in the acquisition of skill. The examination of the interaction of systematic and unsystematic influences in the construction of the perceptual–motor work space is currently a central theoretical and empirical issue.

Search Strategies and the Perceptual–Motor Work Space

The dynamical layout of the perceptual–motor work space is continually evolving qualitatively and quantitatively due to the continuous nature of the organism–environment interaction. Paradoxically, the act of searching the work space itself leads to changes in the structure of the space, and the structure of the space may specify the qualitative nature of the search employed. This apparently intricate relation between attractor dynamics and exploratory behavior contributes to the nonstationarity (changing dynamics) of the dynamical interface of the perceptual–motor work space.

A search strategy refers to the way in which the performer explores the perceptual–motor work space. The central idea is that the search strategy reveals the systematic and unsystematic components to the pathway taken through the multidimensional state space that maps perception and action. The search behavior can lead to the organization and subsequent reorganization of attractor dynamics in the perceptual–motor work space and the resultant qualitative and quantitative properties of the movement forms that support action.

Numerous search strategies have been uncovered in a variety of physical and biological systems, many of which appear common across systems. An important category distinction in exploratory behavior differentiates between *local* (continuous) and *global* (discontinuous) search stategies. This framework may be useful to the organism for characterizing the distinctive nature of the search problem and for adaptively operating in the boundary regions of a readily constructed attractor dynamic (such as a learned movement skill) and in attempting to construct a new attractor regime (one that supports a never-before-produced movement form). A systematic experimental analysis of the strategic searches in the perceptual–motor work space while individuals are in different stages of learning movement skills has not yet been undertaken. It is hypothesized, however, that there is a relation between the search behavior in the perceptual–motor work space and the orderly changes noted previously in the outcome score and movement dynamics that occur with practice.

In searching for task-relevant solutions to the coordination and control of movement, the learner is bounded by what has been called the *dual-control problem*. This is the problem of discovering the dynamic characteristics of the system while at the same time trying to control the system. It is the problem of searching for and constructing in the perceptual–motor work space new attractor regions and the confronting of probable regions of instability, while at the same time trying to preserve (for system integrity considerations) some overall level of stability of the system. Many examples of this dual-control problem come readily to mind. Consider learning to ride a bicycle while at the same time trying not to fall, an infant's learning to walk while at the same time trying not to fall, or a pilot's learning to fly an airplane while at the same time trying not to crash the plane. The costs of movement instabilities (falling, crashing, and so on) may well determine the degree to which the learner approaches the instability boundaries of the attractor regions of the perceptual–motor work space that support action. The irony is that learning the instabilities of the system may well be the best strategy of learning the stabilities of a new movement form. The degree to which this learning strategy is implemented will be influenced by the costs of system instability and the benefits of realizing a new system configuration.

In closing this section, I deem it reasonable to propose that the concept of search strategies could provide the foundations of a theory of practice for motor-skill acquisition. Surprisingly, there is currently no theory of motor learning that accommodates the construct of practice, in spite of the centrality of practice to motor learning. One reason for this state of affairs is that most motor-learning studies researchers have not considered the changes in the movement and outcome relations either *between* individual trials in a discrete task-practice sequence or *within* the performance of a continuous task trial. Rather, the search strategy of the learner is masked in the averaging of data over trials and individuals. Bernstein reiterated a point he had advanced in other writings, namely, that practice is repetition without repetition, but the subtle implications of this statement have not been systematically examined.

Bernstein outlined two key hypotheses in regard to strategies of practice. First, he clearly specified the importance of establishing, early in practice, the correct movement pattern and not straying from this as a goal. Second, after the learner's having developed the appropriate qualitative properties of the movement pattern, he suggested that variations of the quantitative output be purposefully designed (task manipulations) to give the learner a variety of experiences in relation to the movement dynamics. A particular consequence of this variability of practice is that it broadens the sensory input experienced by the individual, a critical aspect for developing corrections at the various levels of the system and the resultant expressions of dexterity. These two hypotheses in regard to practice strategies have been emphasized over the years by many other theorists and practitioners of motor skills. A theory of practice should be a central feature of theorizing about coordination, control, and skill of physical activity, but the propositions that are central to such a theory remain elusive.

Augmented Information and the Facilitation of Search Strategies

It is quite evident that a learning strategy of self-discovery enables many learners to achieve considerable success in a number of physical activities and tasks. That is, the information naturally available in the organism–environment interaction is often sufficient to specify to the learner the appropriate coordination and control solution for the given task demands and the search strategy to realize this goal. However, self-discovery through the information naturally available can also lead to inefficient and ineffective searches, and, in some situations, the appropriate coordination solution or task goal may never be realized. This is particularly the case in the learning of certain ontogenetic activities, such as those in music and sport, in which the realization of an advanced coordination and control solution for particular facets of an activity can be illusory to some learners.

Augmented information is that information not normally available to the learner when learning and performing the task. It is information that is augmented to that normally available in the organism–environment interaction during practice of the task. The increasing technological developments make the distinction of natural and augmented information a fine line and a matter of definition, particularly in person–machine interactions: Information that is construed as augmented one day can subsequently be permanently built into the system of future machine designs and thus become, in essence, natural information the next day. Bernstein had little to say about the role of augmented information in motor-skill acquisition, except for emphasizing the general point that information for movement modifications is important in motor learning.

There are a number of different types of augmented information and media through which that information can be conveyed. It is important to distinguish between the nature of the information conveyed and the mechanism for conveying the information, because often the same information can be presented to a learner in a number of different ways. Thus, the medium for conveying information, such as videotape, does not necessarily provide direct intuitive clues about the information that is available or transmitted.

There appear to be at least three categories of augmented information used to facilitate motor learning and performance. These categories include prescriptive information, information feedback, and transition information. These information categories can be considered in a common augmented-information framework in which the augmented information provides the support for facilitating the search of the perceptual–motor work space, the construction of attractor dynamics, and the realization of the task goals.

Prescriptive Information. Prescriptive augmented information provides information about the to-be-achieved, end-state movement kinematics. The information can specify the relative, absolute, and common motion components of a to-be-achieved coordination and control solution to the task demands. This information (or elements of it) is most typically conveyed by either or both oral instructions and a demonstration of a behavioral outcome of a to-be-achieved coordination and control solution. The demonstration can be presented via some medium such as film or videotape or live by an instructor.

The presentation of prescriptive augmented information for the acquisition of movement skills is common in dance, sports, and music activities. Its use is based on the intuitive perspective that such information is effective for learning and that "a picture is worth a thousand words." The empirical evidence in support of such a proposition is not as compelling as the intuition, however, a fact that suggests subtle interactions between the effects of this category of information, the nature of the skill, and the skill level of the performer.

One problem is that a demonstration displays only the kinematics of the motion, which is the product of both the active and passive forces of the system. It would seem that the larger the role of the reactive forces in producing a given coordination solution the less likely that a demonstration will have immediate effects on learning. Bernstein also proposed that the process of observation cannot develop the appropriate sensory corrections for movement control, which are very important in bringing about change in movement. The central problem of which prescriptive information is useful or essential to the learner in regard to the end-state dynamics is still an open theoretical and empirical issue.

Information Feedback. This category of augmented information provides information about some past state or states of the movement dynamics produced by the learner in an evolving movement sequence or on a just-completed movement trial. Information feedback can be provided about any absolute, relative, or common motion property, but there are principles about the most useful information to provide. *Concurrent* information feedback provides information about prior states of the still-ongoing movement sequence. *Terminal* information feedback provides information about earlier movement properties or their consequences (movement outcome) on completion of the trial. Bernstein emphasized the role of sensory corrections in motor-skill acqusition but in regard to the self-discovery conditions of learning without augmented information feedback.

A major challenge is understanding the nature of *what* information feedback is appropriate for each learner at each stage of learning a skill. Information feedback has been shown to strongly influence the learning and performance of movement skills. The emerging principle is that for movement tasks with one or two degrees of freedom, the degrees of freedom contained in the information should match the degrees of freedom requiring constraint in the task. However, the problem of what information feedback is appropriate in the learning of whole-body actions is more profound because many informational properties of the action may be considered. In tasks requiring the coordination of many biomechanical degrees of freedom, information feedback is often not very direct about the nature of the change that needs to be made on the next trial. Consequently, for many tasks, information feedback does not constrain the search sufficiently for the learning of new coordination modes and leads to less effective and less efficient learning than has been apparent in investigations of the learning of single-limb tasks under the same information-feedback conditions.

Transition Information. A category of augmented information that has not been studied systematically is that of transition information. Transition information relates directly to the change in the coordination and control solution that must occur at some future time of the ongoing trial or on the next trial in a learning sequence. This type of information would appear to be particularly useful in the acquisition of a new set of relative motions or movement form for the task at hand. Transition information specifies a to-be-achieved property of a coordination and control solution that should be searched for in the upcoming movement trial, but in the act of the learner's realizing that goal, a transition to another coordination and control solution emerges. Thus, transition information is not prescriptive information, because it is not prescribing the to-be-achieved end-state dynamics of the to-be-learned movement skill; nor is it information feedback, because it does not provide information about past movement states and their goals realized. Rather, it provides information more *directly* than either prescriptive or feedback information about the change in movement coordination and control. Theoretically, transition information may be viewed as a control parameter that facilitates the search through the perceptual–motor work space for the realization of a task-relevant coordination and control solution, and it may appear unrelated to the to-be-achieved end-state dynamics.

Information and Search Strategies. A key issue for a theory of motor learning is how to integrate the concept of information into the Bernstein coordination problem and the changing regulation of redundant degrees of freedom. The categories of augmented information just outlined provide different forms of information to the learner and support the information naturally available for motor learning and control in the organsim–environment interaction. Augmented and natural information are rarely considered cohesively in a theoretical framework, but augmented information can be usefully viewed as information that facilitates the search for task-relevant coordination and control solutions. The respective categories of information provide different types and degrees of constraint on the search behavior and the emergent channeling of the task-relevant movement dynamics. In practice, instructors tend to intertwine the use of each of these categories of information, according to the nature of the task and the skill level of the performer, to facilitate motor learning.

In general, then, augmented information acts as an environmental constraint to action. The different categories of information provide varying boundary conditions to the search through the perceptual–motor work space in the realization of new task goals. How information facilitates exploratory behavior in motor learning is an integral part of coming to terms with Bernstein's problems of learning to regulate redundant degrees of freedom and practice as repetition without repetition.

RETENTION OF ACTION SOLUTIONS

Clues about the learning of movement coordination and control solutions to action may be gleaned from a characterization of the retention of action solutions. In other words, unraveling the relations between trial-to-trial and session-to-session coordination and control solutions should provide some insight into the nature of the systematic and unsystematic changes in movement and its outcome over time. Indeed, a general indication that someone has learned a skill is his or her ability to reproduce it at some later time after the initial learning session.

The facility of individuals to reproduce action solutions at some later time depends on a number of factors: the nature of the task, the stage of learning of the performer, the duration of the retention interval, and the kind of movement experiences that the individual has engaged in during the retention interval. As Bernstein remarked, once the essential elements of a task are learned, many movement skills apparently are remarkably well retained, even over extended periods of nonspecific practice on the task. For example, normal, healthy people do not seem to forget how to ride a bicycle, play a musical instrument, or perform a particular activity of daily living. This is not to say that there is not some performance decrement or change in movement organization over a retention interval; it means, rather, that the essence of the skill is preserved. In other words, many of the essential properties of the movement sequence appear to be persistent over time whereas the less essential properties tend to fluctuate to some degree or even to disappear.

The persistent movement properties relate to the organization of the relative motions of the body and limbs in relation to the environmental demands. A moment's reflection will suggest that this observation depends on the earlier definition that activities are defined or characterized by a set of relative motions. If the respective set of relative motions were not preserved, then one would or could not say that a given action solution had been retained. In other words, one would not be able to recognize the repetitive production over time of such activities as walking, running, throwing, and so on. On the other hand, one might imagine that although certain fundamental coordination solutions are well preserved over time other, perhaps less stable solutions, are not. In certain activities, such as violin playing, gymnastics, or ice-skating, the more fundamental and stable action sequences may be reliably preserved over time, but the more advanced and possibly less stable coordination modes may not be. Thus, the general observation that motor skills are well retained over time, a position that Bernstein endorsed, can perhaps be compromised by the nature of the task or action under consideration and the level of detail of the observation.

As outlined previously, ideas about the retention of action solutions have typically rested on theoretical propositions regarding the representation in memory of movement and action. The failure to reproduce an action solution at some subsequent retention test has traditionally been interpreted as the loss in memory over the interval of the appropriate representation for the movement sequence. This memory loss results from either the fading of the memory representation over extended time periods or interference with the representation due to engagement in other activities. Indeed, the term *forgetting* implies that some change or loss has occurred in the memory representation of the action at hand, thus giving rise to the performance decrement over a retention interval. Bernstein did not extend his perspective on dexterity directly to these issues about the nature of representations in memory, but his theoretical framework clearly endorses the importance of memory for movement and sensory corrections.

The ecological approach to motor-skill learning emphasizes, however, the task-specific construction of action solutions. Moreover, this perspective gives less emphasis to representation of the many degrees of freedom providing the basis for movement reproduction and more to the appropriate *construction* of the task-relevant action solution. It is not that there is no representation for action but rather that the search is for a low-dimensional solution to the harnessing of the many degrees of freedom, a view consistent with a dynamical interpretation of the coordination of information and movement. In this approach, intention is considered another boundary condition or constraint to action rather than a set of prescriptions for the organizational details of movement dynamics.

The ability to produce an environmental or task-relevant scaling of a given coordination mode appears to be the movement property that changes the most over extended retention intervals. Over short retention intervals this performance or organization change has been referred to as *warm-up decrement*, because a short practice session quickly allows the performer to recalibrate (conduct a local search of the attractor dynamic?) the organization of the system to the task demands. The longer the retention interval is, the more likely that longer practice sessions are required to recapture previously produced levels of task-relevant, motor-system organization and movement outcome.

The constraints to action change over time, and this change itself can require a different coordination and control solution to the same task goal. For example, properties of the organism change, such as strength, flexibility, endurance, information transmission speed, and so on. Structural and functional changes of the organism may substantially influence the constraints to action and the attractor layout of the perceptual–motor work space. Thus, certain changes apparent over time in the coordination and control solution to the task may not be due to forgetting at all but rather to the natural adaptation to the changing confluence of constraints to action.

TRANSFER TO NEW TASK DEMANDS

In a general, and perhaps trivial, sense, there is always transfer to a different confluence of constraints in the conduct of action, because there is continual change to some greater or lesser degree in the organismic and environmental constraints to action. *Transfer* classically refers, however, to the influence of one task on the learning or performance of another task. Thus, transfer is traditionally viewed within the bounds of changing task constraints and the influence of realizing one action goal on the facility and adeptness of realizing another action goal.

Positive transfer occurs when engagement in a particular task facilitates the learning or performance of another task. *Negative transfer* occurs when practice on one task negatively influences the learning or performance of another task. No transfer occurs when performance on one task has no influence on the learning or performance of another task. It is apparent that positive, negative, and no transfer are common consequences of the learning and retention of movement skills.

The assessment of the probability of transfer occurring between two or more tasks usually depends on an analysis of the similarity of both the task constraints and the resultant movement organization typically produced in the execution of the tasks. In traditional psychological parlance, this is referred to as the similarity of the *stimulus* and *response* components, respectively. The similarity of the stimulus and response has formed the basis for various descriptive frameworks for predicting the type and degree of transfer between tasks. The prediction of a high probability of positive transfer is usually predicated on the high similarity of both the stimulus and response components in the respective tasks. A high probability of negative transfer is typically projected to occur when a different response is required to a similar stimulus. Beyond these extreme degrees of task similarity and dissimilarity, the type and degree of transfer is typically projected to vary in a nonlinear fashion over the different gradations of stimulus–response similarity.

A major problem with this account of transfer is its predication on a weak account of what the stimulus and response dimensions actually are. For example, how does one formally assess response similarity? And, without this assessment in place, how can one formally and reliably predict transfer? Furthermore, the current understanding of the task constraints on actions and their relationship across tasks is very poor. As Bernstein noted, predictions of transfer from motor task to motor task often are not particularly successful practically or relevant theoretically. Bernstein sketched an approach to transfer (positive and negative) based on his conceptualization of levels of movement construction and the degree of involvement of automatisms in the tasks being performed.

The promise of the approach to motor learning and control developed in this chapter is that the issue of transfer may be more usefully predicated on a consideration of attractor dynamics in the perceptual–motor work space. In other words, an analysis of the attractor dynamics supporting each task will afford an understanding of the common and distinct dynamical regimens that support the movement forms in each action. A key issue for movement transfer is the development of principles that specify the transition out of and into attractor regimens. Transitions between attractor dynamics is a major area of investigation in the acquisition of movement skill, an area that might also provide the dynamical basis for considering transfer between different task constraints. Similarly, an understanding of the search strategies used in exploratory behavior as a function of the attractor dynamics of the perceptual–motor work space may lead to principled predictions about the nature and probability of systematic changes between task constraints.

It should be evident that the concepts of learning, retention, and transfer are intimately related because they all concerned with the *change* in movement and skill that occurs over time. To put it another way, the accommodation to changing conditions and constraints on action is, in effect, a reflection of what is called learning, retention, and transfer. The facility with which an individual realizes these demands across a wide range of conditions is what Bernstein called dexterity.

CONCLUDING COMMENTS

Bernstein's profound insights regarding the degrees-of-freedom problem capture the central issue for the coordination and control of movement dynamics. However, the organization of the motor system in the harnessing of the degrees of freedom for task-relevant solutions and the changes in that organization over time that are interpreted as learning, retention, and transfer are driven by the pickup and utilization of information for action. The ecological approach to perception and action proposes that the problem of motor learning can be viewed as the discovery of the dynamical laws that organize information and movement dynamics in the support of action.

In this volume Bernstein developed several parts of his broad theoretical framework for the coordination, control, and skill of physical activity. A key element advanced in this text is the evolutionary perspective to the neurophysiological account of the levels of movement construction that support movement and action. This framework offers several biologically based hypotheses about the nature of the change over time in the organization of movement coordination and control. A major contribution of this text is that the behavioral aspects of actions and goals are placed in a coherent framework, along with his earlier published ideas of movement coordination and control.

Dexterity is the emergent property of action par excellence for Bernstein, and this possibly generalized idea of skill may now find a more important place in the learning, retention, and transfer of movement coordination and control than it has in the recent past. The development of this perspective to coordination, control, and skill will require a principled approach to intention, attention, and information in motor skill acquisition—all concepts that Bernstein highlighted the importance of but did not develop theoretically. The contemporary ecological approach to perception and action has taken up this theoretical and empirical challenge with the strategy of realizing this goal in a fashion that is consistent with the natural laws of dynamics.

FURTHER READING

Bernstein, N. (1967). *The coordination and regulation of movements.* New York: Pergamon.

Cutting, J. E., & Proffitt, D. R. (1982). The minimum principle and the perception of absolute, common, and relative motions. *Cognitive Psychology, 14,* 211–246.

Fowler, C. A., & Turvey, M. T. (1978). Skill acquisition: An event approach with special reference to searching for the optimum of a function of several variables. In G. E. Stelmach (Ed.), *Information processing in motor control and learning* (pp. 1–40). New York: Academic Press.

Gibson, J. J. (1979). *The ecological approach to visual perception.* Boston: Houghton Mifflin.

Greene, P. H. (1969). Seeking mathematical models for skilled actions. In D. Bootzin & H. C. Muffley (Eds.), *Biomechanics (Proceedings of the First Rock Island Arsenal Biomechanics Symposium).* New York: Plenum.

Haken, H., Kelso, J. A. S., & Bunz, H. (1985). A theoretical model of phase transitions in human hand movements. *Biological Cybernetics, 51*, 347–356.

Kugler, P. N., & Turvey, M. T. (1987). *Information, natural law, and self-assembly of rhythmic movement: Theoretical and experimental investigations.* Hillsdale, NJ: Lawrence Erlbaum Associates.

Newell, K. M. (1991). Motor skill acquisition. *Annual Review of Psychology, 42*, 213–237.

Newell, K. M., Kugler, P. N., van Emmerik, R. E. A., & McDonald, P. V. (1989). Search strategies and the acquisition of coordination. In S. A. Wallace (Ed.), *Perspectives on the coordination of movement* (pp. 85–122). Amsterdam: North–Holland.

Newell, K. M., & McDonald, P. V. (1992). In American Academy of Physical Education (Ed.), *Enhancing human performance in sport: New concepts and developments.* Champaign, IL: Human Kinetics.

Newell, K. M., & McDonald, P. V. (1994). Learning to coordinate redundant biomechanical degrees of freedom. In S. Swinnen, H. Heuer, J. Massion, & P. Casaer (Eds.), *Interlimb coordination: Neural, dynamical, and cognitive constraints* (pp. 515–536). New York: Academic Press.

Newell, K. M., Morris, L. R., & Scully, D. M. (1985). Augmented information and the acquisition of skill in physical activity. In R. L. Terjung (Ed.), *Exercise and Sport Sciences Reviews, 13*, 235–262.

Schoner, G. (1989). Learning and recall in a dynamic theory of coordination patterns. *Biological Cybernetics, 62*, 39–54.

Turvey, M. T. (1990). Coordination. *American Psychologist, 45*, 938–953.

Turvey, M. T., & Kugler, P. N. (1984). An ecological approach to perception and action. In H. T. A. Whiting (Ed.), *Human motor actions: Bernstein reassessed* (pp. 373–412). Amsterdam: North–Holland.

Vereijken, B., van Emmerik, R. E. A., Whiting, H. T. A., & Newell, K. M. (1992). Free(z)ing degrees of freedom in skill acquisition. *Journal of Motor Behavior, 24*, 133–142.

Zanone, P. G., & Kelso, J. A. S. (1992). Evolution of behavioral attractors with learning: Nonequilibrium phase transitions. *Journal of Experimental Psychology: Human Perception and Performance, 18*, 403–421.

The Primacy of Action in Development

Edward S. Reed
Franklin & Marshall College

Blandine Bril
École des Hautes Études en Sciences Sociales, Paris

In this chapter, we focus on Bernstein's account of motor learning, because we believe that it is especially in this part of his theorizing that Bernstein was most radical and provocative, offering ideas that are still "ahead of their times" in many ways. The account of motor learning offered in *On Dexterity and Its Development* carries the seeds of a radical shift in how to think about the acquisition of skill. For Bernstein, functional actions are primary, and the control of movements and postures are secondary. Movements are not the building blocks of action; instead, the control of movements is one of the results of the development of action. Although we are convinced that this insight about the primacy of action is fundamental for any successful functional theory of action, it is still the case that the majority of textbooks and theorists in the field of motor control and development resist such a radical approach (Schmidt, 1982).

We argue that a theory placing action as primary in development is the only kind that can really help theorists to begin to understand how many of the important, culturally specific skills that characterize human beings have evolved and developed. After situating Bernstein's *On Dexterity* in its historical and theoretical context, we briefly describe how the traditional kinds of accounts of motor development emphasize movements and repetitions of movement as the basic factor in development and skill acquisition. After this, we show how Bernstein, in *On Dexterity*, began to turn such theories "on their heads." Following this, we offer some suggestions concerning how an action-based theory of development may be very useful in helping theorists to understand one of the fundamental problems of psychological science: why and how human cultures develop their own specific patterns of everyday activities and skills.

SITUATING ON DEXTERITY
IN ITS HISTORICAL CONTEXT

Two books were written at the end of the 1940s, which together should have changed the face of psychology. Both of these books offered naturalistic approaches to basic psychological processes, which, prior to that time, had been treated in highly abstract ways, often torn out of their functional context. In one of these books, James J. Gibson's *Perception of the Visual World* (1950), the author argued for developing a "ground" theory of visual perception to replace previous theories, which he dubbed "air" theories. Gibson wanted to know how human visual perception functions in realistic, everyday situations, where the ground is always below us and the air above us. Previous theories of vision, beginning as they do with an analysis of the visual stimulus as rays of light producing points of stimulation on the retina, are literally about seeing what is up in the air. Gibson countered this with an account of seeing along the ground. Of course, the "air theorists" Gibson criticized responded that seeing along the ground is just made up of combinations of ray-type stimuli. Over the course of four decades now, this debate is still raging: Can theorists begin psychological science with atomistic accounts of psychological processes and develop models of their combination, or should theorists attempt to discover at the outset some of the typical patterns within which these processes have emerged (Reed, 1988)?

Had Bernstein's *On Dexterity* been published as scheduled, around 1950, it would have offered a powerful companion piece to Gibson's emerging ecological analysis of perception. The key idea in Bernstein's book is essentially that theorists need what might be called a "ground theory of movement" as well as one of perception. Dexterity is not a property of movements as such, as Bernstein emphasized, but a property of movements in situations. In a sense, one cannot move dexterously; one can only solve a motor problem dexterously. (For Bernstein, dance and gymnastics were important special cases in which the motor problem was one of creating a specific pattern of movement and posture.) Thus, the student of movement control cannot analyze a given movement, such as running, in the abstract and then apply this analysis unchanged to running in a situation—they are two different actions (essay 7).

It is worthwhile to compare Bernstein's *On Dexterity* (or Gibson's, 1950, *Visual World*) to several other important psychology books of that era. Hebb's *Organization of Behavior* (1949), Ashby's *Design for a Brain* (1952), and Miller, Galanter, and Pribram's (1960) *Plans and the Structure of Behavior* are all roughly contemporaneous with Bernstein's book, and all made major contributions to the study of behavior. Yet, in none of these is there anything approaching the scope or rigor of Bernstein's analysis of behavior. Remarkably, there is not a single passage in all three of these important books that offers a detailed, empirically based analysis of an everyday skill. It is a surprising fact that there is very little sustained description of any behavior in these books. For example, the few descriptions of behavioral activities in Miller et al.'s *Plans* all turn out to be "docudramas" describing what the authors *imagined* such behaviors to be, independent of any serious empirical investigation. Similarly, although evolution and development are *mentioned* in these books, there is no sustained use of evolutionary or developmental concepts. Subsequent psychologists seem to have followed what these texts *did* (as opposed to what they *said*), acting as if scientific analysis of the context and development of naturalistic behavior were irrelevant or impossible.

In contrast to these formative books of the cognitive revolution, Bernstein's *On Dexterity* is replete with detailed and empirically based analyses of all sorts of everyday skills and actions, often with extensive use of developmental and evolutionary concepts to help the reader understand the actions. Bernstein gave theorists a real behavioral science, one that is serious about both science and behavior. His analysis is rigorous and always empirically informed, and the focus never wavers from real behaviors in real contexts. Interestingly, it is also behavioral analysis refreshingly independent of *behaviorism*. The theory that action can be reduced to stimulus and response had no hold on Bernstein (indeed, behaviorism had less hold on Bernstein at that time than it did on Gibson; see Reed, 1988). Bernstein showed us how one can analyze behavior in physical terms without downplaying the meaningfulness of embodied action—an approach that has yet to be developed within mainstream American psychology.

FROM THE THEORY OF MOVEMENT TO THE THEORY OF ACTION: DEEPENING BERNSTEIN'S ANALYSIS

The parallel between Gibson's (1950) *Visual World* and Bernstein's *On Dexterity* extends even to the limitations of both books. In his book, however radical in certain aspects of its conception, Gibson still clung to a number of traditional tenets of perception theory. In particular, although Gibson recognized that his "ground theory" of perception required a complete revision of the concept of sensory inputs in perception theory, he was unwilling or unable at that time to go so far. Mainstream physiology at that time seemed to require perceptionists to assume that perceiving is based on the very atomistic responses of sensory receptors to physical stimulation, such as a somatosensory response to a poke to the skin. It was only after trying to apply the *Visual World* theory in a number of different contexts that Gibson (1966) was forced to turn traditional perceptual theory upside down, as it were, and suggest that these sensory inputs and their associated subjective states are *by-products* of the activity of perceiving. It is this activity that is primary, and it is only through specialized training and attention that a person can even notice the sensations and sensory inputs.

Bernstein's *On Dexterity*, like Gibson's (1950) *Visual World*, also contains a theoretical analysis the implications of which are far more radical than anything articulated in the text. (Because it was never published, and because of the many constraints on Bernstein's subsequent career, it is unclear whether Bernstein himself would have developed some of these radical ideas as far as we do here. It is interesting to note, however, that Bernstein began to call for a "physiology of activity" in the late 1950s, for example, as in Bernstein, 1984, 1988.) The concept of dexterity itself, as developed by Bernstein, seems to imply the need for an analysis in which actions are primary and in which movements and postures are consequences of the activities of the organism. Yet, especially in the phylogenetic and ontogenetic analyses, Bernstein did not deviate from traditional theories in which actions are considered to be constructed out of movements. The contrast can be stated in a precise form: If movements in different contexts are truly different, as Bernstein repeatedly claimed, then what would appear to be learned when one learns to act is just that, the action, not any of the particular movements (or, as Bernstein himself put it, one learns the process of solving motor problems). Hence, what Bernstein called Level D, the level of actions, is, in fact, primary and not built up from the various levels of movement and posture he described. Instead, those levels (A–C) that he claimed are developmentally and phylogenetically more primitive might be better understood not as movements but as simpler forms of action, which the nervous systems at those levels of development tend to carry out.

From our point of view, the ability to construct, coordinate, and modulate movements regardless of the functional context of the organism is itself one of the most sophisticated achievements of human action systems. The time and effort required for skill in this area—as manifested in athletic and dance skills, discussed by Bernstein—strongly suggest that the ability to "fractionate" actions into postures and movements in a controlled way is one of the most sophisticated of human achievements. In fact, it is difficult for the nimblest of circus animals or young children to learn to make precise movements or postures; they are often taught by the expedient of having them learn to act in just such a manner that tends to entail the desired movement or posture. Theorists have always been taught that "movements" are—even *must be*—the building blocks of actions. It is intellectually bracing to have this text of Bernstein's, in which he began to suggest that the sophisticated control of particular movements characteristic of human skills is, in fact, a *consequence* of action development, not its basis.

BERNSTEIN'S ACCOUNT OF ACTION DEVELOPMENT: REPETITION WITHOUT REPETITION

Most theories of motor development have been built on a very few premises. These premises have seemed to be obviously true, and a considerable amount of experimental research can be interpreted in accordance with these premises. It is Bernstein's greatest achievement in *On Dexterity* to have challenged the very foundations of these traditional theories. These theories are built on the following basic premises:

- Movements are the units of actions.
- Movements are either the results of central nervous system commands or reflexive.
- Movements are more likely to be repeated when they become associated with pleasurable feelings or outcomes.
- The repetition of movements, leading to changes in the frequency of given movements, is the central mechanism in action learning.
- Together these assumptions make up what one might call "associative hedonism"—the idea that associating positive states are what drive motor learning.

One can use such a theory to generate a scenario to explain almost any kind of action learning or development. Certainly one finds these sorts of explanations throughout the literature. For example, Asanuma and Arissian (1984) wrote, "When a subject is trained to pursue a specific movement, the practice produces vigorous circulation of impulses in particular corticoperipheral loops related to that movement. Repeated practice results in an increased efficiency of synaptic transmission in these loops" (p. 224). But is repetition of *movement* really so important in *action* development? Is the mechanistic association of movements with feelings or outcomes really so important as well? The twin ideas that repetition of movement and association of movement with positive hedonic states carve out pathways in the central nervous system are basic to all existing theories of motor development—but Bernstein soundly rejected this whole approach.

Bernstein occasionally summarized his theory of motor learning with the enigmatic phrase, "repetition without repetition." If one understands what this means, it serves as a key for unlocking a whole new way of thinking about behavior. Bernstein's always emphasized that absolute repetition of a movement pattern is not possible because of the inherent variability and complexity of the environment (Reed, 1984). A given pattern of muscle excitation will cause different patterns of limb and body movement when an animal encounters varying circumstances in its environment. This variability is not "noise" for the nervous system, according to Bernstein, but a fundamental environmental fact that exerts selection pressure on the evolution of nervous systems.

Yet, for the traditional theory of motor learning, such variability *is* noise, because it is assumed that what the animal must do when it learns an action is repeat certain behaviors until a specific neural pathway is well established. Bernstein countered this idea with a very striking argument: "It is very wrong to identify the elaboration of a skill with the beating a neural path in the brain. The coefficient of efficacy of this method would be outrageously low, for example, to spend hundreds of thousands of kilogram-meters of work on numerous repetitions of a pole vault in order to move a few molecules of the brain that had been blocking the neural path" (essay 6).

Thus, in the traditional theory of motor development it is *assumed* that the purpose of repetition is the establishment of neural paths, an assumption that is doubly unrealistic because of the impossibility of creating precise repetitions of neural or behavioral activity in different contexts (Edelman, 1993) and because of the manifest inefficiency of this scheme. In contrast, Bernstein *hypothesized* that repetition has an ecological function. Repetition, Bernstein insisted, is characteristic of motor learning because one must repeat actions many times in order to solve a motor problem. "Repetitive solutions . . . are also necessary because, in natural conditions, external conditions never repeat themselves. . . . Consequently, it is necessary to gain experience relevant to all various modifications of a task. . . . for the animal not to be confused by future modifications of the task and external conditions" (essay 6).

This concept of motor learning implies a new definition of what is learned and a new definition of motor skill, which Bernstein provided: "Motor skill is not a movement formula and certainly not a formula of permanent muscle forces imprinted in some motor center. Motor skill is an ability to solve one or another type of motor problem" (essay 6). Motor skill is thus defined ecologically—as the ability of an organism to encounter the range of environmental variations for a given motor problem and to learn to solve them adaptively. Obviously some species (or some individuals) will be able to handle wider ranges of variability than will others, but learning any motor skill, according to this definition, implies learning to solve a motor problem in a real environment, a process that involves the animal's managing to find a solution across at least some variation in circumstances. Inspired by Bernstein, a number of psychologists began in the 1970s to define action as the ability of an animal to control its changing relationship with the environment (Fowler & Turvey, 1978; Reed, 1982; Turvey, 1977).

Nevertheless, despite all the variability and change in an animal's relation to its environment, there are patterns of repetition that are important. Moreover, as we emphasize later, human learning is especially characterized by forms of cultural organization that allow the child or other learner to repeat aspects of an activity many times. As Bernstein pointed out, however, "Adherents to the view that exercise leads to beating a trail or imprinting a certain trace onto the central nervous system, somehow, have never paid attention to an important fact. A human starts learning a movement because he or she cannot do it." At the beginning of learning a skill "there is nothing to be beaten" or, worse, "the only thing available for imprinting is wrong, clumsy movements" (essay 6).

A good example of how actions begin to be learned before humans can do them is the development of reaching. As Von Hofsten (1979) showed, children begin to reach for moving objects before they are 3 months old. Yet the movement pattern of these reaches is totally different from mature reaches and even radically different from the more mature reaches of a 6- or 9-month-old. The early reaches include many phases of acceleration–deceleration–acceleration because the child's control over the arm is very "wobbly." But repetition of these incorrect patterns by no means imprints a version of this pattern; on the contrary, all normal children reorganize their reaching so that almost the entire displacement of the hand is accomplished by a single acceleration–deceleration phase, added to which is one additional deceleration–acceleration phase to make a final adjustment of position. Moreover, this change in *movement* organization is, at least in part, the result of a reorganization and development of dynamic *postural* control, which enables the child to move his or her arm more smoothly because the potential disbalancing effects of those movements are taken into account (Rochat, 1992).

Exactly the same analysis could be applied to learning to walk. In a longitudinal study, Bril and Breniere (1992, 1993) suggested that the main problem the young toddler has to face is the mastering of dynamic disequilibrium. The solution adopted at the onset of walking is very different from that used by adults: Infants tend to use a large base of support, small steps, high frequency of stepping, negative acceleration of the center of mass at foot contact, and no heel strike. Improved postural control results in the modification of these patterns over the course of development.

We think Bernstein's insight applies to almost all important aspects of action development: What develops is never a movement pattern, and the repetition of one movement pattern is by no means a guarantee that that pattern will be imprinted or more likely to occur in future. On the contrary, in learning an action one repeats, "not the means for solving a given motor problem, but the process of its solution, the changing and improving of the means" (essay 6). This is what "repetition without repetition" means: What one learns is how to solve a motor problem or how to act. This knowledge is learned by repetition, not by repeating patterns of movement, but rather by repeating the process of solving the motor problem.

The twin assumptions that repetition *must be* repetition of movements and therefore *must* beat a pathway in the nervous system follow from theorists' treating the nervous system as a mechanical system. Traditionally, psychologists and others who have studied motor behavior have tended to treat the nervous system as an input–output mechanism. However, the nervous system is much more accurately modeled as a self-organizing, dynamic system in which alterations in the activities of a single part may cause radical reorganization of the whole (Edelman, 1993; Kugler, Kelso, & Turvey, 1982; Fogel, 1993; Reed, 1989; Thelen & Smith, 1994).

It is fascinating to note that Bernstein seemed to have anticipated even this relatively late-20th-century concept of organization. He recognized that certain patterns and processes involved in repeated activities would tend to be repeated, and others would tend not to be repeated, depending on whether or not the activities tend to contribute to the dynamic stability of the system: "Even if it were possible, at the cost of considerable effort, to perform an unstable, self-destructing movement pattern, it is certainly, absolutely unrealistic to repeat it consecutively several times" (essay 6). The very capacity to repeat a movement pattern is an *achievement* of the organism, not something one can merely assume to be the basis for learning! Furthermore, "stable forms [of action] have all the prerequisites for being easily reproducible and, therefore, should be easily memorized. The result is that bad, unsuccessful movements are not fixed in memory, whereas successful solutions to motor problems tend to be firmly remembered" (essay 6). Bernstein stated that this tendency is an instance of the behaviorists' "law of effect," but it is really a radical reinterpretation of that so-called law. As we mentioned earlier, the traditional law of effect was based on the idea that a positive affective state would be associated with certain movements and that this association would be the cause of the increased probability of those movements occurring. Bernstein's position is that there are intrinsic, dynamic properties of some solutions to motor problems (*not* movements alone) and that it is the relative stability of these dynamics that is the cause of the increased probability of that solution's being repeated. Bernstein treated learning as a change in the probability of a process's recurring and changing in efficiency, not in the probability of a movement's recurring (Kugler et al., 1982; Thelen & Smith, 1994).

We extend Bernstein's argument in one important way. We emphasize that the ability to find dynamically stable solutions to motor problems in human life is rarely an individual matter. Even such biologically basic activities as eating and walking are always and everywhere learned with at least some help from other people. Caretakers of infants always structure the environment of the infants, frequently intervening directly in the infant's action patterns. Human infants thus do not "discover" motor problems on their own, in an inanimate environment. Specific motor problems are in many cases called to the infant's attention or even thrust upon the infant by one or more caretakers in what we call a *field of promoted action*. It is because human adults promote specific motor problems for infants—often before the child is capable of solving that problem— that human action development takes the course that it does. Bernstein's account of motor learning and his revised law of effect help explain why different human cultures provide very different fields of promoted action to their children and, yet, why a number of more or less invariant human activity patterns can be found cross-culturally.

THE CULTURAL SELECTION OF ACTION, MOVEMENT, AND POSTURE

As Gibson (1979/1986) noted, the ecological niche of a species can be understood as a set of opportunities for useful or meaningful action, opportunities that he labeled *affordances* (p. 128). Those affordances that are more common or important for individuals of that species will constitute a set of motor problems that all members of that species must be capable of solving in some way. However, in social animals, such as human beings, for which explicit instruction, observational learning, and various patterns of apprenticeship are ubiquitous, the niche itself is partially structured by the activities of members of the evolving population. That is, the probability of a developing animal's encountering a given affordance can be markedly raised or lowered by the actions of its caretakers. In addition, the frequency of such encounters can also be changed by the caretakers. Finally, the functional importance of the encounter can be significantly modulated by the caretakers (e.g., the mother cat may encourage her kittens to learn how to catch mice, but she will not force them to rely entirely on their own skill for obtaining nourishment).

The description of the niche for a developing member of a social species must thus include a realistic assessment of these significant facts of the "populated environment" (Gibson, 1982, p. 411). We suggest the following analysis (a modification of Reed, 1993) for helping to track these social factors in development.

At the level of individual action and interaction there are innumerable, particular behaviors by which one individual calls the attention of another individual to an affordance or even makes a particular affordance more easily accessible to the other. With regard to human action development these individual acts of *scaffolding* (Bruner, 1983; Rogoff, 1990) are of fundamental importance. The cultural organization of human life is so pervasive that even such "biological" skills as eating and walking typically develop along the path that they do in large part because of acts of scaffolding. We believe it would be a truly exceptional case for a human being to acquire the skill of walking without some older individual's having been repeatedly involved in the infant's acquisition of an erect posture, alternate foot placement, and the maintenance of visual attention on the region to which the infant is heading.

Human infants, then, do not inhabit the complete ecological niche for our species. On the contrary, infants will be *selectively exposed* to only a subset of that niche, to certain selected opportunities for experience and action. This selected subset of the niche we call the *field of promoted action*. Although each child probably inhabits a unique field of promoted action, it is very likely that fields of promoted action will tend to be organized in characteristic ways by each culture. Thus, although most human caretakers of infants can and do engage in scaffolding activities, the affordances emphasized, their frequency, and their significance are likely to vary in systematic ways from one culture to the next. Rogoff (1990) provided a striking illustration of this. In many rural villages, very young children are allowed to handle and use real tools, including sharp ones, such as machetes. Rogoff illustrates this point with a picture of an 11-month-old using a machete to cut open some fruit—an action not at all uncommon in some rural cultures but virtually unheard of in "advanced," industrial parts of the world.

We emphasize that what we are describing is a field of *promoted action*, not just a field of *preferred affordances*. Although adult intervention often merely highlights the existence or desirability of a given affordance, many instances of adult intervention go beyond the mere offering of an opportunity and extend to the organizing or constraining of the process of solving a motor problem as well. For example, in India and in many African cultures, the hand involved in wiping oneself after defecation cannot be used for eating. Hence, from a young age, children in these cultures not only never see adults using their left hands to eat but are also explicitly stopped if and when they attempt to use their left hands for this task and constrained to using only their right hands for eating. Thus, even toddlers in these cultures typically have developed a strong habit of using the left hand for one task and the right for another.

Bernstein's modified law of effect can be read as a hint that, by encouraging certain postures, a caretaker can ensure that one particular developmental path (out of many possible paths) is taken for a given skill. We speculate that the encouragement and modeling of special postures (such as setups for a task, or follow-throughs) are an important source of cultural diversity in the organization of action.

On the basis of this analysis, we suggest that the structure of a culture's field of promoted action can be analyzed along the following dimensions:

- *Intensity.* How strongly promoted or prohibited a given opportunity—or the acton itself—for a given age group in a give cultural setting affordance or action is.

- *Extensity.* How widespread or frequent are encounters with a given affordance. With increasing globalization, one can find instances of culturally specific artifacts far from their origin (see Wolf, 1982, for some surprising examples). On the other hand, it is one thing for a child to see chopsticks, for example, a few times while growing up and another thing to see them used every day by almost every adult with whom one comes into contact.

- *Propriety.* There are often social rules about who may do what with what objects and in what circumstances. In a populated environment, motor problems not only must be solved expediently but also in the way acknowledged to be appropriate by that culture (Reed, 1988).

• *Development.* The field of promoted action of any culture is also organized developmentally, as a function of what is considered to be proper for a child of a given age. Gustafson, Green, and West (1979) showed that Western mothers adapt and change the games they play with 6- to 12-month-old infants, emphasizing very different skills across this period of time.[1]

THE CULTURAL ECOLOGY OF HUMAN ACTION DEVELOPMENT

Human beings often introduce their offspring to motor problems before the child can possibly solve that motor problem in an autonomous manner. This feature seems to be universal for all fields of promoted action. As Bernstein emphasized, human beings begin to learn motor skills well before they can actually accomplish the tasks to be learned. An extreme example is the use of technological tools, such as mobile "walkers" for nonlocomoting infants (Gustafson, 1984). However, in every culture caretakers seem to have a tendency to teach infants how to sit erect, reach, walk, and talk—and to perform many other skills—significantly before the child could be expected to accomplish those skills on her or his own. Indeed it may frequently be the case that the caretaker's scaffolding activity is necessary for any of these actions to be functionally meaningful. In these cases, the child's learning an action is thus accomplished by a progressive withdrawal of the caretaker's scaffolding activities and a complementary development of the child's ability to use the affordances at hand. Rogoff (1990) refers to this process as *bridging*. We would add that the concept of bridging fits in very well with Bernstein's emphasis that what is learned when a skill is acquired is typically the process of solving the motor problem, not the abstract movements that might accompany the mature adult's solution to the problem. We would also add that there are likely to be cases in which the child's learning to use an affordance is *slowed down* by scaffolding, because bridging is delayed or inadequate.

Smooth and efficient solutions to motor problems tend to emerge from focused and extensive practice, as Bernstein emphasized with his modification of the law of effect. If human action systems are built on the principles of self-organizing dynamics—as seems to be the case (Thelen & Smith, 1994)—then repetition without repetition will tend to lead to the production of stable, smooth, and efficient solutions to motor problems. Even here, however, culture plays an important role. Not only do cultures bias the kinds of motor problems to which children are exposed and the frequency of that exposure but they also play a role

---

[1] What is seen as developmentally appropriate varies not only with the age of the child but also, in all known cultures, with gender. Furthermore, specific cultures may have other ways of differentiating what is appropriate treatment (e.g., differential treatment by caste, race, handedness, etc.). The organization of populations of children in fields of promoted action might well be called "the developmental niche" of children in that culture, as Super and Harkness (1986) have suggested.

in biasing the dynamics of the movements and postures used by children in different tasks. Studies of cross-cultural action development strongly suggest that particular postures are often the target of scaffolding activity: Preparatory postures, dynamic postures (e.g., maintenance of eyes directed to the target of locomotion during walking), and follow-throughs are the common foci for this scaffolding activity. Because almost any given motor problem can be solved in more than one way, the specific postures selected for emphasis by different cultures may well represent different "stable states" of the developing action systems.

POSTURAL DEVELOPMENT WITHIN FIELDS OF PROMOTED ACTION

It has been widely reported in the literature that West African babies are advanced in their motor development, compared to Western European babies (Geber & Dean, 1957; Super, 1981; Werner, 1972). Our data on postural development agree with this finding. Bril and her colleagues (see Bril, 1993, for a review) evaluated infants' stages or levels of postural development according to the following parameters: no independent postural control; control of rolling over; assisted sitting possible; unassisted sitting possible. In all cases, the African children in the study were advanced with respect to their age-matched European counterparts (see Figure 1).[2]

The question we address here is what factors might lead to these different development trajectories. Our evidence strongly suggests that the most important differences between African (Bakongo) and European (French) infants lies in their respective fields of promoted action.

One simple measure of the field of promoted action for a very young infant is the percentage of the time that a child is allowed to lie supine, which all the youngest human infants can do without help. A related measure is the amount of time caretakers spend in supporting or encouraging motor performance. Assessments of this latter measure reveal an immediate and striking finding: Mothers in rural, "underdeveloped" cultures (like the Bakongo) typically encourage what might be called "infant gymnastics" as early as the first week or two of life. These babies are picked up, and their limbs stretched and massaged; they may also be turned upside down and held by a foot or hand (see Figure 2). Such activities

---

[2]Unlike in other studies in this domain, Bril and her colleagues did not simply use periodic observations of what mothers and children happened to be doing at a given time. Instead, a method was developed on the basis of a "time-series" principle. Each child was observed during two successive days between 8–10 hours per day; or, if this was impossible, observations were carried out on 2 nonsuccessive days within the same week. For each child, the results were therefore calculated on approximately 16 or more hours of observations. This method afforded two main advantages: The analysis of the frequencies of appearance of behaviors was more reliable; it allowed an analysis of the duration of the actions and their sequencing in time.

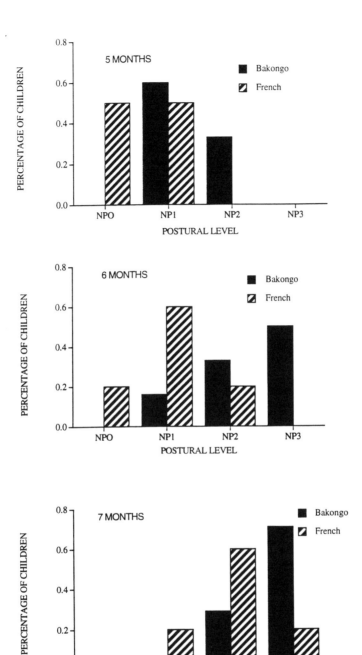

FIG. 1. Postural habits of mother–infant dyads in Mali and France. Based on observations of 15–20 hours/dyad over 2 days. $n = 10$ for Mali; $n = 14$ for France.

STRETCHING

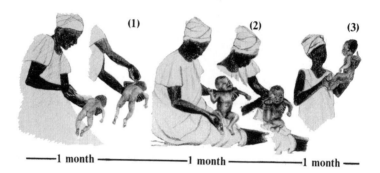

SUSPENSION

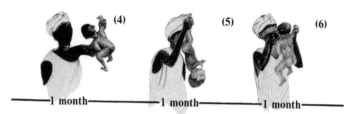

FIG. 2. Bambara baby gymnastics. This drawing illustrates some of the kinetic manipulations and massage techniques used widely among the Bambara for young infants.

are very routine and stylized within these rural communities. In contrast, French babies, and infants in other "developed," industrialized cultures are rarely subjected to such systematic exercise.

We have estimated both the percentage of waking time that young African and European babies are left to lie alone and the percentage of time they are actively handled and given "kinetic stimulation," as we call it (the term is used to include the nonsystematic handling most European babies are subjected to as well as the systematic gymnastics found elsewhere). The contrasts between the two groups are striking (see Figure 3): At every age level, the African babies are less likely to be left alone and unsupported and more likely to be actively stimulated. In fact, our data suggest that at every age, the *most* "left alone" of the African babies is handled *more* than the *least* left alone of the European babies. Also, the *most* "stimulated" European children appear to receive *less* stimulation than the *least* stimulated African babies (see Figure 3). Because these are results with relatively few infants in only two settings, they should be interpreted with caution. However, if such results can be shown to be representative in general of European–African cultural differences, then they offer persuasive evidence that the fields of promoted action with respect to motor performance are extremely different between these two cultures. We emphasize that the Bakongo and Bambara emphases on infant gymnastics appears to be characteristic of many rural communities outside of Africa as well, for example, South India (Reissland & Burghart, 1987) or Great Britain among West Indians living there (Hopkins & Westra, 1989).

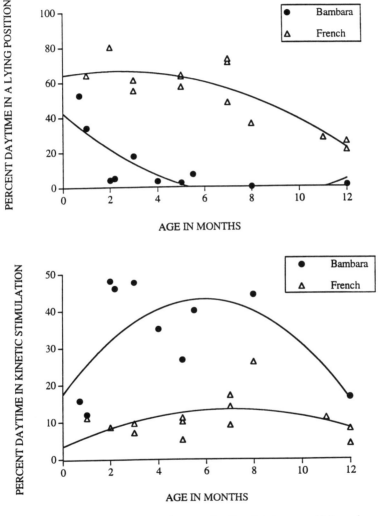

FIG. 3. Motor development in Bakongo and in French infants. n = 10 for each age group of French infants; n = 10 for each age group of Bakongo infants except 6-month-olds (n = 11). Postural levels are defined as follows: Level 1 = Infant cannot sit; Level 2 = Infant can sit with the aid of a single hand; Level 3 = Infant can sit on his or her own; Level 4 = Infant can sit and crawl.

MOTOR PROBLEM SOLVING WITHIN
THE FIELD OF PROMOTED ACTION

The data just reported reflect general differences in basic postural development. One question about such findings that is directly implied by Bernstein's *On Dexterity* is whether such differences affect the development and growth of specific dexterous actions as well as more general motor development. Will the children who are posturally advanced also be advanced in specific motor skills? As adults, humans are so used to being able to act dexterously—to adapt flexibly to many novel circumstances—that it seems obvious that such postural precocity should be beneficial in other skills. However, if Bernstein was correct that dexterous action as such is a special level of neuropsychological functioning, then such accelerated competence in movement and posture will *not* generalize to other skills *unless* it is coupled with development of the capacity to solve motor problems. For example, Hombessa-N'Kounkou (1988) found that Kongo infants were approximately 1–2 months "advanced" over French infants in sitting and standing postural development. In turn, this advancement led to what appeared to be earlier and more advanced reaching skills. However, a careful inspection revealed that much of this "advantage" in reaching shown by the African infants was restricted to arm movements—the grasping skills of the two groups were not very different.

However, there are important instances in which a culture's field of promoted action promotes not only early advanced postural competence but also advanced dexterity. A remarkable example is that action skill of "toilet training"—the ability to control the voiding of both the bladder and bowels dexterously. Variations in the method and timing of toilet training are found in different cultures. These differences seem in large part to be reflective of differences in "folk theories" about child rearing. In many African cultures (Bril, Zack, & Nkounkou-Hombessa, 1989; M. W. DeVries & M. R. DeVries, 1977) as well as in Asian cultures (Jo, 1989), infants are expected to be toilet trained before their first birthday. European as well as American and Japanese cultures, however, have developed a very different attitude toward toilet training. In these industrialized societies, many adults are convinced that sphincter control is maturationally determined, a belief that undermines the idea of early toilet training and promotes the idea that it is unnecessary and perhaps even dangerous for the infant.

French mothers expect their child to be trained at around 2 years for the daytime and about 3 years for the nighttime (Bril et al., 1989; Norimatsu, 1993). West African women insist on a strikingly earlier age, saying that children should be trained before the end of the first year (Bril et al., 1989; M. W. DeVries & M. R. DeVries, 1977). Two different African cultures have been found to have similar methods for training infants in both bladder and bowel control. The adult sits on the ground or on a small stool and places the child so that it sits on the adult's feet, facing the adult. When the infant is very young, she or he

FIG. 4. Bambara toilet-training postures. Special postures used by the Bambara when toilet training young infants.

is maintained by the arms near the shoulders; when older, the child is able to maintain herself or himself with very little help (see Figure 4). A similar position has been observed among the Gujarat in India. The Bambara mother uses this position for both bladder and bowel voiding, whereas the Digo mothers use a position for bladder voiding in which the infant is placed between the mother's legs facing away from her. When the child is in position, the mother associates a noise from the mouth with voiding. In both cultures, the mothers also reported that they learned to read signals from the position, muscle activation, and facial movements of the child. Here again, by being positioned at the right time on the mother's feet, the child is expected to learn to signal his or her needs. The Digo infant is expected to master voiding at around 6 months of age, whereas Bambara children are expected to do so by their first birthday.

This toilet-training method offers a remarkable example of the intricacy of the field of promoted action and the importance of perceptual learning for action development. Several different perceptual systems are used simultaneously by both mother and child (vision, hearing, haptics). The mother not only helps to organize the child's postures and movements but also strives to structure the events around the child, by relating a vocalization to the act of voiding, and further strives to identify information in the child's actions. We can only speculate, but it is reasonable to assume that the child too is looking for information in the mother's activities. Here is a striking example of a basic biological function whose timing, pattern, and intensity of acquisition are literally organized in considerable part by cultural norms.

CONCLUSIONS

Bernstein's *On Dexterity* offers theorists a strikingly new and promising way of thinking about the development of action. First and foremost, Bernstein provided very strong arguments for abandoning a number of the basic assumptions of traditional theories of motor development, theories that are still highly influential. Theorists have been taught for so long that actions *must* develop by repetition of movement patterns and the association of these movements with favorable outcomes and positive stimuli that it comes as something of a shock to reject these assumptions. Yet they simply do not fit the facts: People often begin to develop actions *before* they have acquired the relevant movements and postures; indeed, the learning of a dexterous action often transforms their capacity to control postures and movements.

We have pointed out that Bernstein's concept of dexterity is inherently *ecological*. He repeatedly emphasized that in developing action skills the central nervous system is learning, not to move the body, but to solve motor problems presented to it by external circumstances. These problems vary in their concrete details as the body moves through the environment. A central nervous system that excelled at producing copies of movements would actively harm any normal animal, because it would inevitably produce grossly inappropriate bodily forces in many situations.

To act dexterously, as Bernstein emphasized, is to excel at a process of solving motor problems, not at producing particular movement patterns. We have emphasized that the development of dexterity in humans takes place within a cultural environment, not just in an individual context. Here, we mean that caretakers of infants select opportunities for actions (affordances) and aspects of actions for infants to experience and learn. Some opportunities are emphasized, and some are deemphasized or even prohibited; some activities are supported, and others are not.

There is now striking evidence that this culturally based process of promoting actions plays a major role in the development of dexterity, evidence from a source which Bernstein could not have anticipated. Tomasello, Savage-Rumbaugh, and Kruger (1993) showed that acculturated chimpanzees acquire a great deal of what Bernstein would call dexterity from having their actions develop within a human field of promoted action. Tomasello et al. compared 18-month-old and 30-month-old human children with two groups of chimps. One group of chimps had been raised by other chimps, but the second group of chimps had been raised by humans (and taught a form of language as well). All the groups were tested on how well they could learn to use a novel object merely on the basis of being shown its use. The experimenters recorded not only successful uses of the objects but also whether the child or chimp copied the motor pattern from the one they had observed. The objects and actions tested were chosen to be fairly novel to all the participants: These were either novel objects or novel actions with familiar objects and included such things as a squeegee (wiping foam off a surface) and a reel (open it and reel an object in). In all cases, the human-reared chimps performed far better than the chimp-reared chimps. In fact, the human-reared chimps learned both the action goals and means as well as the human children learned. Furthermore, the human-reared chimps *retained* their skills over a 48-hour period much better than any other group, even the

30-month-old children. Bernstein's *On Dexterity* urges theorists to look at action, not just as movement, but as adaptive and flexible response to a complex environment. The results of Tomasello et al.'s (1993) study shows how powerful a factor the field of promoted action is in the development of dexterity.

Bernstein's *On Dexterity* implies a thoroughly up-to-date research agenda for students of action and its development. On the one hand, researchers need to refine Bernstein's concept of self-organization, to try to understand why developing dynamic action systems exhibit the patterns of self-organization that they do—what we referred to as Bernstein's revision of the law of effect. On the other hand, researchers need to understand how fields of promoted action are organized so the organism can take advantage of these developmental patterns of self-organization, promote certain developmental pathways, and retard others. We end with the suggestion that what can unite these two different directions for research on action is an ecologically informed account of how the developing child learns to detect and use information about the affordances of the environment in regulating her or his pattern of activity.

ACKNOWLEDGMENTS

We thank Herb and Anne Pick, Barbara Rogoff, and especially the editors for very constructive comments on an earlier version of this paper. E. S. Reed thanks B. Bril and L'École des Hautes Études en Sciences Sociales and Paris for supporting a very productive visit there, during which this paper was begun. Reed's work on writing this chapter was in part supported by a Guggenheim fellowship.

REFERENCES

Asanuma, H., & Arissian, K. (1984). Experiments on functional role of peripheral input to motor cortex during voluntary movements in the monkey. *Journal of Neurophysiology, 52,* 212–227.

Ashby, W. R. (1952). *Design for a brain.* New York: Wiley.

Bernstein, N. (1984). *Human motor actions: Bernstein re-assessed.* Amsterdam: North-Holland.

Bernstein, N. (1988). *Bewegungsphysiologie* [Physiology of activity] (2nd ed.). Leipzig: J. Barth.

Bril, B. (1993). *Une approche ecologique de l'acquisition d'habiletes motrices* [An ecological approach to the acquisition of everyday actions]. Habilitation, Université René Descartes—Paris V.

Bril, B., & Breniere, Y. (1992). Postural requirements and progression velocity in young walkers. *Journal of Motor Behavior, 24,* 105–116.

Bril, B., & Breniere, Y. (1993). Posture and gate in early childhood: Learning to walk or learning dynamic equilibrium? In G. Savelsberg (Eds.), *Development of coordination.* Amsterdam: Elsevier.

Bril, B., Zack, M., & Nkounkou-Hombessa, E. (1989). Ethnotheories of development and education: A view from different cultures. *European Journal of Psychology of Education, 4,* 307–318.

Bruner, J. (1983). *Child's talk.* New York: Norton.

DeVries, M. W., & DeVries, M. R. (1977). The cultural relativity of toilet training readiness: A perspective from East Africa.

Edelman, G. (1993). Neural Darwinism: Selection and reentrant signaling in higher brain function. *Neuron, 10,* 115–125.

Fowler, C. A., & Turvey, M. T. (1978). Skill acquisition: An event approach with special reference to searching for the optimum of a function of several variables. In G. Stelmach (Ed.), *Information processing in motor control and learning.* New York: Academic Press.

Geber, M., & Dean, R. F. (1957). The state of development of newborn African children. *Lancet, 272,* 1216–1219.

Gibson, J. J. (1950). *The perception of the visual world.* Boston: Houghton-Mifflin.

Gibson, J. J. (1966). *The senses considered as perceptual systems.* Boston: Houghton-Mifflin.

Gibson, J. J. (1982). Perceiving in a populated environment. In E. Reed & R. Jones (Eds.), *Reasons for realism: Selected essays of James J. Gibson.* Hillsdale, NJ: Lawrence Erlbaum Associates.

Gibson, J. J. (1986). *The ecological approach to visual perception.* Hillsdale, NJ: Lawrence Erlbaum Associates. (Original work published 1979)

Gustafson, G. (1984). Effects of the ability to locomote on infants' social and exploratory behaviors: An experimental study. *Developmental Psychology, 20,* 397–405.

Gustafson, G., Green, J., & West, M. (1979). The infant's changing role in mother–infant games: The growth of social skills. *Infant Behavior and Development, 2,* 301–308.

Hebb, D. O. (1949). *The organization of behavior.* New York: Wiley.

Hombessa-N'Kounkou, E. (1988). *Le développement psychomoteur du bébé congo-lari.* Thesis Université de Paris, V.

Hopkins, B., & Westra, T. (1989). Maternal expectation and motor development: Some cultural differences. *Developmental Medicine and Child Neurology, 31,* 384–390.

Jo, J. S. (1989) *Puériculture coréenne, passé et présent: L'évolution des habitudes de puériculture dans deux vilages coréens* [Korean child-rearing practices: The evolution of child-rearing practices in two Korean villages]. Memoire de Diplôme, École des Hautes Études en Sciences Sociales.

Kugler, P., Kelso, J., & Turvey, M. (1982). On the control and coordination of naturally developing systems. In J. A. S. Kelso & J. E. Clark (Eds.), *The development of movement control and coordination* (pp. 5–78). New York: Wiley.

Miller, G., Galanter, E., & Pribram, K. (1960). *Plans and the structure of behavior.* New York: Holt, Rinehart, & Winston.

Norimatsu, H. (1993). Development of child autonomy in eating and toilet training: One to three year old Japanese and French children. *Early Development and Parenting, 2,* 39–50.

Reed, E. S. (1982). An outline of a theory of action systems. *Journal of Motor Behavior, 14,* 98–134.

Reed, E. S. (1984). From action gestalts to direct action. In H. T. A. Whiting (Ed.), *Human motor actions: Bernstein re-assessed.* Amsterdam: North-Holland.

Reed, E. S. (1988). *James J. Gibson and the psychology of perception.* New Haven: Yale University Press.

Reed, E. S. (1989). The neural regulation of adaptive behavior: An essay on Gerald Edelman's *Neural Darwinism. Ecological Psychology, 1,* 97–117.

Reed, E. S. (1993). The intention to use a specific affordance: A conceptual framework for psychology. In R. H. Wozniak & K. Fischer (Eds.), *Development in context: Acting and thinking in specific environments.* Hillsdale, NJ: Lawrence Erlbaum Associates.

Reissland, N., & Burghart, R. (1987). The role of massage in South Asia: Child health and development. *Social Science Medicine, 25,* 231–239.

Rochat, P. (1992). Self-sitting and reaching in 5- to 8-month-old infants: The impact of posture and its development on early eye–hand coordination. *Journal of Motor Behavior, 24,* 210–220.

Rogoff, B. (1990). *Apprenticeship in thinking: Cognitive development in social context.* New York: Oxford University Press.

Schmidt, R. A. (1982). *Motor control and learning: A behavioral emphasis.* Champaign, IL: Human Kinetics.

Super, C. M. (1981). Behavioral development in infancy. In R. H. Munroe, R. L. Munroe, & B. Whiting (Eds.), *Handbook of cross-cultural human development.* New York: Garland.

Super, C. M., & Harkness, S. (1986). The developmental niche: A conceptualization of the interface of child and culture. *International Journal of Behavioral Development, 9*, 545–569.

Thelen, E., & Smith, L. (1994). *Dynamic systems in development*. Cambridge, MA: MIT Press.

Tomasello, M., Savage-Rumbaugh, S., & Kruger, C. (1993). Imitative learning of actions on objects in children, chimpanzees, and acculturated chimpanzees. *Child Development, 64*, 1688–1701.

Turvey, M. T. (1977). Preliminaries to a theory of action with reference to vision. In R. Shaw & J. Bransford (Eds.), *Perceiving, acting, and knowing*. Hillsdale, NJ: Lawrence Erlbaum Associates.

Von Hofsten, C. (1979). Development of visually directed reaching: The approach phase. *Journal of Human Movement Studies, 5*, 160–178.

Wolf, E. (1982). *Europe and the people without a history*. Berkeley & Los Angeles: University of California Press.

Author Index

Subject Index